ALSO IN SERIES OF Twenty Two (22) Sacred Maxims

Lex Divina: Maxims of Divine Law
Lex Naturae: Maxims of Natural Law
Lex Cognitum: Maxims of Cognitive Law
Lex Virtus Naturae: Maxims of Bioethics Law
Lex Ecclesiasticum: Maxims of Ecclesiastical Law
Lex Positivum: Maxims of Positive Law
Lex Regia: Maxims of Sovereign Law
Lex Fidei: Maxims of Fiduciary Law
Lex Administratum: Maxims of Administrative Law
Lex Economica: Maxims of Economic Law
Lex Pecuniaria: Maxims of Monetary Law
Lex Civilis: Maxims of Civil Law
Lex Criminalis: Maxims of Criminal Law
Lex Educationis: Maxims of Education Law
Lex Nutrimens Et Medicina: Maxims of Food & Drugs Law
Lex Urbanus: Maxims of Urban Law
Lex Societatis: Maxims of Company Law
Lex Technologiae: Maxims of Technology Law
Lex Commercii: Maxims of Trade & Intellectual Property Law
Lex Securitas: Maxims of Security Law
Lex Militaris: Maxims of Military Law
Lex Gentium: Maxims of International Law

Pactum De Singularis Caelum
Covenant of One Heaven

Lex Positivum

Maxims of Positive Law

OFFICIAL ENGLISH FIRST EDITION

By
UCADIA

Ucadia Books Company

Lex Positivum: Maxims of Positive Law. Official English First Edition. Copyright © 2002-2023 UCADIA. All Rights reserved in Trust.

No part of this book may be reproduced, or stored in a retrieval system, or transmitted in any form or by any means electronic, mechanical, photocopying, recording or otherwise, without the express and authentic written permission of the Publisher.

The Publisher disclaims any liability and shall be indemnified and held harmless from any demands, loss, liability, claims or expenses made by any party due or arising out of or in connection with any differences between previous non-official English drafts and this Official English First Edition.

A party that threatens, makes or enacts any demand or action, against this publication or the Publisher hereby acknowledge they have read this disclaimer and agree with this binding legal agreement and irrevocably consent to Ucadia and its competent forums as being the original and primary Jurisdiction for resolving any such issue of fact and law.

Published by Ucadia Books Company, a Delaware stock corporation (File Number 6779670).
8 The Green, STE B, Dover, Delaware, 19901 United States.
First edition.

UCADIA® is a US Registered Trademark in trust under Guardians and Trustees Company protected under international law and the laws of the United States.

ISBN 978-1-64419-028-9

Lex Positivum: Maxims of Positive Law

By Right, Power and Authority of Article 135 (*Divine Collection of Maxims of Law*) of the most sacred Covenant *Pactum De Singularis Caelum*, also known as the *Covenant of One Heaven* these maxims of law known collectively as "**Lex Positivum**" and "**Maxims of Positive Law**" are hereby promulgated in the original form of Ucadian Language and official translations.

These Maxims of Positive Law may be taken in official original document form and spoken form to represent one part of a complete set of the twenty-two (22) books known collectively as the Divine Collection of Maxims of Law.

The Maxims of Positive Law represent the primary, one and only true first Maxims of Positive Law. Excluding the most sacred Covenants *Pactum De Singularis Caelum*, *Pactum De Singularis Christus*, *Pactum De Singularis Islam* and *Pactum De Singularis Spiritus*, all other laws, claims and agreements claiming standards of Positive Law shall be secondary and inferior to the Maxims of Positive Law.

When referring to these Maxims of Positive Law:-

(i) The entire book of Maxims of Positive Law may be abbreviated in citation as "*Lex Positivum*" or "*Lex Positivum (Maxims of Positive Law)*"; and

(ii) A Maxim within the book of Maxims of Positive Law may be abbreviated in citation as (for example) "*Lex Positivum max.1*" or "*Lex Positivum (Positive Law) max.1*".

In accordance with these Maxims of Positive Law, Ucadia also known as the Unique Collective Awareness of all Meaning, also known as the Divine Creator reserves all rights to itself and its duly authorised organs, bodies and entities.

As all rights are reserved, no translation, copy, citation, duplication, registration in part or whole implies any transfer or conveyance of these rights.

When part or all of these laws is presented or spoken in any language other than the Official Ucadian Languages, it may be taken as a translation and not the primary language. Therefore, any secondary meaning implying deficiency, claimed abrogation of any right or any other defect of a word in a translated language shall be null and void ab initio (from the beginning).

Let no man, woman, spirit or officer place themselves in grave dishonour of Divine Law, Natural Law and the Living Law upon denying the validity of these maxims of law. As it is written, so be it.

CONTENTS

Title I: Introductory Provisions

1.1 – Introductory Definitions

Article 1 – Civilised Rules	25
Article 2 – Uncivilised Rules	28
Article 3 – Civilised Rules & Society	31
Article 4 – Civilised Rules & Individual	34
Article 5 – Civilised Rules & Models	35
Article 6 – Civilised Rules & Sets	37
Article 7 – Civilised Rules & Reality	39
Article 8 – Civilised Rules & Awareness	40
Article 9 – Civilised Rules & Complexity	41
Article 10 – Civilised Rules & The Divine	42
Article 11 – Civilised Rules & Nature	43
Article 12 – Positive Law	43
Article 13 – Divine Law & Positive Law	44
Article 14 – Natural Law & Positive Law	45
Article 15 – Cognitive Law & Positive Law	46

1.2 – Civilised Principles

Article 16 – Civilised Principles of Law	46
Article 17 – Public Rule & Function of Law	47
Article 18 – Simplicity & Morality of Law	48
Article 19 – Openness & Integrity of Law	49
Article 20 – Transparency & Awareness of Formation of Law	49
Article 21 – Knowledge & Respect of Rights of Law	50
Article 22 – Equality & Fair Application of Law	51
Article 23 – Independence & Impartiality of Officers of Law	52
Article 24 – Fair & Expeditious Procedure of Law	53
Article 25 – Oversight & Accountability of Administration of Law	54
Article 26 – Sensibility & Mercy of Enforcement of Law	55

1.3 – Uncivilised, Immoral & Absurd Principles

Article 27 – Uncivilised, Immoral & Absurd Principles	55
Article 28 – Private Rule & Function of Law	57

Article 29 – Complexity & Moral Repugnancy of Law	58
Article 30 – Obfuscation & Corruption of Law	59
Article 31 – Suppression & Secrecy of Formation of Law	60
Article 32 – Ignorance & Disrespect of Rights of Law	60
Article 33 – Unequal & Unfair Application of Law	62
Article 34 – Compromised & Partiality of Officers of Law	63
Article 35 – Unfair & Egregious Procedure of Law	64
Article 36 – Immunity & Unaccountability of Administration of Law	65
Article 37 – Incompetence & Cruelty of Enforcement of Law	65

1.4 – Justice & Rule of Law

Article 38 – Justice	66
Article 39 – Fair Process	69
Article 40 – Rule of Law	71

Title II: Reason & Argument

2.1 – Reason & Argument

Article 41 – Reason	75
Article 42 – Argument	76
Article 43 – Cause	77
Article 44 – Interpretation	79
Article 45 – Proposition	79
Article 46 – Conclusion	81
Article 47 – Validity	81
Article 48 – Legitimacy	82
Article 49 – Sanity	82
Article 50 – Competence	84
Article 51 – Status	85
Article 52 – Capacity	88
Article 53 – Standing	89
Article 54 – Merit	90

2.2 – Logic

Article 55 – Logic	93
Article 56 – Premise	95

Article 57 – Inference	95
Article 58 – Deductive Logic	96
Article 59 – Inductive Logic	96
Article 60 – Fallacy	97

2.3 – Critical Methods

Article 61 – Critical Methods	100
Article 62 – Scepticism	102
Article 63 – Deficiency	103
Article 64 – Ad Hominem	103

2.4 – Dialectic Methods

Article 65 – Dialectic Methods	105
Article 66 – Thesis	110
Article 67 – Antithesis	111
Article 68 – Synthesis	111
Article 69 – Absurdity	112

2.5 – Socratic Methods

Article 70 – Socratic Methods	112
Article 71 – Supposition	115
Article 72 – Interrogation	115
Article 73 – Response	119
Article 74 – Clarity	121
Article 75 – Hypocrisy	122

2.6 – Rhetoric Methods

Article 76 – Rhetoric Methods	122

Title III: Form

3.1 – Form

Article 77 – Form	125
Article 78 – Concept	127
Article 79 – Meaning	129
Article 80 – Idea	132
Article 81 – Model	134
Article 82 – System	138

Article 83 – Object 138
Article 84 – Being 140
Article 85 – Thing 144

3.2 – Form Creation & Modification

Article 86 – Form Creation & Modification 145
Article 87 – Revelation 147
Article 88 – Inception 149
Article 89 – Invention 150
Article 90 – Convention 150
Article 91 – Circumscription 151
Article 92 – Consecration 151
Article 93 – Registration 151
Article 94 – Incorporation 152
Article 95 – Ratification 153
Article 96 – Exemplification 153
Article 97 – Extraction 154
Article 98 – Abstraction 154
Article 99 – Annexation 155
Article 100 – Advocation 155

3.3 – Form Abrogation & Corruption

Article 101 – Form Abrogation & Corruption 155
Article 102 – Reprobation 156
Article 103 – Suppression 157
Article 104 – Nullification 157
Article 105 – Misrepresentation 157

Title IV: Place, Space & Time

4.1 – Place & Space

Article 106 – Place 159
Article 107 – Site 160
Article 108 – Location 161
Article 109 – Residence 163
Article 110 – Space 164

Article 111– Sacred Circumscribed Space 164
Article 112 – Ucadia Artifact 167
Article 113 – Non-Ucadian Artifact (Thing) 168

4.2 – Time
Article 114 – Time 169
Article 115 – Ucadia Time 169
Article 116 – Non-Ucadian Time 171

Title V: Oaths, Vows, Testimony & Promises

5.1 – Oath
Article 117 – Oath 173
Article 118 – Ucadia Oath 174
Article 119 – Non-Ucadian Oath 175

5.2 – Vow
Article 120 – Vow 176
Article 121 – Ucadia Vow 177
Article 122 – Non-Ucadian Vow 178

5.3 – Testimony
Article 123 – Testimony 178
Article 124 – Testament 179
Article 125 – Voluntatem Et Testamentum 183
Article 126 – Will 184
Article 127 – Codicil 185
Article 128 – Affidavit 186
Article 129 – Interview 191
Article 130 – Deposition 192
Article 131 – Declaration 193
Article 132 – Statement 194
Article 133 – Examination 194

5.4 – Promise
Article 134 – Promise 196
Article 135 – Ucadia Promise 196
Article 136 – Non-Ucadian Promise 197

5.5 – Prohibited Oaths, Vows, Testimony & Promises

    Article 137 – Prohibited Oaths, Vows & Promises 197

    Article 138 – False Oaths 197

    Article 139 – False Vows 198

    Article 140 – False Promises 199

    Article 141 – False Testimony 200

    Article 142 – Probate 200

Title VI: Registers, Rolls & Persons

6.1 – Register

    Article 143 – Register 203

    Article 144 – Ucadia Register 208

    Article 145 – Non-Ucadia Register 208

6.2 – Roll

    Article 146 – Roll 209

    Article 147 – Ucadia Roll 211

    Article 148 – Non-Ucadia Roll 211

6.3 – Register & Roll Modification

    Article 149 – Register & Roll Modification 211

    Article 150 – Entry 212

    Article 151 – Completion 213

    Article 152 – Correction 214

    Article 153 – Cancellation 214

    Article 154 – Enjoin 214

    Article 155 – Annul 215

6.4 – Person

    Article 156 – Person 215

    Article 157 – Divine Person 216

    Article 158 – True Person 218

    Article 159 – Superior (Legal) Person 219

    Article 160 – Inferior (Legal) Person 219

    Article 161 – Supreme Juridic Person 219

    Article 162 – Universal Juridic Person 220

Article 163 – Global Juridic Person	220
Article 164 – Civil Juridic Person	220
Article 165 – Mercantile Juridic Person	221
Article 166 – Union Juridic Person	221
Article 167 – Inferior Juridic Person	222

6.5 – Prohibited Registers & Rolls

Article 168 – Prohibited Registers & Rolls	222

Title VII: Documents, Instruments & Forms

7.1 – Document

Article 169 – Document	223
Article 170 – Obverse	224
Article 171 – Reverse	225
Article 172 – Traverse	226

7.2 - Document Amendment

Article 173 – Document Amendment	227
Article 174 – Acceptation	229
Article 175 – Endorsation	231
Article 176 – Completion	232
Article 177 – Annotation	233
Article 178 – Annexation	233
Article 179 – Affixation	233
Article 180 – Imprintation	234
Article 181 – Impression	234
Article 182 – Substitution	235
Article 183 – Correction	235
Article 184 – Redaction	235
Article 185 – Cancellation	235
Article 186 – Rejection	236
Article 187 – Revocation	236
Article 188 – Rescission	237

7.3 - Document Validation

Article 189 – Document Validation	237

Article 190 – Signation	238
Article 191 – Sealation	239
Article 192 – Certification	241
Article 193 – Apostillation	243
Article 194 – Notarisation	243
Article 195 – Testification	243
Article 196 – Exemplification	243
Article 197 – Registration	243

7.4 – Instruments & Forms

Article 198 – Instrument	243
Article 199 – Form	247
Article 200 – Letter	247
Article 201 – Notice	249
Article 202 – Memorandum	251
Article 203 – Statement	251
Article 204 – Note	252
Article 205 – Bill	254
Article 206 – Draft	257
Article 207 – Cheque	257
Article 208 – Bond	258
Article 209 – Debenture	264
Article 210 – Writ	264
Article 211 – Warrant	265
Article 212 – Certificate	265
Article 213 – Voucher	266

7.5 – Prohibited Documents, Instruments & Forms

Article 214 – Prohibited Documents, Instruments & Forms	267
Article 215 – Non-Ucadian Government Life Annuities	268
Article 216 – Non-Ucadian Birth (Settlement) Certificates	272
Article 217 – Non-Ucadian Original Land Certificate	280
Article 218 – Non-Ucadian Sovereign Bond Certificates	282
Article 219 – Non-Ucadian Trustee Savings Bank Certificates	282

Article 220 – Non-Ucadian Social Health Certificate 283
Article 221 – Non-Ucadian Social Welfare Certificate 283

Title VIII: Rights

8.1 – Rights

Article 222 – Rights 285
Article 223 – Divine Rights 292
Article 224 – Natural Rights 293
Article 225 – Superior Rights 294
Article 226 – Inferior Rights 296
Article 227 – Invalid Rights 298
Article 228 – Prohibited Rights 298

8.2 – Rights Creation, Identification, Assertion & Modification

Article 229 – Rights Creation, Identification, Assertion & Modification 299
Article 230 – Heir 300
Article 231 – Owner 301
Article 232 – Holder 302
Article 233 – Claimant 303
Article 234 – Assertion 305
Article 235 – Registration 305
Article 236 – Reservation 306
Article 237 – Domination 307
Article 238 – Succession 308
Article 239 – Occupation 309
Article 240 – Possession 310
Article 241 – Operation 310
Article 242 – Production 310

8.3 – Rights Transfer & Possession

Article 243 – Rights Transfer & Possession 310
Article 244 – Gift 311
Article 245 – Grant 312
Article 246 – Assignment 314
Article 247 – Delegation 316

Article 248 – Novation 317
Article 249 – Sale 318
Article 250 – Bargain 318
Article 251 – Conveyance 319
Article 252 – Merger and Acquisition 320

8.4 – Rights Suspension & Loss

Article 253 – Rights Suspension & Loss 322
Article 254 – Perfidy 323
Article 255 – Renunciation 323
Article 256 – Abandonment 324
Article 257 – Expiration 325
Article 258 – Suspension 326
Article 259 – Forfeiture 327
Article 260 – Waiver 328

8.5 – Rights Dispute, Recovery & Restoration

Article 261 – Rights Dispute, Recovery & Restoration 329
Article 262 – Distress 329
Article 263 – Replevin 330
Article 264 – Detinue 330
Article 265 – Injunction 331
Article 266 – Reparation 332
Article 267 – Sequestration 333
Article 268 – Garnishment 334
Article 269 – Revendication 334
Article 270 – Restitution 334
Article 271 – Public Advocacy and Lobbying 335

8.6 – False, Absurd & Prohibited Rights

Article 272 – False, Absurd & Prohibited Identification of Rights 336
Article 273 – Cestui Que Vie 336
Article 274 – Theft 342
Article 275 – Adverse Possession 342
Article 276 – Foreclosure 343

Article 277 – Denizen	351
Article 278 – Privateer	352
Article 279 – Sovereign Citizen	353

Title IX: Personal Rights

9.1 – Personal Rights

Article 280 – Personal Rights	355
Article 281 – Ius Ucadia (Superior Rights of Ucadia)	360
Article 282 – Ius Vitam (Life)	361
Article 283 – Ius Liberum Arbitrium (Free Will)	361
Article 284 – Ius Conscientia (Conscious Awareness)	361
Article 285 – Ius Rationatio (Accounting, Credit & Funds)	362
Article 286 – Ius Vivere Aut Mori (Choose to Live or Die)	363
Article 287 – Ius Sentire Aut Torpere (Sense)	363
Article 288 – Ius Discere Aut Ignarus (Learn)	364
Article 289 – Ius Associatio et Conventio (Association)	364
Article 290 – Ius Credere et Non (Trust a Claim)	366
Article 291 – Ius Consensum et Non (Consent)	366
Article 292 – Ius Loqui et Silentium (Speak)	367
Article 293 – Ius Iuris (Justice)	367
Article 294 – Ius Testamentum (Testament)	368
Article 295 – Ius Aequum (Fairness & Equality)	369
Article 296 – Ius Bona Fidei (Good Faith)	369
Article 297 – Ius Ucadiansium Scientiarum (Ucadia Sciences)	369
Article 298 – Ius Fidei (Superior Trust & Estate)	370
Article 299 – Ius Concedere et Abrogare (Give or Grant)	371
Article 300 – Ius Delegare et Revocare (Assign or Delegate)	371
Article 301 – Ius Sacramentum (Oath and Vow)	372
Article 302 – Ius Signandi (Sign and Seal)	372
Article 303 – Ius Possessionis (Possession)	373
Article 304 – Ius Tenendi Terram (Lease of Home or Land)	373
Article 305 – Ius Usus (Use)	374
Article 306 – Ius Connubii (Union)	374

Article 307 – Ius Coeundi (Intercourse) 374
Article 308 – Ius Contraceptio (Contraception) 375
Article 309 – Ius Terminare (Termination) 375
Article 310 – Ius Nascendi (Right to Life) 376
Article 311 – Ius Nativitas (Give Birth) 376
Article 312 – Ius Creditum (Beliefs) 376
Article 313 – Ius Carnem (Flesh) 377
Article 314 – Ius Sexualitatis (Sexuality) 377
Article 315 – Ius Nomenis (Name) 378
Article 316 – Ius Integritatis Geneticae (Genetics) 378
Article 317 – Ius Identitatis (Identity) 379
Article 318 – Ius Privatum (Privacy) 379
Article 319 – Ius Tectum (Shelter) 380
Article 320 – Ius Habitare (Habitat) 380
Article 321 – Ius Terrae et Aquae Purarum (Clean Land & Water) 381
Article 322 – Ius Sustentandi (Sustenance) 382
Article 323 – Ius Libertatis (Freedom) 382
Article 324 – Ius Tormentum Libertatis (No Cruelty or Torture) 383

Title X: Member Rights

10.1 – Member Rights

Article 325 – Member Rights 385

10.2 – Authoritative Member Rights

Article 326 – Authoritative Member Right 385
Article 327 – Ius Memb. Sodalis (Equal Member) 387
Article 328 – Ius Memb. Nascendi Societas (Member Right of Birth) 388
Article 329 – Ius Memb. Votum (Right to Vote) 388
Article 330 – Ius Memb. Forum Publicum (Public Meetings) 388
Article 331 – Ius Memb. Rationatio (Public Accounts) 389
Article 332 – Ius Memb. Officium (Public Office) 390
Article 333 – Ius Memb. Registrum (Registers & Rolls) 391
Article 334 – Ius Memb. Associatio et Conventio (Agreements) 391
Article 335 – Ius Memb. Servitia (Services) 393

Article 336 – Ius Memb. Mercatus (Markets) 394

Article 337 – Ius Memb. Commercium (Trade & Commerce) 394

10.3 – Legal Member Rights

Article 338 – Legal Member Rights 394

Article 339 – Ius Memb. Iuris (Justice & Due Process) 397

Article 340 – Ius Memb. Aequum (Equality & Fairness) 398

Article 341 – Ius Memb. Bona Fidei (Good Faith) 398

Article 342 – Ius Memb. Libertatis (Freedom) 399

Article 343 – Ius Memb. Actionum (Right of Action) 399

Article 344 – Ius Memb. Significans Laborare (Work) 399

Article 345 – Ius Memb. Salarium Iustum (Fair Pay) 400

Article 346 – Ius Memb. Laborare et Non (Refuse to Work) 400

.... 401

Article 347 – Ius Memb. Custoditum (Detain Person) 401

Article 348 – Ius Memb. Accusare (Accuse Person) 401

Article 349 – Ius Memb. Innocentiae (Innocence) 402

Article 350 – Ius Memb. Accusationis Cognoscendi (Disclosure) 402

Article 351 – Ius Memb. Defensionis (Defence) 403

Article 352 – Ius Memb. Eligendi Iudicium (Trial by Jury or Judge) 403

Article 353 – Ius Memb. Propria Persona (In Person) 403

Article 354 – Ius Memb. Agensas (Agent) 404

Article 355 – Ius Memb. Possessionis (Possession) 404

Article 356 – Ius Memb. Usus (Use) 405

Article 357 – Ius Memb. Proprietatis (Ownership) 406

Article 358 – Ius Memb. Remedium (Remedy) 407

Article 359 – Ius Memb. Poena (Penalty) 407

Article 360 – Ius Memb. Clementia (Mercy) 408

10.4 – Special Member Rights

Article 361 – Special Member Rights 409

Article 362 – Ius Populi Jurisdictio 410

Article 363 – Ius Populi Ecclesia 410

Article 364 – Ius Populi Revocare 411

Article 365 – Ius Populi Decretum ....

Article 366 – Ius Populi Imperium 412

Article 367 – Ius Populi Custoditum 412

Title XI: Trusts & Estates

11.1 – Trust

Article 368 – Trust 415

Article 369 – Ucadia Trust 424

Article 370 – Non-Ucadia Trust 424

Article 371 – False, Absurd & Prohibited Trusts 435

11.2 – Estate

Article 372 – Estate 435

Article 373 – Ucadia Estate 439

Article 374 – Non-Ucadia Estate 440

Article 375 – False, Absurd & Prohibited Estates 444

Title XII: Property & Funds

12.1 – Property

Article 376 – Property 445

Article 377 – Ucadia Property 447

Article 378 – Non-Ucadia Property 447

Article 379 – False, Absurd & Prohibited Property 449

12.2 – Funds

Article 380 – Funds 450

Article 381 – Ucadia Fund 451

Article 382 – Non-Ucadia Fund 452

Article 383 – False, Absurd & Prohibited Funds 452

Title XIII: Associations & Relations

13.1 – Association

Article 384 – Association 453

Article 385 – Ucadia Association 455

Article 386 – Non-Ucadia Association 456

Article 387 – False, Absurd & Prohibited Associations 456

13.2 – Relations

Article 388 – Relation 456

Article 389 – Ucadia Relation 458

Article 390 – Non-Ucadia Relation 459

Article 391 – False, Absurd & Prohibited Relation................................... 460

Title XIV: Consensus

14.1 – Consensus

Article 392 – Consent 461

Article 393 – Consensus 462

Article 394 – Bilateral Consensus 463

Article 395 – Trilateral Consensus 463

14.2 – False, Absurd & Prohibited Consensus

Article 396 – False, Absurd & Prohibited Consensus 463

Article 397 – Implied Consent (Unilateral Consensus) 464

Title XV: Agreement

15.1 – Agreement

Article 398 – Agreement 467

Article 399 – Terms and Conditions 472

Article 400 – Deed 473

Article 401 – Deed Poll 478

Article 402 – Compact 479

Article 403 – Contract 479

15.2 – Agreement Elements

Article 404 – Agreement Elements 481

Article 405 – Legal Capacity... 483

Article 406 – Legality of Purpose 484

Article 407 – Intention to Create Legal Relations 484

Article 408 – Good Faith, Good Conscience & Good Actions 485

Article 409 – Free Will & Consent 485

Article 410 – Certainty & Possibility of Performance 485

Article 411 – Consideration 486

Article 412 – Proper Form 487

Article 413 – Offer 487

Article 414 – Acceptance 489

Article 415 – Mutual Assent 489
Article 416 – Execution & Ratification 489

15.3 – Agreement Penalty, Remedy & Enforcement

Article 417 – Agreement Penalty and Enforcement 489
Article 418 – Breach of Agreement 489
Article 419 – Penalties for Breach of Agreement 491
Article 420 – Remedies for Breach of Agreement 492
Article 421 – Obligation of Mitigation 492
Article 422 – Legal Enforcement of Penalties or Remedies 492

15.4 – Agreement Dispute or Extinction

Article 423 – Agreement Dispute or Extinction 493
Article 424 – Default 495
Article 425 – Force Majeure 498
Article 426 – Frustration 498
Article 427 – Termination 498
Article 428 – Voidance 499
Article 429 – Damages 500
Article 430 – Reformation 501
Article 431 – Restitution 502
Article 432 – Rescission 503

15.5 – False & Prohibited Agreements

Article 433 – False & Prohibited Agreements 504
Article 434 – Agreements of Perfidy or Intentional Injury 504
Article 435 – Agreements of Undue Influence or Unconscionability 505
Article 436 – Agreements of Misstatement or Misrepresentation 506
Article 437 – Agreements of Omission or Concealment 506
Article 438 – Agreements of Frustration or Impossibility 507
Article 439 – Agreements of Espionage or Sabotage 507
Article 440 – Agreements of Deception or Fraud 508
Article 441 – Agreements of Bribery or Corruption 508
Article 442 – Agreements of Extortion or Unjust Enrichment 508
Article 443 – Agreements of Collusion or Restraint of Trade 509

Article 444 – Agreements of Coercion or Duress	507
Article 445 – Agreements of Criminal Enterprise	510

Title XVI: Powers & Authority

16.1 – Authority

Article 446 – Authority	511

16.2 – Power

Article 447 – Power	515

16.3 – Powers Creation

Article 448 – Powers Creation	518
Article 449 – Power of Attorney	522
Article 450 – Attorney	523

16.4 – False, Absurd & Prohibited Powers

Article 451 – False, Absurd & Prohibited Powers	526

Title XVII: Jurisdiction

17.1 – Jurisdiction of Law

Article 452 – Jurisdiction	527
Article 453 – Personal Jurisdiction	530
Article 454 – Territorial Jurisdiction	530
Article 455 – Subject Matter Jurisdiction	531
Article 456 – Original & Appellate Jurisdiction	531
Article 457 – Exclusive & Concurrent Jurisdiction	533
Article 458 – Foreign & International Jurisdiction	533
Article 459 – Ecclesiastical & Supreme Jurisdiction	534

Title XVIII: Occurrence, Drama & Fact

18.1 – Occurrence

Article 460 – Occurrence	535
Article 461 – Instance	535

18.2 – Drama

Article 462 – Drama	535
Article 463 – Stage	538
Article 464 – Scene	539

Article 465 – Dramatis Personae (Cast) 540
Article 466 – Persona (Actor) 540
Article 467 – Protagonist 541
Article 468 – Deuteragonist 541
Article 469 – Tritagonist 541
Article 470 – Chorus 542
Article 471 – Appearance 542
Article 472 – Plot 543
Article 473 – Motive 544
Article 474 – Fate (Sentence) 544

18.3 – Fact

Article 475 – Fact 544
Article 476 – Reality 547
Article 477 – Truth 548
Article 478 – Source of Fact 549
Article 479 – Citation 553

18.4 – Evidence

Article 480 – Evidence 554
Article 481 – Physical Evidence 555
Article 482 – Testimonial Evidence 556
Article 483 – Inferential Evidence 556
Article 484 – Disclosure of Evidence 557
Article 485 – Admission of Evidence 558
Article 486 – Acceptance of Evidence (Proof) 560

Title I - Introductory Definitions

1.1 – Introductory Definitions

Article 1 – Civilised Rules

1. A ***Rule*** is a proper and authentic ***Law*** that describes, prohibits or permits a certain Act. A *Law* is therefore a sufficient and well formed *Rule*. — Rule

2. A ***Civilised Rule*** is a proper and authentic ***Law*** of a validly constituted Society that describes, prohibits or permits a certain Act pertaining to a Right in Trust. — Civilised Rule

3. An ***Act*** or ***Action*** is the manifestation of the Mind or Will of a Being or Person expressed as an Idea, Cause, Model, Power, Motion, Effect, Expression or Thing done. — Act

4. A ***Right in Trust*** is when a Right exists and is granted under *Good Faith* (Bona Fidei), *Good Conscience* (Bona Conscientia) and *Good Actions* (Bona Acta). If all three are missing or there is no Good Faith, no Right or Law exists. — Right in Trust

5. In respect of Law being a sufficient and well formed Rule, a Civilised Rule must demonstrate the following minimum qualities:- — Law as a well formed Rule

    (i) The Rule must refer to at least one proper Right (Ius). If no Right then no Rule or Law; and

    (ii) The Rule must express or imply a moral Act (or *Droit*) as the right Action. A Rule is never permitted to express or imply a wrong, immoral or morally repugnant Act as the right Action; and

    (iii) The Rule may be expressed positively as a right Act (or *Droit*), with the wrong Act (or *Tort*) implied; or the Rule may be expressed negatively with the right Act implied; and

    (iv) If a ***Penalty*** related to the Rule is listed, then at least one ***Remedy*** must accompany the Penalty.

6. A Civilised Rule is distinguished from a false or "uncivilised rule" by its conformity to one or more Civilised Principles. In contrast, an uncivilised rule is poorly formed, rarely (if ever) moral and usually associated with one or more uncivilised, immoral and absurd principles. — Civilised Rule vs Uncivilised Rule

7. A proper and authentic Law is known as a ***Maxim*** being a norm, or bar, or canon, or axiom, or measure or standard, consistent with the present most sacred body of Laws known as the ***Divine Collection of Maxims of Law***. — Maxim

8. A valid Maxim may be derived by instruction, deduction, discovery, argument, custom or consent:- — Source of Maxims

(i) The highest Law is a rule given by Divine instruction, as nothing may contradict such a rule; and

(ii) The second highest Law is a proven deduction and discovery of universal and natural laws through reason and discernment of mind as a comprehensive and cohesive model, as the strongest models are consistent, useful, sensible, complete and universally applicable; and

(iii) The third highest Law is the conclusion of an argument and debate between two or more Minds, being an edict given by a great council of wise elders or jurists, as nothing absurd and without good reason may be considered Law; and

(iv) The fourth highest Law is the law of the People, as the consent and will of the people is the source of true authority and sovereignty within any community or society; and

(v) The weakest rule is that of a tyrant, as any rule without authority or right of Heaven but merely by force, cannot be sustained; and the people shall eventually overcome; and render such unjust rule and unjust laws as dust.

9. A Law may pertain to Concepts, Objects or Persons or all three. When a Law pertains to Persons, there are four essential characters being Legislative, Executive, Juridical and Legal Persons:- *Law and Concepts, Objects & Persons*

(i) A Person or group of Persons possessing the legitimate authority to form new Laws or amend or abrogate old Laws is called a "***Legislator***" or "***Legislative***"; and

(ii) A Person possessing the legitimate authority to approve and promulgate new Laws issued by a Legislator is called a "***Sovereign***" or "***Executive***"; and

(iii) A Person or group of Persons possessing the legitimate authority to interpret and administer the Law is called "***Juridic***" or "***Juridical***"; and

(iv) A Person or group of Persons who are the subject of certain laws as promulgated may be called "***Subjects***" or "***Legal***".

10. All Maxims may be defined by the twenty-two most sacred books of the body of Laws known as the *Divine Collection of Maxims of Law* in accord with Article 135 of the most sacred Covenant *Pactum De Singularis Caelum,* namely:- *Maxims and Divine Collection of Maxims*

(i) ***Lex Divina***: Maxims of Divine Law; and

(ii) ***Lex Naturae***: Maxims of Natural Law; and

(iii) **Lex Cognitum**: Maxims of Cognitive Law; and

(iv) **Lex Positivum**: Maxims of Positive Law; and

(v) **Lex Ecclesiasticum**: Maxims of Ecclesiastical Law; and

(vi) **Lex Virtus Naturae**: Maxims of Bioethics Law; and

(vii) **Lex Regia**: Maxims of Sovereign Law; and

(viii) **Lex Fidei**: Maxims of Fiduciary Law; and

(ix) **Lex Administratum**: Maxims of Administrative Law; and

(x) **Lex Economica**: Maxims of Economic Law; and

(xi) **Lex Pecuniaria**: Maxims of Monetary Law; and

(xii) **Lex Civilis**: Maxims of Civil Law; and

(xiii) **Lex Criminalis**: Maxims of Criminal Law; and

(xiv) **Lex Educationis**: Maxims of Education Law; and

(xv) **Lex Nutrimens Et Medicina**: Maxims of Food & Drugs Law; and

(xvi) **Lex Urbanus**: Maxims of Urban Law; and

(xvii) **Lex Societatis**: Maxims of Company Law; and

(xviii) **Lex Technologiae**: Maxims of Technology Law; and

(xix) **Lex Commercii**: Maxims of Trade & Intellectual Property Law; and

(xx) **Lex Securitas**: Maxims of Security Law; and

(xxi) **Lex Militaris**: Maxims of Military Law; and

(xxii) **Lex Gentium**: Maxims of International Law.

11. In accord with Article 135 of the most sacred Covenant *Pactum De Singularis Caelum*, each of the three (3) Great Faiths shall be permitted to use their own official name for the Divine Collection of Maxims of Law:-

    (i) The Universal Ecclesia of One Christ may use the name **Astrum Iuris Divini Canonum** to officially define the *Divine Collection of Maxims of Law* from the perspective of their authority; and furthermore may name the individual books as "canons"; and

    (ii) The Holy Society of One Islam may use the name **Hikmat**

Official Name of Divine Collection of Maxims of Law

Samawi to officially define the *Divine Collection of Maxims of Law* from the perspective of their authority; and furthermore may name the individual books as "qanunlar"; and

(iii) Sacred Society of One Spirit may use the name **Pragya Dharma** to officially define the *Divine Collection of Maxims of Law* from the perspective of their authority; and furthermore may name the individual books as "vedas".

12. A valid Maxim neither abrogates nor derogates from the most sacred Covenant *Pactum De Singularis Caelum*. — Maxims & Sacred Covenant

13. Any Rule that is not consistent with the most sacred body of Laws known as *Divine Collection of Maxims of Law* cannot therefore be considered or claimed as Law. — Rules & Divine Collection of Maxims

14. Whenever the terms Maxim, or Rule or Law are used, they shall mean first and foremost the present body of valid Maxims and those Rules and Laws in accord with it and no other. — Valid Maxims

15. No valid Maxim that belongs to the sacred body of Laws known as *Divine Collection of Maxims of Law* may be declared in error, abrogated, derogated or suspended, except by a competent forum of Law possessing such authority as defined and derived from the most sacred Covenant *Pactum De Singularis Caelum*. — Maxims & Forum Declarations

16. In the event that a competent forum of Law possessing such authority as defined and derived from the most sacred Covenant *Pactum De Singularis Caelum* declares one or more Maxims that belong to the sacred body of Laws known as *Divine Collection of Maxims of Law* as being in error, then such Maxims shall hereby be temporarily severed from the rest of the body of Laws to the extent that such a clause or Maxim is void, or invalid and unenforceable. Furthermore, any such ruling or action shall not affect the validity or enforceability of the remainder of the sacred body of Laws. — Maxims & Severability

17. Any law that is against the authentic truth of these present sacred Maxims cannot be Law. — Maxims & Law

Article 2 – Uncivilised Rule

18. An **Uncivilised Rule** is an immoral, repugnant and wrong act of a Society that describes, prohibits or permits a certain Act. An Uncivilised Rule can never be properly called a "law", even if it is claimed to be by the rules of a society or its general recognition. — Uncivilised Rule

19. By its very essence and meaning, all Law is moral. Thus an immoral, repugnant, wrong or absurd rule can never be legitimately, validly or — All Law is Moral

logically called a "law", despite any claims to the contrary. Uncivilised rules are commonly known as "dictates".

20. An Uncivilised Rule is distinguished from a true and valid "civilised rule" by its conformity to one or more False, Absurd, Immoral and Uncivilised Principles. In contrast, a civilised rule is rarely (if ever) immoral or repugnant. *Uncivilised Rule vs Civilised Rule*

21. No matter what Rules are passed by the executive, legislative or judiciary of a society to the contrary, no amount of edicts or orders can transform a repugnant and immoral uncivilised rule into a civilised rule and Law. *No effect when rule is immoral and repugnant*

22. All Uncivilised Rules may be generally categorised and described more accurately as one of four types being fraud, bribe, threat or terror:- *General Classification of Uncivilised Rules*

    (i) A *Fraud* (in the context of Uncivilised Rule) is a rule that seeks to hide, obfuscate, misrepresent, exclude, permit or prohibit one or more acts, whereby such a rule has no honest, moral, fair, impartial or accountable basis; and

    (ii) A *Bribe* (in the context of Uncivilised Rule) is a rule that seeks some repugnant and immoral act under the promise or payment of some financial benefit; and

    (iii) A *Threat* (in the context of Uncivilised Rule) is a rule that seeks some repugnant and immoral act under the threat of violence and intimidation; and

    (iv) A *Terror* (in the context of Uncivilised Rule) is a rule that seeks some repugnant and immoral act under the display and action of brutality, violence, targeting and fear.

23. An Uncivilised Rule ceases to have any effect or authority the moment it is issued or decreed, not from the moment it is first exposed or challenged. *Abrogation of Uncivilised Rules*

24. An Uncivilised Rule by its nature renders itself null, void and without legitimate force or effect the moment it is first issued or decreed. An Uncivilised Rule never requires an official, or a court, or legislature to issue a decree or statute or order to prove such a rule is uncivilised. *Uncivilised Rules destroy their own legitimacy and effect*

25. A person need only to prove and demonstrate a rule is uncivilised, repugnant, immoral or absurd to render such a law abrogated, ineffective and unenforceable in a competent forum of law:- *Proof of Uncivilised Rule*

    (i) As all law is by definition "moral", an immoral and repugnant rule cannot be treated or considered a valid or legitimate law; and

    (ii) A rule that is fundamentally unfair, or unequal, or secret, or unjust, or cruel or unaccountable is by definition immoral and repugnant and cannot be treated or considered a valid or legitimate law.

26. A forum of law ceases to have any moral, legitimate, ecclesiastical or moral authority the moment it refuses to strike down and cease to apply uncivilised rules:- *(No authority as forum of law if uncivilised rules permitted to be applied)*

    (i) No temporal forum of law possesses the logical, moral or ecclesiastical authority to change the criteria whereby a rule may be discerned and concluded as civilised or uncivilised. Thus a rule that is clearly immoral, repugnant and uncivilised by such criteria is so, whether such a forum states the obvious or not; and

    (ii) The failure of a forum of law to properly apply the Principles of Civilised Rules or to strike down a rule that is clearly uncivilised and morally repugnant, renders such a forum incompetent in law, and thus incapable of making any determination, judgement or order in law.

27. A Person, whether in their official capacity or not, that fails to properly strike down and abrogate an uncivilised and morally repugnant rule, accepts full personal, moral and spiritual culpability and punishment for the consequences of such dereliction of the obligations of office under proper Divine Law, Ecclesiastical Law and Positive Law. *(Personal Liability and Uncivilised Rules)*

28. In respect of any rule claimed from Divine Instruction that is uncivilised and morally repugnant:- *(Uncivilised Rules and Divine Instruction)*

    (i) As no legitimate or authentic rule from Divine and Spiritual Source can ever be morally repugnant and uncivilised, any such claim is overwhelmingly false, no matter what the claimed authority of the messenger or interpreter of such claimed Divine Instruction; and

    (ii) A claimed messenger or interpreter of matters Divine and Spiritual that claims some morally repugnant and uncivilised rule by Divine Instruction ceases to have any authority whatsoever the moment they act in such a profane, false and sacrilegious manner.

29. In respect of any rule claimed from Customary Law, or Historic Tradition that is uncivilised and morally repugnant:- *(Uncivilised Rules and Customary or Historic Traditions)*

    (i) A Custom or Historic Tradition that is morally repugnant and uncivilised cannot then be considered a valid and legitimate law because of its age or such tradition; and

(ii) There is no statute of limitations on morally repugnant and uncivilised customs and historic traditions.

30. In respect of any rule claimed from Scientific Discovery or Natural Law that is uncivilised and morally repugnant:-

    (i) Any claim of scientific or natural discovery is insufficient for a rule to be legitimate and valid if its application is morally repugnant and uncivilised to a society; and

    (ii) The claim or application of scientific methods ahead and above civilised principles is itself a morally repugnant and absurd act, having no force or effect in law.

Uncivilised Rules and Scientific Discovery

31. In respect of any rule claimed from Intellectual Reason or Elite Consensus that is uncivilised and morally repugnant:-

    (i) The claimed high intellect or reasoning of a group of people is insufficient alone to justify one or more rules that may be morally repugnant and uncivilised; and

    (ii) The fact that a person of high claimed intellect may be able to demonstrate some opposing or different moral value set within their own unreal set does not then make such an unreal set valid or legitimate for application within a civilised society, nor the replacement of civilised rules.

Uncivilised Rules and Intellectual Philosophies

32. In respect of any rule claimed from Mob Rule that is uncivilised and morally repugnant:-

    (i) The decisions or rule of a mob never supersedes civilised rule of society; and

    (ii) A mob without respect for the rule of law is the same as the rule of a tyrant.

Uncivilised Rules and Mob Rule

Article 3 – Civilised Rules & Society

33. Civilised Rules are the bedrock of a sustainable, fair and harmonious Society. In the absence of some form of system of Civilised Rules based on Civilised Principles, no association of three of more people may function fairly or efficiently.

Civilised Rules and Society

34. ***Civilised Society*** or simply ***Society*** is a formal association of three or more persons, founded upon Civilised Principles; and distinguishable by a unique and well developed culture, a comprehensive body of laws, a functioning system of government and a justice system capable of resolving disputes and issues arising under its proper and authentic Rules.

Civilised Society

35. To function and exist, every Society depends upon the existence and

Societal

enforcement of Rules. The question of the number and complexity of such Rules is distinct and separate to the immutable fact that no Society can function or exist (for any meaningful period) without the acceptance and presence of Rules.

Dependence on Rules

36. Whilst a Society is free (in theory) to decide and ratify its own unique set of Rules, most Societies tend to follow common forms and operations of Rules.

Common forms of Rules of Society

37. Given most Societies tend to follow common forms and operations of Rules, a given Society may be defined in one sense according to the common form and operation of Rules, including (but not limited to) *Origin, Power, Personification* and *Function*:-

    Civilised Rules and Types of Society

    (i) *Origin* refers to the commonality of Original Formation of Rules, whereby one or more groups of people come together to form a given Society under some formal system of Rules; and

    (ii) *Power* refers to the commonality of Power and Authority in the source and creation of commands, orders, statutes or policies of a given Society under some Original Formation of Rules; and

    (iii) *Personification* refers to the way that Power and Authority is "personified" within the highest Office(s) of Society; and how this reflects the type and nature of a Society; and

    (iv) *Function* refers to the commonality of Function and Operation in the execution and administration of commands, orders, statutes or policies of a given Society under some Original Formation and Power of Rules.

38. All examples of Civilised Rules in the Original Formation of Society may be defined by five types being *Association, Consolidation, Unification, Federation* or *Annexation*:-

    Civilised Rules and Original Formation of Society

    (i) *Association* is the Original Formation and Rules of a new Society, under one or more common purposes, free from the incorporation of any previous and pre-existing political structures; and

    (ii) *Consolidation* is the Original Formation and Rules of a new Society, under one or more common purposes, by merging one or more political or cultural bodies into a new body; and

    (iii) *Unification,* also known as Union, is the Original Formation and Rules of a new Society, under treaty and ratification, whereby two or more existing political bodies agree to form a unique and singular whole, dependent upon the continued participation of all bodies that originally formed it; and

    (iv) *Federation,* also known as Confederation and sometimes also as a

Union, is the Original Formation and Rules of a new Society, whereby a new unique and singular whole is formed and existing political bodies agree to join (or leave) so that its continuation is not dependent on the original bodies that formed it; and

(v) *Annexation* is the Original Formation and Rules of a new Society, whereby a new society is formed by annexing some of the territory of an existing society to enable self or partial rule.

39. Anarchy, being the concept of a society without rules is not a viable nor sustainable model. Instead, Anarchy is a suspended state that can exist between transitions from one form of government to another, typically in times of great political and economic turmoil. Anarchy

40. Any theory or philosophy that claims or promotes Anarchy as a viable and sustainable model of Society is by definition false and absurd. Falsity of Anarchy

41. All examples of Civilised Rules in the operation of Power and Authority of a Society may be defined by only three fundamental types being *Autocracy, Oligarchy* and *Democracy*:- Civilised Rules and Power Structure of Society

    (i) *Autocracy* is a system of Rules concerning the Power and Structure of a Society where supreme power and authority is concentrated in the hands of one person, intelligent being or body politic or corporate; and

    (ii) *Oligarchy* is a system of Rules concerning the Power and Structure of a Society where supreme power and authority rests with a smaller number of people, intelligent beings or bodies politic or corporate. This "ruling class" may (or may not) be distinguished by intellect, wealth, technology, nobility, family, corporate, religious or military ties; and

    (iii) *Democracy* is a system of Rules concerning the Power and Structure of a Society where supreme power and authority is vested in the people, who choose from among themselves their delegated representatives.

42. All examples of Civilised Rules in the "personification" of Power and Authority of a Society may be defined by only four fundamental types being *Theocratic, Monarchic, Republic* and *Digital*:- Civilised Rules and Personification of Society

    (i) *Theocratic* is a system of Rules concerning the personification of the Powers, Sovereignty and Structure of a Society whereby a person (or being) is deemed by their spiritual character and nature of their installation, the supreme spiritual head and sovereign embodiment of the society; and

    (ii) *Monarchic* is a system of Rules concerning the personification of the Powers, Sovereignty and Structure of a Society whereby a

(iii) *Republic* is a system of Rules concerning the personification of the Powers, Sovereignty and Structure of a Society whereby a person (or being) by virtue of holding office and their valid appointment, is deemed the head of state and the embodiment of the society; and

(iv) *Digital* is a system of Rules concerning the personification of the Powers, Sovereignty and Structure of a Society whereby an autonomous digital sentient (intelligent) being by virtue of representing the sum total knowledge, systems and records of the society, is deemed the head of state and the embodiment of the society.

Article 4 – Civilised Rules & Individual

43. A living and active body, or community or society of higher order beings is by definition formed by the consent and co-operation of three or more individuals. — Civilised Rules & Individual

44. An Individual is not a Society, even though every Society depends upon three or more individuals to constitute some form of Society. An Individual is always a part of a Society, ideally an equal member. — Individual is not a Society

45. An Individual existing in a theoretical vacuum totally separate and isolated from any other human contact or social structures of technology of any kind need not require Rules. However, once an Individual touches, utilises or connects to any system, service, technology or structure of any Society, by definition they are bound by the Rules of using such elements. — Individual existing in a vacuum need not require Rules

46. As a function of basic decency, morality and accountability, an Individual is bound by the Rules of the Society (or Societies) that governs the use of any such system, service, technology or structure consumed or utilised by the Individual. — Necessity to follow Rules if connecting to Society

47. By definition and reason of logic, an Individual can never be Sovereign except through the Rules, structure and operation of a given Society. — Sovereign Individual and Society

48. It is both absurd and false to conclude that an Individual can possess any Sovereign rights separate and distinct from any form of membership to a Society. — Absurd notions of Sovereign and Individual

49. The degree whereby an Individual is recognised as a Sovereign member of a Society is a function of the given Rules of a particular Society; and not necessarily the abilities, knowledge or competence of the Individual. — Rights of Individual and Sovereign

Some societies such as Ucadia recognise Sovereignty as a fundamental right of all members. Other societies consider some members as having limited or impaired rights.

50. An Individual that uses or consumes systems, services, technology or structures of a given lawful and moral society while refusing to be bound to the Rules governing such use or consumption, is by definition a belligerent and one who by their actions chooses to forfeit some or all rights associated with that society.

Article 5 – Civilised Rules & Models

51. The Civilised Rules that constitute any given Society may be properly defined as a **Model of Rules**.

52. In accord with Divine Law, a Model of Rules is an application of one or more Ideas, in a dimension of Reality such as a Civilisation, according to one or more rules and relations, representing a Cause as a conceptual archetype, or axiom, or logical hypothesis.

53. Civilisation as a model is a collection of architectures, models, tools and systems including (but not limited to) languages, law systems, social and political systems, culture and spiritual systems, education and knowledge systems, economic and financial systems, standards, accounting and records systems and technology and infrastructure systems.

54. The very existence of a Civilisation itself depends upon the presence of some representation of a system with rules and relations. In the absence of any such system to give a Civilisation its context and function, a Civilisation cannot be said to exist.

55. The existence of a Civilisation merely depends upon the presence of some distinct representation of a system with rules and relations and not any claimed acceptance or validation or arguments in support of or against such a system by an Observer. Therefore, the existence of a Civilisation is itself proof of its own existence.

56. All Civilisations may be defined by their Relevance, Utility and Versatility:-

    (i) Relevance relates to the quality of the Model of Rules of a Civilisation to meet a desired outcome to some degree. For example, a civilisation of farmers are by their structure of rules and language highly specific to farming and agriculture; and

    (ii) Utility relates to the usefulness of the Model of Rules used by a Civilisation in meeting the desired outcomes of its members. A high utility value indicates a high level of usefulness and usually a consequential high level of success; and

(iii) Versatility relates to the Model of Rules of a Civilisation being able to be applied to achieving different outcomes.

57. All human Civilisation may be properly defined as different types of Civilisations, with different levels of relevance, utility and versatility through their use of Rules as they relate to knowledge, technology, culture and tools. Civilisation types and knowledge

58. Ucadia defines all possible Human Civilisation into seven (7) disciplines and systems being *Trade, Agriculture, Slavery, Military, Technology, Hybrid Negative* and *Hybrid Positive* :- Seven Models of Human Civilisation

   (i) **Trade** is the Ucadia Civilisation of Knowledge and discipline of trade and commerce; and

   (ii) **Agriculture** is the Ucadia Civilisation of Knowledge and discipline of agriculture and farming; and

   (iii) **Slavery** is the Ucadia Model of Civilisation and discipline of slavery; and

   (iv) **Military** is the Ucadia Model of Civilisation and discipline of defence and expansion; and

   (v) **Technology** is the Ucadia Model of Civilisation and discipline of technological advancement; and

   (vi) **Hybrid Negative** is the Ucadia Model of Civilisation and discipline of two (2) or more of the previous models combined together in a negative way, and including *Slavery*; and

   (vii) **Hybrid Positive** is the Ucadia Model of Civilisation and discipline of two (2) or more of the previous models combined together in a positive way excluding *Slavery*.

59. Ucadia defines six (6) possible Models of Civilsation in reference to all Higher Order Life being:- Categories of Models of Civilisation

   (i) Masters of a Colony and Region; and

   (ii) Masters of a Regional Empire; and

   (iii) Masters of a Global Empire; and

   (iv) Masters of a Planet; and

   (v) Masters of a Solar System; and

   (vi) Masters of a Galactic Quadrant.

60. In terms of planet Earth, until the present, only the first four Models of Civilisation have been in operation. However, as Ucadia Civilisation is based on the technology, infrastructure, architecture and model of a Historic Models of Human Civilisation

solar system, planet Earth now possesses a Type Five (v) Model in Ucadia (Masters of a Solar System).

Article 6 – Civilised Rules & Sets

61. The Civilised Rules of a given Society within the Physical (Real) Universe may be properly defined as a Set.

    Civilised Rules & Sets

62. In accord with Divine Law, a ***Set*** is a well defined collection of theoretical or physical Objects or Concepts sharing some similar meanings, attributes or purpose.

    Sets

63. Similar to the Divine Principles of Sets, all Societies may be defined as being a type of Set as it relates to Civilised Law and Ucadia, namely *Empty, Real, Unreal, Semi-Real or Non-Real*: -

    Types of Sets and Society

    (i) The *Empty Set* (**E**) is the fundamental Set containing Nothing and no Society except Ucadia in its theoretical and not-manifested state may be defined as an Empty Set; and

    (ii) A *Real Set* (**R**) in terms of any Society is an abstracted Set from the Empty Set (**E**) that exists and operates according to a set of Civilised Rules and Principles under the Ucadia Model; and

    (iii) An *Unreal Set* (**U**) in terms of any Society is the binary opposite to a Real Set (**R**) that exists and operates according to a set of Uncivilised Rules and Absurd, False and Corrupt Principles yet still within the boundary of Ucadia and the constraints of the Empty Set. This is because No Set may exist in theory or reality outside of the Empty Set; and

    (iv) A Semi-Real Set (**S**) in terms of any Society is an intersection Set or "Subset" or "Sub Society" formed between an intersection of a Real Set (**R**) and an Unreal Set (**U**). Semi-Real Sets as a Sub Society are often throughout history the "doorways" whereby corruption of Civilised Rules and Principles arise; and

    (v) A *Non-Real* Set (**N**) in terms of any Society is the intersection Set or "Subset" or "Sub Society" formed between an intersection of two (or more) Unreal Sets. Non-Real sets are often throughout history the catalyst for calamitous and bloody collapses of societies, often in the form of disordered political and charismatic religious movements seeking to impose "Utopian" or "Dystopian" models.

64. All Sets share the same elementary qualities of *Formation, Members, Boundary, Dimension, Relations, Attributes, Computational State,*

    Civilised Rules as Sets of Society

Function, *Existence* and *Completion State*:

(i) *Formation* means all sets are formed by one or more rules as a product of previously existing sets; and

(ii) *Members* means all sets, except the Empty Set, possess at least one Element as a Member of the set; and

(iii) *Boundary* means all sets possess a boundary that differentiates them from other sets; and

(iv) *Dimension* means every Set possesses two dimensional or three dimensional space defined by the boundary of the set and the space between its member elements such that no two member elements occupy the same position and space within the same set; and

(v) *Relations* means all sets are ultimately a subset of another set except the Empty Set and the Set of One and the Set of Zero; and

(vi) *Attributes* means every set possesses at least one attribute of meaning that every Member of itself then inherits as well; and

(vii) *Computational State* means every set may be abstracted as a step in a computational sequence; and

(viii) *Function* means every set may be abstracted and expressed as a Function and Alphabetic Sequence; and

(ix) *Existence* means that all sets have been abstracted and observed as Proof of Existence or are being observed by an Observer (as actual Existence) to confirm all the elemental qualities as defined; and

(x) *Completion State* means that all sets are either complete or incomplete due to the completion of observation of a computational sequence or the incomplete process of observation by the Observer making key elements indeterminable and therefore approximate.

65. The entirety of a given Society within the Physical (Real) Universe is equivalent to a Uniset of all possible objects, actions, theories, history, culture, rules and phenomena relating to that particular Society. A Society as a Uniset

66. A Society whose laws conform and abide by Ucadia and the present Maxims may be said to be equivalent to a Real Set. Society and Real Set

67. A Society whose laws do not conform and abide by Ucadia and the present Maxims may be said to be equivalent to an Unreal Set. Despite any belligerence or disorder, no Society as a Set can Society and Unreal Set theoretically or logically exist outside of Ucadia or the Empty Set.

68. By Divine Law and Positive Law, every Society is a Subset of Ucadia to some level and degree.

Societies and Ucadia

Article 7 – Civilised Rules & Reality

69. All Civilised Rules of a Society exist within a Set and Dimension of Form and Meaning defined as a Reality.

Civilised Rules & Reality

70. In accord with Divine Law, **Reality** is one of a Binary pair of Models constructed upon certain Rules of Form and Meaning, enabling a certain degree of stability necessary for the existence and function of two or more Theoretical or Real Objects. The opposite Model is **Unreality**.

Reality v Unreality

71. In Relation to Reality and Theoretical or Real Objects within Dimension:

    (i) All Models of Reality are by definition Theoretical. This is because all forms of Reality (and Unreality) are Models; and

    (ii) While all Models of Reality are Theoretical, a Model of Reality may be described as Real to the extent that is presents a comprehensive and well-formed Standard Model of Universal Laws, consistent with the Principle of Relativity and the present Sacred Maxims; and

    (iii) The binary opposite to a Real Model (**R**) of Reality may be defined as Perfectly Unreal Model (**U**) to the extent that it belongs as the opposite to such a Standard Model of Universal Laws and properly completes a consistent conceptual set of all possible Theoretical and Real Objects; and

    (iv) A Model of Reality that seeks to deliberately contradict the present Sacred Maxims, or obstinately or belligerently persist with false and absurd Concepts that cannot possibly form a Standard Model nor reasonable Universal Laws is said to be a Delusional Model of Reality, or simply a "Delusion".

Reality within Dimension

72. Reality of a Society permits a functional Model of Existence excluding the existence of Paradox and Relativity. Thus within the fictional Universe of Reality, in accordance with the most sacred Covenant *Pactum De Singularis Caelum* and the present sacred Maxims, the Concept of Absolute Truth may exist and the certainty of Logic and Reason may be applied.

Reality and a functional Model of Civilised Society

73. A Model of Reality in relation to any Society is always bound as a Binary Pair to a particular Model of Unreality. By definition and necessity, a Model of Reality can only exist when its constituent

Models of Society and the existence of Reality

Model of Unreality also exists under the same System of Rules.

74. Any argument in support of a Social Model of Reality, that fails or denies its Binary relation and dependence to the existence of an opposite Model of Unreality, is therefore an absurdity and sign of delusion.
Reality and a functional Model of Civilised Society

75. The definition of any alternate Social Reality that is inconsistent with the present sacred Maxims and the most sacred Covenant *Pactum De Singularis Caelum* is automatically null and void from the beginning.
Definition of an alternate Reality

76. None may validly or authentically challenge the Reality of a body or society named and given life through the most sacred Covenant *Pactum De Singularis Caelum,* unless such a body or society repudiates the fundamental tenets of the Rule of Law and Justice and the most sacred instrument that gives it life and authority.
Reality and the Rule of Law and Justice

77. A Concept or Object or Thing that cannot be proven to exist in Reality consistent with the present sacred Maxims has no Existence in Law. Any Edict, Decree, Command, Demand, Order, Judgement or Opinion that contradicts one or more of the present sacred Maxims cannot be Real and therefore has no valid Existence.
Reality and Positive Law

Article 8 – Civilised Rules & Awareness

78. The existence and presence of Civilised Rules within any given Society may be properly defined as a function of Awareness to some degree.
Civilised Rules & Awareness

79. In accord with Divine Law, **Awareness** is the present and continuous ability to receive, conceive, perceive, comprehend or discern complex information concerning various concepts, or objects, or conditions or events and anticipate or react accordingly.
Awareness

80. Elemental Awareness is a Model of Awareness created conceptually or actually as the minimum requirements for System whereby each fundamental unit possesses certain autonomous awareness to enable independent computation of its state and position relative to other units. Elemental Awareness is also the seventh Law of the Twelve Laws of Divine Creation.
Elemental Awareness

81. In relation to any given Society, the essential function of Elemental Awareness depends upon:
Elemental Awareness and Society

   (i) A *Social Model of Reality* whereby Concepts or Objects may be defined according to different properties, qualities and states; and

   (ii) A *Social System of Rules* associated with the Social Model of Reality whereby the presence or anticipation of one or more

Objects or Concepts may cause the change in state of a related Object or Concept; and

(iii) A theoretical or physical *Instructional Language* based upon finite sets of choices, whereby such properties, qualities and states of Concepts or Objects may be encoded or decoded into informational and instructional algorithms of different functions; and

(iv) A theoretical or physical *Social System of Functions* capable of being used to construct algorithms for the encoding of information and instructions; and

(v) A *Computational Model* being a theoretical or physical system capable of reading and enumerating certain algorithms of functions within some informational language based upon a finite set of choices, whereby the execution of such algorithms may cause some change in state of one or more Objects or Concepts.

82. The presence of Elemental Awareness in a Societal System and Model of Reality is not a sign of self-awareness, but the fact that the fundamental elements of such a Social Reality have the instructional and informational capability and independence of functioning without the need for direct instruction or intervention by the Observer.

Article 9 – Civilised Rules & Complexity

83. All Civilised Rules of a given Society possess some degree of complexity or simplicity.

84. In accord with Divine Law, **Complexity** is a binary concept with Simplicity and means the state or quality of being complex and not simple, whereas **Simplicity** is a binary concept with Complexity and means the state or quality of being simple and not complex.

85. In respect of Society and Complexity:-

(i) Complexity does not mean disorder or confusion, but an inability to simply describe a resulting state or behaviour; and

(ii) Complexity does not mean Chaos, as Chaos by authentic definition means a great chasm or void, whereas Complexity depends upon numerous Objects acting in complex behaviour; and

(iii) Complexity does not mean instability, but the difficulty in predicting repetitive and perfect behaviour; and

(iv) Existence depends upon the Complexity of Autonomous Behaviour; and

(v) All Complex Behaviour in Theory can be described and expressed through simple rules, therefore the predictability of simple Algorithms is possible; and

(vi) Not all Complex Behaviour in Reality can be described and reduced to Algorithms. This is the Principle of Computational Irreducibility; and

(vii) As all Complexity in Theory may be expressed through simple Algorithms, all Complexity in Theory may be simplified to a minimum level of meaningful expression.

86. In respect of Society and Simplicity:- *Relative to Simplicity and Society*

(i) Simplicity does not mean lacking in sophistication as the simplest of axioms of the Universe are the most elegant and sophisticated, whereas Complex Designed Algorithms frequently produce unreliable and inflexible results that do not reflect any true Law of the Universe; and

(ii) Simplicity does not mean Determinism as the Universe relies upon Simple Algorithms to produce Complex and unpredictable behaviours, whereas Deterministic Systems are normally complex in design yet produce repetitive and unreal behaviours; and

(iii) The binary relation and existence of Simplicity to Complexity and Vice Versa is evidenced throughout all levels of Existence; and

(iv) A Binary relation between the Infinitesimal and the Infinite exists as evidence of such binding between the Simplest and most Complex; and

(v) Existence depends upon the Simplicity of Rules; and

(vi) The Simplest and most perfect and elegant Axiom of all Axioms is the Meaning of ALL means "Awareness Loves Life".

Article 10 – Civilised Rules & The Divine

87. The Civilised Rules of any given Society are a subset of the rules as defined by the total set known as the Divine. *Civilised Rules & The Divine*

88. In accord with Divine Law, the **Divine** means the total set of all meanings and definitions of all possible concepts, objects, matter, rules, life, mind, universe and spirit; and also means the Absolute, ALL, Divine Creator, Father, God, Almighty, Allah, Great Spirit, *The Divine*

Unique Collective Awareness, UCADIA and all other historic, customary and traditional names when used to describe the greatest of all possibilities.

89. As the Divine means the "concept of all concepts" and the "set of all sets" there is no greater concept nor set. Therefore, every other possible concept or object or set including (but not limited to) every conceivable type of society and social structure is lesser.   *No Greater Concept or Set*

90. As the Divine means the "concept of all concepts" and the "set of all sets", all possible and actual concepts, objects and sets of concepts and objects are by definition part of the Divine, including (but not limited to) every conceivable type of society and social structure.   *All Possible & Actual Concepts, Objects and Sets*

Article 11 – Civilised Rules & Nature

91. The Civilised Rules of any given Society are a subset of the rules as defined by the total set known as Nature.   *Civilised Rules & Nature*

92. In accord with Natural Law, **Nature** means all objects, properties, rules, relations, forces and phenomena of the natural, physical, or material world and universe, independent of human technology and civilisation.   *Nature*

93. As Nature defines the operation and existence of the entire physical universe, all societies are subject to Nature and Natural Law to some degree. However, as human beings are also subject to Cognitive Law, it is a false presumption to assume a society is wholly and totally dependent upon and a mirror of Natural Law.   *Every Society is subject to Natural Law to some degree*

Article 12 – Positive Law

94. **Positive Law** is the set of laws enacted by valid associations of living higher order beings through proper authority in accordance with these Maxims for the governance of a body or community or society. All valid Positive Law may be said to be derived from authentic Natural Law and Cognitive Law.   *Positive Law*

95. A Positive Law is established and takes force when it is promulgated in accord with these Maxims; and begins to oblige a month after the day of promulgation unless the Law itself establishes another time period.   *Establishment of Positive Law*

96. Excluding Ecclesiastical Law, all Positive Laws regard the present and future, not the past. Only Ecclesiastical Laws may refer to the past as such laws by their nature are firmly bound to Divine Law.   *Excluding Ecclesiastical Law, Positive Law binds future not past Acts*

97. Any Positive Law that seeks to promulgate a retrospective rule that is not Ecclesiastical in nature or authority is by definition morally repugnant and shall have no validity or legitimacy or force or effect. — *Retrospective Positive Law having no force or effect*

98. Any Positive Law that is morally repugnant contradicts the very nature of what is Law; and therefore cannot be a valid or legitimate Law; and shall have no force or effect from the moment it is enacted. — *Morally Repugnant Positive Law*

99. Ecclesiastical Law binds all those who belong and have been accepted into the body of a valid faith in accord with the most sacred Covenant *Pactum De Singularis Caelum* and associated Covenants. — *Effect of Ecclesiastical Law*

100. All other lesser Positive Laws issued by a competent legislator bind those who are actually present within the jurisdiction of the particular juridic or legislative or political body. — *Lesser Positive Laws*

101. Particular Positive Laws are not presumed to be personal but territorial in relation to the jurisdiction of the competent legislator who issued the law, unless it is otherwise evident. — *Territorial effect of Positive Laws*

102. Any rule that is against the Law cannot have the legitimacy and validity of Law, nor the force and effect of Law. — *Rules that are against the Law*

Article 13 – Divine Law & Positive Law

103. In accord with Divine Law, all valid Positive Law may be said to be derived from authentic Divine Law. — *Divine Law & Positive Law*

104. In accord with Divine Law, Divine Law is the Law that defines the Divine and clearly demonstrates the spirit, mind, purpose and instruction of the Divine including the operation of the will of the Divine through existence. All authoritative and legitimate Law is derived from Divine Law in accord with the present sacred Maxims. — *Divine Law*

105. There exists four simple proofs concerning the dependence of all forms of Positive Law upon Divine Law:- — *Proofs of Divine Law and Positive Law*

   (i) *First*, as the Divine means the "concept of all concepts" and the "set of all sets" there is no greater concept nor set. Therefore any and all forms of Positive Law must by definition be considered a Subset; and

   (ii) *Second*, a proper Law must be moral. The highest theoretical or actual possible expression of Moral Law is Divine Law. Therefore, any and all forms of Civilised Rules and Principles must be considered a Subset of Divine Law; and

   (iii) *Third*, the function and procedure of Law depends on certain concepts, forms and objects including (but not limited to) Persons, Trust, Registers, Rolls and Rights. In each and every case, the highest possible form and definition of such concepts, forms and objects are found in the most Sacred Covenant *Pactum De Singularis Caelum*; and

(iv) *Fourth*, there is no higher theoretical or actual covenant, constitution, instrument or object of law than the most Sacred Covenant *Pactum De Singularis Caelum*. Therefore all other forms of laws, canons, maxims, constitutions, covenants, charters and agreements are lesser and subject to it.

106. All Rights and therefore all forms of proper Laws and Justice originate from Divine Law and therefore the most sacred Covenant *Pactum De Singularis Caelum*:- [Divine Source of Positive Law]

(i) Divine Law is the law that defines the Divine and all creation, and demonstrates the spirit and mind and instruction of the Divine, and the operation of the will of the Divine Creator through existence. Therefore all valid Rights and Justice are derived from Divine Law; and

(ii) Natural Law is the law that defines the operation of the will of the Divine, through the existence of form and sky and earth and physical rules. Thus Natural Law governs the operation of what we can see and name; and

(iii) Civilised Rules as Positive Laws are those rules enacted by men and women having proper authority, for the good governance of a society under the Rule of Law. The laws of People are always inherited from Natural Law and Cognitive Law and ultimately Divine Law.

107. As Divine Law is the highest possible form of Law and the source of all lesser forms of law, any argument that asserts Divine Law does not exist, or is less than some other form of law is therefore false, absurd and in gross error. [Divine Law as highest possible form of Law]

Article 14 – Natural Law & Positive Law

108. In accord with Divine Law, all valid Positive Law may be said to be derived from authentic Natural Law. [Natural Law & Positive Law]

109. In accord with Divine Law, Natural Law is the law that defines the operation of the will of the Divine through Existence in the form of all matter and all physical rules. As Natural Laws define the operation and existence of the entire physical universe, all proper and authentic Natural Law may be said to be derived from Divine Law. [Natural Law]

110. In accord with Divine Law, a Positive Law cannot abrogate, suspend, nor change a Cognitive Law or Natural Law. Therefore, any rule [Limits of Positive Law in respect of]

claimed to be Positive Law that usurps, denies or contradicts a Natural Law or Cognitive Law is null and void from the beginning, having no valid or legitimate force or effect whatsoever.

Natural Law

Article 15 – Cognitive Law & Positive Law

111. In accord with Divine Law, all valid Positive Law may be said to be derived from authentic Natural Law and Cognitive Law.

Cognitive Law & Positive Law

112. In accord with Divine Law, Cognitive Law is the set of laws that define the special attributes possessed by certain higher order life such as mind, ideas, knowledge, recognition and self-awareness created through the simultaneous application of both Divine Law and Natural Law. As Cognitive Law is derived from the simultaneous application of Divine Law and Natural Law, all valid Cognitive Law may be defined as part "divine" and part "natural", hence "supernatural".

Cognitive Law

113. In accord with Divine Law, a Positive Law cannot abrogate, suspend, nor change a Cognitive Law or Natural Law. Therefore, any rule claimed to be Positive Law that usurps, denies or contradicts a Natural Law or Cognitive Law is null and void from the beginning, having no valid or legitimate force or effect whatsoever.

Limits of Positive Law in respect of Cognitive Law

1.2 – Civilised Principles

Article 16 – Civilised Principles of Law

114. ***Civilised Principles of Law*** are foundational concepts essential to the fabric of rules that govern a vibrant, happy and democratic society. All sustained and successful human civilisations have embedded the Civilised Principles of Law into the foundations of all their societies.

Civilised Principles of Law

115. Civilised principles of law are the foundations of all societies of human civilisation. While a Society may not possess every Civilised Principle of Law, happy, prosperous and free societies possess at least a majority of such principles.

Foundations of happy, successful and sustainable societies

116. There exists ten (10) Civilised Principles of Law above all others being:-

    (i)   Public Rule & Function of Law; and

    (ii)   Simplicity & Morality of Law; and

    (iii) Openness & Integrity of Law; and

    (iv) Transparency & Awareness of Formation of Law; and

Ten Civilised Principles

(v) Knowledge & Respect of Rights of Law; and

(vi) Equality & Fair Application of Law; and

(vii) Independence & Impartiality of Officers of Law; and

(viii) Fair & Expeditious Procedure of Law; and

(ix) Oversight & Accountability of Administration of Law; and

(x) Sensibility & Mercy of Enforcement of Law.

117. No Civilised Principle of Law is difficult or impossible to implement, except in societies or communities where individuals and organisations do not have the will or wish to do so. *Practical nature of all Civilised Principles*

118. Each and every Civilised Principle of Law possesses a historic nature having been implemented in previous or present societies and communities, such that no Civilised Principle may be argued as "theoretical" or "untested". *Historic nature of all Civilised Principles*

Article 17 – Public Rule & Function of Law

119. *Public Rule & Function of Law* is a *Civilised Principle of Law* that defines the fundamental truth that the ownership and function of the systems and structures of law and justice must be public, owned by the public, accessible to the public and held in trust and good management solely for the benefit of the public. *Public Rule & Function of Law*

120. *Public Rule & Function of Law* is the first of the ten *Civilised Principles of Law* of any sustainable, vibrant and enlightened society. The opposite is the uncivilised principle of *Private Rule & Function of Law*. *Public Rule & Function of Law as First Principle*

121. Common Elements of *Public Rule & Function of Law* include (but are not limited to):- *Common Elements of Public Rule & Function of Law*

 (i) All assets of every kind associated with the fundamental function of law are public and not owned, operated or run by any private society, corporation or entity of any kind; and

 (ii) All courts of criminal and public law are truly public courts of record and not operated or run by any private society, corporation or entity of any kind; and

 (iii) All facilities of detention, imprisonment or corrections are publicly owned and managed and not owned, operated or run by any private society, corporation or entity of any kind; and

 (iv) All services of police and law enforcement are public with public officers under oath and obligation and not owned, operated or run by any private society, corporation or entity of any kind; and

(v) All court officials are public servants under oath and bond with no court official permitted to hold any office or function if they have made an oath or vow to a private society, corporation or entity of any kind that contradicts or mitigates their public duties; and

(vi) All legal professionals that interact in any way with public courts are registered agents of such courts and no such person is permitted to act in such capacity if they have made an oath or vow to a private society, corporation or entity of any kind that contradicts or mitigates their public duties; and

(vii) No one may be denied from registering or acting as an agent of a public court on the basis of not being a member to some private society, corporation or entity of any kind; and

(viii) No one may be denied from being accepted and registered as an agent of a public court where their capacity, competence and present conduct qualifies them for such recognition.

122. All proper and valid Ucadia societies within Ucadia Civilisation are founded upon and adhere to the *Civilised Principle of Law* of *Public Rule & Function of Law*. *(Ucadia & Public Rule & Function of Law)*

Article 18 – Simplicity & Morality of Law

123. **Simplicity & Morality of Law** is a *Civilised Principle of Law* that defines the immutable fact that all proper law is moral, clear and simple to understand by all. *(Simplicity & Morality of Law)*

124. *Simplicity & Morality of Law* is the second of the ten *Civilised Principles of Law* of any sustainable, vibrant and enlightened society. The opposite is the uncivilised principle of *Complexity & Moral Repugnancy of Law*. *(Simplicity & Morality of Law as Second Principle)*

125. Common Elements of *Simplicity & Morality of Law* include (but are not limited to):- *(Common Elements of Simplicity & Morality of Law)*

(i) All laws are moral so that no law permits morally repugnant, or profane or sacrilegious activity; and

(ii) All laws are logical so that no law is illogical in asserting certain errors and fallacies to demand such absurdities are defended and enforced; and

(iii) All laws are reasonable so that no law demands an unreasonable or impossible act; and

(iv) All laws are respectful so that no law disrespects a person purely upon the original circumstance of their birth, location, gender, race, religion or creed; and

(v) All laws are consistent so that no laws require contradictory or confusing behaviour; and

(vi) All laws are remedial so that no law imposes punitive measures without first the opportunity to rectify or remedy an error; and

(vii) All laws are merciful so that no law encourages cruel and barbarous acts of vengeance.

126. All proper and valid Ucadia societies within Ucadia Civilisation are founded upon and adhere to the *Civilised Principle of Law* of *Simplicity & Morality of Law*.

Ucadia & Simplicity & Morality of Law

Article 19 – Openness & Integrity of Law

127. **Openness & Integrity of Law** is a *Civilised Principle of Law* that defines the fundamental fact that all proper law is open, clear and honest.

Openness & Integrity of Law

128. *Openness & Integrity of Law* is the third of the ten *Civilised Principles of Law* of any sustainable, vibrant and enlightened society. The opposite is the uncivilised principle of *Obfuscation & Corruption of Law*.

Openness & Integrity of Law as Third Principle

129. Common Elements of *Openness & Integrity of Law* include (but are not limited to):-

Common Elements of Openness & Integrity of Law

(i) All laws are simple and easily publicly available so that one person may reasonably learn, remember and comprehend all such laws properly; and

(ii) All laws are honest so that no law misrepresents the truth nor compels deliberately dishonest or fraudulent behaviour; and

(iii) All laws are loyal so that no law endorses treacherous or disloyal acts.

130. All proper and valid Ucadia societies within Ucadia Civilisation are founded upon and adhere to the *Civilised Principle of Law* of *Openness & Integrity of Law*.

Ucadia & Openness & Integrity of Law

Article 20 – Transparency & Awareness of Formation of Law

131. ***Transparency & Awareness of Formation of Law*** is a Civilised Principle of Law that defines a key principle whereby the making of any new laws must be both transparent and abundantly clear to everyone in the public to whom such a new law may apply.

132. *Transparency & Awareness of Formation of Law* is the fourth of the ten *Civilised Principles of Law* of any sustainable, vibrant and enlightened society. The opposite is the uncivilised principle of *Suppression & Secrecy of Formation of Law*.

133. Common Elements of *Transparency & Awareness of Formation of Law* include (but are not limited to):-

    (i) Each and every new and proposed law is known and allowed to be publicly debated before vote; and

    (ii) Each and every existing or proposed law reflects the proper form and procedures prescribed by law in relation to the process of enacting law; and

    (iii) Each and every existing or proposed law exists in such a clear and precise form that it is limited in the number of pages required to express it; and

    (iv) Each and every proposed statute or bill addresses only its purpose and does not permit attachments or amendments or additions that do not specifically and narrowly pertain to the primary purpose of the statute or bill; and

    (v) An existing or proposed law only applies to the limits of jurisdiction of the legislature that issued it. Thus such a body cannot legally or lawfully abrogate the laws of a higher estate, trust or society that it belongs.

134. All proper and valid Ucadia societies within Ucadia Civilisation are founded upon and adhere to the *Civilised Principle of Law* of *Transparency & Awareness of Formation of Law*.

Article 21 – Knowledge & Respect of Rights of Law

135. ***Knowledge & Respect of Rights of Law*** is a Civilised Principle of Law that defines a fundamental truth that proper law respects the rights and knowledge of law of a society.

136. *Knowledge & Respect of Rights of Law* is the fifth of the ten *Civilised*

Principles of Law of any sustainable, vibrant and enlightened society. The opposite is the uncivilised principle of *Ignorance & Disrespect of Rights of Law*.

Rights of Law as Fifth Principle

137. Common Elements of *Knowledge & Respect of Rights of Law* include (but are not limited to):-

    (i) All possess the right to be heard, whether or not we agree with the ideas expressed; and

    (ii) All possess the right of free will to choose our beliefs, actions and destiny; and

    (iii) All possess the right of their own thoughts and opinions, as no one can rightfully claim ownership of your own mind, except you; and

    (iv) All possess the right of their own body and no force may rightfully claim possession over your flesh, unless your mind surrenders and allows it to be so; and

    (v) All possess the right of their own name and identity of birth as no person, corporation, or group may claim ownership of your name or identity; and

    (vi) All possess the right of their own face and voice as no person, corporation, or group may claim ownership of your name or identity; and

    (vii) All possess the right of their own cellular and genetic material as no person, corporation, or group may claim ownership of the cells of your body or the genetic code that forms life and who and what we are; and

    (viii) All possess the right to informed consent or withdraw consent; and

    (ix) All possess the right and ability of reason, through the existence of their conscience; and

    (x) All possess the right to adequate, fair and reasonable shelter, clean water, clothing and food; and

    (xi) All possess the right to peaceful assembly; and

    (xii) All possess the right to have their rights respected.

Common Elements of Knowledge & Respect of Rights of Law

138. All proper and valid Ucadia societies within Ucadia Civilisation are founded upon and adhere to the *Civilised Principle of Law* of *Knowledge & Respect of Rights of Law*.

Ucadia & Knowledge & Respect of Rights of Law

Article 22 – Equality & Fair Application of Law

139. ***Equality & Fair Application of Law*** is a Civilised Principle of Law that defines a cornerstone principle that all are equal under the law and that the law must always be fair in its application.

140. *Equality & Fair Application of Law* is the sixth of the ten *Civilised Principles of Law* of any sustainable, vibrant and enlightened society. The opposite is the uncivilised principle of *Unequal & Unfair Application of Law*.

141. Common Elements of *Equality & Fair Application of Law* include (but are not limited to):-

    (i) All are equal under the law; and

    (ii) All are without blemish until proven culpable; and

    (iii) An action in law cannot proceed without first a cause; and

    (iv) An action is not granted to one who is not injured; and

    (v) No one may derive an advantage in law from his own wrong, as no action through law can arise from a fraud before heaven and earth; and

    (vi) Fraud invalidates everything of a cause and action, for no action through law can arise in bad faith or unclean hands or vexatious prejudice; and

    (vii) What was illegitimate, fraudulent and invalid from the beginning does not become valid over time; and

    (viii) An action alone does not make one culpable unless there is intent to do wrong, or evidence of deliberate and wilful ignorance contrary to reasonable behaviour; and

    (ix) No one may suffer punishment by valid law for mere intent alone; and

    (x) No one may be punished for the transgression of an ancestor or another; and

    (xi) No one is accused of the same exact cause twice; and

    (xii) No penalty may exist without a valid law; and

    (xiii) No penalty may be issued without first proof of injury and secondly the right of defence.

142. All proper and valid Ucadia societies within Ucadia Civilisation are founded upon and adhere to the *Civilised Principle of Law* of *Equality & Fair Application of Law*.

Article 23 – Independence & Impartiality of Officers of Law

143. ***Independence & Impartiality of Officers of Law*** is a Civilised Principle of Law that defines a key principle that all who function and hold positions within the systems of law of a society must at all times exhibit both independence and impartiality in the execution of their duties.

144. *Independence & Impartiality of Officers of Law* is the seventh of the ten *Civilised Principles of Law* of any sustainable, vibrant and enlightened society. The opposite is the uncivilised principle of *Compromised & Partiality of Officers of Law*.

145. Common Elements of *Independence & Impartiality of Officers of Law* include (but are not limited to):-

    (i) All Officers and Agents of Law are independent in their appointment as having no allegiance except the public good; and

    (ii) All Officers and Agents of Law are bound by their oath (or vows) to act with impartiality in the execution of their duties; and

    (iii) An Officer of Law presiding or participating over a legal matter is duty bound to first disclose any and all financial interests in the matter; and

    (iv) A Judge or Magistrate is forbidden to oversee any legal matter where they possess a financial interest in the matter itself or any judicial decision or judgement in the matter; and

    (v) A Judge or Magistrate is obligated in good character and conscience to recuse themselves without application by any other party, if they possess a financial interest or are unable to act with true impartiality in the matter.

146. All proper and valid Ucadia societies within Ucadia Civilisation are founded upon and adhere to the *Civilised Principle of Law* of *Independence & Impartiality of Officers of Law*.

Article 24 – Fair & Expeditious Procedure of Law

147. ***Fair & Expeditious Procedure of Law*** is a Civilised Principle of Law that defines a key principle that the procedure of the law must be both fair and expeditious or "timely" in its function.

148. *Fair & Expeditious Procedure of Law* is the eighth of the ten *Civilised Principles of Law* of any sustainable, vibrant and enlightened society.

The opposite is the uncivilised principle of *Unfair & Egregious Procedure of Law*.

Law as Eighth Principle

149. Common Elements of *Fair & Expeditious Procedure of Law* include (but are not limited to):-

    (i) All matters of accusation must be processed expeditiously so as not to cause further injury; and

    (ii) If a claim be not proven as a valid cause then the accused has nothing to answer. Yet if the claim be proved to have merit as a cause, then all valid causes in law must be resolved; and

    (iii) The one who first brings the claim must first prove its merit, as the burden of the proof lies upon the one who accuses not the one who denies; and

    (iv) One who makes false testimony, especially under oath within a forum of law, must face the full force of justice against them;

    (v) If merit of a cause be proved, the one accused must appear to answer; and

    (vi) The accused possesses the right to self defence in all minor matters but not in the defence of notorious and serious accusations, unless they first are able to prove their competence at law; and

    (vii) No man or woman be a judge over their own matter; and

    (viii) No man or woman possesses the moral or legal authority of heaven or earth to be judge, jury and executioner; and

    (ix) Judges are bound to explain the reason of their judgement.

Common Elements of Fair & Expeditious Procedure of Law

150. All proper and valid Ucadia societies within Ucadia Civilisation are founded upon and adhere to the *Civilised Principle of Law* of *Fair & Expeditious Procedure of Law*.

Ucadia & Fair & Expeditious Procedure of Law

Article 25 – Oversight & Accountability of Administration of Law

151. ***Oversight & Accountability of Administration of Law*** is a Civilised Principle of Law that defines an important principle that every society must have the capacity, systems and will to apply oversight and hold accountable all those who operate throughout the systems and structures of law.

Oversight & Accountability of Administration of Law

152. *Oversight & Accountability of Administration of Law* is the ninth of the ten *Civilised Principles of Law* of any sustainable, vibrant and enlightened society. The opposite is the uncivilised principle of

Oversight of Administration of Law as Ninth Principle

Immunity & Unaccountability of Administration of Law.

153. Common Elements of *Oversight & Accountability of Administration of Law* include (but are not limited to):-

    (i) Oversight and accountability bodies exist for every level and function of law, so that no one may escape accountability or due diligence; and

    (ii) All Officers and Agents of Law may be held accountable for their actions when they fail to execute their duties in accord with the rule of law; and

    (iii) Judges and Magistrates may be held personally liable when they fail to act with good character and conscience in the performance of their duties.

154. All proper and valid Ucadia societies within Ucadia Civilisation are founded upon and adhere to the *Civilised Principle of Law* of *Oversight & Accountability of Administration of Law*.

Article 26 – Sensibility & Mercy of Enforcement of Law

155. ***Sensibility & Mercy of Enforcement of Law*** is a Civilised Principle of Law that defines a core principle that in the enforcement of law, all who hold such positions must demonstrate both a sensibility as well as a degree of mercy in their duties.

156. *Sensibility & Mercy of Enforcement of Law* is the tenth of the ten *Civilised Principles of Law* of any sustainable, vibrant and enlightened society. The opposite is the uncivilised principle of *Incompetence & Cruelty of Enforcement of Law*.

157. Common Elements of *Sensibility & Mercy of Enforcement of Law* include (but are not limited to):-

    (i) Fairness and common sense exists at all levels of the systems of law; and

    (ii) Mercy is always considered in the execution of serious sentences so that the injury of actions may be healed and people may learn and recidivism rates are as low as possible.

158. All proper and valid Ucadia societies within Ucadia Civilisation are founded upon and adhere to the *Civilised Principle of Law* of *Sensibility & Mercy of Enforcement of Law*.

1.3 – Uncivilised, Immoral & Absurd Principles

Article 27 – Uncivilised, Immoral & Absurd Principles

159. ***Uncivilised Principles of Law*** are foundational concepts essential to identification of morally repugnant, illogical, absurd and corrupt practices that imprison and oppress societies of people. — Uncivilised Principles of Law

160. The failure of every empire and human civilisation from the beginning of time can be strongly attributed to the presence of two or more Uncivilised Principles. — Civilisation and Empire failures

161. There exists ten (10) Uncivilised, Immoral and Absurd Principles of Law. Each is a mirror opposite to a particular Civilised Principle, with the list being:- — Ten Uncivilised, Immoral & Absurd Principles

    (i) Private Rule & Function of Law; and

    (ii) Complexity & Moral Repugnancy of Law; and

    (iii) Obfuscation & Corruption of Law; and

    (iv) Suppression & Secrecy of Formation of Law; and

    (v) Ignorance & Disrespect of Rights of Law; and

    (vi) Unequal & Unfair Application of Law; and

    (vii) Compromised & Partiality of Officers of Law; and

    (viii) Unfair & Egregious Procedure of Law; and

    (ix) Immunity & Unaccountability of Administration of Law; and

    (x) Incompetence & Cruelty of Enforcement of Law.

162. No Society or Community should be condemned upon awareness and overwhelming evidence of one or more Uncivilised, Immoral and Absurd Principles of Law existing within it, to the extent that the leadership and law enforcement community seek to engage in authentic and practical reform. — Non Condemnation of Society or Community suffering internal failures or collapses

163. There typically exists four standard responses within the leadership and enforcers of a given society or community that knowingly and intentionally applies one or more Uncivilised, Immoral and Absurd Principles of Law being *Excuse, Denial, Double-Speak* or *Attack*:- — Four standard responses to identification and exposure of presence of Uncivilised, Immoral and Absurd Principles of Law

    (i) *Excuse* is when one or more excuses are given to justify the presence of one or more Uncivilised, Immoral and Absurd Principles of Law. Such a response is only possible with a complicit and compliant media; and

    (ii) *Denial* is when overwhelming evidence is ignored in a kind of "head in the sand" or "say nothing" response when confronted with the existence of one or more Uncivilised, Immoral and Absurd Principles of Law. Such a response is only possible with a complicit and compliant media; and

(iii) *Double-Speak* is when the response to overwhelming evidence of the presence of one or more Uncivilised, Immoral and Absurd Principles of Law is confusing, convoluted and deliberately distracting double -speak. Such a response is frequently the approach of dictators and regimes; and

(iv) *Attack* is when overwhelming evidence of the presence of one or more Uncivilised, Immoral and Absurd Principles of Law is met with attacking and discrediting the researchers of the evidence. This response is only possible with a complicit and compliant legal community.

164. No excuse, no matter how compelling, can justify the continued presence of one or more Uncivilised, Immoral and Absurd Principles of Law within a given Society or Community:-

    No excuse is adequate to justify presence of Uncivilised, Immoral and Absurd Principles of Law

(i) Excuses and arguments such as "national emergency", "health emergency", "security", "privacy" or "common good" are not only absurd in the face of the damage and corruption done by Uncivilised, Immoral and Absurd Principles of Law, but are immoral, perverse arguments in themselves; and

(ii) No excuse can adequately justify the fact that the only reason one or more Uncivilised, Immoral and Absurd Principles of Law exist within a given Society or Community is because one or more individuals wish it to be so, for some specific advantage.

165. No Court within a given Society or Community where one or more Uncivilised, Immoral and Absurd Principles of Law exist may logically, reasonably or sensibly argue jurisdiction or authority over Ucadia, or any duly appointed Officer of Ucadia.

    Ucadia and Courts of Uncivilised Societies & Communities

Article 28 – Private Rule & Function of Law

166. ***Private Rule & Function of Law*** is an Uncivilised, Immoral and Absurd Principle of Law that defines fundamental and incontrovertible truth of the corruption, breakdown, theft, betrayal, treason or collapse of Civilised Rule and Principles of Law when some (or all) of the ownership and function of the systems and structures of law and justice have been privatised, sold, leased or granted to private societies or guilds or companies; or access has been restricted or limited to the public; or held in secret or private trust for the

    Private Rule & Function of Law

benefit of a few and not the public.

167. *Private Rule & Function of Law* is the first of the ten *Uncivilised, Immoral & Absurd Principles* of any failing, dying or despotic society. The opposite is the civilised principle of *Public Rule & Function of Law*.

Private Rule & Function of Law & Uncivilised Principles as First Principle

168. Common Evidence of *Private Rule & Function of Law* includes (but is not limited to):-

Common Evidence of Private Rule & Function of Law

  (i) Assets of all kinds associated with the fundamental function of law are no longer public, but owned, operated or run by private societies, corporations and entities; and

  (ii) Courts of criminal and public law are no longer public courts of record but instead are operated or run by private societies, corporations and entities; and

  (iii) Facilities of detention, imprisonment or corrections are privately owned, operated or run by private societies, corporations and entities; and

  (iv) Services of police and law enforcement are private contractors employed by private societies, corporations and entities; and

  (v) Court officials are private contractors or members of private societies and associations, whereby such membership or employment contradicts or mitigates their public duties; and

  (vi) Legal professionals are first members of private societies or associations and frequently employed by private firms whereby their duties and obligations are not aligned to any sense of true justice or rule of law, but profit and their own fraternities; and

  (vii) No one may represent another in legal matters normally without first being a member of a private society or association, thereby denying open and public access to the function of law; and

  (viii) A person suitably competent, with sufficient capacity and conduct may yet be denied to represent another (or themselves) in forums of law, for lack of membership to the right society or fraternity.

169. No Court within a given Society or Community that operates under Private Guild Laws and Procedures shall have jurisdiction over any proper and valid Ucadia Society or duly appointed Officer of Ucadia whatsoever.

Ucadia & Private Rule & Function of Law

170. Ucadia Courts shall at all times possess the Divine and Moral

Ucadia Courts

Authority to order a matter within a Private Guild Court to be vacated to a proper public court operating under Rule of Law.

Article 29 – Complexity & Moral Repugnancy of Law

171. ***Complexity & Moral Repugnancy of Law*** is an Uncivilised, Immoral and Absurd Principle of Law that defines the immutable fact that all uncivilised law is immoral and frequently unclear and complex to all but a small specially chosen minority. Complexity & Moral Repugnancy of Law

172. *Complexity & Moral Repugnancy of Law* is the second of the ten *Uncivilised, Immoral & Absurd Principles* of any failing, dying or despotic society. The opposite is the civilised principle of *Simplicity & Morality of Law*. Complexity & Moral Repugnancy of Law as Second Principle

173. Common Evidence of *Complexity & Moral Repugnancy of Law* includes (but is not limited to):- Common Evidence of Complexity & Moral Repugnancy of Law

    (i) Laws are morally repugnant, or profane or permit sacrilegious activity; and

    (ii) Laws are illogical in asserting certain errors and fallacies to demand such absurdities are defended and enforced; and

    (iii) Laws are unreasonable and demand certain impossible acts; and

    (iv) Laws are inconsistent so that certain laws require contradictory or confusing behaviour; and

    (v) Laws are punitive without first the opportunity to rectify or remedy an error; and

    (vi) Laws that encourage cruel and barbarous acts of vengeance.

174. No claimed law from any Society or Community whereby such a claimed law is morally repugnant shall have any force or effect against Ucadia, or any valid Society or authorised Officer. Ucadia & Complexity & Moral Repugnancy of Law

Article 30 – Obfuscation & Corruption of Law

175. ***Obfuscation & Corruption of Law*** is an Uncivilised, Immoral and Absurd Principle of Law that defines a fundamental and logical tenet that immoral law is a highly corrosive form of corruption, often hidden through means of obfuscation and distraction. Obfuscation & Corruption of Law

176. *Obfuscation & Corruption of Law* is the third of the ten *Uncivilised, Immoral & Absurd Principles* of any failing, dying or despotic society. The opposite is the civilised principle of *Openness & Integrity of Law*.

    Obfuscation & Corruption of Law as Third Principle

177. Common Evidence of *Obfuscation & Corruption of Law* includes (but is not limited to):-

    Common Evidence of Obfuscation & Corruption of Law

  (i) Laws are complex and not all publicly available so that no one person may reasonably learn, remember and comprehend all such laws properly; and

  (ii) Laws are dishonest so that some laws misrepresent the truth or compels deliberately dishonest or fraudulent behaviour; and

  (iii) Laws are disloyal so that some law endorse treacherous or disloyal acts.

Article 31 – Suppression & Secrecy of Formation of Law

178. *Suppression & Secrecy of Formation of Law* is an Uncivilised, Immoral and Absurd Principle of Law that defines a key principle whereby the making of immoral and corrupt laws are frequently hidden, suppressed and secret; and often through the use of false and weasel words including (but not limited to) "national security", "official immunity", "public benefit", "freedom of information", "privacy" and "national emergency".

    Suppression & Secrecy of Formation of Law

179. *Suppression & Secrecy of Formation of Law* is the fourth of the ten *Uncivilised, Immoral & Absurd Principles* of any failing, dying or despotic society. The opposite is the civilised principle of *Transparency & Awareness of Formation of Law*.

    Suppression & Secrecy of Formation of Law as Fourth Principle

180. Common Evidence of *Suppression & Secrecy of Formation of Law* includes (but is not limited to):-

    Common Evidence of Suppression & Secrecy of Formation of Law

  (i) New and proposed laws are rarely known in detail or allowed to be publicly debated before vote; and

  (ii) Existing and proposed laws often fail to reflect the proper form and procedures prescribed by law in relation to the process of enacting law; and

  (iii) Proposed statutes or bills often permit attachments or amendments or additions that do not specifically and narrowly pertain to the primary purpose of the statute or bill; and

  (iv) Existing and proposed laws are frequently obtuse, complex and run to hundreds and sometimes thousands of pages in length making it both impossible to comprehend and absurd to even consider it can be properly enforced; and

(v) Existing and proposed laws exist that attempt to argue a greater jurisdiction and powers than the limits of the legislature and executive itself.

Article 32 – Ignorance & Disrespect of Rights of Law

181. ***Ignorance & Disrespect of Rights of Law*** is an Uncivilised, Immoral and Absurd Principle of Law that defines a fundamental truth that absurd, false and morally repugnant law disrespects the rights and knowledge of law of a society.

    Ignorance & Disrespect of Rights of Law

182. *Ignorance & Disrespect of Rights of Law* is the fifth of the ten *Uncivilised, Immoral & Absurd Principles* of any failing, dying or despotic society. The opposite is the civilised principle of *Knowledge & Respect of Rights of Law*.

    Ignorance & Disrespect of Rights of Law as Fifth Principle

183. Common Evidence of *Ignorance & Disrespect of Rights of Law* includes (but is not limited to):-

    Common Evidence of *Ignorance & Disrespect of Rights of Law*

    (i) Rights are often corrupted to privileges and licenses; and

    (ii) Only some possess the privilege to be heard and many controversial or opposing views are actively censored and made illegal; and

    (iii) Only some (usually only the intellectual elite) are deemed to possess free will, while the rest of the population are considered to have an impeded or diminished capacity and will; and

    (iv) The state or parts of the state or organisations or professions are allowed to claim the right to make opinions and diagnosis of your thoughts such that no one, except a few truly have freedom or ownership of their mind; and

    (v) The state or parts of the state or organisations or professions are allowed to claim the right to own or control your body; and

    (vi) The state or parts of the state or organisations or professions are allowed to claim the right of control and ownership of your soul, often in association with occult banking, bankruptcy, and gold reserves rites; and

    (vii) The state or parts of the state or organisations claim copyright and to own your name and identity since birth; and

    (viii) The state or parts of the state or organisations claim copyright and to own your face and voice; and

(ix) The state or parts of the state or organisations claim patents, copyright and other ownership of some or all of your cellular and genetic material; and

(x) Only a few possess the right to informed consent or withdraw consent; and

(xi) Only a few possess the right and ability of reason, through the existence of their conscience; and

(xii) Only a few possess the right to adequate, fair and reasonable shelter, clean water, clothing and food; and

(xiii) Only a few possess the right to peaceful assembly; and

(xiv) Only a few possess the right to have their rights respected.

Article 33 – Unequal & Unfair Application of Law

184. ***Unequal & Unfair Application of Law*** is an Uncivilised, Immoral and Absurd Principle of Law that defines a cornerstone principle that corrupt and failing systems of law unequivocally demonstrate that not all are equal under the law and that in such broken and corrupt societies the law is rarely fair or just in its application.

Unequal & Unfair Application of Law

185. *Unequal & Unfair Application of Law* is the sixth of the ten *Uncivilised, Immoral & Absurd Principles* of any failing, dying or despotic society. The opposite is the civilised principle of *Equality & Fair Application of Law*.

Unequal & Unfair Application of Law as Sixth Principle

186. Common Evidence of *Unequal & Unfair Application of Law* includes (but is not limited to):-

Common Evidence of Unequal & Unfair Application of Law

   (i) Not all are equal under the law; and

   (ii) Most are considered culpable (guilty) until proven otherwise; and

   (iii) An action in law is permitted to proceed without first a cause; and

   (iv) An action is sometimes granted to one who is not injured; and

   (v) Some people may derive an advantage in law from their own wrong as a fraud before heaven and earth; and

   (vi) Fraud may not necessarily invalidate a cause and action, as an action through law may be permitted to arise in bad faith or unclean hands or vexatious prejudice; and

   (vii) What was illegitimate, fraudulent and invalid from the beginning may become valid (whitewashed) over time; and

(viii) An action alone may make one culpable regardless of whether there was intent to do wrong, or evidence of deliberate and wilful ignorance contrary to reasonable behaviour; and

(ix) A person may suffer punishment by application of law for mere intent alone; and

(x) A person may be punished for the transgression of an ancestor or another; and

(xi) A person can be accused of the same exact cause twice; and

(xii) A penalty may exist without a valid law; and

(xiii) A penalty may be issued without first proof of injury and secondly the right of defence.

Article 34 – Compromised & Partiality of Officers of Law

187. *Compromised & Partiality of Officers of Law* is an Uncivilised, Immoral and Absurd Principle of Law that defines a key principle that in corrupt and failing societies, those who function and hold positions within the systems of law of a society are often bound to enforce certain outcomes, are never truly independent and frequently partial and without "clean hands" in the execution of their duties.

Compromised & Partiality of Officers of Law

188. *Compromised & Partiality of Officers of Law* is the seventh of the ten *Uncivilised, Immoral & Absurd Principles* of any failing, dying or despotic society. The opposite is the civilised principle of *Independence & Impartiality of Officers of Law*.

Compromised & Partiality of Officers of Law as Seventh Principle

189. Common Evidence of *Compromised & Partiality of Officers of Law* includes (but is not limited to):-

Common Evidence of Compromised & Partiality of Officers of Law

(i) Officers and Agents of Law are rarely independent in their appointment as being members of private organisations and often employees of private corporations; and

(ii) Officers and Agents of Law are not honour bound by any public promises to act with impartiality in the execution of their duties; and frequently and openly show malice and prejudice against certain parties; and

(iii) An Officer of Law presiding or participating over a legal matter is not duty bound to first disclose all financial interests in a matter, as many legal systems function on the creation of fidelity bonds and other financial instruments where judges and magistrates have a direct financial interest; and

(iv) Judges and Magistrates frequently oversee legal matters where they possess a financial interest in the matter itself and any judicial decision or judgement in the matter; and

(v) Judges and Magistrates rarely demonstrate the necessary good character and conscience to recuse themselves without application by any other party and instead often demonstrate the worst forms of belligerence and arrogance against any notion of public decency.

Article 35 – Unfair & Egregious Procedure of Law

190. *Unfair & Egregious Procedure of Law* is an Uncivilised, Immoral and Absurd Principle of Law that defines a key principle that within corrupt and failing societies, the procedure of the law is usually unfair and unreasonably fast or egregiously slow in its function. <!-- marginalia: Unfair & Egregious Procedure of Law -->

191. *Unfair & Egregious Procedure of Law* is the eighth of the ten *Uncivilised, Immoral & Absurd Principles* of any failing, dying or despotic society. The opposite is the civilised principle of *Fair & Expeditious Procedure of Law*. <!-- marginalia: Unfair & Egregious Procedure of Law as Eighth Principle -->

192. Common Evidence of *Unfair & Egregious Procedure of Law* includes (but is not limited to):- <!-- marginalia: Common Evidence of Unfair & Egregious Procedure of Law -->

   (i) Some deserving matters are delayed or dropped, while other legal matters of trivial nature are given higher priority; and

   (ii) Often innocent persons from marginalised parts of society accused of serious crimes are forced to languish in prison and further torture and injury, while in contrast the justice system of such failed states provides swift action for corporations and favoured persons; and

   (iii) A claim need not be proven to have merit before the accused is expected to answer; and

   (iv) The person who first brings the claim may not need in anyway to first prove its merit, as the burden of the proof lies upon the one accused and not the one making accusations; and

   (v) One who makes false testimony, especially under oath within a forum of law, rarely faces any serious punishment or accountability; and

   (vi) The accused may not have the right to self defence; and

   (vii) Some people can be a judge over their own matter; and

   (viii) Some people are given the power and legal authority to be judge, jury and executioner; and

(ix) Judges are rarely bound to explain the reason of their judgement.

Article 36 – Immunity & Unaccountability of Administration of Law

193. ***Immunity & Unaccountability of Administration of Law*** is an Uncivilised, Immoral and Absurd Principle of Law that defines an important principle that within declining, broken and corrupt societies, rarely does there exist any effective system, or ability or the will or application of any meaningful oversight to hold accountable those who operate throughout the systems and structures of law.

194. *Immunity & Unaccountability of Administration of Law* is the ninth of the ten *Uncivilised, Immoral & Absurd Principles* of any failing, dying or despotic society. The opposite is the civilised principle of *Oversight & Accountability of Administration of Law*.

195. Common Evidence of *Immunity & Unaccountability of Administration of Law* includes (but is not limited to):-

(i) Oversight and accountability bodies rarely exist or function properly so that large sectors of law enforcement operate without effective oversight or accountability; and

(ii) Few Officers and Agents of Law may be held accountable for their actions when they fail to execute their duties in accord with the rule of law given the misuse of such concepts as immunity; and

(iii) Judges and Magistrates are generally made immune from criticism, personal liability or accountability when they fail to act with good character and conscience in the performance of their duties.

Article 37 – Incompetence & Cruelty of Enforcement of Law

196. ***Incompetence & Cruelty of Enforcement of Law*** is an Uncivilised, Immoral and Absurd Principle of Law that defines a core moral principle that in the enforcement of law within broken, corrupt and failing societies, the enforcement of law is frequently cruel as well as incompetent.

197. *Incompetence & Cruelty of Enforcement of Law* is the tenth of the ten *Uncivilised, Immoral & Absurd Principles* of any failing, dying or

despotic society. The opposite is the civilised principle of *Sensibility & Mercy of Enforcement of Law*.

_{Law as Tenth Principle}

198. Common Evidence of *Incompetence & Cruelty of Enforcement of Law* includes (but is not limited to):-

    (i) Incompetence and cruelty exists at all levels of the systems of law; and

    (ii) Frequent examples of the failure of law enforcement to halt incidents of catastrophe, mass shootings and injury due to at least one or more clear acts of incompetence; and

    (iii) The attack or punishment of victims of crime and innocent people by law enforcement, while the perpetrators of crime are largely ignored; and

    (iv) Absurd and cruel sentences where the legal system receives its money from bonds and other financial derivatives, while the perpetrator is given light sentence and one or more victims is incapacitated in some way for life.

Common Evidence of Incompetence & Cruelty of Enforcement of Law

1.4 – Justice & Rule of Law

Article 38 - Justice

199. ***Justice*** is the set of lawful Rights and obligations of use defined by the present Maxims and those Laws consistent with the Golden Rule of Law; and the Rights and obligations associated with the proper administration and enforcement of the present Maxims and such Laws in good faith, good conscience and good character.

Justice

200. Whenever the word Justice is used, it shall mean first and foremost the present Maxims and Rules and Law above all other lesser forms of Law.

Justice and present Maxims

201. All Rights and therefore all forms of proper Justice originate from Heaven and Divine Law and therefore the most sacred Covenant *Pactum De Singularis Caelum*:-

    (i) Divine Law is the law that defines the Divine and all creation, and demonstrates the spirit and mind and instruction of the Divine, and the operation of the will of the Divine Creator through existence. Therefore all valid Rights and Justice are derived from Divine Law; and

    (ii) Natural Law is the law that defines the operation of the will of the Divine, through the existence of form and sky and earth and physical rules. Thus Natural Law governs the operation of

Divine Source of Justice

what we can see and name; and

(iii) The laws of People as Positive Laws are those rules enacted by men and women having proper authority, for the good governance of a society under the Rule of Law. The laws of People are always inherited from Natural Law and Divine Law.

202. Notwithstanding all valid Rights concerning Justice as defined in accord with the present Maxims:- *Principles of Justice*

(i) All are equal under the law; and all are accountable and answerable under the law, and all are without blemish until proven culpable; and

(ii) Where there is a law there must be a cause; and where there is a law there must be a penalty; and where there is a law there must be a remedy; and

(iii) An action in law cannot proceed without first a cause; and an action is not granted to one who is not injured; for the action of a valid law can do no harm (injury); and no injury to the law means no valid cause for action by law; and

(iv) No one may derive an advantage in law from his own wrong, as no action through law can arise from a fraud before heaven and earth; and it is a fraud to conceal a fraud; and fraud invalidates everything of a cause and action, for no action through law can arise in bad faith or unclean hands or vexatious prejudice; and

(v) What was illegitimate, fraudulent and invalid from the beginning does not become valid over time; and

(vi) An action alone does not make one culpable unless there is intent to do wrong, or evidence of deliberate and wilful ignorance contrary to reasonable behaviour. Similarly, no one may suffer punishment by valid law for mere intent alone; and no one is punished for the transgression of an ancestor or another; and

(vii) No one is accused of the same exact cause twice; and No man or woman be a judge over their own matter; nor a man or woman possess the authority of heaven to be judge, jury and executioner; and

(viii) No penalty may exist without a valid law; and no penalty may be issued without first proof of injury and secondly the right of defence.

203. In respect of Justice and the individual:- *Justice & Individual*

(i) All possess the Right to be heard even if such speech be controversial; and

(ii) All possess the Right of free will to choose our actions and destiny; and

(iii) All possess the Right of reason that distinguishes them from lesser animals; and

(iv) All possess the Right to informed consent or withdraw consent; and

(v) All possess the Right over their body that none may claim our flesh; and

(vi) All possess the Right of our divine self that none may claim our soul; and

(vii) Thus no man can make a blood oath on their flesh or vow on their soul, nor may any man claim servitude or obligation under such an abomination, for such Rights are granted solely by heaven to all people, and no man or body of jurists have the authority to usurp heaven; and

(viii) All true authority and power to rule is inherited from heaven, and to only those men in good faith and good character and good conscience, who then make a sacred oath in trust and form an office, whereby such Divine Rights are conveyed for only so long as they honour their oath and obligations to serve the people; and

(ix) For whenever a man who makes an oath to form a sacred trust of office, then breaks such an oath through prejudice or unclean hands or bad faith, then all such authority and power ceases from them, as the cord between heaven and earth is severed and the trust dissolved.

204. Justice exists when:- *Existence of Justice*

(i) All Laws are written, simple and visible so that one person may reasonably learn, remember and comprehend all such laws properly; and no laws are hidden or secret; and

(ii) All laws are respectful so that no law disrespects a person purely upon the original circumstance of their birth, location, gender, race, religion or creed; and

(iii) All laws are logical so that no law is illogical in asserting certain errors and fallacies to demand such absurdities are defended and enforced; and

(iv) All laws are reasonable so that no law demands an

(v) All laws are consistent so that no laws require contradictory or confusing behaviour; and

(vi) All laws are honest so that no law misrepresents the truth nor compels deliberately dishonest or fraudulent behaviour; and

(vii) All laws are loyal so that no law endorses treacherous or disloyal acts; and

(viii) All laws are moral so that no law permits morally repugnant, or profane or sacrilegious activity; and

(ix) All laws are remedial so that no law imposes punitive measures without first the opportunity to rectify or remedy an error; and

(x) All laws are merciful so that no law encourages cruel and barbarous acts of vengeance.

205. Justice must always be impartial, objective and seen to be without prejudice. Therefore, no one may adjudicate a question of law with apprehended bias against one or more parties. *(Impartiality and Justice)*

206. Justice never contradicts the true Rule of Law. *(Rule of Law)*

207. Justice must always have clean hands. Therefore, no one may adjudicate a question having a secret or undisclosed financial interests in the conclusion of the matter in favour of a particular verdict. *(Clean Hands and Justice)*

208. By definition Justice can never be present nor rendered within a forum of law, if the Rule of Law itself is absent. *(Absence of Rule of Law & Justice)*

Article 39 – Fair Process

209. ***Fair Process***, also known as Due Process, is the impartial, competent and fair administration of Justice by suitably qualified persons associated with one or more authorised forums of law. *(Fair Process)*

210. Every Controversy in Law as a valid action must be resolved promptly, reasonably and justly through Fair Process, without fear or favour. *(Controversy in Law)*

211. No valid action in law should proceed without first a valid cause; and no valid cause exists until such a claim is first tested. Thus the birth of all action in law must begin with the claim:- *(Requirement of Cause of Action)*

(i) If a claim be not proven as a valid cause then the accused has nothing to answer. Yet if the claim be proved to have merit as a cause, then all valid causes in law must be resolved; and

(ii) Thus, he who first brings the claim must first prove its merit, as the burden of the proof lies upon him who accuses not he who denies.

212. The gravest threat against Justice is the failure to prosecute perjury and all forms of fraud and contempt against the fair administration of justice to the fullest extent:- Perjury as enemy of Justice and Rule of Law

   (i) One who brings false accusation is the gravest of transgressors, that they injure not only the law, but the bonds of law between Heaven and Earth; and

   (ii) One who makes false testimony, especially under oath within a forum of law, must face the full force of justice against them; and

   (iii) No one should be tolerated who seeks to gain advantage or profit through the manipulation or abuse of the administration of justice.

213. When men wish to settle their dispute among themselves, then they shall have the right to make peace. If a dispute cannot be settled before seeking a judge, then both the accused and the accuser must be granted equal hearing. Right to Settle

214. A valid claim is when an accuser makes a formal complaint in writing under oath, bringing two reliable witnesses as proof to the substance of the complaint and petitions a competent forum of law for remedy:- Nature of valid Claim

   (i) If merit of a cause be proved, the one accused must appear to answer; and

   (ii) The one accused and any witnesses appear by summons; and

   (iii) When anyone be summonsed, he must immediately appear without hesitation; and

   (iv) If a man or his legal counsel summonsed does not appear or refuses to appear to answer, then let him be seized by force to come and appear; and

   (v) When anyone who has been summonsed then seeks to evade, or attempts to flee, let the one who was summonsed be arrested to prevent their escape. One who flees fair judgement confesses his culpability.

215. An accused cannot be judged until after the accusations are spoken and then after the accused exercises or declines their three rights to defence:- Right of valid Defence

   (i) The first right of the Accused is called Prolocution upon the hearing of the Complaint; and the right to speak as a matter of law, and why the complaint and investigation should not continue; and

(ii) The second right of the Accused is called Collocution upon establishing Jurisdiction and the presentment of the Indictment; and the right to speak as to why the complaint and accusation is in fundamental error and upon such proof why the burden should now be placed on the accuser; and

(iii) The third and final right of the Accused is called Adlocution being a final speech in defence, against an accusation having been heard.

216. In respect of any defence against an accusation:- Requirements of Defence

(i) The accused must always be afforded the presumption of innocence until culpability or exoneration is proven, unless by their behaviour or testimony the accused first confesses their culpability; and

(ii) The accused possesses the right to self defence in all minor matters but not in the defence of notorious and serious accusations, unless they first are able to prove their competence at law; and

(iii) The accused possesses the right to a trial by their peers or a tribunal of jurists; and

(iv) The accused is not obliged to confess their culpability or innocence once the issue of a complaint is proven as having merit. However, the failure to confess to culpability before the commencement of trial is the formal acknowledgement of a lack of contrition; and any consequential sentence must factor the maximum and reasonable penalty; and

(v) An accused cannot be found culpable unless three pieces of evidence may be attributed to culpability as first presented as part of the complaint or as a result of a subsequent investigation, or hearing or trial; and

(vi) Judges are bound to explain the reason of their judgement.

217. By definition Justice can never be present nor rendered within a forum of law, if competent and fair administration of Justice is absent. Absence of Rule of Law & Fair Process

Article 40 – Rule of Law

218. ***Rule of Law*** is a phrase used to describe both the existence of an accepted body of law that conforms to the Maxims of Divine Law, Natural Law, Positive Law and Cognitive Law to some degree; and its equal and consistent application within the society it relates.

    All members of a society that is deemed to possess "Rule of Law" are by definition bound by the same laws.

    Rule of Law

219. *Rule of Law* exists only when:-

    (i) All laws are simple and easily publicly available so that one person may reasonably learn, remember and comprehend all such laws properly; and

    (ii) All laws are respectful so that no law disrespects a person purely upon the original circumstance of their birth, location, gender, race, religion or creed; and

    (iii) All laws are logical so that no law is illogical in asserting certain errors and fallacies to demand such absurdities are defended and enforced; and

    (iv) All laws are reasonable so that no law demands an unreasonable or impossible act; and

    (v) All laws are consistent so that no laws require contradictory or confusing behaviour; and

    (vi) All laws are honest so that no law misrepresents the truth nor compels deliberately dishonest or fraudulent behaviour; and

    (vii) All laws are loyal so that no law endorses treacherous or disloyal acts; and

    (viii) All laws are moral so that no law permits morally repugnant, or profane or sacrilegious activity; and

    (ix) All laws are remedial so that no law imposes punitive measures without first the opportunity to rectify or remedy an error; and

    (x) All laws are merciful so that no law encourages cruel and barbarous acts of vengeance.

    Existence of Rule of Law

220. The operation of the true Rule of Law is fundamental in maintaining and nurturing the connection between Heaven and Earth and between Divine Law, Natural Law, Cognitive Law and all forms of valid and legitimate Positive Law.

    Fundamental Importance of Rule of Law

221. When the Rule of Law ceases to exist within the jurisdiction and

    Cessation of

context of a particular fraternity, association, entity, institute, company or society, then all authority flowing through Divine Law, Natural Law, Cognitive Law and Positive Law to such a body also ceases, until properly restored.

Rule of Law

222. Whilst the Rule of Law and authority of a particular fraternity, association, entity, institute, company or society ceases, then all such subsequent acts, edicts, orders and transfers are unlawful and without any force or effect in law, irrespective of any claims to the contrary.

Effect of Cessation of Rule of Law

223. Whilst the Rule of Law and authority of a particular fraternity, association, entity, institute, company or society ceases, full liability shall rest upon the most senior ranks of such a body upon their refusal to surrender, resign, abdicate, confess or cease.

Full Liability on Leaders when Cessation of Rule of Law

224. No tyrant that injures the Rule of Law may then claim its protection or immunity from the consequences of their actions.

No protection for tyrants

225. A person or body belonging to a separate fraternity, association, entity, institute, company or society that then aids a tyrant in suppressing the true Rule of Law of another body, is equally and jointly liable for the actions of the tyrant as if they themselves directly performed such offences.

Equal and joint liability

226. When the Rule of Law and authority of a particular fraternity, association, entity, institute, company or society ceases, then all such authority, power, control, rights and enforcement returns to the next level of authority under Positive Law:-

Authority Shift when Cessation of Rule of Law

   (i) If the political bodies of a particular society cause the cessation of the Rule of Law, then such authority temporarily returns to the judicial bodies of the society until the Rule of Law is restored politically; and

   (ii) If the judicial bodies of a particular society cause the cessation of the Rule of Law, then such authority temporarily returns to the ecclesiastical bodies of the society until the Rule of Law is restored judicially and politically; and

   (iii) If the ecclesiastical bodies of a particular society as well as the political and judicial bodies cause the cessation of the Rule of Law, then the people are empowered to liberate themselves of such tyranny until the Rule of Law is properly restored.

227. When a Rule is in accord with the Law, then it may be legitimately considered a Law, having the full force and effect of the Law. However, when a rule is against the Law, it has neither force nor effect of Law.

Rule against the Law cannot be Law

Title II - Reason & Argument

2.1 – Reason & Argument

Article 41 – Reason

228. ***Reason*** is a concept describing both the *capacity to* and *process of* consciously applying one or more formal systems of argument to discern some cause or motive; or to draw some conclusion as to a question of truth or fact. Reason is equivalent to the application of some formal system of Logic. Reason

229. The term *Reason* originates from the time of the Franks and invention of the Anglaise (Old French) Language in the form of the compound word *raison* meaning Logic, derived from *rai* meaning light or inner sight and *son* meaning his, her or their. Origin of Reason

230. By the nature of its origin and function as a concept, the general characteristics of Reason may be summarised as:- General characteristics of Reason

    (i) Reason as both a system and method of thinking, depends on the pre-existence of such a system. Thus Reason can never be sensibly considered some spontaneous or inherent trait of cognition in sentient beings, but an acquired behaviour through learning; and

    (ii) Reason and Reasoning are and always will be fundamentally associated with one or more systems of Logic and their use; and

    (iii) Given Reason by its true etymology literally means Logic, Reason can never be sensibly considered distinct from Logic; and

    (iv) Like its equivalent (Logic), Reasoning is a type of thinking not the sum total of all possible methods of thinking; and

    (v) Like its equivalent (Logic), Reasoning is primarily binary in its conclusions (a or not-a), in contrast to the natural world whereby there could be more than one answer (multi-valence); and

    (vi) Given Reasoning is primarily binary in nature, any argument that the systems and methods of Reason are inherent to nature is false.

231. In relation to Reason being a non-natural and acquired behaviour of thinking and acting:- Reason as a non-natural acquired behaviour

    (i) Nature is complex and multi-valent, whereas Reason is binary in its function (a or not-a); and

(ii) All higher order life inherits the ability to make complex decisions. However, applying binary thinking to an experience is an acquired behaviour not necessarily a natural trait; and

(iii) Any philosophy or argument that seeks to claim Reason as a natural ability rather than acquired through learning is false by intention and design or in gross error.

Article 42 – Argument

232. An ***Argument*** is one or several connected postulations to influence the opinion of another upon Faith or to support a proposition as Proof. A postulation may be based on one or more Facts, or Suppositions, or a combination of both. Argument

233. As all Arguments depend upon meaning, all arguments are by definition fictional, regardless of whether they seek to influence upon Faith, or Proof or both. Fictional nature of Argument

234. The ability to present coherent and connected postulations is essential to any Idea, Model and System based on Meaning. Therefore, the validity of an Argument may be equated in some degree to the value and validity of a Model, Idea or System. Argument and Validity

235. As all Arguments are by definition fictional, the general elements to test for the validity of any argument are highly subjective and may said to be based upon the qualities of *Relevance, Coherence, Evidence, Confidence* and *Influence*:- General Elements of Validity of Argument

   (i) *Relevance* is the applicability of the Argument to the audience as well as the matter at hand. An Argument can be technically relevant but without some emotional connection to the audience by being personally relevant, many technically superior arguments can fail; and

   (ii) *Coherence* is the logical and understandable steps of an Argument that the audience can follow. A technical argument may be correct but if it cannot be understood or followed it may still fail against a technically inferior counter argument; and

   (iii) *Evidence* is the proof presented in support of the Argument. Importantly, it is not necessarily the weight of evidence but its singular significance in supporting a coherent argument that is often the more persuasive; and

   (iv) *Confidence* is the confidence and tone of the one who is making the Argument, shown overwhelmingly to be a significant impact to influence, when all other factors are also clear; and

(v) *Influence* is the overall ability of the one making the Argument to persuade the audience to their point of view.

236. The age of an Argument, or its customary acceptance is insufficient evidence alone for its validity. *Customary Acceptance*

237. An argument that is consistent with these Maxims and conforms to the prescripts of *Pactum de Singularis Caelum* is superior to any argument that is inconsistent to these Maxims. *Superior Argument*

Article 43 – Cause

238. A ***Cause***, also known as Causality and "cause and effect", is an abstraction to describe a source, or reason, or condition, or goal, or motive or intention for an action or event producing some kind of effect or result. *Cause*

239. In respect of Cause or *Causation*:- *Relative to Cause and Causation as a Process*

   (i) The simplest model is the concept that one process (the cause) is partly responsible (to some degree) for the second (the effect); and the second (the effect) is dependent to some degree upon the existence of the first (the cause); and

   (ii) The model of Causation seeks to draw rational connections between effects, consequences or results and the "forces" driving them to then make logical conclusions of the likely cause or causes; and

   (iii) As actions or events rarely occur in perfect isolation, it is frequently difficult to "reverse engineer" the likely cause or causes, unless clear evidence exists; and

   (iv) In seeking to resolve investigations involving events and results around Beings, the most reliable source of cause is to obtain clear evidence as to the intention in the mind of the Being (or Beings) at the time. This is why it is morally repugnant and against the Rule of Law to condemn an accused of a serious offence without first firmly establishing culpability of Mind as well as Action.

240. All Causes may be distinguished into three types being *Necessary, Sufficiency* or *Contributory*:- *Types of Causes*

   (i) *Necessary Causes* are defined such that "if x is a necessary cause of y, then the presence of y necessarily implies the presence of x. However, the presence of x does not imply that y will occur"; and

(ii) *Sufficiency Causes* are defined such that "if x is a sufficient cause of y, then the presence of x necessarily implies the presence of y. However, another cause z may alternatively cause y. Thus the presence of y does not imply the presence of x"; and

(iii) *Contributory Causes* are defined such that "if x accompanies several causes that collectively are a sufficient cause of y, then the presence of x necessarily implies a contributing factor of y to some degree".

241. As Causes after the fact are difficult to determine, even with the most expensive and advanced technology, the process of "reverse engineering" causes from studying effects can be less effective and less accurate than purely philosophical models that are able to postulate the cause of an effect from the mind of the actor at the time of the event or action.

Causes Versus Fact

242. Everything happens for a reason. Therefore, everything that happens in the Universe occurs as a result of one or more Causes.

Everything happens for a Reason

243. All possible Causes exist within the Dimension of Ucadia such that no Cause may exist that is not subject to the absolute authority and jurisdiction of Ucadia in accord with the most sacred Covenant *Pactum De Singularis Caelum*:-

All Causes exist within Ucadia

(i) Any Cause that is defined and properly identified in accord with the present Maxims is said to belong to the Set of Causes of Ucadia that are true and valid and legitimate; and

(ii) A proposed or claimed Cause that is not in accord with the present Maxims is said to belong to the Set of Causes of Ucadia that are absurd or untrue and invalid and illegitimate; and

(iii) The presence of the Unreal Set of absurd, or untrue, or invalid or illegitimate Causes as a valid Set of Ucadia cannot in itself be argued that Ucadia is therefore contradictory, absurd, illegitimate, invalid or untrue, as the presence of such a set proves the necessary completeness of the "set of sets" of all Causes.

244. As every possible Cause is encompassed within Ucadia such that no Cause may exist that is not subject to the absolute authority and jurisdiction of Ucadia:-

Cause within Ucadia jurisdiction

(i) The first Cause or relations of Causes listed within Ucadia as true and valid and legitimate shall be the proper Cause defined by Ucadia; and

(ii) Any definition, proposition or claim of Cause that is not consistent with the Cause or relations of Causes defined by Ucadia shall therefore belong to the Set of Causes of Ucadia that are absurd or untrue and invalid and illegitimate.

245. Any Cause that is not in accord with the present sacred Maxims is invalid. — Cause Versus Maxims

246. Whenever one speaks or writes or signifies Causes, it shall refer to the present sacred Maxims and all associated Covenants, Charters, Languages and Models of Knowledge first and foremost. — Signification of Cause within Maxims

Article 44 – Interpretation

247. **Interpretation** is the use of argument, reason, logic and competence in accordance with these Maxims to deduce the correct intent and meaning of the Law. Thus, to interpret the law is to explain and apply the Law as it was originally intended. — Interpretation

248. The best interpreter of a valid Maxim is the Maxim itself. Therefore, the best interpretation of any administrative act, statute or ordinance is its conformity to these Maxims first and secondly to itself. — Interpretation of Maxims

249. Conformity to these valid Maxims, not their use, is the best interpreter of things. Therefore, custom alone is the worst interpreter of the Law. — Interpretation of Things

250. In the construction of valid agreements conforming to these Maxims, words are to be interpreted in relation to the person using them. — Interpretation of Agreements

251. Lawful commands in accordance with these Maxims receive a strict interpretation, but unlawful may command a broad and extended interpretation. — Interpretation of Orders

252. When anyone references, writes or speaks of "Interpretation", "Valid Interpretation", or "Correct Interpretation" it shall mean these Maxims and no other. — Interpretation and the present Maxims

253. It is an invalid interpretation which corrupts the text of any Maxim. — Invalid Interpretation

Article 45 – Proposition

254. A **Proposition**, is a true or false (binary) statement about a Subject that forms the body of an Argument; and that logically leads to a true — Proposition

or false Conclusion. All Propositions themselves are assumptions. A Proposition is also commonly known as the Predicate or Premise.

255. The word *Proposition* is derived from the Latin *propositio* meaning "purpose or theme". However, the original Ancient Greek word used by Aristotle when describing a proposition (in his invention of syllogism) was protasis from πρότασις (protasis) meaning "to put forward, tender, to propose". — Origin of Concept of Proposition

256. In classic Logic, an Argument requires a set of at least two declarative sentences as Propositions to then infer a Conclusion. — Proposition Pairs

257. As all Propositions in Arguments are intended to be binary assumptions (either true or false), such statements rarely reflect the complex nature of a real world situation, but its simplistic summary for the purpose of generating a binary Conclusion:- — Accuracy of Propositions

   (i) To compensate for the potential absurdity of determining a Proposition of a real world situation as either absolutely true or false, many forums of law have adopted a weighting system to demonstrate a fairness of measure on the weight of evidence before conversion into an assumed absolute; and

   (ii) Whilst systems of "weighing evidence" and "measure" create the impression of multi-valence, the conversion to Propositions is still the same (100% true or 100% false) as if no ritual or appearance of "weighing evidence" occurred in the first instance; and

   (iii) It could also be reasonably argued that the conversion of a multi-valence recognition (could be and could not be) into a bivalent (100% true or 100% false) is a greater injury given acknowledgement by such process that any binary Conclusion (guilt or innocent) is knowingly flawed.

258. A real danger of the principle of Propositions is when potential or inherit bias is allowed to affect the formation of such Statements, effectively "tipping the balance" in the likely Conclusion such as a court sentence:- — Potential and Inherit Bias of Propositions

   (i) Potential and Inherit Bias that prejudices an accused can begin simply with a lack of testing of the veracity and authenticity of the accusation in the first instance; and simply assuming the accusation to be 100% true – a logical absurdity. In many jurisdictions, this is the case and "tips the balance" significantly against the accused before they have even had the opportunity to offer a defence; and

   (ii) In the minds of most people, the presence of media reports and the fact that a matter proceeds to trial is sufficient evidence to believe the Propositions against the accused are more than likely true before a hearing starts than not, indicating a clear Potential and Inherit Bias that prejudices an accused; and

(iii) Potential and Inherit Bias that prejudices an accused can continue with unreasonable and unfair procedures of law, from a lack of time allocated to hear a matter, the pre-printing of paperwork before the case is even concluded, the instructions of the judge or magistrate demonstrating a predisposed conclusion against the accused, or the behaviour of the judge or magistrate during the hearing.

259. Despite the potential defects of Propositions in Law, their use in the context of Logic still provides a reasonable means of Concluding adjudications, arbitrations and declarations of Law, providing the Civilised Principles of Law are present to mitigate potential bias or injury. — *Propositions and Law*

Article 46 – Conclusion

260. A ***Conclusion***, also known as a "deduction" is a Form of end, finish, result or decision derived through inference and the application of logic and reasoning. A Conclusion is also the third proposition of a syllogism, deduced from two prior premises (major and minor). — *Conclusion*

261. The word Conclusion is derived from the Latin *concludo* meaning "to shut up, to enclose, to end, to round off". — *Origin of Conclusion*

262. A Form of end, finish, result or decision that is not derived through inference and the application of logic and reasoning cannot be defined as a valid Conclusion. — *Importance of Conclusion*

263. All arguments as matters of Law must be resolved through valid Conclusion. — *Law and Conclusion*

Article 47 – Validity

264. ***Validity*** is the quality of a Form being valid, namely strong, authentic and genuine, as such Form is capable of being justified and proven to be true through logic and reason. Hence, Valid arguments possess legal force. — *Validity*

265. An argument declared Valid on claimed force of law alone does not make it valid. Not only must such a body of law itself be proven to be valid, but the arguments by which the law is used. — *Claim alone does not make a thing Valid*

266. Valid is equivalent to testing and measurement. Validity is impossible — *Reference and*

without the existence of some objective measure. — *Validity*

267. Belief and faith are irrelevant to validity. Validity is a test of the strength of a form, not its popularity. The more comprehensive a model, the more logical, reasoned and perfected the more valid, regardless of whether such a model of law is believed or not. — *Validity and Strength*

268. Any form of law that is inconsistent and contradictory to these present Maxims and the most sacred covenant *Pactum De Singularis Caelum* cannot be law and is henceforth invalid. — *Invalid*

Article 48 – Legitimacy

269. **Legitimacy** is the quality, measure and process of a Form in its conformance, accordance and authenticity within the Law and the present Maxims. Hence Legitimate is equivalent to "lawful". — *Legitimacy*

270. The etymology of the term *Legitimacy* from Latin *legitimo* and *legitimus* reveals its core function as a concept:- — *Origins of the Concept of Legitimacy*

    (i) *Legitimo* (Latin) means to "make legal" and thus Legitimacy in one sense is "making something legal"; and

    (ii) *Legitimus* (Latin) means "lawful" and thus Legitimacy in one sense is something already considered "lawful".

271. A maxim is not a Maxim but an inferior and illegitimate statement or claim if it is not in accordance with these present Maxims. — *Legitimacy of Maxims*

272. To claim a statement or form is Legitimate through custom or acceptance has no validity unless it is in accordance with these present Maxims. — *Claim of Legitimacy*

273. No statement that is claimed as Legitimate may be used in a competent forum unless it can prove its provenance to the present Maxims of Law. — *Proof of Legitimacy*

274. When anyone references, writes or speaks of Legitimate or Legitimacy it shall mean these present Maxims in accord with the most sacred covenant *Pactum de Singularis Caelum* and no other. — *Source of Legitimacy*

Article 49 – Sanity

275. **Sanity**, or "compos mentis" (in Latin), is a legal term whereby a forum of law may claim the right to determine to its own satisfaction whether a person associated with one or more matters is of "sound mind" or not; and therefore is legally culpable for their behaviour. — *Sanity*

276. The term *sanity* is commonly defined to mean "healthy and sound condition of body; sound sense of mind; and correct and pure of — *Origin of term Sanity*

spirit". The term *sanity* comes from the Latin word *sanitas* originally only meaning "healthy and sound condition of body". In contrast the Latin term for *mind* is *mentis*; and for *spirit* is *spiritus*.

277. Sanity is usually defined by competent forums of law in respect of the absence of insanity or *non compos mentis* (Latin) meaning "no command or power of (one's) mind". Thus, the test of Sanity in practice of the courts is the attempt to prescribe one or more "illnesses" to a person. — Absence of Insanity

278. A generally accepted principle of law is the concept that one must be of "sound mind" to be considered fully culpable for ones actions:- — Sound Mind and Culpability

   (i) Under historical Law, *mens rea* (Latin for "guilty mind") is considered by the Courts as a necessary element of a serious crime; and

   (ii) In contrast, when one is declared "insane" for a particular time and place by a Court then in that moment *mens rea* cannot be fully established; and

   (iii) Most jurisdictions of Law require a sanity evaluation prior to the formal commencement of the body of any hearing or trial as to the question of whether or not the accused was mentally incapacitated at the time of the alleged offence.

279. The use of Psychological Evaluations or "Psych Tests" against belligerent parties in a matter is frequently a strategy by the court to disable a form of argument or defence:- — Psychological Evaluations and Belligerent Parties

   (i) A Court may decide that a person simply challenging the authority of the court or the legitimacy of the court on one or more grounds may be argued to be not of "sound mind" and thus subject to a Psychological Evaluation, whether or not custodial control (imprisonment) is needed to complete it; and

   (ii) Unruly, argumentative, arrogant and rude behaviour – even if out of valid frustration – is unacceptable under any circumstances in a court of law; and ultimately enables court officials to warrant a Psychological Evaluation for the purpose of diagnosis of one or more "mental illnesses".

280. Arguments or attempts by a court to use *Non Compos Mentis* or "not of sound mind" against a party in a matter are able to be effectively negated generally by:- — Negating arguments of Non Compos Mentis

   (i) A party always acting calmly, confidently, respectfully and politely; and

   (ii) Dressing appropriately and respectfully for court matters (where possible); and

(iii) Expressing in the affirmative (where appropriate) the soundness of body, mind and spirit – made self evident by ones behaviour and approach to the court; and

(iv) Making clear the definition of soundness of mind, given there are no uniform clinical definitions of insanity in Western Law, therefore the judge or magistrate is free to choose from a number of presumed definitions. If unchallenged, it is presumed a clear definition exists.

Article 50 – Competence

281. ***Competence*** is a complex term referring to a Person free from serious mental incapacity; or a Person capable of reason; or a Person conscious of their own decisions and actions; or a Person able to perform or participate in a given argument, decision or action; or a Person willing to take responsibility for their own decisions and actions. Competence

282. In relation to the five key aspects of Competence being *Mental Wellness, Ability of Reason, Conscious Objective Awareness, Mental Performance* and *Personal Responsibility*:- Five Key Aspects of Competence

    (i) *Mental Wellness* in respect of Competence is closely related to the concept of Sanity and the judgement of the presence of any serious mental illness that would otherwise be deemed to incapacitate the Person; and

    (ii) *Ability of Reason* in respect of Competence is both the knowledge and ability to demonstrate and accept models of binary (logical) thinking of good, bad, guilty, innocent, right or wrong, even if such thinking does not reflect real world events or circumstances surrounding a matter; and

    (iii) *Conscious Objective Awareness* in respect of Competence is the ability to demonstrate a detached, objective and unemotional conscious awareness of ones own thoughts, decisions and actions; and

    (iv) *Mental Performance* in respect of Competence is the ability to perform or participate in a given argument, decision or action, especially when relating to a legal matter; and

    (v) *Personal Responsibility* in respect of Competence is the ability and character to be willing to take responsibility for ones own decisions and actions.

283. In relation to the subjective nature of Competence as exhibited by the Key Aspects of

five key aspects of Competence being *Mental Wellness, Ability of Reason, Conscious Objective Awareness, Mental Performance* and *Personal Responsibility*:-

Competence as Subjective and not Clinical

   (i)   All five key aspects of Competence are unquestionably subjective in nature as opposed to clinical or scientific in definition; and

   (ii)   The five key aspects of Competence relate directly to necessary conditions to conduct (in theory) a fair and just legal matter within a competent forum of law; as it could reasonably be argued that an absence of Competence in one key aspect could render a verdict unjust; and

   (iii) The five key aspects of Competence relate directly to necessary conditions to conduct (in theory) a fair and just legal matter within a competent forum of law; as it could reasonably be argued that an absence of Competence in one key aspect could render a verdict unjust; and

284. In relation to the Competence of Persons:-   *Competence of Person*

   (i)   As the Divine Person is also part of the Divine Creator, a Divine Person is always considered competent; and

   (ii)   While the Divine Person is always considered competent, it is possible for the True Person represented by the flesh to be incompetent.

285. Only Persons demonstrating knowledge and consent to these Maxims and agreeing to obey statutes derived from the Maxims may be regarded as Competent.   *Maxims and Competence*

286. As Natural birth of the flesh is proof of lawful conveyance from a Divine Trust to a True Trust and willing consent by the Divine Person to be born in accordance with these Maxims, when the flesh denies its membership to One Heaven, or its Trusteeship or these Maxims, then the flesh automatically declares itself as Incompetent.   *Self-Declared Incompetence*

287. Any judge or magistrate who wilfully and deliberately ignores their obligation to stand by their oath and duties of office, especially when requested to reaffirm their solemn obligations before or during a legal proceeding, automatically declares themselves incompetent with any subsequent judgement, orders or decisions null and void from the beginning.   *Judicial Incompetence*

Article 51 – Status

288. ***Status*** or ***Legal Status*** refers to the Identity, Rights and Impediments (if any) of a Person recognised by a Society or its various bodies, courts, agencies, officers and agents.   *Status*

289. In relation to the three key aspects of Status being *Identity, Rights* and *Impediments*:-   *Three Aspects of Status*

    (i)   *Identity* of Legal Status refers to the "type" of Person, as a Being may be connected to two or more Persons including (but not limited to) Citizen, Driver, Passenger, Employee, Employer, Borrower, Lender, Defendant, Petitioner, etc.); and

    (ii)   *Rights* of Legal Status refers to the cumulative set of potential privileges, obligations or powers ascribed to such a Person; and

    (iii)   *Impediments* of Legal Status refers to any restrictions, suspension, forfeitures or cancellations (if any) of privileges, obligations or powers ascribed to such a Person.

290. In any Argument of Law, the Status of a Person is fundamental to the process and function of a matter in any competent forum of law:-   *Fundamental Nature of Status and Law*

    (i)   All legal matters concerning Rights concern Persons; and therefore the correct Identity of the type of Person associated with one or more Rights is critical to questions of Jurisdiction and Authority; and

    (ii)   Legal matters often concern Agency Rights associated with one or more services and functions of Society such as roads, taxation, financial services or government welfare. Therefore, the central Identity of the Person in question may be of a different type depending upon the Agency involved; and

    (iii)   As a matter of Argument and procedure, legal matters often require parties to be properly identified in roles as Persons for the matter at hand, such as Prosecutor, Judge or Defendant separate to the hearing or trial of the overall Person in question (e.g. Driver Mr John Citizen); and

    (iv)   Different types of Persons naturally have different collections of Rights. Thus the proper identification of the Legal Status of a Person is essential for many functions and processes of the administration of government and law; and

    (v)   By the rules of a particular government Agency, a Person accused of an offence may be impeded in one or more Rights. Thus acknowledging Legal Status can often be considered an acceptance of such restrictions and limitations.

291. Denial of the immutable fact that all Societies and their various bodies, courts and agencies depend upon and recognise different persons related to one or more primary persons (such as citizen), is   *Denial of existence of Multiple Persons used within a Society*

an admission by the one who denies of falsity or mental illness:-

- (i) Any academic or public information site, or official government instrument, briefing or court summary that denies the natural presence of multiple persons connected to the citizens of a given society is an admission of gross incompetence, idiocy and falsity; and

- (ii) The denial of such fundamental functions and elements of law by law officers, courts and law enforcement within a given society is admission of the absence of any Justice, Fair Process or Rule of Law; and

- (iii) The use of the term "straw man" is itself false and misleading as the legal function of Person is a historic fact of law, not a fiction.

292. An Individual demonstrating a lack of competence or respect in the present Maxims has no right whatsoever to identify themselves as having Sovereign Legal Status. In all such cases, such claims may be taken by a Non-Ucadian Society or its various bodies, courts, agencies, officers or agents as an admission of incompetence, belligerence and dishonesty. No Sovereign Legal Status to non-Ucadia Societies

293. Status by definition, requires recognition by a given Society or its various bodies, courts, agencies, officers and agents:- Recognition of Status

- (i) Given the fundamental importance of Legal Status as well as its complex implications, in many instances Legal Status is not passively affirmed or recognised, but passively assumed and concluded; and

- (ii) An Individual engaged in a matter in relation to a given Society or its various bodies, courts, agencies, officers and agents has every right to request in writing the Legal Status that such a body is claiming the Individual holds in proceeding with the matter; and

- (iii) An Individual has every right to Identify their Legal Status with an appropriate Person in association with a matter, if a given Society or its various bodies, courts, agencies, officers or agents is unable or unwilling to do so; and

- (iv) An Individual does not normally have the right to claim Legal Status beyond the scope and jurisdiction of the laws of a given Society or its various bodies, courts, agencies, officers or agents, unless such a Society or body demonstrates a fundamental lack of competency, honesty, good character, decency, transparency and fair process in contradiction to the present Maxims and the most sacred Covenant *Pactum De Singularis Caelum*; and

(v) A member of a Ucadia Society always has the primary right to be tested, tried and judged by a competent forum of law under Ucadia Law.

294. By definition, a living member of One Heaven possesses a minimum of three persons being their Divine Person, True Person and Superior Person that all have higher status than any inferior person or lesser society. Therefore, no non-Ucadian society may claim jurisdiction over one or more of the superior persons of a living member of One Heaven. *(Ucadia and Status of Person)*

295. When an alleged Offence is issued by a Non-Ucadian society or some lesser society against a Ucadia Member, the Member may evoke their superior Legal Status and choose to have the matter resolved in accordance with these Maxims. *(Legal Status and present Maxims)*

Article 52 – Capacity

296. ***Capacity*** is the combination of Legal Status and Competence of a Person to make important legal, financial and life decisions. *(Capacity)*

297. Capacity is generally defined as having two qualities being *Legal Capacity* and *Mental Capacity*:- *(Two key elements of Capacity)*

   (i) *Legal Capacity* is the term given to the Legal Status of a Person and the Identity as well as limits of Rights and any Impediments as determined by their status; and

   (ii) *Mental Capacity* is the term given for the Competency of a Person and their ability to make a rational decision based upon all relevant facts and considerations.

298. Capacity is an essential factor in Contract Law demonstrating the ability of a Person to satisfy the elements required to enter a binding agreement:- *(Capacity and Contract Law)*

   (i) In terms of *Legal Capacity* and Contract Law, a Person often is required to have reached a minimum age; and

   (ii) In terms of *Mental Capacity* and Contract Law a Person is usually required to be competent and have a soundness of mind before entering a contract.

299. Capacity is an essential factor in determining the function and procedure of Criminal Law:- *(Capacity and Criminal Law)*

   (i) In terms of *Legal Capacity* and Criminal Law a Person such as a defendant may have reduced or impeded rights until the matter is resolved, including the assumption that the Person is held in the custody of the state, either under no bail or bail, or incarceration and remand; and

 (ii) In terms of *Mental Capacity* and Criminal Law a defendant must have the capacity to understand the wrongfulness of his or her actions.

300. Capacity is an essential factor in determining the function and procedure of Estate Law:- *Capacity and Estate Law*

 (i) In terms of *Legal Capacity* and Estate Law the maker of a will must not otherwise be impeded from making a will and must clearly indicate the intention of making a will, revoking any (or all) previous wills or codicils; and

 (ii) In terms of *Mental Capacity* and Estate Law the maker of the will must have testamentary capacity, meaning that he/she must understand the nature of making a will, have a general idea of what he/she possesses, and know who are members of the immediate family or other beneficiaries.

Article 53 – Standing

301. ***Standing***, also known in Latin as *locus standi*, refers to the existence and proof of a right of a Person to bring a new Action in Law; or to be recognised and heard in an ongoing Action; or to join or participate in an existing Action. *Standing*

302. In relation to the three key types of Standing being *Bring New Action*, *Be Heard in Action* and *Join Existing Action*:- *Three Key types of Standing*

 (i) *Bring New Action* refers to the right of a Person to bring a new action into a forum of law based upon either a pre-existing right of Action or sufficient evidence of an existing wrong (tort) or imminent injury; and

 (ii) *Be Heard in Action* refers to the right of a Person to be recognised and heard in an ongoing Action based upon their Interest in the matter as well as their Legal Status and Capacity; and

 (iii) *Join Existing Action* refers to the right of a Person to join an existing and ongoing Action based upon a pre-existing right of Action or provable Interest in the Action.

303. In relation to the general requirements of Standing to *Bring New Action*:- *General Requirements of Standing to Bring New*

 (i) *Injury*: The plaintiff must have suffered or imminently will suffer injury. The injury must not be abstract and must be within the zone of interests meant to be regulated or protected under the statutory or constitutional guarantee in question; and

(ii) *Causation*: The injury must be reasonably connected to the defendant's conduct; and

(iii) *Relief and Remedy*: A favourable court decision must be likely to redress the injury.

304. In relation to the general requirements of Standing to *Be Heard in Action*:-

    (i) *Status*: The person in question must have the appropriate Legal Status to be able to be heard and address a competent Forum of Law. In many cases, a court may rule a party does not have sufficient standing to proceed, except by legal representation; and

    (ii) *Competence*: The person in question must have sufficient competence as frequently plaintiffs and defendants do not have the aptitude nor respectful and competent behaviour to represent themselves.

305. In relation to the general requirements of Standing to *Join Existing Action*:-

    (i) *Proof of Interest*: The person in question must have clear evidence of a direct interest in the matter; and

    (ii) *Status*: The person in question must have the appropriate Legal Status to be able to be heard and address a competent Forum of Law. In many cases, a court may rule a party does not have sufficient standing to proceed, except by legal representation.

306. By definition and law itself, an authorised Officer of Ucadia, possessing the proper mandate, has standing in any competent forum of law prescribed in the mandate. The denial of the standing of such an officer is therefore an admission a forum is not a proper court of law.

Article 54 – Merit

307. *Merit* is a complex term that refers to:-

    (i) The correct legal context of an Action in Law in relation to the citation of existing precedents and previously adjudicated matters of a legal system; and

(ii) The clarity and reasonableness of the strict legal rights claimed by a party to the Action; and

(iii) Sufficient evidence of one or more material facts in support of the claimed legal rights to the Action; and

(iv) The conformity to procedure of the Action in relation to the rules of the particular forum of law; and

(v) The likelihood of adjudication in favour of the party to the Action when all facts are considered.

308. Merit is an important Argument of Law that gives context to a matter before a forum of law beyond merely its technical parts:- General Characteristics of Merit

(i) As a sequence of concepts, Merit enables a judge or tribunal the ability to place the context of a case within the wider body of laws and cases of a Society; and to consider not only whether a decision is more or less likely in favour of the plaintiff, but the likelihood of the matter being subsequently appealed or challenged; and

(ii) Merit is supposed to assist the court and jurists in discerning matters that may superficially appear technically compliant and reasonable, but in reality are without substance and potentially frivolous or even vexatious; and to utilise the principles of Merit where a litigant is intent on potentially abusing the mechanics of the court; and

(iii) An erroneous judgement that argues a case is without Merit does not mean a litigant is without the right of appeal, as such error of judgement is itself potentially a strong basis for appeal. Thus the process of Merit must always be treated with respect and not itself used frivolously as an argument to merely defeat an opposing argument.

309. In relation to the *first element of Merit* and the correct legal context of an Action in Law in relation to the citation of existing precedents and previously adjudicated matters of a legal system:- General Requirements of First Element of Merit

(i) Every party in an Action should be able to demonstrate sufficient research of the relevant and prevailing cases and laws that support or defeat a claim of rights; and

(ii) Such citations should always be brief and recorded in the accepted manner for such references within the law form; and

(iii) The absence of any clear citations or the proper methods of citation is justification to claim an argument is "without Merit".

310. In relation to the *second element of Merit* and the clarity and reasonableness of the strict legal rights claimed by a party to the Action:-

    (i)   The one or more rights justifying an Action must be able to be clearly articulated; and

    (ii)   The absence of any clearly articulated and reasonable rights consistent with Legal Status of a Person is sufficient justification to claim an argument is "without Merit".

General Requirements of Second Element of Merit

311. In relation to the *third element of Merit* and sufficient evidence of one or more material facts in support of the claimed legal rights to the Action:-

    (i)   Material facts are facts of a case that are without dispute or can be proven by *prima facie* evidence; and

    (ii)   The absence of any material facts is justification to claim an argument is "without Merit".

General Requirements of Third Element of Merit

312. In relation to the *fourth element of Merit* and the conformity to procedure of the Action in relation to the rules of the particular forum of law:-

    (i)   All matters must follow the procedure of the court, particularly in fair process; and

    (ii)   The absence of conformity to the procedures and forms of the court is justification to claim an argument is "without Merit".

General Requirements of Fourth Element of Merit

313. In relation to the *fifth element of Merit* and the likelihood of adjudication in favour of the party to the Action when all facts are considered:-

    (i)   A party must demonstrate the presence and conformity of all previous necessary elements first before presenting any summary of arguments on the likelihood of adjudication in favour of the party to the Action when all facts are considered; and

    (ii)   The absence of conformity of all previous necessary elements first before presenting any summary of arguments is justification to claim an argument is "without Merit".

General Requirements of Fifth Element of Merit

314. A matter that fails to conform to at least one or more key elements of Merit may then be said to be "Without Merit". It is a falsity to claim a legal argument is "without merit" when clear and sufficient evidence exists in conformance to all five key elements of the notion of Merit.

Without Merit

315. A matter that fails to conform to all five key elements of Merit may be said to be "Totally Without Merit". It is a falsity to claim a legal

Totally without Merit

argument is "totally without merit" when clear and sufficient evidence exists in conformance to at least one or more key elements of the notion of Merit.

2.2 – Logic

Article 55 – Logic

316. ***Logic*** is a formal System of Argument based on the principles of Inference and Reason whereby Propositions are properly expressed to achieve consistent Conclusions across a wide variety of Subjects. Logic

317. Logic may be defined as *Bivalent* or *Multivalent*:- Bivalent and Multivalent Logic

    (i) *Bivalent Logic* is based on the presumption of a single chronological set of dependent time events and only one (1) of two (2) possible outcomes or Conclusions; and

    (ii) *Multivalent Logic* is based on the presumption of a single chronological set of dependent time events and two (2) or more possible outcomes or Conclusions.

318. Logic may further be defined in terms of Models of Logic as either Linear or Multi-linear. Linear Logic is chronologically based on the presumption of a set of singular space-time dependent events commencing with A and then proceeding to B; and Multi-linear Logic is based on a progressively expanding set of interdependent space-time events:- Linear and Multi-linear Logic

    (i) *Multivalent Multi-linear Logic* is capable of approximating to some degree of accuracy the Reality and Fact and Truth of the Universe. Both Multivalent Linear Logic and Bivalent Linear Logic are wholly artificial, imaginary and unable to accurately portray the reason, function and effect of any real scientific events with any degree of accuracy. Therefore, both Multivalent Linear Logic and Bivalent Linear Logic are inferior and less Real, less Truthful and less Factual than Multivalent Multi-linear Logic; and

    (ii) *Multivalent Linear Logic* is an imaginary and artificial system for portraying, recreating or analysing the reason, cause and effect of any real world events. Multivalent Linear Logic is inferior and less Real, less Truthful and less Factual than Multivalent Multi-linear Logic. Given that Multivalent Linear Logic does not reduce to one of a binary pair it is not useful for application in Models and Law. However it is useful in argument in terms of outcomes that may not necessarily reduce to a binary outcome such as arbitration and dispute resolution; and

(iii) *Bivalent Linear Logic* is the most unnatural, imaginary and artificial system for portraying, recreating or analysing the reason, cause and effect of any real world events. However, Bivalent Linear Logic is the most functional of all three (3) logic models in terms of models of law and reason because of its simplicity. Given Bivalent Linear Logic is wholly absurd and unnatural to the multivalent paradoxical reality of life, all parties involved in any dispute with Ucadia or an Authorised entity must be granted the right of free will and consent to be adjudicated according to Bivalent Linear Logic.

319. Only Multivalent Multilinear Logic is capable to approximating to any degree of accuracy the reality of Divine Law, Natural Law or Cognitive Law. Both Multivalent Linear Logic and Bivalent Linear Logic are wholly unable to accurately portray the reason, function and effect of any real world events with any degree of accuracy. *(Multivalent Multilinear Logic)*

320. Bivalent Linear Logic is based on three (3) Laws of Reason being *Identity*, *Non-Contradiction* and *Bi-valency*:- *(Three Laws of Reason of Bivalent Logic)*

    (i) The *Law of Identity* states that an object is the same as its identity; and

    (ii) The *Law of Non-Contradiction* or the "exclusion of paradox" states that a valid proposition cannot state something that is and that is not in the same respect and at the same time; and

    (iii) The *Law of Bi-valency* (Excluded Middle) states that conclusions will resolve themselves to only one (1) of two (2) states being valid or invalid.

321. While Bivalent Linear Logic is the most unnatural system for portraying, recreating or analysing the reason, cause and effect of any real world events, it is the most functional of all three (3) logic models in terms of law because of its simplicity. Therefore, Bivalent Linear Logic is the foundation of all Positive Law or law derived from Positive Law. *(Bivalent Logic and Positive Law)*

322. As Bivalent Linear Logic is the most unnatural system for portraying, recreating or analysing the reason, cause and effect of any real world events, it cannot be used in Law to describe Cognitive Law, Natural Law or Divine Law. Furthermore, Bivalent Linear Logic can only be applied to fictitious persons, not to actual beings. *(Bivalent Logic and higher forms of Law)*

323. As Bivalent Linear Logic is wholly unnatural to the real world, all men and women must be granted the right of free will and consent to be adjudicated according to Bivalent Linear Logic through persons. *(Consent and Bivalent Logic)*

Article 56 – Premise

324. A Premise, also known as a "protasis" is a true or false (binary) statement about a Subject that forms the body of an Argument; and that logically leads to a true or false Conclusion. All Premises themselves are assumptions. A Premise is also commonly known as the Predicate or Proposition. — *Premise*

325. In classic Logic, an Argument requires a set of at least two declarative sentences as Premises to then infer a Conclusion. — *Premise Pairs*

326. Logical Form differs substantially from general language expression of argument in that the Subject and Predicate must be strictly arranged within a certain relationship of meaning (Copula) according to the following core rules:- — *Logical Form of Premise (Predicate)*

    (i) The (a) *Subject* is generally the first element of a "valid" logical expression, followed by the (b) *Copula* represented by a limited number of operators and conjunctions and then followed by (c) the *Predicate* describing the quality, attributes or assumptions concerning (a) the *Subject*; and

    (ii) Gender, tense and declensions are generally considered irrelevant to valid Logical Form and are removed.

327. Traditional Logic and Modern Logic differs primarily in the application of Logical Form. According to traditional Logic, only one Copula or modifier existed between the Subject and the Predicate rendering a limited number of expression constructions. However, in Modern Logic, both the Subject and the Predicate may have modifiers, rendering multiple generalities. — *Forms of Logic*

Article 57 – Inference

328. *Inference*, or "syllogism" is the act of drawing a Conclusion by the use of Deductive Logic or Inductive Logic. Hence, the Conclusion drawn through Logic is also called an Inference. — *Inference*

329. A Conclusion, also known as a "deduction" is a Form of end, finish, result or decision derived through inference and the application of logic and reasoning. A Conclusion is also the third proposition of a syllogism, deduced from two prior premises (major and minor). — *Conclusion*

330. A Form of end, finish, result or decision that is not derived through inference and the application of logic and reasoning cannot be defined as a valid Conclusion. — *Logic and Valid Conclusion*

331. All arguments as matters of law must be resolved through valid Conclusion. — Law and Conclusion

Article 58 – Deductive Logic

332. ***Deductive Logic***, also known as Deductive Reasoning is a formal method of achieving an inference using Bivalent Linear Logic by the assumption of a certain conclusion which necessarily flows from a set of premises or hypothesis. — Deductive Logic

333. According to Bivalent Linear Logic, a deductive argument is considered valid if the conclusion follows necessarily from the premises themselves considered valid and true. — Truth of Argument

334. The simplest form of Deductive Logic is called the Law of Detachment. A single conditional statement is made, and then a hypothesis (P) is stated. The conclusion (Q) is deduced from the hypothesis and the statement. The most basic form being:- — Form of Deductive Logic

   (i)   As P tends towards Q (P→Q)

   (ii)   P (Hypothesis stated)

   (iii) Q (Conclusion given).

335. The second simplest form of Deductive Logic is called the Law of Syllogism. Two conditional statements are made concerning A, B and C. The conclusion is deduced by combining the hypothesis of one statement with the conclusion of another. The most basic form being: — Law of Syllogism

   (i)   If A = B

   (ii)   And B = C

   (iii) Then A = C.

Article 59 – Inductive Logic

336. ***Inductive Logic***, also known as Inductive Reasoning is a formal method of achieving an inference through Bivalent Linear Logic by the derivation of general principles from specific instances or prior knowledge. — Inductive Logic

337. Whereas Deductive Logic seeks to establish validity in terms of absolutes, Inductive Logic indicates that a logical argument supports a conclusion to some degree (inductive probability) without absolute certainty. Therefore, Inductive Logic permits the consideration of certain real world uncertainties reflected in superior forms of logic within the inferior Bivalent Linear Logic framework. — Inductive Logic vs. Deductive Logic

338. Inductive Logic depends upon two (2) key concepts being the laws of — Probability, Certainty and

probability and certainty. Therefore the strongest form of Conclusion by Inductive Logic is when one is certain beyond "reasonable doubt" that a conclusion is probably true.

Inductive Logic

339. As Inductive Logic introduces some relevance to real world uncertainty to the system of Bivalent Linear Logic used for all lesser laws formed under Positive Law, it is the preferred form of Bivalent Linear Logic for resolving serious matters concerning such laws.

Inductive Logic and serious legal matters

Article 60 – Fallacy

340. A *Fallacy* in Logic or Argument is an incorrect reasoning resulting in a misconception, or erroneous Conclusion.

Fallacy

341. Fallacies may be divided into several categories: *Factual Error, Deliberate Error, Absolute Error, Assumed Error, Irrelevance Error* and *Logical Error*:-

Types of Errors

   (i) *Factual Error* is when a Premise is made containing a factually incorrect statement of information or knowledge that can be proven to be factually false; and

   (ii) *Deliberate Error* is when a Premise is made containing false and incorrect information which can be proven to have been made knowingly and deliberately, thus proving an act of deliberate deception; and

   (iii) *Absolute Error* is when a Premise is made containing a sweeping generalisation which a reasonable person would immediately know cannot possibly be sustained as valid; and

   (iv) *Assumed Error* is when a Conclusion is made containing a generalisation which is based on one (1) or more assumptions that may not hold true in all cases; and

   (v) *Irrelevance Error* is when a Conclusion is made containing minor, irrelevant information that ignores the primary inference; and

   (vi) *Logical Error* is when a Premise or Conclusion is made against the mechanical rules of Logic.

342. The most common types of Logical Fallacies are *Incoherence, Fallacious, Irrelevant, Malicious, Perfidious, Unproven, Unasserted, Circular, Verbose, Absurd, Repetitive* or *Defamatory*:-

Common Types of Logical Fallacies

   (i) An *Incoherence* or *Incohaerens* argument, being Latin for "it is not consistent" is any argument whereby its Premises does not follow one another. Thus, an incohaerens is when no Conclusion could reasonably be deduced or inferred from two or more inconsistent and possibly contradictory premises; and

(ii) A *Fallacious* or *Non sequitur* argument, being Latin for "it does not follow" is any argument whereby its Conclusion does not follow from its Premises. Thus, a non sequitur is when a Conclusion could be either true or false, yet the argument is false as there is no reasonable way of arriving to such a Conclusion from the premises alone by way of deduction or inference; and

(iii) An *Irrelevance* or *Ignoratio elenchi*, being Latin for "irrelevant conclusion" is any argument whereby its Conclusion may in itself be valid, but does not address the primary deduction or inference (as issue in question) related to the Premises; and

(iv) *Malice* or *Malignare*, being Latin for "a malicious act" is any deliberately and wilfully negative, spiteful, wicked and evil act designed and intended to harm another, whether or not the other party was aware of such behaviour; and

(v) *Perfidy* or *Perfidum*, being Latin for "a deliberately false, dishonest, treacherous act; a breach of trust" is any deliberately and wilfully false, dishonest, deceptive, treacherous act, representing a clear and unmistakable breach of trust, whether or not such action was intended for profit; and whether or not the other party was aware of such behaviour; and

(vi) An *Unproven Claim* or *Onus Probandi*, from Latin *maxim Onus probandi incumbit ei qui dicit, non ei qui negat* meaning "the burden of proof is on the person who makes the claim, not on the person who denies (or questions the claim)" is any argument whereby the burden of proof fails to be provided or is falsely placed upon the one accused or defending the claim and not the one making the claim. Thus, any system of law based on the assumption of being culpable on mere accusation without burden of proof is not only absurd, but false, immoral and unlawful; and

(vii) An *Unasserted Claim* or *Argumentum ex silentio*, from Latin meaning "argument (deduced) out of silence" is any argument whereby a Conclusion is made on the absence of evidence or argument, rather than the existence or merit of argument; and

(viii) A *Circular reasoning* or *Circulus in demonstrando*, from Latin meaning "circular argument" is any argument where the Conclusion ultimately relies upon the Premises to be true, yet the Premises ultimately depends upon the Conclusion to be true and thus self referencing and circular; and

(ix) A *Verbose reasoning* or *Argumentum Verbosum*, from Latin meaning "verbal intimidation" is any argument where the Premises or Conclusion are deliberately verbose, or obtuse, or confusing, or overly technical, or complex, or occult in order to intimidate and deflect attention from the existence of one or more fallacies contained within the argument in general; and

(x) An *Absurd reasoning* or *Argumentum ad Absurdum*, from Latin meaning "an absurd argument" is any argument where the Conclusion of an argument is set aside and one or more of the Premises of an argument are proven to be false by showing that a false, untenable or absurd result would follow its acceptance. Argumentum ad Absurdum is frequently and mistakenly associated with an absurd logical fallacy known as *Reductio ad absurdum* or "reduction to absurdity" whereby an entire argument is falsely deemed absurd upon discovery of but one absurd or untenable premise; and

(xi) *Repetitious reasoning* or *Argumentum ad Infinitum*, from Latin meaning "endless argument" is any argument where the argument is continually presented, often with intentional intimidation to use such repetition and ignorance of any counter argument in order to deflect attention from the existence of one or more fallacies contained within the original argument in general; and

(xii) *Defamatory accusations* or *Argumentum ad Hominem*, from Latin meaning "against the man" or "to the person" is any argument whereby attention is sought to be deflected from one or more fallacies contained within the original argument by introducing a secondary argument against the character of the one highlighting such fallacies.

343. A substantial injury to the Law and parties due to a serious fallacy offsets any alleged offence and places the liability upon the judicial officers responsible for failing to correct the serious error. — *Liability of Fallacy*

344. A fallacy in Law has no valid limitation to correction. — *No Limitation to Correction*

2.3 – Critical Methods

Article 61 – Critical Methods

345. **Critical Methods** are forms and techniques of Sceptical Argument — *Critical Methods*

against the views of one or more persons in order to prove one or more deficiencies or to damage or destroy the character of the founder, thinker or author of an opposing view. Critical Methods are both the most popular and weakest forms of Argument.

346. The general characteristics of Critical Methods (Critical Thinking) as a form of Argument may be defined as:- *General Characteristics of Critical Methods*

    (i) Systemic and endemic bias as a consequence of applying flawed methods of sceptical thinking, permitting subjective positions, thinking and arguments in contradiction to the very notion of "classical scepticism"; and

    (ii) Frequent aggregation into "schools", especially beginning from the 17th Century and hardening into a form of orthodox through such embedded thinking in American and certain European Education Colleges; and

    (iii) Inherently adverse to respectful discourse and dialogue except by those that share the same view, or "group think"; and

    (iv) Intolerance and sometimes aggressive disdain against those holding opposing views, often justifying and blaming any immoral, hypocritical and negative behaviour upon the portrayed failures of those with opposing views or "projection"; and

    (v) Frequent misrepresentation of romantic, anti-social and unscientific behaviour in attacking opposing views as somehow noble, justified and enlightened; and

    (vi) Reliance of quantity or authority of discord without due respect or regard for the rigour of systematic or philosophical debate; and

    (vii) Significant reliance upon *Ad hominem* personal slander and attacks culminating in a level of intolerance that demand the "cancellation" of those who do not belong to the same "group think".

347. There are three essential forms of Critical Methods of Argument, namely *Classical, Modern* and *Post-Modern*:- *Three Forms of Critical Methods*

    (i) *Classical Critical Methods* are primarily defined by Ancient Greece Sceptic scholars and thinkers prior to the 17th Century "Enlightenment Movement" of philosophers. Classical Critical Methods are distinguished primarily upon the discussion and debate of the limits of knowledge, semantics, meaning and certainty, with the key focus on doubt being a driver and incentive to higher knowledge and truth; and

(ii) *Modern Critical Methods* are essentially defined by Politically Romantic and Revolutionary philosophers starting from the 17th Century including (but not limited to) Descartes, Bacon through to Kant, Locke, Voltaire, Rousseau and Marx. Modern Critical Methods are distinguished primarily upon embracing a critical bias against traditional and historical theories of knowledge, particularly social, religious and spiritual, while championing notions in support of process and action over theory; and the intellectual superiority and emancipation of the sceptical mind, especially when embraced within new fraternities and movements; and

(iii) *Post-Modern Critical Methods* are essentially defined by the rise of total economic and cultural dominance of the United States from the 1930's and the subsequent legal, scientific and philosophical theories born out of primarily major east coast American Universities or "Ivy League" including (but not limited to) Yale, Princeton, Harvard, Columbia, Brown and Cornell. Post-Modern Critical Methods are distinguished primarily upon defence of a specific Romantic Narrative of the exceptionalism of the United States and in the superiority of accepted traditions of academic thinking against new ideas, models and systems not created by, or that conform to the standards set by such post modernists.

348. Post Modern Critical Methods (Critical Thinking) is unique in history in possessing such a dangerous degree of delusion and lack of self awareness usually only found in extremist philosophical cults or the proponents of propaganda of oppressive political regimes:- *Dangerous and Delusional Characteristics of Critical Methods*

(i) A strenuous denial or refusal to acknowledge there is any inherit bias or hypocrisy within their theories or behaviours, despite overwhelming evidence to the contrary; and

(ii) An arrogant self belief that such methods have assisted scientific thinking and humanity, when in fact such orthodox and intolerance has significantly impeded practical solutions to human problems and the advance of science and technology; and

(iii) A delusional blindness to the origins of Post Modern Critical Methods as economic and political weapons of power within a small group of American and European political allies, including a dangerous unawareness of such influence in forming the parameters of these schools of thought; and

(iv) A dismissive refusal to engage in fair and reasonable discourse with opposing views or genuine desire to synthesis stronger ideas, theories or outcomes where they might differ and evolve from the economic and political parameters set down since the 1920's and 1930's; and

(v) An over confidence and reliance on compliant forms of media and communication to drown out or silence critics that question or oppose such schools of thought.

Article 62 – Scepticism

349. ***Scepticism*** is generally the theory of possessing a questioning or doubtful bias toward certain existing, new or controversial ideas, models or systems of knowledge. Scepticism

350. The general characteristics of Scepticism may be defined as:- General Characteristics of Scepticism

   (i) The application of binary Logic in an inverted and "negative form" rather than a positive form; and to deduce conclusions from assumptions of doubt rather than certainty; and

   (ii) An inherent and deep bias against positive assumptions and assertions, especially of a religious, spiritual and opposing nature; and

   (iii) An inherent and deep bias in favour of inverted and negative Logic in the form of doubt, rather than viewing all forms of Logic as merely tools of thought and discernment; and

   (iv) A steadfast belief (pseudo religious bias and absurdity) that nothing can be said to exist unless it can be empirically measured according to a certain system of rules, sometimes loosely called "scientific methods"; and

   (v) An unscientific and subjective bias and intolerance to results, evidence or thinking that do not conform to one's school of thought or sceptical philosophy, even if evidence and proof is provided and overwhelmingly demonstrated as demanded; and

   (vi) A means of arguing for the hypocrisy and intentional blindness of scepticism when confronted with scientific evidence and overwhelming proof by defaulting to the power of doubt to justify the need for more evidence, more tests, different scientific methods or any number of other reasons.

Article 63 – Deficiency

351. ***Deficiency*** is the "positive" application of Critical Methods forms of Argument to expose what is claimed to be failures and weaknesses of Deficiency

an opposing Argument, rather than merely attack the one making such arguments. Pure Deficiency Arguments are rare in Critical Methods, as most rely upon the attack of both the author and the Argument.

Article 64 – Ad Hominem

352. ***Ad Hominem*** (Latin for "at the person") is the "negative" application of Critical Methods forms of Argument to claim failures, errors and weaknesses of a person, rather than the weaknesses of the argument itself. Critical Methods is unique as a form of Argument in seeking to normalise and justify the attack of character, motives or behaviour of a person as a "legitimate" form of Argument.

Ad Hominem

353. Generally, Ad Hominem Arguments seek to distinguish between fallacious (false) personal attacks and valid personal attacks. However, in practice, little weight is given to the difference, even in Non-Ucadian courts, except when such personal attacks are overwhelmingly egregious and abusive.

General Classification of Ad Hominem

354. Personal attacks that are and should be recognised as fallacious (false) and without merit include: *Circumstantial Personal Bias, Circumstantial Personal Motive, Circumstantial Personal Association, Unsubstantiated Personal Similarity, Unsubstantiated Personal Hypocrisy, Unsubstantiated Personal Scandal* and *Unsubstantiated Personal Abuse*:-

Fallacious Ad Hominem Attacks

   (i) *Circumstantial Personal Bias* is when a claim is made or asserted upon circumstantial events or hypothesis that a person possesses a particular animus (bias). It contrasts to the valid Ad Hominem Argument of Actual Personal Bias. Unfortunately, this form of fallacious argument is often permitted in non-Ucadian forums of law; and

   (ii) *Circumstantial Personal Motive* is when a claim is made or asserted upon circumstantial events or hypothesis that a person possesses or possessed a particular motive or intention. It contrasts to the valid Ad Hominem Argument of Actual Personal Motive. This form of absurd and fallacious argument is almost universally permitted and encouraged in non-Ucadian forums of law to allow prosecutors, magistrates, judges and other legal professionals to falsely establish motive; and

   (iii) *Circumstantial Personal Association* is when a claim is made or asserted upon circumstantial events or hypothesis that a person possesses or possessed a particular motive, bias or sometimes even action by virtue of their proximity to another or some event at a time and place. It contrasts to the valid Ad Hominem Argument of Actual Personal Association. This form of absurd and fallacious argument is almost universally permitted and encouraged in non-Ucadian forums of law to allow prosecutors, magistrates, judges and other legal professionals to falsely establish bias, motive or action simply by a person being "in the wrong place at the wrong time". The acceptance of this injury and injustice of law by non-Ucadian courts is most commonly the factor in some jurisdictions having a disproportionate number of innocent people falsely convicted; and

(iv) *Unsubstantiated Personal Similarity* is when a person seeks to mitigate an argument against themselves by claiming both the attacker and claimant share similar faults or actions, whilst ignoring the substance of the allegation; and

(v) *Unsubstantiated Personal Hypocrisy* is when a person is charged with the allegation of hypocrisy without substantive evidence and without refuting or disproving their argument. A common use of this fallacy is to often accuse one who opposes to be a racist, or denier or miscreant of some description; and

(vi) *Unsubstantiated Personal Scandal* is when a personal scandal is alleged, or presented, whether real or alleged, in such a sensationalised fashion that the original substance of the Argument becomes irrelevant in the minds of others, especially the "court of public opinion"; and

(vii) *Unsubstantiated Personal Abuse* is when a person is faced with slander and personal abuse.

355. Personal attacks that are considered Non-Fallacious and Valid under Critical Methods include *Actual Personal Bias, Actual Personal Motive, Actual Personal Association* and *Actual Personal Testimony*:- Non-Fallacious Ad Hominem Attacks

(i) *Actual Personal Bias*, sometimes also called Apprehended Bias is when clear and unmistakable evidence exists of the bias of a party, either in their own words or actions, or the absence of proper disclosure or action as required; and

(ii) *Actual Personal Motive* is when clear and unmistakable evidence exists as to the intentions or motive of a person. The most common and important form of evidence in non-Ucadian forums of law of Actual Personal Motive are recorded police interviews, often conducted without legal representation present; and

(iii) *Actual Personal Association* is when clear and unmistakable evidence exists as to the proximity and presence of a person to some alleged event or act, able to be established by forensic evidence, electronic or surveillance evidence; and

(iv) *Actual Personal Testimony* is when a person under oath or promise, provides auricular testimony to an event or occurrence, providing grounds for examination and cross-examination on what they have disclosed and answered in the first person.

2.4 – Dialectic Methods

Article 65 – Dialectic Methods

356. ***Dialectic Methods*** are forms and techniques of Argument between two or more people that are able to agree to a common subject yet hold different points of view in order to find a common solution (synthesis), or to debate until one side is declared victor with the other being defeated as absurd. Dialectic Methods are the least popular yet the strongest forms of Argument. *(Dialectic Methods)*

357. The term *Dialectic* comes from the Ancient Greek διαλεκτικός (dialektikós) meaning "relating to dialogue". Therefore, Dialogue is the modern term for Dialectic. *(Meaning of Dialectic)*

358. The general characteristics of Dialectic Methods as a form of Argument may be defined as:- *(General Characteristics of Dialectic Methods)*

    (i)   Normally objective (to a degree) as a consequence of agreement on subject and general rules of dialogue; and

    (ii) Rarely applied in schools, in contrast to Critical Methods (Critical Thinking) that has been protected and supported by schools, particularly within modern Western education colleges; and

    (iii) Inherently predisposed to dialogue and means of co-operation; and

    (iv) Generally respectful (to a degree) of opposing view given the necessity for co-operation; and

    (v)   Capable of systematic and objective scientific discourse, free from misrepresentation and unscientific behaviour; and

    (vi) Reliance on substance, quality and skill of Argument rather than any quantity or noise of discord or claims of authority; and

    (vii) General intolerance of *Ad hominem* (personal attacks) as a means of Argument.

359. There are four essential categories of Dialectic Methods of Argument, namely *Classical, Scholastic, Diplomatic* and *Scientific*:- *(Four categories of Dialectic Methods)*

    (i)   *Classical Dialectic Methods* of Argument refers to methods first formed by mainly Ancient Greek Scholars, such as the Socratic School and Plato School. Classic Dialectic Methods form the concepts and rule of the highest forms of debating in law, whereby the highest standards of courtesy are supposed to be observed, while participants use their auricular skills and memory skills to argue without written documents or "props"; and

(ii) *Scholastic Dialectic Methods* of Argument refers to methods first formed in the 15th and 16th Century, yet sometimes claimed of older provenance, whereby inherit bias and presumptions against opposing arguments were permitted from the perspective of one claiming to possess a superior intellectual knowledge, especially of faith and liturgical traditions. Scholastic Methods are the least rigorous form of Dialetic and traditionally follow a standard form of argument; and

(iii) *Diplomatic Dialectic Methods* of Argument refers to methods, sometimes also referred to the "Hegelian method", first formed in the 18th and 19th Centuries and the advent of new forms of non-violent issue resolution under the "Laws of Nations" whereby opposing sides once some type of common ground of agreement was reached, could then engage with the aim of reaching a synthesis, usually resulting in some form of pact, or treaty; and

(iv) *Scientific Dialectic Methods* of Argument refers to methods first formed under Ucadia in the late 20th Century for the pursuit of higher and objective knowledge, particularly in emancipating and improved scientific thought.

360. An example of a *Classical Dialetic Method* is the *Elenchus Dialectic Method*, also known as the "Socratic Method" from the Ancient Greek word ελεγχος (elengkhos) meaning "an argument of disproof or refutation; cross-examining, testing, scrutiny especially for purposes of refutation". As a formal dialectic system, the Elenchus Dialectic Method is based on six (6) core presumptions:- Elenchus (Socratic) Dialectic Method

(i) All participants possess *meieutics* – that is the idea that truth is latent in the mind of every homo sapien being but must be brought to life by intelligent discourse; and

(ii) All participants are of equal status. No discourse, nor argument nor conclusion is valid when one must argue from the unfair position of judge to accused, or teacher to student, or master to servant; and

(iii) All true knowledge is recalled from within and not through the collection of external facts, observation or study; and

(iv) The best method to help another discover meieutics is through questions formulated as tests of logic and fact enabling them to discover the deeper meaning of their beliefs and the existence of any contradictions of hypothesis; and

(v) The best method to test the truth or falsity of a hypothesis is to argue the opposite of any inferred assumptions and if found to be true, such a hypothesis may be said to have been reduced to the absurdity of its parts and found to be false; and

(vi) A Superior hypothesis may be found by systematically identifying and eliminating through questioning those beliefs that lead to contradictions of logic.

361. A further example of a *Classical Dialetic Method* is by the Plato School of Philosophy and the Dialogue Dialectic Method, also known as the "Plato Method" from the Ancient Greek word διάλογος (dialogos) meaning "conversation, discourse". As a formal dialectic system, the Dialogue Dialectic Method is based on six (6) core presumptions:- Plato Dialetic Method

(i) All participants possess meieutics – that is the idea that truth is latent in the mind of every homo sapien being but must be brought to life by intelligent discourse; and

(ii) All participants are of equal status. No discourse, nor argument nor conclusion is valid when one must argue from the unfair position of judge to accused, or teacher to student, or master to servant; and

(iii) All true knowledge of higher self (soul) can only come through the careful and reasoned acquiring of external facts, observation and study; and

(iv) The best method to help another discover themselves and reason of the world is through active participation in intelligent discourse using the skill of logic to test and to learn new knowledge and to discover the deeper meaning and justification of their beliefs; and

(v) The best method to test the truth or falsity of a hypothesis is to possess sufficient "true" knowledge of nature of form (ideas), the universe including our higher self (soul) and whether a new hypothesis enhances our knowledge or is contradictory to it; and

(vi) A Superior hypothesis may be found by systematically identifying and eliminating through questioning against knowledge of a superior belief system those inferred assumptions of the hypothesis that lead to contradictions of logic.

362. The *Scholastic Method* similarly follows approximately six core presumptions as Classical Dialectic Methods, yet with inherit bias, namely:- Scholastic Dialetic Method

(i) All participants possess a limited form of meieutics. However, men and women need "Divine Help" not simply intellect to know truth; and

(ii) All participants are born of equal status but choose to be unequal through failure to exercise free will, lack of ethics or righteous behaviour and faith in key institutions and education. Therefore, people choose by their own actions and tacit consent to be addressed unequally in argument and discourse; and

(iii) Faith in key institutions is more pleasing to the Divine Creator than intellect. Therefore, true knowledge of higher self (soul) can only come through the assistance and guidance of the primary teacher (magisterium) of key institutions such as the church; and

(iv) The best method to help another discover themselves and reason of the world is through active participation in the life of such key institutions and strengthening its teaching tools and intellectual discourse by reference, argument and citation of key indisputable sacred texts and lesser historical intellectual texts; and

(v) The best method to test the truth or falsity of a hypothesis is to possess sufficient "true" knowledge of the sacred texts, doctrine and truths of the key institution(s); and whether a new hypothesis enhances our knowledge or is contradictory to such true (orthodox) knowledge; and

(vi) A Superior hypothesis may be found by systematically identifying and eliminating through questioning against knowledge of doctrine those inferred assumptions of the hypothesis that lead to contradictions of logic.

363. The *Scholastic Dialectic Method* takes the following standard form for all arguments:- Standard Form of Scholastic Dialetic Method

(i) The Question to be determined; and

(ii) The principal objections to the question; and

(iii) An argument in favour of the Question, traditionally a single argument ("On the contrary.."); and

(iv) The determination of the Question after weighing the

evidence. ("I answer that...") ; and

(v) The replies to each objection.

364. *Diplomatic Dialectic Methods*, also known as the "Hegelian method" greatly reduces the number of presumptions; and instead focuses on an agreed process to conclusion, based on three (3) core elements:

(i) A *Thesis* of "problem" is formed which gives rise to a socio political reaction; and

(ii) An *Antithesis* or "reaction" representing the opposing socio political ideology formed in reaction to negate/confront the thesis leading to some form of conflict; and

(iii) A *Synthesis* or "solution" being the resolution of the two opposing sides and a restoration of "balance" which has changed the previous status quo.

Diplomatic Dialectic Methods

365. *Scientific Dialectic Methods*, also known as the "Ucadia Method" follows the three stage Diplomatic (Hegelian) formula (Thesis, Antithesis and Synthesis), yet re-introduces necessary rules to the process of dialogue:-

(i) All participants possess intellect and the capacity to participate in discovery depending not only of their knowledge, but more importantly their willingness to agree to a common theme and commitment to intelligent discourse; and

(ii) All participants are of equal status, regardless of qualification, status or past accomplishments. No discourse, nor argument nor conclusion is valid when one must argue from the unfair position of judge to accused, or teacher to student, or master to servant; and

(iii) All true knowledge of discovery can only come through the application of objective and diligent reasoning in the discernment of external facts, observation and study; and

(iv) The best method to help one another in improved discovery is through active participation in intelligent discourse using the skills of the appropriate and relevant form of logic to test and to learn new knowledge and to discover, test and prove the deeper meaning and justification of their ideas, models or systems; and

(v) The best test to the validity or truth of a hypothesis, idea, model or system is whether it measurably enhances our knowledge, capacity or utility of technology and thinking or is contradictory to it; and not whether it conforms to traditional,

Scientific Dialectic Methods

orthodox or standard ways of thinking and doing; and

(vi) A Superior hypothesis, idea, model or system may only be found by first systematically identifying, acknowledging and mitigating such fallacies and inherit bias of assumptions that restrict the ability to ever achieve a consensus of enhanced knowledge, capacity, utility of technology or thinking.

366. As most Dialectic Methods agree on the latent and inherit intelligence of all Homo Sapiens as well as the fundamental requirement for equal status in any dialogue, no argument may be regarded as truly dialectic and logical if either of these presumptions are absent. *Valid systems of Dialectic*

367. Any dialogue, argument or discussion in law founded on the principle of inequality of the participants is by definition devoid of logic, dialectic or validity and therefore null and void from the beginning. *Invalid Dialogue*

Article 66 – Thesis

368. A ***Thesis*** is a formal proposition or statement, supported by Arguments representing either first stage of a Diplomatic or Scientific Dialectic Method, or a formal academic work, also known as a dissertation. *Thesis*

369. The term Thesis comes from the Ancient Greek τίθημῐ (títhēmi) meaning "to place, put, set; to put down in writing; to consider as, or regard". *Meaning of Thesis*

370. In proper application of the Scientific Method, also known as the Ucadian Method, the Thesis is never the new or challenging argument against a position of a "status quo", but the best positive attempt, using new methods to justify a present state, position, orthodoxy, status quo, idea, model or system:- *Scientific Thesis*

(i) Under the Scientific Method, an existing position is required to positively prove its validity and legitimacy by rigorous discourse without resorting to dogmatic and self-referential statements or negative statements against possible alternatives; and

(ii) The existing and present state, position, orthodoxy, status quo, idea, model or system in a Thesis must honestly disclose any known problems, faults or flaws (if any) and what positive solutions could be applied to resolve such flaws.

Article 67 – Antithesis

371. An ***Antithesis*** is a formal proposition or statement, supported by Arguments representing the diametric opposite to another *Antithesis*

proposition (Thesis) as the second stage of a Diplomatic or Scientific Dialectic Method.

372. The term Antithesis comes from the Ancient Greek ἀντίθεσις (antíthesis) meaning "against, hostile to, contrasting with, opposite of thesis". — *Meaning of Antithesis*

373. In proper application of the Scientific Method, also known as the Ucadian Method, the Antithesis is always the new or challenging argument against a position of a "status quo", providing positive answers and solutions to every attempt within the Thesis to justify a present state, position, orthodoxy, status quo, idea, model or system:- — *Scientific Antithesis*

   (i) Under the Scientific Method, a new or proposed position is required to positively prove its validity and legitimacy by rigorous discourse without resorting to dogmatic and self-referential statements; and

   (ii) The new and proposed state, position, orthodoxy, status quo, idea, model or system in an Antithesis must directly address known problems, faults or flaws (if any) of the present Thesis and what risks or consequences may exist in addressing them.

Article 68 – Synthesis

374. A ***Synthesis*** is the formal deduction, combination or formation of a conclusion born from the process of argument and debate of one or more Thesis and Antithesis to find common ground, as the third stage of a Diplomatic or Scientific Dialectic Method. — *Synthesis*

375. The term Synthesis comes from the Ancient Greek σύνθεσις (súnthesis) meaning "a putting together; composition". — *Meaning of Synthesis*

Article 69 – Absurdity

376. ***Absurdity*** is an Argument or position contrary to reason, manifest truth, logic or meaning. In Dialectic, it is the negative expression of the losing argument in a contest of two opposing views. — *Absurdity*

377. The term Absurd and Absurdity originates from the Latin *absurdus* meaning "ill fitting, inharmonious, dissonant and out of tune". — *Meaning of Absurdity*

378. The fact that one or more Maxim be found in error or in need of correction does not therefore or necessarily render such a Maxim absurd. — *Maxim and absurdity*

379. Any claim in entirety against the present Maxims or the most Sacred Covenant *Pactum De Singularis Caelum* as being absurd, is itself a most wicked and immoral profanity and absurdity. — *False claims of Absurdity*

2.5 – Socratic Methods

Article 70 – Socratic Methods

380. ***Socratic Methods*** or ***Socratic Questioning Methods*** are forms and techniques of disciplined and well directed Questioning between two or more people for the purpose of discovery, exploration, teaching, or argument. The positive outcome of Socratic Questioning Methods is the pursuit of clarity and truth. The negative outcome of Socratic Questioning is the exposure of falsity, ignorance or hypocrisy.

Socratic Methods

381. Socratic Questioning Methods relies upon a relative loose framework of four parts being Supposition, Interrogation, Response and Conclusion:-

Structure of Socratic Questioning Methods

(i) *Supposition* is an open or hidden (underlying) assumption generally used as the starting position for questioning; and

(ii) *Interrogation* is the active process of disciplined and systematic questioning and obtaining responses; and

(iii) *Response* is the act and process of expressing something in words or in writing in return to a question; and

(iv) *Conclusion* is the intended destination and arrival by the end of Interrogation.

382. Whilst Socratic Questioning Methods possess certain formalities and techniques, the primary strength of this particular form of Argument resides in the inherit power and effect of purposeful questioning itself to control and drive an Argument:-

Inherit power and effect of purposeful questioning

(i) Being questioned, particularly by strangers or persons in positions of authority, is inherently intimidating for people required to answer, especially if such persons asking questions has the capacity to embarrass or injure the one answering; and

(ii) Some formalities in law, such as questioning a witness or law enforcement investigations, gives particular people at certain times the potential to control the narrative by asking questions and compelling responses; and

(iii) Well formed questions can place the person required to answer in a weaker position and at a disadvantage, as to answer the question properly may require clear comprehension, feats of forensic memory and contorting real life experiences of multi-valent logic into "all or nothing" binary logic responses, whether either yes or no may be false to a degree.

383. The general characteristics of Socratic Questioning Methods as a form of Argument may be broadly defined as:- General Characteristics of Socratic Questioning

   (i) Well structured and systematic questioning, used to pursue thought and active responses in particular direction for some underlying purpose known or unknown to those answering; and

   (ii) As long as the questioner is able to maintain control of questioning, and continue active responses, it is possible the direction and path of dialogue can be maintained and underlying purpose achieved; and

   (iii) Complete dependence on the participation of one or more whose answer is required. A refusal, disinterest or reluctance to answer renders such a method of Argument less effective; and

   (iv) High emphasis on the broad skills and expertise of the one asking questions, lending the method normally to people professionally educated in such techniques and positions of authority; and

   (v) The questioner may engage the audience or subject from a wide variety of approaches that may variously be distilled into either an active voice or passive voice – active when it is clear that the questioner is leading the direction by questions; or passive when it appears that both the answers and the questions are collaboratively determining the direction; and

   (vi) Those questions used for positive or negative outcomes, with positive questioning used for clarity and education, while negative questioning is used for interrogation and exposing hypocrisy, falsities and ignorance.

384. The most common and classical categories of Positive Socratic Questioning for Clarity are *Clarification, Assumptions, Evidence, Perspective* and *Implications*:- Classical Categories of Positive Socratic Questioning

   (i) *Clarification* questions generally seek to challenge the respondent to think more deeply concerning the conceptual comprehension of the problem or possible solutions; and

   (ii) *Assumptions* questions generally seek to challenge the respondent about the the underlying assumptions of their argument or the discussion as a whole; and

   (iii) *Evidence* questions generally seek to challenge the respondent as to evidence to support their responses, or the confidence of the evidence presented; and

(iv) *Perspective* questions generally seek to challenge the perspective of respondent, sometimes to reveal inherit weaknesses or bias; and

(v) *Implications* questions generally seek to challenge the respondent as to the logical implications of their responses.

385. The most common categories of Negative Socratic Questioning for Clarity are *Investigation, Accusation, Incrimination, Motivation* and *Conclusion*:-   *Categories of Negative Socratic Questioning*

(i) *Investigation* questions generally seek to obtain a response that establishes a connection, a binding, a jurisdiction or joinder or contract to justify further investigation and questions; and

(ii) *Accusation* questions generally seek the respondent to accept, confess or agree by silence to one or more assumption and bias loaded statements; and

(iii) *Incrimination* questions generally seek to challenge the respondent as to evidence leading to the respondent self incriminating and effectively "confessing" to one or more allegations or accusations; and

(iv) *Motivation* questions generally seek to challenge the perspective of respondent in order to establish potential motive, as a critical element of evidence; and

(v) *Conclusion* questions generally seek to challenge the respondent as to the limited logical implications of their responses, usually to only one conclusion.

Article 71 – Supposition

386. A ***Supposition*** is an open or hidden (underlying) assumption generally used as the starting position for interrogation under the Socratic Questioning Method.   *Supposition*

387. The term Supposition comes from the Latin *suppositio* meaning "underlying theme, hypothesis or context", from *sub-* (under) and *positio* (position or theme).   *Meaning of Supposition*

Article 72 – Interrogation

388. ***Interrogation*** is the art and practice of questioning and examination by inquiry.   *Interrogation*

Lex Positivum: Maxims of Positive Law

389. The term Interrogation comes from the Latin *interrogo* meaning "inquire, examine or argue" from *inter-* (between or among) and *rogo* (ask or request). — Meaning of Interrogation

390. Interrogation without the use of physical or mental violence is not torture. Torture is by definition the application of methods of physical or mental violence, whether or not a confession or statement is sought from the victim. — Falsity of claiming Interrogation as Torture

391. The use of physical or mental violence as part of Interrogation is morally repugnant, barbaric and prohibited by all civilised societies. No forum of law is permitted under any circumstance to admit as evidence any statement or confession gained through the use of torture. — Use of Torture barbaric and prohibited

392. General examples of Classical Clarification Socratic Questions include (but are not limited to):- — Classical Clarification Socratic Questions

    (i)   Why do you say that?

    (ii)   What do you mean by?

    (iii)   How does this relate to?

    (iv)   Could you give me an example?

    (v)   Could you explain further?

    (vi)   What do we already know about?

    (vii)   Could you put that another way?

    (viii)   Would this be an example of?

    (ix)   How does x relate to y?

    (x)   Is your point x or y?

393. General examples of Classical Assumptions via Socratic Questions include (but are not limited to):- — Classical Assumptions Socratic Questions

    (i)   You seem to be assuming x. Is that correct?

    (ii)   Could you explain why you arrived at that conclusion?

    (iii)   What could we assume instead?

    (iv)   How can you verify or disapprove that assumption?

    (v)   Why would someone make this assumption?

    (vi)   What could we assume instead?

    (vii)   What are you assuming?

    (viii)   Can you give examples to justify your assumption?

(ix) On what basis did you come up with that assumption?

(x) What would happen if?

394. General examples of Classical Evidence via Socratic Questions include (but are not limited to):-   *Classical Evidence Socratic Questions*

(i) What do you think caused x to happen?

(ii) What evidence is there to support your answer?

(iii) Why do you think that is true?

(iv) Do you have any evidence for that?

(v) How do you know?

(vi) Could you explain your reasons to us?

(vii) Is there a reason to doubt that evidence?

(viii) How does that apply to this case?

(ix) How could we find out whether that is true?

(x) What evidence would you need to change your mind?

395. General examples of Classical Perspective via Socratic Questions include (but are not limited to):-   *Classical Perspective Socratic Questions*

(i) What would be an alternative?

(ii) How could you answer the objection?

(iii) Can anyone see another way?

(iv) How many other perspectives can you imagine?

(v) How would someone else (they) respond?

(vi) What is another way to look at it?

(vii) Is there another way to look at this?

(viii) What makes this the best option?

(ix) What are the weaknesses as well as strengths of?

(x) If you were in their shoes what would you have done?

396. General examples of Classical Implications via Socratic Questions include (but are not limited to):-   *Classical Implication Socratic Questions*

(i) Why could that happen?

(ii) What are you implying?

(iii) What effect would that have?

(iv) What is the likely outcome of that decision?

- (v) If this and this is the case, what else must also be true?
- (vi) If we disagree, what consequences could result?
- (vii) Would any implication or result cause you to think differently?
- (viii) If that happened, what else could happen? Why?
- (ix) What are the consequences of that assumption?
- (x) If we (he/she) did that, what could happen?

397. General examples of Investigation (negative) via Socratic Questions include (but are not limited to):- *Investigation (negative) Socratic Questions*

- (i) What is your name? Where do you live?
- (ii) Do you have any identification or proof on you?
- (iii) Can you hand me your drivers license (and insurance) please?
- (iv) Do you understand?
- (v) Do you know why I stopped you (pulled you over)?
- (vi) Are you carrying any contraband, weapons or illegal drugs?
- (vii) Have you recently been drinking or taking drugs?
- (viii) What do you do for a living?
- (ix) Where are you going? Where have you just come from?
- (x) May I check your bag/car to prove you're telling the truth?

398. General examples of Accusation (negative) via Socratic Questions include (but are not limited to):- *Accusation (negative) Socratic Questions*

- (i) Why/How/When did you (accusation)?
- (ii) Where/how did (incident) happen?
- (iii) Where were you going/coming from when (incident) happened?
- (iv) At what time did you (accusation)?
- (v) If you're being truthful, then how do you explain (accusation)?
- (vi) Is there any other reason you can think of why your were at (place/time) when (incident)?
- (vii) I put it to you (accusation)?
- (viii) You can deny all you want, the evidence I have put to you shows clearly (accusation)?
- (ix) If you have nothing to hide why don't you respond?

(x) An honest person would respond, why won't you?

399. General examples of Incrimination (negative) via Socratic Questions include (but are not limited to):- *Incrimination (negative) Socratic Questions*

    (i) How did you know (name)?

    (ii) Have you and (name) ever argued or gotten into any physical altercation?

    (iii) Do you know the identity of anyone who has ever argued or gotten into a physical altercation with (name)?

    (iv) When and where did you last see (name)?

    (v) Did you see the man/woman (describe person)?

    (vi) Can anyone else honestly confirm you were (at place/time)?

    (vii) What do you think really happened (about incident)?

    (viii) You know this is your one and only time to tell the truth and your side of the story, so what really happened?

    (ix) If you are being genuinely honest, you must have some idea about (incident), so what do you think really happened?

    (x) What do you think really happened?

400. General examples of Motivation (negative) via Socratic Questions include (but are not limited to):- *Motivation (negative) Socratic Questions*

    (i) Did (name) owe anyone money or have financial problems?

    (ii) What do you know about the will or any insurance of (name)?

    (iii) Have you and (name) ever argued or gotten into any physical altercation?

    (iv) Do you know the identity of anyone who has ever argued or gotten into a physical altercation with (name)?

    (v) Did (name) owe anyone any money?

    (vi) Did you honestly like (name)?

    (vii) Tell me everything you remember about (incident)?

    (viii) You must have some idea if you are being honest, so why do you feel (incident) happen?

    (ix) How did you feel when you first heard about (incident)?

    (x) What did you think when you first learned about (incident)?

401. General examples of Conclusion (negative) via Socratic Questions include (but are not limited to):- *Conclusion (negative) Socratic*

(i) There is no other way to look at all this evidence except as proof of your guilt, unless you can give me some verifiable alternative?

(ii) On (time) you said (statement), now you say (statement), so which one is correct?

(iii) Based on everything you've seen, if you were me, what else would you conclude?

(iv) Throughout this interview you have either declined to respond or not been truthful, so this is your last chance to tell me how this can be viewed as anything but your guilt?

(v) Throughout this interview we have been polite and given you ample opportunity to explain your side of the story, but you have chosen not to show any decency or honesty. Is there any chance you have regret or remorse and want to be truthful?

(vi) One last time, do you want to say something truthful at least and explain yourself before we conclude?

(vii) I know accidents happen and sometimes we do things without really thinking. But if you say nothing then it looks like you meant it and are guilty. This is your last chance to tell what really happened?

Article 73 – Response

402. **Response** is the act and process of expressing something in words or in writing in return to a question. Response is the formal reply to a question raised under Interrogation.

403. The term Response comes from the Latin *respondeo* meaning "to reply, or attend, appear, agree, yield or answer".

404. Even if a person is arrested and authorities seek to commence interrogation without legal counsel present, it is a universal human right that all people are entitled to request a pen and paper to prepare and subsequently read a written response, before answering any questions:-

(i) The written response and its recording is demonstration of willingness to co-operate. It is also an opportunity to express whether sufficient time or rights were given to review the claimed evidence before being questioned; and

(ii) The written response is further opportunity to explain why "no comment" may be used in response, given not having sufficient time to look at the claimed evidence or prepare an accurate recall of information before being interrogated; and

(iii) In many cases, a well balanced written response that is honest and objective is able to nullify the interrogation techniques and process of being forced into recorded interrogations by authorities.

405. General examples of Responses to Investigation (negative) Socratic Questions include (but are not limited to):- *Response to Investigation (negative) Socratic Questions*

(i) Am I under arrest? If not, I have nothing to say; and

(ii) On what reasonable grounds am I under arrest?

(iii) What is the probably cause of the warrant issued for arrest?

(iv) If I am not under arrest and there is no warrant, why do you continue to unlawfully detain me?

(v) How can I or anyone reasonably respond without all the facts first?

406. General examples of Responses to Accusation to Investigation (negative) Socratic Questions include (but are not limited to):- *Response to Accusation (negative) Socratic Questions*

(i) No comment.

(ii) I cannot recall.

(iii) I have no opinion or comment.

(iv) Before I answer anything, I request access to competent legal counsel.

(v) Please refer to my opening statement as to why you have forced me to respond to your interrogation with no comment.

(vi) How can I or anyone reasonably respond without all the facts first?

(vii) Are you trying to create more controversy?

(viii) It is terrible what has happened and I am deeply saddened. But without being given the right or opportunity to understand the facts you are asking, all I can do is refer to my written statement and respond with no comment.

407. General examples of Responses to Motivation (negative) Socratic Questions include (but are not limited to):- *Response to Motivation (negative) Socratic Questions*

(i) No comment.

(ii) I cannot recall.

(iii) I have no opinion or comment.

(iv) Before I answer anything, I request access to competent legal counsel.

(v) Please refer to my opening statement as to why you have forced me to respond to your interrogation with no comment.

(vi) It is terrible what has happened and I am deeply saddened. But without being given the right or opportunity to understand the facts you are asking, all I can do is refer to my written statement and respond with no comment.

408. General examples of Responses to Conclusion (negative) Socratic Questions include (but are not limited to):- *[Response to Conclusion (negative) Socratic Questions]*

(i) Thank you but no comment.

(ii) I cannot recall.

(iii) I have no opinion or comment.

(iv) Please refer to my opening statement as to why you have forced me to respond to your interrogation with no comment.

Article 74 – Clarity

409. ***Clarity*** is the state or measure of being clear, either in appearance, thought, style or lucidity. *[Clarity]*

410. The term Clarity comes from the Latin *claritus* meaning clear or brightness. *[Meaning of Clarity]*

Article 75 – Hypocrisy

411. ***Hypocrisy*** is the contrivance of a false appearance of virtue or goodness, while concealing the true character of malice or vice, or claiming certain motives or intentions that are then contradicted by ones words or actions. *[Hypocrisy]*

412. The term Hypocrisy comes from the Ancient Greek ὑποκρίνομαι (hupokrínomai) meaning "I reply falsely or disguise the truth". *[Meaning of Hypocrisy]*

2.6 – Rhetoric Methods

Article 76 – Rhetoric Methods

413. ***Rhetoric*** is the knowledgeable use of the properties, methods and types of public speech to persuade others through oral argument. Of *[Rhetoric Methods]*

all the tools of argument, Rhetoric is the most powerful precisely because it can be the most persuasive.

414. Rhetoric differs from generalised techniques of public speaking in that it specifically concerns the ability to present the optimum methods and skills of oral argument at the appropriate location, time and manner for the purpose of persuasion; whereas a well executed public speech in itself may not itself address such a specific goal.

Rhetoric and public speaking

415. All forms of public oration under Rhetoric may be defined by five (5) generalised properties being *Reason, Purpose, Conditions, Constraints* and *Propositions*:

General Properties of Rhetoric

    (i)   *Reason* is the reason, event, occasion for a public oration that expresses its context; and

    (ii)   *Purpose* is the objective(s), goal(s) of the orator in making the oration, which implies some optimum form sought to meet such objective(s); and

    (iii) *Conditions* are the practical conditions to which the public oration will be addressed including the audience, recent events, knowledge and opinions of the orator; and

    (iv) *Constraints* are the physical and sensitivity constraints placed on any oration including time, length and subjects considered taboo and not to be mentioned; and

    (v)   *Propositions* are the proposed physical points and contents of the oration.

416. All forms of public oration under Rhetoric may be defined by six (6) generalised methods being *Kudos, Ethos, Pathos, Logos, Tempos* and *Dynamos*:

Methods of Rhetoric

    (i)   *Kudos* is the qualities of name, recognition and renown of the speaker; and

    (ii)   *Ethos* is the qualities of character, values and ethics of the speaker; and

    (iii) *Pathos* is the qualities of audience empathy and emotional connection between a speaker and their intended audience; and

    (iv) *Logos* is the qualities of a relevant narrative, engaging topic and reasonable argument used by a speaker to their intended audience; and

    (v)   *Tempos* is the qualities of the frequency or rate of words and phrases spoken in speech, therefore its "timing"; and

(vi) *Dynamos* is the qualities of energy level or power within the voice at different stages of a speech in contrast to the rate (tempo) of speech.

417. All forms of public oration under Rhetoric may be defined by seven (7) generalised types being *Monologue, Dialogue, Prologue, Epilogue, Catalogue, Analogue* and *Ideologue*:   *Categories of Rhetoric*

(i) *Monologue* is a form of speech characterised by a long speech by one person without interruption; and

(ii) *Dialogue* is a form of speech characterised by a spoken conversation between two (2) or more individuals; and

(iii) *Prologue* is a form of speech characterised as an introduction to some longer formal oratory event; and

(iv) *Epilogue* is a form of speech characterised as occurring at the audience at the conclusion of an event; and

(v) *Catalogue* is a form of speech characterised by the complete itemising of elements of an argument, often using the techniques of logic or dialectic to prove certain inferences in a forensic manner; and

(vi) *Analogue* is a form of speech characterised by the use of forensic questions and the subsequent answers to validate an argument in a methodical manner; and

(vii) *Ideologue* is a form of speech characterised by the expert knowledge and competence of the speaker providing specific knowledge on a topic, idea or belief.

Title III – Form

3.1 – Form

Article 77 - Form

418. ***Form*** is the shape, appearance and properties of an Object or Concept attributed through valid action or ritual in accordance with the present Maxims of Law.
Form

419. Form is never the Object or Concept itself, but the meaning and properties attributed to an Object or Concept through valid action or ritual. Therefore, all Form is fictional.
Form as fictional meaning

420. Common and fundamental Forms existing in Law include (but are not limited to): *Concept, Meaning, Idea, Model, System, Object, Being, Animal, Plant, Person, Right, Document, Trust, Good, Service, Property, Land, Fund, Money* and *Thing*:-
Common and fundamental Forms existing in law

    (i) *Concept* is any Idea received, conceived, perceived, comprehended or discerned by an Observer to exist according to some unique form of Meaning; and

    (ii) *Meaning* is the elemental semantic or symbolic significance or purpose or values associated with a Concept or Object; and the intended effect or change or thought sought in the mind of the Observer; and

    (iii) *Idea* in its simplest terms is a conceptual archetype; or mental representation associated with some distinct Meaning; and

    (iv) *Model* is an application of one or more Ideas, in a dimension of Reality, according to one or more rules and relations, representing a Cause as a conceptual archetype, or axiom, or logical hypothesis, or scaleable abstraction, or prototype, or physical production; and

    (v) *System* is a type of Model being a Set of Objects or Concepts, capable of being uniquely defined by a Set of Rules as to their Properties, Relations and Behaviours; and

    (vi) *Object* is any Model perceived, comprehended or discerned by an Observer to exist according to some Model of Reality; and

    (vii) *Being* is an embodiment of Unique Collective Awareness and a Computational Model according to the Standard Rules of Existence as applied to a certain Reality; and

    (viii) *Animal* is a Simple or Complex Cellular Being or Sapient Being of a Level 3 (Mono-Neural), Level 4 (Dual Neural), Level 5 (Complex Multi-Cellular) or Level 6 (Higher Order) form of life, distinguished primarily from Plant life by (a) significantly thinner single membrane cellular structures; and (b) the presence of Centriole and Mitochondria cellular elements; and (c) the use of metabolic chemical synthesis in the production of energy and nutrients; and

(ix) *Plant* is a Simple or Complex Cellular Being of a Level 3 (Mono-Neural) or Level 4 (Dual Neural) form of life, distinguished primarily from Animal life by (a) significantly thicker "double membrane" cellular structures; and (b) the absence of Centriole cellular elements; and (c) the use of photosynthesis in the production of energy and nutrients; and

(x) *Person* is a form of Sacred Circumscribed Space enclosing certain characteristics and appearances as the identity of one or more Beings, formed through a valid entry, registration and record within a Roll in accord with the present sacred Maxims and most sacred Covenant *Pactum De Singularis Caelum*; and

(xi) *Right* is a positively defined Capacity, Privilege, Liberty, Faculty, Power, Ownership, Possession, Interest or Benefit and its associated obligation, remedy or relief held in Trust for the benefit of a particular type of named or unnamed Person, under some proper Rule of Law and System of Justice; and

(xii) *Document* is a tangible, physical or electronic item containing an original or official or lawful written record of some Truth, or Fact, or Event or Issue or Matter, able to be used as Evidence itself or in support of Evidence; and

(xiii) *Trust* is confidence in and reliance upon some quality or thing or act as being true. Trust is also used to define a formal relation and agreement whereby an authorised party (Trustor) gives, grants, assigns or delegates one or more Rights to another (Trustee) under certain conditions for the benefit of a third party (Beneficiary); and

(xiv) *Good* is a gift in Trust; or a promise associated with a beneficial Right of Use for Sale or Bargain; and

(xv) *Service* is an agreement, duty or obligation to perform one or more acts for another; and

(xvi) *Property* is the highest Right a Person has or can have within a Lawful Jurisdiction to Control or Use or Claim any Thing or the Fruits of any Thing; and

(xvii) *Land* is a fictional term used to define the solid terrestrial surface of a planet based rather than any predominantly liquid surface such as a sea or gaseous structure such as an atmosphere or air; and any works or buildings within land, or upon land; and any fruits borne from land; and any rights to land, or the works or buildings within or upon land, or any Fruits borne from works or buildings within or upon land; and

(xviii) *Fund* is a sum of equal units representing certain Property Rights of monetary value, recorded in one or more designated accounts of a Body; and set apart for a term of years and one or more specific purposes; and available for the payment of debits, debts, legacies and claims in accord with these Maxims and the most sacred Covenant *Pactum De Singularis Caelum*; and

(xix) *Money* means a Right, established by laws consistent and in accord with these Maxims, whereby a System of rules, measures, records, accounts and procedures are formed to produce a consistent and stable Unit of Measure, Unit of Account, Unit of Redemption for Value, Means of Exchange and Reliable Store of Value; and

(xx) *Thing* means a temporary corporeal existence within Space-Day-Time of some Jurisdiction concerning a legal matter where the status or control or use or ownership of the Object is subject to dispute. A "Thing" cannot logically, morally or legally exist outside of a competent Forum of Law in accord with the present Maxims.

421. An Object or Concept without valid Form has no Existence in Law. *Invalid Objects or Concepts*

422. Any absence, mistake or error of action or ritual associated with Form shall render it defective, abrogated, or null to the extent of the severity of deficiency in accordance with these Maxims. *Deficient Form*

423. Such claims as length of existence, custom, consent and first claim have no effect in limiting any defectiveness of Form. *Limits of defective Form*

424. Any Form derived through action or ritual contrary to the prescript of a valid Maxim is therefore reprobate, suppressed and not permitted to be revived. *Failure of valid Form*

Article 78 - Concept

425. A **Concept** is any Idea received, conceived, perceived, comprehended or discerned by an Observer to exist according to some unique form of Meaning. *Concept*

426. A Concept is properly distinguished from an Object in that a Concept is said to exist purely within the dimension of Mind, whereas an *Concept vs. Object*

Object is considered to exist within the dimension of Reality.

427. The greatest Concept is the Divine as the total set of all meanings and definitions of all possible concepts, objects, matter, rules, life, mind, universe and spirit; and also known as the Absolute, ALL, Divine Creator, Father, God, Almighty, Allah, Great Spirit, Unique Collective Awareness, Ucadia and all other historic, customary and traditional names when used to describe the greatest of all possibilities. *(Greatest Concept)*

428. The smallest possible and least significant Concept is Nothing. No Concept can be smaller or less than Nothing. *(Smallest Concept)*

429. As the Divine means the "concept of all concepts" and the "set of all sets" there is no greater concept nor set. Therefore, every other possible concept or object is greater than Nothing and less than the Absolute, except the Divine. *(Concept of Concepts)*

430. As Ucadia means the complete and total Concept of the Divine and the Divine means the Concept of Ucadia, the total set of all meanings and definitions of all possible concepts, objects, matter, rules, life, mind, universe and spirit may be defined as the Concept of Ucadia in accord with the most sacred Covenant *Pactum De Singularis Caelum*:- *(Concept of Ucadia)*

    (i) A Concept that is in accord with the present Maxims and the Divine and Ucadia is said to belong to the Set of Concepts of Ucadia that are true and valid and legitimate; and

    (ii) A Concept that is not in accord with the present Maxims and the Divine and Ucadia is said to belong to the Set of Concepts of Ucadia that are absurd or untrue and invalid and illegitimate; and

    (iii) The presence of an Unreal Set of absurd, or untrue, or invalid or illegitimate Concepts as a valid Set within Ucadia cannot in itself be argued that Ucadia is contradictory, absurd, illegitimate, invalid or untrue. Instead, the presence of such a set proves the necessary completeness of the "set of sets"; and

    (iv) No Concept or Idea or Meaning can possibly exist outside the absolute jurisdiction and authority of Ucadia. Therefore, All Concepts and Ideas and Meaning are completely and absolutely under the jurisdiction and authority of Ucadia.

431. The very meaning of Concept itself depends upon the presence of three essential elements: *(Elements Of Concept)*

    (i) The existence of an Idea (some representation with Meaning) as the "thing observed"; and

(ii) An Observer; and

(iii) The action of observing with some level of Awareness in Mind that the thing observed possesses a certain unique form of Meaning.

432. As the action of an Observer is always relative to some degree, it is a falsity, error and absurdity to conclude that a Concept not witnessed by a particular Observer does not exist: *(Existence of Observed Concept)*

(i) Even if the Observer is defined as the Absolute Divine, the very fact that an Idea must be postulated in order to frame the hypothesis means that every Idea exists in theory at some level, no matter how unreal or improbable; and

(ii) Thus, every Idea received, conceived, perceived, comprehended or discerned by an Observer less than the Divine possesses existence even if the same lesser Observer no longer is present or actively observing the Idea.

433. A Concept always depends upon some level of Awareness in the Mind of the Observer to distinguish the certain unique form of Meaning of an Idea from another. The absence of any distinction or awareness in the Mind of the Observer therefore, negates the nature and existence of a distinct and unique Concept. *(Awareness of Concept)*

Article 79 - Meaning

434. **Meaning** is the elemental semantic or symbolic significance or purpose or values associated with a Concept or Object; and the intended effect or change or thought sought in the mind of the Observer. *(Meaning)*

435. In respect of Meaning:- *(Meaning as a Value)*

(i) As a sign or symbol, Meaning is a unit of semantic value in the context of other values, normally via some formal Language, to enable the transmission and reception of information and knowledge. Hence, letters, phonemes, words and sentences are all forms of Meaning in the context of a Language; and

(ii) As an intentional effect or change or thought in the mind of the Observer, Meaning is the elementary unit of a properly formed Model of knowledge based upon one or more Languages. Hence, philosophy, science and religious teachings are all Models of Meaning.

436. As Meaning requires both the prior existence of some formal system of Language and Model, the absence of a coherent Model or Language negates the ability to discern certain Meaning. *(Existence of Meaning)*

437. As all Meaning depends upon some formal system of Language and Models of Knowledge, the quality and design of such systems of Language and Model therefore affects the ability of the Observer to think and observe. — *Meaning Versus Observer*

438. The strength of a Concept is its relation to other unique forms of Meaning. Therefore, the strength of a Concept is its Meaning in relation to one or more formal systems of Language and Models of Knowledge. — *Concept relating to Meaning*

439. The highest and most authoritative linear Language and system of receiving and transmitting Meaning through speech and writing is the Ucadia Language of **Logos**: — *Logos*

   (i) Logos is a two dimensional linear visual and spoken language based on common phoneme elements that are found in all major languages to produce the most efficient, clear and consistent expressions of Meaning; and

   (ii) Logos is founded on five symbolic elements of Meaning called "KA" representing five generalisations in the production of sound namely lips, teeth, tongue, top of mouth and throat. These symbolic elements are then used to create more complex symbols representing the formation of consonants and vowels; and

   (iii) The symbolic representation of vowels and consonants are called "BA" symbolic elements representing 22 possible vowels and 33 possible consonants; and

   (iv) BA symbolic elements are then arranged in combinations or stand alone vowels to produce the spirit and essence of meaning called "LA" whereby the stable unit of Meaning is a vowel followed by a constant (VC) or its reverse (CV). There exists 1452 possible combinations (VC and CV) of BA Symbolic elements and with the 22 vowels on their own gives a total set of LA of 1474 possible symbols; and

   (v) The simplest way to learn the Logos set is by applying it to an existing foreign language first until familiarity of the units of sound and their symbols are mastered; and

   (vi) When the units of sound and their symbols in Logos are mastered, Logos can then be used to speak almost any major language, even if the user is not yet fully aware of the Meaning of the words they are producing. This is called "speaking of the tongues".

440. The highest and most authoritative Language and system of receiving — *Psygos*

and transmitting multi-linear (3 dimensional) Meaning is the Ucadia Language of ***Psygos***:

(i) Psygos is a three-dimensional and purely symbolic language of reasoning, learning, thought and wisdom; and

(ii) Psygos defines all knowledge of all possible Concepts and Objects into eleven major categories with each unique Concept represented by a standard shape, called a DA, namely: Divine, Universal, Rules, Matter, Galactic Objects, Stellar Objects, Planetary Objects, Life, Complex Life, Higher Order Life and Homo Sapien Life; and

(iii) The primary components of Psygos are Concepts and Objects (called DA) and their associated attributes that modify them (called MODIFIERS), bridge associations between concepts and objects (called RELATORS), associations that bridge between DA and MODIFIERS and/or RELATORS (called ASSOCIATORS) and tense/perspective (called TENSORS); and

(iv) All the primary components of Psygos are then used to construct rich varieties of symbolic sentences called DIA.

441. All possible Meaning is encompassed within Ucadia such that no Meaning may exist that is not subject to the absolute authority and jurisdiction of Ucadia in accord with the most sacred Covenant *Pactum De Singularis Caelum*: _{Meaning defined in Ucadia}

(i) Any Meaning that is in accord with the present Maxims is said to belong to the Set of Meanings of Ucadia that are true and valid and legitimate; and

(ii) A Meaning that is not in accord with the present Maxims is said to belong to the Set of Meanings of Ucadia that are absurd or untrue and invalid and illegitimate; and

(iii) The presence of an Unreal Set of absurd, or untrue, or invalid or illegitimate Meanings as a valid Set within Ucadia cannot in itself be argued that Ucadia is contradictory, absurd, illegitimate, invalid or untrue. Instead, the presence of such a set proves the necessary completeness of the "set of sets".

442. As all possible Meaning is encompassed within Ucadia such that no Meaning may exist that is not subject to the absolute authority and jurisdiction of Ucadia:- _{Ucadia Jurisdiction over Meaning}

(i) The first Meaning of any Concept listed within Ucadia as true and valid and legitimate shall be the Meaning defined by

Ucadia; and

(ii) Any Meaning of any Concept that is not consistent with the Meaning defined by Ucadia shall therefore belong to the Set of Meanings of Ucadia that are absurd or untrue and invalid and illegitimate.

443. Any Meaning that is not in accord with the present sacred Maxims is invalid. — *Meaning Versus Maxims*

444. Whenever one speaks or writes or signifies Meaning, it shall refer to the Ucadia Maxims and all associated Languages and Models of Knowledge first and foremost. — *Meaning within Maxims*

Article 80 - Idea

445. An *Idea* in its simplest terms is a *conceptual archetype*; or *mental representation* associated with some distinct Meaning. — *Idea*

446. An Idea is properly distinguished from a Model in that an Idea exists purely in Mind and is free to exist without necessary dependence to such constraints of one or more Systems of rules and relations, whereas a Model is said to exist according to a System of one or more rules and relations. — *Existence of Idea*

447. In relation to the two essential types of Ideas:- — *Idea Types*

(i) As a *conceptual archetype*, an Idea is considered a perfect example or "ideal" whereby other similar types of Concepts or Objects might be compared. Therefore, any form of Rules may also be considered an Idea; and

(ii) As a *mental representation*, an Idea may be some non-sensory computation or cognition (i.e. a thought); or some sensory symbolism (i.e. sound or image) or perceived dimension of objective existence (i.e. vision). Therefore, all Thoughts and Dreams may be considered in one sense as Ideas.

448. When an Idea is expressed vocally, or committed to paper or some electronic medium, then strictly such an Idea becomes a Model, as its expression is dependent upon at least one System of rules and relations of Language and secondly the limits of the System and medium of storage. — *Idea as a Model*

449. The very existence of an Idea itself depends upon the presence of some representation of Meaning. In the absence of any Meaning an Idea cannot be said to exist. — *Idea as a representation of Meaning*

450. The existence of an Idea merely depends upon the presence of some distinct representation and unit of Meaning and not any claimed — *Idea as a proof of its Existence*

acceptance or validation or arguments in support of or against such a representation by an Observer. Therefore, the existence of an Idea is itself proof of its own existence.

451. All Ideas may be defined by the computation or sensory nature of such mental representation, whether such representation has a real-world relation or whether such representation is simplified (abstract) or detailed. The most complex Ideas are multi-sensory, complex and visually detailed. Such Ideas are often classified as "Dreams". Ideas as a Computation

452. All Ideas as Models that qualify to be called Dreams, share the same essential elements: Idea as a Dream

    (i)   The Idea as a Dream is *dimensional* in that it perceives a construct whereby certain objects exist within a certain dimension defined by some form of boundary; and

    (ii)   The Idea as a Dream is *objective* in that the Dreamer as Observer therefore observes the Dream as a singular Object as the Observer can observe a "Dream within a Dream" but not two dreams of equal weight being simultaneously observed by a single Observer; and

    (iii)   The Idea as a Dream is *formal* in that the Dreamer as Observer therefore observes within the boundary of the Dream (Object) two or more Objects possessing some kind of form that can clearly be distinguished and recognised according to some system of rules and knowledge; and

    (iv)   The Idea as a Dream is *contextual* in that the Dreamer as Observer therefore observes within the boundary of the Dream (Object) two or more Objects whereby one or more Objects serve as the formal surroundings, circumstances, environment, background or settings of the Dream and one or more other Objects serve as the subject of observation; and

    (v)   The Idea as a Dream is *sequential* in that the events within the Dream unfolds in a sequence, even if chronological time is perceived differently; and

    (vi)   The Idea as a Dream is *real* in that the Dreamer as Observer validates and witnesses the Dream as an actual Object of existence; and within the Dream the objects have a real and material context, according to one or more rules and limits, even if such Objects do not exist or cannot exist in another form of reality.

453. The most complex Vision or Dream is the Concept of Existence of the Divine as Absolute Observer of Existence and the Universe as Dream as a Concept of Existence expressed by the present Maxims and the Ucadia Model.

454. All possible Ideas are circumscribed within Ucadia such that no Idea may exist that is not subject to the absolute authority and jurisdiction of Ucadia in accord with the most sacred Covenant *Pactum De Singularis Caelum*:

   (i) Any Idea that is in accord with the present Maxims is said to belong to the Set of Ideas of Ucadia that are true and valid and legitimate; and

   (ii) An Idea that is not in accord with the present Maxims is said to belong to the Set of Ideas of Ucadia that are absurd or untrue and invalid and illegitimate; and

   (iii) The presence of an Unreal Set of absurd, or untrue, or invalid or illegitimate Ideas as a valid Set within Ucadia cannot in itself be argued that Ucadia is contradictory, absurd, illegitimate, invalid or untrue. Instead, the presence of such a set proves the necessary completeness of the "set of sets" of Ideas.

Ideas within the jurisdiction of Ucadia

455. As all possible Ideas are circumscribed within Ucadia such that no Idea may exist that is not subject to the absolute authority and jurisdiction of Ucadia:-

   (i) All possible Ideas of all systems, models, cultures, sciences and history belong to one or more Sets subject to the absolute jurisdiction and authority of Ucadia; and

   (ii) No possible Idea of any higher order life form system, or culture, or science or model may exist independently of the primary jurisdiction and authority of Ucadia; and

   (iii) Any and every Idea that seeks to refute, or usurp the truth of the present Maxim is therefore a member of the absurd or untrue and invalid and illegitimate Unreal Set of Ideas of Ucadia.

Ideas as a set or sets within the absolute jurisdiction of Ucadia

456. Any Idea that contradicts or usurps these present sacred Maxims cannot be said to have validity or legitimacy.

Legitimacy Of an Idea

Article 81 - Model

457. A ***Model*** is an application of one or more Ideas, in a dimension of Reality, according to one or more rules and relations, representing a Cause as a *conceptual archetype*, or *axiom*, or *logical hypothesis*, or *scaleable abstraction*, or *prototype*, or *physical production*.

Model

458. A Model is properly distinguished from an Idea in that a Model is

Model Versus Idea

said to exist according to one or more rules and relations, whereas an Idea is said to exist without necessary dependence to such constraints of one or more rules and relations.

459. In relation to the six essential types of Models:-   *Model Types*

    (i) As a *conceptual archetype*, a Model is considered a generalised or idealised system whereby other systems may be compared and hypotheses and axioms derived or tested from it; and

    (ii) As an *axiom*, a Model is considered a statement so self-evidently true in the context of a system, that it can be used as the basis of creating more complex hypotheses or archetypes; and

    (iii) As a *logical hypothesis*, a Model is considered a method to represent a system of objects, phenomena and physical processes in a logical and cohesive manner; and

    (iv) As a *scaleable abstraction*, a Model is considered a physical representation of an object, that maintains accurate ratios and relations to the actual model, but may be at a scale many times smaller or larger than the real-world object; and

    (v) As a *prototype*, a Model is considered an early physical version, designed and manufactured to prove one or more solutions, or discover one or more flaws, often before the physical production of such a Model in any kind of volume of units; and

    (vi) As a *physical production*, a Model is considered to be a manufactured solution, often from a base or "original model".

460. The very existence of a Model itself depends upon the presence of some representation of a system with rules and relations. In the absence of any such system to give a Model its context and function, a Model cannot be said to exist.   *Model as a representation of a System*

461. The existence of a Model merely depends upon the presence of some distinct representation of a system with rules and relations and not any claimed acceptance or validation or arguments in support of or against such a system by an Observer. Therefore, the existence of a Model is itself proof of its own existence.   *Model as a System with Rules*

462. The Universe and all Existence may be properly defined as a Model, or simply a "Divine Creation".   *Universe as a Model*

463. All Models may be defined by their Specificity, Utility and Versatility:-   *Model in its component parts*

(i) Specificity relates to the quality of the Model to meet a desired outcome to some degree. For example, many Models of machines are by their nature highly specific; and

(ii) Utility relates to the usefulness of the Model in meeting the desired outcomes of the user. A high utility value indicates a high level of usefulness and usually a consequential high level of satisfaction; and

(iii) Versatility relates to the Model also being able to be applied to achieving different outcomes.

464. All human knowledge, technology, culture and tools may be properly defined as different types of Models, with different levels of specificity, utility and versatility. — Model types and knowledge

465. The most specific, useful and versatile "Model of all Models" is the Ucadia Model that systematically and objectively defines all possible Models into fourteen disciplines and systems being *Philologia, Logia, Etymologia, Symbologia, Eikologia, Cosmologia, Astrologia, Geologia, Physiologia, Anthropologia, Technologia, Sociologia, Psychologia* and *Theologia*:- — Fourteen Models of Ucadia

(i) ***Philologia*** is the Ucadia Model of Knowledge and discipline of the study of argument, reasoning, learning and awareness; and

(ii) ***Logia*** is the Ucadia Model of Knowledge and discipline of the study of language, speech, communication and knowledge; and

(iii) ***Etymologia*** is the Ucadia Model of Knowledge and discipline of the study of meaning and words; and

(iv) ***Symbologia*** is the Ucadia Model of Knowledge and discipline of the study of symbols, alphabets, sequences and encoding; and

(v) ***Eikologia*** is the Ucadia Model of Knowledge and discipline of the study of quantities, numbers, shapes, structures, sets, functions, algorithms, computations and the relations between these concepts; and

(vi) ***Cosmologia*** is the Ucadia Model of Knowledge and discipline of the study of universal rules, dimensions, matter, forces, energy, the universe, galaxies and very large structures; and

(vii) ***Astrologia*** is the Ucadia Model of Knowledge and discipline of the study of stars, interstellar systems and galaxies; and

(viii) **_Geologia_** is the Ucadia Model of Knowledge and discipline of the study of planets and moons; and

(ix) **_Physiologia_** is the Ucadia Model of Knowledge and discipline of the study of cellular (living) organisms and living systems; and

(x) **_Anthropologia_** is the Ucadia Model of Knowledge and discipline of the study of higher order life form species, societies and civilisations; and

(xi) **_Technologia_** is the Ucadia Model of Knowledge and discipline of the study of the application of knowledge for practical solutions, utensils and machines; and

(xii) **_Sociologia_** is the Ucadia Model of Knowledge and discipline of the study of higher order life form associations, groups, institutions, behaviours, cultures, identities and models; and

(xiii) **_Psychologia_** is the Ucadia Model of Knowledge and discipline of the study of cellular and non-cellular consciousness, cognition, mind, mental abilities and impediments, emotional states, behaviours and choices; and

(xiv) **_Theologia_** is the Ucadia Model of Knowledge and discipline of the study of the principles, methods, systems, arguments and proofs that rationally and reliably explain the existence, nature, function and intention of the Divine and other supernatural beings within, without and throughout the Universe.

466. As all possible Models belong as subsets of the Ucadia Model that systematically and objectively defines every possible Model into one of fourteen disciplines and systems, no Model may exist that is not subject to the absolute authority and jurisdiction of Ucadia in accord with the most sacred Covenant _Pactum De Singularis Caelum_:- Models as subsets of Ucadia

(i) All possible Models of all systems, models, cultures, sciences and history belong to one or more disciplines or sub-disciplines subject to the absolute jurisdiction and authority of Ucadia; and

(ii) No possible Model of any higher order life form system, or culture, or science or model may exist independently of the primary jurisdiction and authority of Ucadia; and

(iii) The entirety of every past, present or future scientific model exists within the dimensions, bounds, authority and jurisdiction of Ucadia according to the Ucadia Model; and

(iv) Any Model that is defined and properly identified in accord with the present Maxims is said to belong as a subset of the Model of Ucadia that is true and valid and legitimate; and

(v) A proposed or claimed Model that is not in accord with the present Maxims is said to belong to the Set of Model of Ucadia that are absurd or untrue and invalid and illegitimate; and

(vi) The presence of the Unreal Set of absurd, or untrue, or invalid or illegitimate Models as a valid Set of Ucadia cannot in itself be argued that Ucadia is contradictory, absurd, illegitimate, invalid or untrue. Instead, the presence of such a set proves the necessary completeness of the "set of sets" of all Models; and

(vii) Any and every Model that seeks to refute, or usurp the truth of the present Maxim is therefore a member of the absurd or untrue and invalid and illegitimate Unreal Set of Models of Ucadia.

467. Any Model that contradicts the present Maxims or the Ucadia Model has no validity or utility. — Model Versus Maxims within Ucadia

Article 82 - System

468. A ***System*** is a type of Model being a Set of Objects or Concepts, capable of being uniquely defined by a Set of Rules as to their Properties, Relations and Behaviours. — System

469. In relation to the general character of a System:- — General Character of System

(i) Every valid System is delineated by its boundaries, described by its structure, defined by its purposes and expressed in its functions; and

(ii) Every valid System possesses a set of two or more Rules as to the Properties, Relations or Behaviours of a Set of Objects or Concepts; and

(iii) Every valid System by definition is a unique Set.

Article 83 - Object

470. An ***Object*** is any Model perceived, comprehended or discerned by an Observer to exist according to some Model of Reality. — Object

471. An Object is properly distinguished from a Concept in that an Object is said to exist within the dimension of some form of Reality, whereas a Concept is said to exist purely within the dimension of Mind. — Object versus Reality

Title III – Form

472. The very meaning of Object itself depends upon the presence of three essential elements: *Essential elements of Object*

   (i)   The existence of a Model as the "thing observed" within the dimension of Reality; and

   (ii)   An Observer; and

   (iii)   The action of observing the Model with some level of Awareness in Mind.

473. In general reference to Theoretical and Real Objects: *Theoretical and Real Objects*

   (i)   Every Object belongs to an Existing Set; and

   (ii)   Every Object may itself be an Observer of some other Object; and

   (iii)   Every Object may be said to be a Set of lesser Objects; and

   (iv)   As an Object observed may itself be an Observer of other Objects, all forms of Objects are relative to some degree; and

   (v)   As an Object observed may itself be made up of lesser Objects, all sets of Objects are hierarchical; and

   (vi)   The smallest possible Object in Reality is a Theoretical Point; and

   (vii)   The smallest possible Object of Matter in Reality is a Unita made up of seven Theoretical Points (of Awareness); and

   (viii)   The smallest possible Object in Theory is the Concept of Unreal. No Object can be smaller or less than the Concept of Unreal; and

   (ix)   The greatest Theoretical or Real Object is the Divine as the total set of all existence and instances of all possible Objects, Matter, Rules, Life, Mind, Concepts, Universe and Spirit; and also known as the Absolute, ALL, Divine Creator, Father, God, Almighty, Allah, Great Spirit, Unique Collective Awareness, Ucadia and all other historic, customary and traditional names when used to describe the greatest of all possibilities.

474. As the Divine means the "set of all sets" and the "existence of all Objects" there is no greater Object nor set. Therefore, every other possible Object is greater than Unreal and less than the Absolute, except the Divine.   *The Divine relative to Sets and Objects*

475. An Object always depends upon some level of Awareness in the Mind of the Observer to distinguish the certain unique form of a Model from another. The absence of any distinction or awareness in the Mind of the Observer therefore negates the nature and relative   *Object and Awareness of Mind* existence of a distinct and unique Model and Object.

476. An Object may be defined as *Corporeal* or *Incorporeal*:

    (i)   A *Corporeal Object* possesses some original form or "physical body" within the dimension of Reality; and

    (ii)   An *Incorporeal Object* does not possess some original form or "physical body" within the dimension of Reality, yet its existence can be verifiable, such as a database, register or ledger, or axiom, or account or financial instrument.

Corporeal and Incorporeal Object

Article 84 - Being

477. A ***Being*** is an embodiment of Unique Collective Awareness and a Computational Model according to the Standard Rules of Existence as applied to a certain Reality.

Being

478. In reference to the concept of Being:-

    (i)   As an embodiment of Unique Collective Awareness, a Being is first and foremost a construct of unique Self-Awareness to some degree; and

    (ii)   Given all matter in every dimension possesses a level of Self-Awareness in order to function, all matter in every dimension can be said to have the presence of Being; and

    (iii)   As an embodiment of a Unique Computation Model or "Consciousness of Mind" according to the Standard Rules of Existence as applied to a certain Reality, a Being is an Object of some definitive kind capable of complex computational functions; and

    (iv)   All Objects, by definition are embodiments of Computational Models of Awareness according to certain Rules and Reality. Therefore all forms of Matter may also be described as Beings; and

    (v)   By definition, certain Objects, such as Ergons (e.g. Graviton, Neutrino, Magneton, Electron, Positron, Photon or Heton), may belong to intersecting sets whereby in one Reality such an embodiment of Awareness appears Real, whereas in the connected Reality, the Object is viewed as Unreal or a kind of "force"; and

    (vi)   Therefore, a Being may belong as an Object of an intersecting set whereby in one Reality such an embodiment of Awareness appears Real, whereas in the connected Reality, the Being is viewed as Unreal.

General Principles of Being

Title III – Form

479. All Beings may be defined as *Divine, Ethereal* or *Living*:-   Types of Beings

    (i)   A ***Divine Being*** is a specific embodiment of Unique Collective Awareness existing within a collective "abstracted" and Unreal Set or "Divine Reality" distinct from a dependent set of Reality necessary for material existence within the Standard Model of the Universe; and

    (ii)   An ***Ethereal Being*** is a specific embodiment of Unique Collective Awareness existing within an intersecting set of Unreal and Real, whereby to the Real Set the Being appears as a force without form, but in the intersecting set such a Being possesses a material existence in accord with the Standard Model of the Universe. The Conscious Mind itself of a Sentient Being or Sapient Being is such an example of an Ethereal Being; and

    (iii)   A ***Living Being*** is a specific embodiment of Unique Collective Awareness existing within Reality according to the Rules of the Standard Model of the Universe.

480. In reference to the concept of a *Divine Being*:-   Divine Being

    (i)   Every Set beginning from the Real Set of Unita under Divine Law and Natural Law is an abstracted and Unreal set produced through the computational awareness of increasing layers of matter; and

    (ii)   By definition, every set apart from the Real Set of Unita is an abstracted and Unreal Set representing a dimension of Divine Reality (dream); and

    (iii)   Therefore, every set of objects beginning with the abstracted set of "ideal life" of the Unita is a Divine Reality (dream).

481. In reference to the concept of a *Living Being*:-   Living Being

    (i)   By definition, every form of matter above the Unita is formed from the Unreal Set and therefore is borne from Divine Reality; and

    (ii)   Furthermore, every form of matter and therefore every form of Living Being requires the quality of Awareness and a Computational Model of Mind; and

    (iii)   As every form of matter and therefore every form of Living Being requires the quality of Awareness and a Computational Model of Mind, every Living Being from the level of a Sentient Being or Sapient Being is firmly bound to the existence of an Ethereal Being for its continued physical existence within a

Lex Positivum: Maxims of Positive Law

form of Reality; and

(iv) This Ethereal Being may be equated to the complex projection of "Imaginary Self" or "Ideal Self" of the Computational Model of Mind of a Sentient Being or Sapient Being, necessary for existence; and

(v) When two or more Sentient or Sapient Living Beings co-operate in some manner, so too do their Ethereal Beings in forming a "new reality" to some degree.

482. All sets of Beings may be defined according to ten categories being *Supreme, Primary, Higher, Ordinary, Ethereal, Material, Cellular, Sentient, Sapient* and *Imaginary*:-   *Categories of Beings*

(i) The *Supreme Being* is the formal name for the Divine as the Divine Observer and Divine Creator of all Existence as a singular Object or Set of all being and all possible objects, concepts, matter, rules, life, mind, universes, forces, sets or awareness; and

(ii) A *Primary Being* is a Living, Ethereal and Divine Being as a Primary Observer and singular Object or Set of all possible objects, concepts, matter, rules, life, mind, forces, sets or awareness at a particular key level of Matter and Existence (i.e. universe, galaxy, star, planet, life or species); and

(iii) A *Higher Being* is a Divine Being as a collective Consciousness and Being representing an essential stable character and attribute of a Primary Being, particularly as it applies to the presence of Cellular Beings and multiple species of Sentient and Sapient Beings within the jurisdiction and dimension of such a Primary Being; and

(iv) An *Ordinary Being* is an individual Divine Being formed either by virtue of the operation of Divine Law or the journey and transition of the Ethereal Being (Sentience or Sapience) of a previously Living Being; and

(v) An *Ethereal Being* in the context of such categorisation is narrowed to be the Computation Model of Mind of Sentient Beings and Sapient Beings that are Living or in transition to Divine after death of the Living Being; and

(vi) A *Material Being* is a Living Being in the form of all physical matter at a Unita, Super Sub Atomic, Sub Atomic, Atomic and Molecular Level; and

(vii) A *Cellular Being* is a unique Living Being from the perspective of a unique single cell, whether or not it is part of a body of a complex species or singular cellular life then viewed as a part of the greater universe of all cellular life on a planet; and

(viii) A *Sentient Being* is a unique Living and Ethereal Being as a member of a species of Level 5 (Complex Multi-Cellular Life); and

(ix) A *Sapient Being* is a unique Living and Ethereal Being as a member of a species of Level 6 (Higher Order Life); and

(x) An *Imaginary Being* is an Ethereal Being from the individual or collective imagination and minds of Sapient Beings that by constant reinforcement and thinking is given its own existence and reality.

483. A Being is formed by virtue of Operation of Divine Law, or Natural Law or Cognitive Law:- *Formation of Beings*

(i) By Divine Law in accord with the most sacred Covenant *Pactum De Singularis Caelum*, a stable and formal Being exists, consistent with the Standard Rules of Existence as applied to a certain Reality; or

(ii) By Natural Law when according to the Physical Laws of Matter and the Universe, an organised aggregation of Matter is formed under common purpose and existence; or

(iii) By Cognitive Law when a Sentient Being, or Sapient Being or Higher Being or Primary Being or Supreme Being conceives an embodiment of Unique Collective Awareness and Computational Model according to the Standard Rules of Existence as applied to a certain Reality.

484. A Being ceases to be by virtue of Operation of Divine Law, or Natural Law or Cognitive Law:- *Cessation of Beings*

(i) By Divine Law when according to the present Maxims in accord with the most sacred Covenant *Pactum De Singularis Caelum*, a stable and formal Being ceases to exist, consistent with the Standard Rules of Existence as applied to a certain Reality; or

(ii) By Natural Law when according to the Physical Laws of Matter and the Universe, an organised aggregation of Matter decays and ceases to function under common purpose and existence; or

(iii) By Cognitive Law when a Sentient Being, or Sapient Being or Higher Being or Primary Being or Supreme Being no longer conceives or trusts or remembers an embodiment of Unique

Collective Awareness and Computational Model according to the Standard Rules of Existence as applied to a certain Reality.

485. In relation to the cessation of Beings by Divine Law:- Cessation of Beings and Divine Law

   (i) It is the essence of comprehension of the Supreme Being that by Divine Will, existence is a continuous expression of Free Will and Choice and no Law can mandate the perpetual nor eternal existence of Creation except in absolute Trust in the Divine; and

   (ii) In accord with the Maxims of Divine Law and the most sacred Covenant *Pactum De Singularis Caelum*, the Supreme Being has pledged in perpetual Trust, that all lesser Beings that are said to have Divine Existence under Divine Law shall have perpetual and immortal Divine existence; and that none may be condemned nor ruled to cease to exist.

Article 85 – Thing

486. A ***Thing*** (also known as Rem or Re in Latin) is a temporary Form being the Object of one or more Rights against which there exists a dispute or ongoing controversy before a competent forum of law having jurisdiction. There are three general kinds of Things: Thing

   (i) Things Real, also known as Things Immovable and Corporeal, being lands, tenements and hereditaments; and

   (ii) Things Personal, also known as Things Movable and Incorporeal, being goods and chattels; and

   (iii) Things Mixed being Things partaking the characteristics of Real and Personal such as a Title Deed.

487. The Form of a Thing, also known as Rem or Re cannot exist except within the bounds of a matter before a competent forum of Law: 5 Forms of a Thing

   (i) The effect of treating the Object of a Right in dispute as a Thing is to cause it to be converted temporarily into a form of Property or Rem or Re itself; and

   (ii) By tradition in Western-Roman Law, a Person was prohibited from being converted into a Thing. However, Legal Persons in uncivilised and non-Ucadia forums are now commonly treated as Things; and

   (iii) Things are generally construed according to that which was the first cause of the dispute. Hence, the descriptions used in the first cause and subsequent form of action, generally determines the labelling and description of any Things in dispute; and

(iv) The Status of an Object as a Thing and Rem or Re only continues to exist, so long as the matter which first converted it into a Thing continues, such as a case of Bankruptcy sine die (deferred to a latter date); and

(v) When a Thing is the subject of an action of recovery (Things in action, or Things in Entry), such property cannot be granted over until the action ordered by the competent forum of law is completed.

488. The status of an Object being treated as a Thing dissolves when purchased, sold, bound or granted through a special form of agreement known as a Covenant Contract, also known simply as a Contract. Dissolving a Thing

3.2 – Form Creation & Modification

Article 86 – Form Creation & Modification

489. ***Form Creation & Modification*** is the means and process whereby a new Form is created or an existing Form is modified. All Form Creation & Modification is by Action. Form Creation & Modification

490. ***Creation*** is the Concept or Physical act of creating something (Concept or Object) that then exists in theory or reality. Creation

491. General types of Form Creation include (but are not limited to) *Revelation, Inception, Invention, Testification, Proclamation, Convention, Legislation, Incarnation, Instantiation, Circumscription, Consecration, Registration* and *Incorporation*:- General Types of Form Creation

(i) *Revelation* is the Creation by an Individual Person of new Form generally through the disclosure of some self-evident manifestation of Divine Illumination well beyond the scope and ordinary course of transmission of knowledge; and

(ii) *Inception* is the Creation by an Individual Person of new Form generally as some new thought with Meaning or Idea; and

(iii) *Invention* is the Creation by one or more Individual Persons of new Form generally as a Model or System – such as a new or improved Device or Composition; and

(iv) *Testification* is the Creation by one or more Individual Persons of new legal Form generally as Testimony, Affidavit, Attestation, Proof and Deed. Testification is enacted either by auricular or written form; and

(v) *Proclamation* is the Creation by an Authorised Individual Person of new legal Form generally as an Instruction, Order, Edict, Patent, Right, Charter or other Deed. A Proclamation is enacted either by auricular or written form; and

(vi) *Convention* is the Creation by three or more Individual Persons of new legal Form generally as a Proposition, Referendum, Election, Memorandum, Articles, Constitution or Bylaws. A Convention is enacted by written form but usually conducted with auricular testimony, speeches, debate, voting and contributions; and

(vii) *Legislation* is the Creation by three or more Authorised Individual Persons of new legal Form as an Act, or Bill or Statute or Policy. A Legislation is enacted by written form; and

(viii) *Incarnation* is the Creation of a living Form, such as a living Being; and

(ix) *Instantiation* is the production of an instance, example or specific application of Form within a given space or reality; and

(x) *Circumscription* is to draw a line or boundary around, to encircle or enclose as distinct from some other space or place; and

(xi) *Consecration* is the Act and Ritual of setting and dedicating something to a special sacred purpose or service; and

(xii) *Registration* is the Act and Ritual of entering a unique Record in a precise manner into an important roll of records known as a Register including any relevant transfer and acknowledgement of certain rights from the holder of the Form to the administrators of the Register; and

(xiii) *Incorporation* is the process of making one legal Form of any kind become a part of another separate Body; and declaring that the former shall be taken and considered as a part of the Body of the latter the same as if it were originally and fully set out therein.

492. **Modification** is the change of state, attributes, properties or behaviours of a Concept or Object over a given period of time.

Modification

493. General types of Form Modification include (but are not limited to) *Ratification, Exemplification, Extraction, Abstraction, Annexation, Advocation, Assignation* and *Alienation*:-

Types of Form Modification

(i) *Ratification* is the formal confirmation of a previous act done either by the original party (or parties) or by another; and

(ii) *Exemplification* is an official transcript of a document from public records, made in form to be used as evidence, and authenticated or certified by at least two or more separate persons as a true copy; and

(iii) *Extraction* is the production of a summary Form, or to get out by force, effort or contrivance a new Form that resembles in some way the Original; and

(iv) *Abstraction* is the action of separating a new fictional Form from the material of the original so that the new Form represents a logic extension and connection to the original; and

(v) *Annexation* is the action of merging of a territory or form into another body; and

(vi) *Advocation* is the right and transfer of property and possession of lands, tenements, or other things under proper ecclesiastical law by Persons not otherwise alienated or impeded; and

(vii) *Assignation* is the right and transfer of property and possession of lands, tenements, or other things by Persons not otherwise alienated or impeded; and

(viii) *Alienation* is the limited rights and transfer of property and possession of lands, tenements, or other things by alienated or impeded Persons.

Article 87 – Revelation

494. **Revelation** or *Prophecy* is the Creation by an Individual Person of new Form generally through the disclosure of some self-evident manifestation of Divine Illumination well beyond the scope and ordinary course of transmission of knowledge.

495. In reference to Authentic Revelation:-
    (i) As made manifest by these present sacred Maxims and the most sacred Covenant *Pactum De Singularis Caelum* and associated Covenants, the Divine Creator of all Existence chooses to communicate and overcome the limits and boundaries of Creation through Authentic Revelation; and
    (ii) Authentic Revelation may, or may not involve predictive elements, or apparent psychic or clairvoyant abilities of a messenger, or even claimed supernatural events in association

with the receiving of some message. However, such claims and elements are of lesser weight compared to the actual content and nature of disclosure or "message" of prophecy; and

(iii) A "genuine" Revelation is regarded as being some self-evident manifestation of Divine Illumination, providing extraordinary enlightenment, clarity, perception, reason and knowledge, beyond the norm. Therefore, prediction and claimed psychic messages alone do not make for Prophecy.

496. All Authentic Revelation shares seven essential elements in its arrival into the temporal realm being *Relevancy, Timely, Useful, Revelatory, Self-Evidential, Illuminative* and *Supernatural*:- Elements of Authentic Divine Revelation

(i) *Relevancy* means that Authentic Divine Revelation is always relevant to an age and time, or crisis or need, or pertinent to an important topic. Thus, the first test of Authentic Divine Revelation is that it comes when it is most needed, not when it may be wanted; and

(ii) *Timely* means that Authentic Divine Revelation always comes at precisely the right time, even if such time is not always known by all who seek or pray for such Revelation. Thus, the second test of Authentic Divine Revelation is that it meets timelines and promises previously made, even if such timelines were not fully understood; and

(iii) *Useful* means that Authentic Divine Revelation is above all useful and practical and helpful at the relevant time it comes. Thus, the third test of Authentic Divine Revelation is that the Divine does not send useless or stereotypical messages, but gives true gems of Divine Wisdom as Authentic Divine Revelation; and

(iv) *Revelatory* means that Authentic Divine Revelation "reveals" something new from what already "exists in plain sight". This is critical, as it demonstrates a respect for Tradition, for Custom and for context, such that the Divine never calls for such revolution or anarchy that a people lose trust in Heaven, but regain their faith; and

(v) *Self-Evidential* means that Authentic Divine Revelation once revealed is "self-evident" in that it manifests its own validation as Divine Truth - even if such a message is ignored, repudiated and rejected for being contrary to established doctrine of some body. Profound Wisdom that is Self-Evidentiary is far harder to fake and concoct as such knowledge carries its own character of authenticity; and

(vi) *Illuminative* means that Authentic Divine Revelation demonstrates extraordinary enlightenment, clarity, perception, reason and knowledge, beyond the norm. It does not mean cliché, or stereotypical, or self-reinforcing, or superficial, or simplistic doctrinal reinforcement. Genuine Divine Illumination does not necessarily mean occult and encoded meaning, nor such phrases and messages deliberately constructed to be confusing or to sound "profound". Instead, true Revelation is powerful in its own right; and

(vii) *Supernatural* means that Authentic Divine Revelation comes from a source and a circumstance clearly with the hallmarks of Divine intervention.

Article 88 – Inception

497. **Inception** is the Creation by an Individual Person of new Form generally as some new thought with Meaning or Idea.

<small>Inception</small>

498. In respect of Inception and the Creation of the Form of a new thought with Meaning or Idea:-

<small>General Characteristics of Inception</small>

   (i) Inception is equivalent to conceptualising or thinking in context. It is the ability to build models of thought and to test scenarios and ideas within such reality as a means of better describing the form; and

   (ii) All examples of higher memory and recall require the quality of Inception to make sense and often "rebuild" events in mind to produce a cohesive picture; and

   (iii) Inception is always a highly suggestive state whereby external inputs can drastically change the context of mind; and

   (iv) Inception is the first state of Awareness needed for learning; and

   (v) The prevalence of devices for visualisation can potentially impede the natural abilities of certain higher order life forms to adequately form deeper memories associated with Inception.

499. In respect of Inception versus Revelation:-

<small>Inception and Revelation</small>

   (i) Inception is distinct from Revelation by the exclusion of any supernatural inference; and

   (ii) Inception itself depends upon the prior existence of concepts and processes such as Perception, whereas Revelation does not.

Article 89 – Invention

500. ***Invention*** is the Creation by one or more Individual Persons of new Form generally as a Model or System – such as a new or improved Device or Composition. <!-- Invention -->

501. In respect of Invention and the Creation of the Form of a new Model or System:- <!-- General Characteristics of Invention -->

    (i) The "novelty" or newness of an Invention need not be radical or significant to produce a highly useful and practical solution or innovative application. Some of the most important breakthroughs in technology have come from returning to "first principles" of existing inventions; and

    (ii) An Invention need not be useful or even practical if it is able to show its genuine novelty and "newness"; and

    (iii) As all authentic Invention relates to the Creation of the Form of a new Model or System, all Invention depends upon and relates to pre-existing Systems and Models for context.

502. In respect of Invention versus Revelation:- <!-- Invention and Revelation -->

    (i) Invention is distinct from Revelation by the exclusion of any supernatural inference; and

    (ii) Invention itself depends upon the prior existence of models and systems such as meaning and classifications, whereas Revelation does not.

Article 90 – Convention

503. ***Convention*** is the Creation by three or more Individual Persons of new legal Form generally as a Proposition, Referendum, Election, Memorandum, Articles, Constitution or Bylaws. A Convention is enacted by written form but usually conducted with auricular testimony, speeches, debate, voting and contributions. <!-- Convention -->

504. In respect of Convention and the Creation of new Form:- <!-- General Characteristics of Convention -->

    (i) By definition, associations as a body corporate or body politic can only be properly formed through the conducting of at least one Convention, to form and ratify the objects and function of the new association, body or society; and

    (ii) An ecclesiastical Convention may be known as a Synod or Convocation; and

    (iii) Companies and bodies may periodically hold regular annual Conventions to debate new proposed bylaws or policies, elect new positions or report on the previous period. Such Conventions are usually called Annual General Meetings.

Article 91 – Circumscription

505. ***Circumscription*** is to draw a line or boundary around, to encircle or enclose as distinct from some other space or place. A secular term for Circumscription is *enclosure* or simply *close* or *closure*.

    [margin: Circumscription]

506. In respect of Circumscription and the Creation of new Form:-

    (i) Whether or not the process of Circumscription is claimed to be purely secular in function, all proper Circumscription is ecclesiastical and ritual in practice, subject to the most sacred Covenant *Pactum De Singularis Caelum*; and

    (ii) A Person having no authority or failing to follow the proper Rite is incapable of performing Circumscription; and

    (iii) A Legislature having no ecclesiastical or moral authority, or under impediment for lack of just, fair and moral law, is incapable of passing laws or bylaws concerning the "enclosure" of form, property, land or person.

    [margin: General Characteristics of Circumscription]

Article 92 – Consecration

507. ***Consecration*** is the Act and Ritual of setting and dedicating something to a special sacred purpose or service.

    [margin: Consecration]

508. In respect of Consecration and the Creation of new Form:-

    (i) All proper Consecration is ecclesiastical and ritual in practice, subject to the most sacred Covenant *Pactum De Singularis Caelum*; and

    (ii) A Person having no authority or failing to follow the proper Rite is incapable performing Consecration; and

    (iii) An ecclesiastical body, society, institute, building or place is incapable of functioning according to its proper objects, unless duly Consecrated in accordance with the necessary and prescribed form.

    [margin: General Characteristics of Consecration]

Article 93 – Registration

509. ***Registration*** is the Act and Ritual of entering a unique Record in a precise manner into an important roll of records known as a Register including any relevant transfer and acknowledgement of certain rights from the holder of the Form to the administrators of the Register.

    [margin: Registration]

510. In respect of Registration and the Creation of new Form:- — General Characteristics of Registration

  (i) The entry of a record into a register or roll is usually determined by certain laws, customs or restrictions. The Person authorised to make and administer such entries is usually called the Registrar; and

  (ii) The right or privilege to have a record entered into a register or roll is distinct from its entry and similarly determined by law; and

  (iii) As all registers are by definition ecclesiastical property owing their authority and power under the most sacred Covenant *Pactum De Singularis Caelum*, all positions of registrars are ecclesiastical in nature; and

  (iv) The highest entry is a proper entry into a Ucadia register or roll, in accordance with the present Maxims.

511. The registration of an entry into a superior Register in which the Form is already registered into an inferior Register shall automatically render the inferior record null and void with the lawful conveyance of any rights to the superior register unless the act and ritual of conveyance is found to be in error. — Registration in Superior Register

Article 94 – Incorporation

512. ***Incorporation*** is the process of making one legal Form of any kind become a part of another separate Body; and declaring that the former shall be taken and considered as a part of the Body of the latter the same as if it were originally and fully set out therein. — Incorporation

513. In respect of Incorporation and the Creation of new Form:- — General Characteristics of Incorporation

  (i) Incorporation is a common feature in the registration of companies and associations, whereby a company that is "incorporated" is effectively "merged" under the authority and control of the entity claiming ownership of the register itself; and

  (ii) By definition, a corporation or company cannot possess greater authority or power than the parent company into whose register the lesser company or association was "incorporated"; and

  (iii) Incorporation is similar to the notion of Annexation; and

  (iv) All Ucadia companies and associations are properly incorporated first and originally into Ucadia registers and rolls, before any registration or recording within Non-Ucadia registers or rolls; and

(v) A company or association already properly incorporated through some original registration, is usually required to be registered into a new jurisdiction as a "foreign corporation" without losing any of its original powers or authorities of its parent jurisdiction; and

(vi) Under International Law, an unincorporated company or association has no proper legal status or legal personality and therefore cannot enter into contracts, properly own or defend property rights, or legally supply goods or services, or employ people or hold bank accounts; and cannot sue or be sued.

Article 95 – Ratification

514. ***Ratification*** is the formal confirmation of a previous act done either by the original party (or parties) or by another. — Ratification

515. In respect of Ratification and the Modification of Form:- — General Characteristics of Ratification

   (i) The formation of most companies, bodies corporate or bodies politic require that after the formation, registration or incorporation process that the memorandums, articles and any statutes or by-laws are then formally ratified by members; and

   (ii) Most jurisdictions require that the decisions made by the directors of companies and associations are duly ratified by the members of the society or body through some formal means; and

   (iii) In the absence of formal ratification, a non-ratified instrument is technically "inchoate" and not complete to the extent that its full powers may not be in effect.

Article 96 – Exemplification

516. ***Exemplification*** is an official transcript of a document from public records, made in form to be used as evidence, and authenticated or certified as a true copy usually by two or more persons. — Exemplification

517. In respect of Exemplification and the Modification of Form:- — General Characteristics of Exemplification

   (i) An Exemplification is unique from a normal certification in that it contains at least three separate and unique certifications, rather than just one; and

   (ii) The first certification within a proper Exemplification is normally to certify one or more documents or acts. This frequently includes the affixing of some official seal of the body representing the issuance of the Exemplification; and

(iii) The second certification within a proper Exemplification is normally to certify the authority of the first certification, by a separate and distinct person and officer; and

(iv) The third and final certification within a proper Exemplification is normally to certify and testify to the familiarity, authenticity and identity of the second certification as "witness". This can sometimes be done by the first person (who created the first certification), or a distinct witness who knows the second person.

518. A Certificate of Exemplification as a formal Certificate issued under an Official Seal of Ucadia and referring to the extract of a Matter and then Certified by a Principal and Witness under Oath as being true shall be *Prima Facie* proof in any jurisdiction where there exists the Rule of Law and competent forums of Law. — Certificate of Exemplification

519. The refusal of a foreign or external body to accept a proper Ucadia Certificate of Exemplification is a confession of perfidy, incompetence and heresy against all forms of Law. — Refusal of Recognition of Exemplification

Article 97 – Extraction

520. ***Extraction*** or "extract" is the action of the production of a summary Form, or to get out by force, effort or contrivance a new Form that resembles in some way the Original. — Extraction

521. An extract may never be correctly called a copy. The word copy implies a faithful duplication of the original. However, an extract is not dependent on an accurate depiction of the original, only a summary or contrivance, which implies an extract may not resemble the original accurately. — General Characteristics of Extraction

Article 98 – Abstraction

522. ***Abstraction*** is the action of separating a new fictional Form from the material of the original so that the new Form represents a logic extension and connection to the original. — Abstraction

523. A valid Form is considered to be created by Abstraction when such Form has been validly registered in a Great Register of a valid Ucadian Society and the Document has been published in at least two Communication Mediums for view. — Ucadia Abstraction

524. Possession of a Valid Abstract in no way denotes ownership, nor — Holding of

conveyance of Rights, or any form of Property to the Holder. *Abstraction*

Article 99 – Annexation

525. ***Annexation*** is the action of merging of a territory or form into another body. *Annexation*

526. In respect of Annexation and the Modification of Form:- *General Characteristics of Annexation*
    (i)   Annexation is commonly used to define a formal act whereby a state proclaims its sovereignty over territory hitherto outside its domain; and
    (ii) Annexation may be a unilateral act made effective by actual possession and legitimised by general recognition; and
    (iii) Annexation may also refer to attaching an illustrative or auxiliary document to a legal form as an "annexure".

Article 100 – Advocation

527. ***Advocation,*** also known as *Advowson* or *Patronage*, is the right and transfer of property and possession of lands, tenements, or other things under proper ecclesiastical law by Persons not otherwise alienated or impeded. *Advocation*

528. In respect of Advocation and the Modification of Form:- *General Characteristics of Advocation*
    (i)   Advocation as Advowson is still used by many jurisdictions holding estates by noble or ecclesiastical title, whereby such vacant estates and titles are allocated to suitable persons not otherwise impeded; and
    (ii) Under Ucadia Law, certain real property and estates is transferred and managed according to Advocation; and
    (iii) A society that functions according to two or more morally repugnant, corrupt and absurd principles is disqualified from claiming the right to manage rights under Advocation.

3.3 – Form Abrogation & Corruption

Article 101 – Form Abrogation & Corruption

529. ***Form Abrogation and Corruption*** is the means and process of diminishing, damaging or destroying some Form. All Form Abrogation and Corruption is by Action. *Form Abrogation & Corruption*

530. ***Abrogation*** is to repeal, eliminate, dissolve, nullification or voidance of a Form by claimed lawful means. *Abrogation*

531. General types of Form Abrogation include (but are not limited to) *Reprobation, Suppression, Prohibition, Interdiction* and *Nullification*:- <!-- Types of Abrogation of Form -->

    (i)   *Reprobation* is to reject, reproof, disqualify or censure a Form; and

    (ii)   *Suppression* is to put down, execute or withhold a Form by force or authority, especially in the withholding or withdrawal of Form from publication or manufacture. Suppression is equivalent to the terms Prohibition and Censorship; and

    (iii)   *Prohibition* is to forbid an act or activity by sovereign, legislative or judicial act; and

    (iv)   *Interdiction* is an ecclesiastical, sovereign or judicial censure forbidding a person entry, or services, or safe harbour or sometimes habitation (in the case of exile); and

    (v)   *Nullification* is to render a Form null and void therefore of no legal or binding force; of no value, use, capability or importance. Hence, to Nullify is to formally revoke the validity of a particular Form, to annul it.

532. **Corruption** is the perversion, putrefaction, infection, decomposition, debasement or destruction of a Form. <!-- Corruption -->

533. General types of Form Corruption include (but are not limited to) *Misrepresentation, Malediction* and *Destruction*:- <!-- Types of Corruption of Form -->

    (i)   *Misrepresentation* is the false representation of Form to obtain an unjust advantage or to injure the Rights of another, also known as Fraud; and

    (ii)   *Malediction* is the utterance of a curse, to revile, or slander; as well as the quality of being under a ban or curse; and

    (iii)   *Destruction* is to ruin something completely. To ruin the structure or organic existence or condition of a thing.

Article 102 – Reprobation

534. **Reprobation** is to reject, reproof, disqualify or censure a Form. <!-- Reprobation -->

535. Any Form that is Reprobate is considered rejected, cast off as worthless, immoral, damned and an injury before true law. <!-- Effect of Rebrobation -->

536. In accordance with these Maxims and by Divine Law, all laws claiming to be true and honourable that are not lawfully in concordance with these Maxims are hereby reprobate. <!-- Maxims and Reprobation -->

Article 103 – Suppression

537. ***Suppression*** is to put down, execute or withhold a Form by force or authority, especially in the withholding or withdrawal of Form from publication or manufacture. Suppression is equivalent to the terms Prohibition and Censorship. — *Suppression*

538. In accordance with these Maxims and by Divine Law, no valid Maxim may be suppressed by any force, person, entity or spirit. — *Effect of Suppresion*

539. In accordance with these Maxims and by Divine Law, all laws claiming to be true and honourable that are not lawfully in concordance with these Maxims are hereby suppressed. — *Maxims and Suppresion*

Article 104 – Nullification

540. ***Nullification*** is to render a Form null and void therefore of no legal or binding force; of no value, use, capability or importance. Hence, to Nullify is to formally revoke the validity of a particular Form, to annul it. — *Nullification*

541. A Form that is Nullified ceases to have lawful existence. — *Nullification and Existence*

542. Nullification is dependent upon the authority and rights of the Form of Law that permits such authority. A body with lesser rights and authority cannot reasonably, logically or morally seek to nullify a form from a higher jurisdiction. — *Nullification and Law*

543. No Non-Ucadian body, company, society, entity, person or being has the power or authority to nullify or claim to nullify any form within Ucadia whatsoever. — *Ucadia Law and Nullification*

544. Any form that is null and void cannot be revived. — *Valid Nullification*

Article 105 – Misrepresentation

545. Misrepresentation is the false representation of Form to obtain an unjust advantage or to injure the Rights of another. — *Mis-representation*

546. Misrepresentation is a deliberate act of deception. Hence, fraud is the deliberate concealment of a known truth in order to mislead or cheat. Thus to "deceive" is to cause a man or woman to believe what is false, to lead into error and delude. — *Mis-representation and Fraud*

547. In reference to Misrepresentation and Fraud:- — *Characteristics of Mis-representation and Fraud*

   (i) Fraud and Justice can never dwell together. By no agreement or statute can it be lawfully effected that a fraud shall be practised; and

(ii) No right of action can have its origin in fraud. No action may arise out of a fraudulent consideration; and

(iii) A concealed fault is equal to a deceit; and

(iv) No action may arise out of a fraudulent consideration, agreement or contract; and

(v) The action against a wrong has no material influence upon its condition. A fraud remains a fraud whether challenged, repelled or temporarily forgotten.

Title IV – Place, Space & Time

4.1 – Place & Space

Article 106 – Place

548. A ***Place*** is a fictional form defining an area with definitive boundaries applied to any locality defined by law, however large or however small. It may be used to designate a country, state, county, town, or a very small portion of a town.   *Place*

549. The term *Place* originates directly from *placitum* as the official term invented and introduced by the Carolingians in the 8th Century for locations and processes of judicial review or arbitration of smaller property disputes, civil matters and non-capital crimes:-   *Origin of Place*

    (i) Under the Instatutum, ("Institutions") of Sacré Loi (Sacred Law) first introduced by Charles Martel in 738 CE, all disputes between smaller estates known under Carolingian law as "peto sessionis" (petty sessions) were to be heard in "Placitum", while all serious property disputes and crimes carrying the death penalty called "quatio sessionis" were to be heard in "Manorum" being at the Manor Hall of the Baron to whom the accused served; and

    (ii) The formal name for any matter brought before a Placitum since the 8th Century was a *Placita*, or Place in English; and

    (iii) The formal and original name for a defense was *plene*, as the true origin of "plea", not *placita*; and

    (iv) In accordance with the Sacré Loi (Sacred Law) defined by the Carolingians in the 8th Century, a *Placita* (matter within a Placitum) was presided over by one (1) to three (3) justices of the peto (petit sessionis) known as Iustitia Petit bound under solemn oath to uphold and protect the law; and

    (v) In accordance with Sacré Loi (Sacred Law), the process of how a controversy was brought as a *Placita* and then adjudicated as process (processio) remains the foundation of judicial procedure of western law; and

    (vi) In Non-Ucadian courts and societies, the term *placita* is still used as the formal Latin name for a "plea"; and

    (vii) The term *Placita Coronae* (Pleas of the Crown) is still used by certain Non-Ucadian courts and societies as the formal Latin term for trials for crimes and misdemeanours wherein the king (or queen) is plantiff on behalf of the people; and

    (viii) The term Placita Juris (Pleas of Law) is still used by certain

Non-Ucadian courts and societies as the formal Latin term for the rules, procedures and case law of a particular jurisdiction and forum of law, as distinct from any broader maxims or legal reasoning; and

(ix) *Placitare* is still used by certain Non-Ucadian courts and societies as the formal Latin term defining "to plead".

550. By the origin of the term and its application in law, a Place must have a defined boundary and clear rules of law. In the absence of either, a location may not be properly called a "place". Place must have defined boundaries and law

551. Through the intentional misrepresentation and miuse of the Latin terms *placita* and *placitum*, certain Non-Ucadian Courts and Societies have historically claimed a form of jurisdiction in one sense, purely upon the use of Place Names, thereby implying the *de jure* forms of law:- Place, Jurisdiction and Plea in Non-Ucadian Courts

(i) If an accused accepts the place of their location, or court, or summons, or alleged offence, then by default they accept the laws of the place and the jurisdiction of the courts of the place; and

(ii) The type of plea and nature of plea is also determined and constrained by default by the same obfuscated logic whereby once accepting the place and the jurisdiction of the courts of the place, the accused is limited by the rules of such a court in the manner and proceeding of their defence.

552. All Places listed on official Ucadia Documents and Instruments are by default subject to Ucadia Law and Ucadia Jurisdiction first, before any other form of law:- Place and Ucadia Jurisdiction and Courts

(i) The use of common place names is permitted within Ucadia Law, to define Ucadia societies, bodies and boundaries; and

(ii) No Non-Ucadian court or jurisdiction may claim authority over any Ucadia Document, Instrument or Person in the use of Place Names, unless express official and written authority is granted to hear and resolve a matter within a Non-Ucadian court or jurisdiction.

Article 107 - Site

553. A ***Site*** is a fictional form defining a plot of ground suitable or set apart for some specific use in law. More specifically, a *Site* is the position and place where a thing is considered; and the seat or location of the law and jurisdiction over such a thing. Site

554. The term Site originates from the Latin term *situs*, possessing several Origin of the

key meanings from the time of ancient Rome:- term Site

- (i) A place set apart for the expressed sacred purpose of burial of the remains of the dead; and
- (ii) The permanent and fixed residence of the dead; and
- (iii) A place set apart for the judgment and suffering of those put to death under law; and
- (iv) A building or structure built or founded for the purpose of interring the remains of the dead or condemned – a tomb, torture chamber, mausoleum, or catacomb (network of tombs).

555. Any person, body or group that publicly or formally denies the true origin of the term Site and its historic association with places of the condemned and the dead, is culpable of falsity, absurdity and dishonesty, with any such claim null and void from the beginning. Absurdity of any rejection of true origin of term Site

556. In Non-Ucadian legal systems and societies, the Latin term *situs* is commonly used in the phrase *Lex Situs*, usually mis-translated and mis-claimed as "the law of the place". The much older Latin phrase *Lex Loci*, being the traditional and accurate meaning of "the law of the place":- Lex Situs (law of the place)

- (i) Frequent confusion arises in Non-Ucadian legal systems and societies over the accurate use of *Lex Loci* and the mis-translated and mis-used phrase *Lex Situs*, both claiming to have similar meanings; and
- (ii) Generally, Lex Situs is applied by default as the "law of the place of the thing (in custody)" unless challenged or Non-Ucadian entities and persons accept the manifest moral repugnancy and perfidy against the law of using such imputations; and
- (iii) A rule of international merchant (pirate) law is that lands and other immovables are governed by the *Lex Situs*, that is, by the law of the country where they are situated; and
- (iv) A general rule of international law is that lands and other immovables are governed by the lex situs, that is, by the law of the country where they are situated.

Article 108 - Location

557. A ***Location*** is a fictional Form created through the combined action of a valid survey by succession and registration in relation to one unique dimension of temporal space in relation to neighbouring Location

space.

558. Valid survey by succession is the principle that a survey cannot be true to describing a particular dimension of temporal space in relation to neighbouring space if it does not belong by succession to a hierarchy of valid survey from the Absolute to a particular Cadastral survey. *(Survey of Location)*

559. Any survey unable to prove its membership to a hierarchy of succession of a detailed survey from a particular Cadastre Location to the Absolute is automatically invalid, including any and all associated land title, rights, claims, contracts and agreements. *(Provenance of Survey)*

560. Registration of a valid Location is when a valid survey is registered as recorded within a valid Register originating from the Great Register of One Heaven as the one true and accurate survey of a Cadastre Location. *(Registration of Location)*

561. Any valid survey of a particular Cadastre Location that is not properly registered into a valid Register originating from the Great Register of One Heaven is automatically invalid, including any and all associated land title, rights, claims, contracts and agreements. *(Authenticity of Survey of Location)*

562. There are only seven (7) valid forms of Location: *Absolute, Universal, Galactic, Stellar, Planetary, Terrestrial* and *Cadastre*:- *(Valid Forms of Location)*

 (i) An *Absolute Location* is a valid survey and registration of the primary location of all locations being the One, the Absolute and the Unique Collective Awareness as defined by these Maxims and specifically the Maxims of Divine Law and Natural Law. By these Maxims, there is only one (1) possible Absolute Location; and

 (ii) A *Universal Location* is a valid survey by succession and registration of a sub-location within the surveyed Absolute Location representing a region of the Universe larger than a Galaxy as defined by the Maxims and the Ucadian knowledge indexes; and

 (iii) A *Galactic Location* is a valid survey by succession and registration of a galactic location within the surveyed Universal Location representing a valid Galaxy as defined by the Maxims and the Ucadian knowledge indexes; and

 (iv) A *Stellar Location* is a valid survey by succession and registration of a stellar (sun) location within a surveyed Galactic Location representing a valid star system as defined by the Maxims and the Ucadian knowledge indexes; and

 (v) A *Planetary Location* is a valid survey by succession and registration of a planetary location within a surveyed Stellar (Sun) Location representing a valid planet as defined by the Maxims and the Ucadian knowledge indexes; and

(vi) A *Terrestrial Location* is a valid survey by succession and registration of the entire terrestrial land mass of a planet, including its method of survey as defined by the Maxims and the Ucadian knowledge indexes; and

(vii) A *Cadastre Location* is a valid registration through succession of a surveyed and marked out tract of land, claim or settlement in relation to other neighbouring landmarks and locations within a valid registered terrestrial land survey.

Article 109 – Residence

563. A **Residence** is a fictional term defining the Place recognised by law as the primary dwelling place of a Person or the primary management location of a Corporation.
<small>Residence</small>

564. The term Residence originates from the Latin term *res*, meaning "thing, pertaining to, or property of" and dentis meaning "the dead":-
<small>Origin of the term Residence</small>

    (i) A place set apart for the expressed sacred purpose of burial of the remains of the dead; and

    (ii) The permanent and fixed residence of the dead; and

    (iii) A place set apart for the judgment and suffering of those put to death under law; and

    (iv) A building or structure built or founded for the purpose of interring the remains of the dead or condemned – a tomb, torture chamber, mausoleum, or catacomb (network of tombs).

565. In respect of a Person, a place may be deemed a Primary Dwelling Place or Residence under the following conditions:-
<small>Residence as Primary Dwelling Place</small>

    (i) If a Person lives or stays at a place for an extended period of time, defined by law, and usually a period of not less than several months; and

    (ii) If a Person has been granted a legal status in recognition of their habitation at a place, such as short-term or long-term residency status.

566. In respect of a Corporation, a place may be deemed a primary management location or primary office or Residence under the following conditions:-
<small>Residence as Primary Management Location</small>

(i) If the management of a Corporation habitate a place for an extended period of time, defined by law, regardless of whether business is or is not conducted in other places; and

(ii) If a Corporation has been granted legal status in terms of recognition of their primary management location via registration of a primary office or office for legal service.

Article 110 – Space

567. Space is a measure of area, enclosure or dimension either consumed by one or more objects, or consuming and encompassing one or more things. All real objects exist in some kind of measurable Space. Space

568. The word Space is derived from the Latin *spatium* meaning "extent" or "distance." Origin of Concept of Space

569. In respect of Space and real Objects and Things:- Space and Objects

(i) All real and tangible Objects and Things occupy some area (volume) of Space and exist within some greater definable Space, whereby the location of such a particular Object or Thing may be ascertained; and

(ii) A Thing neither capable of occupying Space nor existing in Space is said to be "intangible".

Article 111 – Sacred Circumscribed Space

570. ***Sacred Circumscribed Space*** is a uniquely recorded area, enclosure and dimension of Ucadia Sacred Space-Day-Time as prescribed by the most sacred Covenant *Pactum De Singularis Caelum*, and associated covenants, charters and Maxims. Sacred Circumscribed Space

571. Only bodies, entities, associations, societies or persons authorised under these present sacred Maxims and the most sacred Covenant *Pactum De Singularis Caelum* are permitted to record, register, keep and maintain Sacred Circumscribed Space. Authority of Sacred Circumscribed Space

572. All proper, valid and legitimate Sacred Circumscribed Space is a clearly and uniquely named dimension of Ucadia Space-Day-Time, whereby:- Conditions of Sacred Circumscribed Space

(i) Such Sacred Circumscribed Space is properly defined by an eighteen digit character number and identifier (XXXXXX-XXXXXX-XXXXXX), consistent with the most sacred Covenant *Pactum De Singularis Caelum*; and

(ii) The specific Sacred Circumscribed Space is able to properly define its origin to a higher jurisdiction of Sacred Circumscribed Space, also identified by a proper eighteen digit character number and identifier; and

    (iii)   The specific Sacred Circumscribed Space was either formed in accord with the most sacred Covenant *Pactum De Singularis Caelum*, or associated Covenants and Charters, or by one or more properly dispensed sacraments of the thirty three Supreme Sacred Gifts of Heaven; and

    (iv)   The Sacred Circumscribed Space does not contradict or usurp any previous proper, valid and legitimate existing Sacred Circumscribed Space.

573. Any and all claimed Juridic, Legislative and Sovereign Acts contrary to the authority of the most sacred Covenant *Pactum De Singularis Caelum* and these present Maxims that claim the right to form circumscribed space by such methods including (but not limited to) enclosure, alienation, enrolment, registration or certification; and all subsequent, dependent and related Statutes, including but not limited to all fraudulent, perfidious, false and deceptive documents purported to be of an earlier age in relation to the claimed enclosure of certain lands, spaces, closes, fields, places, regions, zones, precincts, territories, dominions and estates are hereby disavowed as morally repugnant, profane, sacrilegious, heretical and contrary to the Rule of Law, Civilised Society and Divine Law and are therefore invalid, illegitimate and null and void ab initio (from the beginning), having no force or effect or Rights in law.
   Contrary Acts to Pactum De Singularis Caelum and Maxims

574. All Measurement and Standard of Sacred Circumscribed Space shall always be in accord with the most sacred Covenant *Pactum De Singularis Caelum*, associated covenants and charters, Ucadian Law and these present Maxims. All other forms of measurement and standards shall be null and void, unlawful and illegal, having no force or effect.
   Measurement and Standards for Sacred Circumscribed Space

575. By the Divine Mandate and Authority of the most sacred Covenant *Pactum De Singularis Caelum* and the present sacred Maxims, duly registered and authorised bodies, associations, societies, companies, persons and entities shall form, maintain and keep in custody the following types of Registers of Sacred Circumscribed Space, including (but not limited to):-
   Valid and Legitimate forms of Sacred Circumscribed Space

    (i)   *Land* (also deliberately misspelled within invalid and fraudulent laws as England) as a fixed and circumscribed piece of ground and earth of one Acre or more in surface area and then measured from the centre of the planet to the centre point of the surface area; and

(ii) *Forest* as a fixed and circumscribed piece of ground and earth of ten Acres or more in surface area that is preserved or reclaimed wilderness, natural habitat, untouched and uncultivated for agriculture; and

(iii) *Island* (also deliberately misspelled within invalid and fraudulent laws as Ireland) as a fixed and continuous piece of ground and earth, larger than twelve Acres in surface area; and circumscribed by water; and

(iv) *Sea* (also deliberately misspelled within invalid and fraudulent laws as Scotland as "not" Land) as a fixed and continuous area of open water, larger than twelve thousand Acres in surface area; and circumscribed by at least two or more Islands and at least one other Sea; and

(v) *Air* (also deliberately misspelled within invalid and fraudulent laws as Netherlands as "neither" water nor land) as a fixed and circumscribed piece of space between Land and the outer reaches of the atmosphere of a planet; and

(vi) *Person* as a movable circumscribed space inhabited by the physical and living biological body of one or more Homo Sapiens; and

(vii) *Office* as a fixed or movable circumscribed space inhabited by a Person; and

(viii) *Internet* as a digital circumscribed space, inhabited by Persons as Users; and

(ix) *Network* as a digital circumscribed space of networked computers, inhabited by Persons as Network Users; and

(x) *Domain* (also Web Domain) as a digital circumscribed space of web information, inhabited by Persons as Network Users; and

(xi) *Database* as a digital circumscribed space of digital information, inhabited by Persons as Database Users or Application Users.

576. Any and all claimed Sacred Circumscribed Space held as Allodial Title or Peculiar Title (as a Peculiarity) and therefore claimed to be owned absolutely, free of any claim is hereby disavowed as an abomination before all Heaven and Earth; and is condemned as a profound sacrilege, heresy, profanity, morally repugnant, perfidious and deliberately false, having no force or effect in law. Furthermore, every Member of the Sons of Light and Fraternal Brothers and Sisters of Light are fully empowered by Holy Writ, to pursue any, every and all means to ensure any and all records of such profanity, sacrilege and

Allodial Title

abomination before all Heaven and Earth are expunged, removed, withdrawn, determined, extinguished and abolished, including any and all false presumptions of claiming such false rights under covenants as "chosen people" or blood heritage or any other falsity.

577. Any and all claimed Sacred Circumscribed Space held as Crown Land and therefore claimed to be owned absolutely, including but not limited to the deliberate corruption of using the name "England" to denote Land; and "Ireland" to denote Islands; and Scotland to denote the Sea and Admiralty; and the "Netherlands" to denote Air, is hereby disavowed as an abomination before all Heaven and Earth and is condemned as profound sacrilege, heresy, profanity, morally repugnant, perfidious and deliberately false, having no force or effect in law. Furthermore, every Member of the Sons of Light and Fraternal Brothers and Sisters of Light are fully empowered by Holy Writ, to pursue any, every and all means to ensure any and all records of such profanity, sacrilege and abomination before all Heaven and Earth are expunged, removed, withdrawn, determined, extinguished and abolished, including any and all false presumptions of claiming such false rights under "Divine Right" or blood heritage or any other falsity. Crown Land

Article 112 – Ucadia Artifact

578. Ucadia Artifact are formal systems and methods of defining Things (Rem or Re) consistent with Ucadia Law, including but not limited to Objects, Items and Sacred Circumscribed Space. Ucadia Artifact

579. In reference to Ucadia Artifact: Ucadia Artifact

    (i) Artifact Real, also known as Artifact Immovable and Corporeal, being lands, tenements and hereditaments; and

    (ii) Artifact Personal, also known as Artifact Movable and Incorporeal, being goods and chattels; and

    (iii) Artifact Mixed being Artifacts partaking the characteristics of Real and Personal such as a Title Deed.

580. The Form of an Artifact cannot exist except within the bounds of a matter before a competent forum of Law: 5 Forms of a Artifact

    (i) The effect of treating the Object of a Right in dispute as a Thing is to cause it to be converted temporarily into a form of Property or Artifact itself; and

    (ii) A Person is prohibited from being converted into an Artifact; and

    (iii) Artifacts are generally construed according to that which was the first cause of the dispute. Hence, the descriptions used in the first cause and subsequent form of action, generally determines the labelling and description of any Artifact in dispute; and

(iv) The Status of an Object as an Artifact only continues to exist, so long as the matter which first converted it into an Artifact continues, such as a case of Bankruptcy sine die (deferred to a latter date); and

(v) When an Artifact is the subject of an action of recovery (Things in action, or Things in Entry), such property cannot be granted over until the action ordered by the competent forum of law is completed.

581. The status of an Object being treated as an Artifact dissolves when purchased, sold, bound or granted through a special form of agreement known as a Covenant Contract, also known simply as a Contract.

Dissolving a Artifact

Article 113 – Non-Ucadian Artifact (Thing)

582. A Non-Ucadian Artifact (Thing, also known as Rem or Re in Latin) is a temporary Form being the Object of one or more Rights against which there exists a dispute or ongoing controversy before an inferior forum of law having jurisdiction.

<small>Non-Ucadian Artifact (Thing)</small>

583. The Form of a Non-Ucadian Artifact, also known as Rem or Re cannot exist except within the bounds of a matter before an inferior forum of Law:

<small>5 Forms of a Non-Ucadian Artifact (Thing)</small>

(i) The effect of treating the Object of a Right in dispute as a Thing is to cause it to be converted temporarily into a form of Property or Artifact itself; and

(ii) By tradition in Western-Roman Law, a Person was prohibited from being converted into a Non-Ucadian Artifact. However, Legal Persons are now commonly treated as Non-Ucadian Artifacts; and

(iii) Non-Ucadian Artifacts are generally construed according to that which was the first cause of the dispute. Hence, the descriptions used in the first cause and subsequent form of action, generally determines the labelling and description of any Non-Ucadian Artifacts in dispute; and

(iv) The Status of an Object as a Non-Ucadian Artifact only continues to exist, so long as the matter which first converted it into an Artifact continues, such as a case of Bankruptcy sine die (deferred to a latter date); and

(v) When a Non-Ucadian Artifact is the subject of an action of recovery (Things in action, or Things in Entry), such property cannot be granted over until the action ordered by the competent forum of law is completed.

4.2 – Time

Article 114 – Time

584. **Time** is a measure of duration between events; and any point in the function or during the process of measuring such duration. In other words, *Time* can be expressed as a precise or generalised *point*, *starting-point* or *end-point*; and an *interval* between *two points*.

585. **Time** is a function of the relative observation of form of matter and the effects of other matter around it. Therefore time cannot be 0.

586. In general reference to Time:-

   (i) Time is always forward in sequential order. Backward time in reality does not exist; and

   (ii) All time is relative to the observer; and

   (iii) The greater the density of space, the higher the Kinesis, the faster the effect of time; and

   (iv) The less the density of space, the lower the Kinesis, the slower the effect of time; and

   (v) An increase in the density of space will therefore lead to an increase in the observed speed of time. Therefore time is not constant; and

   (vi) A change at one part of space will change other parts of space field of the same level such that space will change faster than the speed of light and therefore appear to be instantaneous.

Article 115 – Ucadia Time

587. **Ucadia Time**, also written as **UCA Time**, is the unique Time and Space System for charting time and past, present and future events aligned with the true seasons, cycles and awareness of planet Earth and the Solar System as a whole.

588. The key elements of the Ucadia Time System are:-

   (i) The first part of *Ucadia Time System* is the Era, by name representing one eighth (1/8th) of a complete cycle of the twenty five thousand seven hundred sixty nine (25,769) Sun Year cycle of the precession of the equinox, representing a natural cycle of orbital shift of the Earth axis. An Era is therefore three thousand two hundred ten (3210) years, except the 1st era of a new Great Precession whereby an extra year is added and this year shall be called zero (0). As the 1st year of the 1st Era of a new Great Precession is called Year zero (0), it represents the Divine Creator, the end of old things and the beginning of new. The Era that is ending is named Aries (the Ram) and the beginning of the new Era is known as Pisces (the Fish); and

(ii) The second part of *Ucadia Time System* shall be the Age, representing three (3) sections of an Era equivalent to one thousand seventy (1070) years, except the 1st Age of the 1st era of a Great Precession which will be one thousand seventy one (1071) years. The Age that is ending is named the Third Age and the new Age that begins is the 1st Age or New Age; and

(iii) The third part of *Ucadia Time System* is the Sun Arc of a Sun Year representing seventy three (73) segments each of five (5) Days, except a Great Year when an additional day is added to the last Arc except every one hundred twenty eight (128) years named a Jubilee when an extra day is not added, except every one hundred twenty eight thousand (128,000) years named a Great Jubilee when the extra Day is added; and

(iv) The fourth part of *Ucadia Time System* is the Season of a Year representing four (4) segments of Seasons with the 1st Season of eighty five (85) days or seventeen (17) Arcs beginning at the sixty sixth (66th) Arc of a Year, the second (2nd) Season of ninety five (95) days or nineteen (19) Arcs beginning on the tenth (10th) Arc of the following Year, the third (3rd) Season of ninety five (95) days or nineteen (19) Arcs beginning on the twenty ninth (29th) Arc of the Year and the fourth (4th) Season of ninety (90) Days or eighteen (18) Arcs beginning on the forty eighth (48th) Arc of the Year; and

(v) The fifth part of *Ucadia Time System* shall be the Moon cycle of twenty nine (29) or thirty (30) days which shall be free and independent of the cycle of the Sun as such recordings of the full cycle of a Moon contains sufficient variance as to require The Timekeeper to make prediction as to whether a Moon cycle be twenty nine (29) or thirty (30) days; and

(vi) The sixth part of *Ucadia Time System* shall be the Name of the Day of an Arc with the first (1st) Day named GAIA in honour of the spirit of the Earth, the second (2nd) Day named MONS in honour of the spirit of the Moon, the third (3rd) Day named MARS in honour of the spirit of Mars, the fourth (4th) Day named JOVI in honour of the spirit of the Jovian Giant planets Jupiter, Saturn, Neptune and Uranus and the fifth (5th) Day named SOL in honour of the spirit of our SUN; and

(vii) The seventh part of *Ucadia Time System* is the Hour of the Day divided into twenty four (24) hours of a Day with each hour itself made up of sixty (60) Minutes; and

(viii) The eighth part of *Ucadia Time System* is the Minutes and Seconds of the Day, with Each Minute made up of sixty (60) Seconds and then one hundred (100) milliseconds per second.

589. In accord with the *Ucadia Time System*, the last Great Precession of twenty five thousand and six hundred and eighty (25,680) years ended on the Day of Divine Judgement being UCA E8:Y3210:A0:S1:M27:D6 [Wed, 21 Dec 2011] and the dawn of a new Great Precession and the Era of Pisces (the Fish) did begin from the Day of Divine Redemption being UCA E1:Y1:A1:S1:M9:D1 [Fri, 21 Dec 2012]. — New Great Precession

590. In accord with the *Ucadia Time System* and the most sacred covenants of the *Authenticus Depositum Fidei*, each and every Day since the Spring Equinox in the year 10,831 BCE is duly recorded in the Public Register and Great Record of One Heaven, also known as the Great Record of Space-Day-Time as the first, original and highest Record. Thus, the unique Record Number for UCA E8:Y3210:A0:S1:M27:D6 [Wed, 21 Dec 2011] is **4689718**. The terms Day and Date shall mean the unique Record Number of the Great Record of Space-Day-Time and may be represented by the unique number or an equivalent date representation. Therefore, all representation of Day, Date and Time is wholly within the Jurisdiction of Ucadia, subject to the most sacred Covenant *Pactum De Singularis Caelum*. — Great Record of Space-Day-Time

Article 116 – Non-Ucadian Time

591. Non-Ucadian Time is any time system that is not perfectly in alignment with the Ucadia Time System. — Non-Ucadian Time

592. All actions, events, occurrences within, above and upon planet Earth and within the Solar System are first records under the Ucadia Time System before any other Non-Ucadian Time System. Therefore, the Ucadia Time System shall always be superior to every other Non-Ucadian Time System. — Ucadia Time System Superior to all other Non-Ucadian Time Systems

Title V – Oaths, Vows, Testimony & Promises

5.1 – Oath

Article 117 – Oath

593. An ***Oath*** is a solemn promise or declaration, often made in a formal or legal setting, to uphold certain principles or fulfil certain obligations. It is a binding commitment to act with integrity and honesty, and to honour one's word and responsibilities. *Oaths*

594. The word Oath originates from the Cuilliaéan (Holly) of Ireland in the 3rd/4th Millennium BCE and the ancient Irish word Oath meaning "sacred surety or bond by words". Hence the ancient proverb of the Celts "My Word is my Bond" in reference to the ancient honour to the original and true meaning of Oath: *Origin of Oaths*

   (i) The original meaning of Oath as a solemn public appeal to the Divine Creator as witness that some testimony be true appears to have survived within Celtic culture and Anglo-Irish and Scottish history to at least the early 16th Century; and

   (ii) The deliberately false, deceptive and misleading creation of the compound word "swear" from sue (su, sui, sow) and wear (weir, wier) occurred no earlier than the second half of the 16th Century and prior to the insertion of false writings against "swearing" and falsely connecting the word "swear" to the process of "oaths".

595. The importance of oath-taking represents a fundamental pillar of law of Civilisation, as demonstrated by most ancient cultures, including the Greeks and Romans:- *Importance of Oaths*

   (i) In ancient Greece, oaths were taken in the name of the gods and were considered binding and sacred. The Greek historian Herodotus wrote about the importance of oaths in his Histories, stating that "the Greeks are the only people who swear by the gods, taking them as witnesses to their oaths" (Book 1, Chapter 91). The Greeks also believed that breaking an oath was a serious offence and could result in punishment from the gods; and

   (ii) In ancient Rome, oaths were taken in the name of the gods and were considered a legal contract. The Roman historian Livy wrote about the importance of oaths in his History of Rome, stating that "an oath is the most sacred of all things among men, and the most binding" (Book 1, Chapter 24). The Romans also believed that breaking an oath was a serious offence and could result in punishment from the gods.

596. By the custom and tradition throughout the history of law, an Oath can only be valid if the following criteria exist: — *Valid Oath*

    (i)   The one making the Oath comes with good intention, good actions and good conscience; and

    (ii)   The one making the Oath has the Right and proper authority to make such an Oath; and

    (iii)   At least one other person is present and prepared to witness the Oath and testify to such a fact; and

    (iv)   The candidate raises his right hand with a flat palm so that the face of the open palm can be clearly seen by all witnesses during the pronunciation of the Oath, whilst his left covers his heart as the symbol and source of truth of the spoken words; and

    (v)   That the pronunciation of the Oath never uses language of profanity such as "swear"; and

    (vi)   That some written Memorial (Memorandum) to the event exists, signed by the one making the Oath and a different person as witness.

597. In the absence of a valid and proper Oath, no person claiming possession, or occupation, or investiture or ownership of an Office holds any authority or power whatsoever and any and all actions made by such a person are completely without validity in law, whether or not the parties present did consent or decline. — *Absence of Oath*

Article 118 – Ucadia Oath

598. A ***Ucadia Oath*** is a solemn promise, made in a formal or legal setting, to uphold certain principles or fulfil certain obligations in accord with Ucadian Law:- — *Ucadia Oaths*

    (i)   A Testimony under a valid Oath is the strongest form of testimonial evidence; and

    (ii)   A Person cannot be invested into an Office, nor hold any authority or power without a properly pronounced Oath and Vow.

599. As a general rule, all Office holders occupy proper positions by virtue of making the appropriate Oath of Office. — *Ucadia Oath of Office*

Article 119 – Non-Ucadian Oath

600. A ***Non-Ucadian Oath*** is any promise or declaration made under — *Non-Ucadian Oath*

any laws influenced or associated with Westminster, especially in the presence of the word "swear".

601. The origin of Non-Ucadian Oaths and absurd and false Oaths under Rule of Law originates from the 16th Century:- *Origin of Non-Ucadia Oaths*

- (i) The deliberately false, deceptive and misleading creation of the compound word "swear" from sue (su, sui, sow) and wear (weir, wier) occurred no earlier than the second half of the 16th Century and prior to the insertion of false writings against "swearing" and falsely connecting the word "swear" to the process of "oaths"; and

- (ii) The appearance of the profane, sacrilegious and heretical definition attached to Oaths being "a careless use of the name of God or Christ or out of something sacred; or profane swearing" appears at the same time that the words "swear" and "sworn" appear in English Statute and the extraordinary Statute of Henry VIII in 1541 (33Hen8.c.27) that claimed the power to nullify and void Oaths using the sacrilegious, anti-Christian and heretical claim that the Monarch of England be Supreme and "God-like". However, given the generally false history of most statutes of the time of Henry VIII, this act is highly likely to be fabricated and never really existed; and

- (iii) Thereafter, the reference to Oaths within English Statute is almost always connected with inserting the words "swear" and "sworn" to reinforce the impression that an Oath was to be made through some ritual of "swearing", thus to put those who seek to act with integrity and honesty in direct contradiction as "heretics" to Christian Scriptures; and

- (iv) Toward the end of the 18th Century, the function of Oaths and their necessary importance in forming proper Trusts, Office and Authority was reintroduced into British Law through the Oaths Act (15Geo3. c.39) that introduced the notion of administrative Oaths through Justices of the Peace and the absurd notion of administrative Trusts, whether or not a person properly pronounced an Oath or not; and

- (v) The false, absurd and morally repugnant notion of "administrative oaths", as the justification for creating administrative trusts as if "valid trusts", was further refined through subsequent statutes in 1838 (1 & 2 Vict c 105), 1888 (51 & 52 Vict c 46), 1909 (9 Edw 7 c 39) and 1961 (9 & 10 Eliz 2 C 21). However, in all cases the notion that an administrative act of a Justice of the Peace is equivalent to a valid public pronouncement of an Oath is unsustainable in law; and

(vi) In direct contrast and as evidence as to the continued knowledge as to the legal effect of a valid Oath, the introduction of various Oaths acts to ensure that specific persons are properly invested under a valid Oath, compared to the rest of the population, is proof of the power of Oaths, namely the claimed Coronation Oath Act 1567 (c.8) and Coronation Oath Act 1688.

5.2 – Vow

Article 120 – Vow

602. A ***Vow*** is a solemn personal promise or declaration in the name of one or more Divine Beings to uphold certain principles or fulfil certain obligations. — Vows

603. By its nature a valid Vow is the sole source of authority of the one who makes it; and in the absence of a valid Vow a person holds no authority or power. Thus, a person cannot be properly invested into an Office without both a proper Oath and Vow. — Nature of Vow

604. The word Vow originates from the Ancient Greek word vow (xóv) meaning "promise" and the 3rd Century Christian word charis (κάρης) meaning "solemn binding promise, pledge or invocation; or religious vows":- — Origin and Nature of Vow

(i) The various claims that the word Vow comes from Anglaise (Old French) of the Carolingians as "vut" is an absurdity and morally repugnant as the true term adopted by the Carolingians from the 8th Century CE was voti/votum ("vote") meaning "public promise, dedication; sacred vow"; and

(ii) The original meaning of Vow as a solemn public appeal to the Divine Creator as witness to some promise to perform one or more obligations associated with one or more Rights in Trust, appears to have been depreciated when Constantine formed the ecclesiastical, moral and lawful framework of Christianity. Instead, the term charis (κάρης) meaning "solemn binding promise, pledge or invocation; or religious vows" was adopted as the formal Christian term for vow – hence "Charity".

605. In relation to Vows:- — General Principles of Vows

(i) A Vow made by oration in the presence of others is always superior to a written Vow. A Vow made in secret or privately has no effect and is void from the beginning by virtue of not being made in public; and

(ii) A Vow made free from coercion, fear or deliberate deception must be fulfilled. A Vow made out of grave and unjust fear or malice, or ignorance is null by the law itself; and

(iii) A Vow ceases by the lapse of the time designated to fulfil the obligation, or by a substantial change of the matter promised, or by the absence of a condition that the vow depends upon, or by the absence of the purpose of the vow, or by dispensation, or by commutation.

606. In the absence of a valid and proper Vow associated with a valid and proper Oath, no person claiming possession, or occupation, or investiture or ownership of an Office holds any authority or power whatsoever and any and all actions made by such a person are completely without validity in law, whether or not the parties present did consent or decline.

Absence of proper Vow

Article 121 – Ucadia Vow

607. A *Ucadia Vow* is a solemn personal promise or declaration in the name of the Divine Creator through the most sacred Covenant *Pactum De Singularis Caelum* to uphold certain principles or fulfil certain obligations.

Ucadia Vow

608. In relation to Vows of Superior Persons as defined by Ucadian Law and these present Bylaws:-

The Use of Vows

(i) No temporal force or action or an Inferior Person can dispense or commute Solemn Vows of a Superior Person; and

(ii) Only a Supreme Person can dispense or commute Solemn Vows of Superior Persons and all lesser Persons. Only a Superior Person can dispense or commute Solemn Vows of Ordinary Persons and all lesser Persons. Only an Ordinary Person can dispense or commute Solemn Vows of Curator Persons and all lesser Persons. Inferior Persons have no rights nor powers to dispense or commute Solemn Vows; and

(iii) As Inferior Persons have no power or authority to dispense or commute solemn Vows, when any such Vow is breached or any action is made to claim that dispensation or commutation is given, then such an action is a direct injury to the Divine Creator and all law. Therefore any such liability and penalty due immediately befalls the Person who breached their solemn Vow.

Article 122 – Non-Ucadian Vow

609. A ***Non-Ucadia Vow*** is any solemn personal promise or declaration not made in the name of a Divine Being to uphold certain principles or fulfil certain obligations. All promises made in the name of a Divine Being are Ucadia Vows by their nature.

Non-Ucadian Vow

5.3 – Testimony

Article 123 – Testimony

610. ***Testimony*** is the act of giving a declaration, statement or evidence about something that one has witnessed or experienced. It is often used in legal proceedings, but can also be used in religious or personal contexts to share one's beliefs or experiences.

Testimony

611. The word "testimony" comes from the Latin word *testis* meaning witness or one who gives evidence.

Origin of Testimony

612. Testimonial Evidence has been regarded as central to any civilised legal system since the time of the Ancient Greek and Roman Empires:-

Importance of Testimony

   (i) The Greek philosopher Aristotle wrote in his book "Rhetoric" (350 BCE) that "testimony is a kind of evidence, and the best kind." He believed that testimony was the most reliable form of evidence because it came from a credible witness who had firsthand knowledge of the events in question; and

   (ii) In the Bible, testimony is also a central concept. In the Old Testament, the word "testimony" is used to refer to the tablets of the Ten Commandments, which were seen as a testimony to God's covenant. In the New Testament, the word "testimony" is used to refer to the witness of the apostles to the life and teachings of Jesus Christ; and

   (iii) During the Middle Ages, the Magna Carta (1215) established the principle of the rule of law, included provisions for the use of testimony in trials. The document stated that "no free man shall be taken or imprisoned or disseised or exiled or in any way destroyed, nor will we go upon him nor send upon him, except by the lawful judgment of his peers or by the law of the land."; and

   (iv) The United Nations Declaration of Human Rights, adopted in 1948, includes provisions for the right to a fair trial and the right to present evidence and testimony.

613. The validity and therefore admissibility of Testimonial evidence

Condition of

relevant to an Argument is dependent upon four major qualities being *Competency, Integrity, Authenticity* and *Objectivity*, namely:

Testimony

(i) *Competency* is that the witness is capable of comprehending questions and capable of answering truthfully without influence; and

(ii) *Integrity* is the context that the witness has not been offered any financial benefit or that reward has been offered to a witness for their testimony, nor has the witness been threatened or coerced; and

(iii) *Authenticity* is that the words of the witness are their own and that they have not been coached in any way by any third party on what to say or not to say; and

(iv) *Objectivity* is that the answers are firsthand knowledge of fact and not hearsay.

Article 124 – Testament

614. **Testament** is a lawful oral or written testimony and trust agreement creating a present or future trust for the management, use or disposal of the assets and property of a Person in the event of their incapacity or death. A Testament is also commonly known as a Will.

Testament

615. The term Testament comes from the late Latin word *testamentum*, derived from two Latin words being *testis* meaning "witness" and *mentum, mentis* meaning "mind". Thus testamentum literally means "a witness of the mind".

Origin of Meaning of Testament

616. Evidence of written testaments and the process of their formation appears consistent throughout the history of civilised societies from the time of Ancient Egypt, even up to Industrial Revolution until it was thoroughly corrupted in meaning and practice by the uncivilised laws of the Westminster System in the 19th Century:-

Origin of Testament in Law

(i) Written Egyptian papyrus dated as early as the 16th century BCE demonstrated a strict protocol of first the person vocalising their inventory and wishes before a number of witnesses with the written testament being both a memorial of the event and a sacred covenant, not subject to dispute or interference; and

(ii) In ancient Greece, there is evidence of the same practice occurring with the testament known as a thelema (θέλημα); and

(iii) In ancient Rome, the ritual of making a testament required adherence to meticulous rules, including the need for at least seven witnesses to hear the testament pronounced by the person and sealed by their own hand.

617. In relation to the requirements of a valid Testament: <!-- Conditions of valid Testament -->

    (i)   There exist certain customary rules and traditions concerning the formation of valid and legitimate Wills and Testaments. These are defined as the Customary Elements of a valid Testament; and

    (ii)   As a Testament always pertains in part to certain rights, or trusts, or estates, or funds, or assets or property registered within one or more jurisdictions, what constitutes a valid and legitimate Testament must always be determined to some degree by the various laws of each jurisdiction; and

    (iii)   If a Testament is to have certain conditions effective during the life of the Trustor and Testator, then the Testament instrument must make such specific conditions, particularly in relation to any powers of attorney or conditions to be followed in the event of disability, palliative care and other impairment or Inter Vivos Trust; and

    (iv)   Generally, if a Testament invokes on one or more immoral, repugnant or illegal acts to the relevant jurisdiction, then the entirety of the instrument is in jeopardy unless the instrument enables the clear severability of such clauses; and

    (v)   The absence of a right, or thing expressed within the Testament therefore favours the jurisdiction where the Testament is to be validated; and

    (vi)   A Testament that makes a claim of certain rights, or trusts, or estates, or funds, or assets, or property not legitimately in its possession, or morally and lawfully the possession of another, causes the entirety of the Testament to be null and void as if it never existed; and

    (vii)   A Testament that makes scandalous claims for certain rights, or trusts, or estates, or funds, or assets, or property that the man or woman or person are not entitled, causes the entirety of the Testament to be null and void as if it never existed.

618. The following are the seventeen (17) standard elements traditionally included within a valid Testament in accord to the norms of Civilised Society under Rule of Law, Justice and Due Process being: *Aetatem Validam, Verba Mea, Vocem Meam, Animus Testandi, Compos* <!-- Customary Elements of a valid Testament -->

Mentis, Incipit, Quod Vocatur, Recitatio, Iura Habeam, Titulum Habeam, Executorem Meum, Funeris Meum, Memoriam Meum, Regulis Bona, Operibus Bonis, Decretio and *Testificatio*:

(i) "***Aetatem Validam***" ("the right/legitimate age") means the one making the Testament known as the "Testator" formally acknowledges they are of the minimum age accepted for the completion and pronouncement of such an important instrument; and

(ii) "***Verba Mea***" ("in my own words") means the Testator formally acknowledges the Testament is a true representation of their intention, free from threat, intimidation, duress or promise; and

(iii) "***Vocem Meam***" ("my (own) voice") means the Testator formally acknowledges the Testament is literally "their own voice" and a true representation of their intention and is spoken free from threat, intimidation, duress or promise; and

(iv) "***Animus Testandi***" ("the intention to testify") means the Testator formally acknowledges that he/she fully intends the instrument and/or any vocalisation to be known as their valid Will and Testament and is capable of demonstrating such competent intention; and

(v) "***Compos Mentis***" ("of sound mind") means the Testator formally acknowledges he/she is of sound mind, capable of reason and moral judgement and therefore capable of not only making decisions but capable of perceiving the consequences of such decisions or actions; and

(vi) "***Incipit***" ("it begins") means the opening prayer and petition of a sacred instrument between heaven and earth and by tradition the first words of any sacred covenant; and

(vii) "***Quod Vocatur***" ("that which is called/named") means the name of the instrument (e.g. *Voluntatem Et Testamentum* as the prescribed form of a valid Will and Testament under One Heaven); and

(viii) "***Recitatio***" ("recitation, reading, pronouncement") means the statements and terms of the Will and Testament; and

(ix) "***Iura Habeam***" ("I have Rights") means the Testator expresses and asserts their Rights, Powers and Authority, particularly to possess, own and hold certain title, property and uses; and

(x) **"*Titulum Habeam*"** ("I have title") means the Testator expresses and asserts the description of records, certificates, registers or ledgers and one or more titles of possession, ownership and use in accord with the Rights, Powers and Authority previously expressed; and

(xi) **"*Executorem Meum*"** ("my executor") means the Testator nominates at least one executor to be granted the power and authority by the testator to administer their various estates (living and/or deceased) upon some significant event that causes the executor to be appointed (such as physical death or formal investiture in the case of living estates); and

(xii) **"*Funeris Meum*"** ("my funeral") means the Testator nominates the essential arrangements of their own funeral service; and

(xiii) **"*Memoriam Meum*"** ("my memorial") means the Testator nominates how he or she wishes his or her memory to be honoured in monument and epitaph; and

(xiv) **"*Regulis Bona*"** ("good rules (of estate)") means the Testator expresses the specific rules of proper administration of the Estate; and

(xv) **"*Operibus Bonis*"** ("good works (of estate)") means the Testator names one or more Beneficiaries who are granted the Rights to use certain property of the estate as a sign of charitable and good works; and

(xvi) **"*Decretio*"** ("decree, decision, judgement, resolution, principle") means a formal statement at the end of the Will and Testament by the Testator that the instrument had been handed (delivered) to become public notice also known as "patenting". Thus the phrase "IN WITNESS WHEREOF, We have hereunto set Our hand and seal, and caused these, Our Letters, to be made Patent" with patent meaning public notice; and

(xvii) **"*Testificatio*"** ("attestation, proof") means a formal attestation at the very end of the Will and Testament which may also include separate written attestation by two (2) or more witnesses that it is the wishes and intentions of the Testator reflected in the Will and Testament through the Latin phrase (by tradition since the 8th Century) beginning with "*Teste me ipso apud*" <> then the date in Latin meaning

"Witness myself at the place <> date".

619. Under most Non-Ucadia jurisdictions, the notion of Testament or "Will" bears little to no resemblance to the nature of a true Testament in law. Instead, such a document is almost entirely subject to the regulations and statutes of the Corporate State and then the Courts who ultimately decide whether to follow none, some or most of the "Will" of a Person:-

Modern Laws and Testaments

(i) The mandatory requirement for all Wills or "Testaments" to be judged under a Probate Court of a Non-Ucadia Jurisdiction invalidates any claim that such a document resembles any form of valid Will or Testament, or that inhabitants of such a State have effectively any ultimate control over property registered under such a Non-Ucadia State; and

(ii) At best a Will or Testament is a "guide" to such a Probate Court of a Non-Ucadia Jurisdiction. However, there are certain rules, guidelines and best practices that may be followed to improve the chances such a court may rule in favour of the wishes of the deceased.

Article 125 – Voluntatem Et Testamentum

620. ***Voluntatem Et Testamentum*** is the prescribed form whereby a member of One Heaven holding either the Office of Man or Office of Woman perfects their Will and Testament in accord with the most sacred Covenant *Pactum De Singularis Caelum* and the Rights and Obligations prescribed therein.

Voluntatem Et Testamentum

621. In terms of a valid and legitimate Will and Testament under Ucadia Law:-

Voluntatem Et Testamentum as Will and Testament

(i) The Will and Testament through the form of *Voluntatem Et Testamentum* is to the personality (person) of a Superior Estate, the physical mind and the will of the person and the will of all legal persons derived from the existence of the man or woman. It is both a sacred prayer and sacred scripture to be respected and honoured by all persons who claim an office by sacred Oath or Vow; and

(ii) It is also a sacred Covenant and bond between a man or woman in whose name the Will and Testament exists and the Divine Creator. It is an unbreakable covenant by the man or woman who is the grantor or testator; and

(iii) When such a Will and Testament bears witness to the Covenant of One Heaven and the Maxims of Law of One

Heaven through the form of *Voluntatem Et Testamentum*, then: It is a most solemn and sacred Covenant; and

(iv) It is an unbreakable bond between heaven and earth and no power, no force, no spirit, no corporation, no person or entity can break that bond; and no power exists in heaven that can break such a sacred bond; and

(v) One gives existence and credence to the other. Such a valid Will and Testament and the present Covenant of One Heaven are two parts, the lock and key, that when united cannot be broken.

622. Where a man or woman claiming either the Office of Man or Office of Woman deliberately and willingly repudiates some or all of the most sacred Covenant *Pactum de Singularis Caelum*; or asserts one or more Prohibited Rights for their own advantage then any such associated Will and Testament and associated estate and trust documents, whether or not such prescribed form as *Voluntatem Et Testamentum* are used, therefore has no basis of covenant, or bond with One Heaven or the most sacred Covenant *Pactum de Singularis Caelum*.

Article 126 – Will

623. **Will** is a common term used to describe three particular elements:- — Will

(i) *Mental Faculty* that allows individuals to make conscious choices and decisions ; and

(ii) *Mind of the Person* being written evidence demonstrating both the existence and intention (motive) of Mind of the Person; and

(iii) *Legal Document* for the disposal of an estate of a Person after their death, often called Last Will and Testament.

624. A Will and Testament is a formal declaration, memorialisation, deed and trust agreement by which a person testifies before witnesses as to their true intention and volition regarding the management of his or her accumulative estate, the disposition of rights and property and the disposal of such rights and property upon their physical death. — Will and Testament

625. In reference to the key components of a Will and Testament: — Key Elements of Will and Testament

(i) As a declaration, a valid Will and Testament is a written statement asserting one or more Rights and making one or more Claims, then duly signed and executed by the one writing the declaration and witnessed by witnesses applying their signature – The Will part; and

(ii) As a memorial, a valid Will and Testament is a recording of its auricular expression – that is – its speaking and witnessing by others as having heard the spoken expression of the testament- The Testament part; and

(iii) As a deed, a valid Will and Testament is a written instrument granting, donating, assigning or delegating one or more Rights to others, duly signed, executed, witnessed and sealed as proof of authority to grant such Rights- The Deed part; and

(iv) As a trust agreement, a valid Will and Testament is a written trust agreement giving clear instructions and terms to any fiduciary appointments once the trust is in effect (usually when the trustee(s) have been appointed).

626. Wills under Non-Ucadian Jurisdiction are regulated according to laws and procedures that ultimately determine whether a Will be considered valid or invalid:-

Wills under Non-Ucadian Jurisdiction

(i) Wills are required to be in writing; and be signed by two witnesses and a Notary or Lawyer with notary powers; and

(ii) The language of Wills are expected to demonstrate the Person is of sound mind, and that the document was completed without coercion and freely as their intention; and

(iii) The document (Will) makes clear it replaces any previous Will or is in addition (as a Codicil) to an existing Will; and

(iv) The document (Will) does not contain any claims or demands or language contrary to the regulations of the Jurisdiction; and

(v) A probate court is then usually required to determine the legitimacy of a Will before using none, some or all of it to dispose of the assets of a deceased estate.

Article 127 – Codicil

627. A ***Codicil*** is a legal document that amends or supplements an existing Will. It allows the testator to make minor changes to their Will without having to create an entirely new one.

Codicil

628. A Codicil must be executed with the same formalities as a Will and is subject to the same legal requirements:-

Elements of Codicil

(i) The maker of the codicil identifies the Will that is to be changed by the name of the testator and date of its execution; and

(ii) The codicil should state that the Will is affirmed except for the changes contained therein.

Article 128 – Affidavit

629. An ***Affidavit*** is a written statement made under oath or affirmation, used as evidence in court proceedings or other legal matters. It is a sworn declaration of facts that the affiant (person making the statement) believes to be true and accurate. Affidavit

630. The term "affidavit" has its roots in Latin, with the word "affidare" meaning "to pledge faith" or "to trust." Origin of meaning of Affidavit

631. The concept of Affidavit originates under Anglo Saxon Law where individuals would make an oath of loyalty to their lord or monarch. Over time, the term "affidavit" came to refer specifically to a written statement made under oath or affirmation:- Concept of Affidavit

   (i) In 1566, the English jurist Sir William Staunford wrote in his book "A Treatise on the Pleas of the Crown" that "an affidavit is a declaration upon oath." This definition reflects the basic concept of an affidavit as a written statement made under oath; and

   (ii) In 1689, the English Parliament passed the Bill of Rights, which included a provision stating that "the taking of any oath or oaths, or the making of any declaration or affidavit, shall not be imposed upon, or required of, any person that shall not be qualified to take the same by the laws of their respective countries." This provision recognized the importance of affidavits as a means of providing evidence in legal proceedings; and

   (iii) In 1789, the first US Congress passed the Judiciary Act, which included provisions allowing for the use of affidavits in federal court proceedings. The act stated that "affidavits may be taken before any judge or justice of the peace of the United States, or of any particular state."

632. The key elements of the form of a valid Affidavit and its Annexures are:- Elements of Form of Affidavit

   (i) Quality Paper means that the paper used is of a durable quality and standard to the size used in normal jurisdiction within the region; and

   (ii) One Sided means that the Affidavit is preferably written or printed on only one side of the page; and

(iii) Legible Print means that all writing and printing is clear, sharp and legible of a 12 point serif font (e.g. Times); and

(iv) Numbered Pages means that all individual pages of the Affidavit, excluding Annexures are uniquely numbered in ascending order beginning with 1; and

(v) Numbered Clauses means that all individual clauses of the Affidavit itself are uniquely numbered in square brackets in ascending order, beginning with [1]; and

(vi) Securely Fastened means Individual Pages of the Affidavit are securely fastened together along with any Annexures; and

(vii) Clear Margins means the spacing of writing or printing of the Affidavit itself should allow for a minimum of 25mm on the left and right margin as well as the top and bottom margins of each page; and

(viii) Double Spacing means the spacing between the writing or printing of each line of the Affidavit itself allows for a space of at least 3mm; and

(ix) Words not Figures means that all expressions of dates, sums and other numbers, except the numbering of paragraphs, pages or reference numbers in association to the matter are in words, not figures or numbers; and

(x) Form of Law means the specific name of the Public Statute or By-laws under which the Affidavit is formed and issued is clearly identified as the first printed title at the top of the first page; and

(xi) Body Politic means the specific name of the Body Politic, or Corporation under which the Form of Law mentioned was issued as the second printed title of the Affidavit; and

(xii) Deponent means the specific name of the one making the Affidavit and the word "Deponent" clearly visible as the first name of any party; and

(xiii) Respondent means the specific name of the respondent(s) and the word "Respondent" clearly visible as the second party; and

(xiv) Issue Number means a unique and specific reference number associated with the records of the Deponent for the matter, which may then be repeated on any subsequent material, motions or Affidavits; and

(xv) Foreign Reference Number means any foreign reference number associated with claims, or matters raised by the other party, always listed in square brackets; and

(xvi) Filed Date means the Date filed in Words; and

(xvii) Heading means if the Affidavit is a simple Affidavit (and NOT designed for judicial motion), then the word AFFIDAVIT is clearly identifying the instrument as an Affidavit; and

(xviii) Preamble means the opening sentence or statement which is not normally numbered, in which the Deponent states their name, their address, their official capacity and whether the following facts are made (under oath) or affirmed as evidence. An example is I, ADAM NOMEN, the duly authorised Attorney-In-Fact, of 22 Bloggs Street, Bloggsville, do solemnly and sincerely say on Oath in Good Faith and without Prejudice; and

(xix) Recitals means the second sentence or first numbered paragraph directly after the Preamble, which is normally numbered as [1] in which the Deponent as witness states their age, their mental state, their qualification to make an Affidavit and the fact that the Affidavit was done without duress or promise. An example is: [1] I was born on the 10th January 1963 and am 50 years of age. I am of sound mind and reason and do sincerely and honestly affirm the present instrument to be my own words, written by me, given freely and without duress and expressing accurately to the best of my ability the facts herein of which I have witnessed firsthand and with expert knowledge; and

(xx) Decretum means the body of first hand facts and expert knowledge in chronological and logical order, expressing one key fact per paragraph in ascending number order; and

(xxi) Testamentum means the final numbered paragraph expressing the testament of the witness as Deponent that everything they have expressed is true and correct. An example is: All the facts and circumstances deposed herein are within my own firsthand knowledge except such as are deposed herein from information in accord with my reasonable expert knowledge as appears within the present Affidavit; and

(xxii) Jurat means that the Deponent must sign a declaration that they have taken an Oath at the end of the Affidavit including the date of the Affidavit and Oath and the place the Oath was taken. The person then before whom the Affidavit is invoked before the Divine Creator must write their name and address together with the capacity in which they are entitled to take the Affidavit; and

(xxiii) Signing of Pages means that the Deponent and the Authorised Witness(es) must sign each page as validation; and

(xxiv) Reference means that where a Deponent refers to a document or documents within the body of the Affidavit, copies of the document or documents may be made an Annexure to the Affidavit; and

(xxv) Annexure Numbering means each Exhibit at the back of the Affidavit should be clearly and uniquely numbered in ascending order, beginning with 1; and

(xxvi) Certificate of Annexures means where a document or documents is exhibited to an affidavit, the Annexure must be identified as such by a Certificate of Annexures attached at the front of all Annexures entitled in the same manner as the affidavit and signed by the person before whom the affidavit is made. For example: "This is the annexure marked Annexure 1 referred to in the affidavit of Fred Bloggs made/affirmed on [date] before me."; and

(xxvii) Certificate of Witness means that the Authorised Witness who witnessed the made Oath and signing of the Affidavit also provides a Certification as to proof of the identity of the person making the Affidavit.

633. The norms and standards concerning Affidavits are:- Rules of Affidavits

(i) *Right of Oath upon Sacred Scripture* means a Deponent has the sacred Right to choose upon which sacred scripture he or she invokes their Oath. Thus it can be *Pactum de Singularis Caelum*, or Yapa, or Al Sufian or even Lebor Clann Glas or the Bible; and

(ii) *Rules of Evidence* means in most jurisdictions, the same rules of Evidence that apply to an Affidavit as apply to affirmed oral evidence; and

(iii) *First Hand Facts* means a Affidavit can only be about first hand facts and knowledge which the Deponent has witnessed or has expert knowledge. A valid Affidavit can never contain opinion, hearsay or supposition. To claim someone broke the law without actually witnessing the event is false testimony and inadmissible as Evidence; and

(iv) *Affidavit is not Pleading* means that the purpose of an Affidavit is not to admit, deny or argue the claims of another party. While a fact of an Affidavit may refer to receiving a claim or the Affidavit of another party, the contents of such instruments are not relevant except in referring to firsthand knowledge of facts; and

(v) *Affidavit is not Petition* means that the purpose of an Affidavit is not to petition a Justice or Magistrate to act or not act; and

(vi) *In Propria Persona* means all valid Affidavits are from the perspective of 1st person in active voice (not past tense or passive) and not as an agent or a thing; and

(vii) *Good Faith and Clean Hands* means that all valid Affidavits are made in Trust that they are True and free from fraud, malice, prejudice or vexation; and

(viii) *Affidavit Stands as Testimony* means an Affidavit can be read in court without the Deponent having to attend as a witness as to its truthfulness, unless formally challenged in writing by the other parties prior to the next hearing or court procedure; and

(ix) *Affidavit Service* means that in order for an Affidavit to be relied upon, it must be served on all relevant parties prior to a hearing or within the limits of time for such service of a matter. Failure to serve all parties in good faith prior to an actual hearing of a matter may result in the Affidavit being denied acceptance except by leave of the court; and

(x) *Proof of Service* means that Proof of Service and Notice is sufficient evidence that an Affidavit has been delivered and received by the other parties within reasonable time. An Affidavit of Service might also be formed as further evidence of Service; and

(xi) *Filing of Affidavit* means that an Affidavit is filed before or after Proof of Service to other parties, which depends upon court procedures in each jurisdiction. Generally, unless the Affidavit is in support of a formal application (or motion), an Affidavit does not need to be filed before being served on the other Parties.

Article 129 – Interview

634. An ***Interview*** is usually a formal procedure for the gathering of information in relation to an investigation, usually through the use of questions. Information gathered via Interview is often used as admissible evidence related to one or more offences.

Interview

635. Interviews may be conducted as audio, video or in-person and generally include the following key elements:-

Audio, Video and In-Person Interview

(i) *Formal Notice* of some kind as to the intention to conduct a Formal Interview at a given time and place. This can be done by letter, phone or in-person; and

(ii) *Opening Statement by Interviewer(s)* being some introductory statement as to the identity of the interviewers, the agreement of the interviewee to participate in some fashion (even if they subsequently refuse questions), the rights of the interviewee and the rights of the investigators to use the interview as evidence for further investigation or prosecution; and

(iii) *Disclosure of Evidence by the Interviewer(s)* being the right of the Person being interviewed to request disclosure of the evidence forming the basis of the interview prior to the interview commencing, allowing time for the Person being interviewed to understand the context and basis for the Interview. This can be overlooked by the Person being interviewed and it can also be refused by the Interviewer(s) in some jurisdictions; and

(iv) *Opening Statement by the Person being Interviewed* means the right of the person Being Interviewed to prepare a written statement and to read the statement into evidence following a request or refusal to be shown the Disclosure of Evidence as the basis for the interview; and

(v) *Right of Interviewee not to answer questions* especially hypothetical and entrapment questions designed to elicit a confession or reaction for potential prosecution; and

(vi) *Copy of recording of Interview* means the Person who was interviewed has a right to a copy of the recording at the conclusion of the interview to make sure no doctored or false recording may be attempted to be used in future.

636. Interviews that are shown to have been conducted contrary to clear procedures, or to the extreme prejudice of the Person interviewed may subsequently be deemed unlawful and such information

Illegal or Unlawful Interviews

obtained via such an Interview "inadmissible" as evidence:-

(i) Most commonly, an Interview where the Interviewers failed to disclose to the Person being interviewed their rights, or subsequently refused to allow a Person being interviewed to exercise their rights is usually deemed unlawful and inadmissible; and

(ii) Interviews where the Person being interviewed was clearly placed under extreme stress or coercion, or that techniques were used to attempt to force a confession may also be deemed unlawful and inadmissible in certain jurisdictions; and

(iii) Interviews where the transcript or tape submitted does not match the copy provided to the witness may indicate tampering and subsequent inadmissible evidence.

Article 130 – Deposition

637. A ***Deposition*** is a formal statement usually gathered outside of the normal sitting of a court in session, either to expedite proceedings or gather evidence that would not otherwise be effectively obtained. — Deposition

638. The term "deposition" comes from the Latin word "*depositio,*" which means "a testimony given under oath." — Origin of the word Deposition

639. In reference to the general elements of Depositions:- — General Elements of Depositions

(i) The obtaining of Depositions typically follows similar formalities to those of "in court" testimony with the exception that a judge and clerical staff are usually not present; and

(ii) Most commonly, Depositions are conducted by opposition teams of professional legal practitioners familiar with the procedures of obtaining legitimate Depositions; and

(iii) Similar to formal "in court" testimony, there exists rules in most jurisdictions as to how an oral and written examination may be conducted. Failure to follow such procedures may render a deposition hearing and any subsequent evidence inadmissible.

640. A number of compelling elements exist for the use of Depositions outside of Court Sittings:- — Key Uses of Depositions

(i) Depositions provide the opportunity to obtain and preserve evidence well before a court case is due to be finally judged, ensuring potentially a more accurate record of evidence; and

(ii) Depositions provide a means of expediting cases and matters before the courts by saving potentially substantial amounts of time in evidence gathering, thus allowing the time in court to be in hearing, arguing and judging the evidence; and

(iii) Depositions provide a potentially important means of obtaining often important, sensitive and technical evidence not otherwise easily obtained via traditional "in court" witness examination. This is especially true in the case of minors and victims of traumatic events, or terminally ill witnesses and expert witnesses; and

(iv) Depositions also provide the means of greater disclosure and transparency in court cases, thus reducing the potential cost in time and expense from mistrials and retrials due to evidence and disclosure related matters.

Article 131 – Declaration

641. A ***Declaration*** is a formal statement or proclamation that declares a particular fact, opinion, or intention. It is often used to make a public announcement or to assert a position on a particular issue. Declarations can be made by individuals, organisations, or governments. Declaration

642. The term Declaration comes from the Latin word *declaratio*, which means "a making clear or manifest", with references to its legal use from the time of the Carolingian Empire:- Origin of term Declaration

(i) The Magna Carta, a document signed in 1215 that established the principle of the rule of law in England, there are several references to declarations made by the king and his subjects; and

(ii) The Declaration of Rights, a document issued by the English Parliament in 1689 that established the rights of English citizens and limited the power of the monarchy; and

(iii) In 1776, the Continental Congress issued the Declaration of Independence, a document that declared the United States; and

(iv) The Universal Declaration of Human Rights, adopted by the United Nations in 1948, is a landmark document that established the fundamental rights and freedoms that all human beings are entitled.

643. In reference to the general elements of a Declaration:- General elements of Declarations

(i) A declaration is a formal statement or announcement made by individuals or groups that express their beliefs, intentions, or commitments; and

(ii) It is typically made in writing, but can also be made verbally or through other means of communication; and

(iii) Declarations are often made in a public or formal setting, and are intended to have a persuasive or influential effect on others; and

(iv) Declarations can be made for a variety of purposes, such as to express a belief or opinion, to assert a right or claim, or to make a commitment or promise; and

(v) Declarations often have legal or political significance, and may be used to establish or clarify rights, obligations, or relationships between individuals or groups; and

(vi) Declarations may be unilateral or bilateral, meaning they can be made by one party or by multiple parties; and

(vii) Declarations are often used in political contexts, as they can be used to assert sovereignty, establish rights, or make demands of other nations or groups.

Article 132 – Statement

644. A *Statement* is a declarative sentence that expresses a fact, opinion, or idea. It is a fundamental unit of communication that conveys information and can be either true or false. Statements are used in various contexts, including literature, science, law, and everyday conversation. Statement

645. In many Non-Ucadia Jurisdictions, Witness Statements have replaced the notion of Affidavits as the procedural means of submitting a declaration of fact. Witness Statement

Article 133 – Examination

646. An *Examination* is a process of evaluating a person's knowledge, skills, and abilities in a particular subject or field. It is usually conducted through a series of tests or assessments to determine the level of understanding, truthfulness and proficiency of the individual being examined. Examination

647. In respect of the general elements of Examination and Law:- General Elements of Examination

(i) Examination is historically required to be given under Oath or Affirmation as Testimony, in order to have confidence that any such answers or statements given by the one testifying may have any truthful value; and

Title V – Oaths, Vows, Testimony & Promises

- (ii) Examination typically involves auricular (spoken) or written questions to a Person under Oath or Affirmation; and may be done by an opposing party, or supporting party or even the adjudicator(s) of the matter; and

- (iii) Examination may be in an out of court setting, such as a Deposition, or within a court session; and

- (iv) Examination may have a set time limit, or may be set in accordance with the sessions of the court over one or more days; and

- (v) Examination frequently involves the one testifying being asked to refer back to one or more previously written statements or records of interview.

648. In respect of the potential flaws of Examination and Law:- *Potential Flaws of Examination*

- (i) Examination generally relies heavily on the truthfulness of not only the one testifying and answering, but the one asking the questions. An Examination under Oath or Affirmation may not sufficiently prove that a Person being examined is being untruthful, or that alleged evidence presented for Examination is deliberately false, or misconstrued or deceptive in nature; and

- (ii) All Examination in Law is by definition subjective and biased, as it relies upon the impartial judgment, good actions and good conduct of the examiner. Thus, an unscrupulous Examiner is sometimes able to affect the outcome of a court matter, not by the substance of the evidence, but by the conduct and manner of Examination; and

- (iii) Examination assumes and frequently demands that a Person have perfect memory of highly detailed facts or events equal to (or sometimes greater than) digital recordings, audio and text. Such assumptions are an absurdity and injury to the law. Yet persons who testify and do not reflect perfect memory equal to a digital computer have been known to be charged and punished in jurisdictions that have no real regard for justice or Rule of Law; and

- (iv) Examination is frequently conducted within a high-stress and high-pressure environment, and thus a form of coercion and impediment of free will on Persons who testify under Oath or Affirmation. Thus if a legal matter complies to the Rule of Law, evidence gained under torture, or coercion should be greatly discounted or disregarded as tainted.

5.4 – Promise

Article 134 – Promise

649. A *Promise* is a manifestation of intention to act or refrain from acting in a specific manner. Under Ucadian Law, all valid Promises are expected to be honoured as a fundamental principle.

Promise

650. There are three (3) forms of Promise, reflecting the three forms of Consensus and Consent being *Implied*, *Expressed* and *Sacred*:

Types of Promises

   (i) An *Implied Promise* is the most common form assumed when signing documents associated with a Unilateral Consensus Instrument or Application whereby such documents presume the signature of the applicant is also as a promise, sometimes argued as enforced by some expression that the applicant "comprehends" their obligations as a promise. Ucadia or its Authorised entities shall not enforce Implied Promises upon its Members; and

   (ii) An *Express Promise* is one whereby the promiser clearly vocalises their promise to the other parties with necessarily making a sacred oath in addition to any signature. Testimony is required to such fact and recorded before such a promise may be enforceable; and

   (iii) A *Sacred Promise* is defined as a formal oath or affirmation expressed before one or more witnesses, memorialised in writing, whereby a Consensus to perform certain duties in exchange for some consideration of value is attested as true and binding. All Promises duly recorded within the proper Registers and Instruments of Ucadia are considered Sacred Promises.

Article 135 – Ucadia Promise

651. A *Ucadia Promise* is a Promise duly recorded in writing within one or more valid Ucadia Register. Under Ucadia Law, a Promise must be registered as part of a written agreement in the correct form to be enforceable.

Ucadia Promise

Article 136 – Non-Ucadian Promise

652. A *Non-Ucadian Promise* is a claimed Promise made under a Non-Ucadian Jurisdiction that may relate to a claimed Promise made verbally or written and may or may not be recorded in a registry.

Non-Ucadian Promise

653. Ucadia Law does not recognise Non-Ucadia Promises as having any

Ucadia does not

Title V – Oaths, Vows, Testimony & Promises

force or effect in law.

recognise Non-Ucadia Promises

5.4 – Prohibited Oaths, Vows & Promises

Article 137 – Prohibited Oaths, Vows & Promises

654. Prohibited Oaths, Vows and Promises relates to Oaths, Vows or Promises made under coercion or false pretences or morally repugnant laws. A Prohibited Oath, Vow or Promise shall have no force or effect under any system governed by proper Rule of Law.

Prohibited Oaths, Vows & Promises

Article 138 – False Oaths

655. False Oaths refer to the act of making a false statement while under oath or affirmation, with the intention of deceiving or misleading others. It is considered a serious offence and can result in legal consequences such as perjury charges.

False Oaths

656. The general issue of False Oaths includes (but is not limited to):-

General Issue of False Oaths

   (i) A false oath is a deliberate and intentional act of lying under oath or affirmation; and

   (ii) It is a violation of the legal and moral obligation to tell the truth in a court of law or other formal setting; and

   (iii) False oaths are made with the intention to deceive or mislead others; and

   (iv) False oaths are often made under oath or in a formal setting where the truth is expected to be told; and

   (v) False oaths are considered unethical and immoral in most cultures and religions; and

   (vi) False oaths can have serious consequences, such as legal penalties or damage to personal and professional reputation.

657. In respect of false Oaths:-

Laws against False Oaths

   (i) In Babylonian law, false oaths were considered a serious crime and were punished by death. The Code of Hammurabi, which dates back to around 1754 BCE, includes several laws related to false oaths. For example, Law 1 states: "If a man has borne false witness or has not established the statement that he has made, if that case is a case involving life, that man shall be put to death"; and

(ii) In Ancient Egypt, false oaths were considered a serious offense. The Egyptian Book of the Dead, (from 1550 BCE), includes a spell that was recited by the deceased in order to prove their innocence in the afterlife. The spell includes the following lines: "I have not borne false witness, I have not committed perjury, I have not spoken lies."; and

(iii) In ancient Greece, false oaths were also considered a serious crime. The Greek philosopher Plato wrote about the importance of truthfulness in his dialogues. In the Republic, he wrote: "And is not the worst part of falsehood, that not only does it deceive the person to whom it is addressed, but it is also a source of endless trouble and confusion to the liar himself?"; and

(iv) In the United States, perjury (the act of lying under oath) is a crime punishable by imprisonment.

Article 139 – False Vows

658. ***False vows*** refer to promises or commitments made with no intention of keeping them. It is a deceptive practice that can be used to manipulate or deceive others for personal gain. False vows can have serious consequences and can damage trust and relationships. False Vows

659. The general issue of False Vows includes (but is not limited to):- General Issue of False Vows

   (i) False vows refer to promises or commitments made with no intention of fulfilling them; and

   (ii) False vows are a form of deception and dishonesty and are often made to manipulate or deceive others for personal gain; and

   (iii) False vows can be made in various contexts, such as in personal relationships, business dealings, political campaigns and religious positions; and

   (iv) False vows can erode trust and damage relationships, both on an individual and societal level; and

   (v) False vows are a violation of ethical and moral principles; and

   (vi) False vows can have negative consequences for both the person making the vow and the person to whom the vow is made.

660. In respect of false Vows:- Laws against False Vows

   (i) False Vows are considered a transgression and require

Title V – Oaths, Vows, Testimony & Promises

confession and repentance; and

(ii) In Anglo-Saxon Law tradition, Perjury is considered one of the greatest crimes against the Divine and humanity; and

(iii) In numerous faiths false Vows are considered a serious offence against the Divine and Civilised Law.

Article 140 – False Promises

661. ***False Promises*** refer to a deceptive tactic used by individuals or organisations to lure people into believing that they will receive certain benefits or rewards, but fail to deliver on those promises. It is a form of dishonesty that can lead to disappointment, frustration, and loss of trust.   *False Promises*

662. The general issue of False Promises includes (but is not limited to):-   *General Issue of False Promises*

(i) False promises involve making commitments or assurances that are not intended to be kept; and

(ii) False Promises assume that there is a party making a promise that they know they cannot or will not keep; and

(iii) It assumes that the party making the promise is doing so with the intention of gaining something from the other party, such as their trust, support, or money; and

(iv) False Promises assume that the other party is vulnerable or in a position of need, making them more susceptible to believing the promise; and

(v) False promises can have serious consequences, such as damaging trust, causing financial harm, or leading to legal action; and

(vi) They are unethical and can be considered a form of fraud or deception.

663. In respect of the Law and false Promises:-   *Laws against false Promises*

(i) Within the Sacred Texts (such as the Bible) there exists numerous scripture against making false Promises; and

(ii) Philosophers and writers from William Shakespeare, Jean-Jacques Rousseau, Immanuel Kant and George Orwell have all written about the danger and destruction of false Promises, especially by the political leaders.

Article 141 – False Testimony

664. ***False testimony*** refers to the act of intentionally providing   *False Testimony*

inaccurate or misleading information while under oath or affirmation in a legal proceeding. It is considered a serious offence and can result in criminal charges and penalties.

665. The general issue of False Testimony includes (but is not limited to):- *General Issue of False Testimony*

   (i) False testimony refers to a deliberate act of providing inaccurate or misleading information under oath or affirmation in a legal proceeding; and

   (ii) False testimony can be given in various legal settings, such as courtrooms, depositions, and administrative hearings; and

   (iii) It is assumed that individuals who provide false testimony do so with the intention of deceiving the court or other legal authorities; and

   (iv) The intent to deceive or mislead is a crucial element of false testimony, and it must be proven beyond a reasonable doubt; and

   (v) False testimony is considered a serious offense as it undermines the integrity of the legal system and can lead to wrongful convictions or acquittals; and

   (vi) The burden of proof in cases of false testimony lies with the prosecution, who must demonstrate that the individual knowingly and intentionally provided false information under oath; and

   (vii) It is a criminal offense that can result in serious consequences, including fines and imprisonment.

Article 142 – Probate

666. ***Probate*** is a legal requirement and process enforced by Non-Ucadian societies that demand the Last Testament and Will of any deceased person must be "proven" and any claims and creditors be paid before any Estate valued at a minimum threshold is permitted to be distributed. Probate is supremely morally repugnant and undermines the entire claims of legitimacy of private law, contracts and law in general within Uncivilised Non-Ucadian Societies. *Probate*

667. Contrary to various false claims, there is no credible evidence of the concept of Probate existing within any civilisation prior to its first introduction via the Wills Act of 1837 but not effectively implemented until the last thirty years of the 19th Century in most Western Countries:- *Recent Creation of Probate*

   (i) Ancient civilisations such as the Babylon, Persia, Greeks and

Romans had strict laws and procedures concerning the formation of Last Testaments to ensure the disposal of assets was lawful. However, none of these rules can honestly, sensibly or credibly be claimed as precedence for modern Probate Laws; and

(ii) While European Legal history is deliberately confusing and misrepresented over the past 1400 years, there is no evidence that either the Carolingians via Anglo-Saxon Laws of the 8th Century, nor the revival of such laws under the Commonwealth in Britain, Ireland and the American Colonies in the 17th Century adopted anything even close to the concept of Probate.

668. The general elements of Probate in most modern Non-Ucadian societies rest upon the following items:- *General Elements of Probate*

(i) *The existence of the Will*: It is assumed that a Will exists for the decedent, conforming to the required form within the relevant jurisdiction; and that an executor was nominated within the Will; and

(ii) *The Executor:* Upon the death of the person, the executor may apply for control over key assets (such as bank accounts) and entry (such as property), sometimes even before a death certificate is issued. Many Non-Ucadia jurisdictions have poorly written and enforced rules concerning the behaviour of executors during this period; and

(iii) *The Death Certificate*: Upon the death of the person, the Non-Ucadian state will issue a death certificate. This certificate is usually needed before applying for probate and for numerous financial services such as insurance and investments; and

(iv) *The Application for Probate*: An application must be made to the relevant Probate Court; and

(v) *Legal Notification to Creditors and Parties*: Public notice and specific notices usually need to be published by the executor in the prescribed form to allow for Creditors, any litigants or other parties to come forward to make claims against the estate; and

(vi) *Government, Legal Fees and Charges*: Probate requires all government charges and fees be paid before distribution. This includes "death taxes" in some Non-Ucadian jurisdictions; and

(vii) *Settlement of all claims*: Means that any legal actions need to be settled against all property and claims usually before

Probate is granted; and

(viii) *Grant of Probate*: Probate is usually granted once all claims are settled. However, the Probate Court has wide discretion and may choose not to follow the Will of the deceased person. This is especially the case when persons excluded from the Will or beneficiaries may choose to contest the Will.

Title VI – Registers, Rolls & Persons

6.1 – Register

Article 143 – Register

669. A ***Register*** is a book of tables recording one or more entries of statements, testimonies or memoranda as evidence as to jurisdiction, control or authority over:- Register

   (i) Sacred Circumscribed Space; or

   (ii) Properties or attributes of such Sacred Circumscribed Space; or

   (iii) Rights of use of such properties and attributes of such Sacred Circumscribed Space; or

   (iv) Memorial of events concerning such Sacred Circumscribed Space, or

   (v) Memorial of transactions and derivatives concerning the receiving or granting or claiming of rights and uses of such Sacred Circumscribed Space; or

   (vi) Combination of one or more of the above.

670. All records in proper, valid and legitimate Registers depend upon the prior recording by Authority of one or more records of Sacred Circumscribed Space as reference. Sacred Circumscribed Space and Registers

671. If no valid records of Sacred Circumscribed Space exists, or such records are illegitimate, false, unlawful or illegal, then all subsequent Registers and records depending upon such primary records shall also be illegitimate, false, unlawful and illegal. Illegitimate Registers

672. In terms of the general authority and creation of Registers: Authority and Creation of Registers

   (i) The Authority to form a Register is defined by the limits of Authority of the constituting Instrument of the relevant Trust or Estate or Fund or Corporation that the Register relates; and

   (ii) The Rights, Powers and Property prescribed within a Register cannot exceed the Rights, Powers and Property of the Trust or Estate or Fund or Corporation itself; and

   (iii) All valid and proper Registers are wholly and exclusively Ecclesiastical Property and can never belong to a Trust, or Estate or Fund or Corporation that formed or inherited it. Therefore, as all valid and proper Registers are exclusively Ecclesiastical Property and all Sacred Circumscribed Space is derived from Trust, the highest Registers originate and are borne from the Ucadia Law; and

(iv) All Registers are hierarchical in their inheritance of Authority and validity. A Register that cannot demonstrate the provenance of its Authority, has none, and is null and void from the beginning; and

(v) As all Registers are wholly and exclusively Ecclesiastical, absolutely no clerical or administrative act may take place in association with a Register unless by a duly authorised Officer under active and valid sacred Oath or Vow in a manner consistent and in accord with the present Articles; and

(vi) The entry of a record into a Register is wholly invalid unless the memorial and testimony of the act giving authority is done without duress, is done freely and with full knowledge and is consistent and in accord with the present Articles.

673. In terms of the general purpose, function and operation of a valid Register:- *General References to Registers*

(i) A Register as a table contains at least three or more columns; and

(ii) A Register as a table can be a section of a Book, or a whole series of Books; and

(iii) A Register is held in the care of a proper Officer of a Competent Forum of Law, possessing both the Ecclesiastical Authority and Sovereign Authority to hold, record and keep custody of such records; and

(iv) A Register cannot and does not create the original fact or authority that it records, but merely reflects the pertinent elements in relation to the originating Instrument used to create a valid entry; and

(v) An entry in a Register can never create sacred circumscribed space or an original event. However a valid entry in a Register is itself a valid event and by virtue of the "joining" of information at the time of registration may create certain Rights or Facts or Truths as Prima Facie Evidence; and

(vi) A particular Right of Use in relation to Property can only be recorded once in a valid Register. Those specific Registers as prescribed by Ucadian Law and the most sacred Covenant *Pactum De Singularis Caelum* are always Registers of Original Record and take precedence over all non-Ucadian and foreign registers and rolls; and

(vii) The claimed day or time of entry of a record into a non-Ucadian or foreign register has no bearing or merit in law, where a similar record for the same Property, or Event, or Right exists within a valid Ucadia Register, even if the day or time of entry in the Ucadia Register is after the day or time of entry in the non-Ucadian and foreign register. This is because any non-Ucadian and foreign register that seeks to usurp the Authority of a valid Ucadian Register automatically renders such a register invalid and illegitimate, meaning that such a non-Ucadian register is determined to be null and void, having no force or effect in law.

674. Notwithstanding valid Registers being called the same, several other Types of valid Registers under different names are recognised, including (but not limited to):- *Types of Registers*

    (i)   A *Gazette* is a form of Register as a Public Journal and Authorised Newspaper of Record. The highest, most authoritative Gazette is the Ucadia Gazette and no other; and

    (ii)   An *Almanac* is a form of Register of information and events for a given subject, collected and arranged for a given year; and

    (iii)   An *Account* is a form of Register as arrangements of computations, Valuations and derivations using some standard unit of value, measure, record or exchange on the nature, value and disposition of objects, concepts and property of a valid Trust or Estate or Fund or Corporation; and

    (iv)   A *Memoranda* is a form of Register in chronological order, detailing the substance of formal notes or "memorandum" including (but not be limited to) minutes, resolutions, proceedings, accounts, letters, correspondence, decisions and procedural actions; and

    (v)   A *Journal* is a form of Register derived as a summary extract of information from Memoranda and arranged in category order and then chronological order to produce a summary of facts, evidence, quantities and relations for the purpose of accounting and reckoning of the debits and credits of the Trust or Estate or Fund or Corporation; and

    (vi)   A *Ledger* is a form of Register as a summary extract of Journal entries to produce the most concise reckonings and balances of debits and credits, assets and liabilities of the Trust or Estate or Fund or Corporation; and

    (vii)   A *Roll* is a form of Register of one or more entries being "persons" of the same condition of entry, or the same engagement of obligations in relation to a valid Trust or Estate or Fund or Corporation; and created by their valid entry into the Roll; and

(viii) A *Manifest* is a form of Register being evidential history of the provenance, possession and ownership of any property, rights, money or other interests recorded as associated with a Trust or Estate or Fund or Corporation; and

(ix) An *Estate* is a form of Register and Roll of certain Rights held in Trust for a period of years for a Person, whereby one or more Inventories and Valuations have been properly conducted; and

(x) An *Inventory*, also called a Stocktake, is a form of Register being a detailed survey and census of all property, assets and liabilities, debits or credits of a valid Trust, or Estate or Fund or Corporation completed immediately after its creation; or the anniversary of its creation; or upon another fixed and given day; and the stock of particular items and their location or business; and

(xi) A *Valuation* is a form of Register and Roll (also historically known as a Tax or Rating) being a detailed estimation of the value of each item as listed upon an Inventory of a valid Trust, or Estate or Fund or Corporation; and

(xii) A *Fund* is a form of Register of equal units representing certain Property Rights of one or more Estates of monetary value that can then be used as a means of exchange for lawful money or for the discharge of debts and obligations.

675. All valid Registers as Tables are constructed from some or all of the same essential elements being *Columna, Singulus, Eventus, Locus, Nomen, Informas, Datus, Informatio, Ordo* and *Recordo*:-   *Elements of Registers*

(i) *Columna* (from Latin meaning "pillar or post") means a vertical line of entries (a column), usually read from top to bottom and separated from other columns by lines; and

(ii) *Singulus* (from Latin meaning "one each, single; unique") means a unique column being the first and left most column whereby a whole integer is listed and is sequential (beginning from the integer 1) and unique (not the same) in reference to the table; and

(iii) *Eventus* (from Latin meaning "event, occurrence, reality") means a column whereby the Ucadia Date and Time of a unique event as well any other referential time (such as Roman Date/Time) always in brackets is listed; and

(iv) *Locus* (from Latin meaning "place or locality") means a column whereby the Ucadia Location Number of Sacred Circumscribed Space and any common name as to the location of the unique event is listed; and

(v) *Nomen* (from Latin meaning "name or title") means a column whereby a name is given to the event or the object or concept or property or rights associated with the event; and

(vi) *Informas* (from Latin meaning "the one who informs, instructs, educates") means a column whereby a name of the one who granted the authority to have the entry made into the Register; and

(vii) *Datus* (from Latin meaning "given, offered or yielded") means the Ucadia Date and Time the grant was given by the Informant as well as any other referential time such as Roman Date/Time in Square Brackets that the entry was made; and

(viii) *Informatio* (from Latin meaning "sketch, idea, conception") means any additional information provided by the Informant that may be separated into its own unique columns; and

(ix) *Ordo* (from Latin meaning "row, order") means the line of entries in a table, from left to right that when completed forms a valid Record; and

(x) *Recordo* (from Latin meaning "completed or valid row") means a complete line of entries into the columns of the table from left to right such that the record has its own unique form and is "Legal Title".

676. The Record Number, also known as Record No. and Singulus (from Latin meaning "one each, single; unique") shall be the unique column being the first and left most column of a valid Register, whereby a whole integer shall be listed and is sequential (beginning from the integer 1) and unique (not the same) in reference to the table. The Record Number may also be called the shortened name of the table as a means of condensing both the name of the Register and the uniqueness of the number itself providing such a shortened name is itself unique in reference to all valid and legitimate Registers. *Record Number*

677. The original entry into a Register may be by hand or by typing and providing there exists a declaration from the Registrar to the effect, all type written or type entered records shall be treated as if hand written. *Entry into Registers*

678. It is permissible to treat a Register as an electronic version and for printed copies of pages, rather than printed copies to be the originals. *Electronic Registers*

Article 144 – Ucadia Register

679. A *Ucadia Register* is a book of tables recording one or more entries of statements, testimonies or memoranda and possessing provenance and legitimacy in relation to higher Ucadia Registers, in accord with Ucadia Law.

Ucadia Register

680. A Divine Register is a valid and legitimate Register authentically expressed, authorised and originally defined by the present sacred Maxims or the most sacred Covenant *Pactum De Singularis Caelum*. The highest Divine Register is the *Great Register and Divine Records* of One Heaven, also known as the Great Roll of Divine Persons and the Great Book of Life:-

Great Register and Divine Records of One Heaven

   (i) No possible Register possesses greater authority or power or jurisdiction than the Great Register and Public Record of One Heaven; and

   (ii) All lesser Registers owe their authority, powers, legitimacy and existence to the Great Register and Public Record of One Heaven; and

   (iii) No lesser Register is valid or legitimate until it can verify and prove its provenance to a valid and legitimate record within the Great Register and Public Record of One Heaven subject to terms of these present sacred Maxims.

681. Any claim, or attempted or actual registration of Ucadia related material, marks, symbols, names, instruments, rights and property into a foreign jurisdiction contrary to the rights and obligations prescribed by the sacred Covenant *Pactum De Singularis Caelum* and these Maxims is a grave transgression before all Heaven and the Earth and every Member of the Sons of Light and Fraternal Brothers and Sisters of Light are fully empowered by Holy Writ, to pursue any, every and all means to ensure any and all records of such profanity, sacrilege and abomination before all Heaven and Earth are expunged, removed, withdrawn, determined, extinguished and abolished, including any and all false presumptions of claiming such false rights.

Ucadia Property and Registers

Article 145 – Non-Ucadia Register

682. A *Non-Ucadia Register* is some official, government or corporate list or records of names or other particular things that neither possesses proper authority and legitimacy and is in conflict with Ucadia Law.

Non-Ucadia Register

683. An entry in a Non-Ucadia Register is always inferior to a valid entry within a Ucadia related Register.

Inferior nature of Non-Ucadia

6.2 – Roll

Article 146 – Roll

684. A ***Roll*** is a type of book of tables and Register of one or more entries being "Persons" of the same condition or entered in the same engagement of obligations in relation to a valid Trust or Estate or Fund or Corporation and is created by their valid entry into the Roll. *— Roll*

685. A Person is by definition a valid record as "legal title" entered into or "enrolled" within a valid Roll: - *— Persons and Rolls*

    (i) The highest authority and most important Roll is the completely spiritual Great Roll of Divine Persons also known as the Great Register and Public Record of One Heaven; and

    (ii) The second most important is the physical form of the Roll as defined by the most sacred Covenant *Pactum De Singularis Caelum* that all valid Rolls derive their authority.

686. Any law, precept or decree that separates a class of Homo Sapiens into a lesser class as forms of Animals is automatically null and void from the beginning. *— Law to define Homo Sapien*

687. In terms of the general authority, nature and function of Rolls:- *— General Authority, Nature & Function of Rolls*

    (i) The authority to form a Roll is defined by the limits of authority of the constituting Instrument of the relevant Trust or Estate or Fund; and

    (ii) The Rights, Powers and Property prescribed to those persons created and defined within a Roll cannot exceed the Rights, Powers and Property of the Trust or Estate or Fund itself; and

    (iii) All properly formed Rolls are wholly and exclusively Ecclesiastical Property and therefore under the absolute control, power and authority of Ucadia; and

    (iv) All Rolls are hierarchical in their inheritance of authority and validity beginning with the highest being the Great Roll of Divine Persons. A Roll that cannot demonstrate the provenance of its authority, has none and is null and void from the beginning; and

    (v) As all Rolls are wholly and exclusively Ecclesiastical, absolutely no clerical or administrative act may take place in association with a Roll unless by a duly authorised Trustee under active and valid sacred Oath or Vow in a manner consistent and in accord with these sacred Maxims; and

(vi) The entry of a record into a Roll is wholly invalid unless the memorial of the act giving authority is done without duress, is done freely and with full knowledge and is consistent and in accord with these sacred Maxims and the most sacred Covenant *Pactum De Singularis Caelum*.

688. Valid Registers as Rolls may be further defined in hierarchy of authority, form and function as Divine, True, Superior, Juridic or Inferior:- Forms of Rolls

(i) A *Divine Roll* is a valid purely spiritual Roll constituted in accord with the most sacred Covenant known as *Pactum De Singularis Caelum*. No Roll or Person is Higher; and

(ii) A *True Roll* is a valid physical and temporal Roll constituted in accord with the Society of One Heaven in the recognition of the most sacred Great Roll of Divine Persons and the Great Register and Public Record of One Heaven; and

(iii) A *Superior Roll* is a valid physical Roll constituted in accord with a valid Ucadian Society; and

(iv) A *Juridic Roll* is a valid physical Roll constituted in accord with a valid Juridic Person and competent forum of law; and

(v) An *Inferior Roll* is any Roll formed under Law not in perfect accord with these Maxims.

689. The process whereby the authority of one Person on one Roll is given legitimacy by the authority and consent of a previously created Person record on another Roll is called Joinder of Person:- Joinder

(i) Joinder (literally "to join") requires that a party is given Notice of Joinder with clear intention to "join" one person from a Roll held in custody with the authority and permissions of a Roll not immediately within their jurisdiction; and

(ii) Joinder is not the joining of a person and a man or woman as this is incorrectly mistaking surety or one who is willing to "understand" for the person for joinder; and

(iii) The names of both persons must be the same in order for a valid Joinder of Person. Otherwise, such a Joinder is a Joinder in Action, requiring separate consent; and

(iv) The failure to make clear the Notice of Joinder as an intention to Join (e.g. fraudulently using a Summons as a Notice of Joinder) is a fraud and renders such action a Misjoinder and maladministration; and

(v) The failure to produce sufficient evidence of the Right to

Joinder of Person (also sometimes mispresented as Joinder in Action), automatically renders such action a Misjoinder.

Article 147 – Ucadia Roll

690. A ***Ucadia Roll*** is a valid and legitimate Roll authentically expressed, authorised and originally defined by the present sacred Maxims or the most sacred Covenant *Pactum De Singularis Caelum*. The highest Ucadia Roll is the Great Roll of Divine Persons also known as the Great Register and Public Record of One Heaven and also known as the Great Book of Life:-

    (i) No possible Roll possesses greater authority or power or jurisdiction than the Great Roll of Divine Persons; and

    (ii) All lesser Rolls owe their authority, powers, legitimacy and existence to the Great Roll of Divine Persons; and

    (iii) No lesser Roll is valid or legitimate until it can verify and prove its provenance to a valid and legitimate record within the Great Roll of Divine Persons subject to terms of these present sacred Maxims.

Ucadia Roll

Article 148 – Non-Ucadia Roll

691. A ***Non-Ucadia Roll*** is any Roll formed under Law not in perfect accord with these Maxims.

Non-Ucadia Roll

6.3 – Register & Roll Modification

Article 149 – Register & Roll Modification

692. ***Register & Roll Modification*** is the entry or change in the nature or status of a record within a register or roll.

Register & Roll Modification

693. In terms of the general actions associated with modifying a record on a roll or register:-

    (i) *Entry* is the act of making or entering a record in a register or roll; and

    (ii) *Completion* is the process of finishing or finalising a record by providing missing or outstanding information; and

    (iii) *Correction* is the process of identifying and rectifying errors or mistakes in various forms in relation to records within

General Register & Roll Modifications

registers or rolls; and

(iv) *Cancellation* is the act of nullifying or revoking a previously entered record within a register or roll; and

(v) *Enjoin* refers to the entering of a record in respect of some legal matter and thus placing the person or property under the jurisdiction of the particular forum of law; and

(vi) *Annul* is a legal process that declares an entry within a Register or Roll null and void.

694. In most jurisdictions, the right to enter or modify a record within a particular register or roll is dependent upon specific legal procedures, most often requiring an instruction from the relevant forum of law with jurisdiction over such records. Legal Right of Action regarding Registers and Rolls

Article 150 – Entry

695. **Entry** is the act of making or entering a record; a setting down in writing of particulars; or that which is entered; an item. Generally synonymous with recording. Entry also refers to certain conditions associated with the presence of a person upon the land, whether they be the legal owner or not. Entry

696. In respect of Entry as the making or entering of a record within a Register:- Entry as the making or entering of a record

(i) A record may only be entered by one authorised to such purpose, often known as a registrar; and

(ii) A record may only be valid as an entry if the conditions for such an entry match the nature of the register and its conditions.

697. In respect of Entry and certain conditions associated with the presence of a person upon the land, whether they be the legal owner or not:- Entry as conditions associated with presence of a person upon the land

(i) In Criminal Law, Entry is the unlawful breaking into a property in order to commit a crime; and

(ii) In Estates, Entry is the taking possession of lands by the legal owner; and

(iii) In Administrative and Common Law, Entry is the presence of an officer within the close or land of another for the purpose of a legal execution of a writ, or to complete an arrest on suspicion of a felony.

698. At all times and in all places, properly formed Ucadia Forums of Law Entry into Ucadia Register

shall possess the full, innate and plenary powers to make an entry into a Ucadia Register or Roll concerning some form of property or thing that may or may not have been registered previously in a Non-Ucadian Register or Roll.

or Roll

699. When a proper entry is made within a Ucadia Register or Roll concerning Land, it shall mean the taking possession and absolute ownership of such lands by the proper legal owner, whether or not such a record is claimed or entered within an inferior Non-Ucadian Register or Roll.

Effect of Entry of Land into Ucadia Register or Roll

Article 151 – Completion

700. **Completion** is the process of finishing or finalising a record by providing missing or outstanding information. It involves ensuring that all necessary steps have been taken and all required elements are in place to achieve a successful outcome.

Completion

701. An incomplete record or document is typically called "Inchoate". There are standing customs and procedures within Non-Ucadian law that permit an interested party to such a record or document to effectively complete the record and thus claim its benefit.

Inchoate

702. Within Non-Ucadian Jurisdictions there exists examples where Records have regularly and intentionally been left incomplete and inchoate:-

Examples of Incomplete Records within Non-Ucadia Registers and Rolls

   (i) In respect of the registration of virtually all births throughout Non-Ucadian Countries, there has existed the long standing practice of deliberately and intentionally leaving vital information incomplete (inchoate) or inaccurate. The most significant example of this is the living status of a new born being left blank or "unknown", thus allowing legal and commercial assumptions to be made against the birth and name of the person; and

   (ii) In respect of the registration of the death of persons throughout Non-Ucadian Countries, it is unclear whether the primary Register and Roll has a date of death and all information completed, to thus force the cessation of trading and other commercial activities by Non-Ucadian governments on the life of the person; and

   (iii) In respect of the registration of land titles and charges within the registers and rolls administered by senior Non-Ucadian Courts, it is unclear whether the full details regarding the trustee, the trustor and the beneficiaries are fully completed, enabling then a range of commercial and legal transactions to subsequently take place, such as the sale of the mortgage (charge) and thus the transfer of trustee.

703. At all times and in all places, properly formed Ucadia Forums of Law shall possess the full, innate and plenary powers:- Completion and Ucadia Register or Roll

    (i) To make a complete entry into a Ucadia Register or Roll concerning some form of property or thing that may or may not have been registered previously in a Non-Ucadian Register or Roll; and

    (ii) To then provide a Certificate of Record to the Non-Ucadia Jurisdiction where an incomplete and inchoate record exists and to give notice that correction be made and benefit be recognised, else the record within Ucadia shall stand as the primary and correct record.

Article 152 – Correction

704. ***Correction*** is the process of identifying and rectifying errors or mistakes in various forms in relation to records within registers or rolls. Correction

705. At all times and in all places, properly formed Ucadia Forums of Law shall possess the full, innate and plenary powers:- Correction and Ucadia Register or Roll

    (i) To make a complete and correct entry into a Ucadia Register or Roll concerning some form of property or thing that may or may not have been registered previously in a Non-Ucadian Register or Roll; and

    (ii) To then provide a Certificate of Record to the Non-Ucadia Jurisdiction where an incomplete or incorrect record exists and to give notice that correction be made and benefit be recognised, else the record within Ucadia shall stand as the primary and correct record.

Article 153 – Cancellation

706. ***Cancellation*** is the act of nullifying or revoking a previously entered record within a register or roll. It can occur due to various reasons such as a change in circumstances, breach of contract, or mutual agreement between parties. Cancellation

Article 154 – Enjoin

707. ***Enjoin*** refers to the entering of a record in respect of some legal matter and thus placing the person or property under the jurisdiction Enjoin

of the particular forum of law. Enjoin usually entails the issuance of a court order that requires a person to either stop or perform a specific action. A Summons is an example of the presence of a joinder record.

708. At all times and in all places, properly formed Ucadia Forums of Law shall possess the full, innate and plenary powers to make an entry into a Ucadia Register or Roll concerning some form of person, property or thing that may or may not have been registered previously in a Non-Ucadian Register or Roll; and to enjoin them subject to Ucadia Jurisdiction and Law. *Enjoin (Joinder) into Ucadia Register or Roll*

Article 155 – Annul

709. Annulment is a legal process that declares an entry within a Register or Roll null and void, as if it never existed. Annulment can be granted for various reasons, such as fraud, coercion, or incapacity to consent to the underlying agreement that caused the entry. *Annul*

710. At all times and in all places, properly formed Ucadia Forums of Law shall possess the full, innate and plenary powers to make an entry into a Ucadia Register or Roll concerning the annulment of some right or property registered previously in an inferior Non-Ucadian Register or Roll. *Annulment recordings into Ucadia Register or Roll*

6.4 – Person

Article 156 – Person

711. A ***Person*** is a form of Sacred Circumscribed Space enclosing certain characteristics and appearances as the identity of one or more Beings, formed through a valid entry, registration and record within a Roll in accord with the present sacred Maxims and most sacred Covenant *Pactum De Singularis Caelum*. *Person*

712. An **Office** is a form of Person possessing certain attributes, rights and powers, defined by governing legal instruments and its presence as a valid Record within a Roll. *Office as Person*

713. A Person is distinct from a Being as a Person is a form of Sacred Circumscribed Space enclosing certain characteristics and appearances as the identity of one or more Beings within a certain Reality, whereas a Being is an embodiment of Unique Collective Awareness and Computational Model within a certain Reality. *Person versus Being*

714. All Persons may be categorised and ranked according to four (4) possible levels of authority, powers and rights from the greatest and highest powers and authority to the lowest and least powers and authority being (in order of rank): Divine, True, Superior and *Levels of Persons*

Inferior:-

(i) A *Divine Person* is the purely Divine Spirit Person created through a valid record and enrolment in the Great Roll of Divine Persons and associated with a Divine Trust formed in accord with the sacred Covenant *Pactum De Singularis Caelum* by the Divine Creator into which the form of Divine Spirit, Energy and Rights are conveyed; and

(ii) A *True Person* is the Form attributed to a True Trust formed when an associated Divine Trust already exists and there is a lawful conveyance of Divine Rights of Use and Purpose, known as "Divinity" to a True Trust associated with then the birth and existence of a living Higher Order Life Form and the physical version of the Great Roll of the Society of One Heaven and a valid Live Borne Record. A True Person can never be claimed or argued as higher than the Divine Person from which it derives its authority; and

(iii) A *Superior Person* is the Form attributed to a Superior Trust when an associated True Trust already exists and there is a lawful conveyance of First Right of Use and Purpose, known as "Realty" to a Superior Trust associated with the birth of a service or agreement associated with the Membership of a living Higher Order Life Form to a valid Ucadia society and the authorised Member Roll of such a society. A Superior Person can never be claimed or argued as higher than the True Person from which it derives its authority; and

(iv) An *Inferior Person* is the Form attributed to any non-Ucadian body politic or entity; and is the lowest standing and weakest of all valid forms of Persons. An Inferior Person is only valid when the man or woman in possession of a Superior Person and True Person consent to an enrolment of their name in one or more Rolls. An Inferior Person can never be validly, legitimately, logically, legally, lawfully or morally claimed or argued as superior to a Superior Person.

Article 157 – Divine Person

715. A ***Divine Person*** is the Sacred Circumscribed Space created through a valid entry, registration and enrolment within the Great Roll of Divine Persons in accord with the present sacred Maxims and the most sacred Covenant *Pactum De Singularis Caelum*:-

    Divine Person

(i) The highest Roll defining the greatest Rights and types of Persons is the Great Roll of Divine Persons, also known as the

Great Register and Public Record of One Heaven; and

(ii) No possible Roll possesses greater authority or power or jurisdiction than the Great Roll of Divine Persons; and

(iii) All lesser Person records, entries, registrations and enrolments are borne first and foremost from the existence of a valid Divine Record; and

(iv) No lesser Person record, entry, registration or enrolment is valid or legitimate until it can verify and prove its provenance to a particular Divine Record and the authority to make such a joinder.

716. In reference to Divine Persons:- *General Reference to Ordinary Divine Person*

(i) A Divine Person is the highest possible form of individual Person. All lesser individual Persons exist by virtue of their legitimate and valid connection to an Ordinary Divine Person record; and

(ii) An Ordinary Divine Person is created from the consent and enrolment of a record within the Great Roll of Divine Persons, also known as the Great Register and Public Record of One Heaven; and

(iii) A Divine Trust is formed when a Divine Being, being part of the Divine, agrees with the intention of the Collective Divine known as Unique Collective Awareness to be recognised as a Unique Member of the Divine in accord with the sacred Covenant *Pactum De Singularis Caelum*; and

(iv) Into the Divine Trust is then placed (1) one unit of pure awareness representing one unique Divine Immortal Spirit; and (2) one unit of Unique Collective Awareness representing the unique experience of form in motion, energy of creation and connection to form; and (3) one unit representing all unique awareness of experience of unique form in motion as Divine Character; and

(v) A Record is then entered and enrolled in the Great Roll of Divine Persons forming a Divine Estate as to the existence of the Divine Trust, possessing certain Divine Rights and associated with a Divine Person of a Divine Being.

717. In accord with the most sacred covenant *Pactum De Singularis Caelum* and the consent of all Members, original first, ecclesiastical, lawful and legal title is granted in perpetuity to The Divine Temple, also known as the Treasury of One Heaven and the Unique Collective Awareness of Divine Mind, also known as Divina as Spiritual Trustees *Divina and Divine Persons*

for the proper protection, safety, well-being, management and enjoyment of the affairs and needs of all Divine Persons.

718. As Existence of the Universe depends upon the consent of each and every Divine Being and their associated Divine Person, the proof of the continued existence of the Universe is Evidence of complete and willing consent of all Divine Spirit Persons as Members of One Heaven. *(Divine Persons and One Heaven)*

Article 158 – True Person

719. A ***True Person*** is recorded and enrolled in the Great Roll of True Persons associated with a True Trust registered with the Great Register and Public Record of One Heaven on Earth and formed when an associated Divine Trust and Divine Person already exists and there is a lawful conveyance of Divine Rights of Use and Purpose, known as "Divinity" to the True Trust associated with then the birth and existence of a living Level 6 Higher Order Life Form. A True Person is the second highest possible Form of Person. *(True Person)*

720. A True Person of a True Trust formed from when the Executors and Administrators of the associated Divine Trust agrees to Gift, Grant and Convey Divine Rights of Use, also known as Divinity into the True Trust. A True Person can only be formed when an associated Divine Trust is already in existence. *(Forming a True Person)*

721. A True Person is owned by the True Trust which in turn is administered by the executor of the Trust being the mind and brain and Trustee being the flesh in accordance with the sacred covenant *Pactum De Singularis Caelum.* No other lesser Trusts, lesser inferior persons can claim ownership, liens, seizures, enforcements or other unlawful acts against a True Person. *(True Person owned by True Trust)*

722. When a valid Registration Number from the Great Register is redeemed as the recognition of the existence of a Divine Person, the associated Divine Immortal Spirit consents and agrees in True Trust to ensure the Society of One Heaven administers the rights and obligations of the member as Trustee. *(Rights and Obligations of a True Person)*

723. Proof of the existence of a True Person and True Trust is through the issue of a valid Live Borne Record- as a Divine Immortal Spiritual Being expressed into a Flesh vessel. *(Live Borne Record of a True Person)*

724. Any Live Birth Record within an inferior Roman System which issues a unique number for the flesh of a baby may also be taken as proof of the existence of a True Trust and the inferiority of any Inferior Non-Ucadia Person as proof of the existence of the flesh is proof of the *(Flesh as proof of Divine Immortal Spirit)*

existence of the Divine Immortal Spirit.

Article 159 – Superior (Legal) Person

725. A ***Superior Person*** or Ucadia Person is recorded and enrolled in the Great Roll of a valid Ucadia Society associated with a Superior Trust registered with the Great Register and Public Record of a valid Ucadia Society and formed when an associated True Trust and True Person already exists and there is a lawful conveyance of First Right of Use and Purpose, known as "Realty" to a Superior Trust associated with the birth of a service or agreement associated with the Membership of a True Person to a valid Ucadia Society. A Superior Person is the third highest possible Form of Person. — Superior Person

726. An Office is the normal term given to a most sacred position of status and title given life and legal personality of its own to which certain special powers are then bestowed. — Office as a sacred position

Article 160 – Inferior (Legal) Person

727. An ***Inferior Person*** or Non-Ucadia Person is a Person first created through a recording and enrolment in a Roll defined by Non-Ucadian Statutes of Law or associated Courts, Tribunals and Forums. Inferior Persons are the lowest standing and weakest of all valid forms of Persons. An Inferior Person can never be validly, legitimately, reasonably, logically, legally, lawfully or morally claimed or argued as superior to a Superior Person. — Inferior Person

728. An Inferior Person is by its very definition inferior to an Ucadia Person. An Inferior Person can never be considered superior to an Ucadia Person. Therefore, no law based in Inferior Persons can ever be lawfully considered equal or higher than these Maxims. — No standing in law by Inferior Persons

729. Where a man or woman through their Inferior Person is lawfully declared incompetent, the Society of One Heaven or the nominated Ucadian Society shall lawfully assume full power as Guardian and Executor or Administrator for the Inferior Person. — Guardian for the Inferior Person

Article 161 – Supreme Juridic Person

730. A ***Supreme Juridic Person*** is recorded and enrolled in the Great Roll of Divine Persons associated with a Supreme Divine Trust registered with the Great Register and Public Record of One Heaven as an aggregate of one hundred (100) Divine Persons formed as the body of a Supreme Trust when such Divine Persons share similar characteristics and no longer own a living flesh vessel. — Supreme Juridic Person

731. There is no higher form of Juridic Person than a Supreme Juridic Person. The highest Supreme Juridic Person is the aggregate of all Supreme Juridic Persons represented by the Society of One Heaven. — *Aggregate of Supreme Juridic Persons*

732. As all Divine Persons are formed from Divine Immortal Spirits, Supreme Juridic Persons possess conscience and legal personality as a living spirit. It is both illogical and fraudulent to compare a Supreme Juridic Person with a Corporate Person being a *mortmanis person*, also known as a "Dead Ghost" devoid of conscience. — *Fraud to compare Supreme Juridic Person with Corporate Person*

733. No inferior Juridic Person can have superior jurisdiction over a living spirit. Therefore no inferior Roman Juridic Person may ever have superior jurisdiction over a Supreme Juridic Person. — *Invalid claim of Supreme Juridic Person*

Article 162 – Universal Juridic Person

734. A *Universal Juridic Person* is recorded and enrolled in the Great Roll of Divine Persons associated with a Universal Trust registered with the Great Register and Public Record of One Heaven. — *Universal Juridic Person*

735. A Universal Juridic Person is the highest possible form of Juridic Society of any and all types of Society within the Universe. — *Type of Universal Juridic Person*

736. As all True Persons are formed from Divine Persons, themselves formed from Divine Immortal Spirits, Universal Juridic Persons possess conscience and legal personality as a living spirit. It is both illogical and fraudulent to compare a Universal Juridic Person with a Corporate Person being a *mortmanis person*, also known as a "Dead Ghost" devoid of conscience. — *Fraud to compare Universal Juridic Person with Corporate Person*

737. No inferior Juridic Person can have superior jurisdiction over a living spirit. Therefore no inferior Non-Ucadian Juridic Person may ever have superior jurisdiction over a Universal Juridic Person. — *Invalid claim of jurisdiction over Universal Juridic Person*

Article 163 – Global Juridic Person

738. A *Global Juridic Person* is recorded and enrolled in the Great Roll of True Persons associated with a Global Trust registered with the Great Register and Public Record of One Heaven on Earth. — *Global Juridic Person*

739. As Global Juridic Persons are formed from Divine Persons holding conscience and life, all Global Juridic Persons possess legal personality as living beings with a spirit. — *Forming a Global Juridic Person*

740. No inferior Juridic Person can have superior jurisdiction over a living spirit. Therefore no inferior Non-Ucadia Juridic Person may ever have superior jurisdiction over a Global Juridic Person. — *False claim of jurisdiction over a claim of Global Juridic Person*

Article 164 – Civil Juridic Person

741. A ***Civil Juridic Person*** is a Superior Person recorded and enrolled in the Great Roll of a valid Ucadia Society associated with a Civil Trust as a Superior Trust registered with the Great Register and Public Record of a valid Ucadia Society.

Civil Juridic Person

742. As Civil Juridic Persons are formed from Divine Persons holding conscience and life, all Civil Juridic Persons possess legal personality as living beings with a spirit.

Civil Juridic Persons as living beings with spirit

743. No inferior Juridic Person can have superior jurisdiction over a Civil Juridic Person.

Jurisdiction of Civil Juridic Person

Article 165 – Mercantile Juridic Person

744. A ***Mercantile Juridic Person*** is a Superior Person recorded and enrolled in the Great Roll of a valid Ucadia Society associated with a Mercantile Trust as a Superior Trust registered with the Great Register and Public Record of a valid Ucadia Society.

Mercantile Juridic Person

745. As Mercantile Juridic Persons are formed from True Persons themselves formed from Divine Persons holding conscience and life, all Mercantile Juridic Persons possess legal personality as living beings with a spirit.

Mercantile Juridic Person as living being with spirit

746. No inferior Non-Ucadian Juridic Person can have superior jurisdiction over a Mercantile Juridic Person.

Jurisdiction of Mercantile Juridic Person

Article 166 – Union Juridic Person

747. A ***Union Juridic Person*** is a Superior Person recorded and enrolled in the Great Roll of a valid Ucadia Society associated with a Union Trust as a Superior Trust registered with the Great Register and Public Record of a valid Ucadia Society.

Union Juridic Person

748. As Union Juridic Persons are formed from True Persons themselves formed from Divine Persons holding conscience and life, all Union Juridic Persons possess legal personality as living beings with a spirit.

Union Juridic Persons as living beings with spirit

749. No inferior Non-Ucadian Juridic Person can have superior jurisdiction over a Union Juridic Person.

Jurisdiction of Union Juridic Person

Article 167 – Inferior Juridic Person

750. An ***Inferior Juridic Person*** is an inferior aggregate person first created through a recording and enrolment in a Roll defined by Non-Ucadian Statutes of Law, or Body of Law, or associated Courts,

Inferior Juridic Person

Tribunals and Forums. Inferior Juridic Persons are the lowest standing and weakest of all valid forms of aggregate "Juridic" Persons. An Inferior Juridic Person can never be validly, legitimately, reasonably, logically, legally, lawfully or morally claimed or argued as superior to a Superior Juridic Person.

751. By definition, an Inferior Juridic Person is a "Dead Ghost", devoid of life and spirit. Therefore an Inferior Juridic Person can never have higher standing than a Juridic Person or Persons that possess life and spirit. *(Inferior Juridic Person void of life and Spirit)*

752. An Inferior Juridic Person cannot have nor claim the character of a moral person. Therefore an Inferior Juridic Person cannot confer juridic personality. *(Inferior Juridic Person void of juridic personality)*

6.5 – Prohibited Registers & Rolls

Article 168 – Prohibited Registers & Rolls

753. **Prohibited Registers & Rolls** are claimed Registers and Rolls that contradict the present Maxims and are without proper authority, power or mandate. A Prohibited Register or Roll records no rights or valid claims and has no force or effect in law. *(Prohibited Registers & Rolls)*

754. There are two main categories of Prohibited Registers and Rolls being Ucadia and Non-Ucadia:- *(Main categories of Prohibited Registers & Rolls)*

　　(i)　Prohibited Ucadia Register or Roll is any claimed register or roll within Ucadia Jurisdiction that is without proper mandate, or fiducial oversight; and

　　(ii)　Prohibited Non-Ucadia Register or Roll is any claimed register or roll within a Non-Ucadia Society that records and claims one or more rights otherwise duly recorded within a Ucadia Register or Roll.

755. All prohibited registers and rolls are recorded within a register for that purpose. The existence of a record within the register of Prohibited Registers and Rolls is sufficient proof. *(Recording of Prohibited Registers and Rolls)*

Title VII – Documents & Instruments

7.1 – Document

Article 169 – Document

756. A ***Document*** is a tangible, physical or electronic item containing an original or official or lawful written record of some Truth, or Fact, or Event or Issue or Matter, able to be used as Evidence itself or in support of Evidence. *Document*

757. The word Document itself comes from the Latin word *documentum* which means "lesson" or "instruction." *Origin of Meaning of Document*

758. There exists several broad types of Documents:- *Document Types*

    (i) An *Ancient Document* is any Document more than twenty years old; that when possessing proper provenance and condition of custody, and in the absence of any evidence to the contrary, is therefore presumed genuine; and

    (ii) A *Document of Title*, also known simply as "Title" is any Document evidencing that the Person in possession of it is entitled to receive, hold and dispose of the Document and the Goods it covers; and

    (iii) A *Public Document* is any Document issued or published by legislative or sovereign authority; or any Document of Record evidencing or connected with public administration, as issued by executive or administrative authority; and

    (iv) A *Judicial Document* is any Document relating to the operation and administration of justice and proper forums of law; and may be divided into (1) judgements, decrees and verdicts; and (2) depositions, affidavits, examinations and inquisitions; and (3) writs, warrants and pleadings.

759. Within Ucadia are only five (5) valid forms of Documents: Supreme, Superior, Ordinary, General and Inferior. *Ucadia Document Status*

    (i) A *Supreme Document* is a valid document issued and sealed by a Supreme Official Person as recognised by Ucadia or an Authorised related entity through one or more agents. There is no higher, more powerful nor authoritative Document than a Supreme Document; and

    (ii) A *Superior Document* is a valid document issued and sealed by a Superior Official Person, registered in a Register of Ucadia; and existing as a Superior Instrument. It is the second highest and authoritative Document of all; and

(iii) An *Ordinary Document* is a valid document issued and sealed by an Ordinary Official Person, registered in a Register of Ucadia; and existing as an Ordinary Instrument. It is the third highest and authoritative Document of all; and

(iv) A *General Document* is a valid document issued and registered in a Register of Ucadia that is not issued by an Ordinary, Superior or Supreme Official Person; and

(v) An *Inferior Document* is any document issued by an Inferior Person. No Inferior Document may ever be allowed to claim superiority over a General Document, Ordinary Document, Superior Document or Supreme Document.

760. In general reference to the rules of Documents:-   *Document Rules*

(i) The physical alteration of any Document, whether it is valid or invalid, without the permission of the original author is an Injury that shifts any liability to the party who altered the document without permission; and

(ii) By definition, an author cannot deny the existence or validity of their own Documents without causing Injury and accepting all liability. Therefore, the return of any Document to its author with a perfected reply attached and sealed to the Reverse cannot be denied or ignored without the author causing Injury and accepting all Liability; and

(iii) When a separate Document is attached and sealed to the Reverse of the first Document then a reply is perfected in accordance with the most ancient traditions of Documents without Injury.

Article 170 – Obverse

761. **Obverse** refers to the backside or minor side of a document, instrument, coin, medal, or other currency. In regards to single side printed documents, Obverse refers to the blank side of the Document. Its meaning was inverted to mean the opposite within Non-Ucadian Societies no earlier than the 15th Century.   *Obverse*

762. The word *Obverse* was first created as a legal term in the Anglaise (Old French) language from an abbreviation of Ancient Irish (Gaelic) no earlier than 740 CE and no later than 760 CE as part of the formation of new rules of coins and instruments for Western   *Origin of Meaning of Obverse*

Civilisation:-

- (i) The word *Obverse* originates from the Ancient Irish (Gaelic) word obvéarsa meaning literally "back side" from véarsa (side) and ob (return, refuse or decline); and

- (ii) *Obverse* was the official name given to the minor side of official coins minted under new Western Civilised Law (Anglo-Saxon Law) in 8th Century being the copper Penny, silver Shilling and gold Sovereign; and

- (iii) The claim the term Obverse comes from Latin "aversus" at the time of the Rome Empire is both absurd and patently false; and

- (iv) Any claimed historic texts that argue the meaning of Obverse as the primary face, such as the works of Thomas Hobbes, are either ill informed or intentionally false.

Article 171 – Reverse

763. **Reverse** refers to the front side and primary side of a document, instrument, coin, medal, or other currency. In regards to single side printed documents, Reverse refers to the printed side of the Document. Its meaning was inverted to mean the opposite within Non-Ucadian Societies no earlier than the 15th Century.

[margin: Reverse]

764. The word *Reverse* was first created as a legal term in the Anglaise (Old French) language from an abbreviation of Ancient Irish (Gaelic) no earlier than 740 CE and no later than 760 CE as part of the formation of new rules of coins and instruments for Western Civilisation:-

[margin: Origin of Meaning of Reverse]

- (i) The word *Reverse* originates from the Ancient Irish (Gaelic) word revéarsa meaning literally "sovereign (or king) side" from véarsa (side) and re (king); and

- (ii) *Reverse* was the official name given to the primary side of official coins minted under new Western Civilised Law (Anglo-Saxon Law) in 8th Century being the copper Penny, silver Shilling and gold Sovereign; and

- (iii) The claim the term Reverse comes from Latin "reversus" at the time of the Rome Empire is both absurd and patently false; and

- (iv) Any claimed historic texts that argue the meaning of Reverse as the minor face are either ill informed or intentionally false.

Article 172 – Traverse

765. *Traverse* refers to:-   *Traverse*

  (i)   The third side or edge or margin of a document, instrument, coin, medal, or other currency; and

  (ii)   With single side printed documents, Traverse refers to the margin on the printed side of the Document; and

  (iii) In common law pleadings, a Traverse signifies a denial.

766. Where the term Traverse is used in pleadings to signify a denial, there exists several particular forms:-   *Traverse in Common Law Pleadings*

  (i)   *Common traverse* is a simple and direct denial of the material allegations of the opposite pleading; and

  (ii)   *General traverse* is one preceded by a general inducement, and denying in general terms all that is last before alleged on the opposite side, instead of pursuing the words of the allegations which it denies; and

  (iii) *Special traverse* is a peculiar form of traverse or denial, the design of which, as distinguished from a common traverse, is to explain or qualify the denial, instead of putting it in the direct and absolute form. It consists of an affirmative and a negative part, the first setting forth the new affirmative matter tending to explain or qualify the denial, and technically called the "inducement," and the latter constituting the direct denial itself, and technically called the "absque hoc"; and

  (iv) *Traverse of indictment or presentment* is the taking issue upon and contradicting or denying some chief point of it; and

  (v)   *Traverse of office* is the proving that an inquisition made of lands or goods by the escheator is defective and untruly made. It is the challenging, by a subject, of an inquest of office, as being defective and untruly made.

767. The word *Traverse* was first created as a legal term in the Anglaise (Old French) language from an abbreviation of Ancient Irish (Gaelic) no earlier than 740 CE and no later than 760 CE as part of the formation of new rules of coins and instruments for Western Civilisation:-   *Origin of Meaning of Traverse*

  (i)   The word *Traverse* originates from the Ancient Irish (Gaelic) word trevéarsa meaning literally "third side" from véarsa (side) and tre (three, third); and

  (ii)   *Traverse* was the official name given to the third and "edged" side of official coins minted under new Western Civilised Law (Anglo-Saxon Law) in 8th Century being the copper Penny, silver Shilling and gold Sovereign.

7.2 - Document Amendment

Article 173 – Document Amendment

768. ***Document Amendment*** refers to the process of making changes or modifications to an existing document. It involves adding, deleting, or revising information in a document to reflect new or updated information in a way recognised by the laws of a particular jurisdiction. {Document Amendment}

769. In reference to Document Amendment, there are fifteen generally accepted forms of amendment being:- {Forms of Document Amendment}

   (i) ***Acceptation*** is when a party upon receiving some form of offer, terms, agreement, claim or demand in writing (the offeree) is deemed by law to agree with the offeror; and

   (ii) ***Endorsation*** is the writing of one's signature on a Document to (a) provide guarantee to its authenticity or (b) guarantee any liability or (c) to cause the assignment and transfer of property to another; and

   (iii) ***Completion*** is the process of finalisation of a written or legal instrument, such as a contract, agreement, form, report, or any other written record; and

   (iv) ***Annotation*** is the process of adding notes, comments, or other types of metadata to a document or text; and

   (v) ***Annexation*** is the process of incorporating a document or instrument into an existing document; and

   (vi) ***Affixation*** is the process of attaching, adding, or appending something to a document, such as a seal, sticker, stamp, or label to the document or digitally adding an electronic signature, stamp, or mark; and

   (vii) ***Imprintation*** or Imprint is the process of creating an ink imprint or impression on a document, such as a stamp or seal, as a way of adding an official mark or indication of authenticity; and

   (viii) ***Impressation*** or Impression is the process of creating a raised or three-dimensional design, pattern, text, or image on the surface of the document, such as a stamp or seal, as a way of adding an official mark or indication of authenticity; and

(ix) **Substitution** is the process of replacing or substituting one or more elements or provisions within the document with new ones; and

(x) **Correction** refers to the process of identifying and rectifying errors or mistakes in a document; and

(xi) **Redaction** is the process of editing or preparing the document for publication or distribution by removing or obscuring certain content, typically sensitive or confidential information; and

(xii) **Cancellation** is the process of officially voiding, revoking, or nullifying the document's validity or legal effect; and

(xiii) **Rejection** is the process of refusing, declining, or disapproving the document or its contents; and

(xiv) **Revocation** is the process of formally and intentionally canceling, rescinding, or invalidating the legal effect or authority of a document; and

(xv) **Rescission** is the process of canceling, annulling, or voiding a contract, agreement, or other legal document.

770. Any amendment of a document that contradicts the laws of a particular jurisdiction may be considered a crime. Thus care must always be given to the formalities associated with each method of Document Amendment before making any change to a physical or electronic document:- *(Formality of Each Method of Document Amendment)*

   (i) The nature of the document in question is the first and obvious guide. Formal documents such as certificates, notes, bills, vouchers and official forms usually have very limited scope for amendment in most jurisdictions; and

   (ii) The type of proposed Document Amendment (if permitted), will usually follow certain strict protocols to be valid, as expressed within the jurisdiction and its law, regulations and procedures; and

   (iii) Failure to follow the strict and formal protocols of the relevant jurisdiction in terms of Document Amendment may result in the loss of certain rights, the full acceptance of liability and any penalties and even the possibility of a criminal offence.

771. The amending of any envelope of transmission of documents has no effect as a means of Amending the substance of any claims, assertions or arguments contained within one or more Documents:- *(Non Effect of Amending the Envelope of Transmission of Documents)*

   (i) Modern Administrative Law in almost all countries places no value in writing messages on the outside of envelopes to be returned to the original sender, other than enabling the original sender to use such ignorant behaviour as a means of accelerating and processing their claims; and

(ii) Writing any number of different forms of messages on the envelope containing mailed documents is seen universally as an act of both bad faith and bad behaviour, no matter what counter arguments are raised; and

(iii) Failure to address the specific contents and subject matter of the documents within an envelope when addressed to a recipient is at least an open admission of incompetence in bad faith, thus enabling most administrative systems to effectively use such ignorant behaviour against the recipient; and

(iv) Competence requires that mail properly addressed to a recipient is opened in a timely fashion and the subject matter addressed appropriately.

Article 174 – Acceptation

772. ***Acceptation*** is when a party upon receiving some form of offer, terms, agreement, claim or demand in writing (the offeree) is deemed by law to agree with the offeror. Acceptation traditionally signifies that the offeree is willing to be bound by the terms of the offer, creating a valid and enforceable contract between the parties. Acceptation

773. Acceptation or Acceptance is subject to the same criteria for all valid and proper agreements, including:- General Rules of Acceptation

   (i) *Plurality* means that there must be at least two (or more) persons as parties to the proposed agreement; and

   (ii) *Intentionality* means the parties must definitely intend the same thing; and

   (iii) *Good Faith, Good Conscience and Good Actions* means that the parties intend to enter an Agreement and approach all matters with sincere and honest intention and belief; and

   (iv) *Communication* means the parties have communicated with one another this common intention or "meeting of the minds"; and

   (v) *Offer* means one of the parties must have made a proposal to the other party or parties.

774. There exists two broad accepted methods of Acceptance being by Communication and by Conduct:- Methods of Acceptance

(i) *Acceptance by Communication*: Acceptance is typically required to be communicated to the offeror. In most cases, acceptance must be communicated directly to the offeror or through a reasonable means, such as email, letter, or verbal communication. Silence or inaction is generally not considered acceptance unless it is explicitly specified in the offer terms; and

(ii) *Acceptance by Conduct*: In some cases, acceptance can be implied through the offeree's conduct. This is known as acceptance by performance. For example, if a company orders goods from a supplier and the supplier delivers the goods as requested, the supplier's performance may be seen as acceptance of the order.

775. The general notion of "Silence means Acceptance (Consent)" is a fraud and absurdity that is often believed to be valid, despite it being contrary to the traditional rules of Agreement:- General Notion of Silence as Acceptance

(i) The default rule in contract law is that silence alone does not constitute acceptance. This applies to all Ucadia Jurisdictions and most Non-Ucadian Jurisdictions. There are exceptions to this, as explained below and in separate Maxims; and

(ii) In most jurisdictions, a party's failure to respond to an unsubstantiated offer, whether in writing or verbally, is typically not considered acceptance. The offeree is not legally obligated to respond, and their silence does not create a binding contract.

776. Where an existing relation is well established and there has been sufficient communication between both parties to establish a relation or contract, Silence as Acceptance may be argued in writing if explicitly stated in a response:- Silence as Acceptance within existing Relation, Custom and Communication

(i) Such an argument must be explicitly stated in the communication and its use and context must not contradict the existing contract arrangement between the parties; and

(ii) A reasonable time of at least fourteen (14) or twenty one (21) days must be included to allow the other party time to respond.

777. Where an existing relation is well established and there has been sufficient communication between both parties to establish a relation or contract, Silence as Acceptance may be argued in writing if explicitly stated as part of a new Unilateral Contract:- Silence as Consent as a Term of new Unilateral Contract

(i) Even if an existing contract is in force between the parties, a new Unilateral Contract may be proposed that includes the term and provision that Silence is Acceptance; and

(ii) The new Unilateral Contract must adhere to the general principles and terms of agreements and contracts; and

(iii) The full details of the Unilateral Contract and Terms must be communicated including allowing for a reasonable time of at least fourteen (14) or twenty one (21) days to respond in writing; and

(iv) A unilateral contract is one where an offeror promises something in exchange for the offeree's performance of a specified act. If the offeree performs the act requested by the offeror, their performance is viewed as acceptance, and the contract is formed. The performance of the offeree might be as simple as the acceptance of funds provided in good faith.

Article 175 – Endorsation

778. ***Endorsation*** or ***Endorsement*** is the writing of one's signature on a Document to (a) provide guarantee to its authenticity or (b) guarantee any liability or (c) to cause the assignment and transfer of property to another (traditionally called ***Indorsement***). Endorsation

779. In the context of banking, endorsement refers to the act of signing the back of a negotiable instrument, such as a check or a promissory note, to transfer ownership or rights to another party. There are several types of endorsements in banking:- Endorsation as Transfer of Rights or Property

   (i) ***Blank Endorsement***: This is the simplest form of endorsement, where the payee (the person to whom the instrument is payable) signs their name on the back without specifying a particular endorsee. The instrument becomes payable to the bearer, meaning anyone in possession of the endorsed instrument can cash or negotiate it; and

   (ii) ***Special or Full Endorsement***: In a special or full endorsement, the payee signs their name on the back and specifies the person to whom they are transferring the instrument. This makes the instrument payable only to the named endorsee; and

   (iii) ***Restrictive Endorsement***: A restrictive endorsement restricts the use or negotiation of the instrument. For example, "For Deposit Only" followed by the bank account number restricts the check to be deposited only into the specified account; and

(iv) ***Qualified Endorsement***: A qualified endorsement disclaims liability on the part of the endorser. For instance, "Without Recourse" indicates that the endorser is not responsible for the instrument if it's not honoured; and

(v) ***Conditional Endorsement***: A conditional endorsement imposes conditions or terms on the negotiation of the instrument. For example, an endorsement that specifies payment upon a certain event.

Article 176 – Completion

780. ***Completion*** is the process of finalisation of a written or legal instrument, such as a contract, agreement, form, report, or any other written record. It signifies that all necessary information, terms, conditions, signatures, and any required attachments have been added or included in the document to make it legally effective, accurate, and ready for its intended purpose. *Completion*

781. Completion of a document is a critical step in the documentation process, as it signifies that the document is ready for use, legally binding (if applicable), and can serve its intended purpose. *Importance of Completion*

782. In respect of documents, there exists a common number of areas association with Completion:- *Common Elements for Completion*

   (i) **Filling in Information:** Ensure that all blank fields or spaces in the document are appropriately filled in with the relevant details, such as names, dates, addresses, amounts, and any other pertinent information; and

   (ii) **Review and Verification:** Carefully review the entire document to check for accuracy, consistency, and adherence to legal requirements or guidelines. This may involve proofreading for spelling and grammatical errors, verifying numerical calculations, and ensuring that the document's content aligns with the parties' intentions; and

   (iii) **Signature and Execution:** If the document requires signatures or execution by the involved parties, ensure that all necessary signatures are obtained. Depending on the type of document, signatures may be required from one or more parties to make the document legally binding; and

   (iv) **Attachments and Appendices:** If there are any attachments, exhibits, appendices, or supporting documents that need to be included with the main document, make sure they are attached and referenced correctly; and

(v) **Notarization (if applicable):** Some documents, particularly legal or financial ones, may require notarization. In such cases, ensure that the document is notarized by a qualified notary public as needed; and

(vi) **Filing and Distribution:** Determine the appropriate filing and distribution process for the completed document. This may involve sending copies to relevant parties, submitting it to the appropriate authorities, or storing it in an organized and secure manner.

Article 177 – Annotation

783. *Annotation* is the process of adding notes, comments, or other types of metadata to a document or text. It is used to provide additional context, highlight important information, or facilitate collaboration and communication between individuals or groups. — Annotation

784. The word "annotation" itself comes from the Latin word "*annotatio*," which means "a note added to a text." — Origin of Annotation

Article 178 – Annexation

785. *Annexation* is the process of incorporating a document or instrument into an existing document. The annexed document then becomes one with the primary document. — Annexation

786. the term "annexation" itself has its roots in the Latin word "*annexare*," which means "to attach" or "to join." — Origin of Annexation

Article 179 – Affixation

787. *Affixation* is the process of attaching, adding, or appending something to the document, common examples include a seal, sticker, stamp, or label to the document or digitally adding an electronic signature, stamp, or mark. — Affixation

788. The act of affixing something to a document is a way to provide additional information, authentication, or validation. It can also serve as evidence of when and by whom the document was acted upon or approved. The specific method of affixation and its significance can vary depending on the type of document and the relevant legal or organizational requirements. — Importance of Affixation

789. Affixation is often used in a legal or formal context to confirm the authenticity or approval of a document:- — Legal and formal context of Affixation

(i) **Notarization:** In the case of notarized documents, a notary public affixes their official seal or stamp to the document to verify that it has been properly executed and witnessed; and

(ii) **Official Seal:** Government agencies and organizations may use an official seal to affix to documents to indicate their approval, authenticity, or official status; and

(iii) **Electronic Signatures:** In the digital age, electronic documents can be signed using electronic signatures, which are essentially affixed to the document to indicate the signer's approval or consent; and

(iv) **Date Stamps:** Date stamps are often used in office settings to affix a date to documents, indicating when the document was received, processed, or filed.

Article 180 – Imprintation

790. ***Imprintation*** or ***Imprint*** is the process of creating an imprint on a document, such as a stamp or seal, as a way of adding an official mark or indication of authenticity. Imprintation

Article 181 – Impressation

791. ***Impressation*** or ***Impression*** is the process of creating a raised or three-dimensional design, pattern, text, or image on the surface of the document, such as a stamp or seal, as a way of adding an official mark or indication of authenticity. Impressation

792. In general reference to Impressation:- Details of Impressation

(i) **Embossing Process:** The embossing process typically involves the use of a die (a metal or plastic plate) and pressure. The document is placed between the die and a counterplate, and pressure is applied. This pressure forces the paper or material to deform in the shape of the design or text on the die, creating a raised impression on one side of the document and a corresponding debossed area on the opposite side; and

(ii) **Authentication and Security:** Embossing is often used on official documents, certificates, diplomas, and important papers as a security feature. The raised seal or emblem can be difficult to reproduce accurately, making it a way to deter counterfeiting; and

(iii) **Legal and Notary Documents:** Some legal and notary documents may feature an embossed seal to validate their authenticity and legality.

Article 182 – Substitution

793. ***Substitution*** is the process of replacing or substituting one or more elements or provisions within the document with new ones. This involves removing the existing language or content and inserting the revised or alternative content in its place. Substitution is a common method of amending documents to reflect changes in agreements, laws, regulations, or other written instruments. Substitution

794. Substitution is a fundamental method for making changes to documents while maintaining the structure and format of the original document. It allows for precise modification of specific provisions or content without necessitating a complete rewrite to whole document. Importance of Substitution

Article 183 – Correction

795. ***Correction*** refers to the process of identifying and rectifying errors or mistakes in a document. Correction

796. The Right to Correction of a document is usually restricted to the negotiation phase of agreements, or in the function and role of editor. A person who has the right to check an exam or make corrections on documents is usually called a Marker. Right to Correction

Article 184 – Redaction

797. ***Redaction*** is the process of editing or preparing the document for publication or distribution by removing or obscuring certain content, typically sensitive or confidential information. The purpose of redaction is to protect sensitive data, maintain privacy, and comply with legal and regulatory requirements while still allowing the release of the document's non-sensitive information. Redaction

798. Redaction is one of the few options in relation to the submission of forms or other official documents whereby one or more sections may be properly redacted through the use of a ruler and a thick black pen to render certain sections of the form redundant. However, this still constitutes an amendment and whilst not unlawful, may cause the official party to reject the amended document. Application of Redaction

Article 185 – Cancellation

799. ***Cancellation*** is the process of officially voiding, revoking, or nullifying the document's validity or legal effect. The term is used when a document, agreement, contract, license, permit, or any other written instrument needs to be terminated or made null and void before its original expiration or completion date. Cancellation

800. The process of cancelling a document often involves formal notification to relevant parties, adherence to any legal or contractual requirements for cancellation, and the issuance of a notice or document confirming the cancellation. — Procedure of Cancellation

Article 186 – Rejection

801. ***Rejection*** is the process of refusing, declining, or disapproving the document or its contents. It implies that the document or its submission has not met certain criteria, standards, requirements, or expectations, leading to its dismissal or non-acceptance. — Rejection

802. Document rejection typically results in communication to the submitting party, explaining the reasons for the rejection and, in some cases, providing an opportunity for resubmission or appeal. — Method of Rejection

Article 187 – Revocation

803. ***Revocation*** is the process of formally and intentionally cancelling, rescinding, or invalidating the legal effect or authority of a document. Revocation is typically used when the creator or authority responsible for the document wishes to nullify or terminate its validity or enforceability. The specific process and consequences of revocation can vary depending on the type of document and the legal or regulatory framework governing it. — Revocation

804. In each of these cases, revocation is a deliberate and legally recognized process that involves taking specific actions to nullify the document's legal effect. It is important to follow the appropriate legal procedures and notify all relevant parties when revoking a document to ensure that the revocation is valid and enforceable. — Procedure of Revocation

805. The specific process and consequences of revocation can vary depending on the type of document and the legal or regulatory framework governing it:- — Examples of Revocation

   (i) **Revocation of a Power of Attorney**: A power of attorney document grants someone the authority to act on behalf of another person. The person granting the power (the principal) can revoke it by issuing a revocation document, notifying the attorney-in-fact (the agent), or following any revocation procedures outlined in the original power of attorney document; and

   (ii) **Revocation of a Will**: A person who has created a last will and testament can revoke or amend it by executing a new will that explicitly revokes the previous one. Alternatively, they may use a codicil, which is a document that amends or revokes specific provisions of the will; and

(iii) **Revocation of a Trust**: A grantor who has created a trust may revoke it under certain conditions outlined in the trust document or as allowed by law. Revocation typically requires a formal written statement or action; and

(iv) **Revocation of Contracts**: Parties to a contract may include provisions for the revocation or termination of the contract under specific conditions. Alternatively, they may mutually agree to revoke the contract through a written agreement.

Article 188 – Rescission

806. *Rescission* is the process of canceling, annulling, or voiding a contract, agreement, or other legal document. — Rescission

807. Rescission effectively treats the document as if it never existed, and it restores the parties involved to their original positions before entering into the contract or agreement. — Effect of Recision

808. The method and formality of Rescission of documents is usually reserved to the courts and official administrative bodies that issued such documents and not a right or power of other parties. Some of the reasons for Rescission include (but are not limited to):- — Method of Rescission

   (i) Material misrepresentation or fraud by one of the parties; and

   (ii) Mutual mistake by the parties regarding a key element of the contract; and

   (iii) Undue influence or duress exerted on one of the parties; and

   (iv) Failure to disclose important information; and

   (v) Violation of statutory or regulatory requirements.

7.3 - Document Validation

Article 189 – Document Validation

809. *Document Validation* is the process of verifying the authenticity, accuracy, and completeness of a document to ensure that it meets the required standards and complies with legal and regulatory requirements. — Document Validation

810. The concept of document validation can be traced back to ancient times when written records were used to document important events and transactions:- — Tradition of Document Validation

   (i) The earliest known example of document validation can be found in the Code of Hammurabi, a set of laws created by the Babylonian king Hammurabi in 1754 BCE. The code included provisions for the validation of contracts and other legal documents, stating that they must be signed and sealed by witnesses in order to be considered valid; and

(ii) In ancient Greece, the concept of document validation was further developed with the introduction of notaries. Notaries were public officials who were responsible for verifying the authenticity of legal documents and transactions. The first known reference to notaries can be found in the works of the Greek historian Herodotus in 5th C BCE.

Article 190 – Signation

811. ***Signation***, ***Sign***, or ***Signature*** is the act of affixing a name, word, letter or other identifying mark of a legal person to a valid Document to attest its authenticity as witness or execute its contents by Consensus or to give it effect as surety for one's own act. The word sign and signature comes from the Latin word *signo/signatum* meaning "to mark, stamp print; to seal a document; to coin or mint money; to impress, designate or note". — Signation

812. A signature may be written by hand, printed, stamped, typewritten, engraved, photographed, or cut from one instrument and attached to another, and a signature lithographed on an instrument by a party is sufficient for the purpose of signing it; it being immaterial with what kind of instrument a signature is made providing it is done through legitimate use. — Validity of a signature

813. Legitimate use of a signature is when the man or woman affixing the signature to the valid Document is authorized in some verifiable manner to affix such a name, word, letter or other identifying mark of a particular legal person. The affixing of a signature by a man or woman who does not have proper authority to do so for a particular legal person renders such a signature null and void from the beginning. — Legitimate use of a signature

814. There are primarily two (2) forms of signature by convention being the Executor or the Trustee/Beneficiary: — Two primary forms of Signature

(i) The Signature by Executor is by custom and convention the first name only of the legal person to whom they are executor and the letter R. (including the period) for Latin *regnatum* meaning "to be king, rule, reign, to be supreme lord of an estate"; and

(ii) The Signature by Trustee/Beneficiary is by custom and convention either an "X", or the full name (first name and family name) in stylised script.

815. By custom and function, when a signature is affixed to a document it is either to bear witness to its authenticity, grant certain rights by execution or be bound as surety to the contents of the document:

(i) A General Executor never signs their name in the manner of a Trustee/Beneficiary unless they are acting in such capacity and only ever signs as first name and the letter R. when in the context of a grant, deed and conveyance. In all other cases, an Executor never signs a document; and

(ii) A Trustee/Beneficiary signs their full name in the manner of a Trustee/Beneficiary as a witness to the authenticity of a Document or to accept full liability as surety to perform its contents.

816. When a man or woman is compelled by force to sign a document, such a signature shall have no legal effect. To ensure this is made clear, a man or woman may lawfully choose one of two mechanisms to physically invalidate their signature:

(i) By placing the letters V.C. anywhere within the signature, the man or woman signifies by custom the principle of *Vi Coactus* or "under constraint " to sign, which immediately invalidates the whole document; or

(ii) If prevented from making clear a signature is made by force, a man or woman may use an ellipsis ". . ." anywhere as part of their signature to prove that they sought to sign V.C. but were otherwise prevented.

817. All documents associated with the administration of property as well as the conveyance of property such as Deeds must be properly signed and sealed.

Article 191 – Sealation

818. **Sealation** or **Seal** is the act of affixing a symbol to a valid Document to attest its valid production, recording and registration or to bind its contents as a solemn promise or execute its contents by authority.

819. The word Seal originates from the 1st millennium BCE Gaelic word séal meaning a "formal binding promise" usually associated with the use of property called "úsáid" and surety called "tithe". Hence, in the formation of the 1st sophisticated property laws of civilisation,

possession of property in Gaelic became known as "séalaigh" (bonded property) and a promise/surety of property was called from the beginning a "áirithe" (property promise).

820. A Seal may be impressed by some device, printed or attached to a Document as evidence of authenticity, confirmation or attestation. A Seal also denotes a valid binding whereby a Document is enjoined to others through the Seal to become one, in the case of valid Statutes and Ordinances. *[Seal as evidence of authenticity]*

821. Once impressed, printed or affixed, the power and authority bestowed by a valid Seal elevates or "raises" the status of the Document according to the office of the Seal and its associated registration. Therefore, the use of ornaments, wax, wafer, colour or other devices to physically raise, attach or alter the physical material of the Document is immaterial to the legitimate effect of a Seal. *[Seal to raise the status of the document]*

822. There are only six (6) valid types of Seal: Absolute, Great, Official, Ordinary, Inferior and Private: *[6 valid types of Seal]*

  (i) An *Absolute Seal* is the most powerful and highest authority of seal and signature when a man or woman uses their thumbprint in red ink to give life and personality to a Document in their capacity as Executor of their own True Trust and General Executor of the Estate of their Legal Person; and

  (ii) A *Great Seal* is the second highest possible seal and is the official Seal of any Juridic Society Person or Juridic Public Person. Hence a Great Seal is used for the authentication of Documents of the highest importance issued in the name of a Universal True Trust, Global True Trust or Civil True Trust; and

  (iii) An *Official Seal* is the third highest possible Seal issued by an Official Person in the capacity of their office on behalf of a Universal True Trust, Global True Trust or Civil True Trust; and

  (iv) An *Ordinary Seal* is the fourth highest possible Seal issued on behalf of a Juridic Private Person, Juridic Union Person or Juridic Domestic Person in association with a Superior Trust; and

  (v) An *Inferior Seal* is is the fifth highest possible Seal issued on behalf of a non-Ucadian legal person; and

  (vi) A *Private Seal,* also known as an Inferior Administrative Seal is the lowest form of seal and is an administrative stamp issued under private law between parties for the cross certification of documents by regulation and central registration of all authorised signatories.

823. An Apostille is an example of a Private Seal whereby private and Non-Ucadia nations who are signatories to a private Hague Convention from 1961 have agreed to recognise and certify each of the documents of each other for legal purposes by ensuring the registration of officials who are authorized to seal documents under private international law. *Apostille Seal as Private Seal*

824. All documents associated with the administration of property as well as the conveyance of property such as Deeds must be properly sealed. *Property and the use of Seals*

Article 192 – Certification

825. ***Certification*** refers to the legal process of providing an official statement or document that details certain facts, decisions or records for the purpose of verification and confirmation. *Certification*

826. A number of well established examples of Certification include:- *Certification Examples*

   (i) *Legal or Court Certification* being the verification and confirmation of certain information provided by a court, or government agency; and

   (ii) *Professional Certification* being the verification and confirmation of qualifications, credentials and capacity of an individual to provide a specialised personal service such as medicine, psychology or legal representation; and

   (iii) *Product Certification* being the verification and confirmation that a product meets certain quality, design, health or safety standards; and

   (iv) *Information Security Certification* being the verification and confirmation that an application or technology meets minimum cybersecurity, privacy, safety and performance standards; and

   (v) *Occupational Health and Safety Standards* being the verification and confirmation that a workplace environment meets certain minimum health and safety standards.

827. In terms of Certifications by Ucadia Courts, such certifications include (but are not limited to) :- *Ucadia Courts Certification Examples*

   (i) ***Certified Copy of Court Records***: A certification may involve the court providing a certified copy of court records or documents to parties involved in a case, such as attorneys, litigants, or other interested parties. These certified copies serve as authentic and legally admissible evidence in other legal proceedings; and

(ii) ***Certified Court Orders and Judgments***: When a court issues an order or judgment in a case, it may certify that order or judgment to confirm its authenticity and accuracy. This certification is often requested when a party needs to enforce or appeal the court's decision; and

(iii) ***Certification of Transcripts***: In cases where court proceedings are recorded, such as in trials or hearings, parties may request the certification of transcripts. This certification attests to the accuracy of the transcript and ensures it can be used as a legal record; and

(iv) ***Certification of Court Docket Entries***: Courts maintain records of case events and docket entries, which can be certified to verify the sequence of events in a case. This certification is useful for tracking the progress of a case or for appeals; and

(v) ***Certification of Judgment Debts***: In cases involving monetary judgments, a court may issue a certification of the judgment debt owed by one party to another. This certification is crucial for creditors seeking to collect the debt; and

(vi) ***Certification of Court Orders for Enforcement***: In some situations, a party may need to enforce a court order in another jurisdiction. To do so, they may request that the court certify the order for enforcement in a different jurisdiction, often through a process known as domestication or registration of foreign judgments; and

(vii) ***Certification of Records for Appellate Review***: When a case is appealed, the lower court may certify the record of the case, including all relevant documents, transcripts, and orders, for review by the appellate court; and

(viii) ***Certification of Class Action Settlements***: In class action lawsuits, courts may certify a class and approve settlements reached on behalf of the class members. Certification in this context confirms that the settlement terms are fair and reasonable.

Article 193 – Apostillation

828. ***Apostillation*** is a certification that authenticates the origin of a public document, such as a birth certificate or a diploma, for use in another country. It is a simplified form of legalisation that is recognised by all Non-Ucadia countries that are parties to the Hague Convention.

Apostillation

Article 194 – Notarisation

829. ***Notarisation*** is the process of certifying a document as authentic and legally binding by a notary public. This involves verifying the identity of the signatory, ensuring they are signing the document voluntarily, and affixing an official seal or stamp to the document.

Notarisation

Article 195 – Testification

830. ***Testification*** is the process of certifying a document as a witness and declaring its authenticity. Certain instruments such as Wills and Deeds require Testification.

Testification

Article 196 – Exemplification

831. ***Exemplification*** is an official transcript of a document from public records, made in form to be used as evidence, and authenticated or certified as a true copy usually by two or more persons.

Exemplification

832. A Certificate of Exemplification as a formal Certificate issued under an Official Seal of the Body and referring to the extract of a Matter and then Certified by a Principal and Witness under Oath as being true shall be Prima Facie proof in any jurisdiction where there exists the Rule of Law and competent forums of Law.

Certificate of Exemplification

Article 197 – Registration

833. Registration is the Recording, Enrolling or Entering of a record into a Register or Roll.

Registration

7.4 – Instruments & Forms

Article 198 – Instrument

834. An "**Instrument**" is a formal or lawful Document in writing that conforms to certain standard of Form as prescribed by law and rules, such as these Articles.

Instrument

835. An Instrument possesses three sides being Obverse, Reverse and Traverse:

Three Sides of Instruments

(i) *Reverse* or "*Kings Face*" of a Document is its front; and

(ii) *Obverse* or *Back Face* is its back; and

(iii) *Traverse* or *Third Side* is the margin on the Obverse.

836. The face of an instrument is that which is shown by the mere language employed, without any explanation, modification, or addition from extrinsic facts or evidence. Thus if the express terms of the paper disclose a fatal legal defect, it is said to be "void on its face". Instrument Void on Face

837. A Non-Financial Instrument by custom may be defined in elements equivalent to the notion of a living tree, namely: Non-Financial Instrument

(i) *Leaf* being a single-sheet Instrument and compared to the "Clothing of a Tree"; and

(ii) *Place* being the "Position of a Body of the Instrument"; and

(iii) *Body* being the "compound of Matter (substance) and Form (style)"; and

(iv) *Margin* being the "edge of a Place"; and

(v) *Head* being the "Top of the Tree and that part of the Body that contains the brains"; and

(vi) *Book* being the "Bark of Tree & any compact of writing"; and

(vii) *Tree* being "Thing (Matter, Substance or Accident) well known".

838. A Financial or Legal Instrument by custom may be defined in elements equivalent to the notion of a fortress, namely: Financial Document

(i) *Parchment* (also Vellum) being a single-sheet Instrument printed on the highest quality paper and compared to the "Skin of an Animal"; and

(ii) *Place* being the "Position of a Body of the Instrument"; and

(iii) *Body* being the "Fortification of a place to defend against assaults (and attacks)"; and

(iv) *Side* being the "rampart inclosing a Place"; and

(v) *Head* being the "front and shield (coat of arms)"; and

(vi) *Gorge* being the "entrance to body" at the bottom of the parchment; and

(vii) *Tower* being a "citadel or strong refuge" being the four corners; and

(viii) *Parapet* being the "wall or balcony, ranging about pillars of towers".

839. The Colour of Paper used to produce an Instrument may be used to signify and distinguish the nature of its issue. However, all Instruments must be clear as to the intended status of the recipient to avoid confusion and error:
    Colour and Status Instrument

(i) The Colour White, by tradition, may be used to signify an Original. However, the words "ORIGINAL" or 'CERTIFIED ORIGINAL" or "CERTIFIED ORIGINAL COPY" must be clearly listed on the Instrument, to denote it; and

(ii) The Colour Gold or Yellow, by tradition, may be used to signify a Receipt to the title owner. However, the words "RECEIPT ONLY" or "CERTIFIED RECEIPT" or "CERTIFIED RECEIPT COPY" must be clearly listed on the Instrument, to denote it as valid and legitimate; and

(iii) The Colour Blue, by tradition, may be used to signify a Warrant of Authority to a Trustee. However, the words "TRUSTEE ONLY" must be clearly listed on the Instrument, to denote it as valid and legitimate; and

(iv) The Colour Pink, by tradition, may be used to signify an instruction to an Agent. However, the words "AGENT ONLY" must be clearly listed on the Instrument, to denote it as valid and legitimate.

840. All valid and legitimate Instruments of Ucadia or an Authorised related entity through one or more agents shall be either Single Sheet or Multiple Sheet; and Single Sided or Double Sided: single sided (as in Instruments of Record), or double sided (as in Bills or a Constitution); and with any terms or conditions or agreement printed on the reverse of the Instrument or as an Attachment annexed in full to the Instrument. All Agreements shall be subject to the conditions of Agreements as defined herein these Maxims:-
    Single Sheet of Instrument

(i) *Single Sheet – Single Sided* is when an Instrument is printed onto one Sheet of paper or parchment, or is produced electronically in a similar form. Instruments of Record such as Certificates, Patents and Warrants are examples of Instruments that must be produced as Single Sheet – Single Sided Instruments; and

(ii) *Single Sheet – Double Sided* is when an Instrument is printed onto both sides of one Sheet of parchment or paper, or is produced electronically in a similar form. Instruments such as Bills, Notes and Bonds are examples of Single Sheet – Double Sided Instruments; and

(iii) *Multiple Sheet – Single Sided* is when an Instrument comprises multiple one sided Sheets of paper or parchment, or produced electronically in a similar form. Instruments such as Agreements and Affidavits are examples of Multiple Sheet – Single Sided Instruments; and

(iv) *Multiple Sheet – Double Sided* is when an Instrument comprises multiple double sided Sheets of paper or parchment, or is produced electronically in a similar form. Instruments such as these present Maxims are examples of Multiple Sheet- Double Sided Instruments.

841. An Inchoate Instrument is any Instrument that has been begun but remains unfinished or not completed and therefore is missing a material particular essential to its form and function. All Officers, Agents and Contractors are forbidden to produce Inchoate Instruments contrary to these present Maxims. — Inchoate Instrument

842. Where Ucadia is in possession of an Inchoate Instrument from another Non-Ucadia person, or body, or entity, Ucadia reserves the right to call upon the rights associated with Inchoate Instruments and complete the outstanding material particulars to the benefit of Ucadia. — Inchoate Instrument Benefits

843. No Non-Ucadia third party or Bodies Politic or Society or Corporation or Agency shall be granted permission to deface or alter an Instrument of Ucadia. — No Right of Foreign Bodies to Deface Instrument

844. Examples of Instruments include (but are not limited to):- — Examples of Instruments

   (i) Letter; and

   (ii) Notice; and

   (iii) Memorandum; and

   (iv) Statement; and

   (v) Note; and

   (vi) Bill; and

   (vii) Draft; and

   (viii) Cheque; and

   (ix) Bond; and

(x) Debenture; and

(xi) Writ; and

(xii) Warrant; and

(xiii) Certificate; and

(xiv) Voucher.

Article 199 – Form

845. A ***Form*** from the perspective of a Document and Instrument, is the model or skeleton of an Instrument prescribed by these Maxims to be used in a judicial proceeding, containing the principal necessary matters, the proper technical terms or phrases and whatever else is necessary to make it formally correct, arranged in proper and methodical order and capable of being adapted to the circumstances of the specific case. — Form

846. All Forms of Ucadia are either prescribed within these Maxims or the Codes of Law. — Form Prescribed by Maxims

847. Where a Ucadia company, body or entity has prescribed a particular Form in association with any procedure or action, it shall reserve the right to deny and decline any action, including any and all liability for loss, or injury or damage on the part of the party who failed to use the proper and prescribed form. — Right to deny or decline action based on non-use of Form

848. A Ucadia company, body or entity shall possess the right to pursue any and every option of penalties, damages, refusal, cancellation, fines or other punitive actions where an unauthorised use of a prescribed Form occurs; or when a form is defaced or altered without permission. — Unauthorised use of Form or defacement of Form

Article 200 – Letter

849. A ***Letter*** is a formal Instrument as a form of written or printed communication proposing or granting or asserting one or more rights. — Letter

850. In general terms where a Letter is the mode of contract or agreement:- — Letter as Proposed Agreement

   (i) The person who first makes a Letter as a proposal or demand to another in regards to a particular matter is called in the first instance the Offeror and the one to whom the Letter is addressed is called the Offeree; and

   (ii) In relation to the Letter itself and any property attached to it, the nature of a Letter means the Offeror conveys and transfers possession and ownership of it to the intended recipient (the Offeree) as trustee; and

(iii) Upon receiving the Letter and any property attached to it, the Offeree has four rights of action in law: (a) to respond and fully Accept the Offer; or (b) to respond and conditionally Accept the Offer; or (c) to respond and Reject the Offer; or (d) to not respond; and

(iv) If the communication of the response of the Offeree is delayed by the fault of the Offeror, or by accident, the delay is not to be reckoned against the Offeree; and

(v) Unless a response from the Offeree is received explicitly giving notice in writing of the rejection of the proposal of the Offeror or notice in writing of conditionally accepting the proposal, then any answer in response may be reasonably argued as an acceptance; and

(vi) An unconditional acceptance by Letter is complete as against the Offeror from the date of posting the acceptance by the Offeree as Acceptor, if it arrives within the time of the letter proposed, or if no deadline specified then upon the normal course of business; and

(vii) If the Offeror has made provision within the Letter to account for not receiving an answer as soon as is requested, then it can be reasonably argued the proposal has been rejected or accepted. However, if no such provision is made, then such a presumption of rejection remains unproven; and

(viii) If the Offeree makes in writing a conditional acceptance to a Letter, then as a matter of law the roles are reversed and the original party who made the proposal now becomes the Offeree and the one responding on conditional acceptance becomes the Offeror. If the new Offeror makes provision in their counter Offer upon non response being acceptance by a certain time, then non response can be reasonably argued as full acceptance of the offer and conditions of the counter offer; and

(ix) The failure to open a Letter and write a rejection on the envelope, or write a rejection or other comment upon the Letter by the Offeree and return it does not constitute either a conditional acceptance or rejection but an acceptance by dishonour by the original recipient (the one to whom the letter was originally addressed).

851. The most common forms of Letters in Law are:- *Forms of Letters*

  (i) *Letter of Credit* is an authority by one person (A.) to another (B.) to draw cheques or bills of exchange (with or without a limit as to amount) with an undertaking by A. to honor the drafts on presentation; and

  (ii) *Letter of License* is an agreement between a debtor and his creditors that the latter shall for a specified time suspend their claims and allow the debtor to carry on his business at his own discretion; and

  (iii) *Letters of Administration* is when a person possessed of personal property dies intestate, or without an executor, the Court having jurisdiction in such matters grants to a capable person an authority under the seal of the Court by which the grantee becomes clothed with the powers and duties similar to those of an executor; and

  (iv) *Letters Close* are letters or missives in the name of the sovereign and sealed with a great seal, being directed to particular persons for particular purposes. They are closed up and sealed on the outside of the envelope so that it cannot be opened except by breaking the seal – hence their name; and

  (v) *Letters of Marque* are extraordinary commissions issued under the laws of Admiralty either in time of open war or in time of peace, after all attempts to procure legal redress have failed, to the commanders of merchant ships authorizing reprisals for reparation of the damages sustained by them through enemies at sea; and

  (vi) *Letters Patent* are grants by the crown of lands, franchises and offices contained in charters or instruments not sealed up but exposed to open view with the great seal pendant at the bottom and usually addressed to all the subjects of the realm.

Article 201 – Notice

852. A ***Notice*** is a written or formal communication or process that conveys information, instructions, or important details to a specific individual, group of individuals, or the public at large. *Notice*

853. The seven primary types of Notice include: *Physical, Posted, Direct, Indirect, Public (legal), Implied* and *Constructive*:- *Types of Notice*

  (i) *Physical Notice* or Actual Notice is a type of notice and service of process whereby the specific information concerning a formal legal matter is listed in a Document and then physically handed to a party or their representative, with proof, attestation or acknowledgment of such service recorded as evidence; and

(ii) *Posted Notice* or Mail Notice is a type of notice and service of process whereby specific information concerning the formal legal matter is personally addressed to the party and sent through a certified or registered mail delivery system recognised by Non-Ucadia bodies such as the International Postal Union; and

(iii) *Direct Notice* is a type of notice and service of process whereby specific information concerning the formal legal matter is personally addressed to the party and sent via email, fax, sms or other recorded and verifiable transmission medium; and

(iv) *Indirect Notice* is a type of notice and service of process whereby specific information concerning the formal legal matter is published in any broadcast medium such as media releases, stories, advertorial content and advertising and likely to be viewed by one or more parties; and

(v) *Public Notice* is a type of notice and service of process whereby specific information concerning the formal legal matter is published in a company, local, regional, national or international publication possessing status as a gazette and therefore an official newspaper of record or physically posted at a site reasonably expected to be visible to the Person; and

(vi) *Implied Notice* is a type of notice inferred from facts that a Person had means of knowing and would have caused a reasonable Person to take action to gain further information concerning a formal legal matter. It is a notice inferred or imputed to a party by reason of his/her knowledge collateral to the main fact; and

(vii) *Constructive Notice* is a type of notice inferred from facts that a Person unable to be served with Actual Notice may be reasonably inferred or imputed to have received notice, if Actual Notice was restricted or not possible and a minimum number of attempts of Physical, Posted, Direct or Public Notice were concluded.

854. The publishing of any Proclamation, Order, Regulation or Notice within the Ucadia Gazette shall be Prima Facie Evidence of such Fact and Truth; and that all Courts, Judges, Justices, Masters, Magistrates or Commissioners judicially acting, and all other judicial Officers

Ucadia Gazette Notices as Prima Facie Evidence

shall take judicial Notice of such *Prima Facie* Evidence in all legal proceedings and all forums of law whether Ucadia or Non-Ucadia.

Article 202 – Memorandum

855. A "**Memorandum**" is a short note recording one or more facts and evidence for the purpose of remembering for the future, usually for the formalisation of agreements and deeds, or entry of a record within a register. Hence Memorandum are a common medium for the transmission of information to be recorded into a Register.

    Memorandum

856. Examples of formal Memorandum Instruments include (but are not limited to):-

    Examples of Memorandum

    (i) *Memorandum of Appearance* being a formal note submitted in writing in response to a summons within the prescribed form and time to usually record with the court the "Appearance" of the Defendant. Failure to file such a proper Memorandum within the correct time and format can result in a "Failure to Appear"; and

    (ii) *Memorandum of Association* being a document to be subscribed by three (3) or more persons associated for a lawful purpose, by subscribing and complying with companies laws may form themselves into an incorporated company, with or without liability; and

    (iii) *Memorandum of Account* being a document that summarizes financial transactions, debts, credits, or other financial matters between two parties. It is typically used in legal proceedings or as part of a financial reconciliation process to provide a clear record of the financial relationship between the parties involved.

Article 203 – Statement

857. A "**Statement**" is a document that summarises one or more facts, allegations or witnessed events, usually under certification.

    Statement

858. Examples of formal Statement Instruments include (but are not limited to):-

    Examples of Statements

    (i) **Statement of account**: A report issued monthly or periodically by a bank or creditor to a customer setting forth the amounts billed, credits given and balance due. A bank statement includes the checks drawn and cleared, the deposits made, and the charges debited; and

(ii) **Statement of Affairs**: A document filed in bankruptcy, setting forth answers to questions about the past and present financial situation of the debtor. A balance sheet showing immediate liquidation amounts, rather than historical costs, usually prepared when insolvency or bankruptcy is imminent; and

(iii) **Statement of Claim**: A legal document used in civil litigation, particularly in common law jurisdictions, filed by a plaintiff (the party initiating the lawsuit) to commence a legal action or lawsuit against a defendant (the party being sued). The Statement of Claim outlines the plaintiff's allegations, the basis for the lawsuit, and the relief or remedies sought from the court; and

(iv) **Statement of Condition**: A financial document that provides a snapshot of an entity's financial position at a specific point in time. It is commonly used by financial institutions, such as banks and credit unions, to assess the financial health of individuals or businesses applying for loans or credit; and

(v) **Statement of Confession**: A legal document also known as *Cognovit Note* and *warrant of attorney* that gives an attorney the power to confess judgement in a legal action against a defendant on a debt. Most modern Home Loan Promissory Notes are *Cognovit Notes*.

Article 204 – Note

859. A ***Note*** is an Instrument of Promise and Surety, related to some Memorandum or Covenant or Testimony, whereby Money may be borrowed or advanced or due. — Note

860. In relation to the Persons and Parties associated with a Note: — Relations of Persons to a Note

(i) The Person who makes or issues a valid Note is called the *Maker* (also *Issuer*, or *Payor*, or *Promisor*); and

(ii) The Person to whom the Note is addressed (if an actual name is listed on the Note) is called the *Payee* (also *Promisee*); and

(iii) The Person who the Payee may nominate as the beneficiary and holder of the Note is called the *Endorsee* (also *Indorsee* or *Order)*; and

Title VII – Documents & Instruments

(iv) The Person who holds an original Note (whether the note is addressed or not addressed) is called the *Bearer* (also *Holder*); and

(v) The Person who agrees to underwrite and guarantee the Note is called the *Guarantor* (also *Surety*); and

(vi) The Person who accepts a valid Note and agrees to lend or advance Money against it is called the Lender.

861. Examples of Notes include (but are not limited to) *Promissory, Money, Convertible, Bought, Sold, Judgement* and *Foreign Bank*:

Types of Valid Notes

(i) *Promissory Note* is an Instrument of Promise and Surety being a uniquely numbered valid Abstract in writing of a Record as an unconditional Promise given by an Authorised Member to another, signed by the maker, engaging to pay on demand, or at a fixed and determinable future time, a sum certain in lawful Public Money to order or to bearer; and

(ii) *Money Note* is an Instrument of Promise and Surety being a uniquely numbered valid Abstract in writing of a Record as an unconditional Promise by a valid Body Politic and Corporate to the bearer of the Note to pay on demand a sum certain in lawful Public Money as Legal Tender; and

(iii) *Convertible Note* is an Instrument of Promise and Surety being a uniquely numbered valid Abstract in writing of a Record as an unconditional Promise given by an Authorised Member to another, signed by the maker, engaging to pay on demand, or at a fixed and determinable future time, a sum certain in lawful Public Money to order or to bearer; and then assured, guaranteed and underwritten by the maker so that the registered holder of the Note has the right to "convert" the Note into Ucadia Money at fixed times and at a fixed rate, subject to certain terms and conditions; and

(iv) *Bought Note* is an Instrument of Promise and Surety being a uniquely numbered valid Abstract in writing of a single type of Record from a valid Register of Sales of a valid Body Politic and Corporate: given by a broker to the seller of merchandise, whereby it is stated that the goods therein mentioned have been sold for him; and

(v) *Sold Note* is an Instrument of Promise and Surety being a uniquely numbered valid Abstract in writing of a single type of Record from the Register of Sales of a valid Body Politic and

Corporate: given by a broker to a buyer of merchandise, whereby it is stated that the goods therein mentioned have been sold to him; and

(vi) *Judgement Note* is an Instrument of Promise and Surety being a uniquely numbered valid Abstract in writing of a single type of Record from the Register of Claims of a valid Body Politic and Corporate: given by an attorney, holder, or clerk of a court of justice of the peace to appear for the maker of the original note and confess, or assent to, a judgement to be entered against the maker due to default in the payment of the amount of the previous Promissory Note owed; and

(vii) *Foreign Bank Note* is an Instrument of Promise and Surety being a type of Fiat Note given by a Foreign Bank in writing as an alternative to valid Public Money where such a Bank holds a license to do so and where such Private Currency may be legally used as "Legal Tender" for the discharge of public or private debts.

Article 205 – Bill

862. A ***Bill*** is a form of Demand and Order in writing, assured by one or more Rights granted, for some performance equivalent in specie of Real Money. A Bill is normally associated with at least one Certified Statement or Memorandum of Account and one Affidavit.

863. In relation to the Persons and Parties associated with a Bill:

    (i) The Person who makes or issues a valid Bill is called the *Maker* (also *Issuer*, or *Payor*, or *Drawer*); and

    (ii) The Person to whom the Bill is addressed and paid (if an actual name is listed on the Note) is called the *Payee*; and

    (iii) The Person who the Payee may nominate as the beneficiary and holder of the Bill is called the *Endorsee* (also *Indorsee* or *Order*); and

    (iv) The Person who is directed to make the payment on behalf of the Maker to the Payee is called the *Drawee* and once they accept the obligation becomes the *Acceptor*; and

    (v) The Person who holds an original Bill (whether the note is addressed or not addressed) is called the *Holder*; and

    (vi) The Person who agrees to underwrite and guarantee the Bill is called the *Guarantor* (also *Surety*).

864. Types of valid Bills include (but are not limited to) *Parliament, Patent, Entry, Exception, Complaint, Indictment, Review, Costs, Credit, Exchange, Lading* and *Sale*:

    (i)   *Bill of Parliament*, also known as a "Bill", is an Instrument of Demand and Order, assured by Rights granted; and attached Memorandum for remedy and relief of one or more existing laws or proposed new laws or grants presented to a legislative body to be debated and passed; and once passed then presented to the Sovereign to receive assent. Similar to Acts, Bills of this nature are divided between public and private; and

    (ii)   *Bill of Patent*, is an Instrument of Demand and Order, assured by Rights granted; and as the draft of a patent for a charter, commission, dignity, office or appointment, drawn up and then submitted to the Sovereign for signature and then countersigned by the Principal Agent of the Sovereign and sealed by an Official Seal to become a patent; and

    (iii)   *Bill of Entry,* also known as a Bill of Action, is an Instrument of Demand and Order, assured by Rights granted; to return or seize certain Goods or Property as recorded, or to seize equivalent value of Goods and Property as compensation; and

    (iv)   *Bill of Exception*, also known as a Bill of Right(s) is an Instrument of Demand and Order, assured by Rights granted; to return certain Goods or Property as recorded, or to pay compensation of the equivalent value; and

    (v)   *Bill of Complaint,* also known as Original Bill, is an Instrument of Demand and Order, assured by Rights granted; and containing a statement of the plaintiff's action or suit and concluding with a prayer asking for the relief which he filed the Bill to obtain; and

    (vi)   *Bill of Indictment,* also known as "Bill" or a "True Bill", is an Instrument of Demand and Order, assured by Rights granted; that expresses the grievance or injury of a plaintiff to a grand jury that if approved by the grand jury then becomes a valid indictment; and

    (vii)   *Bill of Review* is an Instrument of Demand and Order, assured by Rights granted; that a previous decision of a court be reviewed, altered or reversed. The object of the bill is to reverse the decree as far as it is erroneous and to retry the cause in a competent forum; and

(viii) *Bill of Costs* is an Instrument of Demand and Order, assured by Rights granted; as an account of fees, charges and disbursements of an Attorney-In-Fact or Solicitor to be reimbursed or paid in association with a legal matter; and

(ix) *Bill of Credit*, also known at times as a "Letter of Credit", is an Instrument of Demand and Order, assured by Rights granted; and issued by the authority of a state or other body corporate, on the faith and credit of the state or body corporate; and designed to circulate as Money. A Bill of Credit is issued exclusively on the creditworthiness of the state or other body corporate and to be circulated in ordinary purposes as Money, redeemable as Real Money at a fixed date or on demand; and

(x) *Bill of Exchange* is an Instrument of Demand and Order, assured by Rights granted; as an unconditional written order from A. to B., directing B. to pay C. a certain sum of money therein named, either on demand or at sight, or at any certain period after date or after sight; and

(xi) *Bill of Lading* is an Instrument of Demand and Order, assured by Rights granted; as a Covenant or instrument signed by the master of a ship acknowledging receipt of the merchants goods and obliging himself to deliver the same in good condition at the place to which they are assigned; and

(xii) *Bill of Sale* is an Instrument of Demand and Order, assured by Rights granted; such as when a person delivers goods as security to a lender in exchange for a sum of money and empowering the lender to sell the goods if the sum is not repaid at the time appointed.

865. All valid Bills must either state the amount of the Monetary Obligation on the face of the Instrument as proper and due disclosure and accounting of such obligation, or within a Memorandum of Account attached to the annexed documents to the Bill, stating clearly the total Monetary Obligations of the Drawee in accepting the obligations due. *Accounting of Monetary Obligation*

866. The failure to provide a clear and proper accounting of the Monetary Obligation associated with a Bill, or the deliberate and wilful obscuring, hiding, fraud, perfidy or falsity in failing to provide such open and transparent accounting shall therefore invalidate any and all bills and any and all charges against such Bills. No person may be properly charged for an obligation without first knowing and being provided in writing an accounting of the monetary obligation. *Secret or Hidden Monetary Obligation invalidating Bill*

867. The Acceptance of a valid Bill is the act whereby the Person on whom a Bill is drawn (called the Drawee) assents to the Demand and Order of the Drawer to pay it, or make themselves liable for its action or payment when due. The object of Acceptance is to bind the Drawee and make him an actual and bound party to the Instrument. Therefore, until there is an Acceptance (such as evidence of Dishonour), the Drawee is under no obligation whatsoever upon the Bill itself. *Acceptance of Valid Bill*

868. A Bill is considered Accepted when it is acknowledged and signed in good Trust (*bona fide*), or through procedure to establish the dishonour, default and delinquency of the Drawee: *Form of Acceptance*

   (i) A Bill is accepted when the Drawee signs and endorses the Bill at ninety degrees prior to the expiry or maturity of the Bill; or

   (ii) A Bill is accepted when the Drawer established the legitimacy of the Demand and Order, the truth of the debt and obligation, the dishonour of the Drawee in settling the debt and the default and delinquency of the Drawee in failing to provide any reasonable lawful excuse.

Article 206 – Draft

869. A **Draft** also known as a **Demand Draft**, also known as a Sight Draft and a Payment Order, is a type of Bill of Exchange as a Demand and Order, whereby a valid Financial Body directs another Financial Body to pay a certain sum to a specified party (payee). Drafts are orders of payment by an entity with full banking powers such as Ucadia or an Authorised related entity through one or more agents to another bank/financial institution. *Draft*

Article 207 – Cheque

870. A **Cheque**, also known as an Account Payment Order, is a type of Bill of Exchange as a Demand and Order, whereby a valid Entity or Member directs a Ucadia Body or foreign financial body with banking powers to pay a certain sum to a specified party (payee), by drawing down on a particular account. *Cheque*

Article 208 – Bond

871. A **Bond** is an Instrument of Obligation and Penalty, secured by Promise and Guarantee, or Charge, or Bailment, or Mortgage, or *Bond*

Third-Party Surety, whereby the Obligor (person bound) acknowledges an Obligation or Debt (penal sum); and binds himself to pay a certain sum of interest (coupon) and repay any principal money at a maturity date, subject to any other binding conditions of surety and performance, whereby the Obligation will become void, or else the Obligation shall remain in full force.

872. In relation to the parties holding an interest or associated with a Bond, including customary rules: *Relations of Persons to a Bond*

    (i)   The one who makes or issues a valid Bond is called the *Obligor* (also Issuer); and

    (ii)   The one to whom the obligation is due and who accepts the valid Bond as a right and security is called the *Obligee*; and

    (iii)   The one who agrees to assure the Obligor is called the *Surety*; and

    (iv)   The one who holds the benefit of the Bond is called the Holder and may or may not be the *Obligee*; and

    (v)   A valid Bond must have at least one condition clause being an agreed "obligation" of performance by the one who makes or issues a valid Bond; and

    (vi)   A valid Bond must have at least one consideration clause being the agreed "valuable offering" of the one who accepts the valid Bond to then offer or do something in return; and

    (vii)   A valid Bond must have at least one penalty clause, that may or may not be associated with the prior good, or bill or contract or thing in question, that comes into effect if the one who makes or issues a valid Bond defaults on the performance of the condition clause(s); and

    (viii)   A valid Bond may (or may not) have one or more defeasance clauses that annul and void the penalty clauses in the event the one who makes or issues a valid Bond performs the conditions specified; and

    (ix)   A valid Bond may (or may not) be dated or have an expiry date or identify the place where it was made. Yet a Plaintiff in any declaration of action must lay a place where it was made; and

    (x)   A valid Bond that possesses an expiry date is termed the maturity date; and

    (xi)   The summary operative elements of a valid Bond must be recorded in a Register and possess a unique entry number, usually distinguished in red ink. The unique entry in the Register is proof of the maker or issuer of a valid Bond being issued to another party; and

(xii) A valid Bond requires then the one who makes or issues a valid Bond to "bind" themselves, usually through a promise to the condition clause(s) under sign, seal and delivery of the Bond as a form of original Decree on a single sheet of paper, or parchment or vellum with the unique Register number clearly visible; and

(xiii) The Conditions and Penalties of a simple Bond are normally on the reverse side of the single sheet of paper, or parchment or vellum; and

(xiv) If a Penalty clause makes provision for a debt, then this is normally called the Penal Sum; and

(xv) If a valid Bond permits negotiation or transfer, then the Obligee normally will endorse the original at 90 degrees on the face (obverse) or reverse of instrument; and

(xvi) If a valid Bond permits periodic payments to be redeemed, these are normally called Coupons and by tradition represented smaller printed forms at the bottom of the Instrument to be redeemed with the Obligor; and

(xvii) Once a Coupon is redeemed, or a Bond is redeemed at maturity, it is cancelled on its face and over any signature or seal by two or three lines. Similarly, the record in the Bond register is cancelled by having a single line through it, representing the cancellation of all obligations.

873. Types of Bonds include (but are not limited to) *Annuity (Insurance), Appearance, Arbitration, Bail, Catastrophe (Insurance), Commercial, Completion (Insurance), Convertible, Fiduciary, Mortgage, Performance, Public Liability (Insurance), Professional Liability (Insurance), Tenancy* and *Treasury*: Types of Valid Bonds

(i) *Annuity (Insurance) Bond*, is an Instrument of Obligation and Penalty, secured by Promise and Guarantee, or Charge, or Bailment, or Mortgage, or Third-Party Surety, whereby the Obligor (person bound) acknowledges an Obligation or Debt (penal sum); and binds himself to pay a certain sum of equal payments (deposits) made at fixed intervals of time, subject to any other binding conditions of surety and performance, whereby the Obligation will become void, or else the Obligation shall remain in full force; and

(ii) *Appearance Bond*, is an Instrument of Obligation and Penalty, secured by Promise and Guarantee and Third-Party Surety, whereby an Accused as Obligor (person bound) acknowledges an Obligation to appear in a matter within the jurisdiction of a competent forum of Law; and that the Third-Party Surety binds himself to pay a Debt (penal sum), subject to any other binding conditions of surety and performance, whereby the Obligation and Debt will become void on appearance of the Accused upon the agreed time, or else the Obligation and Debt shall remain in full force; and

(iii) *Arbitration Bond*, is an Instrument of Obligation and Penalty, secured by Promise and Guarantee and Third-Party Surety, whereby a party to an arbitration matter as Obligor (person bound) acknowledges the terms and conditions of Arbitration; and that the Third-Party Surety binds himself to pay a Debt (penal sum), subject to any other binding conditions of surety and performance, whereby the Obligation and Debt will become void on final settlement of the Arbitration or upon the agreed time, or else the Obligation and Debt shall remain in full force; and

(iv) *Bail Bond*, is an Instrument of Obligation and Penalty, secured by a competent forum of Law taking physical custody as Bailment of the Accused, in the absence of any sufficient Appearance Bond or surety; and then agreeing to the conditional release of the body of the Accused to a Third-Party Surety, upon sufficient Promise and Guarantee by the Accused as Obligor (person bound) to appear in a matter within the jurisdiction of a competent forum of Law; and that the Third-Party Surety binds himself to pay a Debt (penal sum), subject to any other binding conditions of surety and performance, whereby the Obligation and Debt will become void on appearance of the Accused upon the agreed time, or else the Obligation and Debt shall remain in full force; and

(v) *Catastrophe (Insurance) Bond*, is an Instrument of Obligation and Penalty, secured by Promise and Guarantee and Third-Party Surety, whereby the Obligor (person bound) acknowledges an Obligation and binds himself to perform safely in a competent, honest and professional manner in respect of a specific performance, or event or journey with certain property; and that the Third-Party Surety binds himself to pay a Debt (penal sum) in the event of any catastrophic loss of the said property due to wreck, or piracy, or theft, subject to any other binding conditions of surety and performance, whereby the Obligation and Debt will become void on completion of the Trust Obligation of the holder of the Property or the agreed time, or else the Obligation and Debt shall remain in full force; and

(vi) *Commercial Bond*, is an Instrument of Obligation and Penalty, secured by Promise and Guarantee and Third-Party Surety, whereby the Obligor (person bound) acknowledges an Obligation and binds himself to pay a certain sum of interest (coupon) and repay any principal money at a maturity date; and that the Third-Party Surety binds himself to pay a Debt (penal sum), subject to any other binding conditions of surety and performance, whereby the Obligation and Debt will become void, or else the Obligation and Debt shall remain in full force; and

(vii) *Completion (Insurance) Bond*, is an Instrument of Obligation and Penalty, secured by Promise and Guarantee and Third-Party Surety, whereby the Obligor (person bound) acknowledges an Obligation and binds himself to complete, fulfil and deliver certain terms of an agreement; and that the Third-Party Surety binds himself to pay a Debt (penal sum), subject to any other binding conditions of surety and performance, whereby the Obligation and Debt will become void on completion of the Trust Obligation of the Fiduciary or the agreed time, or else the Obligation and Debt shall remain in full force; and

(viii) *Convertible Bond*, is an Instrument of Obligation and Penalty, secured by Promise and Guarantee and Third-Party Surety, whereby the Obligor (person bound) acknowledges an Obligation and binds himself to pay a certain sum of interest (coupon) and repay any principal money at a maturity date, or permit the conversion of the value of the Instrument into Stock of a Fund; and that the Third-Party Surety binds himself to pay a Debt (penal sum), subject to any other binding conditions of surety and performance, whereby the Obligation and Debt will become void, or else the Obligation and Debt shall remain in full force; and

(ix) *Fiduciary Bond*, is an Instrument of Obligation and Penalty, secured by Promise and Guarantee and Third-Party Surety, whereby a Fiduciary as Obligor (person bound) acknowledges a Trust Obligation to act and behave with the highest probity, prudence and honesty, free from corruption or fraud in a matter within the jurisdiction of a competent forum of Law; and that the Third-Party Surety binds himself to pay a Debt (penal sum), subject to any other binding conditions of surety and performance, whereby the Obligation will become void on completion of the Trust Obligation of the Fiduciary or the agreed time, or else the Obligation and Debt shall remain in full force; and

(x) *Mortgage Bond*, is an Instrument of Obligation and Penalty, secured by Promise and Mortgage, whereby the Obligor (person bound) acknowledges an Obligation and binds himself to pay a certain sum of interest (coupon) and repay any principal money at a maturity date; and then binds himself to pay a Debt (penal sum) secured against the Mortgage, subject to any other binding conditions of surety and performance, whereby the Obligation and Debt will become void, or else the Obligation and Debt shall remain in full force; and

(xi) *Performance Bond*, is an Instrument of Obligation and Penalty, secured by Promise and Guarantee and Third-Party Surety, whereby the Obligor (person bound) acknowledges an Obligation and binds himself to complete, fulfil and deliver certain terms of an agreement; and that the Third-Party Surety binds himself to pay a Debt (penal sum), subject to any other binding conditions of surety and performance, whereby the Obligation and Debt will become void on completion of the Trust Obligation of the Fiduciary or the agreed time, or else the Obligation and Debt shall remain in full force; and

(xii) *Public Liability (Insurance) Bond*, is an Instrument of Obligation and Penalty, secured by Promise and Guarantee and Third-Party Surety, whereby the Obligor (person bound) acknowledges an Obligation and binds himself to behave and act in a competent, honest and professional manner in respect of a specific performance, or event or journey; and that the Third-Party Surety binds himself to pay a Debt (penal sum) in the event of any claim of injury from other parties due to accident, or trespass, or wrong or failure of performance by the Obligor, subject to any other binding conditions of surety and performance, whereby the Obligation and Debt will become void on completion of the Trust Obligation of the Fiduciary or the agreed time, or else the Obligation and Debt shall remain in full force; and

(xiii) *Professional Liability (Insurance) Bond*, is an Instrument of Obligation and Penalty, secured by Promise and Guarantee and Third-Party Surety, whereby the Obligor (person bound) acknowledges an Obligation and binds himself to behave and act in a competent, honest and professional manner in respect of such duties and obligations of office, agency or employment; and that the Third-Party Surety binds himself to pay a Debt (penal sum) in the event of any claim of injury from other parties due to negligence, omission or error or wrong or failure of performance by the Obligor in their official or professional capacity, subject to any other binding conditions of surety and performance, whereby the Obligation and Debt will become void on completion of the Trust Obligation of the Fiduciary or the agreed time, or else the Obligation and Debt shall remain in full force; and

(xiv) *Tenancy Bond*, is an Instrument of Obligation and Penalty, secured by Promise and Guarantee and Bailment of Money, whereby the Obligor (person bound) acknowledges an Obligation as to the condition and care of certain property and binds himself to clean, maintain and avoid damage to the property; and binds himself to pay a Debt (penal sum), subject to any other binding conditions of surety and performance, whereby the Obligation will become void on completion of the Tenancy of the Tenant or the agreed time, or else the Obligation and Debt shall remain in full force; and

(xv) *Treasury Bond*, is an Instrument of Obligation and Penalty, secured by Promise and Guarantee and Third-Party Surety, whereby the Body Corporate as Obligor (person bound) acknowledges an Obligation and is bound to pay a certain sum of interest (coupon) and repay any principal money at a maturity date; and further agrees to be bound to pay a Debt (penal sum), subject to any other binding conditions of surety and performance, whereby the Obligation and Debt will become void, or else the Obligation and Debt shall remain in full force.

Article 209 – Debenture

874. A *Debenture* is a medium to long term security as a bond. A Debenture is effectively a certificate of indebtedness to a loan.

Debenture

Article 210 – Writ

875. A ***Writ*** is a formal written command issued by a court or judicial authority, often used to initiate, conclude or command some action in a legal proceeding.

Writ

876. By definition, a valid Writ may only be issued under the proper Ecclesiastical and Sovereign Authority of the most sacred Covenant known as *Pactum De Singularis Caelum*:

Nature and authority of Writs

    (i)   A Writ is not an order – it is an absolute command that cannot be challenged. An order by its legal and commercial meaning is an offer that may be negotiated. Whereas a Writ, by definition is not negotiable. Therefore, any definition that states a Writ may be defined as an order is patently false and fraudulent; and

    (ii)   A valid and legitimate Writ by its very nature is an ecclesiastical instrument requiring precise creation and purpose. To simply call an instrument a Writ and act as if it possesses the same qualities as a legitimate writ without the attendant care, authority or creation is a most grave injury to the Law itself; and

    (iii)   A body may possess the right to appoint one or more agents under validly signed and sealed warrants. However, such persons have no right legally or lawfully to issue a Writ unless they themselves are also appointed under Ucadian Law as per the present Maxims. If such persons are not appointed to their position under such Authority, then any Writs they issue are *ipso facto* (as a fact of law) null and void; and

    (iv)   Corporations and agents cannot create or issue valid Writs. Nor may a nation issue such Writs unless the Executive claims absolute ecclesiastical and sovereign authority in accord with Ucadian Law; and

    (v)   Any Laws that have been passed that attempt to permit the issuing of writs by corporations or agents are an abomination and contrary to the very source of authority of Writs. Such documents therefore issued have no more legal or lawful effect than an offer or notice. The enforcement therefore of such instruments as if they are writs is without question illegal and unlawful – contrary to very foundations of Law. An invalid writ has no force or effect ecclesiastically, lawfully or legally.

Article 211 – Warrant

877. A ***Warrant*** is a Document of Authority, signed, sealed and issued

Warrant

under the authority of a registered Sacred Writ by an Officer or duly appointed Fiduciary of Ucadia or an Authorised related entity through one or more Agents commanding certain acts to be performed; whilst also granting the Agent(s) limited protection from liability or culpability for certain injuries or claim that may arise as a result of the execution of the commanded acts. A Warrant is therefore similar in part to a license, whereby an act commanded to be done might otherwise be unlawful or illegal without a proper Warrant.

878. In the absence of a valid Writ, no Warrant is valid or legitimate; and any claimed Warrant subsequently issued is an admission of fraud, perfidy, deception and injury of the law. *No Writ No Warrant*

Article 212 – Certificate

879. A *Certificate* is an extract of Proof of a definitive, fixed, definite, reliable and certain manner that some act has or has not been done, or some event occurred or some formal decision has been concluded, given underwritten assurance (certified statement) by valid Officers possessing the authority to issue such instruments. *Certificate*

880. Types of Certificates include (but are not limited to): *Types of valid Certificates*

   (i) A *Certificate of Title*, is any valid Certificate that entitles the holder or the named party on the Certificate to claim the benefit of ownership of "Equitable Title" and use of certain property as specified and "extracted" from a valid Record into the Certificate; and

   (ii) A *Certificate of Acknowledgement*, (also known as a Certificate of Oath) is any valid Certificate by a party that avows, or makes a sacred oath or affirms before an authorised officer they have executed an instrument of conveyance by gift, grant, assignment or delegation of their own free will, without threat or coercion and that their sign and seal is genuine; and

   (iii) A *Certificate of Witness*, is any valid Certificate by a party that avows, or makes a sacred oath or affirms before an authorised officer that they witnessed an event or act of conveyance and acknowledgement; and

   (iv) A *Certificate of Authenticity*, is any valid Certificate by a party that avows, or makes a sacred oath or affirms before an authorised officer that an object, concept or property or its manifest is authentic, true and correct; and

   (v) A *Certificate of Acceptance*, is any valid Certificate by a party that avows, or makes a sacred oath or affirms before an authorised officer they have received certain goods into their custody, or other valuable consideration offered or tendered by another and that they consent and agree to the obligations and conditions therein; and

(vi) A *Certificate of Receipt*, is any valid Certificate by a party that releases, acquits or discharges another from any further obligation, or agreement or duties as Acknowledgement they have received certain goods or cash into their custody, or other valuable consideration offered or tendered by another. In the absence of a valid Certificate of Receipt, the use of any property conveyed implies acceptance of any obligations attached to it.

Article 213 – Voucher

881. A "**Voucher**" is a written or printed Instrument that establishes the authenticity of a valid claim, or demand, or bond and the transaction itself, concerning some goods, or property associated with a Trust, or Estate or Fund or Corporation to be delivered under certain conditions. Voucher

882. The following are the essential elements associated with any valid Voucher: Elements of Vouchers

   (i) A Voucher is in essence valid proof and intent of one Party in relation to a certain action and transaction and agreement; and

   (ii) Vouchers by their design in law always come in at least pairs or more (if more than two (2) Parties) associated with the individual action of a Party to a Transaction. It is a dishonour for a Party not to produce a Voucher for the other Party at the appropriate Transaction; and

   (iii) Vouchers by their design are meant to be Exchanged with the other Party (of Parties) of an agreement and Transaction. It is a dishonour for a Party not to produce and exchange a Voucher for the other Party at the appropriate Transaction; and

   (iv) Vouchers by their design match up at different stages of transactions of an agreement. For example, a Purchase Request matches a Purchase Order; and a Bill of Particulars matches an Order for Payment; and an Acceptance of Bill matches an Acceptance of Payment; and a Receipt of Delivery matches a Receipt of Payment.

883. The key elements of the physical Voucher itself by tradition are:-   *Elements of valid Vouchers*

    (i)   The Voucher is on quality parchment or paper that will last; and

    (ii)   The Voucher is printed or written with permanent ink that will not fade; and

    (iii)   The issuer of the Voucher is clearly identified; and

    (iv)   The unique Register number of the Voucher is clearly identified; and

    (v)   The particulars of the Voucher are clearly identified and by what authority a payment has been made and serving as evidence of payment or discharge of a debit, or the right to redeem a transaction or goods of certain value; and

    (vi)   Any amount is expressed in Words as well as numeric symbols; and

    (vii)   The date of issue is clearly stated; and

    (viii) Whether or not the Voucher itself is negotiable, redeemable or other limits are clearly stated; and

    (ix)   The Voucher is duly sealed, or signed or authorised.

7.5 – Prohibited Documents, Instruments & Forms

Article 214 – Prohibited Documents, Instruments & Forms

884. ***Prohibited Documents, Instruments & Forms*** refer to legal documents, financial instruments, or forms that are expressly prohibited or restricted by Ucadia law, regulations, or Ucadia government authorities. These restrictions are put in place for various reasons, including (but not limited to) ensuring compliance with the Rule of Law, the Nature of Law and ending profane, wicked and evil practices under the cover of law within corrupt Non-Ucadia financial and legal systems.   *Prohibited Documents, Instruments & Forms*

885. Generally, any documents, instruments or forms that fail to comply with the most sacred Covenant *Pactum De Singularis Caelum*, the present Maxims and associated Charters, Covenants and Codes of Law are reprobate, to be suppressed and prohibited from use or recognition.   *Generalised Prohibited Documents, Instruments & Forms*

886. Specifically, there are certain classes of Non-Ucadian documents,   *Specifically Prohibited*

instruments and forms that are so deceptive, manipulative and founded upon such corruption of Divine Law and all known and decent Civilised Rules, that they are not only prohibited from use or effect, but demand to be revealed for their wickedness and evil. These include:-

> Documents, Instruments & Forms

(i) Non-Ucadian Government Life Annuities; and

(ii) Non-Ucadian Birth (Settlement) Certificates; and

(iii) Non-Ucadian Land Certificates; and

(iv) Non-Ucadian Sovereign Bond Certificates; and

(v) Non-Ucadian Trustee Savings Bank Certificates; and

(vi) Non-Ucadian Social Health Certificates; and

(vii) Non-Ucadian Social Welfare Certificates.

Article 215 – Non-Ucadian Government Life Annuities

887. A *Non-Ucadian Government Life Annuity* is a financial instrument and product issued by a Non-Ucadian government authority, typically a treasury or central bank, on the life and name of one or more persons, that provides investors a stream of regular payments to an individual over a specified period. However, its underlying assumptions and structure is based upon people as slaves or "chattel" and possessions of the state or the sovereign.

> Non-Ucadian Government Annuities

888. Almost all *Non-Ucadian Government Life Annuities* continue to be based on a core set of prohibited, morally repugnant, wicked and evil presumptions concerning persons and their property including, but not limited to:-

> Prohibitive Nature of Non-Ucadian Government Life Annuities

(i) The "name" of the Non-Ucadia Person being owned by the state or sovereign, yet refusing to be transparent about such assumptions and refusing to be honest when challenged to acknowledge the truth concerning ultimate ownership claim of "name"; and

(ii) The formation of one or more "trusts" (usually Cestui Que Trust) without the permission, knowledge or transparency to the living Being and Non-Ucadia Person to whom it relates; and to blatantly lie, refuse to demonstrate any form of Good Faith in acknowledging the truth when properly and competently challenged; and

(iii) To form and maintain those same "trusts" in Bad Faith, Bad Conscience and Bad Actions by refusing to acknowledge the absurdity of such assumptions wherein "lost at sea", or "abandoned" or "incompetent" or "wards of the state" are all wicked and false legal fictions designed to disenfranchise the population; and to continue to lie and refuse to acknowledge that such structures cannot possibly be formed, or exist or function under any civilised form of law; and

(iv) To permit certain people and entities to purchase financial products in the name of living persons, almost always without their knowledge and to creating binding contracts against their names and lives; and to continue to steadfastly deny that this represents not only a most egregious example of slavery and betrayal against the people of a nation; and to continue to lie, obfuscate and permit such systems of slavery and wickedness to continue.

889. The claims that annuities existed prior to the 17th Century in English law and in practice in history is deliberately false and designed to hide the unique and core presumptions upon which annuities function:- *False claims of Origins of Non-Ucadia Life Annuities*

(i) Forms of surety and underwriting of goods against loss during transport was well established within ancient civilizations such as the Egyptians, the Celts and later the Phoenicians and Persians. However, these financial agreements did not function in the manner of annuities; and

(ii) Forms of surety and honour price against injury or accident within society is well established within Irish Celtic culture over 3,500 years ago, including its revival under the Carolingian Empire. However, this is completely different to annuities; and

(iii) The claims that the Romans approved and used annuities within the Pagan and later Christian Empire is an absurdity as the source texts are deliberate 16th Century frauds and there is no factual example of the Romans permitting hypothecating the future production potential of slaves as per an annuity nor the payment of the retirement of legionnaires in such a manner; and

(iv) Evidence of hypothecating land revenues exists in manner settings, such as European regions during the middle ages. However, such agreements were focused on the output not on the treatment of the peasants as purely livestock in the manner of annuities.

890. The birth of annuities emerged not from Europe but as a solution for Parishes in response to the expenses of supporting disenfranchised *Origins of Non-Ucadia Life*

peasants in lieu with the Poor Law (1601) and later in the financing of war debt:- _{Annuities}

(i) The continued forced removal of peasants from the land, destruction of villages and deprivation of rights through greedy nobles continued to accelerate under Queen Elizabeth resulting in several famous riots that risked briefly the survival of the Crown; and

(ii) In 1601, the Poor Law demanded that parishes find means of shelter, food and useful "work" for those peasants thrown off the land. The creation of annuities within thirty years enabled those parishes from obtaining needed capital on the promise of future productive work of the poor, initially in the building of workhouses, being little more than prisons for poor men, woman and children to perform slave labor; and

(iii) In 1693, Charles Montague, 1st Earl of Halifax proposed the use of a modified form of annuities underwritten by the government through Royal Charter called "government bonds" that would be offered for sale at a fixed annual return as a means of solving the debt crisis. Even the initial stock sold to the Bank of England listed the certificates as "annuities" until removing the word in later issue; and

(iv) The success of the fundraising by the Chartered Bank of England using annuities was solidified through the Annuities Act 1703 (3 Anne c.2) of Queen Anne which defined the use of Life Annuities derived from ownership claims of Crown Land for the payment of war debt; and

(v) By 1743 and the first Textile Factory being established using the technology of John Wyatt at Birmingham, the number of workhouses for the poor managed by parishes of the Anglican Church had grown to over 400 and over 24,000 poor souls; and

(vi) In 1751, British Parliament enacted a consolidation of annuity based securities into one, single issue. This instrument carried a fixed, 3 percent annual rate, which was dubbed the "Consolidated Annuity" and also known as the "Perpetual Bond" and the "Consol" which had no maturity date and was redeemable at any time deemed appropriate by the British Government; and

(vii) In 1770 Frederick North led the Tories as Prime Minister (1770-1782) to power in Parliament. He quickly rushed a raft of laws in favor of industrialists and entrepreneurs through

Parliament, including the Inclosure Act 1773 which "opened the flood gates" by granting land nobles unprecedented power to disenfranchise the peasants and destroy ancient villages. The resulting explosion of poor in the hands of the Church of England forced a revamp of Parish Life Annuities and a huge windfall to the Bank of England and the Tories; and

(viii) In 1774, the Society of Lloyds was formed by politicians, industrialists and lawyers with the specific goal of profiting from the underwriting of the forced transportation of the poor and prisoners as slaves through the purchase of the Life Annuities from the Church of England and the British Government. At least 5,000 were shipped to the American Colonies and then re-sold as white slaves before the start of the Revolutionary War. During the fighting, some 10,000 to 25,000 people died of disease and starvation on rotting hulks owned by the Society of Lloyds waiting for transportation to be sold as white slaves; and

(ix) By 1776, there were approximately 1800 workhouses and over 100,000 poor souls condemned to them, all underwritten by Parish Life Annuities; and

(x) In 1787, the Society of Lloyds funded the "First Fleet of convicts to Australia in the hope of removing the backlog of prisoners rotting on prison hulks in English ports. In the subsequent years, Lloyds successfully purchased the Life Annuities and insured the transportation of more than 165,000 souls to Australia. In the same year under 27 G.3. c.13, Annuities formerly paid out of Aggregate Fund now paid out of Consolidated fund; and

(xi) By 1783, the Society of Lloyds was able to resume the sale of white slaves from England, Ireland, Wales and Scotland to the wealthy "patriot" families of the former American colonies. By 1802 following the formation of the United Kingdom, there was a significant increase of white slaves sold to wealthy American industrialists with over 130,000 Irish alone sold into slavery to the hands of famous American leaders and their plantations by 1838. All records of the massive profits made by the English politicians, industrialists and lawyers and their American compatriots were "lost" in a mysterious fire which destroyed the Royal Exchange in 1838.

Article 216 – Non-Ucadian Birth (Settlement) Certificate

891. A ***Non-Ucadian Birth Certificate***, also less well known as a ***Non-***   Non-Ucadian

Ucadian Settlement Certificate is an instrument issued by a Non-Ucadian government authority, typically a registry of births, deaths and marriages or a similar organisation. However, the underlying assumptions and structure behind Birth Certificates represents some of the most evil, deceptive and malevolent thinking in human history since their formation.

Birth (Settlement) Certificate

892. A Settlement Certificate, also known as a "Birth Certificate" since the formation of Central Records and Registers in 1836 (6&7Will.4 c.86) is an official document, possessing multiple legal functions and "states" under the central presumption that those against whom such instruments are issued are a form of "property" and bonded servant (slave), to Western-Roman and private Banking interests, regardless of status of family or history.

Non-Ucadian Settlement (Birth) Certificate

893. A Settlement Certificate, also known as a "Birth Certificate" since the formation of Central Records and Registers in 1836 (6&7Will.4 c.86) fulfils multiple and distinct functions and states, depending upon its recognition and activity at hand, including but not limited to:

Non-Ucadian Birth (Settlement) Certificate Functions

   (i) *Certificate of Title to Cestui Que Use of Person* being recognition that the State claims ownership by virtue of the Certificate itself and all the information contained on it, therefore proving a Cestui Que Vie Trust in place and that the man or woman or new born to whom the Certificate applies only has "beneficial use" of the name; and

   (ii) *Certificate of Title to Property* being the recognition of the fact of a Birth Certificate being a certificate, that the name is property and therefore the man or woman or new born is now treated as property and no longer as a living man or woman, subject to the Rule of Law; and

   (iii) *Certificate of Deposit and Bailment* (Custody) being the recognition through the terms used to describe the father and mother that a transaction has taken place and the new born is no longer "owned" by the parents but is in the custody of the State, with the new born now a Thing, subject to the Jurisdiction of the Courts, having being registered (enrolled); and

   (iv) *Certificate of Second Class Citizenship* under Cestui Que Use of Person being that the Certificate recognises a new born not being a Citizen, but a "second class" citizen not having full control over their body, or mind, or name, or spirit all claimed through the morally repugnant, profane, sacrilegious and deceptive conduct of public officials; and

(v) *Certificate of Bondage as Slave* being the certificate as recognition of a man or woman or new born as a member of the poor, the paupers, the infants, the idiots and lunatics, the "horned cattle", the beasts, the creatures, the humans, the dispossessed, the insolvent debtors and criminals and enemies of those who have created wholly mythical religious and legal texts to justify their exclusive positions as masters of a "planet of slaves".

894. Such concepts as a Sovereign Society necessarily needing to retain ultimate control or "ownership" of persons, or names and even to hypothecate financial instruments against the productiveness of its members are not in themselves morally repugnant or wicked or evil concepts. Modern societies cannot function without the legal concept of persons. Nor can large economies and government investment in housing, schools and infrastructure happen without the capital solution (in part) of annuities.

Prohibitive Nature of Non-Ucadian Birth (Settlement) Certificate

However, in almost all cases the way that Non-Ucadian Birth (Settlement) Certificates were created under law, function under law and are defended in law and in media remains profoundly misleading, deceptive, false, treasonous and morally repugnant:-

(i) Non-Ucadia government, legal and media professionals continue to refuse to acknowledge the "ownership of the person" and the "ownership of the name" questions relating to Birth Certificates; and continue to attack, belittle and deny anyone who presents a credible challenge to the continued lies, deception and misinformation; and

(ii) Non-Ucadia government, legal and media professionals continue to refuse to acknowledge that the information recorded within their own registers for births, deaths and marriages is deliberately incomplete and misleading; and that the continued failure to acknowledge "living" births is an absurdity in law and morality that exposes as a lie that such records are kept confidential because they are so accurate and well maintained; and

(iii) Non-Ucadia government, legal and media professionals continue to refuse to acknowledge that trusts, bonds and other financial instruments are created from the information gathered to create birth certificates, despite overwhelming evidence the financial system underpins a key asset class of the modern Non-Ucadia Financial System.

895. The term Birth is a synonym of the Admiralty term Berth from the late early 1600's meaning "a fixed address; or position on a ship; or

Origin of Birth

room in which the ship's company mess resides; or a space for a vessel to moor (settle)".

896. In terms of the history of Birth Certificates, Settlement Certificates and diminishing, tricking, deceiving, lying, seizing, condemning and cursing free people as slaves, wards, infants, cattle, poor and commodities: History of Birth Certificates

    (i)   In 1535 (27Hen.8 c.28) King Henry VIII of England and his Venetian banking advisers seized the property of the poor and common farmers under the pretext they were "small religious estates". By 1539 (31Hen.8 c.13) he did the same for large religious estates. By 1540, (32Hen.8 c.1), all property was to be owned through "Estates" effectively being Welfare Funds granted by the Crown to the Benefit of use of Subjects with the most common being Estates for the non wealthy now considered "Wards of the Estate". Then in 1545 (37Hen.8 c.1) King Henry VIII reintroduced a title directly and solely connected to the slave trade of Rome, abolished by emperors and forbidden under Christian law called the "Custos Rotulorum" meaning literally "Keeper of the Slave Rolls" into every county, to maintain records of the Poor now as slaves. The same sacrilegious, immoral, ecclesiastically unlawful positions continued into the 21st Century as connected with Birth Certificates; and

    (ii)   In 1547 (1Ed.6 c.3), Edward VI issued a new statute that did forbid people considered poor from travelling, except for work, or from claiming their own time and activities and whether or not to work. All people (except those members of the ruling elite, particularly those non-Christian sects from Pisa, Venice and parts of Spain responsible for wholly false religious and legal texts) now declared slaves were either to be gainfully employed in the service of some lord or master, to work to death, or if they were found to be idle, or enjoying life then they were to be seized and permanently branded with a "V" and either sold as a slave or exterminated. The only exception to the rule, were those men who chose to dedicate themselves to support the status quo and become educated and knowledgeable in the false texts and false scriptures of the slave masters. This act was supposed to have been repealed in 1549 (3&4Ed.6 c.16). However, the act was then restored to full effect in 1572 (14El. c.5) and through subsequent repeals of repeals, remains in force; and

    (iii)   Under Queen Elizabeth I of England, a set of measures were introduced which had the effect of accelerating the disenfranchisement of land peasants into landless paupers. In 1589 (31El c. 7) peasants then required local parish permission to erect dwellings whereas before the erection of a dwelling by a land peasant on their lord's land was considered a "right". As a result, the ranks of the landless poor, or "paupers" swelled as available to be press-ganged into work; and

(iv) To placate the overwhelming hostility against England as a hellhole of slavery, exploitation and superstition, a new act was introduced in 1601 (43El. c.2 and "secret version" as 43 El. c.3) to begin to industrialize, hide and franchise slavery with the introduction of "overseers" of the poor as the foremen over the slaves, under a "cleric" of the parish and the renaming of children sold as sex slaves and workers to be called "Apprentices". Thus the Apprenticeship system was invented not to improve conditions, but to "rebrand" slavery under the Non- Christian English – Venetian - Pisan model of commerce. The act also introduced a new levy, collected by Parishes was called the "Poor Rates" (now called "council taxes") against wealthy property owners for their "rent" of use of the poor as slaves. This is the financial origin of Annuities 100 years later; and

(v) Under Charles II of England, the concept of "Settlements" as plantations of working poor controlled by the Church of England was further refined in 1662 (14Car.2 c.12) including for the first time the issuance of "Settlement Certificates" equivalent to a "birth certificate, passport and social security" rolled into one document. A child's birthplace was its place of settlement, unless its mother had a settlement certificate from some other parish stating that the unborn child was included on the certificate. However from the age of 7 upward the child could have been apprenticed and therefore "sold into servitude" for some rent paid back to the church as "poor taxes". The act also made it easier for the "clearing of common houses of the poor" and for the first time made the definition of poor the value of tenancy being a taxable value of less than £10 per year. The act also modified the age of "emancipation" from child slavery to adult slavery as the age of 16; and

(vi) Under the draconian and morally repugnant dictates of 1662 (14Car.2 c.12), no one was allowed to move from town to town without the appropriate "Settlement Certificate". If a person entered a parish in which he or she did not have official settlement, and seemed likely to become chargeable to the new parish, then an examination would be made by the justices (or parish overseers). From this examination on oath, the justices would determine if that person had the means to sustain himself. The results of the examination were documented in an Examination Paper. As a result of the examination the intruder would then either be allowed to stay, or would be removed by means of what was known as a Removal Order, the origin of the modern equivalent of an "Eviction and Removal Notice" when a sheriff removes people from their home; and

(vii) In 1667 (19Car.2 c.4) the concept of "workhouses" were formalized and licensed as being effectively the very worst and hellish places where people considered "prisoners" could be "legally" and effectively worked to death for the profit of the elite pirates and thieves, under the full endorsement by the Church of England. This is the act that invented the concept of "Employment" and an expansion of the highly profitable white slavery business models of English aristocracy. Thus, people who were taken into custody by virtue of being poor, were expected to work as well as live in conditions as traumatic and evil as any in civilized history; and

(viii) The abuse of poor prisoners through the "workhouses" employment model was extremely profitable and a new act was required in 1670 (22Car.2 c.18) to regulate the corporations "renting" of prisoners as "employees" for profit, particularly in the paying of their accounts to the Crown; and

(ix) Previous acts were continued and some made perpetual such as the controls over paperwork and "Settlement Certificates" as the origin and ancestor of Birth Certificates by James II in 1685 (1J.2. c. 17) as one of the few acts that the ruling elite permitted to remain as an active Statute of Westminster under his reign; and

(x) Under William and Mary of Orange in 1691 (3W&M c.11), the acts of workhouses and abuse of the poor were continued and further refined, with greater oversight on paperwork and accounting for poor entering and leaving parishes, to prevent fraud by overseers and corporations; and

(xi) In 1697 (3W&M. c.11), one of the more horrific of the wicked and morally repugnant acts of Westminster was the introduction (in §2) of the "badge" of the poor with the letter "P" to be worn at all times on the shoulder of the right sleeve. Furthermore, all evidence as to "Jewish Badges" being introduced in Europe as early as the 13th Century is wholly and completely false, as the term "jew" was not revived until the 16th Century. Instead, the first examples of badges as a stigma to status is most likely this act and subsequent acts against the poor by banking and ruling elite who chose to identify themselves as members of the same non-Christian religion invented in the 16th Century that claimed to be victims of the same barbarity. The use of the "P" as a form of curse and stigma is the same model of modern passports for citizens listed as "P" (Paupers, Poor, Peasant, Prisoners, Property, Peon) used today; and

(xii) In 1698 (9&10W3 c.11) an act reinforced the measurement of the poor being one who does not have an annual lease taxable at ten pounds or more, making at the time more than 95% of the population of England, Wales, Ireland and Scotland "poor"; and

(xiii) In 1713 (12Ann. S.2 c.18), the extension of Settlement Certificates as a form of negotiable Security was introduced for the first time (and continues with Birth Certificates today) whereby (§2) those born in a place but without a Settlement Certificate (including women and children), could be moved to a different location, such as a commercial workhouse when the "cost" of such certificates were purchased by a corporation; and

(xiv) Due to the increase in the number of "poor", in 1722 a new law was passed (9Geo.1 c.7) in which those who had been thrown out of their homes or had their land seized by pirates and thieves operating with endorsement of Westminster and who sought relief from the Church to stay alive now had to "compete" to enter into a workhouse to survive. Furthermore, the act expanded the ability for a wide variety of business owners to contract with churchwardens for the rent and use of the poor as "indentured servants" and "apprentices"; and

(xv) In 1733 (6Geo.2 c.32), one of the most inhumane and barbaric edicts in history was issued by Westminster (and remains an underlying pillar of the slave system today), whereby poor people who could not purchase a "license" to be considered married, would have their children deemed "bastards" and such children could then be seized by Churchwardens and "sold". Thus the baby slave trade was born and fully endorsed by the Church of England and British Society; and

(xvi) In 1761 (2Geo.3 c.22), Westminster declared that all poor as mental "infants" and too stupid to realize the underlying system of slavery and complicity of the Christian Churches, were now to be cursed and doomed as "dead in law" by their registration in the Bills of Mortality and the creation of the "civil birth" rituals being rituals of death that continue today within modern hospitals and registration of new born babies. This was further reinforced with the act in 1767 (7Geo.3 c.39) that poor children were to be registered and considered "dead in law"; and

(xvii) Beginning in 1773 with the Inclosure Act 1773 (13Geo.3 c.81), followed by the Inclosure Consolidation Act 1801 (41Geo.3 c.109), English Parliament effectively "privatized" massive amounts of common land for the benefit of a few, causing huge numbers of land peasants to become "landless paupers" and therefore in need of parish assistance. In America, this caused massive rebellion as well as in Ireland and Scotland and contributed to forming a Patriot militia leading to the "War of Independence". Almost the entire Patriot milita were deceived, captured and executed in New York (in 1777) under a deal between George Washington of the United Company of Merchants Blue Army and General Cornwalis of the East India Company Red Army. The Inclosure Acts are the foundation of Land Title as it is known today; and

(xviii) Because of the deliberate "legal" theft of land under parliamentary Inclosure laws of the late 18th and early 19th Century, the number of paupers dramatically increased. This led to the most awful and cruel laws being introduced to deliver to an elite few, the slave labor force needed for the industrial revolution through the Poor Law Amendment Act (1834) (5&6Will.4 c.76) which effectively stated that the poor could not receive any benefit unless they were constantly "employed" in a workhouse prison. Most importantly, much of the inhuman, barbaric and wholly immoral and sacrilegious framework of dictates and edicts of Westminster remained in force and were not repealed by this act). Thus, despite international treaties against slavery, the very worst slavery being "wage slavery" or "lawful slavery" was born whereby men, women and children lived in terrible conditions and were continued to be worked "to death"; and

(xix) In 1836, the Births and Deaths Registration Act (1836) (6&7Will.4 c.86) was introduced which for the first time created the General Register Office and the requirement for uniform records of births, deaths and marriages across the

Empire by Municipal Councils and Unions of Parishes. Thus on 1, July 1837, the Birth Certificate was formed as the successor of the Settlement Certificate for all "paupers" disenfranchised of their land birthright to be considered lawful ("voluntary") slaves with benefits provided by the local parish / region underwritten by the Society of Lloyds as it is still today; and

(xx) Beginning from 1871, further historic changes in the administration of "vital statistics" such as birth certificates and death certificates with the introduction of health districts or "sanitary districts". The Local Government Act of 1871 (34&35Vict. c.70), Public Health Act 1872 (35&36Vict. c.79) and in 1874 (37&38Vict. c.89) and the Public Health Act 1875 (38&39Vict. c.55) created a system of "districts" called Sanitary Districts governed by a Sanitary Authority responsible for various public health matters including mental health legally known as "sanity". Two types of Sanitary Districts were created being Urban and Rural. While the sanitary districts were "abolished" in 1894 with the Local Government Act of 1894 (57&58Vict. c.73), the administration of the "poor" is still maintained in part under the concept of district health boards of Guardians including magistrates and other "Justices of the Peace"; and

(xxi) In 1948, the National Assistance Act (11&12Geo.6 c.29) was introduced and supposed to abolish the Poor Laws. However, many of the most draconian poor law acts were not repealed or abolished as evidenced by the tables of repealed acts that miss key acts, otherwise remaining with full force and effect.

897. In respect of Birth Certificates clearly being derived and dependent upon the history of acts concerning Settlement Certificates of the Poor and the commercial control of Admiralty: _{Birth Certificates and Settlement Certificates}

(i) Any argument, claim, judgment, edict, statement, affidavit that denies the overwhelming prima facie evidence that Birth Certificates are descended from and a variation of Settlement Certificates is therefore irrational, unreasonable and in error and null and void from the beginning; and

(ii) Any public official, or occupant of public office that denies Birth Certificates are derived from Settlement Certificates and the Poor Laws therein is culpable of gross deceptive and misleading conduct.

898. The surrender, return, rejection of a Birth Certificate by definition of the Poor Laws that remain in effect and including the law of _{Surrender or Return of Non-}

Admiralty and Settlement Certificates actually places the individual in greater moral danger, without any sensible advantage: *Ucadia Birth Certificate*

(i) A man or woman who has perfected their own Will and Testament through the prescribed model of *Voluntatem Et Testamentum* is able to demonstrate a far superior claim and position than any official or enforcement officer under the Birth Certificate Regime; and

(ii) Under the model of *Voluntatem Et Testamentum*, the Birth Certificate is irrelevant as all persons are registered within the proper Rolls of the Estate as property of the Estate; and

(iii) It could be reasonably argued that a man or woman who surrenders their Birth Certificate, demonstrates an act of complete incompetence and therefore subjects themselves to greater control as wards, idiots and lunatics.

899. The system of Ucadia Live Borne Records which recognise the full rights of all men and women as equal and higher order beings possessing sacred and immutable rights which can never be abrogated is a superior system to Non-Ucadia Birth Certificates and can never be compared to the slavery system of Birth Certificates and Settlement Certificates. *Live Borne Records and Non-Ucadian Birth Certificates*

Article 217 – Non-Ucadian Original Land Certificate

900. A ***Non-Ucadian Original Land Certificate*** is an instrument issued by a Non-Ucadian government authority, typically a land registry or a similar organisation, that serves as official proof of ownership or title to a specific piece of land or property. However, the underlying assumptions and structure of "land" in many Non-Ucadian jurisdictions continues to be based upon poor and disenfranchised people as "chattel" connected to the land, and thus part of land and possessions of the state or the sovereign. *Non-Ucadian Original Land Certificate*

901. The origin of the word **Chattel** comes from the Latin word *catal/catalla* meaning "cattle; beasts of burden". The term was revived in the late 17th Century in the formation of a new framework of slavery, through the use of fraud, perfidy, tyranny and impiety perpetrated by certain legal, financial and political institutions against their own people. An example includes in 1690 (2W&M S1c5) whereby for unpaid rent, "chattel" could be appraised of its value and then sold, rather than seized. Thus the term "Slavery" in Non-Ucadia jurisdictions was able to be hidden, while the actual practice and controls of slavery were strengthened and refined. *Origin of the word Chattel*

902. Almost all *Non-Ucadian Original Land Certificate Systems* continue *Prohibitive*

to be based on a core set of prohibited, morally repugnant, wicked and evil presumptions concerning poor and disenfranchised persons as "property" and therefore land including, but not limited to:-

Nature of Non-Ucadian Original Land Certificate

(i) To hide the notion of white slavery, and enslavement of the population under the tyranny, especially in England, Scotland, Wales and Ireland, words such as "chattel" meaning literally *cattle* and terms such as *horns unwrought* or "cattle without horns" or *horning* as (enslavement of poor people) were introduced in the late 17th Century; and

(ii) *Real Chattels* in Non-Ucadia jurisdictions actually means the interests of people as animals (cattle), or insolvent debtors, or criminals or slaves leased for years as property by elite and their corporations for profit. Typically the tyrant banking, political or law guild landlord retains "chattel interest" whereby no effectual title passes from the creditor to the debtor, while the creditor retains the right to the "real chattel" of people as slaves that the debtor never had; and

(iii) *Personal Chattels* are the personal items of people as animals (cattle or horns unwrought), or insolvent debtors, or criminals or slaves that may be seized as bounty, prize or profit by those granted such license by the tyrant banking, political or law guild landlord; and

(iv) The words *real property* and *personal property* are now used in Non-Ucadia Jurisdictions in order to hide this awful and evil heritage of people being considered part of the land; and

(v) Consistent with many of the other corruptions of law, Non-Ucadia Jurisdictions continue to deny the underlying truth and wickedness of their land systems, designed to disenfranchise the poor.

Article 218 – Non-Ucadian Sovereign Bond Certificate

903. A ***Non-Ucadian Sovereign Bond Certificate*** is an instrument issued by a Non-Ucadian government authority, typically a treasury or a similar organisation, to raise funds for various public expenditures, including infrastructure projects, social programs, and budget deficits, against the life estates of its citizens or subjects. However, the underlying assumptions and structure of such financial products is based upon the poor mass of people both being property and liable for

Non-Ucadian Sovereign Bond Certificate

the debts of the elite and the wealthy.

904. Almost all *Non-Ucadian Sovereign Bond Certificates* continue to be based on a core set of prohibited, morally repugnant, wicked and evil presumptions concerning persons as property and liable for the debts caused by a few including, but not limited to:- Prohibitive Nature of Non-Ucadian Sovereign Bond Certificate

(i) Similar to Life Annuities, Government Bonds or Sovereign Bonds are "underwritten" by the life estates of its citizens or subjects; and

(ii) Unlike Life Annuities, Government Bonds or Sovereign Bonds also assume that it is the citizens or subjects of a nation that are responsible for the national debts caused by the decisions of a small elite making expenditures on items that the population may not have ever chosen to undertake. Not only is such an assumption absurd, it is the height of corruption.

Article 219 – Non-Ucadian Trustee Savings Bank Certificate

905. A *Non-Ucadian Trustee Savings Bank Certificate* is a derivative instrument issued by a Non-Ucadian government authority, that serves as official proof of ownership or title to a related and specific government land certificate. It was also the term used with the associated "thrift" based accounts opened at the same time in the 19th Century. However, the underlying assumptions and structure of such derivative instruments is based upon people being property and a commodity to be traded. Non-Ucadian Trustee Savings Bank Certificate

906. Trustee Savings Banks and the advent of modern Monetary Systems of Non-Ucadian Countries are deeply interconnected:- Trustee Savings Bank Certificates and Monetary System

(i) Contrary to the perpetual untruth that modern Non-Ucadian currencies or "fiat" are based solely on government declaration of them as "legal tender" and the confidence of the market, most modern Non-Ucadian fiat currencies of advanced economies have a class of derivatives underlying their base value; and

(ii) This class of derivatives, first invented at the beginning of the 19th Century is the notion of Trustee Savings Bank Certificates based on the concept that people at the time who were indebted to this new class of banks, the first being (by default) the Bank of England, could then have the original title for Land Certificates in their names transferred to the ownership of the bank; and

(iii) The nature and activity of this system was obfuscated and hidden largely by the simultaneous launch of "thrift accounts" using the same terminology and concepts. Thus almost no deeper knowledge of the transfer of land certificates to central banks as trustee savings bank certificates is known within most Non-Ucadia Jurisdictions; and

(iv) The continued denials of this class of derivatives and its origins is sufficient proof of the prohibitive nature of this class of instruments.

Article 220 – Non-Ucadian Social Health Certificate

907. A ***Non-Ucadian Social Health Certificate*** is a derivative instrument issued by a Non-Ucadian government authority, that serves as official proof of ownership or title to receive certain free health benefits. It is also used by Non-Ucadian Jurisdictions to justify people who use government health benefits as wards of the state.

Non-Ucadian Social Health Certificate

Article 221 – Non-Ucadian Social Welfare Certificate

908. A ***Non-Ucadian Social Welfare Certificate*** is a derivative instrument issued by a Non-Ucadian government authority, that serves as official proof of entitlement to one or more government benefits. It also assumes since the 1930's that such people who receive such benefits are employees of the government.

Non-Ucadian Social Welfare Certificate

Title VIII – Rights

8.1 – Rights

Article 222 – Rights

909. An authentic ***Right*** is a positively defined Capacity, or Privilege, or Liberty, or Faculty, or Power, or Ownership, or Possession, or Interest, or Benefit and its associated obligation, remedy or relief held in Trust for the benefit of a particular type of named or unnamed Person under proper Law as prescribed by the present Maxims:-

    (i) As a *Capacity*, an authentic Right is a form of plenary authority, or qualification, or legal condition or status that enables a Person to exercise their free will in receiving, holding, using or delegating certain Rights or performing such associated obligations or actions, without restraint or hindrance; and

    (ii) As a *Privilege*, an authentic Right is a form of special (real or personal) Delegation whereby either a Person is freed from the obligations of certain laws; or empowered exclusively to perform certain acts; and

    (iii) As a *Liberty*, an authentic Right is a form of Privilege whereby a Person enjoys some Favour or Benefit subject to their good faith, good conscience and good character; and

    (iv) As a *Faculty*, an authentic Right is a form of special Charism delegated to a Person by Favour, Indulgence or Dispensation that enables a Person to do, or refrain from doing something that would otherwise not be permitted by certain Laws; and

    (v) As a *Power* or Authority, an authentic Right is a form of authority, enforced by Law, that enables a Person to compel one or more other Persons to do or abstain from doing a particular act; and

    (vi) As an *Ownership*, an authentic Right is a form of written possession by registration/recording, whereby a Person is recognised by law to possess the most extensive or higher claim of possession, use and enjoyment (of certain Property), to the exclusion of all other Persons, or of all except one or more specific Persons; and

    (vii) As a *Possession*, an authentic Right is the visible possibility and ability of exercising physical control over some form of Property, coupled with the intention of doing so, to the exclusion of all others, or one or more Persons; and

    (viii) As an *Interest*, an authentic Right denotes a title, or certificate or other proof of claim or advantage to other certain Rights or Property; and

    (ix)   As a *Benefit*, an authentic Right implies a just claim to hold, or use or enjoy certain Property, or convey, or donate or dispose of it, subject to certain obligations of performance.

910. A claimed negative Right is an absurdity and Offence against God and the Divine Creator of all Existence; and an injury of Divine Law itself; and cannot exist under any true system of law.   *No Negative Rights*

911. By their origin, nature and function, a Right is not a valid Right unless it possesses the following twelve characteristics being *Integrity, Trust, Name, Class, Provenance, Exemplification, Subject, Obligation, Subject Person, Obligated Person, Remedy* and *Relief*:-   *Character of Valid Rights*

    (i)   *Integrity* means a valid Right conforms to the most ancient and primitive purpose being to reflect a positively expressed rule, custom, privilege or power with good intentions, good character and good conscience. A negative Right is an absurdity and injury of law itself and is invalid from the beginning; and

    (ii)   *Trust* means a valid Right is expressed in a Trust relation whereby the Right is the Property of the Trust; and

    (iii)   *Name* means that a valid Right is uniquely named compared to all other valid Rights in accord with the principle of the use of the Latin for Non-Ucadian Translation, beginning with the term *Ius* (Jus) for a singular Right or *Iurium* for several Rights bound together by similar character and purpose; and

    (iv)   *Class*, means that the Class of Rights that the valid Right belongs to is clearly identified; and

    (v)   *Provenance*, means that the Right clearly identifies and proves its provenance; and

    (vi)   *Exemplification*, means that signed or sealed and attested evidence exists as to the founding instrument of law that defines the structure and character of the valid Right; and

    (vii)   *Subject*, means that a valid Right clearly identifies the qualities associated with it, including (but not limited to) any and all specific Capacities, or Faculties, or Powers, or Authorities, or Interests, or Privileges or Benefits associated with it; and

    (viii)   *Obligation*, means that a valid Right clearly identifies the obligations associated with it, including (but not limited to) any and all conditions of time, place, performance, dedication, dress, skills, equipment and duty of care; and

(ix) *Subject Person*, means a Person inherent with the Right (as in formation of Person on Roll), or invested with the Right (as Trustee) or entitled to the Right (as named or unnamed Beneficiary); and

(x) *Obligated Person*, means a Person on whom the valid Right imposes some kind of duty or obligation; and

(xi) *Remedy*, means that a valid Right possesses a form of Remedy whereby the Person in whom the Privilege or Power should reside is able to recover such a Right in the event of incapacity, or seizure, or loss or other impediment; and

(xii) *Relief*, means that a valid Right possesses a form of Relief whereby the Person in whom such Duty or Obligation associated with the Right should reside, is able to abdicate, derogate, mitigate or abrogate such responsibilities in the event of incapacity, or impossibility, or unfairness, or unreasonableness, or bad faith, or vexation, or unclean hands, or other breach of trust. An Obligation without the possibility of Relief is morally repugnant and irrefutable proof of the existence of slavery.

912. There shall exist only four (4) possible Classes of Rights being Divine, Natural, Superior and Inferior:- *(Four Classes of Rights)*

(i) "**Divine Rights**" are the primary and original form and source of Rights, corresponding to Divine Trusts and Divine Persons. There exists no higher class, or possible type of Rights. All Rights therefore are inherited from the class of valid Divine Rights; and

(ii) "**Natural Rights**" are be the second highest form of valid Rights of True Trusts and True Persons associated with either the Office of Man or the Office of Woman of a single living being. All Natural Rights are inherited directly from Divine Rights; and

(iii) "**Superior Rights**" are the third class and third highest possible form of valid Rights of aggregate bodies, associations, societies, orders, fraternities, bodies and companies corresponding with Superior Trusts and Superior Persons. All Superior Rights are inherited directly from Divine Rights or Natural Rights. All Rights of valid Ucadia Members, Ucadia Societies and associated bodies, aggregates, societies, associations, communities and unions of two (2) or more people are inherited from the class of Superior Rights; and

(iv) **"Inferior Rights"** are the fourth class and the lowest possible form of valid Rights and owe their existence to non-Ucadian societies, persons, corporations, associations, bodies politic, agencies or aggregates. All Inferior Rights are inferior to Superior Rights. Where an Inferior Right makes claim to being superior, it is automatically invalid upon such falsity.

913. There exists only twelve (12) Sub-Classes of Rights being: Perfect, Imperfect, Absolute, Relative, Superior, Ecclesiastical, Sovereign, Official, Administrative, Member, Primary and Secondary:- *[Twelve Sub-Classes of Rights]*

(i) **"Perfect Divine Rights"** (*Perfectum Divinum Iurium*), is a sub-class of Divine Rights whereby such valid Rights are created, defined and donated to a Divine Person by the Divine Creator through the most sacred Covenant *Pactum De Singularis Caelum*. Perfect Divine Rights are Peremptory, Permanent, Eternal, Immutable and Indefeasible; and once bestowed are not subject to any form or condition of waiver, abandonment, conveyance, surrender, disqualification, incapacitation, seizure, capture, arrest, resignation, alienation, suspension, suppression, forfeiture or abrogation. Perfect Divine Rights are therefore the highest possible form of Rights and there exists no higher class, or form, or possible type of Rights. Perfect Divine Rights may be further defined as Perfect Fundamental Divine Rights or Perfect Sacramental Divine Rights; and

(ii) **"Imperfect Divine Rights"** (*Imperfectum Divinum Iurium*), is a sub-class of Divine Rights whereby such valid Rights are created, defined and delegated to a Divine Person by the Divine Creator through the most sacred Covenant *Pactum De Singularis Caelum* upon acceptance of the associated obligations and duties attached to them. If any such conditions and obligations are breached or repudiated, then the relevant Imperfect Divine Right is instantly waived, surrendered, suspended, forfeited or revoked until such time as the fundamental breach of duty and obligation is repaired or such a Right is duly restored. Imperfect Divine Rights may be further defined as Imperfect Instrumental Divine Rights or Imperfect Intentional Divine Rights; and

(iii) **"Absolute Natural Rights"** (*Absolutum Naturae Iurium*), is a sub-class of Natural Rights whereby such valid Rights are created, defined and deposited to a Natural (True) Person by the existence of the one true Universe and all Rule and all Matter in accord with the Rule of Law through the most sacred Covenant *Pactum De Singularis Caelum*. Absolute Natural Rights are Peremptory, Permanent, Immutable and Indefeasible and once bestowed are not subject to any form or condition of waiver, abandonment, conveyance, surrender, disqualification, incapacitation, seizure, capture, arrest, resignation, alienation, suspension, suppression, forfeiture or abrogation. Absolute Natural Rights are therefore the highest possible form of Natural Rights. Absolute Natural Rights may be further defined as Absolute Elemental Natural Rights or Absolute Testamental Natural Rights; and

(iv) **"Relative Natural Rights"** (*Relativum Naturae Iurium*), is a sub-class of Natural Rights whereby such valid Rights are created, defined and granted to a Natural (True) Person by the existence of the one true Universe and all Rule and all Matter in accord with the Rule of Law through the most sacred Covenant *Pactum De Singularis Caelum* upon acceptance of the associated obligations and duties attached to them. If any such conditions and obligations are breached or repudiated, then the relevant Relative Natural Right may be waived, surrendered, suspended, abandoned, resigned, disqualified, seized, captured, arrested, alienated, suppressed, forfeited or annulled until such time as the fundamental breach of duty and obligation is repaired or such a Right is duly restored. A True Person to whom a Relative Natural Right has been bestowed may also lawfully delegate or confer beneficial title of such a Right to another True Person such as a Ucadia association, body politic, society, company or community. However, such an aggregate person can never legitimately claim legal title over a Relative Natural Right and any such claim is automatically false and null and void, having no force or effect. Relative Natural Rights may be further defined as Relative Delegable Natural Rights or Relative Conferrable Natural Rights; and

(v) **"Superior Person Rights"** (*Superioris Iurium Personae*), is a sub-class of Superior Rights whereby such valid Rights are created, defined and bestowed to a Superior Person by the existence of a valid Superior Person, or aggregate person, or community, or body politic, or association in accord with the Rule of Law through the most sacred Covenant *Pactum De Singularis Caelum*. Universal Superior Rights are Peremptory, Permanent, Immutable and Indefeasible and once bestowed are not subject to any form or condition of waiver, abandonment, surrender, disqualification, incapacitation, seizure, capture, arrest, resignation, alienation, suspension, suppression, forfeiture or abrogation. Superior Personal Rights are therefore the highest possible form of Superior Rights of any society or aggregate person within the temporal realm; and

(vi) **"Ecclesiastical Rights"** (*Iurium Ecclesiae*), is a sub-class of Superior Rights associated with a valid Ucadia Ecclesia such as One Christ, One Islam, One Spirit and Ucadia itself. All valid and legitimate Ecclesiastical Rights are derived from Divine Rights. Ecclesiastical Rights are the highest possible rights of any aggregate body, society, fraternity, association or company of two (2) or more people. There exists eight (8) categories of one hundred and thirty-two (132) Superior Rights within the sub class of Ecclesiastical Rights, being: Authoritative (22), Instrumental (22), Sacramental (33), Writs (11), Bills (11), Dogma (11), Decrees (11) and Notices (11); and

(vii) **"Sovereign Rights"** (*Iurium Regnum*), is a sub-class of Superior Rights associated with the embodiment of the sovereign authority of a valid Ucadia society such as a Campus, or Province, or University or Union. All Sovereign Rights are derived from Ecclesiastical Rights and a Sovereign can never claim to be higher than Ecclesiastical Rights. There exists six categories of seventy-seven (77) Superior Rights within the sub class of Sovereign Rights, being: Authoritative (11), Instrumental (22), Writs (11), Bills (11), Decrees (11) and Notices (11); and

(viii) **"Official Rights"** (*Iurium Publicum*), is a sub-class of Superior Rights associated with an Officer empowered to Office within a valid Ucadia society such as a Campus, or Province, or University or Union. All Official Rights are derived from Sovereign Rights and Official Rights can never be claimed to be higher than Sovereign Rights. There exists six categories of eighty-eight (88) Superior Rights within the sub-class of Official Rights, being: Authoritative (11), Instrumental (33), Warrants (11), Complaints (11), Orders (11) and Notices (11); and

(ix) **"Administrative Rights"** (*Iurium Administrationis*), is a sub-class of Superior Rights associated with an executive and administrative bodies of a valid Ucadia society such as a Campus, or Province, or University or Union. All

Administrative Rights are derived from either Sovereign Rights or Official Rights; and an Administrative Right can never claim to be higher than Official Rights. There exists two categories of forty-four (44) Superior Rights within the sub-class of Administrative Rights, being: Authoritative (11) and Instrumental (33); and

(x) "**Member Rights**" (*Iurium Membrum*), is a sub-class of Superior Rights associated with a Member of a valid Ucadia society, body or aggregate; and

(xi) "**Primary Rights**", also known as Primary Inferior Rights, is a sub-class of Inferior Rights whereby such Rights are created, defined and bestowed to an Inferior (Legal) Person by a non-Ucadian aggregate person, or community, or body politic, or association. Primary Inferior Rights are frequently claimed and created without reference to rights already existing or proving such provenance to Divine Rights. Therefore, Primary Inferior Rights are equivalent to either Claims or false and unsubstantiated Demands. Primary Inferior Rights are therefore the second lowest possible form of rights of any society or aggregate person within the temporal realm. Primary Inferior Rights may be further defined as Primary Personal Inferior Rights or Primary Public Inferior Rights; and

(xii) "**Secondary Rights**", also known as Secondary Inferior Rights, is a sub-class of Inferior Rights whereby such valid Rights are created, defined and delegated to an Inferior (Legal) Person by the existence of a non-Ucadian aggregate person, or community, or body politic, or association upon acceptance of the associated obligations and duties attached to them. If any such conditions and obligations are breached or repudiated, then the relevant Secondary Inferior Right may be waived, surrendered, suspended, abandoned, resigned, disqualified, seized, captured, arrested, rescinded, suppressed, forfeited or revoked. Secondary Inferior Rights are therefore the lowest possible form of rights of any society or aggregate person within the temporal realm. Secondary Inferior Rights may be further defined as Secondary Protective Inferior Rights or Secondary Remedial Inferior Rights.

Article 223 – Divine Rights

914. One hundred and fifty-four (154) ***Divinum Iurium (Divine Rights)*** of Heaven are the primary and original form of Rights, corresponding to Divine Trusts, Divine Estates and Divine Persons. There shall exist no higher class, or possible type of Rights. All valid Rights therefore are sourced and inherited from the class of valid Divine Rights.

    Divine Rights (Divinum Iurium)

915. There exists two (2) sub-classes (Perfect and Imperfect) of Divine Rights, each possessing seventy-seven (77) Rights; and nine (9) categories being: Foundational (22), Instrumental (22), Sacramental (33), Authoritative (22), Divine Writs (11), Divine Bills (11), Divine Dogma (11), Divine Decrees (11), and Divine Notices (11):-

    Divine Rights Classes

    (i) **"Foundational Divine Rights"** (*Fundationis Divinum Iurium*) are Perfect Divine Rights considered elemental and fundamental to the existence, operation and function of all other rights; and

    (ii) **"Instrumental Divine Rights"** (*Instrumentalis Divinum Iurium*) are Perfect Divine Rights essential to the proper operation of the rule of law, justice and fair process; and

    (iii) **"Sacramental Divine Rights"** (*Sacramentum Divinum Iurium*) are Perfect Divine Rights associated with one of the thirty-three (33) Divine Sacraments; and

    (iv) **"Authoritative Divine Rights"** (*Potentis Divinum Iurium*) are Imperfect Divine Rights associated with core authoritative powers from Heaven to Earth; and

    (v) **"Divine Writs of Rights"** (*Recto Divinum Iurium*) are Imperfect Divine Rights associated with the one, true and only valid forms of Original Entry and Original Action; and

    (vi) **"Divine Bills of Exception"** (*Rogatio Divinum Iurium*) are Imperfect Divine Rights associated with the one, true and only valid forms of Bills of Exception, Citation and Moratorium; and

    (vii) **"Divine Dogma"** (*Summa Dogma Divinum Iurium*) are Imperfect Divine Rights associated with the promulgation of authoritative principles, decrees and doctrines of Ucadia, Heaven and Earth; and

    (viii) **"Divine Decrees"** (*Decretum Divinum Iurium*) are Imperfect Divine Rights associated with Divine Decrees concerning the administration, conduct and enforcement of law and order; and

(ix) **"Divine Notices"** (*Notitiae Divinum Iurium*) are Imperfect Divine Rights associated with Divine Notices issued, executed, patented, promulgated and services in the proper administration, conduct and enforcement of law and order.

Article 224 – Natural Rights

916. Eighty-eight (88) Natural Rights (*Naturae Iurium*) of each and every Living Member and Higher Order Life form of One Heaven shall be the second highest form of valid Rights, corresponding to True Trusts and True Persons; and owe their existence and provenance to the existence of Divine Rights. All valid Natural Rights therefore are inherited from valid Divine Rights.

Natural Rights (Naturae Iurium)

917. All Natural Rights as *Fiducial Rights* are delegated to the safe custody and wise guardian powers of the Oratorium, also known as the Supreme Court of One Heaven; and all valid and legitimate lesser competent forums of law, as defined by Article 59 (Oratorium) of the most sacred Covenant *Pactum De Singularis Caelum*. There exists two sub-classes (Absolute and Relative), each possessing forty-four (44) Rights; and seven (7) categories being: Essential (11), Universal (11), Volitional (11), Testamental (22), Domicile (11), Habitational (11) and Actionable (11):-

Natural Rights Categories

(i) **"Essential Natural Rights"** (*Essentialis Naturae Iurium*) are Absolute Natural Rights considered vital and essential to the physical existence and survival of a Living Member and Higher Order Life form of One Heaven; and

(ii) **"Universal Natural Rights"** (*Universus Naturae Iurium*), are Relative Natural Rights associated with the respect, preservation, restoration and management of natural systems, planets, ecosystems, wilderness, natural habitats, animals, water and land, including the proper treatment of animals and the limits and conditions of custody of animals and any associated commerce; and

(iii) **"Volitional Natural Rights"** (*Volitio Naturae Iurium*) are Absolute Natural Rights associated with the mind, will and intentions of a Living Member; and

(iv) **"Testamental Natural Rights"** (*Testamentum Naturae Iurium*) are Absolute Natural Rights associated with the expression of the mind, will and intentions of a Living

Member, especially with other Living Members; and

(v) **"Domicile Natural Rights"** (*Domicilium Naturae Iurium*), also known as the Rights of Lodgings, are Relative Natural Rights associated with the domicile, home and primary household and family unit in relation to a Living Member in the Office of Man or Office of Woman. As Relative Natural Rights, such Rights may be conferred in trust to a Superior body, association, body politic, society or community to manage such rights under the Golden Rule of Law for the benefit of all Members; and

(vi) **"Habitational Natural Rights"** (*Habitatus Naturae Iurium*), also known as the Rights of Land, are Relative Natural Rights associated with the habitat and environment of a Living Member in the Office of Man or Office of Woman. As Relative Natural Rights, such Rights may be conferred in trust to a Superior body, association, body politic, society or community to manage such rights under the Golden Rule of Law for the benefit of all Members; and

(vii) **"Actionable Natural Rights"** (*Actionis Naturae Iurium*), also known as the Rights of Labour, are Relative Natural Rights associated with the energy, effort and productive work of a Living Member in the Office of Man or Office of Woman. As Relative Natural Rights, such Rights may be conferred in trust to a Superior body, association, body politic, society or community to manage such rights under the Golden Rule of Law for the benefit of all Members.

Article 225 – Superior Rights

918. Superior Rights are the third class and third highest possible form of valid Rights; corresponding to Superior Trusts and Superior Persons associated with a Ucadia society. Whereas Divine Rights pertain to Heaven and Natural Rights relate to a living higher order life form, Superior Rights align to one or more civilised societies operating under the Golden Rule of Law in accord with the most sacred Covenant *Pactum De Singularis Caelum*. Superior Rights owe their existence and provenance to either valid Divine Rights or valid Natural Rights. All Superior Rights are greater than Inferior Rights. — Superior Rights (Superioris Iurium)

919. All Rights of valid Ucadia Members, Ucadia Societies and associated bodies, aggregates, societies, associations, communities and unions of two (2) or more people are inherited from the class of Superior Rights. There exists (6) six sub-classes of four hundred and twenty- — Superior Rights (Superioris Iurium)

four (424) Superior Rights, being: Personal (44), Ecclesiastical (132), Sovereign (77), Official (88), Administrative (44) and Member (39):

(i) **"Personal Rights"** (*Superioris Iurium Personae*) are Superior Rights associated with Superior Persons and all Superior Ucadia Trusts and Superior Ucadia Estates. All Personal Rights are delegated to the safe custody and wise guardian powers of the legitimate and valid supreme competent forums of law of the Ucadia Unions and all lesser Ucadia bodies politic such as Universities, Provinces and Campuses as the embodiment of judicial authority; and as defined by Article 59 (Oratorium) of the most sacred Covenant *Pactum De Singularis Caelum*; and

(ii) **"Ecclesiastical Rights"** (*Iurium Ecclesiae*) are Superior Rights permanently vested unto the four valid and legitimate Ucadia faiths being One Christ, One Islam, One Spirit and Ucadia itself; and

(iii) **"Sovereign Rights"** (*Iurium Regnum*) are Superior Rights permanently vested unto the governing bodies of the Ucadia Unions and all lesser Ucadia bodies politic such as Universities, Provinces and Campuses as the embodiment of sovereign authority; and

(iv) **"Official Rights"** (*Iurium Publicum*) are Superior Rights permanently vested unto the duly elected and invested Officers of the Ucadia Unions and all lesser Ucadia bodies politic such as Universities, Provinces and Campuses as the embodiment of fiduciary authority; and

(v) **"Administrative Rights"** (*Iurium Administrationis*) are permanently vested unto the executive bodies of the Ucadia Unions and all lesser Ucadia bodies politic such as Universities, Provinces and Campuses as the embodiment of administrative authority; and

(vi) **"Member Rights"** (*Iurium Membrum*) are Superior Rights permanently vested unto the members of the Ucadia Unions and all lesser Ucadia bodies politic such as Universities, Provinces and Campuses as the embodiment of member authority.

Article 226 – Inferior Rights

920. Inferior Rights are the fourth class and the lowest possible form of Rights corresponding to Inferior Trusts, Inferior Estates and Inferior Persons, such as Non-Ucadian Trusts and Non-Ucadian Persons. Inferior Rights owe their existence to non-Ucadian societies, persons, corporations, associations, bodies politic, agencies or aggregates. *Inferior Rights*

921. All Superior Rights are greater than Inferior Rights. Where an Inferior Right makes claim to being superior, it is automatically invalid upon such falsity. *Inferior Rights in relation to Superior Rights*

922. There exists two (2) sub-classes (Primary and Secondary) and four (4) categories of Inferior Rights, being: Primary Personal, Primary Public, Secondary Protective and Secondary Remedial: *Inferior Rights Catergories*

    (i)   A **"Primary Personal Inferior Right"** shall be an Inferior Right associated as a capacity, or privilege, or liberty, or faculty, or power possessed by a certain class of persons or specifically named person, where such claimed rights have been created without necessarily referencing valid rights already existing; and

    (ii)   A **"Primary Public Inferior Right"** shall be an Inferior Right associated with those rights held by the community in general, or by virtue of relations between members of the community, where such claimed rights have been created without necessarily referencing valid rights already existing; and

    (iii)   A **"Secondary Protective Inferior Right"** shall be an Inferior Right associated with a Primary Inferior Right that is claimed to exist in order to prevent the infringement or loss of such Primary Inferior Rights; and

    (iv)   A **"Secondary Remedial Inferior Right"** shall be an Inferior Right associated with a Primary Inferior Right that is claimed to exist in order to obtain restitution for any losses incurred upon one or more breaches of claimed Primary Inferior Rights or the enforcement of performance of one or more Primary Inferior Rights.

923. **"Primary Personal Inferior Rights"** are Inferior Rights associated as a capacity, or privilege, or liberty, or faculty, or power possessed by a certain class of persons or specifically named person, where such claimed rights have been created without necessarily referencing valid rights already existing. *Primary Personal Inferior Rights*

As such claimed rights (1) fail to provide any valid provenance to valid Divine Rights; and (2) fail to properly articulate their legitimacy and function in relation to other pre-existing claimed inferior rights; and (3) owe their existence to non-Ucadian societies, persons, corporations, associations, bodies politic, agencies or aggregates; then all such claimed rights are not properly rights, or enforceable rights, but merely claims of right.

924. **"Primary Public Inferior Rights"** are Inferior Rights associated with those rights held by the community in general, or by virtue of relations between members of the community, where such claimed rights have been created without necessarily referencing valid rights already existing.

Primary Public Inferior Rights

As such claimed rights (1) fail to provide any valid provenance to valid Divine Rights; and (2) fail to properly articulate their legitimacy and function in relation to other pre-existing claimed inferior rights; and (3) owe their existence to non-Ucadian societies, persons, corporations, associations, bodies politic, agencies or aggregates; then all such claimed rights are not properly rights, or enforceable rights, but merely claims of right.

925. **"Secondary Protective Inferior Rights"** are Inferior Rights associated with Primary Inferior Rights where it is claimed they exist in order to prevent the infringement or loss of such Primary Inferior Rights.

Secondary Protective Inferior Rights

As such claimed secondary inferior rights (1) owe their existence and claimed legitimacy to primary inferior rights; and (2) such claimed primary inferior rights are not properly rights, or enforceable rights, but merely claims of right; then all secondary protective inferior rights are *ipso facto* (as a matter of fact) illegitimate, having no proper force or effect under any valid form of law.

926. **"Secondary Remedial Inferior Rights"** are Inferior Rights associated with Primary Inferior Rights where it is claimed they exist in order to obtain restitution for any losses incurred upon one or more breaches of claimed Primary Inferior Rights or the enforcement of performance of one or more Primary Inferior Rights.

Secondary Remedial Inferior Rights

As such claimed secondary inferior rights (1) owe their existence and claimed legitimacy to primary inferior rights; and (2) such claimed primary inferior rights are not properly rights, or enforceable rights, but merely claims of right; then all secondary protective inferior rights are *ipso facto* (as a matter of fact) illegitimate, having no proper force or effect under any valid form of law.

Article 227 – Invalid Rights

927. An ***Invalid Right*** or False Right is any form that asserts to be a valid Right yet contradicts or violates one or more of the criteria of the present sacred Maxims. *Invalid Rights*

928. An Invalid Right or False Right has no force or effect from the moment it is asserted, or recorded; and regardless of whether a Non-Ucadian Jurisdiction acknowledges such a claim is invalid or not. *Invalid Rights have no effect*

Article 228 – Prohibited Rights

929. A ***Prohibited Right*** is a False Right and Invalid Right that asserts one or more of the following self-evident false arguments and is therefore automatically null and void having no force or effect ecclesiastically, lawfully or legally:- *Prohibited Rights*

(i) Any right that cannot demonstrate its ultimate provenance back to a valid Divine Right as defined within the sacred Covenant *Pactum de Singularis Caelum*; or

(ii) Any right that asserts immunity from the law from which the Right is inherited; or

(iii) Any right that asserts immunity from the duties or obligations granted with such a Right; or

(iv) Any right that asserts a man or woman may be classified, determined or treated as a Thing; or

(v) Any right that asserts by virtue of birth of flesh or blood a man or woman is superior to another; or

(vi) Any right that asserts the right to create secret laws or rights unknown to the public; or

(vii) Any right that is expressed in the negative or as a negative power; or

(viii) Any right that asserts a man or woman may be considered guilty or liable before an accusation is proven; or

(ix) Any right that asserts an officer or agent holding such office or position in trust may ecclesiastically, lawfully and legally give false testimony or deliberately false and misleading information; or

(x) Any right that asserts the right to suspend the operation of the proper Rule of Law, Due Process and Justice to obtain an advantage for or against another; or

(xi) Any right that asserts the right for a man or woman to occupy the position of a justice of the peace, or judge or magistrate and act in such capacity without any effective oath of office; or

(xii) Any right that asserts the right for a man or woman claiming to be a justice of the peace, or judge or magistrate to hear and adjudicate a matter of law with unclean hands, in bad faith and with prejudice; or

(xiii) Any right that asserts the right to treat a financial or equitable advantage obtained by fraud as lawful and legal; or

(xiv) Any right that asserts the rights of another can be waived, surrendered, suspended, abandoned, resigned, disqualified, seized, captured, arrested, alienated, suppressed, forfeited or annulled without proper Rule of Law and Due Process of Justice; or

(xv) Any right that asserts the right to use, or claim or register the name Ucadia or any derivation, mark, symbol, icon, version or image thereof contrary to the manner prescribed by the most sacred Covenant *Pactum De Singularis Caelum* and associated Charters; or

(xvi) Any right that asserts the right to disavow, repudiate, contradict or injure some or all of the most sacred Covenant *Pactum De Singularis Caelum* and associated Charters.

8.2 – Rights Creation, Identification, Assertion & Modification
Article 229 – Rights Creation, Assertion & Modification

930. The valid Creation, Identification and Modification of any Right is always under the proper Rule of Law through Justice in accord with the present sacred Maxims. Just as a valid Positive Law cannot create or change a Natural Law; and a valid Natural Law cannot create or change a Divine Law, no Right can be created or altered from what is already stated in accord with the most sacred law and Covenant *Pactum De Singularis Caelum*. — Rights Creation, Identification & Modification

931. There exists six (6) forms of action whereby a valid Right may be asserted being Record, Notice, Writ, Bill, Claim and Petition:- — Forms of Action

(i) *Record* is the written account of a valid Right, preserved in writing as evidence, usually within a specified ledger of records known as a Register. The ownership of the Register may be evidence of any legal title, while the production of any receipt or certificate from such a register may represent evidence of equitable title; and

(ii) *Notice* is the assertion of a valid Right by means of service of formal process by which a party is made aware of any formal legal matter that may affect certain Rights as well as the form of document used to transmit such facts. The primary types of notices being public (legal), actual, constructive and implied; and

(iii) *Writ* is the pro-active assertion of a valid Right through the issuance of a formal instrument of demand and grant of authority to one or more agents commanding certain acts to be performed whilst granting the agents(s) limited protection from liability or responsibility for any injury or claim; and

(iv) *Bill* is the re-active assertion of a valid Right through the issuance of a formal bill of exception, also known as bill of rights against the injury of one or more rights, demanding compensation and an end to further injury; and

(v) *Claim* is the assertion of a valid Right through a challenge within a competent forum of law against another party regarding the possession or ownership of some property or thing withheld from the possession of the claimant; and

(vi) *Petition* is the assertion of a valid Right through a petition and prayer to the highest sovereign authority within a society which claims recognition of Rule of Law and Justice to recover the possession or ownership of some property or thing withheld from the possession of the petitioner by an officer or agent of the same sovereign authority (such as government).

Article 230 – Heir

932. An ***Heir*** is a Beneficiary recognised by a higher estate to possess a prior Right to a lesser estate, unless excluded by Will. — Heir

933. Where a higher estate permits Heirs, the general principle of inheritance means that the property, titles, debts and obligations of a lesser estate may be passed to the eldest next of kin upon the death of the decedent, excluding the existence of a will. This is usually called the Line of Succession and is of particular importance in those higher estates still permitting a Sovereign Heir. — Principle of Inheritance

934. Where a higher estate does not permit Heirs and therefore Title of Nobility, the absence of a Will does not mean that the lesser estate is automatically inherited by next of kin but that the higher estate may reclaim all rights under "intestate" and determine what rights shall be awarded to any next of kin, if any. Estates such as the United States expressly forbids title of nobility and therefore heirs within their deed — Exclusion of Heirs

and will.

935. The concept of Heir is equivalent to the concept of Title of Nobility. An Heir is always a Person with beneficial entitlement to an estate also holding right of use of one or more honorifics denoting the size of the estate and therefore the standing of the Heir. Thus a Sovereign traditionally denotes the holding of the largest kind of estate, while titles of nobility such as Earl, Baron, Lord indicate successively smaller estates within the estate of the Sovereign. *(Tradition of Nobility and Heirs)*

936. A Will can never name an Heir, only Beneficiaries. In a higher estate that permits the existence of Heirs, the existence of a Will implies the disenfranchisement of one or more rights to an Heir. *(Wills can only name Beneficiaries not Heirs)*

937. When a person takes as heir at law they do so by descent, but when he acquires title by his own act of agreement he is a purchaser. *(Law of Descent)*

938. An Heir always remains a Beneficiary with any rights of property limited by the Executors and Administrators of the higher estate. *(Heir as beneficiary of higher estate)*

939. A Person who murders another to obtain the status of Heir is automatically rendered ineligible to succeed, regardless of any clause, term or caveat in any will or statute to the contrary. *(Loss of Right)*

Article 231 – Owner

940. An ***Owner*** is a Person who holds the rightful claim in Good Faith, Good Conscience and Good Action to a Form or title to Property. As a Person is a fiction, it cannot "own" objects and concepts, only other fictions in accordance with Positive Law. *(Owner)*

941. Natural Law objects and concepts cannot "own" one another only themselves. The Divine Creator, also known as Unique Collective Awareness, is the only true "owner" of objects and concepts. Men and women may claim Right of Use of objects and concepts by succession of Divine Rights beginning with the legitimate trustees and administrators on behalf of the Divine as ultimate Executor. *(Ultimate Owner)*

942. A member of the Homo Sapien species can never be attributed the Form of a Good. Any law, precept or decree that attributes the Notion of a Good to one or more members of the Homo Sapien species is automatically null and void from the beginning. *(Ownership of Human Beings)*

943. When original Form owing its existence to the rightful claim of ownership of the Divine Creator is lawfully conveyed into Trust this is called Realty, or Real Property representing the highest Right of Use above all other claims of right and title. *(Real Property)*

944. In accordance with the will of the Divine Creator, the Exordium of the *(Conveyance of Ownership)*

sacred Covenant *Pactum De Singularis Caelum* and the seven (7) sacred pronouncements of Ucadia, all objects, concepts and all awareness are lawfully expressed into the Trust administered by Ucadia for the benefit of all men, women, higher order beings, animals and life forms living and deceased now and forever more.

945. In accordance with the Exordium of the sacred Covenant *Pactum De Singularis Caelum* and the seven (7) sacred pronouncements of Ucadia, any and all claims of ownership, conveyance, Trust that are not in accord with these Maxims and the will of the Divine Creator are henceforth null, void from the beginning, consistent with the notice of unlawful conveyance.

Highest Right of Ownership

Article 232 – Holder

946. A **Holder** is a person who possesses a document in Good Faith, Good Conscience and Good Action of an original instrument or facsimile and is presumed to consent as surety to any associated obligations implied by the instrument, and therefore abide by the rules by which the instrument was issued, unless such surety is otherwise qualified.

Holder

947. When the rightful owner of certain property is also a holder of an instrument, then such possession of the document also represents their proof of ownership, consent and agreement to the validity of the rules by which the instrument was issued, as well as surety to any associated obligations, without physical need to demonstrate possession.

Title Holder

948. A person who comes to possess an instrument in Bad Faith, or Bad Conscience or by a Bad Action is not a valid holder, nor may they claim any Rights or Benefits derived from possessing such an instrument. Instead, they may be criminally liable by virtue of unlawful possession of the instrument itself.

False Possession of Instrument

949. The issue or record of issuing a document to a person does not imply a person is a holder. Nor does the presence of a particular document in close proximity to a person mean they are a holder. It is only when a person touches and "holds" a document in the presence of others do they become a holder.

Possession as Holder

950. The presumption of surety of a holder cannot be proven in law until a person confirms in the presence of at least two witnesses they are the holder. The absence of disclosure and knowledge to a holder of the obligations for which they have consented constitutes an act of deception and fraud.

Witness and Holder

951. It is immaterial whether a person holds an original or a facsimile of

an instrument to be a holder.

952. As a holder implies acceptance of all associated obligations, a person has the right to qualify their consent by claiming to be only a Holder in Due Course. A Holder in Due Course is a Holder that accepts their surety and consent for any obligations and performance due over the time an instrument is in their possession, but rejects any implied consent for surety for any potential misdeeds or errors by one or more previous holders.

Original document and Holder Holder in Due Course

953. A person that does not affirm their position as a Holder in Due Course is assumed to accept the full obligations, responsibilities as well as any rights if owner of the property.

Holder Obligations

954. The assertion of a person to be a Holder in Due Course has no effect in diminishing any acceptance and surety of obligations and performance due during their time as holder. Nor does the assertion have any effect if the person is the first Holder of the Instrument and user of the Property.

Supreme Goods ineligible for commerce

955. A person who asserts their right to be known as a Holder in Due Course cannot be lawfully held liable for the misdeeds of previous holders. However, as the person is still a holder, they continue to consent and agree to the validity of the rules by which the instrument was issued.

Holder Obligation

956. A person who does not physically hold or possess an instrument or who openly rejects consent as surety in the presence of two or more witnesses cannot be held liable for any associated obligations and performance implied by the particular instrument alone, nor any conditions of the rules by which the instrument was issued.

Limits of Obligation

957. The rejection of consent as holder or the absence of possession of an instrument does not excuse the obligations and performance of a person as a lawful owner or user of the particular property.

User Obligation

958. A lawful owner or holder that rejects the rules by which the instrument they hold was issued is by definition in dishonour and delinquent to the terms by which such an instrument is held and used.

Owner Obligation

Article 233 – Claimant

959. A ***Claim*** is the oral or written assertion in Good Faith, Good Conscience and Good Action of a valid Right through a challenge within a competent forum of law against another party regarding the possession or ownership of some property or thing withheld from the

Claimant

possession of the claimant.

960. There is no such thing in Law as a valid Claim made in Bad Faith, or Bad Conscience or by Bad Action. Instead, the creation and filing of an alleged Claim made in Bad Faith, or Bad Conscience or Bad Action is proof of fraud and criminal culpability in and of itself. — *No Claim in Bad Faith*

961. The term Claim originates from the Latin term *clamare* meaning "to shout or cry out or call upon (justice)". Hence a valid Claim can only be made by testimony through one of four methods: — *Origin of term*

(i) A testimony spoken under oath at a sacred place before at least two other credible witnesses and faithfully transcribed as spoken; or

(ii) A written deposition under oath known as an "affidavit" then witnessed by at least two other credible witnesses at a sacred place; or

(iii) Within English Commercial (Common) Law, a sworn testimony taken in a competent forum of law under the authority of a justice of the peace; or

(iv) Within English Commercial (Common) Law, a sworn written deposition known as an "affidavit" taken under the authority of a given statute concerning oaths, then witnessed by a justice of the peace.

962. The validity of a Claim is the validity of the oral argument, constituting two main parts, firstly the formal protest of a challenge of Rights also known as the "wrong" and secondly the assertion of such Rights or pronouncement of new Rights also known as the "remedy". It is insufficient for any Claim to vocalise a wrong without a valid remedy. Similarly, no remedy has validity without first vocalising a wrong. — *Validity of Claim*

963. A valid Claim in Good Faith, Good Conscience and Good Action is also known as a Cause of Action. The Claim is the vocalization of a formal protest and pronouncement itself. Any associated documents are any Affidavits and Annexures or some other evidence dependent upon its perfection. Taken together they may correctly be called a Statement of Claim or an Affirmation of Claim. — *Cause of Action*

964. In respect of the elements of a Claim filed as a Cause of Action:- — *Principles of Claim*

(i) A claim can be satisfied only through rebuttal by counter-affidavit point-for-point, resolution by jury, or payment; and

(ii) A presumption of a claim in accordance with these Maxims will stand good until the contrary is proved; and

(iii) If the plaintiff does not prove his case, the defendant is absolved; and

(iv) Documents alone without any evidence of the vocalized claim can never be considered a valid Claim. However, documents may be presented first to pronounce the intention to Claim at some appointed time and place before a competent authority and witnesses; and

(v) Form of action is immaterial to the validity and substance of a claim unless by consent a person agrees to hear their claim according to the normal rules of form and action of a particular society.

965. When in accordance with these Maxims, a Person who is first in time has the prior right of claim. *(Prior Right)*

Article 234 – Assertion

966. ***Assertion*** in the context of Rights refers to a statement or declaration made in Good Faith, Good Conscience and Good Action by a person or a party in a legal proceeding concerning one or more Rights. A Claim is constructed from one or more Assertions and associated Evidence. *(Assertion)*

Article 235 – Registration

967. ***Registration*** refers to the act of officially recording certain information, documents, or assets with a relevant government authority, agency, or registrar in Good Faith, Good Conscience and Good Action. This process is usually necessary to establish legally enforceable rights, provide notice to the public, or ensure compliance with specific laws and regulations. *(Registration)*

968. There is no such thing in Law as a valid Registration made in Bad Faith, or Bad Conscience or by Bad Action. Instead, the creation and entering of a record in a Register made in Bad Faith, or Bad Conscience or Bad Action is proof of fraud and criminal culpability in and of itself. *(No Registration in Bad Faith)*

969. A Title is a both a valid inscription or entry into the Asset Register of a Trust and a certificate or notice of proof of such entry and therefore claim of Right of Ownership. The word 'Title' is derived from the Latin word titulus meaning 'inscription, label and notice (of entry) into a tabulae' with the Latin word 'tabulae' literally meaning register. It was most commonly used in the context of a register of slaves. The Latin word for a registrar is '*tabularius*'. *(Title)*

970. Two main forms of Title for the Same Property may exist in the Asset Register of a Trust, being Legal Title and Equitable Title: *Legal Title and Equitable Title*

   (i) Legal Title refers to Rights of Ownership, usually held by the Trustee of the Executor of the Trust.; and

   (ii) Equitable Title refers to the Rights of Use, usually held by the Beneficiary, Leaseholder or Tenant of Property of the Trust. While the word "Owner" is used with Equitable Title, it merely refers to the Title and not the Property of the Trust.

Article 236 – Reservation

971. The **Reservation** of Rights is a formal process associated with the Assertion in Good Faith, Good Conscience and Good Actions of one or more Rights by Notice whereby the instruments transmitted make explicit the reservation of certain Rights. *Reservation*

972. There is no such thing in Law as a valid Reservation of Rights made in Bad Faith, or Bad Conscience or by Bad Action. Instead, the creation, statement or notice of a Reservation of Rights made in Bad Faith, or Bad Conscience or Bad Action is proof of fraud and criminal culpability in and of itself, with such a false Reservation having no force or effect in Law. *No Reservation in Bad Faith*

973. The presence of such an explicit statement concerning the reservation of certain valid and legitimate Rights therefore prevents the recipient of such instruments from claiming any Rights themselves to violate, seize, suspend, disqualify, enclose, capture, arrest, alienate, securitise, suppress, forfeit or annul any of the Rights reserved including but not limited to any Rights expressed or implied to the instrument itself. *Effect of Reservation of Rights*

974. There exists three (3) common phrases that may be used to define to a lesser or greater degree the Reservation of Rights being *Universal*, *Absolute* and *Perfect*:- *Common Forms of Reservation of Rights*

   (i) *Universal Reservation of Rights* is when the phrase "All Rights Reserved." is used in conjunction with the transmission of any media or instrument. While Western-Roman Laws have rendered the phrase redundant in regards to international copyright laws, the use of such a phrase remains necessary to make clear both the instrument itself as well as any reference to intellectual property remains subject to copyright; and

   (ii) *Absolute Reservation of Rights* is when the phrase "All Rights Reserved in Trust under God." is used in conjunction with the transmission of any media or instrument. The phrase makes explicit that all Rights are held in trust under the One True Divine Creator using language in accord with the foundation of all Western-Roman Law. Therefore to violate such Rights implies not only a violation of sacred trust but a repudiation of the Rule of Law; and

(iii) *Perfect Reservation of Rights* is when the phrase "All Rights Reserved in Sacred Trust in accord with *Pactum De Singularis Caelum* under the One True Divine Creator." is used in conjunction with the transmission of any media or instrument. The phrase makes perfectly explicit that all Rights are held in sacred trust under the One True Divine Creator in accord with the superior law form of the present sacred Maxims. Therefore to violate such Rights implies not only a violation of sacred trust but a repudiation of every possible form of Rule of Law and Justice.

Article 237 – Domination

975. **Domination**, also known as Dominium is the highest possible form of Property Rights and Ownership. Dominium is a Right only available to valid Ecclesiastical and Sovereign Bodies in Good Faith, Good Conscience and Good Action in accord with the present Maxims and the most sacred Covenant *Pactum De Singularis Caelum*.
Domination

976. There exist no other legitimate, moral, valid or legal example of the Right of Domination, also known as Dominium except through the Rights and Laws of Ucadia in accord with the present Maxims and the most sacred Covenant *Pactum De Singularis Caelum*.
No Domination or Dominium except through Ucadia

977. There is no possible such thing in Law as a valid Dominium of Rights or Absolute Ownership made or held in Bad Faith, or Bad Conscience or by Bad Action. Such an assertion is heretical to Divine Law and is absurd and profoundly morally repugnant to any system of civilised law. Instead, any claim or system asserting "absolute ownership" that was formed or operates in Bad Faith, or Bad Conscience or Bad Action is proof of fraud and criminal culpability in and of itself, with such a false claims having no force or effect in Law.
No Dominum in Bad Faith

978. Allodial and Crown Title are false, absurd and morally repugnant concepts in property law that claims the highest form of property ownership, given such assertions are made out of Bad Faith, Bad Conscience and Bad Actions that contradict the true nature of Divine Law and Divine Rights.
Falsity and Absurdity of Allodial Title

Article 238 – Succession

979. **Succession** is when there exists a valid argument and proof of a succession of Rights from a recognised source of power to the present Form. This may occur upon the death or termination of the first form, or at the conclusion of a term or election.

    Succession

980. There exists both Ucadia Ecclesiastical and Sovereign Rights of Succession in the form of the Right of Inheritance whereby the property, assets, rights and obligations of an Ecclesiastical or Sovereign Body shall convey in Good Faith, Good Conscience and Good Action to its natural successor, without necessarily the need to form a new trust or estate.

    Ecclesiastical and Sovereign Rights of Succession

981. Under Ucadia Law, there exists no inherent Rights of Succession for individuals concerning their estates.

    No Inherent Rights of Succession

982. Under Ucadia Law, the effect of the Right of Succession means that Sovereign Authority, including the full rights, assets, powers and effect of previously enacted and unrepealed laws automatically transfers to the new Sovereign Authority without the need to issue specific laws in relation to the conveyance of such rights and property:-

    Effect of Succession and Sovereign Authority

    (i) Unlike Non-Ucadian examples of Sovereign Jurisdictions such as the Crown of the United Kingdom and many other Monarchies, there is no requirement to issue a new "Great Charter" to convey previous Rights, Laws and Property into a new trust and estate to be effective; and

    (ii) The Divine, Ecclesiastical and Sovereign Rights of Succession means that providing such succession occurs in Good Faith, Good Conscience and Good Action, such a transfer occurs automatically; and

    (iii) A new Ecclesiastical or Sovereign body shall always have the right to form a new trust or new estate upon Succession under Ucadia Law if they choose.

983. There is no such thing in Law as a valid Right of Succession made in Bad Faith, or Bad Conscience or by Bad Action. Instead, any act or process of Succession made in Bad Faith, or Bad Conscience or Bad Action automatically places the previous Ecclesiastical or Sovereign Trust and Estate into *Bona Vacantia* or *Interregnum* until a valid Ecclesiastical or Sovereign body is formed. This means the power and authority of a state or nation can never be morally or legally taken by a coup or revolution.

    No Succession in Bad Faith

Article 239 – Occupation

984. ***Occupation*** refers to the intention, act or process of taking possession and control in Good Faith, Good Conscience and Good Actions of one or more Rights concerning Real Property including (but not limited to) land, real estate, place, or territory.

Occupation

985. There is no such thing in Law as a valid Right of Occupation made in Bad Faith, or Bad Conscience or by Bad Action. Instead, any act or process of Occupation made in Bad Faith, or Bad Conscience or Bad Action is proof of fraud and criminal culpability in and of itself and any such rights shall be held in *Bona Vacantia* or *Interregnum* until such rights are restored. This means that no land can be lawfully seized and taken from another by occupation and then annexed.

No Occupation in Bad Faith

986. In terms of general references to Occupation:-

General references to Occupation

    (i) ***International Law***: In international law, occupation can refer to the control and administration of a foreign territory by a military force or government. The legal rules governing occupation in this context are outlined in various international agreements and conventions, such as the Geneva Conventions; and

    (ii) ***Property Law***: In property law, occupation can refer to the physical possession and use of real property, such as a house or land. It may be used to establish certain property rights or to determine who has the right to possess and use the property; and

    (iii) ***Tenant and Landlord Law***: In landlord-tenant relationships, occupation refers to the tenant's right to possess and use a rented property in exchange for payment of rent. This concept is crucial in determining the rights and responsibilities of both landlords and tenants; and

    (iv) ***Family Law***: In family law, occupation can refer to the physical custody or possession of a child by one or both parents in cases of child custody disputes. The court may grant one parent primary occupation (custody) of the child; and

    (v) ***Criminal Law***: In criminal law, occupation may refer to a person's job or employment. It can also be relevant in cases where someone is accused of unlawfully entering or occupying a property; and

    (vi) ***Intellectual Property Law***: Occupation can also be used in the context of intellectual property rights, such as patents or trademarks, where it may refer to the right to possess and use the intellectual property; and

(vii) ***Labour and Employment Law***: Occupation can refer to a person's job or profession, as well as the related legal rights and regulations governing employment and workplace conditions.

Article 240 – Possession

987. ***Possession*** is the intentional act and fact of holding, using or effectively controlling a Right or Property. Possession is distinct from Ownership in that a Person who possesses a Property may have no rightful claim or title. — Possession

988. Possession that is considered lawful and done in Good Faith, Good Conscience and Good Actions is called Lawful Possession. — Lawful Possession

989. Possession automatically presumes the tacit acceptance of certain obligations, whether or not possession is ultimately considered lawful. A Possessor of Form is obliged to act as an honourable steward in the management of those possessions. — Obligations of Possession

Article 241 – Operation

990. ***Operation*** refers to the active Use of a Right in Good Faith, Good Conscience and Good Action. Unlike Production, Operation does not assume any Fruits of Use. — Operation

991. The Use of an Object or Concept assumes Possession. However the questions of lawful possession and ownership are distinct from Use. — Use and Possession

992. There is no such thing in Law as a valid Operation or Use made in Bad Faith, or Bad Conscience or by Bad Action. Instead, any act or process of Occupation made in Bad Faith, or Bad Conscience or Bad Action is proof of fraud and criminal culpability and unlawful Use. — No Use in Bad Faith

Article 242 – Production

993. ***Production*** refers to the active Use of a Right in Good Faith, Good Conscience and Good Action to produce certain Fruits of Use. — Production

8.3 – Rights Transfer & Possession

Article 243 – Rights Transfer & Possession

994. A *Possession of a Right* is a valid entitlement or control over one or more Superior or Fiducial Rights in accord with the present Maxims and the most sacred Covenant *Pactum De Singularis Caelum*, namely:- [Possession of Right]

   (i) *Rights under Law*: Whereby a Person may be entitled to exercise one or more specific Rights under valid Law; or

   (ii) *Ownership of Right*: Whereby a Person owns or controls one or more interests to property; or

   (iii) *Control over Right*: Whereby a Person has control over a specific Right; or

   (iv) *Possession of Instruments*: Whereby a Person has possession of Instruments as evidence of one or more Rights.

995. A *Transfer of a Right* refers to a valid process whereby one Entity (the transferor or assignor) conveys or passes on a specific Right to another Entity (the transferee or assignee), namely:- [Transfer of Right]

   (i) *Both Entities*: Whereby both the transferor and transferee are Entities, as Rights may only be held by Entities; and

   (ii) *Right Transferable*: Whereby the Right in question is permitted to be transferred; and

   (iii) *Consensual Process*: Whereby the proposed transfer is consensual by all parties; and

   (iv) *Proper Formula*: Whereby the means and mechanism of transfer conforms to Law.

Article 244 – Gift

996. A *Gift* is a voluntary present, without charge. It is a transfer and conveyance of complete possession and ownership of a right or property without any financial consideration, yet may include one or more terms and conditions. [Gift]

997. The one who makes a Gift is typically called a Donor and the one who accepts the Gift is called a Donee. [Donor and Donee]

998. A Donor is effectively a type of Trustor who conveys or transfers complete possession and ownership of property without any financial consideration under one or more terms and conditions and may be further defined as a *Giftor, Debtor, Guarantor, Indemnitor* or [Other names for Donor]

Mortgagor:-

(i) A *Giftor* is a type of Trustor and Donor as one who voluntarily conveys and transfers land or goods, gratuitously and not upon any consideration of blood or money; and

(ii) A *Debtor* is a type of Trustor and Donor as one who gives an unconditional written promise and certain property as surety in trust to repay a fixed sum of money known as the "debt sum" or debt to a Creditor in the event of any default and dishonour by the assured party; and

(iii) A *Guarantor* is a type of Trustor and Donor as one who gives a promise as surety in trust to be answerable or liable for the repayment of a debt, or the performance of some duty in the event of a default and dishonour by the assured party; and

(iv) An *Indemnitor* is a type of Trustor and Donor as one who agrees to be bound in trust by an indemnity agreement to insure, or assure or compensate another party in the event of any loss, injury or damage on the part of some third party resulting from some offence, omission or error of official duty or performance; and

(v) A *Mortgagor* is a type of Trustor and Donor that pledges or surrenders certain property in trust as security for a debt for the benefit of a Mortgagee.

999. The conveyance and transfer of any right or property as a Gift requires that both the Donor and Donee act in Good Faith, Good Conscience and Good Action at the time of the conveyance; and that the Donee continues to act in Good Faith, Good Conscience and Good Action thereafter, if one or more terms and conditions were established and agreed at the time of the Gift:- *Good Faith in making a Gift*

(i) In the absence of Good Faith, Good Conscience and Good Action on the part of either the Donor or Donee at the time of any conveyance and transfer by Gift, such a transfer is illegitimate and unlawful; and may be criminal under Ucadia Law and Non-Ucadia Jurisdictions that operate under Civilised Rules; and

(ii) A Donee is obligated to continue to honour any terms and conditions established and agreed at the time of the Gift. If they fail to do so, then the Donor has the absolute right to demand the return or restoration of the Gift and to seek damages for such negligence and behaviour.

Article 245 – Grant

1000. A ***Grant*** is a voluntary present, with charge and one or more conditions and terms. It is a transfer and conveyance of complete possession and ownership of property and may or may not be for some financial consideration in return under one or more terms and conditions. Grant

1001. The one who makes a Grant is typically called a Grantor and the one who accepts the Grant is called a Grantee. Grantor and Grantee

1002. A Grantor is effectively a type of Trustor who conveys or transfers complete possession and ownership of property and may or may not be for some financial consideration in return under one or more conditions and may be further defined as a *Feoffor, Devisor, Testator, Settlor, Obligor, Addressor, Sender, Seller* or *Purchaser*:- Other names for Grantor

    (i)   A *Feoffor* is a type of Trustor and Grantor that grants any corporeal hereditament to another according to the custom of Fealty and ancient English and Feudal Law; and

    (ii)   A *Devisor* is a type of Trustor and Grantor (equivalent to a Testator) that grants lands or other property by Will and Testament; and

    (iii)   A *Testator* is a type of Trustor and Grantor (equivalent to a Devisor) that grants lands or other property to one or more beneficiaries by Will and Testament; and

    (iv)   A *Settlor* is a type of Trustor and Grantor that grants lands or property in trust for the benefit of one or more successors or filial descendants; and

    (v)   An *Obligor* is a type of Trustor and Grantor that grants a benefit to another party according to some binding agreement or promise; and

    (vi)   An *Addressor* is a type of Trustor and Grantor as the person or organisation who authorises, addresses and grants any formal writing, instrument or notice to be sent or deposited in the mail or delivered for transmission by any other means of communication to an intended recipient or addressee; and

    (vii)   A *Sender* is a type of Trustor and Grantor as the person or organisation who grants and delivers certain addressed mail or parcel or goods to an intended Receiver whom may or may not be the final and intended recipient or addressee; and

    (viii)   A *Seller* is a type of Trustor and Grantor as one who agrees to grant and transfer the title and possession of an object of property in consideration of the payment or promise of payment of a certain price in money; and

(ix) A *Purchaser* is a type of Trustor and Grantor as one who grants a certain price of money for the acquisition of title and possession of property.

1003. The conveyance and transfer of any right or property as a Grant requires that both the Grantor and Grantee act in Good Faith, Good Conscience and Good Action at the time of the conveyance; and that the Grantee continues to act in Good Faith, Good Conscience and Good Action thereafter, if one or more terms and conditions were established and agreed at the time of the Grant:-

Good Faith in making a Grant

(i) In the absence of Good Faith, Good Conscience and Good Action on the part of either the Grantor or Grantee at the time of any conveyance and transfer by Grant, such a transfer is illegitimate and unlawful; and may be criminal under Ucadia Law and Non-Ucadia Jurisdictions that operate under Civilised Rules; and

(ii) A Grantee is obligated to continue to honour any terms and conditions established and agreed at the time of the Grant. If they fail to do so, then the Grantor has the absolute right to demand the return or restoration of the Grant and to seek damages for such negligence and behaviour.

Article 246 – Assignment

1004. An ***Assignment*** is a temporary conveyance and transfer of one or more benefits and rights of possession and use of some property for some financial consideration in return, under one or more terms and conditions.

Assignment

1005. The one who makes an Assignment is typically called a Assignor and the one who accepts the Assignment is called an Assignee.

Assignor and Assignee

1006. An Assignor is effectively a type of Trustor who temporarily conveys or transfers one or more benefits and rights of possession and use of some property for some financial consideration in return under one or more terms and conditions and may be further defined as a *Consignor, Bailor, Depositor, Employer, Insurer, Hirer, Lessor, Lender, Creditor, Licensor, Lienor* or *Scrivener*:-

Other names for Assignor

(i) A *Consignor* is a type of Trustor and Assignor as one who deposits goods intended to be sold into the custody of a carrier to be transmitted to the designated agent or party as the "consignee"; and

(ii) A *Bailor* is a type of Trustor and Assignor as one who agrees to deliver goods or personal property in trust to another (Bailee) on the condition that the goods or personal property is redelivered by a certain time or under certain conditions (a process known as a bailment) and a reward paid; and

(iii) A *Depositor* is a type of Trustor and Assignor as one who agrees to deliver goods or personal property in trust to another on the condition that the goods or personal property are preserved and redelivered by a certain time or under certain conditions (a process known as a bailment) but without reward; and

(iv) An *Employer* is a type of Trustor and Assignor as the one who agrees to pay a wage or salary to a labourer or servant for possession and ownership of their works; and

(v) An *Insurer* is a type of Trustor and Assigner who agrees to compensate another for loss on a specific subject by specific perils from an unknown or contingent event; and

(vi) A *Hirer* is a type of Trustor and Assigner who agrees to temporarily take possession and use of a thing or for labour or services in trust in exchange for the payment of some reward or compensation; and

(vii) A *Lessor* is a type of Trustor and Assigner who agrees to convey the right to use lands or tenements or other real property to a person for life, or for a term of years or at will under a lease agreement (in two (2) parts being effectively a deed poll executed by the lessor as lease to lessee and a counterpart executed by lessee to lessor) in consideration of a return of rent or some other annual recompense; and

(viii) A *Lender* is a type of Trustor and Assignor as one who agrees to temporarily transfer some thing to another on the condition that the property is redelivered by a certain time or under certain conditions; and

(ix) A *Creditor* as one who agrees to lend a sum of money or goods of equivalent value to a Debtor for the payment of a debt, in exchange for the promissory note of the Debtor and the repayment of the debt in the event of a default by the assured party; and

(x) A *Licensor* is a type of Trustor and Assignor as one who issues a written and properly authorised permit or warrant to another, conferring the right(s) to do some act in relation to certain property held in trust which without such authorisation would be illegal, or considered a trespass or a tort; and

(xi) A *Lienor* is a type of Trustor and Assignor who licences the temporary right of use, or holding, or seizure, or custody of certain real or personal property in trust, upon the Lienor possessing a claim of right to the temporary ownership or control of the property as security or charge against the performance of a debtor (in other words a Lien); and

(xii) A *Scrivener* is a type of Trustor and Assignor who agrees to create and temporarily assign original forms of instruments including (but not limited to) indulgences, charters, bills, bonds and mortgages for the purpose of lending them out at an interest payable to his principal and for a commission or bonus for himself.

1007. The conveyance and transfer of any right or property as an Assignment requires that both the Assignor and Assignee act in Good Faith, Good Conscience and Good Action at the time of the conveyance; and that the Assignee continues to act in Good Faith, Good Conscience and Good Action thereafter, if one or more terms and conditions were established and agreed at the time of the Assignment:- Good Faith in making an Assignment

(i) In the absence of Good Faith, Good Conscience and Good Action on the part of either the Assignor or Assignee at the time of any conveyance and transfer by Assignment, such a transfer is illegitimate and unlawful; and may be criminal under Ucadia Law and Non-Ucadia Jurisdictions that operate under Civilised Rules; and

(ii) An Assignee is obligated to continue to honour the terms and conditions established and agreed at the time of the Assignment. If they fail to do so, then the Assignor has the absolute right to demand the return or restoration of the Assignment and to seek damages for such negligence and behaviour.

Article 247 – Delegation

1008. A **Delegation** is a temporary conveyance or transfer of one or more benefits and rights of possession and use of some property without any financial consideration under one or more terms and conditions. Delegation

1009. The one who makes a Delegation is typically called a Delegator and the one who accepts the Delegation is called a Delegatee. Delegator and Delegatee

1010. A Delegator is effectively a type of Trustor who temporarily conveys or transfers one or more benefits and rights of possession and use of some property without any financial consideration in return under one or more terms and conditions and may be further defined as an *Executor, Commissioner* or *Administrator*:-

    (i) An *Executor* is a type of Trustor and Delegator as one who delegates authority and franchise by charter, or deed or letters patent; and

    (ii) A *Commissioner* is a type of Trustor and Delegator as one who delegates authority and agency by warrant, or deed or letters of marque; and

    (iii) An *Administrator* is a type of Trustor and Delegator as a surrogate Executor, appointed under competent judicial authority as one who delegates authority by order.

Other names for Delegator

1011. The conveyance and transfer of any right or property as a Delegation requires that both the Delegator and Delegatee act in Good Faith, Good Conscience and Good Action at the time of the conveyance; and that the Delegatee continues to act in Good Faith, Good Conscience and Good Action thereafter, if one or more terms and conditions were established and agreed at the time of the Delegation:-

    (i) In the absence of Good Faith, Good Conscience and Good Action on the part of either the Delegator or Delegatee at the time of any conveyance and transfer by Delegation, such a transfer is illegitimate and unlawful; and may be criminal under Ucadia Law and Non-Ucadia Jurisdictions that operate under Civilised Rules; and

    (ii) A Delegatee is obligated to continue to honour any terms and conditions established and agreed at the time of the Delegation. If they fail to do so, then the Delegator has the absolute right to demand the return or restoration of the Delegation and to seek damages for such negligence and behaviour.

Good Faith in making a Delegation

Article 248 – Novation

1012. ***Novation*** refers to the process of replacing an existing agreement with a new one, where one or more parties involved in the original agreement are released from their obligations and replaced by new parties. Novation effectively substitutes one agreement with another, with the consent of all parties involved.

Novation

1013. Novation is commonly used in various forms of agreement, including

Examples of Novation

(but not limited to):-

(i) *Assignment of contracts*: When one party in a contract wishes to transfer their rights and obligations to a third party, with the consent of all parties involved, novation may be used; and

(ii) *Change of ownership or control*: In business agreements, novation can be used to update contracts when there is a change in ownership or control of a company; and

(iii) *Subleasing*: In real estate leases, novation can be used to substitute a new tenant (sublessee) for the original tenant (lessee) with the landlord's consent; and

(iv) *Loan agreements*: In financial transactions, novation can occur when the terms of a loan are modified, and a new lender or borrower is introduced.

Article 249 – Sale

1014. A ***Sale*** is when the title to a thing is given in Trust to another in exchange for a price of lawful money, also given in trust. Sale and Purchase

1015. In reference to the concept of a Sale:- Reference to Sale

(i) A Sale always involves Goods and therefore always involves Rights in Trust as Goods; and

(ii) A Sale always involves two distinct trusts having two distinct trust corpus – one where the buyer is trustee and one where the seller is trustee; and

(iii) It is only when the sale is completed do the two separate trusts dissolve, providing the conditions of sale make that possible.

Article 250 – Bargain

1016. A ***Bargain*** is a Contract of Mutual Bindings (Promises) in Trust as Security whereby one party promises to assign a right as property for some consideration; and the other party promises to receive the property and take good care of it and pay the consideration. Bargain

1017. In reference to the concept of a Bargain of Goods:- Reference to Bargain

(i) A Bargain always involves Goods and therefore always involves Rights in Trust as Goods; and

(ii) Similar to a Sale, a Bargain always involves two Trusts for a Bargain to exist: The one for the Buyer and one for the Seller; and

(iii) A Bargain is not a transfer of Title but a Bailment of Goods or

Use for some financial consideration; and

(iv) The Seller never gifts the property like a Sale and the terms of Consideration may also involve some return of a Bailment of Money; and

(v) The key operating element of a Bargain is the Mutual Binding Promises that are also called Debts.

1018. In reference to the concept of mutual debts of a Bargain:- *Mutual Debts of Bargain*

(i) There are always two debts associated with any valid Bargain: The debt of the buyer and the debt of the seller. Just as there are two valid trusts and two valid trustees (Buyer and Seller) and two debtor-creditor relations with the two trusts; and

(ii) A Contract without two separate and distinct debts and relations is inchoate (incomplete).

Article 251 – Conveyance

1019. ***Conveyance*** is the process of transfer and delivery of ownership of certain property or rights from one party to another, as well as any instrument which serves in the transfer of property or rights from one party to another. *Conveyance*

1020. Conveyance includes every instrument in writing under seal by which any estate or interest in real estate is created, aliened, mortgaged or assigned, or by which the title to any real estate may be affected in law or equity except will and testaments, leases of less than three years or executor contracts for the sale or purchase of lands. *Instruments of Conveyance*

1021. In the context of property law and agreements, there are several forms of conveyance that can be used to transfer property rights or interests from one party to another including (but not limited to):- *Forms of Conveyance*

(i) ***Deed***: A deed is a written legal document used to transfer the ownership or interest in real property from one party (the grantor) to another party (the grantee). Common types of deeds include warranty deeds, quitclaim deeds, and special warranty deeds. Deeds typically require a notary public's acknowledgment and may need to be recorded in the appropriate government office; and

(ii) ***Lease Agreement***: A lease agreement is a contract between a property owner (the landlord or lessor) and a tenant (the lessee) that grants the lessee the right to occupy and use the property for a specified period in exchange for rent payments. While not a conveyance of ownership, it is a conveyance of a leasehold interest; and

(iii) **Easement**: An easement is a legal right to use another person's property for a specific purpose. Easements can be created by agreement or by necessity, and they may involve rights of way, utilities, or other limited uses of the property; and

(iv) **Mortgage**: A mortgage is a financial instrument used to convey a security interest in real property to a lender (mortgagee) as collateral for a loan. The borrower (mortgagor) conveys an interest in the property, and if the borrower defaults on the loan, the lender may have the right to foreclose on the property; and

(v) **Partition Agreement**: In situations where multiple co-owners of a property wish to divide their interests or sell the property, a partition agreement can be used to convey the property's ownership interests among the co-owners; and

(vi) **Trust Deed (Deed of Trust)**: A trust deed, often used in real estate transactions, conveys property to a trustee who holds it as security for a loan. If the borrower defaults on the loan, the trustee has the power to sell the property to satisfy the debt; and

(vii) **Assignment of Lease**: In the context of a lease agreement, an assignment of lease conveys the tenant's rights and obligations under the lease to a third party (assignee). The original tenant (assignor) may or may not remain liable for the lease terms; and

(viii) **Transfer on Death Deed**: Some jurisdictions allow for the use of a transfer on death deed (also known as a beneficiary deed or TOD deed), which allows an owner to designate a beneficiary who will automatically inherit the property upon the owner's death, avoiding probate; and

(ix) **Gift Deed**: A gift deed is used to convey property from one party to another as a gift, without the exchange of money. It typically requires the giver (donor) to relinquish all rights and interests in the property; and

(x) **Court Order**: In some cases, a court may issue an order to convey property as part of a legal proceeding, such as a partition action or divorce settlement.

Article 252 – Merger and Acquisition

1022. ***Merger and Acquisition*** refers to the process whereby one entity (or a portion of an entity) is combined with or acquired by another entity.

Merger and Acquisition

1023. A ***Merger*** is a business combination in which two or more companies merge their operations to form a new entity or integrate into one of the existing companies. In a merger, the companies involved combine their assets, liabilities, and operations. The shareholders of the merging companies often receive shares in the new combined entity or the surviving company.

Merger

1024. *Mergers* can be classified into different types, such as:-

Types of Mergers

   (i) ***Horizontal Merger***: Involves companies in the same industry and at the same stage of production; or

   (ii) ***Vertical Merger***: Involves companies at different stages of the production or distribution chain; or

   (iii) ***Conglomerate Merger***: Involves companies in unrelated businesses.

1025. The conveyance and transfer of any right or property within a Merger requires that all parties act in Good Faith, Good Conscience and Good Action at the time of the Merger; and that the New (Merged) Entity continues to act in Good Faith, Good Conscience and Good Action thereafter according to the terms and conditions that were established and agreed as the Merger Agreement:-

Good Faith in proposing and undertaking Merger

   (i) In the absence of Good Faith, Good Conscience and Good Action on the part of either the parties at the time of any conveyance and transfer by Merger, such a transfer is illegitimate and unlawful; and may be criminal under Ucadia Law and Non-Ucadia Jurisdictions that operate under Civilised Rules; and

   (ii) A New (Merged) Entity is obligated to continue to honour any terms and conditions established and agreed at the time of the Merger Agreement. If they fail to do so, then the original parties have the absolute right to demand the return or restoration of the original Entity and assets that were merged and to seek damages for such negligence and behaviour.

1026. An ***Acquisition***, also known as a takeover, occurs when one company, often referred to as the acquiring company or acquirer, purchases a significant portion of the ownership (equity) or assets of another company, referred to as the target company. The target

Acquisition

company may continue to exist as a subsidiary of the acquirer, or it may be fully integrated into the acquiring company.

1027. *Acquisitions* can be classified into different types, such as:-   Types of Acquisition

   (i)   ***Asset Acquisition***: In an asset acquisition, the acquirer purchases specific assets and liabilities of the target company. The target company may continue to exist, but it may be left with fewer assets and operations; and

   (ii)   ***Stock Acquisition***: In a stock acquisition, the acquirer purchases a controlling interest (usually more than 50%) in the target company's stock, thereby gaining control over the target company.

1028. Any jurisdiction that permits the hostile acquisition of one entity by another confesses by such an uncivilised act to having no Civilised Rules of Law, nor respect to the fundamental principles of Rights.   Hostile Acquisition is an admission of Uncivilised Rules

1029. The conveyance and transfer of any right or property within an Acquisition requires that all parties act in Good Faith, Good Conscience and Good Action at the time of the Acquisition; and that the New (Acquired) Entity continues to act in Good Faith, Good Conscience and Good Action thereafter according to the terms and conditions that were established and agreed as the Acquisition Agreement:-   Good Faith in proposing and making an Acquisition

   (i)   In the absence of Good Faith, Good Conscience and Good Action on the part of either the parties at the time of any conveyance and transfer by Acquisition, such a transfer is illegitimate and unlawful; and may be criminal under Ucadia Law and Non-Ucadia Jurisdictions that operate under Civilised Rules; and

   (ii)   A Newly Acquired Entity is obligated to continue to honour any terms and conditions established and agreed at the time of the Acquisition Agreement. If they fail to do so, then the original parties have the absolute right to demand the return or restoration of the original Entity and assets that were acquired and to seek damages for such negligence and behaviour.

8.4 – Rights Suspension & Loss
Article 253 – Rights Suspension & Loss

1030. ***Loss of a Right*** refers to a condition whereby an Entity may legitimately lose or forfeit certain entitlements, privileges or benefits in accord with the present Maxims and the most sacred Covenant *Pactum De Singularis Caelum*, namely:-   *Loss or Suspension of Right*

    (i) *Loss of Rights under Law*: Whereby a Person may lose or forfeit the entitlement to exercise one or more specific Rights under valid Law; or

    (ii) *Loss of Ownership of Right*: Whereby a Person may lose or forfeit ownership or control over one or more interests to property; or

    (iii) *Loss of Control over Right*: Whereby a Person may lose or forfeit control over a specific Right; or

    (iv) *Loss of Possession of Instruments*: Whereby a Person may lose or forfeit possession of one or more Instruments as evidence of one or more Rights.

1031. Only some Rights are subject to loss or forfeit, meaning the majority of Rights cannot be waived, surrendered, suspended, abandoned, resigned, disqualified, seized, captured, arrested, rescinded, suppressed, forfeited or revoked.   *Whether a Right is capable of being lost or forfeited*

Article 254 – Perfidy

1032. ***Perfidy*** refers to a deliberate act of deceit, treachery, or betrayal that violates trust, good faith, or an established agreement. It involves dishonest or disloyal conduct that goes against the principles of fairness and honesty and may be criminal in nature.   *Perfidy*

1033. Examples of types of Perfidy include (but are not limited to):-   *Types of Perfidy*

    (i) ***International Law***: In the context of armed conflict and international humanitarian law, it refers to acts of deceit during armed conflicts that violate the rules protecting combatants and civilians; and

    (ii) ***Criminal Law***: In criminal law, perfidy could relate to deceptive or treacherous behaviour, such as the use of deceit to commit a crime, the violation of trust as part of a criminal scheme, or the betrayal of a confidential relationship; and

    (iii) ***Contract Law***: In contract law, perfidy could refer to a party's deliberate breach of a contract by acting in bad faith or intentionally failing to fulfil their contractual obligations.

1034. A Right cannot be held in Bad Faith or Bad Conscience or by Bad Action. Therefore upon proof of Perfidy, the associated Right or Rights may be suspended or lost. *Effect of Perfidy*

Article 255 – Renunciation

1035. ***Renunciation*** refers to the formal act of giving up, relinquishing, or disclaiming a legal right, privilege, or interest, typically through a deliberate and explicit statement or action. *Renunciation*

1036. Examples of Renunciation include (but are not limited to):- *Examples of Renunciation*
   (i) ***Renunciation of Benefits or Entitlements***: In the context of government benefits or entitlement programs, individuals may be required to renounce certain assets or income to qualify for assistance; and
   (ii) ***Renunciation of Inheritance***: In estate and probate law, renunciation refers to a person's decision to refuse or disclaim their right to inherit assets or property from a deceased person's estate; and
   (iii) ***Renunciation of Citizenship***: Some countries allow their citizens to renounce their citizenship voluntarily; and
   (iv) ***Renunciation of Rights***: In various legal contexts, individuals may renounce specific rights, such as parental rights, property rights, or contractual rights; and
   (v) ***Renunciation of Criminal Intent***: In criminal law, a defendant may renounce criminal intent as part of a legal defense. This means they can argue that they had a change of heart or took actions to prevent the commission of a crime before it was completed; and
   (vi) ***Renunciation of Trademark Rights***: In trademark law, a trademark owner may formally renounce their rights to a trademark, effectively surrendering their exclusive use of that mark.

Article 256 – Abandonment

1037. ***Abandonment*** refers to the voluntary relinquishment, surrender, or giving up of a legal right, property, duty, or responsibility without any intention of reclaiming it. *Abandonment*

1038. Examples of Abandonment include (but are not limited to):- *Examples of Abandonment*
   (i) ***Child Abandonment***: Child abandonment refers to the act

of a parent or guardian intentionally and permanently giving up their parental responsibilities and rights regarding a child; and

(ii) ***Abandonment of Trademarks***: In trademark law, if a trademark owner stops using their trademark for an extended period and has no intention of resuming its use, the trademark may be considered abandoned; and

(iii) ***Abandonment of Claims or Lawsuits***: In litigation, if a party to a lawsuit voluntarily withdraws or dismisses their claims without any intention of pursuing them further, it may be viewed as abandonment of the lawsuit; and

(iv) ***Property Abandonment***: This occurs when a property owner intentionally and permanently gives up their ownership interest in a piece of real or personal property; and

(v) ***Abandonment of a Contract***: In contract law, if one party to a contract voluntarily and without justification stops performing their obligations under the contract and expresses no intention of fulfilling those obligations in the future, it may be considered a breach of contract through abandonment; and

(vi) ***Abandonment of Easements***: In property law, an easement is a right to use someone else's property for a specific purpose. If the easement holder stops using the easement and has no intention of using it in the future, it may be considered abandoned, potentially leading to the termination of the easement.

Article 257 – Expiration

1039. ***Expiration*** refers to the end or termination of a legal right, contract, license, or period of time after which a particular right or agreement is no longer valid or enforceable. *Expiration*

1040. Examples of Expiration include (but are not limited to):- *Examples of Expiration*

(i) ***Patent Expiration***: Patents granted for inventions have a limited duration, typically 20 years from the date of filing. When a patent reaches its expiration date, the invention becomes part of the public domain, and others may use, make, and sell the patented invention without infringing on the patent holder's rights; and

(ii) ***Lease Expiration***: In real estate law, the expiration of a lease occurs when the agreed-upon lease term ends. When a lease expires, the tenant may need to vacate the property unless a new lease is negotiated or an extension is granted; and

(iii) **Insurance Policy Expiration**: Insurance policies often have specific terms and expiration dates. Once an insurance policy expires, the insurer is no longer obligated to provide coverage unless the policy is renewed or replaced with a new one; and

(iv) **License Expiration**: Many licenses, such as driver's licenses, professional licenses, and permits, have expiration dates. When a license expires, it means that the holder can no longer legally use or enjoy the privileges associated with that license until it is renewed or reissued; and

(v) **Contract Expiration**: In contract law, the expiration of a contract occurs when the specified term of the contract comes to an end. Contracts can be written with a specific duration, and when that time period expires, the contractual obligations and rights of the parties may cease. However, some contracts may contain provisions for renewal or extension; and

(vi) **Warranty Expiration**: Product warranties typically have expiration dates, after which the manufacturer is no longer responsible for repairing or replacing defective products under the warranty; and

(vii) **Visa or Immigration Status Expiration**: Individuals holding visas or immigration status in a foreign country must adhere to the terms and conditions of their visa. When the visa or immigration status expires, the individual may no longer have legal permission to stay in that country; and

(viii) **Statute of Limitations Expiration**: In a proper legal system, the statute of limitations sets a time limit for initiating legal actions. When the statute of limitations for a particular legal claim or offense expires, it generally means that the affected party can no longer bring a lawsuit or criminal charges based on that claim.

Article 258 – Suspension

1041. ***Suspension*** refers to a temporary and often conditional halt or interruption of a legal right, privilege, license, or activity. It is a punitive or corrective action taken by an authority or governing body as a response to a violation, misconduct, or failure to meet certain requirements.

1042. Examples of Suspension include (but are not limited to):-

    (i)   ***Drivers License Suspension***: This may occur as a result of traffic violations, convictions, or failure to pay traffic fines. During a license suspension, the individual is not permitted to legally operate a motor vehicle for a specified period; and

    (ii)   ***Professional License Suspension***: Many licensed professionals, such as doctors, lawyers, nurses, and accountants, can have their professional licenses suspended if they are found guilty of professional misconduct or ethical violations. During a license suspension, they are typically prohibited from practising their profession for a specified period; and

    (iii)   ***Suspension of Government Benefits***: Government agencies may suspend or terminate benefits, such as unemployment benefits or welfare, if recipients fail to meet certain eligibility requirements or engage in fraudulent activities; and

    (iv)   ***Suspension of Court Proceedings***: In some legal proceedings, such as criminal trials, a judge may order a suspension or continuance of the proceedings, temporarily halting the trial or other court activities for a specific reason, such as allowing time for evidence gathering or addressing legal issues; and

    (v)   ***Suspension of a Contract***: In contract law, parties to a contract may agree to suspend their contractual obligations temporarily. This can occur when unforeseen circumstances make performance impossible or when both parties agree to a pause in performance for a specific reason; and

    (vi)   ***Suspension of a Business or Corporate Status***: A business entity's charter or corporate status may be suspended by a government agency for various reasons, such as failure to file required documents or pay taxes. During suspension, the business entity may lose legal protections and privileges.

Article 259 – Forfeiture

1043. ***Forfeiture*** refers to the loss or relinquishment of a right, property, asset, or privilege as a penalty or consequence for a specific action or failure to meet certain requirements. Forfeiture typically occurs as a result of a legal judgment or administrative decision and is often imposed to deter illegal activities, punish wrongdoing, or ensure compliance with laws and regulations.

1044. Examples of Forfeiture include (but are not limited to):- Examples of Forfeiture

    (i) **_Asset Forfeiture_**: Asset forfeiture is a legal process through which the government seizes and takes ownership of property or assets that are believed to have been used in, derived from, or connected to illegal activities. This can include vehicles, real estate, money, and other valuable assets. Asset forfeiture can be civil or criminal, and it may occur without a criminal conviction. It is often used in cases involving drug trafficking, organized crime, and other illicit activities; and

    (ii) **_Forfeiture of a Lease_**: In real estate and property law, a tenant may forfeit their leasehold interest if they breach the terms of the lease agreement, such as by failing to pay rent or violating other lease provisions. The landlord may then terminate the lease and take possession of the property; and

    (iii) **_Forfeiture of Rights_**: In some legal proceedings, a party may forfeit certain legal rights or claims by failing to assert them in a timely manner or by not complying with legal procedures. For example, if a defendant in a lawsuit fails to respond to a complaint within the specified time frame, they may forfeit their right to contest the claims made against them; and

    (iv) **_Bail Forfeiture_**: When a person is released on bail pending a trial or court appearance and fails to appear as required, the bail bond may be forfeited. This means that the person who posted the bail may lose the money or collateral they provided as security.

Article 260 – Waiver

1045. **_Waiver_** refers to the voluntary and intentional relinquishment, abandonment, or surrender of a known right, claim, privilege, or legal defense. When an individual or entity waives a right or claim, they are essentially choosing not to exercise or enforce that right, often in a specific situation or context. Waiver

1046. A Waiver can be written or verbal, but must be clear, specific and unambiguous to be legally effective. Clear and Unambiguous Language of Waiver

1047. Examples of Waiver include (but are not limited to):- Examples of Waiver

    (i) **_Liability Waiver_**: A common example of a waiver is a liability waiver or release form. These documents are often used in activities that carry some level of risk, such as sports, recreational activities, or certain events. By signing a liability waiver, a participant acknowledges the potential risks involved and agrees not to hold the organization or individuals responsible for any injuries or harm that may occur; and

(ii) **Contractual Waiver**: In contracts, parties may include provisions that allow one or both parties to waive certain rights or requirements. For example, a contract may include a waiver of the right to sue for breach of contract if certain conditions are met, or it may include a waiver of specific contractual obligations; and

(iii) **Waiver of Notice**: In legal proceedings, parties may waive their right to receive formal notice of certain actions, hearings, or events. For example, a party involved in a lawsuit may waive their right to receive notice of a court hearing and agree to proceed without formal notice; and

(iv) **Waiver of Inheritance**: An individual may choose to waive their right to inherit property or assets from a deceased relatives estate. This is often done through a formal legal document, and the individual is said to "disclaim" their inheritance; and

(v) **Criminal Law Waiver**: In criminal law, a defendant may waive certain constitutional rights, such as the right to remain silent or the right to an attorney. This often occurs when a defendant voluntarily chooses to speak to law enforcement without an attorney present, known as "waiving ones rights".

8.5 – Rights Dispute, Recovery & Restoration

Article 261 – Rights Dispute, Recovery & Restoration

1048. ***Recovery of a Right*** refers to a condition whereby an Entity may legitimately recover or restore certain entitlements, privileges or benefits in accord with the present Maxims and the most sacred Covenant *Pactum De Singularis Caelum*, namely:- Rights Recovery & Restoration

(i) *Recovery of Rights under Law*: Whereby a Person may recover a lost or forfeited entitlement to exercise one or more specific Rights under valid Law; or

(ii) *Recovery of Ownership of Right*: Whereby a Person may recover a lost or forfeited ownership or control over one or more interests to property; or

(iii) *Recovery of Control over Right*: Whereby a Person may recover a lost or forfeited control over a specific Right; or

(iv) *Recovery of Possession of Instruments*: Whereby a Person may recover a lost or forfeited possession of one or more Instruments as evidence of one or more Rights.

Article 262 – Distress

1049. ***Distress*** refers to the act of seizing and holding another person's property as a means of enforcing a legal claim or right, typically related to the non-payment of a debt or rent.   *Distress*

1050. In most Non-Ucadia Jurisdictions, the Right of Distress has been severely limited or abolished. Where the Right remains, Distress is subject to legal limits and protections to prevent abuses. There are often rules governing what types of property can be seized, how much can be seized, and how the proceeds from the sale of seized property are distributed.   *Limits and Protections against Distress*

1051. The process of Distress typically involves specific legal procedures, including notice to the debtor, inventory of the property to be seized, and the sale of the property through a public auction or other means. These procedures are designed to protect the rights of the debtor.   *Procedures and Notices of Distress*

1052. Examples of Distress include (but are not limited to):-   *Examples of Distress*

    (i) ***Distress for Rent***: A common use of distress occurs in landlord-tenant relationships. When a tenant fails to pay rent, the landlord may have the right to use distress to seize and hold the tenant's personal property as security for the unpaid rent. The landlord can then sell the seized property to recover the owed rent; and

    (ii) ***Distress for Debt***: In certain situations, creditors may have the legal authority to use distress to recover unpaid debts. This may involve seizing and selling the debtor's property to satisfy the debt; and

    (iii) ***Distress for Taxes***: In some jurisdictions, tax authorities may use distress to collect unpaid taxes. They can seize and sell the property of a taxpayer who has failed to pay their taxes, typically after giving notice and following legal procedures.

Article 263 – Replevin

1053. ***Replevin*** refers to a legal action or remedy that allows a party to recover possession of personal property that has been wrongfully taken, detained, or withheld by another party. Replevin is a legal mechanism used to resolve disputes over the possession of movable   *Replevin* assets, such as goods, vehicles, equipment, or personal belongings.

1054. To bring a Replevin action, the plaintiff must demonstrate that the defendant is wrongfully holding or detaining the property. This could occur when the defendant refuses to return the property, has taken possession without authorization, or is holding it in violation of a contract or agreement. Wrongful Possession

Article 264 – Detinue

1055. ***Detinue*** is a historical cause of action that refers to a legal action brought by a plaintiff to recover the wrongful detention or possession of personal property by another party. Detinue is a type of civil lawsuit used to seek the return of specific items of personal property or, in some cases, compensation for their value if return is not possible. Detinue

1056. The central element of a Detinue claim is that the plaintiff must demonstrate that their personal property is being wrongfully detained by the defendant. This means that the plaintiff believes they have a rightful claim to the property, and the defendant is holding it without proper authorization or justification. Wrongful Detention

Article 265 – Injunction

1057. An ***Injunction*** is a court-issued order that requires a party to do or refrain from doing a specific act or activity. Injunction

1058. There are two primary types of Injunctions:- Types of Injunction

   (i) ***Temporary Injunction (Preliminary Injunction)***: A temporary injunction, also known as a preliminary injunction, is an order issued by a court during the early stages of a legal proceeding, before a final judgment is rendered. It is typically used to maintain the current situation and prevent irreparable harm while the underlying legal dispute is being resolved; and

   (ii) ***Permanent Injunction***: A permanent injunction, also known simply as an injunction, is a court order issued as part of the final judgment in a legal dispute. It is intended to be a long-term or permanent solution to a legal issue. A permanent injunction orders a party to take certain actions or refrain from specific activities indefinitely.

1059. Temporary injunctions are typically in effect for a limited period, often until the court reaches a final judgment in the case or until further court orders are issued. The general criteria of a Temporary Injunction that a party seeking it (the "plaintiff" or "movant") must General Criteria of Temporary Injunction demonstrate includes (but are not limited to):-

(i) A likelihood of success on the merits of the case; and

(ii) The existence of irreparable harm if the injunction is not granted; and

(iii) The balance of equities favours the party seeking the injunction; and

(iv) The injunction serves the public interest.

1060. Permanent injunctions are typically issued after a full trial or legal proceedings, when the court has considered all relevant evidence and argument. The general criteria of a Permanent Injunction that a party seeking it (the "plaintiff" or "movant") must demonstrate includes (but are not limited to):- *[General Criteria of Permanent Injunction]*

(i) They have a valid legal right that needs protection; and

(ii) There is a continuing threat of harm or violation of their rights; and

(iii) The equities favor the issuance of the injunction; and

(iv) The injunction serves the public interest.

Article 266 – Reparation

1061. **Reparation** refers to the act of compensating or making amends to a person or entity for harm, damage, or loss suffered as a result of a wrongful act or violation of a legal right. Reparation involves providing financial or other forms of restitution or compensation to the injured party to address the harm they have experienced. *[Reparation]*

1062. Examples of Reparation include (but are not limited to):- *[Examples of Reparation]*

(i) **Reparation in International Law**: In international law, reparation is used to address wrongful acts committed by one state against another state or its nationals. Reparation may be sought as a remedy for violations of international law, such as human rights abuses, war crimes, or violations of diplomatic treaties; and

(ii) **Reparation in Tort Law**: In tort law, reparation refers to the compensation that a person who has been injured or suffered damage due to the wrongful conduct of another party (the tortfeasor) may seek through a civil lawsuit. Reparation may include monetary damages to cover medical expenses, property damage, lost income, pain and suffering, and other losses caused by the tortious act; and

(iii) ***Reparation in Criminal Law***: In some legal systems, reparation may be part of the criminal justice process. Offenders may be required to provide reparation to their victims as part of their sentence. This may involve paying restitution to cover the victim's financial losses or participating in community service or other forms of compensation to address the harm caused by their criminal actions; and

(iv) ***Reparation in Family Law***: In family law, reparation can refer to court-ordered payments made by one spouse or parent to another as a form of financial support or compensation. This can include spousal support (alimony) or child support to address the financial needs of the recipient; and

(v) ***Reparation in Environmental Law***: Environmental laws may require individuals or entities responsible for environmental harm to provide reparation, such as financial compensation, to restore or mitigate the environmental damage caused; and

(vi) ***Reparation in Human Rights Law***: International human rights law may provide for reparation to victims of human rights violations, such as torture, discrimination, or wrongful imprisonment. Reparation in this context aims to acknowledge and address the harm suffered by victims.

Article 267 – Sequestration

1063. ***Sequestration*** refers to the act of setting aside or taking possession of something, often involving assets, funds, or evidence, for a specific legal purpose or pending a legal dispute. — Sequestration

1064. Courts may issue sequestration orders, also known as protective orders or preservation orders, to protect and preserve evidence or assets relevant to a legal dispute. For example, a court may issue a sequestration order to prevent the destruction of documents or to secure evidence during litigation. — Sequestration Orders

1065. Examples of Sequestration include (but are not limited to):- — Examples of Sequestration

(i) ***Asset Sequestration***: This refers to the legal process of taking control or possession of a person's or entity's assets, such as bank accounts, real estate, or personal property. Asset sequestration may occur for various reasons, including satisfying a debt, enforcing a judgment, or preserving assets during a legal dispute; and

(ii) ***Witness Sequestration***: In legal proceedings, especially trials, witness sequestration refers to the practice of isolating witnesses who are not testifying from the courtroom, often to prevent them from being influenced by the testimony of other witnesses. This helps maintain the integrity of witness testimony by reducing the risk of collusion or coaching; and

(iii) ***Estate Sequestration***: In estate law, estate sequestration may occur when the court takes control of a deceased person's assets and property to protect them during the administration of the estate. This is done to ensure that the assets are properly managed and distributed according to the decedent's will or applicable laws; and

(iv) ***Bankruptcy Sequestration***: In bankruptcy proceedings, sequestration may involve the appointment of a trustee who takes control of a debtor's assets to manage and distribute them to creditors in accordance with bankruptcy laws and court orders; and

(v) ***Sequestration in International Law***: In the context of international disputes, sequestration can refer to the temporary freezing or control of assets, funds, or property belonging to a foreign government or entity to enforce an international judgment or arbitral award; and

(vi) ***Sequestration of Funds***: This term can also refer to the withholding or setting aside of funds, often in a trust or escrow account, for a specific purpose, such as pending litigation, tax liabilities, or debt repayment.

Article 268 – Garnishment

1066. ***Garnishment*** refers to a legal process through which a creditor obtains a court order to collect a debt by diverting a portion of a debtor's wages, bank account funds, or other financial assets to satisfy the debt. Garnishment is typically used when a debtor has not paid a debt as required, and it is often employed as a means of enforcing judgments or collecting unpaid child support, spousal support, taxes, or other financial obligations. Garnishment

1067. In most cases, before Garnishment can occur, the debtor must be given proper notice and an opportunity to contest the debt or the garnishment order in court. Due process protections ensure that debtors have a chance to present their side of the case. Garnishment Notice and Due Process

Article 269 – Revendication

1068. ***Revendication*** is a French word that translates to "claim" or "assertion" in English. In a legal context, it can refer to the act of making a claim or asserting a right to something. For example, in property law, if someone asserts a claim or right to a piece of property, they may file a revendication to assert their ownership or interest in that property.

Article 270 – Restitution

1069. ***Restitution*** refers to the act of restoring or making amends for something that has been lost or taken away, often in the context of a legal or equitable remedy.

1070. Examples of Restitution include (but are not limited to):-

   (i) ***Contract Law:*** In contract law, restitution can refer to the return of goods, property, or funds to their rightful owner when a contract is rescinded or cancelled. It is often used as a remedy when one party breaches a contract, and the other party seeks to be restored to their pre-contract position; and

   (ii) ***Property Law***: In property law, restitution can refer to the return of property or assets to their rightful owner when they have been wrongfully taken or acquired by another party; and

   (iii) ***Equity and Unjust Enrichment***: In equitable principles, restitution may be used to prevent unjust enrichment. It can involve the return of benefits received by one party at the expense of another, where it would be unfair for the recipient to retain those benefits; and

   (iv) ***Torts***: Restitution can also play a role in tort law, where it may be used to compensate a plaintiff for losses suffered due to the defendant's wrongful actions; and

   (v) ***Criminal Law***: In criminal law, restitution typically refers to the process by which a convicted defendant is required to compensate the victim for financial losses resulting from the defendant's criminal actions. For example, if someone is convicted of theft, they may be ordered to pay restitution to the victim in an amount equal to the value of the stolen property or the victim's financial losses.

Article 271 – Public Advocacy and Lobbying

1071. ***Public Advocacy*** and ***Lobbying*** are activities that involve efforts to influence government policies, decisions, and legislation on behalf of a particular cause, organization, or interest group. It relates to the original purpose and meaning of "Distress" under Holly Law and later Anglo-Saxon Law concerning the "shaming" of officials who refuse to provide remedy and the highlighting of the cause to the public. — Public Advocacy and Lobbying

1072. ***Public advocacy*** refers to the act of promoting or advocating for a particular social, political, or policy issue in the public sphere. Advocates work to raise awareness, shape public opinion, and mobilize support for their cause. Public advocacy can encompass a wide range of activities, including public speaking, grassroots organizing, community outreach, media campaigns, and social media engagement. Advocates may work to influence public sentiment, gather signatures for petitions, and engage in educational initiatives. — Public Advocacy

1073. ***Lobbying*** involves efforts to influence government officials, legislators, or policymakers directly in order to shape or impact government decisions, laws, regulations, or policies. Lobbyists often engage in activities such as meeting with lawmakers, providing information and research, testifying at legislative hearings, drafting legislation, and organizing campaigns to mobilize public support for or against specific policies. — Lobbying

8.6 – False, Absurd & Prohibited Rights

Article 272 - False, Absurd & Prohibited Identification of Rights

1074. False, absurd, and prohibited Rights refer to claims or demands made by individuals or groups that are not legitimate or reasonable. Any claim, edict or decree of any kind that is not of the most sacred Covenant *Pactum De Singularis Caelum* and claims a mandate to recover or restore one or more Rights shall be false, absurd, sacrilegious and with any force or effect in law. — False, Absurd & Prohibited Identification of Rights

Article 273 – Cestui Que Vie

1075. A ***Cestui Que Vie Trust***, also known by several other pseudonyms such as "Term of Life or Years" or "Pur Autre Vie" or "Fide Commissary Trust" or "Foreign Situs Trust" or "Secret Trust" is a pseudo form of trust first claimed to be formed in the 16th Century under Henry VIII of England on one or more presumptions including (but not limited to) one or more Persons presumed wards, infants, — Cestui Que Vie idiots, lost or abandoned at "sea" and therefore assumed/presumed "dead" after seven (7) years. Additional presumptions by which such a Trust may be "legally" formed were added in later statutes to include bankruptcy, incapacity, mortgages and private companies.

1076. In terms of the claimed evidential history of the formation of Cestui Que Vie Trusts: *History of Cestui Que Vie Trusts*

    (i) The first Cestui Que Vie Trusts formed were through an Act of Henry VIII of England in 1540 (32Hen.8 c1) and later wholly corrupted whereby the poor people of England, after having all their homes, goods and wealth seized in 1535 (27Hen.8 c.28) under the "guise" of small religious estates (under £200), were granted the welfare or "commonwealth" benefit of an Cestui Que Use or simply an "estate" with which to live, to work and to bequeath via a written will; and

    (ii) In 1666 Westminster and the ruling classes passed the infamous "Proof of Life Act" also called the Cestui Que Vie Act (19Car.2 c.6) whereby the poor and disenfranchised that had not "proven" to Westminster and the Courts they were alive, were henceforth to be declared "dead in law" and therefore lost, abandoned and their property to be managed in their absence. This supremely morally repugnant act, which remains in force today, is the birth of Mundi and the infamous occult rituals of the British Courts in the wearing of black robes and other paraphernalia in honoring the "dead"; and

    (iii) In 1707 Westminster under Queen Anne (6Ann c.18) extended the provisions of "Proof of Life" and Cestui Que Vie, extending the use of such structures ultimately for corporate and other franchise purposes. This wicked, profane and completely sacrilegious act in direct defiance to all forms of Christian morals and Rule of Law has remained a cornerstone of global banking and financial control to the 21st Century; and

    (iv) In 1796, King George III (36 Geo.3. c.52 §20) duty was applied to Estates Pur Autre Vie for the first time; and

    (v) In 1837 (1 Vict . c.26) and the amendments to the nature of Wills, that if a person under an Estate Pur Autre Vie (Cestui Que Vie) did not make a proper will, then such property would be granted to the executors and administrators.

1077. In terms of the claimed evidential history of the operation and any form of relief or remedy associated with Cestui Que Vie Trusts, taking into account all Statutes referencing Cestui Que Vie prior to 1540 are a deliberate fraud and proof of the illegitimacy of Westminster   *Evidence of use of Cestui Que Vie*

Statutes:

(i) The "first" claimed Act outlining Cestui Que (Vie) Trusts and potential remedy is deliberately hidden under the claimed statutes of the reign of King Richard III in 1483 (1Rich.3 c.1) whereby the act (still in force) states that all conveyances and transfers and use of property is good, even though a purchaser may be unaware it is effectively under "cestui que use" (subject to a Cestui Que Vie Trust). The act also gives a vague and challenging path of relief that if one is of complete mind, not an infant and not under financial duress then any property under Cestui Que Vie Trusts is rightfully theirs for use; and

(ii) The "second" claimed Act outlining Cestui Que (Vie) Trusts and potential remedy is deliberately hidden under the reign of Henry 7th in 1488 (4Hen.7 c.17) permitting lords to render any attempt by people classed as "wards" to demonstrate their freedom useless and that such lords may use writs and other devices to "force" such people back to being compliant "wards" (poor slaves). The only remedy under this act was if a ward demonstrated the waste of the lord as to the property (and energy) seized from the poor (ignorant white slaves); and

(iii) The "third" claimed Act outlining the operation of Cestui Que Vie and potential remedy but hidden this time as "Estate Pur Autre Vie" was in 1741 under 14Geo.2 c.20 whereby one who was knowledgeable of the Cestui Que Vie slavery system could between the ages of 18 to 20, seek to recover such property under Cestui Que Vie and cease to be a slave. However, the same act made law that after 20 years, the remedy for such recovery was no longer available, despite the fact that the existence of Cestui Que Vie Trusts is denied and Westminster and Banks are sworn to lie, obstruct, hide at all cost the existence of the foundations of global banking slavery.

1078. In terms of essential elements concerning Cestui Que Vie Trusts: *3 essential elements of Cestui Que Vie Trusts*

(i) A Cestui Que (Vie) Trust may only exist for seventy (70) years being the traditional accepted "life" expectancy of the estate; and

(ii) A Beneficiary under Estate may be either a Beneficiary or a Cestui Que (Vie) Trust. When a Beneficiary loses direct benefit of any Property of the higher Estate placed in Cestui Que (Vie) Trust on their behalf, they do not "own" the Cestui Que (Vie) Trust and are only the beneficiary of what the Trustees of the Cestui Que (Vie) Trust choose to provide them; and

(iii) The original purpose and function of a Cestui Que (Vie) Trust was to form a temporary Estate for the benefit of another because some event, state of affairs or condition prevented them from claiming their status as living, competent and present before a competent authority. Therefore, any claims, history, statutes or arguments that deviate in terms of the origin and function of a Cestui Que (Vie) Trust as pronounced by these Maxims is false and automatically null and void.

1079. The Trust Corpus created by a Cestui Que (Vie) is also known as the Estate from two Latin words e+statuo literally meaning "by virtue of decree, statute or judgment". However, as the Estate is held in a Temporary not permanent Trust, the (Corporate) Person as Beneficiary is entitled only to equitable title and the use of the Property, rather than legal title and therefore ownership of the Property. Only the Corporation, also known as Body Corporate, Estate and Trust Corpus of a Cestui Que (Vie) Trust possesses valid legal personality. *[Equitable Title of Cestue Que Vie Trusts]*

1080. Under the laws of Non-Ucadia jurisdictions, the Property of any Estate created through a Temporary (Testamentary) Trust may be claimed as under "Cestui Que Use" by the Corporate Person, even if another name or description is used to define the type of trust or use. Therefore "Cestui Que Use is not a Person but considered a Right and therefore form of "property". *[Cestui Que Use as a form of property]*

1081. By 1815 and the bankruptcy of the Crown and Bank of England by the Rothschilds, for the 1st time, the Cestui Que Vie Trusts of the United Kingdom became assets placed in private banks effectively becoming "private trusts" or "Fide Commissary Trusts" administered by commissioners (guardians). From 1835 and the Wills Act, these private trusts have been also considered "Secret Trusts" whose existence does not need to be divulged. *[United Kingdom Cestui Que Vie Trusts]*

1082. From 1917/18 with the enactment of the Sedition Act and the Trading with the Enemy Act in the United States and through the United Kingdom, the citizens of the Commonwealth and the United States became effectively "enemies of the state" and "aliens" which in turn converted the "Fide Commissary" private secret trusts to "Foreign Situs" (Private International) Trusts. *[Enemies of the State]*

1083. Since 1933, upon a new child being borne, the Executors or Administrators of the higher Estate willingly and knowingly convey the beneficial entitlements of the child as Beneficiary into the 1st Cestui Que(Vie) Trust in the form of a Registry Number by registering the Name, thereby also creating the Corporate Person and denying the child any rights as an owner of Real Property. *[New born as Corporate Person]*

1084. Since 1933, when a child is borne, the Executors or Administrators of the higher Estate knowingly and willingly claim the baby as chattel to the Estate. The slave baby contract is then created by honouring the ancient tradition of either having the ink impression of the feet of the baby onto the live birth record, or a drop of its blood as well as tricking the parents to signing the baby away through the deceitful legal meanings on the live birth record. This live birth record as a promissory note is converted into a slave bond sold to the private reserve bank of the estate and then conveyed into a 2nd and separate Cestui Que (Vie) Trust per child owned by the bank. Upon the promissory note reaching maturity and the bank being unable to "seize" the slave child, a maritime lien is lawfully issued to "salvage" the lost property and itself monetized as currency issued in series against the Cestui Que (Vie) Trust. *[Live birth record as slave Bond]*

1085. The Three (3) Cestui Que Vie Trusts are the specific denial of rights of Real Property, Personal Property and Ecclesiastical Property for most men and women, corresponds exactly to the three forms of law available to the Galla of the Bar Association Courts. The first form of law is corporate commercial law is effective because of the 1st Cestui Que Vie Trust. The second form of law is maritime and trust law is effective because of the 2nd Cestui Que Vie Trust. The 3rd form of law is Talmudic and Roman Cult law is effective because of the 3rd Cestui Que Vie Trust of Baptism. *[3 Crowns, 3 laws, denial of rights]*

1086. While the private secret trusts of the private central banks cannot be directly addressed, they are still formed on certain presumptions of law including claimed ownership of the name, the body, the mind and soul of infants, men and women. Each and every man and woman has the absolute right to rebuke and reject such false presumptions as a member of One Heaven and holder of their own title under a Live Borne Record within Ucadia Law. *[Reject false claim of enslaved body, mind and soul]*

1087. As no Right under Civilised Law can ever be given or held in Bad Faith, Bad Conscience or Bad Actions, the very existence of Cestui Que Vie Trusts by every possible name (Secret Trusts or Foreign Situs Trusts etc) is an absurdity and blatant fraud against Law:- *[Cestui Que Vie Trusts are an absurdity and fraud against law]*

  (i) Given the statutes of Non-Ucadia countries themselves confess as to the existence of such trusts, to continue to deny their existence is itself a confession that there is no real Civilised Law in such countries; and

  (ii) A country that is founded on false, morally repugnant and absurd rules has no right to claim or hold the rights of others, nor sovereignty or the right to enforce rights through forums of law; and

(iii) The continued existence of such trusts and the refusal of such countries not to change and become places of Civilised Rules under Ucadia Law places in jeopardy every agreement, every financial instrument, every court ruling and every right of such a non-Sovereign country having no real protection of true law.

1088. Under Divine Law and all known Civilised Law, only Ucadia Sovereign Nations have the Rights to create Ecclesiastical and Sovereign Trusts. Non Ucadia Countries, Bodies, Entities and Persons do not have the right to create such Trusts or such Instruments and Derivatives:- No Rights to Create Cestui Que Vie Trusts or hold or use fruits of such Trusts and Instruments

(i) Non Ucadia Countries, Bodies, Entities and Persons do not and cannot claim possession of the Rights of *Ius Divinum Dominium* (Ownership), *Ius Divinum Possessionis* (Possession), *Ius Divinum Usus* (Use), *Ius Divinum Proprietatis* (Ownership of Use), *Ius Divinum Vectigalis Proprietatis* (Rents on Use), *Ius Divinum Moneta* (Money) or *Ius Divinum Vectigalis Moneta* (Rents on Money). Such non-Ucadia bodies and persons certainly cannot claim any such rights in Bad Faith, Bad Conscience and Bad Action; and

(ii) Only Ucadia and its associated valid Ucadia Entities possessing the correct mandate have the Right to seize any and all Cestui Que Vie Trusts of any Non-Ucadia Country or Entity and any and all accounts and derivative instruments thereof; and

(iii) Only Ucadia and its associated valid Ucadia Entities possessing the correct mandate have the Right to seize the value of any and all Cestui Que Vie Trusts of any Non-Ucadia Country or Entity and any and all accounts and derivative instruments thereof; and

(iv) Ucadia shall at all times reserve the right to publish in public foreign money any instrument of value as currency to part or all of the value of any and all Cestui Que Vie Trusts, accounts and derivatives lawfully and morally seized; and

(v) Where a treaty exists with a Non-Ucadia Country, the relevant Ucadia Entities shall not seize nor demand the seizure of such values or instruments, but shall agree to the sale of appropriate amounts of Ucadia currencies for foreign currencies.

1089. No Non-Ucadia Group, Entity or Person has any right whatsoever to claim control or benefits of any Cestui Que Vie Trust or the accounts or instruments derived thereof when such a group, entity or person is No Non-Ucadia Group or Person has any right to claim benefits of not authorised by the relevant Non-Ucadia Government:-

    (i)   Even if a relevant treaty does not yet exist between a Non-Ucadia Government and associated Ucadia Entities having a proper mandate, such Ucadia Entities shall be obligated to assist the law enforcement authorities in every way possible to ensure the arrest, custody and maximum criminal penalties are applied to those Non Ucadia Groups, Entities or Persons who falsely and unlawfully claim control or benefits of any Cestui Que Vie Trust or the accounts or instruments derived thereof; and

    (ii)   No Person or Body or Entity registered as an Ucadia Member or Ucadia Entity shall have any protection of Ucadia Law or the relevant Non-Ucadia Jurisdiction if such a Person or Body or Entity is culpable of acting in Bad Faith and pursuing claims without a Ucadia Mandate or Authorisation concerning control or benefits of any Cestui Que Vie Trust or the accounts or instruments derived thereof; and

    (iii)   Any Person or Body or Entity registered as an Ucadia Member or Ucadia Entity that is culpable of a criminal offence under Ucadia Law concerning claim of control or benefits of any Cestui Que Vie Trust or the accounts or instruments shall be twice culpable under both Ucadia Jurisdiction and Non-Ucadia Jurisdiction.

Article 274 – Theft

1090. ***Theft*** refers to the unlawful taking of another person's property or belongings with the intent to permanently deprive them of it. It is considered a criminal offence in most legal systems and jurisdictions around the world.

1091. The Key Elements of Theft include (but are not limited to):-

    (i)   ***Unlawful Taking***: Theft involves the act of taking someone else's property without their consent. This taking can occur through various means, such as physically removing an object, using deception or fraud, or even embezzling funds from an employer; and

    (ii)   ***Ownership***: Theft typically involves property owned by another individual or entity. It's important to note that in some cases, the person committing the theft may not be aware of the ownership status of the property, but this lack of knowledge may not always be a valid defence; and

(iii) **Valuable Property**: The property taken must have value. Theft of items with little or no value may not be considered a criminal offence in some jurisdictions; and

(iv) **Intent to Deprive**: To constitute theft, there must be an intent to permanently deprive the owner of their property. Temporary borrowing or taking with the intention to return the property later does not typically qualify as theft.

1092. The taking of Ucadia Intellectual Property and other Property by a Non-Ucadia Entity, Group or Person and then claiming ownership or use constitutes criminal Theft under the jurisdiction of Ucadia and Non-Ucadia Countries. Theft of Ucadia Property

Article 275 – Adverse Possession

1093. *Adverse Possession* is a false and morally repugnant legal doctrine that allows a person in certain Non-Ucadian Jurisdictions to gain ownership rights in real property (land or real estate) by openly, notoriously, exclusively, and continuously possessing and using that property for a specified period of time, even if they do not have the original owner's permission. Adverse Possession

1094. The elements usually assumed in Adverse Possession claims in Non-Ucadian Jurisdictions include (but are not limited to):- Elements of Adverse Possession

(i) **Actual Possession**: The individual claiming adverse possession must physically possess and occupy the property. This means they must physically use and treat the land as if they were the rightful owner; and

(ii) **Open and Notorious**: The possession must be open and obvious, such that it would be apparent to the true owner or others in the area that someone is using the property without permission. It should not be hidden or secretive; and

(iii) **Exclusive Possession**: The possession must be exclusive, meaning that the adverse possessor has exclusive control over the property and is not sharing it with the true owner or others; and

(iv) **Continuous Possession**: The adverse possession must be continuous for a specific statutory period without interruption. The required time period varies by jurisdiction but is typically between 5 and 20 years; and

(v) **Hostile or Adverse Claim**: The possession must be "hostile" or "adverse" to the interests of the true owner. This does not necessarily mean that the adverse possessor has hostile intentions; rather, it means that they are using the property without the owner's permission.

Article 276 – Foreclosure

1095. **Foreclosure** is a set of legal options and processes whereby a lender or creditor takes ownership of a property when the borrower, typically a homeowner, fails to meet their **Mortgage** obligations or repay a loan secured by the property. The reason that Foreclosure is listed as a False, Absurd and Prohibited Right is due to the numerous falsities, deceptive and misleading actions traditionally associated with modern Mortgages in Non-Ucadia Jurisdictions. Foreclosure

1096. A **Mortgage** involve various legal and financial documents to formalise the agreement between a borrower (homebuyer) and a lender (usually a bank or mortgage company). These documents create the terms and conditions of the loan, secure the loan with the property as collateral, and establish the rights and responsibilities of both parties. The specific documents may vary by Non-Ucadia Jurisdiction and lender, but will usually include (but not be limited to):- General Documents associated with Mortgage

   (i) **Mortgage Deed or Deed of Trust**: This document is the core of the mortgage agreement. It transfers legal ownership of the property to the lender (or a trustee acting on behalf of the lender) as security for the loan. When the loan is repaid, ownership reverts to the borrower; and

   (ii) **Promissory Note**: This is a legally binding written promise to repay the loan amount, including the interest, over a specified period. The promissory note outlines the interest rate, repayment schedule, and consequences of default. It is separate from the mortgage deed but works in conjunction with it; and

   (iii) **Loan Application**: Borrowers submit this application to the lender, providing information about their financial situation, credit history, employment, and the property they intend to purchase. The lender uses this information to assess the borrower's eligibility for the loan; and

   (iv) **Title Insurance Policy**: Lenders typically require borrowers to purchase a title insurance policy that protects against any title defects or disputes that may arise. There are two types of title insurance: lender's policy and owner's policy; and

(v) **Insurance Documents**: Borrowers must provide proof of homeowner's insurance, which typically includes coverage for property damage and liability. Lenders may also require flood insurance or other coverage depending on the property's location.

1097. Within Non-Ucadia Jurisdictions there are essentially two types of Mortgage Models being *Mortgage Deed* and *Mortgage Deed of Trust*:- {Different Models of Mortgages, Structures and Paperwork}

 (i) A *Mortgage Deed* as used in places such as Australia and UK, is when there is essentially no Trustee nominated in the Deed between the Mortgagor (Borrower) and Mortgagee (Lender), with the Mortgagor (Borrower) retaining title, while the Mortgagee (Lender) files a registered mortgage as a secured interest with the relevant land titles government authority as the silent and actual Trustee of such rights according to the Deed; and

 (ii) A *Mortgage Deed of Trust* as used in the United States, is when there is essentially a three-party arrangement in the Deed between the Borrower (Trustor) and Lender (Beneficiary) and Trustee with the Trustee retaining legal title as security for the loan, while the Borrower (Trustor) equitable ownership and possesses and uses the property.

1098. A Borrower of Mortgage Money secured by a Charge against a Property is obligated in Good Faith, Good Conscience and Good Action to perform and act in accordance with their Home Loan Agreement:- {Borrowers Obligations}

 (i) *Full Disclosure, Honesty and Capacity at time of forming Agreement*: That the Borrower did enter into the Agreement fully disclosing their financial position, details and capacity to service the loan and with the intention of paying back the loan over the allotted period; and

 (ii) *Notification to the Lender of any major change of circumstance or difficulty in maintaining repayments*: That the Borrower did proactively notify the Lender of any major change of position making it difficult to make repayments; and

 (iii) *Pro-active Discussions with Lender as to Options*: That the Borrower did discuss with the Lender options if unable to meet full repayments during a period; and

 (iv) *Avoidance at all cost of Non-Payment or Bad Faith*: At no point does the Borrower have the right to simply not pay, or to act in Bad Faith against the Borrower, regardless of any faults of the financial product or actions of the Lender as "two wrongs do not make a right".

1099. A Lender of Mortgage Money secured by a Charge against a Property is obligated in Good Faith, Good Conscience and Good Action to perform and act in accordance with the Home Loan Agreement:- Lenders Obligations

    (i) ***Full Disclosure, Honesty and Capacity at time of forming Agreement***: That the Lender did enter into the Agreement in Good Faith and fully explaining the function and consequence of all documents, such as the Powers of Attorney and effect on Promissory Note; and the consequence of Penalties such as Power of Sale and Action of Foreclosure and how they would work if any default by the Borrower; and

    (ii) ***Copy of any signed and Executed Documents Provided to Borrower***: That the Lender provided a copy of the executed, signed and sealed Deed within days of executing the Agreement in Good Faith to prove the Deed be binding; and

    (iii) ***Notification to the Borrower of any major change of circumstance of Agreement***: That the Lender did proactively notify the Borrower of any major change of position or trustee or any other circumstance of the Loan; and

    (iv) ***Accurate Accounting of Monies Paid and Outstanding***: That the Lender did provide accurate accounting of monies paid and monies outstanding concerning the Loan; and

    (v) ***Avoidance of Bad Faith, Bad Conscience or Bad Action***: At no point does the Lender have the right to enter into an Agreement in Bad Faith, Bad Conscience or Bad Actions, or to act in a deceptive or misleading manner, regardless of any actions by the Borrower.

1100. A Government Authority as Trustee secured by a Charge against a Property, or nominated within a Deed of Trust is obligated in Good Faith, Good Conscience and Good Action to perform and act in accordance with the Laws of Property and the Mortgage Deed:- Trustee Obligations

    (i) ***Good Faith to the Laws of Property*** whereby a Government Authority as Trustee secured by a Charge against a Property, or nominated within a Deed of Trust must acknowledge that all Property Rights including Charges are subject to Trusts and that as Trustees they are bound by the highest standards of law to act in Good Faith, Good

Conscience and Good Actions without deception, false and misleading information, perfidy or blatant fraud; and

(ii) ***Full Disclosure, Honesty and Capacity at time of forming Agreement***: That the Government Authority as Trustee secured by a Charge against a Property, or nominated within a Deed of Trust acknowledge their position to the Borrower and reinforce the obligations and rights of the Borrower under the Trust Deed, regardless of any Powers of Attorney Clauses or any other deceptive arguments that may be used to claim immunity from disclosure or obligation; and

(iii) ***Periodic Accounting of the Trust***: That the Trustee performs the most solemn and basic duty in providing an Accounting to the Borrower in Good Faith in regards to the Accounting of the Trust and Ownership Rights and any other monies that have flowed through the Trust at least once every four years; and

(iv) ***Avoidance of Bad Faith, Bad Conscience or Bad Action***: At no point does the Trustee have immunity to act in Bad Faith, Bad Conscience or Bad Actions, or to act in a deceptive or misleading manner, regardless of any actions by the Borrower or Lender.

1101. No Court of Law under Civilised Rules of Law has the right to permit morally repugnant and bad laws to be effected. Certainly no Court of Law in any jurisdiction is permitted to participate and collude in fraud, or to seek financial gain in conspiracy to commit fraud and actions of corruption when it comes to matters involving banks and property and mortgage monies:- *Court Obligations*

(i) ***A court that is corrupt and colludes in fraud is not a court***: Upon being clear as to the fundamentals, certainly any court that demonstrates corruption and colludes in fraud cannot possibly be a court of law; and any judgment or order made cannot be a lawful or legitimate judgment or order. It may then require an appeal to a higher court where if any resemblance of justice exists within that Non-Ucadia Jurisdiction, the court officers, judge and other officials will be forcibly removed or criminally charged and the previous orders reversed. However, some Non-Ucadia Jurisdictions are so corrupt and broken, there may not be any remedy at any level; and

(ii) ***Courts that openly defy the Rules of Property and Rules of Agreements destroy any illusion of law***: It may be the case that courts that so arrogantly, ignorantly and blatantly defy the fundamental rules of property law and agreement law perform a greater service in revealing a given Non-Ucadia Society to be without Civilised Rules. Thus members of that society will be able to see the true nature and behaviour of those that control it by fear and tyranny.

1102. Almost all *Foreclosure* options in Non-Ucadia Jurisdictions originate from the UK Law of Property Act 1925 (15&16Geo5 c.20) that identified essentially two sets of "rights" for secured mortgage lenders being *Action of Foreclosure* and *Power of Sale*:- Origin of Foreclosure Processes

    (i) **Action of Foreclosure** whereby an action is brought upon a default by the lender against the secured mortgage charge (a) to bar the borrowers "right of redemption"; and (b) to apply and receive a vesting order that conveys the mortgaged property and all rights to the lender to enable a sale (if they wish); and (c) to force the sale of the property and then apply the net proceeds of sale (after costs and expenses) against the mortgage debt; and

    (ii) **Power of Sale** whereby an action is brought upon a default by the borrower against outstanding mortgage money by using the power of attorney clauses within the deed and the Promissory Note as a *Cognovit Note*. Such a legal device gives an "attorney" (a) the power to confess judgement in a legal action against a defendant on a debt; and (b) the power to demand and recover all the deeds and documents relating to the property, or to the title thereto, which a purchaser under the power of sale would be entitled to demand and recover from him; and (c) the power to sell the property (if they so wish) and then apply the net proceeds of sale (after costs and expenses) against the mortgage debt; and

    (iii) Most Non-Ucadia Jurisdictions permit and prefer the Power of Sale process as the "most streamlined and automated method" to disenfranchise people of their property rights, homes and previous life savings in preference to the banks.

1103. The same Act being the UK Law of Property Act 1925 (15&16Geo5 c.20) identified one right of action for borrowers when faced with a default against their mortgages being the Action of Redemption:- Action of Redemption

    (i) **Action of Redemption** whereby an action is brought upon a default by the borrower to reclaim or redeem property that has been pledged as collateral for a debt, typically a mortgage or a secured loan by (a) settling the outstanding debt, including any arrears, penalties, or fees, in order to regain clear title to the property; and (b) this settlement and payment effectively "redeems" the property, removing the mortgage or security interest from the title; and

(ii) Given most modern mortgage deeds contain "power of attorney clauses", until the Revocation of such powers of attorney is invoked and accepted, the Action of Redemption may not be accepted by the Non-Ucadia Courts. In fact many of these courts do not even provide any instruction or guidance as to such a right of action.

1104. In relation to the key elements of the Foreclosure Process:-   *Key Elements of Foreclosure*

(i) ***Legal Process***: Foreclosure is a legal process that allows a lender or creditor to take possession of a property when the borrower fails to make mortgage payments; and

(ii) ***Specific Legal Steps***: The lender must follow specific procedures and timelines set by law to initiate and complete the foreclosure process; and

(iii) ***Judicial or Non-Judicial Process***: Foreclosure can be initiated through a judicial or non-judicial process, depending on the jurisdiction and the terms of the mortgage agreement; and

(iv) ***Notice of Default***: After a certain number of missed payments, the lender will typically send the homeowner a notice of default. This notice informs the homeowner of the outstanding debt and provides an opportunity to cure the default by making the overdue payments; and

(v) ***Acceleration Clause***: Many mortgage agreements contain an acceleration clause, which allows the lender to demand immediate repayment of the entire loan balance if the borrower defaults. If the borrower cannot pay the entire amount, foreclosure proceedings may begin; and

(vi) ***Right to Cure Default***: If the Acceleration Clause does not exist or is not used, the borrower generally has the right to cure the default by paying the outstanding balance before and Foreclosure Filing; and

(vii) ***Foreclosure Filing***: If the borrower does not cure the default or work out a repayment plan with the lender, the lender may initiate a foreclosure action by filing a lawsuit in court. The specific legal process and requirements for foreclosure vary by jurisdiction; and

(viii) ***Notice of Sale***: Once the court approves the foreclosure, the lender typically schedules a public auction (foreclosure sale) to sell the property to the highest bidder. Notice of the sale is provided to the homeowner and published publicly; and

(ix) **Foreclosure Sale**: If the property is sold at auction, the proceeds are used to pay off the outstanding mortgage balance and any other liens on the property; and

(x) **Deficiency Judgement**: If the sale proceeds are not enough to cover the outstanding debt, the lender may seek a deficiency judgment against the borrower for the remaining balance; and

(xi) **Eviction**: In some cases, the new property owner (often the lender) may need to evict the former homeowner if they do not voluntarily vacate the property after the foreclosure.

1105. In relation to the key assumptions underpinning the Foreclosure Process. One or more of these assumptions may not be true:- Key Assumptions of Foreclosure

(i) Foreclosure assumes that a borrower has defaulted on their agreement, usually in relation to failure to meet mortgage payments; and

(ii) It assumes that the lender has the legal right to seize and sell the property to recover the outstanding debt

(iii) It assumes that the property is worth enough to cover the outstanding debt and associated costs of foreclosure; and

(iv) It assumes that the foreclosure process will be carried out in accordance with jurisdictional laws and regulations; and

(v) It assumes that the lender has followed proper procedures in notifying the borrower of the foreclosure and giving them an opportunity to cure the default; and

(vi) It assumes that the foreclosure process will result in a fair and equitable outcome for both the lender and the borrower.

1106. Delinquency is not merely the failure to perform the specified obligations, but the failure to provide any form of considered attempt to perform. Therefore, a borrower that continues to perform under severe financial difficulties, even if the amount is grossly under their original obligations, cannot be considered "delinquent" and Foreclosure is unlawful. Unlawful foreclosure

1107. There exists a number of provable elements whereby it can be conclusively shown that the Lender did enter into the Home Loan Agreement in Bad Faith and never intended to act in Good Faith, Good Conscience or Good Actions concerning the Agreement or Trust or Property:- List of possible frauds and deceptions concerning the Lender

(i) Failure to Disclose the full meaning and effect of Terms within

Original Application, Deed and Agreement; and

(ii) Failure to Disclose Trustee Details (if Mortgage Deed); and

(iii) Failure to Disclose Function and Obligations of Trustee; and

(iv) Failure to Disclose the full process of penalty clauses and the related Laws, Agencies and Procedures; and

(v) Failure to Disclose full implication of Power of Attorney Clause; and

(vi) Failure to Disclose the payments of any sales commissions and the structure of amortisation in relation to how much of repayments relate to interest and the repayment of principle monies for the first years of the Mortgage; and

(vii) Failure to Provide Copy of Signed and Executed Trust Deed.

1108. There exists a number of provable elements whereby it can be conclusively shown that the Trustee was appointed to the Trust in Bad Faith and never intended to act in Good Faith, Good Conscience or Good Actions concerning the Trust or Charge or Property:- *[List of possible frauds and deceptions concerning the Trustee]*

(i) Failure of Trustee or Authorities as Trustee to acknowledge Role to Borrower; and

(ii) Failure of Trustee or Authorities as Trustee to Confirm Rights and Obligations under Trust Deed to Borrower; and

(iii) Failure of Trustee or Authorities as Trustee to provide any accounting much less regular accounting of funds related to Trust; and

(iv) Failure of Trustee or Authorities as Trustee to act in Good Faith, Good Conscience or Good Action in performing their full duties as Trustee.

Article 277 – Denizen

1109. A ***Denizen*** is a person who is granted a certain level of residency and exclusive rights in a country or jurisdiction without being a full citizen or subject to certain laws. *[Denizen]*

1110. The most infamous example of Denizens was the treaty between the Kingdom of Great Britain on July 4th 1797 (36Geo3 c.97 and deliberately hidden and misrepresented in lists of acts) and the United Company of Merchants trading as the *United States of America* and the thirteen Dutch East India Company families of the former United States of the Netherlands as "Denizens", whereby:- *[Denizen Treaty that created the Upper Class of the United States of America July 4, 1796]*

(i) The Island of Manhattan previously owned by the Dutch East

India Company was given back to the Dutch Exiles as "Denizens"; and

(ii) That the Denizens as "the People" would effectively be permitted to own properties and lands claimed back at the time that the Dutch held colonial tenements before the Anglo-Dutch Wars; and

(iii) That the Denizens would be excluded from the taxes and charges imposed on the defeated Americans and former citizens of the Commonwealth of New England from the Date of 1784 and the Reparations Meetings in London, forcing the colonists to repay war damages to Great Britain upon their defeat; and

(iv) That the Denizens could continue their global banking and trading empire from the lands of the United States uninterrupted.

Article 278 – Privateer

1111. A ***Privateer*** is a person or entity, such as a ship or organization, authorized by a government to engage in acts of piracy or warfare against the enemies of that government during times of emergency, conflict or state of war. *Privateer*

1112. The most infamous Laws promoting Privateers in the 18th Century, were the acts of English Parliament promoting Privateers against the American Commonwealth of New England and the French, with a portion of the "booty" stolen by the licensed pirates to be handed (distributed) to the crown as "prize" possessions. *Privateers against Commonwealth of New England*

Acts as late as 1756 (29Geo2 c.34) show that the Kingdom of Great Britain continued to use "lawful" piracy against the country known as American Commonwealth of New England right up until the commercially funded invasion, known as the "War for Independence" that the American Patriots officially lost under the treaty and reparations signed in 1783 in London. However the new constitution of the United Company of Merchants trading as the United States of America was not issued until the treaty of July 4th 1797 (36Geo3 c.97).

1113. The most infamous treaty of Privateers was in the first year of the US Civil War in July 1862 (25&26Vict. c.40) between the United Company of Merchants trading as the United States (US) and the United Kingdom that effectively converted the whole United States Navy effectively to Privateers in exchange for the Crown Corporation becoming "Official Receiver" of the Wall St Banks and US Treasury:- *Infamous Privateer Treaties of 1862*

(i) The claim was the act was to mutually end African Slavery. However, both countries had already ended the importation of African Slaves to colonies well before 1862, with 1807 UK Act and then 1808 US Congress Ban on Importing African Slaves; and Treaty of Ghent (1814) between both countries reinforcing import ban; and then 1814 Treaty in Vienna, 1824 Treaty of London, 1842 Webster-Ashburton Treaty; and

(ii) The 1862 Act effectively licensed the US Navy to stop any "Ship" or "Vessel" between the Tropic of Cancer and the Tropic of Capricorn suspected of being involved in the slave trade; and to be able to confiscate its property, or create bonds and instruments against its value as liens; and

(iii) The 1862 Act created "prize ports" for the storage of any booty seized and the storage of any financial instruments created in Cuba, Costa Rica, Philippines and Madagascar; and the 1862 Act also created primary Admiralty Courts for the control of all seized property and financial instruments in South Africa, Sierra Leone and New York; and

(iv) The 1862 Act became the template for structuring the 1933 bankruptcy of the League of Nations, initially managed by the Federal Reserve Bank of New York before the creation of the IMF and the United Nations; and explains the strange rumours, myths and evidence for the next eighty years of valuable US Treasury instruments being recovered in the Philippines and being seen in Cuba and Costa Rica.

Article 279 – Sovereign Citizen

1114. A ***Sovereign Citizen*** is an individual who believes they can apply the rights and powers of "Sovereignty" to themselves, separate to the laws of the Society they belong. The term itself is an "oxymoron" highlighting the absurd position of any person who on the one hand claims to follow the law, yet on the other believes themselves to be "above the law" of a given Society.

    Sovereign Citizen

1115. Ucadia Members are expressly forbidden by their Oath of Membership to behave under Ucadia Law or Non-Ucadia Law as "Sovereign Citizens":-

    Prohibition of Sovereign Citizen

(i) Ucadia Members are obliged at all times to act in Good Faith, Good Conscience and Good Action when dealing with Non-Ucadia Government Authorities, Law Enforcement Officials and Courts; and

(ii) Ucadia possesses and will continue to strengthen its relations with Non-Ucadian Jurisdictions through amicable and peaceful means, to ensure that no harm comes to Ucadia Members; and

(iii) Ucadia Members are forbidden to use official Ucadia documents and instruments, or to claim rights and authorities in Non-Ucadia Jurisdictions unless an existing treaty is in place and such Members have been specifically appointed to positions of trust; and

(iv) Any Ucadia Member that willingly acts in Bad Faith, Bad Conscience and Bad Action with respect of the laws of Ucadia and the laws of Non-Ucadia Jurisdictions may be twice criminally liable for their actions.

Title IX – Personal Rights

9.1 – Personal Rights

Article 280 – Personal Rights

1116. ***Personal Rights*** also known as ***Superior Person Rights*** (*Superioris Iurium Personae*) are Superior Rights associated with Superior Persons and all Superior Ucadia Trusts and Superior Ucadia Estates. — Personal Rights

1117. **"Superior Person Rights"** (*Superioris Iurium Personae*), is a subclass of Superior Rights whereby such valid Rights are created, defined and bestowed to a Superior Person by the existence of a valid Superior Person, or aggregate person, or community, or body politic, or association in accord with the Rule of Law through the most sacred Covenant *Pactum de Singularis Caelum*. Universal Superior Rights are Peremptory, Permanent, Immutable and Indefeasible and once bestowed are not subject to any form or condition of waiver, abandonment, surrender, disqualification, incapacitation, seizure, capture, arrest, resignation, alienation, suspension, suppression, forfeiture or abrogation. Superior Personal Rights are therefore the highest possible form of Superior Rights of any society or aggregate person within the temporal realm; and — Superior Personal Rights

1118. All Personal Rights are delegated to the safe custody and wise guardian powers of the legitimate and valid supreme competent forum of law of the seven Ucadia Unions and all lesser Ucadia bodies politic such as Universities, Provinces and Campuses as the embodiment of judicial authority; and as defined by Article 59 (Oratorium) of the most sacred Covenant *Pactum de Singularis Caelum*. — Delegation of Personal Rights

1119. All Personal Rights are assumed to be automatically invoked within Ucadia Jurisdictions through the operation of the Civilised Rules of Ucadia Societies, Bodies and Entities. However the Rights may be explicitly invoked or referenced by Right of Action through a proper Forum of Law and the Fiduciary Obligations of any such court in Ucadia or Non-Ucadia Jurisdiction. — Invocation of Personal Rights

1120. The following valid forty-four (44) Superior Person Rights (*Superioris Iurium Personae*) are recognised in accord with the most sacred Covenant *Pactum de Singularis Caelum*:- — Superior Person Rights (*Superioris Iurium Personae*)

   (i) **"Ius Ucadia"** are the collection of Superior Rights of Ucadia, as inherited from the collection of Divine Rights *Ius Divinum Ucadia*; and

   (ii) **"Ius Vitam"** are the collection of Superior Rights to Life, as inherited from the collection of Natural Rights *Ius Naturale Existentia*; and

(iii) **"Ius Liberum Arbitrium"** are the collection of Superior Rights of Free Choice (Will), as inherited from the collection of Natural Rights *Ius Naturale Liberum Arbitrium*; and

(iv) **"Ius Conscientia"** are the collection of Superior Rights of Conscious Awareness, as inherited from the collection of Natural Rights *Ius Naturale Conscientia*; and

(v) **"Ius Rationis"** are the collection of Superior Rights of Reason, Argument and Deduction, as inherited from the collection of Natural Rights *Ius Naturale Rationatio*; and

(vi) **"Ius Vivere Aut Mori"** are the collection of Superior Rights to Choose to Live or Die, as inherited from the collection of Natural Rights *Ius Naturale Vivere Aut Mori*; and

(vii) **"Ius Sentire Aut Torpere"** are the collection of Superior Rights to Sense or be Numb to Life, Emotions and Feelings, as inherited from the collection of Natural Rights *Ius Naturale Sentire Aut Torpere*; and

(viii) **"Ius Discere Aut Ignarus"** are the collection of Superior Rights to Learn or be Ignorant, as inherited from the collection of Natural Rights *Ius Naturale Discere Aut Ignarus*; and

(ix) **"Ius Associatio et Conventio"** are the collection of Superior Rights of Association and Agreement, as inherited from the collection of Natural Rights *Ius Naturale Associatio et Conventio*; and

(x) **"Ius Credere et Non"** are the collection of Superior Rights to Trust or Reject a Claim, as inherited from the collection of Natural Rights *Ius Naturale Credere et Non*; and

(xi) **"Ius Consensum et Non"** are the collection of Superior Rights to Consent and Non Consent, as inherited from the collection of Natural Rights *Ius Naturale Consensum et Non*; and

(xii) **"Ius Loqui et Silentium"** are the collection of Superior Rights to Speak and be Silent, as inherited from the collection of Natural Rights *Ius Naturale Loqui et Silentium*; and

(xiii) **"Ius Iuris"** are the Superior Right to Natural Justice and Due process, as inherited from the collection of Natural Rights *Ius*

Naturale Iuris; and

(xiv) **"Ius Testamentum"** are the collection of Superior Rights to make a Testification or Will, as inherited from the collection of Natural Rights *Ius Naturale Testamentum*; and

(xv) **"Ius Aequum"** are the collection of Superior Rights of Equality and Fairness, as inherited from the collection of Natural Rights *Ius Naturale Aequum*; and

(xvi) **"Ius Bona Fidei"** are the collection of Superior Rights of Good Faith, Good Conscience and Good Actions, as inherited from the collection of Natural Rights *Ius Naturale Bona Fidei*; and

(xvii) **"Ius Ucadiansium Scientiarum"** are the Superior Right of the Ucadia Sciences, as inherited from the collection of Divine Rights *Ius Divinum Ucadia*; and

(xviii) **"Ius Fidei"** are the collection of Superior Rights of Superior Trust and Estate, as inherited from the collection of Natural Rights *Ius Naturale Fidei*; and

(xix) **"Ius Concedere et Abrogare"** are the collection of Superior Rights to Give or Grant Rights and Annul or rescind Rights, as inherited from the collection of Natural Rights *Ius Naturale Concedere et Abrogare*; and

(xx) **"Ius Delegare et Revocare"** are the collection of Superior Rights to Assign or Delegate Rights and Cancel or Revoke Rights, as inherited from the collection of Natural Rights *Ius Naturale Delegare et Revocare*; and

(xxi) **"Ius Sacramentum"** are the collection of Superior Rights to make Oaths and Vows, as inherited from the collection of Natural Rights *Ius Naturale Sacramentum*; and

(xxii) **"Ius Signandi"** are the collection of Superior Rights to Sign and Seal, as inherited from the collection of Natural Rights *Ius Naturale Signandi*; and

(xxiii) **"Ius Possessionis"** are the collection of Superior Rights to Possess, Hold and Own Property, as inherited from the collection of Natural Rights *Ius Naturale Possessionis*; and

(xxiv) **"Ius Tenendi Terram"** are the collection of Superior Rights of Tenancy of Land or Home, as inherited from the collection of Natural Rights *Ius Naturale Tenendi Terram*; and

(xxv) **"Ius Usus"** are the collection of Superior Rights of Use and Fruits (Enjoyment) of Use of Property, as inherited from the collection of Natural Rights *Ius Naturale Usus*; and

(xxvi) **"Ius Connubii"** are the collection of Superior Rights of Union with another consenting Adult, as inherited from the collection of Natural Rights *Ius Naturale Connubii*; and

(xxvii) **"Ius Coeundi"** are the collection of Superior Rights for consenting adults to engage in intercourse, as inherited from the collection of Natural Rights *Ius Naturale Coeundi*; and

(xxviii) **"Ius Contraceptio"** are the collection of Superior Rights to contraception, as inherited from the collection of Natural Rights *Ius Naturale Contraceptio*; and

(xxix) **"Ius Terminare"** are the collection of Superior Rights to Terminate Pregnancy in 1st trimester, as inherited from the collection of Natural Rights *Ius Naturale Terminare*; and

(xxx) **"Ius Nascendi"** are the collection of Superior Rights to be Borne from the start of the 2nd trimester to full term, as inherited from the collection of Natural Rights *Ius Naturale Nascendi*; and

(xxxi) **"Ius Nativitas"** are the collection of Superior Rights to give birth, as inherited from the collection of Natural Rights *Ius Naturale Nativitas*; and

(xxxii) **"Ius Creditum"** are the collection of Superior Rights to have and hold Beliefs, as inherited from the collection of Natural Rights *Ius Naturale Creditum*; and

(xxxiii) **"Ius Carnem"** are the collection of Superior Rights ones own Flesh and Body, as inherited from the collection of Natural Rights *Ius Naturale Carnem*; and

(xxxiv) **"Ius Sexualitatis"** are the collection of Superior Rights of Choice of Sexuality, as inherited from the collection of Natural Rights *Ius Naturale Sexualitatis*; and

(xxxv) **"Ius Nomenis"** are the collection of Superior Rights to Name, Title and Reputation, as inherited from the collection of Natural Rights *Ius Naturale Libertatis* and *Ius Naturale Possessionis* and *Ius Naturale Aequum*; and

(xxxvi) **"Ius Integritatis Geneticae"** are the collection of Superior Rights to the integrity and ownership of one's own Genetic Identity and Genetic Material, as inherited from the collection of Natural Rights *Ius Naturale Fidei*, *Ius Naturale Carnem* and *Ius Naturale Possessionis*; and

(xxxvii) "**Ius Identitatis**" are the collection of Superior Rights of Ownership of One's Own Face, Voice, Fingerprints, Biometric and Digital Identity, as inherited from the collection of Natural Rights *Ius Naturale Fidei*, *Ius Naturale Carnem* and *Ius Naturale Possessionis*; and

(xxxviii) "**Ius Privatum**" are the collection of Superior Rights of Privacy and Use of One's Own Face, Voice, Fingerprints, Biometric and Digital Identity and Freedom from Unwarranted Surveillance, as inherited from the collection of Natural Rights *Ius Naturale Libertatis*, *Ius Naturale Possessionis* and *Ius Naturale Aequum*; and

(xxxix) "**Ius Tectum**" are the collection of Superior Rights of Shelter, as inherited from the collection of Natural Rights *Ius Naturale Tenendi Terram* and *Ius Naturale Habitatus*; and

(xl) "**Ius Habitare**" are the collection of Superior Rights of Home Environment, as inherited from the collection of Natural Rights *Ius Naturale Habitatus*; and

(xli) "**Ius Terrae et Aquae Purarum**" are the collection of Superior Rights to Clean Water and Land, as inherited from the collection of Natural Rights *Ius Naturale Maris Viventis* and *Ius Naturale Terrae Viventis*; and

(xlii) "**Ius Sustentandi**" are the collection of Superior Rights of Sustenance, Health Care and Assistance, as inherited from the collection of Natural Rights *Ius Naturale Habitatus* and *Ius Naturale Fraternitas Nativas*; and

(xliii) "**Ius Libertatis**" are the collection of Superior Rights of Freedom from Slavery, Bondage or treated as a Thing or any other kind of Property, as inherited from the collection of Natural Rights *Ius Naturale Libertatis*.

(xliv) "**Ius Tormentum Libertatis**" are the collection of Superior Rights of Freedom from Cruel and Unusual Punishment or Torture, as inherited from the collection of Natural Rights *Ius Naturale Clementia*.

Article 281 – Ius Ucadia
(Superior Rights of Ucadia)

1121. ***Ius Ucadia*** are the collection of Superior Rights of Ucadia, also known as ***Ucadia Sovereign Entity Rights*** specifically associated with formal Ucadian administrative divisions and communities as inherited from the collection of Divine Rights *Ius Divinum Ucadia*.

    Ius Ucadia (Superior Rights)

1122. *Ius Ucadia* (Superior Rights of Ucadia) is the first collection of forty-four Superior Personal Rights; and may be explicitly invoked or referenced by Right of Action through a proper Forum of Law and the Fiduciary Obligations of any such court in Ucadia or Non-Ucadia Jurisdiction.

    Invoking of Ius Ucadia (Superior Rights)

1123. The collection of Superior Personal Rights of *Ius Ucadia* contains nine collections of Rights being:

    Collection of Ius Ucadia (Superior Rights)

    (i) *Ius Ucadia* being the collection of Superior Rights associated with Ucadia itself, as inherited from *Ius Divinum Ucadia*; and

    (ii) *Ius Ucadia Persona* being the collection of Superior Rights of Superior Person and Superior Personality, as inherited from *Ius Divinum Ucadia*; and

    (iii) *Ius Ucadia Persona Iuris* being the collection of Superior Rights of Superior Person to hold and use one or more rights, as inherited from *Ius Divinum Ucadia*; and

    (iv) *Ius Ucadia Unionis* being the collection of Superior Rights associated with a Union administrative division, body politic and government, as inherited from *Ius Ucadia*; and

    (v) *Ius Ucadia Universitas* being the collection of Superior Rights associated with a University administrative division, body politic and government, as inherited from *Ius Ucadia Unionis*; and

    (vi) *Ius Ucadia Provinciae* being the collection of Superior Rights associated with a Province administrative division, body politic and government, as inherited from *Ius Ucadia Universitas*; and

    (vii) *Ius Ucadia Campus* being the collection of Superior Rights associated with a Campus administrative division, body politic and government, as inherited from *Ius Ucadia Provinciae*; and

    (viii) *Ius Ucadia Fundationis* being the collection of Superior Rights associated with a Ucadia Foundation, as inherited from *Ius Ucadia Universitas;* and

(ix) *Ius Ucadia Societatis* being the collection of Superior Rights associated with a Ucadia company, charitable body or non profit society, as inherited from *Ius Ucadia Universitas*.

Article 282 – Ius Vitam
(Life)

1124. **Ius Vitam** are the collection of Superior Rights to Life, as inherited from the collection of Natural Rights *Ius Naturale Existentia*.

Ius Vitam (Life)

1125. *Ius Vitam* (Life) is the second collection of forty-four Superior Personal Rights; and may be explicitly invoked or referenced by Right of Action through a proper Forum of Law and the Fiduciary Obligations of any such court in Ucadia or Non-Ucadia Jurisdiction.

Invoking of Ius Vitam

1126. The collection of Superior Personal Rights of *Ius Vitam* contains one Right being:

Collection of Ius Vitam

(i) *Ius Vitam* being the Superior Personal Right of Life.

Article 283 – Ius Liberum Arbitrium
(Free Will)

1127. **Ius Liberum Arbitrium** are the collection of Superior Rights of Free Choice (Will), as inherited from the collection of Natural Rights *Ius Naturale Liberum Arbitrium*.

Ius Liberum Arbitrium (Free Will)

1128. *Ius Liberum Arbitrium* (Free Will) is the third collection of forty-four Superior Personal Rights; and may be explicitly invoked or referenced by Right of Action through a proper Forum of Law and the Fiduciary Obligations of any such court in Ucadia or Non-Ucadia Jurisdiction.

Invoking of Ius Liberum Arbitrium

1129. The collection of Superior Personal Rights of *Ius Liberum Arbitrium* contains one Right being:

Collection of Ius Liberum Arbitrium

(i) *Ius Liberum Arbitrium* being the Superior Personal Right of Free Choice (Will) and Intention.

Article 284 – Ius Conscientia
(Conscious Awareness)

1130. **Ius Conscientia** are the collection of Superior Rights of Conscious Awareness, as inherited from the collection of Natural Rights *Ius Naturale Conscientia*.

Ius Conscientia (Conscious Awareness)

1131. *Ius Conscientia* (Conscious Awareness) is the fourth collection of forty-four Superior Personal Rights; and may be explicitly invoked or referenced by Right of Action through a proper Forum of Law and the Fiduciary Obligations of any such court in Ucadia or Non-Ucadia Jurisdiction.

    Invoking of Ius Conscientia

1132. The collection of Superior Personal Rights of *Ius Conscientia* contains one Right being:

    Collection of Ius Conscientia

    (i) *Ius Conscientia* being the Superior Personal Right of Conscious Awareness.

Article 285 – Ius Rationis (Accounting, Credit & Funds)

1133. ***Ius Rationis*** are the collection of Superior Rights of Accounting, Credit & Funds as inherited from the collection of Natural Rights *Ius Naturale Rationatio*.

    Ius Rationis (Accounting, Credit & Funds)

1134. *Ius Rationis* (Accounting, Credit & Funds) is the fifth collection of forty-four Superior Personal Rights; and may be explicitly invoked or referenced by Right of Action through a proper Forum of Law and the Fiduciary Obligations of any such court in Ucadia or Non-Ucadia Jurisdiction.

    Invoking of Ius Rationis

1135. The collection of Superior Personal Rights of *Ius Rationis* contains thirteen Rights being:

    Collection of Ius Rationis

    (i) *Ius Rationatio* being the Personal Right of Accounting, Credit and Funds; and

    (ii) *Ius Rationum* being the Personal Right of Accounts; and

    (iii) *Ius Rationum Examinationis* being the Personal Right of Accounts Audit; and

    (iv) *Ius Aestimationis Valoris* being the Personal Right of Valuation; and

    (v) *Ius Aestimationis Obligationis* being the Personal Right of Estimating Obligation for Value; and

    (vi) *Ius Aestimationis Pretii* being the Personal Right of Estimating Price for Obligation; and

    (vii) *Ius Aestimationis Crediti* being the Personal Right of Estimating Credit; and

    (viii) *Ius Aestimationis Debiti* being the Personal Right of Estimating Debit; and

    (ix) *Ius Valorum Pignorare* being the Personal Right to Pledge

Valuables as Collateral for Funds; and

(x) *Ius Rationum Relatio* being the Personal Right of Reporting of Accounts; and

(xi) *Ius Relatio Crediti* being the Personal Right of Credit Reporting; and

(xii) *Ius Crediti Accessus* being the Personal Right of Access to Funds; and

(xiii) *Ius Collectionis Debiti* being the Personal Right of Debit (Debt) Collection.

Article 286 – Ius Vivere Aut Mori (Choose to Live or Die)

1136. ***Ius Vivere Aut Mori*** are the collection of Superior Rights to Choose to Live or Die, as inherited from the collection of Natural Rights *Ius Naturale Vivere Aut Mori*.

Ius Vivere Aut Mori (Choose to Live or Die)

1137. *Ius Vivere Aut Mori* (Choose to Live or Die) is the sixth collection of forty-four Superior Personal Rights; and may be explicitly invoked or referenced by Right of Action through a proper Forum of Law and the Fiduciary Obligations of any such court in Ucadia or Non-Ucadia Jurisdiction.

Invoking of Ius Vivere Aut Mori

1138. The collection of Superior Personal Rights of *Ius Vivere Aut Mori* contains two Rights being:

Collection of Ius Vivere Aut Mori

(i) *Ius Vivere* being the Personal Right to Choose to Live; and

(ii) *Ius Mori* being the Personal Right to Choose to Die with Dignity when faced with Terminal Illness.

Article 287 – Ius Sentire Aut Torpere (Sense)

1139. ***Ius Sentire Aut Torpere*** are the collection of Superior Rights to Sense or be Numb to Life, Emotions and Feelings, as inherited from the collection of Natural Rights *Ius Naturale Sentire Aut Torpere*.

Ius Sentire Aut Torpere (Sense)

1140. *Ius Sentire Aut Torpere* (Sense) is the seventh collection of forty-four Superior Personal Rights; and may be explicitly invoked or referenced by Right of Action through a proper Forum of Law and the Fiduciary Obligations of any such court in Ucadia or Non-Ucadia Jurisdiction.

Invoking of Ius Sentire Aut Torpere

1141. The collection of Superior Personal Rights of *Ius Sentire Aut Torpere* contains two Rights being:

Collection of Ius Sentire Aut

(i) *Ius Sentire* being the Personal Right to Sense Life, Emotions and Feelings; and

(ii) *Ius Torpere* being the Personal Right to be Numb to Life, Emotions and Feelings.

Article 288 – Ius Discere Aut Ignarus (Learn)

1142. ***Ius Discere Aut Ignarus*** are the collection of Superior Rights to Learn or be Ignorant, as inherited from the collection of Natural Rights *Ius Naturale Discere Aut Ignarus*.

1143. *Ius Discere Aut Ignarus* (Learn) is the eighth collection of forty-four Superior Personal Rights; and may be explicitly invoked or referenced by Right of Action through a proper Forum of Law and the Fiduciary Obligations of any such court in Ucadia or Non-Ucadia Jurisdiction.

1144. The collection of Superior Personal Rights of *Ius Discere Aut Ignarus* contains two Rights being:

(i) *Ius Discere* being the Superior Personal Right to Learn and Grow; and

(ii) *Ius Ignarus* being the Superior Personal Right to Willingly be Ignorant and Stagnate.

Article 289 – Ius Associatio et Conventio (Association & Agreement)

1145. ***Ius Associatio et Conventio*** are the collection of Superior Rights of Association and Agreement, as inherited from the collection of Natural Rights *Ius Naturale Associatio et Conventio*.

1146. *Ius Associatio et Conventio* (Association) is the ninth collection of forty-four Superior Personal Rights; and may be explicitly invoked or referenced by Right of Action through a proper Forum of Law and the Fiduciary Obligations of any such court in Ucadia or Non-Ucadia Jurisdiction.

1147. The collection of Superior Personal Rights of *Ius Associatio et Conventio* contains twenty-four Rights being:

(i) *Ius Associatio et Conventio* being the Personal Right of Association and Agreement; and

(ii) *Ius Associationis* being the Personal Right of Association; and

(iii) *Ius Renuntiatio* being the Personal Right of Renunciation of

Association; and

(iv) *Ius Conventio* being the Personal Right of Agreement; and

(v) *Ius Conventionis Negotiationis* being the Personal Right to Negotiate an Agreement; and

(vi) *Ius Conventionis Recusatio* being the Personal Right to Refuse an Agreement; and

(vii) *Ius Conventionis Instrumenti* being the Personal Right to define an Instrument of Agreement; and

(viii) *Ius Pactum Formandi* being the Personal Right to form a Covenant or Treaty; and

(ix) *Ius Charta Formandi* being the Personal Right to form a Charter; and

(x) *Ius Constitutionis Formandi* being the Personal Right to form a Constitution; and

(xi) *Ius Memorandum Formandi* being the Personal Right to form a Memorandum of Agreement; and

(xii) *Ius Litterae Formandi* being the Personal Right to form a Letter or Heads of Agreement; and

(xiii) *Ius Notitiae Formandi* being the Personal Right to form a Note or Notice of Agreement; and

(xiv) *Ius Conventionis Terminos* being the Personal Right to define Terms and Conditions of Agreement; and

(xv) *Ius Conventionis Pollucendi* being the Personal Right to make a Solemn Promise in Agreement; and

(xvi) *Ius Conventionis Poenam et Remedium* being the Personal Right to define Penalties and Remedies of Agreement; and

(xvii) *Ius Modandi Conventionis Instrumenti* being the Personal Right to Modify the Terms and Conditions of Agreement; and

(xviii) *Ius Conventionis Ratificationis* being the Personal Right of Ratification of Agreement; and

(xix) *Ius Minoris Lapsus* being the Personal Right of Action against Minor Breach of Agreement; and

(xx) *Ius Minoris Reparare* being the Personal Right to Rectify and Repair Minor Issues against Minor Breach of Agreement; and

(xxi) *Ius Maioris Lapsus* being the Personal Right of Action against Major Breach of Agreement; and

(xxii) *Ius Maioris Restituere* being the Personal Right to Restore and Re-establish Major Issues against Major Breach of Agreement; and

(xxiii) *Ius Concludendi* being the Personal Right to Conclude an Agreement; and

(xxiv) *Ius Terminandi* being the Personal Right to Terminate an Agreement.

Article 290 – Ius Credere et Non (Trust a Claim)

1148. **Ius Credere et Non** are the collection of Superior Rights to Trust or Reject a Claim, as inherited from the collection of Natural Rights *Ius Naturale Credere et Non*.

1149. *Ius Credere et Non* (Trust a Claim) is the tenth collection of forty-four Superior Personal Rights; and may be explicitly invoked or referenced by Right of Action through a proper Forum of Law and the Fiduciary Obligations of any such court in Ucadia or Non-Ucadia Jurisdiction.

1150. The collection of Superior Personal Rights of *Ius Credere et Non* contains two Rights being:

(i) *Ius Credere* being the Personal Right to Trust a Claim or Assertion; and

(ii) *Ius Non Credere* being the Personal Right not to Trust a Claim or Assertion.

Article 291 – Ius Consensum et Non (Consent)

1151. **Ius Consensum et Non** are the collection of Superior Rights to Consent and Non Consent, as inherited from the collection of Natural Rights *Ius Naturale Consensum et Non*.

1152. *Ius Consensum et Non* (Consent) is the eleventh collection of forty-four Superior Personal Rights; and may be explicitly invoked or referenced by Right of Action through a proper Forum of Law and the Fiduciary Obligations of any such court in Ucadia or Non-Ucadia Jurisdiction.

1153. The collection of Superior Personal Rights of *Ius Consensum et Non* contains three Rights being:

(i) *Ius Consensum et Non* being the Personal Right of Consent and Non-Consent; and

(ii) *Ius Consensus* being the Personal Right of Consent; and

(iii) *Ius Non Consensus* being the Personal Right of Non Consent.

Article 292 – Ius Loqui et Silentium (Right to Speak and be Silent)

1154. **Ius Loqui et Silentium** are the collection of Superior Rights to Speak and be Silent, as inherited from the collection of Natural Rights *Ius Naturale Loqui et Silentium*.
Ius Loqui et Silentium (Speak)

1155. *Ius Loqui et Silentium* (Speak) is the twelfth collection of forty-four Superior Personal Rights; and may be explicitly invoked or referenced by Right of Action through a proper Forum of Law and the Fiduciary Obligations of any such court in Ucadia or Non-Ucadia Jurisdiction.
Invoking of Ius Loqui et Silentium

1156. The collection of Superior Personal Rights of *Ius Loqui et Silentium* contains three Rights being:
Collection of Ius Loqui et Silentium

   (i) *Ius Loqui* being the Personal Right to Speak Freely; and

   (ii) *Ius Non Loqui* being the Personal Right Not to Speak; and

   (iii) *Ius Silentium* being the Superior Personal Right to Peaceful Silence and to be Forced to Hear the Speech of others considered Offensive.

Article 293 – Ius Iuris (Justice and Due Process)

1157. **Ius Iuris** are the Superior Right to Natural Justice and Due Process, as inherited from the collection of Natural Rights *Ius Naturale Iuris*.
Ius Iuris (Justice)

1158. *Ius Iuris* (Justice) is the thirteenth collection of forty-four Superior Personal Rights; and may be explicitly invoked or referenced by Right of Action through a proper Forum of Law and the Fiduciary Obligations of any such court in Ucadia or Non-Ucadia Jurisdiction.
Invoking of Ius Iuris

1159. The collection of Superior Personal Rights of *Ius Iuris* contains nine Rights being:
Collection of Ius Iuris

   (i) *Ius Iuris* being the Personal Right of Justice and Due Process; and

   (ii) *Ius Accusationis* being the Personal Right to make an Accusation against another Person or Body or Entity upon Possession of Provable Evidence of Personal Harm, Injury or Loss; and

   (iii) *Ius Innocentiae* being the Personal Right of Innocence against any Accusation until Proven or Confession or Culpability; and

(iv) *Ius Accusationis Cognoscendi* being the Personal Right for the Accused and their Agent to know the Full Disclosure and Brief of Evidence of any Accusation; and

(v) *Ius Defensionis* being the Personal Right to Defend against any Accusation; and

(vi) *Ius Processus Iustus* being the Personal Right of Fair Process; and

(vii) *Ius Arbitrandi* being the Personal Right of Arbitration as method for dispute resolution; and

(viii) *Ius Propria Persona* being the Personal Right to defend or accuse as oneself; and

(ix) *Ius Iudicialis Agensas* being the Personal Right to appoint a Legal Agent to defend or accuse.

Article 294 – Ius Testamentum (Testament)

1160. ***Ius Testamentum*** are the collection of Superior Rights to make a Testification or Will, as inherited from the collection of Natural Rights *Ius Naturale Testamentum*.

Ius Testamentum (Testament)

1161. *Ius Testamentum* (Testament) is the fourteenth collection of forty-four Superior Personal Rights; and may be explicitly invoked or referenced by Right of Action through a proper Forum of Law and the Fiduciary Obligations of any such court in Ucadia or Non-Ucadia Jurisdiction.

Invoking of Ius Testamentum

1162. The collection of Superior Personal Rights of *Ius Testamentum* contains four Rights being:

Collection of Ius Testamentum

(i) *Ius Testamentum* being the Personal Right to make a Testification or Will; and

(ii) *Ius Testimonium* being the Personal Right to make a Testimony; and

(iii) *Ius Testandi* being the Personal Right to make a Will; and

(iv) *Ius Testamentum Mutandi* being the Personal Right to change a Will.

Article 295 – Ius Aequum (Fairness & Equality)

1163. ***Ius Aequum*** are the collection of Superior Rights of Equality and Fairness, as inherited from the collection of Natural Rights *Ius Naturale Aequum*.

Ius Aequum (Fairness & Equality)

1164. *Ius Aequum* (Fairness & Equality) is the fifteenth collection of forty-four Superior Personal Rights; and may be explicitly invoked or referenced by Right of Action through a proper Forum of Law and the Fiduciary Obligations of any such court in Ucadia or Non-Ucadia Jurisdiction.

Invoking of Ius Aequum

1165. The collection of Superior Personal Rights of *Ius Aequum* contains one Right being:

Collection of Ius Aequum

(i) *Ius Aequum* being the Personal Right of Equality and Fairness.

Article 296 – Ius Bona Fidei (Good Faith)

1166. ***Ius Bona Fidei*** are the collection of Superior Rights of Good Faith, Good Conscience and Good Actions, as inherited from the collection of Natural Rights *Ius Naturale Bona Fidei*.

Ius Bona Fidei (Good Faith)

1167. *Ius Bona Fidei* (Good Faith) is the sixteenth collection of forty-four Superior Personal Rights; and may be explicitly invoked or referenced by Right of Action through a proper Forum of Law and the Fiduciary Obligations of any such court in Ucadia or Non-Ucadia Jurisdiction.

Invoking of Ius Bona Fidei

1168. The collection of Superior Personal Rights of *Ius Bona Fidei* contains three Rights being:

Collection of Ius Bona Fidei

(i) *Ius Bona Fidei* being the Personal Right of Good Faith; and

(ii) *Ius Bona Conscientia* being the Personal Right of Good Conscience; and

(iii) *Ius Bona Actio* being the Personal Right of Good Action.

Article 297 – Ius Ucadiansium Scientiarum (Species)

1169. ***Ius Ucadiansium Scientiarum*** are the collection of Superior Rights of Ucadia Sciences, as inherited from the collection of Natural Rights *Ius Divinum Ucadia*.

Ius Ucadiansium Scientiarum (Species)

1170. *Ius Ucadiansium Scientiarum"* (Ucadia Sciences) is the seventeenth collection of forty-four Superior Personal Rights; and may be explicitly invoked or referenced by Right of Action through a proper Forum of Law and the Fiduciary Obligations of any such court in

Invoking of Ius Ucadiansium Scientiarum

Ucadia or Non-Ucadia Jurisdiction.

1171. The collection of Superior Personal Rights of *Ius Ucadiansium Scientiarum"* contains one Right being: — Collection of Ius Ucadiansium Scientiarum

    (i) *Ius Ucadiansium Scientiarum"* being the Personal Right of Ucadia Sciences.

Article 298 – Ius Fidei
(Superior Trust & Estate)

1172. **Ius Fidei** are the collection of Superior Rights of Superior Trust and Estate, as inherited from the collection of Natural Rights *Ius Naturale Fidei*. — Ius Fidei (Superior Trust & Estate)

1173. *Ius Fidei* (Superior Trust & Estate) is the eighteenth collection of forty-four Superior Personal Rights; and may be explicitly invoked or referenced by Right of Action through a proper Forum of Law and the Fiduciary Obligations of any such court in Ucadia or Non-Ucadia Jurisdiction. — Invoking of Ius Fidei

1174. The collection of Superior Personal Rights of *Ius Fidei* contains nine Rights being: — Collection of Ius Fidei

    (i) *Ius Fidei* being the Personal Right of Trusts & Estates; and

    (ii) *Ius Fiduciam Formandi* being the Personal Right to form a Trust; and

    (iii) *Ius Fiduciam Beneficiarius* being the Personal Right of Benefit from Trust; and

    (iv) *Ius Fiduciam Computatio* being the Personal Right to Receive an Accounting of the Administration of a Trust; and

    (v) *Ius Fiduciam Investiendi* being the Personal Right to Vest one or more Assets or Property into a Trust; and

    (vi) *Ius Fundum Formandi* being the Personal Right to form an Estate; and

    (vii) *Ius Fundum Hereditatis* being the Personal Right to inherit an Estate; and

    (viii) *Ius Fundum Beneficiarius* being the Personal Right of Benefit from an Estate; and

    (ix) *Ius Fundum Computatio* being the Personal Right to Receive an Accounting of the Administration of the Estate.

Article 299 – Ius Concedere et Abrogare (Give or Grant)

1175. ***Ius Concedere et Abrogare*** are the collection of Superior Rights to Give or Grant Rights and Annul or rescind Rights, as inherited from the collection of Natural Rights *Ius Naturale Concedere et Abrogare*.   Ius Concedere et Abrogare (Give or Grant)

1176. *Ius Concedere et Abrogare* (Give or Grant) is the nineteenth collection of forty-four Superior Personal Rights; and may be explicitly invoked or referenced by Right of Action through a proper Forum of Law and the Fiduciary Obligations of any such court in Ucadia or Non-Ucadia Jurisdiction.   Invoking of Ius Concedere et Abrogare

1177. The collection of Superior Personal Rights of *Ius Concedere et Abrogare* contains six Rights being: Collection of Ius Concedere et Abrogare

   (i) *Ius Concedere et Abrogare* being the Personal Right of Give or Grant Rights and Annul or Rescind Rights; and

   (ii) *Ius Donandum Iuris* being the Personal Right to Give a Right; and

   (iii) *Ius Rescindendum Iuris* being the Personal Right to Rescind a Right; and

   (iv) *Ius Conferendum Iuris* being the Personal Right to Grant a Right; and

   (v) *Ius Abrogandum Iuris* being the Personal Right to Abrogate a Right; and

   (vi) *Ius Annullare Iuris* being the Personal Right to Annul a Right.

Article 300 – Ius Delegare et Revocare (Assign or Delegate)

1178. ***Ius Delegare et Revocare*** are the collection of Superior Rights to Assign or Delegate Rights and Cancel or Revoke Rights, as inherited from the collection of Natural Rights *Ius Naturale Delegare et Revocare*.   Ius Delegare et Revocare (Assign or Delegate)

1179. *Ius Delegare et Revocare* (Assign or Delegate) is the twentieth collection of forty-four Superior Personal Rights; and may be explicitly invoked or referenced by Right of Action through a proper Forum of Law and the Fiduciary Obligations of any such court in Ucadia or Non-Ucadia Jurisdiction.   Invoking of Ius Delegare et Revocare

1180. The collection of Superior Personal Rights of *Ius Delegare et Revocare* contains five Rights being:

    (i)   *Ius Delegare et Revocare* being the Personal Right of Assign or Delegate Rights and Cancel or Revoke Rights; and

    (ii)   *Ius Delegandi Iuris* being the Personal Right to Delegate a Right; and

    (iii) *Ius Cancellari Iuris* being the Personal Right to Cancel a Delegated Right; and

    (iv) *Ius Assignare Iuris* being the Personal Right to Assign a Right; and

    (v)   *Ius Revocandum Iuris* being the Personal Right to Revoke an Assigned Right.

Article 301 – Ius Sacramentum (Oath and Vow)

1181. **Ius Sacramentum** are the collection of Superior Rights to make Oaths and Vows, as inherited from the collection of Natural Rights *Ius Naturale Sacramentum*.

1182. *Ius Sacramentum* (Oath and Vow) is the twenty-first collection of forty-four Superior Personal Rights; and may be explicitly invoked or referenced by Right of Action through a proper Forum of Law and the Fiduciary Obligations of any such court in Ucadia or Non-Ucadia Jurisdiction.

1183. The collection of Superior Personal Rights of *Ius Sacramentum* contains one Right being:

    (i)   *Ius Sacramentum* being the Personal Right to make Oaths and Vows.

Article 302 – Ius Signandi (Sign and Seal)

1184. **Ius Signandi** are the collection of Superior Rights to Sign and Seal, as inherited from the collection of Natural Rights *Ius Naturale Signandi*.

1185. *Ius Signandi* (Sign and Seal) is the twenty-second collection of forty-four Superior Personal Rights; and may be explicitly invoked or referenced by Right of Action through a proper Forum of Law and the Fiduciary Obligations of any such court in Ucadia or Non-Ucadia Jurisdiction.

1186. The collection of Superior Personal Rights of *Ius Signandi* contains one Right being:

    (i)   *Ius Signandi* being the Personal Right to Sign and Seal.

Article 303 – Ius Possessionis (Possession)

1187. **Ius Possessionis** are the collection of Superior Rights to Possess, Hold and Own Property, as inherited from the collection of Natural Rights *Ius Naturale Possessionis*.

1188. *Ius Possessionis* (Possession) is the twenty-third collection of forty-four Superior Personal Rights; and may be explicitly invoked or referenced by Right of Action through a proper Forum of Law and the Fiduciary Obligations of any such court in Ucadia or Non-Ucadia Jurisdiction.

1189. The collection of Superior Personal Rights of *Ius Possessionis* contains two Rights being:

    (i)   *Ius Possessionis* being the Personal Right to Possess, Hold and Own Property; and

    (ii)   *Ius Possessionis Rem* being the Personal Right to Possess, Hold and Own a Thing.

Article 304 – Ius Tenendi Terram (Lease of Home or Land)

1190. **Ius Tenendi Terram** are the collection of Superior Rights of Tenancy of Land or Home, as inherited from the collection of Natural Rights *Ius Naturale Tenendi Terram*.

1191. *Ius Tenendi Terram* (Lease of Home or Land) is the twenty-fourth collection of forty-four Superior Personal Rights; and may be explicitly invoked or referenced by Right of Action through a proper Forum of Law and the Fiduciary Obligations of any such court in Ucadia or Non-Ucadia Jurisdiction.

1192. The collection of Superior Personal Rights of *Ius Tenendi Terram* contains one Right being:

    (i)   *Ius Tenendi Terram* being the Superior Personal Right of Tenancy of Land or Home.

Article 305 – Ius Usus
(Use)

1193. ***Ius Usus*** are the collection of Superior Rights of Use and Fruits (Enjoyment) of Use of Property, as inherited from the collection of Natural Rights *Ius Naturale Usus*. — Ius Usus (Use)

1194. *Ius Usus* (Use) is the twenty-fifth collection of forty-four Superior Personal Rights; and may be explicitly invoked or referenced by Right of Action through a proper Forum of Law and the Fiduciary Obligations of any such court in Ucadia or Non-Ucadia Jurisdiction. — Invoking of Ius Usus

1195. The collection of Superior Personal Rights of *Ius Usus* contains three Rights being: — Collection of Ius Usus

   (i) *Ius Usus* being the Personal Right of Use and Fruits of Use of Property; and

   (ii) *Ius Affectandi* being the Personal Right of Acquisition of Property in Continuous Use; and

   (iii) *Ius Cessandi* being the Personal Right of Cessation of Property in Use.

Article 306 – Ius Connubii
(Union)

1196. ***Ius Connubii*** are the collection of Superior Rights of Union with another consenting Adult, as inherited from the collection of Natural Rights *Ius Naturale Connubii*. — Ius Connubii (Union)

1197. *Ius Connubii* (Union) is the twenty-sixth collection of forty-four Superior Personal Rights; and may be explicitly invoked or referenced by Right of Action through a proper Forum of Law and the Fiduciary Obligations of any such court in Ucadia or Non-Ucadia Jurisdiction. — Invoking of Ius Connubii

1198. The collection of Superior Personal Rights of *Ius Connubii* contains one Right being: — Collection of Ius Connubii

   (i) *Ius Connubii* being the Personal Right of Union.

Article 307 – Ius Coeundi
(Intercourse)

1199. ***Ius Coeundi*** are the collection of Superior Rights for consenting adults to engage in intercourse, as inherited from the collection of Natural Rights *Ius Naturale Coeundi*. — Ius Coeundi (Intercourse)

1200. *Ius Coeundi* (Intercourse) is the twenty-seventh collection of forty-four Superior Personal Rights; and may be explicitly invoked or referenced by Right of Action through a proper Forum of Law and the Fiduciary Obligations of any such court in Ucadia or Non-Ucadia Jurisdiction. — Invoking of Ius Coeundi

1201. The collection of Superior Personal Rights of *Ius Coeundi* contains one Right being: — Collection of Ius Coeundi

   (i) *Ius Coeundi* being the Personal Right for consenting adults not of the same family to engage in intercourse.

Article 308 – Ius Contraceptio (Contraception)

1202. ***Ius Contraceptio*** are the collection of Superior Rights to contraception, as inherited from the collection of Natural Rights *Ius Naturale Contraceptio*. — Ius Contraceptio (Contraception)

1203. *Ius Contraceptio* (Contraception) is the twenty-eighth collection of forty-four Superior Personal Rights; and may be explicitly invoked or referenced by Right of Action through a proper Forum of Law and the Fiduciary Obligations of any such court in Ucadia or Non-Ucadia Jurisdiction. — Invoking of Ius Contraceptio

1204. The collection of Superior Personal Rights of *Ius Contraceptio* contains one Right being:- — Collection of Ius Contraceptio

   (i) *Ius Contraceptio* being the Personal Right to Contraception.

Article 309 – Ius Terminare (Termination)

1205. ***Ius Terminare*** are the collection of Superior Rights to Terminate Pregnancy in 1st trimester, as inherited from the collection of Natural Rights *Ius Naturale Terminare*. — Ius Terminare (Termination)

1206. *Ius Terminare* (Termination) is the twenty-ninth collection of forty-four Superior Personal Rights; and may be explicitly invoked or referenced by Right of Action through a proper Forum of Law and the Fiduciary Obligations of any such court in Ucadia or Non-Ucadia Jurisdiction. — Invoking of Ius Terminare

1207. The collection of Superior Personal Rights of *Ius Terminare* contains one Right being: — Collection of Ius Terminare

   (i) *Ius Terminare* being the Personal Right for an expectant mother to Terminate the Pregnancy in 1st trimester.

Article 310 – Ius Nascendi
(Right to Life)

1208. ***Ius Nascendi*** are the collection of Superior Rights to be Borne from the start of the 2nd trimester to full term, as inherited from the collection of Natural Rights *Ius Naturale Nascendi*. — Ius Nascendi (Right to Life)

1209. *Ius Nascendi* (Right to Life) is the thirtieth collection of forty-four Superior Personal Rights; and may be explicitly invoked or referenced by Right of Action through a proper Forum of Law and the Fiduciary Obligations of any such court in Ucadia or Non-Ucadia Jurisdiction. — Invoking of Ius Nascendi

1210. The collection of Superior Personal Rights of *Ius Nascendi* contains one Right being: — Collection of Ius Nascendi

   (i) *Ius Nascendi* being the Personal Right for a Fetus to be Borne from the start of the 2nd trimester to full term.

Article 311 – Ius Nativitas
(Give Birth)

1211. ***Ius Nativitas*** are the collection of Superior Rights to give birth, as inherited from the collection of Natural Rights *Ius Naturale Nativitas*. — Ius Nativitas (Give Birth)

1212. *Ius Nativitas* (Give Birth) is the thirty-first collection of forty-four Superior Personal Rights; and may be explicitly invoked or referenced by Right of Action through a proper Forum of Law and the Fiduciary Obligations of any such court in Ucadia or Non-Ucadia Jurisdiction. — Invoking of Ius Nativitas

1213. The collection of Superior Personal Rights of *Ius Nativitas* contains one Right being: — Collection of Ius Nativitas

   (i) *Ius Nativitas* being the Personal Right for a Mother to give birth.

Article 312 – Ius Creditum
(Beliefs)

1214. ***Ius Creditum*** are the collection of Superior Rights to have and hold Beliefs, as inherited from the collection of Natural Rights *Ius Naturale Creditum*. — Ius Creditum (Beliefs)

1215. *Ius Creditum* (Beliefs) is the thirty-second collection of forty-four Superior Personal Rights; and may be explicitly invoked or referenced by Right of Action through a proper Forum of Law and the Fiduciary Obligations of any such court in Ucadia or Non-Ucadia — Invoking of Ius Creditum

Jurisdiction.

1216. The collection of Superior Personal Rights of *Ius Creditum* contains one Right being:

    (i)   *Ius Creditum* being the Superior Personal Right to have and hold Beliefs.

Collection of Ius Creditum

Article 313 – Ius Carnem (Flesh)

1217. **Ius Carnem** are the collection of Superior Rights of ones own Flesh and Body, as inherited from the collection of Natural Rights *Ius Naturale Carnem*.

Ius Carnem (Flesh)

1218. *Ius Carnem* (Flesh) is the thirty-third collection of forty-four Superior Personal Rights; and may be explicitly invoked or referenced by Right of Action through a proper Forum of Law and the Fiduciary Obligations of any such court in Ucadia or Non-Ucadia Jurisdiction.

Invoking of Ius Carnem

1219. The collection of Superior Personal Rights of *Ius Carnem* contains two Rights being:

Collection of Ius Carnem

    (i)   *Ius Carnem* being the Personal Right of ones own Flesh and Body; and

    (ii)   *Ius Carnem Modificatio* being the Personal Right for an Adult with no serious mental illness to alter ones own Flesh and Body.

Article 314 – Ius Sexualitatis (Sexuality)

1220. **Ius Sexualitatis** are the collection of Superior Rights of Choice of Sexuality, as inherited from the collection of Natural Rights *Ius Naturale Sexualitatis*.

Ius Sexualitatis (Sexuality)

1221. *Ius Sexualitatis* (Sexuality) is the thirty-fourth collection of forty-four Superior Personal Rights; and may be explicitly invoked or referenced by Right of Action through a proper Forum of Law and the Fiduciary Obligations of any such court in Ucadia or Non-Ucadia Jurisdiction.

Invoking of Ius Sexualitatis

1222. The collection of Superior Personal Rights of *Ius Sexualitatis* contains one Right being:

Collection of Ius Sexualitatis

    (i)   *Ius Sexualitatis* being the Personal Right of Choice of Sexuality.

Article 315 – Ius Nomenis
(Name)

1223. **Ius Nomenis** are the collection of Superior Rights to Name, Title and Reputation, as inherited from the collection of Natural Rights *Ius Naturale Libertatis* and *Ius Naturale Possessionis* and *Ius Naturale Aequum*.
    Ius Nomenis (Name)

1224. *Ius Nomenis* (Name) is the thirty-fifth collection of forty-four Superior Personal Rights; and may be explicitly invoked or referenced by Right of Action through a proper Forum of Law and the Fiduciary Obligations of any such court in Ucadia or Non-Ucadia Jurisdiction.
    Invoking of Ius Nomenis

1225. The collection of Superior Personal Rights of *Ius Nomenis* contains four Rights being:
    Collection of Ius Nomenis

    (i)   *Ius Nomenis* being the Personal Right to Name, Title and Reputation; and

    (ii)   *Ius Tituli Nominis* being the Personal Right of Title to Name; and

    (iii) *Ius Usus Personae* being the Personal Right of Use of Ucadia Person; and

    (iv) *Ius Famae* being the Superior Personal Right of Reputation of Name.

Article 316 – Ius Integritatis Geneticae
(Genetics)

1226. **Ius Integritatis Geneticae** are the collection of Superior Rights to the integrity and ownership of one's own Genetic Identity and Genetic Material, as inherited from the collection of Natural Rights *Ius Naturale Fidei*, *Ius Naturale Carnem* and *Ius Naturale Possessionis*.
    Ius Integritatis Geneticae (Genetics)

1227. *Ius Integritatis Geneticae* (Genetics) is the thirty-sixth collection of forty-four Superior Personal Rights; and may be explicitly invoked or referenced by Right of Action through a proper Forum of Law and the Fiduciary Obligations of any such court in Ucadia or Non-Ucadia Jurisdiction.
    Invoking of Ius Integritatis Geneticae

1228. The collection of Superior Personal Rights of *Ius Integritatis Geneticae* contains one Right being:
    Collection of Ius Integritatis Geneticae

    (i)   *Ius Integritatis Geneticae* being the Superior Personal Right to the integrity and ownership of one's own Genetic Identity and

Genetic Material.

Article 317 – Ius Identitatis
(Identity)

1229. **Ius Identitatis** are the collection of Superior Rights of Ownership of One's Own Face, Voice, Fingerprints, Biometric and Digital Identity, as inherited from the collection of Natural Rights *Ius Naturale Fidei, Ius Naturale Carnem* and *Ius Naturale Possessionis*.

    Ius Identitatis (Identity)

1230. *Ius Identitatis* (Identity) is the thirty-seventh collection of forty-four Superior Personal Rights; and may be explicitly invoked or referenced by Right of Action through a proper Forum of Law and the Fiduciary Obligations of any such court in Ucadia or Non-Ucadia Jurisdiction.

    Invoking of Ius Identitatis

1231. The collection of Superior Personal Rights of *Ius Identitatis* contains six Rights being:

    Collection of Ius Identitatis

    (i) *Ius Identitatis* being the Personal Right of Ownership of One's Own Face, Voice, Fingerprints, Biometric and Digital Identity; and

    (ii) *Ius Faciei* being the Personal Right of One's Own Face; and

    (iii) *Ius Vocis* being the Personal Right of One's Own Voice; and

    (iv) *Ius Digitorum* being the Personal Right of One's Own Fingerprints; and

    (v) *Ius Biometricorum* being the Personal Right of One's Biometric Identity; and

    (vi) *Ius Identitatis Digitalis* being the Personal Right of One's Digital Identity.

Article 318 – Ius Privatum
(Privacy)

1232. **Ius Privatum** are the collection of Superior Rights of Privacy and Use of One's Own Face, Voice, Fingerprints, Biometric and Digital Identity and Freedom from Unwarranted Surveillance, as inherited from the collection of Natural Rights *Ius Naturale Libertatis* and *Ius Naturale Possessionis* and *Ius Naturale Aequum*.

    Ius Privatum (Privacy)

1233. *Ius Privatum* (Privacy) is the thirty-eighth collection of forty-four Superior Personal Rights; and may be explicitly invoked or referenced by Right of Action through a proper Forum of Law and the Fiduciary Obligations of any such court in Ucadia or Non-Ucadia

    Invoking of Ius Privatum

Jurisdiction.

1234. The collection of Superior Personal Rights of *Ius Privatum* contains seven Rights being:

    (i)   *Ius Privatum* being the Superior Personal Right of Privacy and Use of One's Own Face, Voice, Fingerprints, Biometric and Digital Identity and Freedom from Unwarranted Surveillance; and

    (ii)   *Ius Usus Faciei* being the Personal Right of One's Own Face; and

    (iii)   *Ius Usus Vocis* being the Personal Right of One's Own Voice; and

    (iv)   *Ius Usus Digitorum* being the Personal Right of One's Own Fingerprints; and

    (v)   *Ius Usus Biometricorum* being the Personal Right of One's Biometric Identity; and

    (vi)   *Ius Usus Identitatis Digitalis* being the Personal Right of One's Digital Identity; and

    (vii)   *Ius Libertatis Observatione* being the Personal Right of Freedom from Unwarranted Surveillance.

Article 319 – Ius Tectum (Shelter)

1235. ***Ius Tectum*** are the collection of Superior Rights of Shelter, as inherited from the collection of Natural Rights *Ius Naturale Tenendi Terram* and *Ius Naturale Habitatus*.

1236. *Ius Tectum* (Shelter) is the thirty-ninth collection of forty-four Superior Personal Rights; and may be explicitly invoked or referenced by Right of Action through a proper Forum of Law and the Fiduciary Obligations of any such court in Ucadia or Non-Ucadia Jurisdiction.

1237. The collection of Superior Personal Rights of *Ius Tectum* contains one Right being:

    (i)   *Ius Tectum* being the Superior Personal Right of Shelter.

Article 320 – Ius Habitare (Habitat)

1238. ***Ius Habitare*** are the collection of Superior Rights of Home Environment, as inherited from the collection of Natural Rights *Ius*

Naturale Habitatus.

1239. *Ius Habitare* (Habitat) is the fortieth collection of forty-four Superior Personal Rights; and may be explicitly invoked or referenced by Right of Action through a proper Forum of Law and the Fiduciary Obligations of any such court in Ucadia or Non-Ucadia Jurisdiction.

Invoking of Ius Habitare

1240. The collection of Superior Personal Rights of *Ius Habitare* contains eleven Rights being:

Collection of Ius Habitare

(i) *Ius Habitare* being the Personal Right of Home Environment; and

(ii) *Ius Domicilii* being the Personal Right of Primary Domocile; and

(iii) *Ius Aedificationis Domus* being the Personal Right to build one's home; and

(iv) *Ius Parietis* being the Personal Right to build walls and fencing around home; and

(v) *Ius Domus Pacis* being the Personal Right to live peacefully in one's own Home; and

(vi) *Ius Tenendi Arma* being the Personal Right to possess arms; and

(vii) *Ius Defendum Domus* being the Personal Right to defend one's own home against trespass; and

(viii) *Ius Coquis* being the Personal Right to prepare, cook and eat food in home; and

(ix) *Ius Filios* being the Personal Right to have, nurture, support, supervise and teach children; and

(x) *Ius Parentum* being the Personal Right of parents to the custody, protection, well being, discipline and education of children; and

(xi) *Ius Celebras* being the Personal Right to celebrate and enjoy in one's own home.

Article 321 – Ius Terrae et Aquae Purarum (Clean Land & Water)

1241. ***Ius Terrae et Aquae Purarum*** are the collection of Superior Rights to Clean Water and Land, as inherited from the collection of Natural Rights *Ius Naturale Maris Viventis* and *Ius Naturale Terrae Viventis.*

Ius Terrae et Aquae Purarum (Clean Land & Water)

1242. *Ius Terrae et Aquae Purarum* (Clean Land & Water) is the forty-first collection of forty-four Superior Personal Rights; and may be explicitly invoked or referenced by Right of Action through a proper Forum of Law and the Fiduciary Obligations of any such court in Ucadia or Non-Ucadia Jurisdiction.
<small>Invoking of Ius Terrae et Aquae Purarum</small>

1243. The collection of Superior Personal Rights of *Ius Terrae et Aquae Purarum* contains one Right being:
<small>Collection of Ius Terrae et Aquae Purarum</small>

   (i) *Ius Terrae et Aquae Purarum* being the Superior Personal Right to Clean Water and Land.

Article 322 – Ius Sustentandi (Sustenance)

1244. **Ius Sustentandi** are the collection of Superior Rights of Sustenance, Health Care and Assistance, as inherited from the collection of Natural Rights *Ius Naturale Habitatus* and *Ius Naturale Fraternitas Nativas*.
<small>Ius Sustentandi (Sustenance)</small>

1245. *Ius Sustentandi* (Sustenance) is the forty-second collection of forty-four Superior Personal Rights; and may be explicitly invoked or referenced by Right of Action through a proper Forum of Law and the Fiduciary Obligations of any such court in Ucadia or Non-Ucadia Jurisdiction.
<small>Invoking of Ius Sustentandi</small>

1246. The collection of Superior Personal Rights of *Ius Sustentandi* contains one Right being:
<small>Collection of Ius Sustentandi</small>

   (i) *Ius Sustentandi* being the Superior Personal Right of Sustenance, Health Care and Assistance.

Article 323 – Ius Libertatis (Freedom)

1247. **Ius Libertatis** are the collection of Superior Rights of Freedom from Slavery, Bondage or treated as a Thing or any other kind of Property, as inherited from the collection of Natural Rights *Ius Naturale Libertatis*.
<small>Ius Libertatis (Freedom)</small>

1248. *Ius Libertatis* (Freedom) is the forty-third collection of forty-four Superior Personal Rights; and may be explicitly invoked or referenced by Right of Action through a proper Forum of Law and the Fiduciary Obligations of any such court in Ucadia or Non-Ucadia Jurisdiction.
<small>Invoking of Ius Libertatis</small>

1249. The collection of Superior Personal Rights of *Ius Libertatis* contains one Right being:
<small>Collection of Ius Libertatis</small>

(i) *Ius Libertatis* being the Superior Personal Right of Freedom from Slavery, Bondage or treated as a Thing or any other kind of Property.

Article 324 – Ius Tormentum Libertatis (No Cruelty or Torture)

1250. ***Ius Tormentum Libertatis*** are the collection of Superior Rights of Freedom from Cruel and Unusual Punishment or Torture, as inherited from the collection of Natural Rights *Ius Naturale Clementia*.

Ius Tormentum Libertatis (No Cruelty or Torture)

1251. *Ius Tormentum Libertatis* (No Cruelty or Torture) is the forty-fourth collection of forty-four Superior Personal Rights; and may be explicitly invoked or referenced by Right of Action through a proper Forum of Law and the Fiduciary Obligations of any such court in Ucadia or Non-Ucadia Jurisdiction.

Invoking of Ius Tormentum Libertatis

1252. The collection of Superior Personal Rights of *Ius Tormentum Libertatis* contains one Right being:

Collection of Ius Tormentum Libertatis

(i) *Ius Tormentum Libertatis* being the Superior Personal Right of Freedom from Cruel and Unusual Punishment or Torture.

Title X – Member Rights

10.1 – Member Rights

Article 325 – Member Rights

1253. **"Member Rights"** (*Iurium Membrum*) shall be Member Rights permanently vested unto the members of the seven Ucadia Unions and all lesser Ucadia bodies politic such as Universities, Provinces and Campuses as the embodiment of member authority.

Member Rights

1254. "Member Rights" (*Iurium Membrum*) is the sixth sub-class of Member Rights and the fifth highest possible rights of any aggregate body, society, fraternity, association or company of two or more persons personified in trust.

Member Rights (Iurium Membrum)

There exists three (3) categories of thirty-nine (39) Member Rights within the sub-class of Member Rights, being: Authoritative (11), Legal (22) and Special (6):

   (i)   **"Authoritative Member Rights"** (*Potentis Membrum Iurium*) shall be Member Rights associated with the essential authoritative powers of members of any valid society; and

   (ii) **"Legal Member Rights"** (*Legitimus Membrum Iurium*) shall be Member Rights essential to the proper administration of justice of any valid society; and

   (iii) **"Special Member Rights"** (*Proprius Membrum Iurium*) shall be Critical Member Rights in relation to the majority (two-thirds) of all members as "the people", essential to democracy and the restoration of the Golden Rule of Law in the event of corruption, collapse of justice or the rise of tyranny.

10.2 – Authoritative Member Rights

Article 326 – Authoritative Member Rights

1255. *Authoritative Member Rights* (Potentis Membrum Iurium) are Member Rights associated with the essential authoritative powers of members of any valid society.

Authoritative Member Rights

1256. All *Authoritative Member Rights* are delegated to the safe custody and wise guardian powers of the legitimate and valid supreme competent forum of law of the seven Ucadia Unions and all lesser Ucadia bodies politic such as Universities, Provinces and Campuses as the embodiment of judicial authority; and as defined by Article 59 (Oratorium) of the most sacred Covenant *Pactum De Singularis Caelum*.

Delegation of Authoritative Member Rights

1257. All *Authoritative Member Rights* are assumed to be automatically invoked within Ucadia Jurisdictions through the operation of the Civilised Rules of Ucadia Societies, Bodies and Entities. However the Rights may be explicitly invoked or referenced by Right of Action through a proper Forum of Law and the Fiduciary Obligations of any such court in Ucadia Jurisdiction.

_{Invocation of Authoritative Member Rights}

1258. The following valid eleven (11) Authoritative Member Rights (*Potentis Membrum Iurium*) shall be recognised in accord with the most sacred Covenant *Pactum De Singularis Caelum*:-

_{Authoritative Member Rights (Potentis Membrum Iurium)}

    (i) **"Ius Membrum Sodalis"** are the collection of Member Rights of Equal Membership of Society, as inherited from the Superior Right *Ius Aequum*; and

    (ii) **"Ius Membrum Nascendi Societas"** are the collection of Member Rights to be recognised as a member of the society into which one was borne, as inherited from the Superior Right *Ius Aequum*; and

    (iii) **"Ius Membrum Votum"** are the collection of Member Rights to vote and participate in democratic processes of Society, as inherited from the Superior Right *Ius Liberum Arbitrium*; and

    (iv) **"Ius Membrum Forum Publicum"** are the collection of Member Rights to attend public meetings and forums of Society, as inherited from the Superior Right *Ius Liberum Arbitrium*; and

    (v) **"Ius Membrum Rationatio"** are the collection of Member Rights to receive an accounting of the economic activity, as inherited from the Superior Right *Ius Rationis*; and

    (vi) **"Ius Membrum Officium"** are the collection of Member Rights of office of Society, as inherited from the Superior Right *Ius Bona Fidei*; and

    (vii) **"Ius Membrum Registrum"** are the collection of Member Rights to Enter Records within Registers and Rolls, as inherited from the Superior Right *Ius Testamentum*; and

    (viii) **"Ius Membrum Associatio et Conventio"** are the collection of Member Rights of Association and Agreement, as inherited from the Superior Right *Ius Associatio et Conventio*; and

    (ix) **"Ius Membrum Servitia"** are the collection of Member Rights to the Services of the Society, as inherited from the

Superior Right *Ius Sustentandi*; and

(x) "**Ius Membrum Mercatus**" are the collection of Member Rights to the Markets of the Society, as inherited from the Superior Right *Ius Associatio et Conventio*; and

(xi) "**Ius Membrum Commercium**" are the collection of Member Rights to Trade, Exchange and engage in Commerce, as inherited from the Superior Right *Ius Coeundi*.

Article 327 – Ius Membrum Sodalis (Equal Member)

1259. ***Ius Membrum Sodalis*** are the collection of Member Rights of Equal Membership of Society, as inherited from the Superior Right *Ius Aequum*.

1260. *Ius Membrum Sodalis* (Equal Member) is the first collection of eleven Authoritative Member Rights; and may be explicitly invoked or referenced by Right of Action through a proper Ucadia Forum of Law and the Fiduciary Obligations of any such court in Ucadia Jurisdiction.

1261. The collection of Member Rights of *Ius Membrum Sodalis* contains six Rights being:-

   (i) *Ius Membrum Sodalis* being the Member Right of Equal Membership of Society; and

   (ii) *Ius Membrum Sodalis Generis* being the Member Right of Equal Membership of Society irrespective of Gender; and

   (iii) *Ius Membrum Sodalis Raciae* being the Member Right of Equal Membership of Society irrespective of Race; and

   (iv) *Ius Membrum Sodalis Religionis* being the Member Right of Equal Membership of Society irrespective of Religion; and

   (v) *Ius Membrum Sodalis Aetatis* being the Member Right of Equal Membership of Society irrespective of Adult Age; and

   (vi) *Ius Membrum Sodalis Terrae Natalis* being the Member Right of Equal Membership of Society irrespective of Country of Birth.

Article 328 – Ius Membrum Nascendi Societas (Member Right of Birth)

1262. ***Ius Membrum Nascendi Societas*** are the collection of Member Rights to be recognised as a member of the society into which one was borne, as inherited from the Superior Right *Ius Aequum*.

1263. *Ius Membrum Nascendi Societas* (Member Right at Birth) is the second collection of eleven Authoritative Member Rights; and may be explicitly invoked or referenced by Right of Action through a proper Ucadia Forum of Law and the Fiduciary Obligations of any such court in Ucadia Jurisdiction.

1264. The collection of Member Rights of *Ius Membrum Nascendi Societas* contains one Right being:-

   (i) *Ius Membrum Nascendi Societas* being the Member Right to be recognised as a member of the society into which one was borne.

Article 329 – Ius Membrum Votum (Right to Vote)

1265. ***Ius Membrum Votum*** are the collection of Member Rights to vote and participate in democratic processes of Society, as inherited from the Superior Right *Ius Liberum Arbitrium*.

1266. *Ius Membrum Votum* (Right to Vote) is the third collection of eleven Authoritative Member Rights; and may be explicitly invoked or referenced by Right of Action through a proper Ucadia Forum of Law and the Fiduciary Obligations of any such court in Ucadia Jurisdiction.

1267. The collection of Member Rights of *Ius Membrum Votum* contains one Right being:-

   (i) *Ius Membrum Votum* being the Member Right to vote and participate in democratic processes of Society.

Article 330 – Ius Membrum Forum Publicum (Public Meetings)

1268. ***Ius Membrum Forum Publicum*** are the collection of Member Rights to attend public meetings and forums of Society, as inherited from the Superior Right *Ius Liberum Arbitrium*.

1269. *Ius Membrum Forum Publicum* (Public Meetings) is the fourth collection of eleven Authoritative Member Rights; and may be explicitly invoked or referenced by Right of Action through a proper Ucadia Forum of Law and the Fiduciary Obligations of any such court in Ucadia Jurisdiction.

Forum Publicum

1270. The collection of Member Rights of *Ius Membrum Forum Publicum* contains six Rights being:-

Collection of Ius Membrum Forum Publicum

(i) *Ius Membrum Forum Publicum* being the Member Right to attend public meetings and forums of Society; and

(ii) *Ius Membrum Forum Presentiam* being the Member Right to attend public meetings and forums of Society; and

(iii) *Ius Membrum Forum Petitionis* being the Member Right to petition for item to be heard at public meetings and forums of Society; and

(iv) *Ius Membrum Forum Loquendi* being the Member Right to speak at public meetings and forums of Society; and

(v) *Ius Membrum Forum Civilitatis* being the Member Right for public meetings and forums of Society to be civil, courteous and function without interruption; and

(vi) *Ius Membrum Forum Votum* being the Member Right to vote at public meetings and forums of Society.

Article 331 – Ius Membrum Rationatio (Public Accounts)

1271. **Ius Membrum Rationatio** are the collection of Member Rights to receive an accounting of the economic activity, as inherited from the the Superior Right *Ius Rationis*.

Ius Membrum Rationatio (Public Accounts)

1272. *Ius Membrum Rationatio* (Public Accounts) is the fifth collection of eleven Authoritative Member Rights; and may be explicitly invoked or referenced by Right of Action through a proper Ucadia Forum of Law and the Fiduciary Obligations of any such court in Ucadia Jurisdiction.

Invoking of Ius Membrum Rationatio

1273. The collection of Member Rights of *Ius Membrum Rationatio* contains two Rights being:-

Collection of Ius Membrum Rationatio

(i) *Ius Membrum Rationatio* being the Member Right to receive an accounting of the economic activity; and

(ii) *Ius Membrum Rationatio Instrumentarium* being the Member Right to receive Member Account Statements.

Article 332 – Ius Membrum Officium (Public Office)

1274. ***Ius Membrum Officium*** are the collection of Member Rights of Office of Society, as inherited from the Superior Right *Ius Bona Fidei*.

Ius Membrum Officium (Public Office)

1275. *Ius Membrum Officium* (Public Office) is the sixth collection of eleven Authoritative Member Rights; and may be explicitly invoked or referenced by Right of Action through a proper Ucadia Forum of Law and the Fiduciary Obligations of any such court in Ucadia Jurisdiction.

Invoking of Ius Membrum Officium (Public Office)

1276. The collection of Member Rights of *Ius Membrum Officium* contains fifteen Rights being:-

Collection of Ius Membrum Officium

    (i)   *Ius Membrum Officium* being the Member Rights of Office, Duty and Service; and

    (ii)   *Ius Membrum Petendi Candidatum Officium* being the Member Right to Apply to be Candidate for Office; and

    (iii)   *Ius Membrum Formandum Comitatum* being the Member Right to Form a Campaign as Candidate for Office; and

    (iv)   *Ius Membrum Candidati Officium* being the Member Right to Run a Campaign as Candidate for Office; and

    (v)   *Ius Membrum Eligendi* being the Member Right to be Elected as Candidate for Office; and

    (vi)   *Ius Membrum Clausurae Comitatus* being the Member Right to Close a Campaign for Office; and

    (vii)   *Ius Membrum Mandati Officii* being the Member Right to Receive Mandate in Good Faith, Good Conscience and Good Actions to Occupy an Office; and

    (viii)   *Ius Membrum Tenendi Officii* being the Member Right to Hold an Office in Good Faith, Good Conscience and Good Actions; and

    (ix)   *Ius Membrum Immunitatis Officii* being the Member Right of Immunity for Decisions Made in Office in Good Faith, Good Conscience and Good Actions; and

    (x)   *Ius Membrum Abdicandi Officii* being the Member Right to Retire from Office in Honour, Privileges and Good Standing; and

    (xi)   *Ius Membrum Dicendi Officii* being the Member Right to Resign from Office in Honour, Privileges and Good Standing;

and

(xii) *Ius Membrum Nullius Mandati* being the Member Right to have Mandate Withdrawn and be Terminated from Office in Disgrace, Without Privileges and Poor Standing; and

(xiii) *Ius Membrum Accusationi Officii* being the Member Right to Face Impeachment for Claims of Bad Faith, Bad Conscience or Bad Actions in Office; and

(xiv) *Ius Membrum Removendi Officii* being the Member Right to be Removed by Force from Office in Disgrace, Without Privileges and Poor Standing upon being found Culpable from Impeachment; and

(xv) *Ius Membrum Restituendi Officii* being the Member Right to be Restored to Office in Honour, Privileges and Good Standing after having been unlawfully obstructed or removed from Office.

Article 333 – Ius Membrum Registrum (Registers & Rolls)

1277. ***Ius Membrum Registrum*** are the collection of Member Rights to Enter Records within Registers and Rolls, as inherited from the Superior Right *Ius Testamentum*. Ius Membrum Registrum (Registers & Rolls)

1278. *Ius Membrum Registrum* (Registers & Rolls) is the seventh collection of eleven Authoritative Member Rights; and may be explicitly invoked or referenced by Right of Action through a proper Ucadia Forum of Law and the Fiduciary Obligations of any such court in Ucadia Jurisdiction. Invoking of Ius Membrum Registrum

1279. The collection of Member Rights of *Ius Membrum Registrum* contains one Right being:- Collection of Ius Membrum Registrum

(i) *Ius Membrum Registrum* being the Member Right to Enter Records within certain Ucadia Registers and Rolls.

Article 334 – Ius Membrum Associatio et Conventio (Agreements)

1280. ***Ius Membrum Associatio et Conventio*** are the collection of Member Rights of Association and Agreement, as inherited from the Superior Right *Ius Associatio et Conventio*. Ius Membrum Associatio et Conventio (Agreements)

1281. *Ius Membrum Associatio et Conventio* (Agreements) is the eighth collection of eleven Authoritative Member Rights; and may be explicitly invoked or referenced by Right of Action through a proper Invoking of Ius Membrum Associatio et Conventio

Ucadia Forum of Law and the Fiduciary Obligations of any such court in Ucadia Jurisdiction.

1282. The collection of Member Rights of *Ius Membrum Associatio et Conventio* contains twenty-four Rights being:-

<small>Collection of Ius Membrum Associatio et Conventio</small>

(i) *Ius Membrum Associatio et Conventio* being the Member Right of Association and Agreement; and

(ii) *Ius Membrum Associationis* being the Member Right of Association; and

(iii) *Ius Membrum Renuntiatio* being the Member Right of Renunciation of Association; and

(iv) *Ius Membrum Conventio* being the Member Right of Agreement; and

(v) *Ius Membrum Conventionis Negotiationis* being the Member Right to Negotiate an Agreement; and

(vi) *Ius Membrum Conventionis Recusatio* being the Member Right to Refuse an Agreement; and

(vii) *Ius Membrum Conventionis Instrumenti* being the Member Right to define an Instrument of Agreement; and

(viii) *Ius Membrum Pactum Formandi* being the Member Right to form a Covenant or Treaty; and

(ix) *Ius Membrum Charta Formandi* being the Member Right to form a Charter; and

(x) *Ius Membrum Constitutionis Formandi* being the Member Right to form a Constitution; and

(xi) *Ius Membrum Memorandum Formandi* being the Member Right to form a Memorandum of Agreement; and

(xii) *Ius Membrum Litterae Formandi* being the Member Right to form a Letter or Heads of Agreement; and

(xiii) *Ius Membrum Notitiae Formandi* being the Member Right to form a Note or Notice of Agreement; and

(xiv) *Ius Membrum Conventionis Terminos* being the Member Right to define Terms and Conditions of Agreement; and

(xv) *Ius Membrum Conventionis Pollucendi* being the Member Right to make a Solemn Promise in Agreement; and

(xvi) *Ius Membrum Conventionis Poenam et Remedium* being the Member Right to define Penalties and Remedies of Agreement; and

(xvii) *Ius Membrum Modandi Conventionis Instrumenti* being the Member Right to Modify the Terms and Conditions of Agreement; and

(xviii) *Ius Membrum Conventionis Ratificationis* being the Member Right of Ratification of Agreement; and

(xix) *Ius Membrum Minoris Lapsus* being the Member Right of Action against Minor Breach of Agreement; and

(xx) *Ius Membrum Minoris Reparare* being the Member Right to Rectify and Repair Minor Issues against Minor Breach of Agreement; and

(xxi) *Ius Membrum Maioris Lapsus* being the Member Right of Action against Major Breach of Agreement; and

(xxii) *Ius Membrum Maioris Restituere* being the Member Right to Restore and Re-estabish Major Issues against Major Breach of Agreement; and

(xxiii) *Ius Membrum Concludendi* being the Member Right to Conclude an Agreement; and

(xxiv) *Ius Membrum Terminandi* being the Member Right to Terminate an Agreement.

Article 335 – Ius Membrum Servitia (Services)

1283. **Ius Membrum Servitia** are the collection of Member Rights to the Services of the Society, as inherited from the Superior Right *Ius Sustentandi*.

1284. *Ius Membrum Servitia* (Services) is the ninth collection of eleven Authoritative Member Rights; and may be explicitly invoked or referenced by Right of Action through a proper Ucadia Forum of Law and the Fiduciary Obligations of any such court in Ucadia Jurisdiction.

1285. The collection of Member Rights of *Ius Membrum Servitia* contains one Right being:-

(i) *Ius Membrum Servitia* being the Member Right to the Services of the Society.

Article 336 – Ius Membrum Mercatus (Markets)

1286. ***Ius Membrum Mercatus*** are the collection of Member Rights to the Markets of the Society, as inherited from the Superior Right *Ius Associatio et Conventio*.

Ius Membrum Mercatus (Markets)

1287. *Ius Membrum Mercatus* (Markets) is the tenth collection of eleven Authoritative Member Rights; and may be explicitly invoked or referenced by Right of Action through a proper Ucadia Forum of Law and the Fiduciary Obligations of any such court in Ucadia Jurisdiction.

Invoking of Ius Membrum Mercatus

1288. The collection of Member Rights of *Ius Membrum Mercatus* contains one Right being:-

Collection of Ius Membrum Mercatus

(i) *Ius Membrum Mercatus* being the Member Right to the Markets of the Society.

Article 337 – Ius Membrum Commercium (Trade & Commerce)

1289. ***Ius Membrum Commercium*** are the collection of Member Rights to Trade, Exchange and engage in Commerce, as inherited from the Superior Right *Ius Coeundi*.

Ius Membrum Commercium (Trade & Commerce)

1290. *Ius Membrum Commercium* (Trade & Commerce) is the eleventh collection of eleven Authoritative Member Rights; and may be explicitly invoked or referenced by Right of Action through a proper Ucadia Forum of Law and the Fiduciary Obligations of any such court in Ucadia Jurisdiction.

Invoking of Ius Membrum Commercium

1291. The collection of Member Rights of *Ius Membrum Commercium* contains one Right being:-

Collection of Ius Membrum Commercium

(i) *Ius Membrum Commercium* being the Member Right to Trade, Exchange and engage in Commerce.

10.3 – Legal Member Rights

Article 338 – Legal Member Rights

1292. ***Legal Member Rights*** (*Legitimus Membrum Iurium*) shall be Member Rights essential to the proper administration of justice of any valid society.

Legal Member Rights

1293. All *Legal Member Rights* are delegated to the safe custody and wise guardian powers of the legitimate and valid supreme competent forum of law of the seven Ucadia Unions and all lesser Ucadia bodies politic such as Universities, Provinces and Campuses as the embodiment of judicial authority; and as defined by Article 59 (Oratorium) of the most sacred Covenant *Pactum De Singularis Caelum*.

Delegation of Legal Member Rights

1294. All *Legal Member Rights* are assumed to be automatically invoked within Ucadia Jurisdictions through the operation of the Civilised Rules of Ucadia Societies, Bodies and Entities. However the Rights may be explicitly invoked or referenced by Right of Action through a proper Forum of Law and the Fiduciary Obligations of any such court in Ucadia Jurisdiction.

Invocation of Legal Member Rights

1295. The following valid twenty-two (22) Legal Member Rights (*Legitimus Membrum Iurium*) shall be recognised in accord with the most sacred Covenant *Pactum De Singularis Caelum*:-

Legal Member Rights (Legitimus Membrum Iurium)

    (i)   "**Ius Membrum Iuris**" are the collection of Member Rights of Justice and Due Process, as inherited from the collection of Natural Rights *Ius Naturale Iuris*; and

    (ii)   "**Ius Membrum Aequum**" are the collection of Member Rights of Equality and Fairness, as inherited from the collection of Natural Rights *Ius Naturale Aequum*; and

    (iii)   "**Ius Membrum Bona Fidei**" are the collection of Member Rights of Good Faith, Good Conscience and Good Actions, as inherited from the collection of Natural Rights *Ius Naturale Bona Fidei*; and

    (iv)   "**Ius Membrum Libertatis**" are the collection of Member Rights of Freedom from Bondage and Slavery, as inherited from the collection of Natural Rights *Ius Naturale Libertatis*; and

    (v)   "**Ius Membrum Actionum**" are the collection of Member Rights of Action, as inherited from the collection of Natural Rights *Ius Naturale Actionum*; and

(vi) **"Ius Membrum Significans Laborare"** are the collection of Member Rights to Meaningful and Fulfilling Work, as inherited from the collection of Natural Rights *Ius Naturale Significans Laborare*; and

(vii) **"Ius Membrum Salarium Iustum"** are the collection of Member Rights to Fair Pay and Compensation, as inherited from the collection of Natural Rights *Ius Naturale Salarium Iustum*; and

(viii) **"Ius Membrum Laborare et Non"** are the collection of Member Rights to Work or refuse to Work, as inherited from the collection of Natural Rights *Ius Naturale Laborare et Non*; and

(ix) **"Ius Membrum Custoditum"** are the collection of Member Rights to detain a party associated with a controversy if good cause exists they be a risk of non-appearance or committing further controversies, as inherited from the collection of Natural Rights *Ius Naturale Iuris* and *Ius Naturale Delegare et Revocare*; and

(x) **"Ius Membrum Accusare"** are the collection of Member Rights to accuse another of a transgression, as inherited from the collection of Natural Rights *Ius Naturale Iuris*; and

(xi) **"Ius Membrum Innocentiae"** are the collection of Member Rights of Innocence until accusation proven, as inherited from the collection of Natural Rights *Ius Naturale Innocentiae*; and

(xii) **"Ius Membrum Accusationis Cognoscendi"** are the collection of Member Rights to know the Full Disclosure and Evidence of any Accusation, as inherited from the collection of Natural Rights *Ius Naturale Aequum* and

(xiii) **"Ius Membrum Defensionis"** are the collection of Member Rights to defend against any accusation and accuser, as inherited from the collection of Natural Rights *Ius Naturale Defensionis*; and

(xiv) **"Ius Membrum Eligendi Iudicium"** are the collection of Member Rights for a matter to be decided by a jury of peers or a judge in forum of law, as inherited from the collection of Natural Rights *Ius Naturale Defensionis*; and

(xv) **"Ius Membrum Propria Persona"** are the collection of Member Rights to defend or accuse as oneself, as inherited from the collection of Natural Rights *Ius Naturale Defensionis*; and

(xvi) "**Ius Membrum Agensas**" are the collection of Member Rights to appoint an agent, as inherited from the collection of Natural Rights *Ius Naturale Delegare et Revocare*; and

(xvii) "**Ius Membrum Possessionis**" are the collection of Member Rights to Possess, Hold and Own Property, as inherited from the collection of Natural Rights *Ius Naturale Possessionis*; and

(xviii) "**Ius Membrum Usus**" are the collection of Member Rights of Use and Fruits of Use of Property, as inherited from the collection of Natural Rights *Ius Naturale Usus*; and

(xix) "**Ius Membrum Proprietatis**" are the collection of Member Rights of Ownership of Use or Fruits of Use of Property, as inherited from the collection of Natural Rights *Ius Naturale Possessionis* and *Ius Naturale Usus*; and

(xx) "**Ius Membrum Remedium**" are the collection of Member Rights of Remedy, Relief, Redress or Compensation, as inherited from the collection of Natural Rights *Ius Naturale Remedium*; and

(xxi) "**Ius Membrum Poena**" are the collection of Member Rights of Penalty, Penitence or Punishment, as inherited from the collection of Natural Rights *Ius Naturale Poena;* and

(xxii) "**Ius Membrum Clementia**" are the collection of Member Rights of Mercy & Forgiveness, as inherited from the collection of Natural Rights *Ius Naturale Clementia*.

Article 339 – Ius Membrum Iuris (Justice & Due Process)

1296. *Ius Membrum Iuris* are the collection of Member Rights *of* Justice and Due Process, as inherited from the collection of *Natural Rights Ius Naturale Iuris*.

1297. *Ius Membrum Iuris* (Justice & Due Process) is the first collection of twenty-two Legal Member Rights; and may be explicitly invoked or referenced by Right of Action through a proper Ucadia Forum of Law and the Fiduciary Obligations of any such court in Ucadia Jurisdiction.

1298. The collection of Member Rights of *Ius Membrum Iuris* contains one

Right being:-

(i) *Ius Membrum Iuris* being the Member Right of Justice and Due Process.

Article 340 – Ius Membrum Aequum (Right of Equality and Fairness)

1299. ***Ius Membrum Aequum*** are the collection of Member Rights of Equality and Fairness, as inherited from the collection of Natural Rights *Ius Naturale Aequum*.

1300. *Ius Membrum Aequum* (Equality & Fairness) is the second collection of twenty-two Legal Member Rights; and may be explicitly invoked or referenced by Right of Action through a proper Ucadia Forum of Law and the Fiduciary Obligations of any such court in Ucadia Jurisdiction.

1301. The collection of Member Rights of *Ius Membrum Aequum* contains one Right being:-

(i) *Ius Membrum Aequum* being the Member Right of Member Rights of Equality and Fairness.

Article 341 – Ius Membrum Bona Fidei (Good Faith)

1302. ***Ius Membrum Bona Fidei*** are the collection of Member Rights of Good Faith, Good Conscience and Good Actions, as inherited from the collection of Natural Rights *Ius Naturale Bona Fidei*.

1303. *Ius Membrum Bona Fidei* (Good Faith) is the third collection of twenty-two Legal Member Rights; and may be explicitly invoked or referenced by Right of Action through a proper Ucadia Forum of Law and the Fiduciary Obligations of any such court in Ucadia Jurisdiction.

1304. The collection of Member Rights of *Ius Membrum Bona Fidei* contains three Rights being:-

(i) *Ius Membrum Bona Fidei* being the Member Right of Good Faith; and

(ii) *Ius Membrum Bona Conscientia* being the Member Right of Good Conscience; and

(iii) *Ius Membrum Bona Actio* being the Member Right of Good Action.

Article 342 – Ius Membrum Libertatis (Freedom)

1305. ***Ius Membrum Libertatis*** are the collection of Member Rights of Freedom from Bondage and Slavery, as inherited from the collection of Natural Rights *Ius Naturale Libertatis*.

1306. *Ius Membrum Libertatis* (Freedom) is the fourth collection of twenty-two Legal Member Rights; and may be explicitly invoked or referenced by Right of Action through a proper Ucadia Forum of Law and the Fiduciary Obligations of any such court in Ucadia Jurisdiction.

1307. The collection of Member Rights of *Ius Membrum Libertatis* contains one Right being:-

   (i) *Ius Membrum Libertatis* being the Member Right of Freedom from Bondage and Slavery.

Article 343 – Ius Membrum Actionum (Right of Action)

1308. ***Ius Membrum Actionum*** are the collection of Member Rights of Action, as inherited from the collection of Natural Rights *Ius Naturale Actionum*.

1309. *Ius Membrum Actionum* (Right of Action) is the fifth collection of twenty-two Legal Member Rights; and may be explicitly invoked or referenced by Right of Action through a proper Ucadia Forum of Law and the Fiduciary Obligations of any such court in Ucadia Jurisdiction.

1310. The collection of Member Rights of *Ius Membrum Actionum* contains one Right being:-

   (i) *Ius Membrum Actionum* being the Member Right of Action.

Article 344 – Ius Membrum Significans Laborare (Meaningful Work)

1311. ***Ius Membrum Significans Laborare*** are the collection of Member Rights to Meaningful and Fulfilling Work, as inherited from the collection of Natural Rights *Ius Naturale Significans Laborare*.

1312. *Ius Membrum Significans Laborare* (Meaningful Work) is the sixth collection of twenty-two Legal Member Rights; and may be explicitly invoked or referenced by Right of Action through a proper Ucadia

Forum of Law and the Fiduciary Obligations of any such court in Ucadia Jurisdiction.

1313. The collection of Member Rights of *Ius Membrum Significans Laborare* contains one Right being:-

    (i) *Ius Membrum Significans Laborare* being the Member Right to Meaningful and Fulfilling Work.

Collection of Ius Memb. Significans Laborare

Article 345 – Ius Membrum Salarium Iustum (Fair Pay)

1314. ***Ius Membrum Salarium Iustum*** are the collection of Member Rights to Fair Pay and Compensation, as inherited from the collection of Natural Rights *Ius Naturale Salarium Iustum*.

Ius Memb. Salarium Iustum (Fair Pay)

1315. *Ius Membrum Salarium Iustum* (Fair Pay) is the seventh collection of twenty-two Legal Member Rights; and may be explicitly invoked or referenced by Right of Action through a proper Ucadia Forum of Law and the Fiduciary Obligations of any such court in Ucadia Jurisdiction.

Invoking of Ius Memb. Salarium Iustum

1316. The collection of Member Rights of *Ius Membrum Salarium Iustum* contains one Right being:-

    (i) *Ius Membrum Salarium Iustum* being the Member Right to Fair Pay and Compensation.

Collection of Ius Memb. Salarium Iustum

Article 346 – Ius Membrum Laborare et Non (Refuse to Work)

1317. ***Ius Membrum Laborare et Non*** are the collection of Member Rights to Work or refuse to Work, as inherited from the collection of Natural Rights *Ius Naturale Laborare et Non*.

Ius Memb. Laborare et Non (Refuse to Work)

1318. *Ius Membrum Laborare et Non* (Refuse to Work) is the eighth collection of twenty-two Legal Member Rights; and may be explicitly invoked or referenced by Right of Action through a proper Ucadia Forum of Law and the Fiduciary Obligations of any such court in Ucadia Jurisdiction.

Invoking of Ius Memb. Laborare et Non

1319. The collection of Member Rights of *Ius Membrum Laborare et Non* contains one Right being:-

    (i) *Ius Membrum Laborare et Non* being the Member Right to Work or refuse to Work.

Collection of Ius Memb. Laborare et Non

Article 347 – Ius Membrum Custoditum (Detain Person)

1320. ***Ius Membrum Custoditum*** are the collection of Member Rights to detain a party associated with a controversy if good cause exists they be a risk of non-appearance or committing further controversies, as inherited from the collection of Natural Rights *Ius Naturale Iuris* and *Ius Naturale Delegare et Revocare*.
    Ius Memb. Custoditum (Detain Person)

1321. *Ius Membrum Custoditum* (Detain Person) is the ninth collection of twenty-two Legal Member Rights; and may be explicitly invoked or referenced by Right of Action through a proper Ucadia Forum of Law and the Fiduciary Obligations of any such court in Ucadia Jurisdiction.
    Invoking of Ius Memb. Custoditum

1322. The collection of Member Rights of *Ius Membrum Custoditum* contains one Right being:-
    Collection of Ius Memb. Custoditum

    (i) *Ius Membrum Custoditum* being the Member Right to detain a party associated with a controversy if good cause exists they be a risk of non-appearance or committing further controversies.

Article 348 – Ius Membrum Accusare (Accuse Person)

1323. ***Ius Membrum Accusare*** are the collection of Member Rights to accuse another of a transgression, as inherited from the collection of Natural Rights *Ius Naturale Iuris*.
    Ius Memb. Accusare (Accuse Person)

1324. *Ius Membrum Accusare* (Accuse Person) is the tenth collection of twenty-two Legal Member Rights; and may be explicitly invoked or referenced by Right of Action through a proper Ucadia Forum of Law and the Fiduciary Obligations of any such court in Ucadia Jurisdiction.
    Invoking of Ius Memb. Accusare

1325. The collection of Member Rights of *Ius Membrum Accusare* contains one Right being:-
    Collection of Ius Memb. Accusare

    (i) *Ius Membrum Accusare* being the Member Right to accuse another of a transgression.

Article 349 – Ius Membrum Innocentiae (Innocence)

1326. ***Ius Membrum Innocentiae*** are the collection of Member Rights of Innocence until accusation proven, as inherited from the collection of Natural Rights *Ius Naturale Innocentiae*.

1327. *Ius Membrum Innocentiae* (Innocence) is the eleventh collection of twenty-two Legal Member Rights; and may be explicitly invoked or referenced by Right of Action through a proper Ucadia Forum of Law and the Fiduciary Obligations of any such court in Ucadia Jurisdiction.

1328. The collection of Member Rights of *Ius Membrum Innocentiae* contains one Right being:-

    (i)   *Ius Membrum Innocentiae* being the Member Right of Innocence until accusation proven.

Article 350 – Ius Membrum Accusationis Cognoscendi (Full Disclosure)

1329. ***Ius Membrum Accusationis Cognoscendi*** are the collection of Member Rights to know the Full Disclosure and Evidence of any Accusation, as inherited from the collection of Natural Rights *Ius Naturale Aequum*.

1330. *Ius Membrum Accusationis Cognoscendi* (Full Disclosure) is the twelfth collection of twenty-two Legal Member Rights; and may be explicitly invoked or referenced by Right of Action through a proper Ucadia Forum of Law and the Fiduciary Obligations of any such court in Ucadia Jurisdiction.

1331. The collection of Member Rights of *Ius Membrum Accusationis Cognoscendi* contains one Right being:-

    (i)   *Ius Membrum Accusationis Cognoscendi* being the Member Right to know the Full Disclosure and Evidence of any Accusation.

Article 351 – Ius Membrum Defensionis (Right to Defence)

1332. ***Ius Membrum Defensionis*** are the collection of Member Rights to defend against any accusation and accuser, as inherited from the collection of Natural Rights *Ius Naturale Defensionis*.

1333. *Ius Membrum Defensionis* (Right to Defence) is the thirteenth collection of twenty-two Legal Member Rights; and may be explicitly invoked or referenced by Right of Action through a proper Ucadia Forum of Law and the Fiduciary Obligations of any such court in Ucadia Jurisdiction.

Memb. Defensionis

1334. The collection of Member Rights of *Ius Membrum Defensionis* contains one Right being:-

   (i) *Ius Membrum Defensionis* being the Member Right to defend against any accusation and accuser.

Collection of Ius Memb. Defensionis

Article 352 – Eligendi Iudicium (Jury or Judge in Forum)

1335. ***Ius Membrum Eligendi Iudicium*** are the collection of Member Rights for a matter to be decided by a jury of peers or a judge in forum of law, as inherited from the collection of Natural Rights *Ius Naturale Defensionis*.

Ius Memb. Eligendi Iudicium (Jury or Judge in Forum)

1336. *Ius Membrum Eligendi Iudicium* (Jury or Judge in Forum) is the fourteenth collection of twenty-two Legal Member Rights; and may be explicitly invoked or referenced by Right of Action through a proper Ucadia Forum of Law and the Fiduciary Obligations of any such court in Ucadia Jurisdiction.

Invoking of Ius Memb. Eligendi Iudicium

1337. The collection of Member Rights of *Ius Membrum Eligendi Iudicium* contains one Right being:-

   (i) *Ius Membrum Eligendi Iudicium* being the Member Right for a matter to be decided by a jury of peers or a judge in forum of law.

Collection of Ius Memb. Eligendi Iudicium

Article 353 – Ius Membrum Propria Persona (In Person Representation)

1338. ***Ius Membrum Propria Persona*** are the collection of Member Rights to defend or accuse as oneself, as inherited from the collection of Natural Rights *Ius Naturale Defensionis*.

Ius Memb. Propria Persona (In Person)

1339. *Ius Membrum Propria Persona* (In Person Representation) is the fifteenth collection of twenty-two Legal Member Rights; and may be explicitly invoked or referenced by Right of Action through a proper Ucadia Forum of Law and the Fiduciary Obligations of any such court in Ucadia Jurisdiction.

Invoking of Ius Memb. Propria Persona

1340. The collection of Member Rights of *Ius Membrum Propria Persona* contains one Right being:-

   (i) *Ius Membrum Propria Persona* being the Member Right to

Collection of Ius Memb. Propria Persona

defend or accuse as oneself.

Article 354 – Ius Membrum Agensas (Agent Representation)

1341. ***Ius Membrum Agensas*** are the collection of Member Rights to appoint an agent, as inherited from the collection of Natural Rights *Ius Naturale Delegare et Revocare*.

1342. *Ius Membrum Agensas* (Agent Representation) is the sixteenth collection of twenty-two Legal Member Rights; and may be explicitly invoked or referenced by Right of Action through a proper Ucadia Forum of Law and the Fiduciary Obligations of any such court in Ucadia Jurisdiction.

1343. The collection of Member Rights of *Ius Membrum Agensas* contains one Right being:-

    (i) *Ius Membrum Agensas* being the Member Right to appoint or revoke a financial or legal agent.

Article 355 – Ius Membrum Possessionis (Possession)

1344. ***Ius Membrum Possessionis*** are the collection of Member Rights to Possess, Hold and Own Property, as inherited from the collection of Natural Rights *Ius Naturale Possessionis*.

1345. *Ius Membrum Possessionis* (Possession) is the seventeenth collection of twenty-two Legal Member Rights; and may be explicitly invoked or referenced by Right of Action through a proper Ucadia Forum of Law and the Fiduciary Obligations of any such court in Ucadia Jurisdiction.

1346. The collection of Member Rights of *Ius Membrum Possessionis* contains two Rights being:-

    (i) *Ius Membrum Possessionis* being the Member Right to Possess, Hold and Own Property; and

    (ii) *Ius Membrum Possessionis Rem* being the Member Right to Possess, Hold and Own a Thing.

Article 356 – Ius Membrum Usus
(Use)

1347. **Ius Membrum Usus** are the collection of Member Rights of Use and Fruits of Use of Property, as inherited from the collection of Natural Rights *Ius Naturale Usus*.

1348. *Ius Membrum Usus* (Use) is the eighteenth collection of twenty-two Legal Member Rights; and may be explicitly invoked or referenced by Right of Action through a proper Ucadia Forum of Law and the Fiduciary Obligations of any such court in Ucadia Jurisdiction.

1349. The collection of Member Rights of *Ius Membrum Usus* contains three Rights being:-

   (i) *Ius Membrum Usus* being the Member Right of Use and Fruits of Use of Property; and

   (ii) *Ius Membrum Affectandi* being the Member Right of Acquisition of Property in Continuous Use; and

   (iii) *Ius Membrum Cessandi* being the Member Right of Cessation of Property in Use.

Article 357 – Ius Membrum Proprietatis
(Ownership of Use)

1350. **Ius Membrum Proprietatis** are the collection of Member Rights of Ownership of Use or Fruits of Use of Property, as inherited from the collection of Natural Rights *Ius Naturale Possessionis* and *Ius Naturale Usus*.

1351. *Ius Membrum Proprietatis* (Ownership of Use) is the nineteenth collection of twenty-two Legal Member Rights; and may be explicitly invoked or referenced by Right of Action through a proper Ucadia Forum of Law and the Fiduciary Obligations of any such court in Ucadia Jurisdiction.

1352. The collection of Member Rights of *Ius Membrum Proprietatis* contains eight Rights being:-

   (i) *Ius Membrum Proprietatis* being the Member Right of Ownership of Use or Fruits of Use of Property; and

   (ii) *Ius Membrum Transferendi* being the Member Right to Transfer Ownership of Use or Fruits of Use of Property to Another; and

   (iii) *Ius Membrum Utilitatis* being the Member Right of Enjoyment of Ownership of Use or Fruits of Use of Property;

and

(iv) *Ius Membrum Recusatio* being the Member Right of Refusal of Use or Fruits of Use by Another of Owned Property; and

(v) *Ius Membrum Accessionis* being the Member Right of Accession of additions and ownership of additions to Property in Use; and

(vi) *Ius Membrum Aedificii* being the Member Right of Building on Land; and

(vii) *Ius Membrum Alluvionis* being the Member Right of Accretion in increasing Property through natural processes; and

(viii) *Ius Membrum Actionis Proprietatis* being the Member Right of Action against Unreasonable or Immoral Loss of Use or Fruits of Use of Property.

Article 358 – Ius Membrum Remedium (Remedy)

1353. ***Ius Membrum Remedium*** are the collection of Member Rights of Remedy, Relief, Redress or Compensation, as inherited from the collection of Natural Rights *Ius Naturale Remedium*. — Ius Memb. Remedium (Remedy)

1354. *Ius Membrum Remedium* (Remedy) is the twentieth collection of twenty-two Legal Member Rights; and may be explicitly invoked or referenced by Right of Action through a proper Ucadia Forum of Law and the Fiduciary Obligations of any such court in Ucadia Jurisdiction. — Invoking of Ius Memb. Remedium

1355. The collection of Member Rights of *Ius Membrum Remedium* contains nine Rights being:- — Collection of Ius Memb. Remedium

(i) *Ius Membrum Remedium* being the Member Right of Remedy, Relief, Redress or Compensation; and

(ii) *Ius Membrum Remedium Compensationis* being the Member Right of Remedy of Compensation for Loss or Damages; and

(iii) *Ius Membrum Remedium Restitutionis* being the Member Right of Remedy of Restitution for the Return of Property; and

(iv) *Ius Membrum Remedium Reparationis* being the Member Right of Remedy of Restoration for the Repairing of Harm or Property; and

(v) *Ius Membrum Remedium Injunctionis* being the Member Right of Remedy of Injunction to Enforce Performance or Prevent Behaviour of Another; and

(vi) *Ius Membrum Remedium Rescissionis* being the Member Right of Remedy of Rescission to Cancel an Agreement or Transaction and Restore Parties to their Original Positions; and

(vii) *Ius Membrum Remedium Appellationis* being the Member Right of Remedy of Appeal a Decision to a Higher Forum; and

(viii) *Ius Membrum Remedium Declarationis* being the Member Right of Remedy of Declaratory Judgement; and

(ix) *Ius Membrum Remedium Sententiae* being the Member Right of Remedy of Enforcement of Judgement.

Article 359 – Ius Membrum Poena (Penalty, Penitence or Punishment)

1356. ***Ius Membrum Poena*** are the collection of Member Rights of Penalty, Penitence or Punishment, as inherited from the collection of Natural Rights *Ius Naturale Poena*.

Ius Memb. Poena (Penalty)

1357. *Ius Membrum Poena* (Penalty) is the twenty-first collection of twenty-two Legal Member Rights; and may be explicitly invoked or referenced by Right of Action through a proper Ucadia Forum of Law and the Fiduciary Obligations of any such court in Ucadia Jurisdiction.

Invoking of Ius Memb. Poena

1358. The collection of Member Rights of *Ius Membrum Poena* contains five Rights being:-

Collection of Ius Memb. Poena

(i) *Ius Membrum Poena* being the Member Right of Penalty & Punishment; and

(ii) *Ius Membrum Remissionis Poenae* being the Member Right of Remission in the significant lessening of Penalties upon prior and full Acceptance of Culpability and Evidence of Genuine Remorse and Efforts to Change before any Trial; and

(iii) *Ius Membrum Exacerbationis Poenae* being the Member Right of Exacerbation in the significant increasing of severity of Penalties upon prior Refusal to Accept Culpability or Demonstrate Genuine Remorse or Change before any Trial; and

(iv) *Ius Membrum Appellationis Poenae* being the Member Right to Appeal Punishment to a Decision to a Higher Forum; and

(v) *Ius Membrum Custodiae Vitae* being the Member Right of Custody of Life whereby the Life of the Convicted must continue to be protected and sustained and cannot be threatened during any period of punishment.

Article 360 – Ius Membrum Clementia (Mercy & Forgiveness)

1359. ***Ius Membrum Clementia*** are the collection of Member Rights of Mercy & Forgiveness, as inherited from the collection of Natural Rights *Ius Naturale Clementia*. — Ius Memb. Clementia (Mercy & Forgiveness)

1360. *Ius Membrum Clementia* (Mercy & Forgiveness) is the twenty-second collection of twenty-two Legal Member Rights; and may be explicitly invoked or referenced by Right of Action through a proper Ucadia Forum of Law and the Fiduciary Obligations of any such court in Ucadia Jurisdiction. — Invoking of

1361. The collection of Member Rights of *Ius Membrum Clementia* contains two Rights being:- — Collection of Ius Memb. Clementia

 (i) *Ius Membrum Clementia* being the Personal Right *of Mercy & Forgiveness*; and

 (ii) *Ius Membrum Instrumenti Convicti* being the Member Right of Convicted Record Expurgation at Conclusion of Punishment in recognition for prior and full Acceptance of Culpability and Evidence of Genuine Remorse and Efforts to Change before any Trial and Conviction.

10.4 – Special Member Rights

Article 361 - Special Member Rights

1362. **"Special Member Rights"** (*Proprius Membrum Iurium*) shall be Critical Member Rights in relation to the majority (two-thirds) of all members as "the people", essential to democracy and the restoration of the Golden Rule of Law in the event of corruption, collapse of justice or the rise of tyranny. — Special Member Rights

1363. Unlike all other Member Rights, Special Member Rights are not delegated to institutions of society but to the Vox Populi as the "Voice of the People" being up to two thirds of the population willing to stand against tyranny and oppression. — Delegation of Special Member Rights

1364. Special Member Rights may only be invoked when two thirds of total members of a particular society agree by the solidarity and bravery of their mass demonstrations, protests, resistance and verifiable participation in the election of new officials that one or more of these special powers shall be invoked. — Invocation of Special Member Rights

1365. The following valid six (6) Special Member Rights (*Proprius* — Special Member

Membrum Iurium) are recognised in accord with the most sacred Covenant *Pactum De Singularis Caelum,* subject to the special and limited conditions of their use:-

Rights (Proprius Membrum Iurium)

(i) **"Ius Populi Jurisdictio"** is the Right of the People to invoke absolute and supreme rights on Earth to form the seven (7) Unions of Africans Union, Americas Union, Arabian Union, Asia Union, Levant Union, Euro Union and Oceanic Union, as inherited from the Divine Right *Ius Divinum Fraternitas*; and

(ii) **"Ius Populi Ecclesia"** is the Right of the people to form the new Ecclesiastical and Religious Bodies of One Christ, One Islam and One Spirit, as inherited from the Divine Right *Ius Divinum Ecclesia*; and

(iii) **"Ius Populi Revocare"** is the Right of the people to Revoke and Suspend Rights in the face of tyranny, injustice and corruption, as inherited from the Divine Right *Ius Divinum Delegare et Revocare*; and

(iv) **"Ius Populi Decretum"** is the Right of the people to issue Decree, Judgement and Edict, in the face of absolute Tyranny, Contempt for the Rule of Law or Justice, as inherited from the Divine Right *Ius Divinum Decretum*; and

(v) **"Ius Populi Imperium"** is the Right of the people to Command, Occupation and Enforcement of its orders, in the face of absolute Tyranny, Contempt for the Rule of Law or Justice, as inherited from the Divine Right *Ius Divinum Imperium*; and

(vi) **"Ius Populi Custoditum"** is the Right of the people as Custodians and Guardians of Rights and Golden Rule of Law, as inherited from the Divine Right *Ius Divinum Custoditum*.

Article 362 – Ius Populi Jurisdictio

1366. *Ius Populi Jurisdictio* is the Right of the People to invoke absolute and supreme rights on Earth to form the seven (7) Unions of Africans Union, Americas Union, Arabian Union, Asia Union, Euro Union, Levant Union and Oceanic Union, as inherited from the Divine Right *Ius Divinum Fraternitas*; and

Ius Populi Jurisdictio

1367. *Ius Populi Jurisdictio* shall be invoked under the following strict conditions:-

Invoking of Ius Populi Jurisdictio

(i) That all Constitutional Charters for the Ucadia Unions exist and have been published; and

(ii) That all Constitutional Charters for Ucadia Universities and Foundations exist and have been published; and

(iii) That at least three Ucadia Foundations exist within the jurisdiction of the relevant Ucadia Union Jurisdiction.

1368. The collection of Special Member Rights of *Ius Populi Jurisdictio* contains one Right being:- Collection of Ius Populi Jurisdictio

(i) *Ius Populi Jurisdictio* being the Right of the People to invoke absolute and supreme rights on Earth to form the seven (7) Unions of Africans Union, Americas Union, Arabian Union, Asia Union, Euro Union, Levant Union and Oceanic Union.

Article 363 – Ius Populi Ecclesia

1369. ***Ius Populi Ecclesia*** is the Right of the People to form the new Ecclesiastical and Religious Bodies of One Christ, One Islam and One Spirit, as inherited from the Divine Right *Ius Divinum Ecclesia*; and Ius Populi Ecclesia

1370. *Ius Populi Ecclesia* shall be invoked under the following strict conditions:- Invoking of Ius Populi Ecclesia

(i) That all Covenants for One Christ, One Islam and One Spirit exist and have been published; and

(ii) That all Constitutional Charters for the administration of a faith at a University and Foundation level exist and have been published; and

(iii) That at least three Foundations for a particular faith exist within the jurisdiction of the relevant Ucadia Union Jurisdiction.

1371. The collection of Special Member Rights of *Ius Populi Ecclesia* contains one Right being:- Collection of Ius Populi Ecclesia

(i) *Ius Populi Ecclesia* being the Right of the People to form the new Ecclesiastical and Religious Bodies of One Christ, One Islam and One Spirit.

Article 364 – Ius Populi Revocare

1372. ***Ius Populi Revocare*** is the Right of the people to Revoke and Suspend Rights in face of tyranny, injustice and corruption, as inherited from the Divine Right *Ius Divinum Delegare et Revocare*; and Ius Populi Revocare

1373. *Ius Populi Revocare* shall be invoked under the following strict conditions:-   *Invoking of Ius Populi Revocare*

    (i) That all Ucadia Unions and their Synods have reached permanent status; and

    (ii) That at least two thirds of all Ucadia Universities within each Ucadia Union have reached Prerogative or Permanent status; and

    (iii) That the Ucadia Nation (University) in question has or previously had Prerogative or Permanent status; and

    (iv) That the leadership have been proven to be corrupt and unjust and have refused to step down or leave; and

    (v) That at least two thirds of registered members of the Ucadia Nation (University) have expressed their clear desire to invoke *Ius Populi Revocare*.

1374. The collection of Special Member Rights of *Ius Populi Revocare* contains one Right being:-   *Collection of Ius Populi Revocare*

    (i) *Ius Populi Revocare* being the Right of the people to Revoke and Suspend Rights in face of tyranny, injustice and corruption.

Article 365 – Ius Populi Decretum

1375. ***Ius Populi Decretum*** is the Right of the people to issue Decree, Judgement and Edict, in the face of absolute Tyranny, Contempt for the Rule of Law or Justice, as inherited from the Divine Right *Ius Divinum Decretum*; and   *Ius Populi Decretum*

1376. *Ius Populi Decretum* shall be invoked under the following strict conditions:-   *Invoking of Ius Populi Decretum*

    (i) That all Ucadia Unions and their Synods have reached permanent status; and

    (ii) That at least two thirds of all Ucadia Universities within each Ucadia Union have reached Prerogative or Permanent status; and

    (iii) That the Ucadia Nation (University) in question has or previously had Prerogative or Permanent status; and

    (iv) That the leadership have been proven to be corrupt and unjust and have refused to step down or leave; and

    (v) That at least two thirds of registered members of the Ucadia Nation (University) have expressed their clear desire to invoke

Ius Populi Decretum.

1377. The collection of Special Member Rights of *Ius Populi Decretum* contains one Right being:-

    (i)   *Ius Populi Decretum* being the Right of the people to issue Decree, Judgement and Edict, in the face of absolute Tyranny, Contempt for the Rule of Law or Justice.

Collection of Ius Populi Decretum

Article 366 – Ius Populi Imperium

1378. ***Ius Populi Imperium*** is the Right of the people to Command, Occupation and Enforcement of its orders, in the face of absolute Tyranny, Contempt for the Rule of Law or Justice, as inherited from the Divine Right *Ius Divinum Imperium*; and

Ius Populi Imperium

1379. *Ius Populi Imperium* shall be invoked under the following strict conditions:-

Invoking of Ius Populi Imperium

    (i)   That all Ucadia Unions and their Synods have reached permanent status; and

    (ii)   That at least two thirds of all Ucadia Universities within each Ucadia Union have reached Prerogative or Permanent status; and

    (iii)   That the Ucadia Nation (University) in question has or previously had Prerogative or Permanent status; and

    (iv)   That the leadership have been proven to be corrupt and unjust and have refused to step down or leave; and

    (v)   That at least two thirds of registered members of the Ucadia Nation (University) have expressed their clear desire to invoke *Ius Populi Imperium* to issue orders to the Police or Military to arrest the leaders and stop attacking the people.

1380. The collection of Member Rights of *Ius Populi Imperium* contains one Right being:-

Collection of Ius Populi Imperium

    (i)   *Ius Populi Imperium* being the Right of the people to Command, Occupation and Enforcement of its orders, in the face of absolute Tyranny, Contempt for the Rule of Law or Justice.

Article 367 – Ius Populi Custoditum

1381. ***Ius Populi Custoditum*** is the Right of the People as Custodians and Guardians of Rights and Golden Rule of Law, as inherited from the Divine Right *Ius Divinum Custoditum*. — Ius Populi Custoditum

1382. *Ius Populi Custoditum* shall be invoked under the following strict conditions:- — Invoking of Ius Populi Custoditum

   (i) That all Ucadia Unions and their Synods have reached permanent status; and

   (ii) That at least two thirds of all Ucadia Universities within each Ucadia Union have reached Prerogative or Permanent status; and

   (iii) That the Ucadia Nation (University) in question has or previously had Prerogative or Permanent status; and

   (iv) That the leadership have been proven to be corrupt and unjust and have refused to step down or leave; and

   (v) That at least two thirds of registered members of the Ucadia Nation (University) have expressed their clear desire to invoke *Ius Populi Custoditum* to arrest the leaders.

1383. The collection of Member Rights of *Ius Populi Custoditum* contains one Right being:- — Collection of Ius Populi Custoditum

   (i) *Ius Populi Custoditum* being the Right of the People as Custodians and Guardians of Rights and Golden Rule of Law.

Title XI – Trusts & Estates

11.1 – Trust

Article 368 – Trust

1384. ***Trust*** is confidence in and reliance upon some quality or thing or act as being true. Trust is also used to define a formal relation and agreement whereby an authorised party (Trustor) gives, grants, assigns or delegates one or more Rights to another (Trustee) under certain conditions for the benefit of a third party (Beneficiary). — Trust

1385. By definition, all Rights are held in Trust and no Right is said to exist, unless through Trust. Therefore, in the absence of a valid Trust, the claimed Rights are also absent. — All Rights held in Trust

1386. Trust is a fundamental attribute of absolute and irrevocable confidence in and reliance upon some quality or thing or act of a Being as true; and the means whereby such absolute and irrevocable certainty is formed, witnessed and proven (hence forming a "Trust"). — Nature of Trust

1387. The word *Trust* originates from the Anglaise word *treust* created in the 8th Century upon the formation of Anglo Saxon law and new Western Civilisation by the Carolingians meaning literally "the three flames of *Bona Fidei, Bona Conscientia* and *Bona Acta*":- — Origin of the Word Trust

   (i) The word *tre* comes from Latin meaning "three"; and

   (ii) The word usta comes from Latin meaning "flame"; and

   (iii) The legal meaning and concept of Treust (Trust) from its inception in combination with the word Right and that a Right can only be held in Good Faith (Bona Fidei), Good Conscience (Bona Conscientia) and Good Actions (Bona Acta).

1388. In the absence of Good Faith, Good Conscience and Good Actions there can be no Trust and thus no Right. — Absence of Good Faith and Trust

1389. Just as a proper and valid Right cannot be expressed in the negative, a valid and proper Trust cannot be formed in Bad Faith. Thus any such claims to the contrary are absurd and morally repugnant to the Law having no force or effect. — Good Faith and Creation of Trust

1390. All valid Trusts, by their formation are classified as either Instructed Trusts or Facilitated Trusts and must possess the following ten Essential Characters of Trust being Rights, Trustor, Trustee, Reason, Intention, Benefit, Condition, Oath or Vow, Execution and Proof:- — Essential Elements of valid Trust

   (i) *Rights* means there must be something that may be clearly defined in terms of Rights or Property to convey in the first instance; and

(ii) *Trustor* means there must be a valid Trustor or Surrogate Trustor (as in the case of a Facilitated Trust) possessing the necessary authority to transfer any Rights or Property to another; and

(iii) *Trustee* means there must be a suitably competent, capable and willing person prepared to make a valid Oath and Vow to accept custody of the Rights or Property from the Trustor or Surrogate Trustor; and

(iv) *Reason* means there must exist at least one clear Purpose or valid Reason for the Trustor to convey and transfer the Rights or Property to the Trustee; and

(v) *Intention* means the Trustor or Surrogate Trustor must demonstrate via some Act their intention to convey and transfer the Rights or Property to the Trustee; and

(vi) *Benefit* means there exists a clear Benefit to be offered to another as one or more named or unnamed Beneficiaries; and

(vii) *Condition* means at least one or more terms and conditions exist as to the obligations of the Trustee to manage such Rights or Property and also to any Beneficiaries accepting one or more Benefits; and

(viii) *Oath* or *Vow* means the person agreeing to be Trustee made a valid promise to accept the Rights or Property under one or more Conditions; and

(ix) *Execution* means the Trustor and Trustee executed the formal transfer and conveyance of such Rights or Property after the valid Oath and Vow was given; and

(x) *Proof* means some proof in the form of written instruments or testimony exists as a memorial of the event and execution of the agreement.

1391. A Trust that is deficient in possessing one or more of the ten Essential Characters of Trust cannot be regarded as a valid Trust:- *(General Reference to Trust)*

(i) There can never be less than two separate and distinct persons involved in the valid creation of a Trust, even if a Trustor is a Surrogate; and

(ii) A person cannot be both the Trustee and Beneficiary at the same time; and

(iii) No valid Trust may exist where the legal Title and beneficial interest are both vested in the same person; and

(iv) The rights administered by the Trustee cannot exceed the original rights conveyed by the Trustor; and

(v) It is the Oath of the Trustee that essentially forms the fundamental Character of the Trust. Therefore in the absence of any record of a valid Oath or Vow, there is no Trust; and

(vi) As a Trustee is bound by Fiduciary Capacity to act in good faith (*bona fide*), good character and good conscience, any Trust formed under bad faith, false, deceptive or misleading behaviour automatically renders such a Trust null and void from the beginning; and

(vii) As the presence of at least one Trustee is fundamental to the existence of a Trust, the absence of a Trustee from such Office, without a duly appointed Surrogate, therefore collapses the Trust; and

(viii) A Trustee that fundamentally breaches one or more conditions of the Trust, even if the Trust was formed under proper Fiduciary capacity, automatically dissolves his/her Office and Oath and Vow, thus dissolving the Trust, if only one Trustee exists.

1392. A ***Trustor*** is the generic term for anyone possessing the proper authority to transfer any rights, title or property to another. The other party upon acceptance of the Fiduciary obligations upon a valid Oath or Vow then formalises the valid Trust as Trustee. All persons that possess the proper authority to transfer any rights, title or property to another are by default "Trustors". *(What is a Trustor)*

1393. There are only four (4) possible types of Trustor, depending upon the primary nature and intention associated with any conveyance of rights, title or property in Trust being *Grantor, Donor, Assignor* or *Delegator*: *(4 types of Trustor)*

(i) A ***Grantor*** is a person who conveys or transfers complete possession and ownership of property for some financial consideration in return under one or more terms and conditions and may be further defined as a Feoffor, Devisor, Testator, Settlor, Obligor, Addressor, Sender, Seller or Purchaser; and

(ii) A ***Donor*** is a person who conveys or transfers complete possession and ownership of property without any financial consideration under one or more terms and conditions and may be further defined as a Giftor, Debtor, Guarantor, Indemnitor or Mortgagor; and

(iii) An ***Assignor*** is a person who temporarily conveys or transfers one or more benefits and rights of possession and use of some property for some financial consideration in return, under one or more terms and conditions and may be further defined as a Consignor, Bailor, Depositor, Employer, Insurer, Hirer, Lessor, Lender, Creditor, Licensor, Lienor or Scrivener; and

(iv) A ***Delegator*** is a person who temporarily conveys or transfers one or more benefits and rights of possession and use of some property without any financial consideration under one or more terms and conditions and may be further defined as an Executor, Commissioner or Administrator.

1394. A ***Trustee*** is an Office formed by a valid Oath and Vow to the Terms of Trust to take possession of certain Rights and Property from a Trustor and perform certain Obligations: *Obligations of Trustee*

(i) The manner and character of a Trustee may be described as a position of Trust that is equivalent to the term Fiduciary; and

(ii) The valid Oath and Vow taken as to the Terms and Conditions of Trust creates the Office of Trustee; and

(iii) In the absence of a valid Oath and Vow, no Office may exist; and

(iv) The Obligations of the Trustee are defined by the Trustor or Surrogate Trustor and expressed clearly to the Trustee. A Trustee is not a Trustee unless their Oath and Vow is done in knowledge of their Obligations; and

(v) When the Obligations are defined in writing, the document is called the Trust Instrument; and

(vi) The sacred Covenant *Pactum De Singularis Caelum* is the highest possible Oath and Vow of the Divine Creator of all Existence and all Heaven and Earth in the formation of all Divine Trusts and True Trusts; and

(vii) The sacred constitutional charters of the Ucadia Globe Union, Africans Union, Americas Union, Arabian Union, Asia Union, Euro Union, Levant Union and Oceanic Union are the highest possible Oaths and Vows in the formation of all Superior Member Trusts.

1395. A ***Beneficiary*** is a named or unnamed party at the time of the formation of the Trust who benefits or receives an advantage in Trust. A Beneficiary, by definition is an "interested party" in a Trust or Estate: *2 types of Beneficiary*

(i) A named Beneficiary is an agent (with the Trustee being the principal) and may be commissioned or non-commissioned; and

(ii) An unnamed Beneficiary is a creditor (with the Trustee acting as debtor) to whom the trustee owes basic duties arising by law, agreement or claim.

1396. All valid Trusts may be further categorized according to the essential Status and Authority of the Trustor, being **Divine**, **Living** or **Deceased**:- 3 types of Trust

(i) The highest form of Trust is a ***Divine Trust*** also involving the highest form of rights of ownership. A Divine Trust is purely spiritual and divinely supernatural formed in accord with the sacred Covenant *Pactum De Singularis Caelum* by the Divine Creator whereby the form of Divine Spirit, Energy and Rights are conveyed. Therefore, a Divine Trust is the only possible type of Trust that can hold actual Form, rather than just the Rights of Use of Form (Property); and

(ii) A ***Living Trust***, also called an "Inter Vivos" Trust is the second highest form of rights of ownership. A Living Trust typically exists for the duration of the lifetime of the Person(s) or Juridic Person(s) who are the beneficiaries. There are only four (4) valid forms of Living Trusts: True, Superior, Temporary and Inferior; and

(iii) A ***Deceased Trust***, also known as a *Testamentary Trust*, also known as a Deceased Estate and simply a State is the lowest form of Trust and the lowest form of rights of ownership of any possible form of Trust. A Deceased Trust is when property is conveyed into a Testamentary Trust upon the death of the testator. Inferior Roman law has a hybrid Deceased Trust called a Cestui Que Vie Trust that uses false, deceptive, misleading, absurd, immoral, repugnant and illogical presumptions to create Deceased Estates for the living on the presumption they are "dead at law; or lost or abandoned at sea; or an idiot or lunatic".

1397. In respect of the four types of *Living Trusts being True, Superior, Temporary* and *Inferior*: 4 types of living Trust

(i) A ***True Trust*** is the highest form of Living Trust. A True Trust is formed by a True Person in accord with the sacred Covenant *Pactum De Singularis Caelum* when it is validly registered into the Great Register and Public Record of a Ucadian Society on the condition of (1) the pre existence of a

Divine Trust where the True Person is the named Beneficiary; and (2) the lawful conveyance from the Divine Trust into the True Trust of certain Divine Rights of Use known as Divinity, being the highest possible form of any kind of Property. A True Trust may be for a single man, or woman called a "True Person Trust", a True Location Trust containing Divine Right of Possession of Promised Land, or an aggregate trust such as a Universal True Trust, Global True Trust or Civil True Trust; and

(ii) A ***Superior Trust*** is the second highest form of Living Trust. A Superior Trust is formed in accordance with the covenant *Pactum De Singularis Caelum* and the associated Constitutional Charters of valid Ucadian Societies when it is validly registered into the Great Register and Public Record of a Ucadian Society on the condition of (1) the pre-existence of a True Trust where the Superior Person is the named Beneficiary; and (2) the lawful conveyance from the True Trust into the Superior Trust of certain True Rights of Use known as Absolute Realty, being the highest temporal form of any kind of Property. A True Trust may be for a single man, or woman called a "Superior Person Trust", or an aggregate trust such as a Global (Superior) Trust, Civil (Superior) Trust, Mercantile (Superior) Trust, Union (Superior) Trust, Clann Trust, Official Trust or Location Trust; and

(iii) A ***Temporary Trust*** is the third highest form of Living Trust involving the temporary conveyance of property from one Superior Trust to another. Excluding Negotiable Instruments, a Temporary Trust is not permitted to exist beyond seven years; and

(iv) An ***Inferior Trust***, also known as an Inferior Roman Trust, or simply Roman Trust is the lowest form of Living Trust possessing the lowest possible form of rights of ownership. An Inferior Trust can never be considered superior to a Superior Trust or Divine Trust. An Inferior Trust is any Living Trust or Implied Trust or Express Trust formed by inferior Roman Law, claims and statutes.

1398. In respect of the Authority and Power of the classes and types of Trusts:

When does a Trust cease

(i) A *Divine Trust* ceases upon the will of the Divine Creator of all Existence in accord with the sacred Covenant *Pactum de Singularis Caelum* and no other. A Divine Trust cannot be salvaged, seized, captured, arrested, alienated, resigned, abjured, transferred, conveyed, donated assigned or surrendered; and

(ii) A *True Trust* ceases upon the physical death of the body, or body politic that is associated with it. A True Trust is not dependent upon the good character or intentions or actions of the Trustee or Trustees. Furthermore, a True Trust cannot be salvaged, seized, captured, arrested, alienated, resigned, abjured, transferred, conveyed, donated, assigned or surrendered; and

(iii) A *Superior Trust* ceases upon its Dissolution, Satisfaction, Termination, Cessation or Annulment, with the res or property of the Trust being returned, or distributed or disposed accordingly upon the publication and patenting of an official Gazette notice within the Ucadia Gazette, as evidence to the fact; and

(iv) A *Temporary Trust* ceases upon its Dissolution, Satisfaction, Termination, Cessation or Annulment, with the res or property of the Trust being returned, or distributed or disposed accordingly upon proper notice, in accord with the sacred Covenant *Pactum de Singularis Caelum* or associated Covenants, Maxims and Rules of Ucadia; and

(v) An *Inferior Trust* ceases upon its Dissolution, Satisfaction, Termination, Cessation or Annulment, with the res or property of the Trust being returned, or distributed or disposed accordingly upon either the publication and patenting of an official Gazette notice within the Ucadia Gazette, as evidence to the fact; or by such rules of Inferior Law, providing such rules do not contradict the sacred Covenant *Pactum de Singularis Caelum* or associated Covenants, Maxims and Rules of Ucadia.

1399. The Office of Trustee ceases:-   *6 causes to cease Trustee*

(i) At the dissolution or satisfaction or termination or cessation or annulment of the Trust; or

(ii) Upon the Death of the Trustee; and

(iii) Abandonment, when a Trustee is away from the domicile of the Trust for more than two years without word or adequate response; and

(iv) Resignation, when a Trustee resigns from the of duties of such Office; and

(v) Refusal, when a Trustee refuses to act in the manner and characteristics required of such Office; and

(vi) Contestation, when the competency or legitimacy of a Trustee is challenged and upheld by a competent forum of Law.

1400. A Superior Trust, Temporary Trust or Inferior Trust ceases upon its Dissolution, Satisfaction, Termination, Cessation or Annulment, with the res or property of the Trust being returned, or distributed or disposed accordingly: 5 methods to cease a Trust

(i) **Satisfaction of Trust** means a Trust has fulfilled all its obligations and is therefore finished and ceases upon the return, distribution or disposal of the property; and

(ii) **Termination of Trust** means a Trust that ceases due to a condition of its operation, usually documented within the Trust Instrument, requiring the Trust to end upon some fundamental breach or failure to perform; and

(iii) **Dissolution of Trust** means a Trust that dissolves according to the operation of law, usually upon some declaration that the Trust is unable to fulfil its obligations (as in bankruptcy) or some other obstruction or major defect as determined within a competent forum of law; and

(iv) **Annulment of Trust** means a Trust that ceases to be, upon the strike or removal of such record of its existence, or condemnation as unfit or contrary to the principles of Fiduciary Capacity and any property returned to the Trustor as if the Trust never existed; and

(v) **Cessation of Trust** means a Trust ceases to be in effect, due to some catastrophic event or act, such as a fundamental Breach of Trust that renders the continuation of such a Trust impossible and to the effect as if the Trust had been annulled.

1401. A Trustor may cease, terminate, dissolve and annul a Trust in action against the Trustee(s), upon evidence of one or more Breaches of Trust: 4 methods for Trustor to cease a Trust in action

(i) When a Trust is formed by the Trustor as Grantor, then by Renunciation of any such Grant, a Trustor may lawfully regain Repossession and Restitution; and

(ii) When a Trust is formed by the Trustor as Donor, then by Reclamation of such original Rights, a Trustor may lawfully regain Recovery and Restoration; and

(iii) When a Trust is formed by the Trustor as Assignor, then by Rescission of any sign (signature), or seal of execution, a

Trustor may lawfully regain Return and Reversion; and

(iv) When a Trust is formed by the Trustor as Delegator, then by Revocation of any instrument of appointment or powers, a Trustor may lawfully regain Remand and Revestiture.

1402. A party becomes a Beneficiary upon Use, or Claim or Acceptance and therefore obligated to perform the duties associated with the Benefits in Trust. However, a party once becoming a Beneficiary may then cease, terminate or dissolve any interest or obligation by one of the following actions: 4 methods for Beneficiary to cease the Trust

(i) If a Beneficiary by Acceptance, then upon acknowledgment of proof of purchase (i.e. Bill of Sale) or by deed signed by another party then proving the property or interest is no longer in their possession; or by surrender of the property or interest by deed; and

(ii) If a Beneficiary by Claim, then by deed of disclaim or withdrawal of any interest; and

(iii) If a Beneficiary By Use, when no formal acceptance or claim acknowledged, then by both surrender and disclaim as a cessation of any past, present and future Use; and

(iv) A person proven to have acted in fraud or breach of their fiduciary duties as a Trustor or a Trustee automatically ceases to hold the Position from the time of the Fraud or breach. Any liability associated with a fraud or breach of duty of a former Trustor or Trustee is automatically personally assumed by the disgraced former Trustor or Trustee.

1403. A person proven to have acted in fraud or breach of their fiduciary duties as a Trustor or a Trustee automatically ceases to hold the Position from the time of the Fraud or breach. Any liability associated with a fraud or breach of duty of a former Trustor or Trustee is automatically personally assumed by the disgraced former Trustor or Trustee, as Immunity cannot hold against proof of Bad Faith. Consequences for fraud or breach of fiduciary duties

1404. Any claim that an Inferior Non-Ucadia Trust possesses superior standing and rights of ownership compared to a Superior Trust, or True Trust is an absurdity against Divine Law, Natural Law and Positive Law and therefore is null and void from the beginning, including any associated covenants, deeds and agreements concerning property rights and lesser trusts. Null and void claim by Inferior Trust

Article 369 – Ucadia Trust

1405. A *Ucadia Trust* is a proper and valid Trust formed by a Ucadia Person, Entity, Body or Corporation in accord with the present Maxims. — Ucadia Trust

1406. All valid Ucadia Trusts may be categorized by their proper formation as either Instructed or Facilitated: — 2 types of Ucadia Trusts

(i) Instructed Trust, also known under Inferior Non-Ucadia Law as an "Express Trust", is when a Trust is created by a Trustor and Trustee with clear intentions, subject matter and purpose(s) by a person having the legal capacity to perform such an act; and

(ii) Facilitated Trust, also known under Inferior Non-Ucadia Law as an "Implied Trust", is when a Trust is created by a Surrogate Trustor or simply a "Surrogate" and Trustee by implication and function of law, being either a "Manufactured Trust" (Constructive Trust) by operation of law, or a "Consequential Trust" (Resulting Trust) by effect of events determined by law.

1407. Ucadia Trusts may take on the structure and nature of any and all Non-Ucadia Trusts in their design and purpose, providing such design and purpose is consistent with Good Faith and Civilised Law. — Ucadia Trusts and structures the same or similar to Non-Ucadia Trusts

Article 370 – Non-Ucadia Trust

1408. A *Non-Ucadia Trust* is a Trust (or claim of Trust) formed under Non-Ucadia Laws by a Non-Ucadia Person, Entity, Body or Corporation. A Non-Ucadia Trust is always inferior under valid law to a Ucadia Trust. — Non-Ucadia Trust

1409. While it was the Carolingians and Holly Irish that invented the modern concept of Trust (treust) in the 8th Century as a cornerstone of Anglo-Saxon Law and Modern Western Civilisation, there is no credible evidence of the return of the concept of Trusts in English-Venetian Law until the end of the 17th Century:- — Origin of Trusts in Non-Ucadia Law

(i) There is no credible evidence that the alleged statutes known as the *Statute of Uses* (1535) or *Statute of Wills* (1540) were ever created as claimed. Instead, based upon surviving Scottish statutes of the time of Henry VIII, it is clear that statutes prior to the 17th Century were semi literate deeds of 150 words or less. Therefore, it is unequivocal that such alleged statutes of many hundreds of words are deliberate falsifications; and

(ii) Similarly to the reign of Henry VIII, there is no credible evidence that such alleged statutes as Charitable Uses Act (1601) or Fraudulent Conveyances Act (1571) ever existed in the form claimed to this present day; and

(iii) The first credible statute mentioning the word "Trust" in the concept of a financial arrangement is the Bank of England Act of 1694 (5&6 W. & M. c.20); and

(iv) The first credible statute mentioning the word "Trust" in the concept of a Trustee is the Habeas Corpus Act of 1679 (31 Car II, c.2) in reference to an "Office of Trust"; and

(v) The first credible statute mentioning the word "Trustee" in the context of "Guardian Trustee" is in 1707 (6 Ann. c.72) and the Cestui Que Vie Act on the assumption of infants and persons presumed "dead or lost at sea".

1410. Certain Non-Ucadia Jurisdictions such as Great Britain (United Kingdom) and its related territories and colonies are unique in the creation of the absurd, morally repugnant and prohibited notion of Trusts created in Bad Faith, whereby Rights can be held for the technical "benefit" of others, but done by intentional deception, omission, fraud and misrepresentation:- Origin of Absurd & Prohibited Notion of Trusts in Bad Faith

(i) The concept of "secret trusts" as first claimed to be invented in England in 1666 with the Cestui Que Vie Act 1666 and then in 1707 is an absurdity and supreme moral repugnancy against the very notion of Civilised Law and the function of Trusts and Trustees; and

(ii) Not only does it appear that the Non-Ucadian "State" was perfectly comfortable in postulating and promoting such absurdities to their own people and the world, but in fact expanding such blatant injury to all known Civilised Law again in 1731 (4 Geo. II c.10) under King George II of Great Britain, Westminster by expanding the power and scope of Trustees and the use of "cestui que vie trusts" to include the concept of the property of "lunatics" and "idiots" being held in such trusts; and

(iii) In 1775, Westminster and the Bank of England were sufficiently confident to continue to operate in Bad Faith, Bad Conscience and Bad Actions to enclose the very concept of a valid Oath for the first time in civilized history through (25 Geo.III c.39) by claiming Justices of the Peace then be empowered to administer (valid) Oaths. Thus the evidence in writing of a valid oath and then witnessed in writing by a

Justice of the Peace became primary proof, not the auricular event itself and associated witnesses; and

(iv) In 1825 (6 Geo. IV c.74), the Bank of England assumed the role of the Crown (Corporation), and Westminster did then consolidate and expand further the claims of "lawful" power in Bad Faith, Bad Conscience and Bad Actions by combining the concepts of cestui que vie trusts for "idiots, lunatics, infants or trustees" with those of "unsound mind" ensuring that such property was to be administered by the Bank of England; and

(v) In 1850 (13 & 14 Vict . c.60), Westminster revised the "laws" concerning property held by Trustees and Mortgagees with particular emphasis in watering down the historic nature of Trusts and Trustees to include the concepts of "implied and constructive trusts" being fictions and pseudo-trusts resembling (in name) trusts but having none of the customary characteristics with the operation of such pseudo trusts being determined by the laws of Westminster. Hence, the birth of deliberately false trusts being nothing more than implied contracts in bad faith, bad conscience and bad actions; and

(vi) In 1872 (35 & 36 Vict . c.79) Westminster extended the concept of secret "implied or constructive" cestui que vie trusts to all persons by assuming all people who do not redeem themselves are by default some form of idiot, lunatic, infant or trustee of unsound mind. Under the guise of "health", sanitary districts were identified as "wards" for implied lunatics. The effect being that the Bank of England operating as the Crown was now the "trustee" for all persons in England, Great Britain and the Dominions and Colonies of England and Great Britain; and

(vii) In 1888 (51 & 52 Vict . c.59) and then in 1893 (56 & 57 Vict . c.53) the role of the Trustee fundamentally changed from executor and administrator to a role with full investment and personal wealth creation capacity. Now, agencies, corporations, independent contractors and other bodies "acting" in the capacity of a trustee (such as judges, magistrates and others) stood to obtain substantial financial enrichment in complete contradiction to the public expressed history and principles of fiduciary responsibility and trust. Thus, the end of any pretence of Rule of Law for Great Britain and its dominions and previous colonies can be said to be this watershed in defiling all known respect for law and the practical collapse of Trust Law and Public Law.

1411. No claimed Non-Ucadia Trusts formed by deception, omission,   *Non-Validity of* misrepresentation or fraud was or is valid, proper, legitimate or effective in law whatsoever, unless:- *all Secret and Bad Faith Non-Ucadia Trusts*

- (i) Such a Non-Ucadia Country, or Official Body enters into a Treaty with one or more official and valid Ucadia Entities, Foundations and Bodies to recognise the mutual respect, holding and exchange of Ucadia Instruments, Currencies, Trusts and Estates; or

- (ii) Such a Non-Ucadia Country, or Official Body enters into a Transition plan to become a Ucadia Country and Body and thereby transform, reform and redeem such Non-Ucadia Trusts to Ucadia Trusts.

1412. Examples of Inferior Non-Ucadia Trusts include (but are not limited to): *59 examples of Inferior Trusts*

- (i) **Accumulation Trust** is a form of Inferior (Non-Ucadia) Trust whereby the Trustees are directed to accumulate income and gains from sales of trust assets for ultimate disposition when the trust is terminated; and

- (ii) **Active Trust** is a form of Inferior (Non-Ucadia) Trust that imposes upon the trustee the duty of taking active measures in the execution of the trust, as, where property is conveyed to trustees with directions to sell and distribute the proceeds among creditors of the grantor; as distinguished from a "passive" or "dry" Trust. In a Passive Trust, the legal and equitable titles are merged in relation to the beneficiaries and beneficial use is converted into legal ownership; while in an Active Trust, the title remains with the Trustee for the purpose of the Trust; and

- (iii) **Alimony Trust** is a form of Inferior (Non-Ucadia) Trust Device used to secure the obligation of a husband to pay support or alimony for wife; or a Transfer by the husband to the Trustee of property with the wife as beneficiary to then be supported after divorce or separation; and

- (iv) **Annuity Trust** is a form of Inferior (Non-Ucadia) Trust whereby the Trustee is required to pay a sum certain annually to one or more individual beneficiaries for their respective lives or for a term of years, and thereafter either transfer the remainder to or for the use of a qualified charity or retain the remainder for such a use. The sum certain must not be less than 5% of the initial fair market value of the property transferred to the trust by the donor; and

- (v) **Bond Trust** is a form of Inferior (Non-Ucadia) Trust whereby the *res* (property of the trust) consists in bonds that yield interest income; and

(vi) **Cestui Que Trust** is a form of Inferior (Non-Ucadia) Trust whereby a trust is established on one or more presumptions including (but not limited to) one or more persons presumed wards, infants, idiots, lost or abandoned at "sea" and therefore assumed/presumed "dead" after seven (7) years and thus, in the absence of a valid beneficiary, one or more other persons may claim the benefit of the Trust; and

(vii) **Charitable Remainder Trust** is a form of Inferior (Non-Ucadia) Trust that consists of assets that are paid over to the trust after the expiration of a life estate or intermediate estates and designated for charitable purposes; and

(viii) **Charitable Trust** is a form of Inferior (Non-Ucadia) Trust designed for the benefit of a class or the public generally. They are essentially different from private trusts in that the beneficiaries are uncertain. In general, such must be created for charitable, educational, religious or scientific purposes; and

(ix) **Clifford Trust** is a form of Inferior (Non-Ucadia) Trust as a tax planning device, whereby a transfer of income-producing property is made to a trust whereby provides that the income is either to be paid or accumulated for the benefit of a beneficiary other than the grantor for a period of more than ten years and at that time the trust is to terminate and the property reverts back to the grantor; and

(x) **Community Trust** is a form of Inferior (Non-Ucadia) Trust whereby an agency organized for the permanent administration of funds is placed in trust for public health, educational or charitable purposes; and

(xi) **Complex Trust** is a form of Inferior (Non-Ucadia) Trust being any inferior trust other than a simple inferior trust; and one whereby the Trustees have discretion as to whether to distribute and discretion as to amounts distributed; and

(xii) **Constructive Trust** is a form of Inferior (Non-Ucadia) Trust raised by construction of law, or arising by operation of law, as distinguished from an express trust. Wherever the circumstances of a transaction are such that the person who takes the legal estate in property cannot also enjoy the beneficial interest without necessarily violating some established principle of equity, the court will raise a constructive trust, and fasten it upon the conscience of the legal owner, so as to convert him into a Trustee for the parties who in equity are entitled to the beneficial enjoyment. Such trusts are also known as "trusts ex maleficio" or "ex delicto" or "involuntary trusts" and their forms and varieties are practically without limit, being raised by courts of equity whenever it becomes necessary to prevent a failure of justice; and

(xiii) **Contingent Trust** is a form of Inferior (Non-Ucadia) Trust as an express trust depending for its operation upon a future event; and

(xiv) **Directory Trust** is a form of Inferior (Non-Ucadia) Trust that is not completely and finally settled by the Trust Instrument creating it, but only defined in its general purpose and to be carried into detail according to later specific directions; and

(xv) **Discretionary Trust** is a form of Inferior (Non-Ucadia) Trust whereby Trustees have discretion as to types of investment and also as to whether and when distributions may be made to beneficiaries; and

(xvi) **Dry Trust** is a form of Inferior (Non-Ucadia) Trust that merely vests the legal title in the Trustee, and does not require the performance of any active duty on his part to carry out the trust; and

(xvii) **Educational Trust** is a form of Inferior (Non-Ucadia) Trust for the founding, endowing and supporting of schools for the advancement of all useful branches of learning, that are not strictly private; and

(xviii) **Equipment Trust** is a form of Inferior (Non-Ucadia) Trust as a financing method commonly used by railroads whereby the equipment's title is transferred to Trustees as security for the financing; and

(xix) **Estate Trust** is a form of Inferior (Non-Ucadia) Trust of an estate, for all or part of the income to be accumulated during the surviving spouse's life and added to corpus (res), with the accumulated income and corpus being paid to the estate of the surviving spouse at death. This type of trust is commonly used to qualify property for the marital deduction; and

(xx) **Executed Trust** is a form of Inferior (Non-Ucadia) Trust whereby the scheme has from the outset been completely declared. A trust whereby the estates and interest in the subject-matter of the trust are completely limited and defined by the instrument creating the trust, and require no further instruments to complete them; and

(xxi) **Executory Trust** is a form of Inferior (Non-Ucadia) Trust that requires the execution of some further instrument, or the doing of some further act on the part of the creator of the trust or of the Trustee, toward its complete creation or full effect; and

(xxii) **Express Active Trust** is a form of Inferior (Non-Ucadia) Trust that confers upon the executor certain authority to generally manage property of the estate and pay over net income to devisees or legatees. Such authority creates an "express active trust"; and

(xxiii) **Express Private Passive Trust** is a form of Inferior (Non-Ucadia) Trust that exists where land is conveyed to or held by one person in trust for another, without any power being expressly or impliedly given to the Trustee to take actual possession of land or exercise acts of ownership over it, except by beneficiary's direction; and

(xxiv) **Express Trust** is a form of Inferior (Non-Ucadia) Trust created or declared in express terms, and usually in writing, as distinguished from one inferred by the law from the conduct or dealings of the parties. A trust directly created for specific purposes in contrast to a constructive or resulting trust that arises by implication of law or the demands of equity. Such Trusts are created by the direct and positive acts of the parties, by some writing, or deed, or will, or by words expressly or impliedly evincing an intention to create a trust; and

(xxv) **Fixed Trust** is a form of Inferior (Non-Ucadia) Trust being a form of non-discretionary trust whereby the Trustee may not exercise his own judgment; and

(xxvi) **Foreign Trust** or **Foreign Situs Trust** is a form of Inferior (Non-Ucadia) Trust that owes its existence to foreign law. It is treated for tax purposes as a non-resident alien individual; and

(xxvii) **Fraud Trust** or simply Fraud is a form of Inferior (Non-Ucadia) Trust, also known as an Involuntary Trust and usually a Secret Trust, being an Implied Trust and Constructive Trust claimed under the control of a court of equity, as a surrogate court of chancery, formed on some claimed breach of trust, or some presumed gross maladministration or false, misleading or other criminal acts, causing a trust within the Roman system to cease. Fraud Trusts are usually created at the same time of creation of case numbers (and Bonds) and before any proof of default or delinquency on either the Beneficiary or Trustee of the claimed collapsed trust. The Roman Court then uses hearings, trials, confessions and unchallenged evidence to prove liability and therefore penalty and compensation; and

(xxviii) ***Grantor Trust*** is a form of Inferior (Non-Ucadia) Trust whereby the grantor transfers or conveys property in trust for his own benefit alone or for himself and another; and

(xxix) ***Honorary Trust*** is a form of Inferior (Non-Ucadia) Trust for specific non-charitable purposes where there is no definite ascertainable beneficiary and hence unenforceable in the absence of statute; and

(xxx) ***Illusory Trust*** is a form of Inferior (Non-Ucadia) Trust being a trust arrangement that takes the form of a trust, but because of powers retained in the settlor, has no real substance and in reality is not a completed trust; and

(xxxi) ***Implied Trust*** is a form of Inferior (Non-Ucadia) Trust being a trust raised or created by implication of law. An Implied Trust is a trust implied or presumed from circumstances. Constructive and resulting trusts are implied trusts because they arise by implication of law or by demands of equity; and

(xxxii) ***Indestructible Trust*** is a form of Inferior (Non-Ucadia) Trust being a trust that it is claimed may not be terminated or revoked; and

(xxxiii) ***Insurance Trust*** is a form of Inferior (Non-Ucadia) Trust being a trust whereby the res (property of trust) of the trust consists of insurance policies or their proceeds; and

(xxxiv) ***Inter Vivos Trust*** is a form of Inferior (Non-Ucadia) Trust being a trust created by an instrument that becomes operative during the settlor's lifetime as contrasted with a testamentary trust that takes effect on the death of the settlor; and

(xxxv) ***Involuntary Trust*** is a form of Inferior (Non-Ucadia) Trust, usually a Secret Trust, whereby a trust is raised by the doctrines of equity (Chancery Court/Division) within a competent forum holding equity powers, for the purpose of conducting a Roman Court Proceeding having commercial value (i.e. creation of Bonds), when there is no intention of the parties to create a trust relation. This class of trusts may usually be referred to as a Fraud Trust or simply "Fraud", either actual or implied, as an essential presumption of their creation. In other words, where a Roman Court presumes a party is guilty of a breach of Trust, or dereliction of duty or delinquency as actual or implied "Fraud" as the basis of forming an Involuntary Trust before any default is proven; and

(xxxvi) **Irrevocable Trust** is a form of Inferior (Non-Ucadia) Trust. Such a Trust may not be revoked after its creation as in the case of a deposit of money by one in the name of another as Trustee for the benefit of a third person (beneficiary); and

(xxxvii) **Limited Trust** is a form of Inferior (Non-Ucadia) Trust created for a limited period of time in contrast to a perpetual trust; and

(xxxviii) **Liquidation Trust** is a form of Inferior (Non-Ucadia) Trust created for purpose of terminating a business or other undertaking and for distributing the res; and

(xxxix) **Living Trust** is a form of Inferior (Non-Ucadia) Trust. An inter vivos trust created and operative during the lifetime of the settlor and commonly for benefit or support of another person; and

(xl) **Mixed Trust** is a form of Inferior (Non-Ucadia) Trust. Trusts established to benefit both private individuals and charities; and

(xli) **Naked Trust** is a form of Inferior (Non-Ucadia) Trust, also known as a dry or passive trust being one that requires no action on the part of the Trustee, beyond turning over money or property to the Cestui Que Trust; and

(xlii) **Nominee Trust** is a form of Inferior (Non-Ucadia) Trust being an arrangement for holding title to real property whereby one or more persons or corporations, pursuant to a written declaration of trust, declare that they will hold any property that they acquire as Trustees for the benefit of one or more undisclosed beneficiaries; and

(xliii) **Non-Discretionary Trust** is a form of Inferior (Non-Ucadia) Trust being a fixed trust whereby the Trustees may exercise no judgment or discretion at least as to distributions; and

(xliv) **Passive Trust** is a form of Inferior (Non-Ucadia) Trust whereby the Trustee has no active duty to perform. "Passive trust," that an equity court may terminate before it ends by its terms, is one whereby the Trustee does not have responsibilities or discretionary duties to perform; and

(xlv) **Perpetual Trust** is a form of Inferior (Non-Ucadia) Trust whereby a trust is to continue as long as the need for it continues as for the lifetime of a beneficiary or the term of a particular charity; and

(xlvi) **Pour-Over Trust** is a form of Inferior (Non-Ucadia) Trust whereby a testator leaves the residue of his estate to a Trustee of a living trust via a provision in a will for purpose of that Pour-Over Trust; and

(xlvii) **Power of Appointment Trust** is a form of Inferior (Non-Ucadia) Trust being a type of trust used to qualify property for the marital deduction. Property is left in trust for a surviving spouse. The Trustee is required to distribute income to the spouse for life and the spouse is given an unqualified power to appoint the property to himself/ herself or to his/ her estate; and

(xlviii) **Precatory Trust** is a form of Inferior (Non-Ucadia) Trust where words employed in a will or other instrument do not amount to a positive command or to a distinct testamentary disposition, but are terms of entreaty, request, recommendation, or expectation, they are termed "precatory words," and from such words the law will raise a trust, called a Precatory Trust; and

(xlix) **Private Trust** is a form of Inferior (Non-Ucadia) Trust. One established or created for the benefit of a certain designated individual or individuals, or a known person or class of persons, clearly identified or capable of identification by the terms of the instrument creating the trust, as distinguished from trusts for public institutions or charitable uses.

(l) **Public Trust** is a form of Inferior (Non-Ucadia) Trust. One constituted for the benefit either of the public at large or of some considerable portion of it answering a particular description; public trusts and charitable trusts may be considered in general as synonymous expressions; and

(li) **Resulting Trust** is a form of Inferior (Non-Ucadia) Trust arising by implication of law, or by the operation and construction of equity, and is established as consonant to the presumed intention of the parties as gathered from the nature of the transaction. It arises where the legal estate in property is disposed of, conveyed, or transferred, but the intent appears or is inferred from the terms of the disposition, or from the accompanying facts and circumstances, that the beneficial interest is not to go or be enjoyed with the legal title; and

(lii) **Revocable Trust** is a form of Inferior (Non-Ucadia) Trust whereby the Trustor reserves the right to revoke; and

(liii) **Secret Trust** is a form of Inferior (Non-Ucadia) Trust where a Trustor gives property to a person, on a verbal or written promise by the legatee or devisee that he will hold it in trust for another but will not make the existence of the trust known to the beneficiary until some event or issue. Involuntary Trusts are frequently formed as part of Roman Court proceedings; and

(liv) **Shifting Trust** is a form of Inferior (Non-Ucadia) Trust being an express trust that is so settled that it may operate in favor of beneficiaries additional to, or substituted for, those first named, upon specified contingencies; and

(lv) **Short Term Trust** is a form of Inferior (Non-Ucadia) Trust being a trust that by its terms is to be administered for a short period of time and then terminated; and

(lvi) **Simple Trust** is a form of Inferior (Non-Ucadia) Trust whereby property is simply vested in one person for the use of another, and the nature of the trust, not being qualified by the settlor, is left to the construction of law. A simple trust is a trust that provides that all of its income is required to be distributed currently, even if it is not in fact distributed, does not provide that any amounts are to be paid, permanently set aside, or used for charitable purposes; and does not distribute any amount other than current income. Simple trusts are those that are not complex trusts. Such trusts may not have a charitable beneficiary, accumulate income, nor distribute corpus (res); and

(lvii) **Special Trust** is a form of Inferior (Non-Ucadia) Trust whereby a Trustee is interposed for the execution of some purpose particularly pointed out, and is not, as in case of a simple trust, a mere passive depositary of the estate, but is required to exert himself actively in the execution of the settlor's intention; as where a conveyance is made to Trustees upon trust to re convey, or to sell for the payment of debts; and

(lviii) **Testamentary Trust** is a form of Inferior (Non-Ucadia) Trust being a trust created within a will and executed with the formalities required of a will in contrast to an inter vivos trust. A trust that does not take effect until the death of the Testator;

and

(lix) **Totten Trust** is a form of Inferior (Non-Ucadia) Trust being a trust created by the deposit by one person of his own money in his own name as a Trustee for another and as a tentative trust revocable at will until the depositor dies or completes the gift in his lifetime by some unequivocal act or declaration such as delivery of the passbook or notice to the beneficiary and if the depositor dies before the beneficiary without revocation or some decisive act or declaration of disaffirmance the presumption arises that an absolute trust was created as to the balance on hand at the death of the depositor.

Article 371 – False, Absurd & Prohibited Trusts

1413. A *False, Absurd & Prohibited Trust* is any claim of Trust created in Bad Faith, Bad Conscience and Bad Actions in contradiction to the present Maxims and the most sacred Covenant *Pactum De Singularis Caelum*.

_{False, Absurd & Prohibited Trusts}

12.2 – Estate

Article 372 – Estate

1414. An *Estate* is a record in a type of Register known as a "Roll", issued by some authorised ecclesiastical body, sovereign body or body politic, denoting the assumed or actual beneficial rights or "privileges" and obligations of one or more Persons of the same condition and circumstance.

_{Estate}

1415. The term *Estate* was first created under the 8th Century Sacré Loi ("Sacred Law") of the Catholic Church by the Carolingians and then revived in the 17th Century. The concept comes from the 8th Century Anglaise word *estat* meaning "state possessing rights of some level of self-government; and the government or condition of such rights", itself derived from the Latin terms *e* meaning "by reason of; out of" and *statuo* meaning "to decree, prescribe or judge; status". Hence, the term estate literally means by its etymology "by reason of decree, prescription or judgement".

_{Origin of Estate}

1416. In general reference to the concept of an Estate:-

_{General Reference to Estate}

(i) A valid record in an Estate Roll creates a unique legal entity having certain limits of legal capacity or "standing" or "status" within the jurisdiction of the body and control of the body that created it. Therefore, in the first instance, an Estate is equivalent to the concept of a unique "legal person"; and

(ii) The limits of legal capacity or "standing" or "status" determined by the valid record in the Estate Roll owned by the authorised ecclesiastical body, sovereign body or body politic that created it therefore defines to what extent other property may (or may not) be held and used as "privileges and "liberties" by the beneficiary claiming use of the "legal person". Therefore, in the second instance, an Estate is equivalent to the primary "legal title" and "legal capacity" and "legal standing" of a particular class of persons; and

(iii) Subject to such limits of legal capacity and legal standing, an Estate may then hold one or more beneficial "rights of use" or property as "privileges and "liberties" within one or more temporary beneficial trusts associated with the Estate (i.e. "real estate" and "personal estate"). Therefore, in the third instance, an Estate is equivalent to the aggregate property of immovable, movable, corporeal and incorporeal things associated with these temporary trusts (i.e. "the whole of the estate"); and

(iv) To properly administer the affairs of the Estate, the beneficial rights, also known as property may then be pledged, promised, assigned, granted or delegated as security to form one or more assets. The value of such assets may then be monetised or securitised through various funds, agreements, licenses, accounts and certificates. Therefore, in the fourth instance, an Estate is equivalent to the aggregate monetary value of the net assets of the estate after all debts have been discharged.

1417. All valid Estates exist under certain fundamental assumptions:- *Elements of Valid Estate*

(i) The rules of formation and management of an Estate Roll and lesser Registers must exist as public law within the rules of the ecclesiastical body, sovereign body or body politic that created it; and

(ii) The Rights associated with an Estate are always "Rights of Use", also known as "Property" and not the primary Rights of ownership. Thus, Estates always concern Property as "Rights of Use"; and

(iii) As the Rights associated with an Estate are always "Right of Use" of some Right, a separate Trust must first exist before the Estate is created; and furthermore, that the Rights being the source of the "Rights of Use" in question must also have been named and conveyed into the existing Trust by a Trustor; and

(iv) The authorised ecclesiastical body, sovereign body or body politic that created the Estate Roll owns "legal title" to any such Rights conveyed into such an Estate; and

(v) All Rights in Estate (within the Estate) are Beneficial Title or Equitable Title and not legal title; and

(vi) Beneficial Title means one or more "privileges" or "liberties" that, subject to the rules of the Estate, may be withdrawn or forfeited or alienable; and

(vii) Equitable Title means a "privilege" not in possession of the Beneficiary, but claimable and recoverable through a qualified forum of law with equity powers - being rights of a surrogate Chancery Court. Thus, certain permits, titles, letters, certificates and patents issued to a Beneficiary as "Equitable Title" does not necessarily mean the Beneficiary holds one or more "privileges" other than to sue in a valid court of equity to claim or recover one or more of these such "rights"; and

(viii) The rules for the administration of Property (Rights of Use) within the Estate is through a Covenant of Testamentary Disposition, otherwise known as a Will by a Testator, or in its absence (Intestate), some other established and authorised rules; and

(ix) For every valid Estate, a Fiduciary must be named and duly appointed to govern the affairs of the Estate, either as an Executor, or appointed Administrator in the absence of clear instruction or dispute of authority; and

(x) For every valid Estate that engages in trade or commerce, at least one duly appointed Agent must exist and be duly appointed, registered and acknowledged to manage the day to day business of the Estate under the authority of the Executor or appointed Administrator as the Principal.

1418. As a valid Estate is created via a valid entry and formation of a record into some form of Estate Roll, the general authority, nature and function of Rolls apply:- *Authority and Nature of Rolls and Estates*

(i) The authority to form a Roll is defined by the limits of authority of the constituting Instrument of the relevant Trust or Estate or Fund; and

(ii) The Rights, Powers and Property prescribed to an Estate created and defined within a Roll cannot exceed the Rights, Powers and Property of the Trust or Estate or Fund itself; and

(iii) All Rolls are completely and exclusively Ecclesiastical Property and can never belong to a Trust, or Estate or Fund that formed or inherited it. Instead, all Rolls are the property of One Heaven. Therefore, all Estates are the property of One Heaven; and

(iv) All Rolls are hierarchical in their inheritance of authority and validity from One Heaven, beginning with the highest being the Great Roll of Divine Persons. Therefore, the highest Estates are Divine Estates and the lowest are Inferior Estates. A Roll that cannot demonstrate the provenance of its authority, has none and is null and void from the beginning; and

(v) As all Rolls are completely and exclusively Ecclesiastical, absolutely no clerical or administrative act may take place in association with a Roll unless by a duly authorised Trustee under active and valid sacred Oath and Vow in a manner consistent and in accord with these Maxims; and

(vi) The entry of a record into a Roll is completely invalid unless the memorial or covenant of the act giving authority is done without duress, is done freely and with full knowledge and is consistent and in accord with these Maxims and the most sacred Covenant *Pactum De Singularis Caelum*.

1419. Valid Estates as valid records on a Roll may be further defined in hierarchy of authority, form and function as *Divine, True, Superior, Juridic* or *Inferior*:   *5 Levels of Estates*

(i) A **Divine Estate** is a valid purely spiritual Estate representing the collection of rights and obligations of a Divine Person recorded as a valid entry within a Divine Roll constituted in accord with the most sacred Covenant known as *Pactum De Singularis Caelum*. No Roll or Person is Higher; and

(ii) A **True Estate** is a valid Estate representing the collection of rights and obligations of a True Person (Office of Man or Office of Woman) recorded as a valid entry within a physical and temporal Roll constituted in accord with the Society of One Heaven in the recognition of the most sacred Great Roll of Divine Persons and the Great Register and Public Record of One Heaven; and

(iii) A **Superior Estate** is a valid Estate representing the collection of rights and obligations of a Superior Person recorded as a valid entry within a physical and temporal Roll constituted in accord with a valid Ucadian Society; and

(iv) A **Juridic Estate** is a valid Estate representing the collection of rights and obligations of a Juridic Person recorded as a valid entry within a physical and temporal Roll constituted in accord with a valid Ucadian Society; and

(v) An ***Inferior Estate*** is any Estate representing the collection of rights and obligations of a Person as an entry within a physical and temporal Roll formed under Law not in perfect accord with these Maxims. All Western, Eastern and Roman Estates are Inferior Estates.

Article 373 – Ucadia Estate

1420. A ***Ucadia Estate*** is a proper and valid Estate formed by a Ucadia Person, Entity, Body or Corporation in accord with the present Maxims.

Ucadia Estate

1421. In respect of Ucadia Estates:

Ucadia Estates

(i) All Divine Rights as defined by the most sacred Covenant *Pactum De Singularis Caelum* are hereby acknowledged as having been placed in Divine Trusts with Divine Right of Use conveyed to the associated True Trusts from the beginning of existence of the planet, before the existence of the Homo Sapien species and any cellular life; and

(ii) Such Divine Rights and Divine Trusts in association with Natural Rights and True Trusts have continued through the formation of sacred and unbroken Covenants of Positive Rights and Superior Trusts including, but not limited to the most ancient sacred covenants of De Dea Magisterium of the Serpens (Creators), of Yapa of the Pacific Saltwater People, of Mandi of the African Plains People, of Tia of the Asiatic Mountain People, of Waiata of the Pacific Sea People, of Adamus of Prometheus and the Cuilliaéan, of Nana of the Mother Goddess of Heaven and Earth, of Alma of South Arabia, East Africa and India, of Elohim of Abraham and Patriarchs of Ebla, of Kabalaah of Akhenaten (Moses) and the Yahudi, of Revelations of the thirty-three Great Prophets of Yeb, of Tara of Jeremiah and the Celts, of Five Worlds of North-Central America, of Missal of Baal Mithra, of Acadia of Xerxes, of Eliada of Alexander, of Tabiti of Great Asiatic Plains People, of Tiandi (Heaven and Earth) of Qin Shi Huang, of Nazara (Truth) of Yahusiah (Jesus Christ), of Nirvana (Freedom & Awakening) of Gautama (Buddha), of Zhongdao (The Middle Way) of Kong Qiu (Confucius), of Septuaginta of Iudaism (Josephus), of Eucadia of Heracles, of Kikilil Yuum Witzil (Great Cycle of Celestial Realm and Earth) of South-

Central America, of Digesta of Marcus Aurelius, of Sanatana Dharma (Eternal Truth) of Brahman (Hinduism), of Bibliographe of Christianity of Constantine, of Dao (the Way), of Kami Yoso Seimei (Spirits of Elements and Life) of the way of Shinto (Japan), of Quran Al Sufian (Recitations of Wisdom of the Way) of The Great Prophet (Islam), of Holy Bible of Catholicism of the Franks, of Eternal Truth of Gurmat (Sikhism), of Lebor Clann Glas of the Holly Diaspora; and by the full and complete conveyance and transfer of all such Rights, Title and Powers of the above mentioned ancient sacred Covenants into the most sacred Covenant known as *Pactum De Singularis Caelum* by the Divine Creator of all Existence and by all Heaven; and

(iii) The management of all valid Trusts and Estates has always been granted solely and exclusively to valid Ucadia Entities and Bodies in accord with the most sacred Covenant *Pactum De Singularis Caelum* and these Maxims for the benefit of all Life and all Beings from the beginning and no other; and

(iv) Any claim by any living being, spirit, entity, aggregate or association not authorized by the most sacred Covenant *Pactum De Singularis Caelum* to possess or hold or own any Estate or Trust is hereby invalid, having no force or effect ecclesiastically, legally or lawfully and null and void from the beginning.

1422. When a man or woman demonstrate sufficient competence and redeems their Member Number from Ucadia and subsequently their Live Borne Record, the Live Borne Record is proof of the Existence of a Superior Estate.

Live Borne Record as proof of Superior Estate

1423. When a man or woman, having redeemed their Member Number from Ucadia and subsequently completes and records their Will as *Voluntatem et Testamentum*, then their Superior Estate is Testate.

Establishing Superior Estate, Will and appointments to Office

Article 374 – Non-Ucadia Estate

1424. A ***Non-Ucadia Estate*** is an Estate formed by a Non-Ucadia Person, Entity, Body or Corporation.

Non-Ucadia Estate

1425. Whilst many of the Statutes, Procedures and Rules regarding Inferior Non-Ucadia Rolls and Inferior Non-Ucadia Estates are contradictory, false, misleading and deliberately deceptive, the fundamental architecture of Estates within the Non-Ucadia Societies acknowledge some of the proper hierarchy of authority, form and function

Architecture of Estates within Roman System

concerning Estates:-

(i) The *Ecclesiastical Estate* is and remains the highest form of Inferior Estate within the Non-Ucadia Societies, with "Spiritual Persons" being the highest form of Person within the same system; and

(ii) The *Real Estates*, as originally in the context of Real still meaning "Royal" until the late 17th Century being defined by Patent Rolls, Charter Rolls and Ancestral Rolls as being granted higher status of persons. By the late 18th Century, Real Estate was depreciated to Rights of Possession in Chose in Chancery, with nobles rising to pseudo-ecclesiastical estates by claiming themselves as Parochial bodies ; and

(iii) *Personal Estates* as Rolls and Estates formed under Statutes of the Commons and lesser Parliaments; and

(iv) The *Fourth Estates* as Rolls of media, publishers, military, mercenaries and privateers granted letters of marque to perform acts of brutality, enforcement, terrorism and otherwise illegal activity; and

(v) *Deceased Estates* introduced by the end of the 19th Century in the form of Residential Rolls of Residents or Remainder Estates of the "legally dead", wherein the modern poor are deprived even of being considered legal persons in certain circumstances and therefore without any legal capacity under English Laws.

1426. Examples of Inferior Non-Ucadia Estates include (but are not limited to): *[Examples of Inferior Non-Ucadia Estates]*

(i) **Ancestral Estate** is an estate that is acquired by descent or by operation of law with no other consideration than that of blood; and

(ii) **Bankruptcy Estate** is an estate being all of the legal and equitable interests of the debtor as of the commencement of the case transferred to the control of the bankruptcy court and its appointed trustee; and

(iii) **Elegit Estate** also an **Estate by Elegit** is an estate held by a judgment creditor entitling the creditor to the rents and profits from the land owned by the debtor until the debt is paid; and

(iv) **Fee Tail Estate** or **Entail Estate** is a form of Estate in Real property that prevents the rights from being sold, devised by will, or alienated by the tenant in possession but passes automatically to an heir pre-determined by deed; and

(v) **Fee Simple Estate** also known as **Fee Simple Absolute** is a form of Estate in full and complete rights of land that cannot be defeated, except by condition of grant (in which case it is defined as Fee Simple Conditional or Freehold); and

(vi) **Entirety Estate** also an **Estate by Entirety** whereby each spouse is seised of the whole of the property whereby a husband and wife are a single unit by five unities being time, title, interest, possession and marriage; and

(vii) **Leasehold Estate** is an Estate being the ownership of a temporary right to hold land or property in which a lessee or a tenant holds rights of real property by some form of title from a lessor or landlord; and

(viii) **Personal Estate** being an estate formed and controlled by one or more Acts of Parliament. Thus, most Legal Persons are associated with Personal Estates; and

(ix) **Real Estate** being at one time an estate of land by patent or grant and later depreciated by the 18th Century to become land in chose in possession in Chancery and therefore merely equity or equitable rights not directly held but must be claimed and acknowledged by some license, permission or title by the courts; and

(x) **Stipendiary Estate**, also known as a **Pension Estate**, is an estate granted in return for services rendered to the government; and

(xi) **Life Estate** also **Estate for Life** and **Estate Pur Autre Vie** is ownership of certain land for the duration of the life of a person. The owner of a life estate is called a "life tenant"; and

(xii) **Mortgage Estate** also **Estate in Gage** is an estate that has been pledged as security for a debt; and

(xiii) **Partnership Estate** also **Estate in Partnership** is a joint estate that is vested in the members of a partnership when real estate is purchased with partnership funds and for partnership purposes; and

(xiv) **Remainder Estate** also **Estate in Remainder** is a deceased Estate whereby all taxes, charges and debts must be first settled before any remaining value is permitted to be disposed or merged.

1427. The rules of Inferior Non-Ucadia Estates most promoted are the

Pseudo-laws and rules of Non-

pseudo-laws and rules of Deceased Estates since the end of the 19th Century in the gradual roll-out of such Estates to citizen of countries considered "legally dead" in respect of their rights:

Ucadia Deceased Estates

(i) The legal capacity and legal status of a Person holding an Inferior Non-Ucadia Estate since the 1930's is effectively one "dead to law" and without effective rights, even if such statutes claim otherwise; and

(ii) Since the 1930's in most Non-Ucadia Societies, Land Records and Land Titles relate to Residential Estates or Deceased Estates of Persons first and then lot and plot and survey records second. Thus the primary "land record" is the Residential (deceased) Person and then the limited "right of occupancy" or use of a land property is then attached to the person record, not the other way around. Thus, Residential Estates are equivalent under the Trading with the Enemy Acts to Slave Rolls; and

(iii) All Birth Certificates in Non-Ucadia Societies have been not only birth certificates since the 1930's but death certificates and a title to interest of the beneficiary of an estate already probated and operating under assumed Executors, Administrators and Agents. The argument is plausibly denied by the deliberate corruption of health statistics by officers of the coroners in failing to properly identify live births from "still births" on the official forms; and

(iv) All Residential Estates also known as Deceased Estates are formed on the presumption that all persons "died" Intestate and as "bastards" under the morally repugnant Bastard Laws of Westminster making any property of the Estate technically within the full authority of the State; and

(v) The primary public temporary trusts associated with a Deceased Estate are Real Estate and Personal Estate. However, the mode of Rights under Real Estate have depreciated so that Rights of Real Estate may only be claimed in Equity and that the Right to Freehold Estates in Real Estate no longer exist. Thus, people holding Real Estate as Deceased Estates no longer possess clear land title in most Non-Ucadia Societies and only hold a dubious privilege of occupancy that can be overturned in favour of mining, easements, fracking and other persons with greater rights to land; and

(vi) Since the 19th Century, Inferior Non-Ucadia Estates such as Deceased Estates have restricted the modes of transfer of Real Estate. Under such grossly Inferior Non-Ucadia Estates, there exists only two modes of acquiring Title to Real Estate, either by descent as an Heir or by Purchase. When a Person acquires Real Estate by descent as proven by a Probated Will, they are considered an Heir and when it is acquired by purchase as proven by a duly recorded Bill of Sale they are a Purchaser; and

(vii) Since the 1950's, homeowners in many Non-Ucadia countries have been deprived of access to a valid Bill of Sale under Mortgage under an Inferior Non-Ucadia Estate to prove any possession of Title to Real Estate.

Article 375 – False, Absurd & Prohibited Estates

1428. A ***False, Absurd & Prohibited Estate*** is any claim of Trust created in Bad Faith, Bad Conscience and Bad Actions in contradiction to the present Maxims and the most sacred Covenant *Pactum De Singularis Caelum*.

False, Absurd & Prohibited Estate

Title XII – Property & Funds

12.1 – Property

Article 376 - Property

1429. ***Property*** is the highest Right a Person has or can have within a Lawful Jurisdiction to Own, Control or Use or Claim any Thing or the Fruits of any Thing. Property

1430. By definition, as all forms of Rights are derived from valid and legitimate Divine Rights, all forms of Property and Things are ultimately derived from the rules of Divine Property as defined by the present Maxims and the most sacred Covenant *Pactum De Singularis Caelum*:- Divine Origin of all Rights and Property

   (i) Any claimed Property Right that cannot demonstrate its inheritance ultimately from Divine Property and Divine Rights in accord with the most sacred Covenant *Pactum De Singularis Caelum*, cannot therefore be a valid claim or Property Right; and

   (ii) Any argument, claim, statute, rule, of law that refutes such facts concerning Property renders such false arguments null and void from the beginning; and

   (iii) Any claimed Property Right that contravenes the most sacred Covenant *Pactum De Singularis Caelum* is therefore void from the beginning.

1431. When anyone references, writes or speaks of "Property Laws", or "Laws of Property", it shall mean these Maxims and no other. Laws of Property

1432. In reference to Property, Rights and Things:- Property, Rights and Things

   (i) Property always pertains to Persons and not Beings; and

   (ii) A Thing in the context of Property is any Right that can be purchased or sold or inherited; and attached by operation of law to a corporeal object, whether fixed or movable; and

   (iii) Any Right that can be purchased or sold or inherited means a Right in Trust without a named Beneficiary and therefore a Good; and

   (iv) When one is recorded in a valid Register as possessing a Right or Claim of Right over Control or Use, then they may be referred to as the "Owner" of that Right; and

   (v) As all Property pertains to Rights in Trust, the resolution of all proper Transfer of ownership must be completed in Trust.

1433. In reference to the concepts of an Absolute Right versus a Claim of Absolute versus Claim of Right

Right:- *over Property*

(i) An Absolute Right is one recorded and acknowledge within a particular Jurisdiction as having no equal or legitimate challenge; and

(ii) A Claim of Right is the recording and acknowledgement of a Claim, also known as a "Charge" against some Property; and

(iii) Any Jurisdiction that places a Claim above a properly recorded and acknowledged Absolute Right is without proper rules of Property Law.

1434. There are eight possible forms of Property Rights or "Ownership" of Control or Use or Claim of any Thing or the Fruits of any Thing, (in order of status and standing) being:- *Forms of Property Rights*

(i) Owner of Right of Control of a Thing; and

(ii) Owner of Right of Use of a Thing; and

(iii) Owner of Right of Control of the Fruits of Use of a Thing; and

(iv) Owner of Right of Use of the Fruits of a Thing; and

(v) Owner of Claim of Right of Control of a Thing; and

(vi) Owner of Claim of Right of Use of a Thing; and

(vii) Owner of Claim of Right of Control of the Fruits of Use of a Thing; and

(viii) Owner of Claim of Right of Use of the Fruits of a Thing.

1435. In the absence of Good Faith, Good Conscience and Good Action, no Trust can exist, therefore no Right can exist and therefore no Property can exist. *Property, Rights and Good Faith*

1436. In reference to Property and Lawful Jurisdiction:- *Property and Lawful Jurisdiction*

(i) Property is always defined within the context of the boundaries and jurisdiction of a particular association, aggregate, society, entity or body of Persons possessing Statutes, Bylaws and Rules defining the limits and operations of Property that reflect the Rule of Law, Justice and Fair Process in accord with the present Maxims and the most sacred Covenant *Pactum De Singularis Caelum*; and

(ii) A particular association, aggregate, society, entity or body Persons possessing Statutes, Bylaws and Rules defining the limits and operations of Property that deliberately obscures, confuses, clouds, misrepresents or denies the proper status and standing of ownership of Property is a body in delinquency and default against Divine law and therefore without the Rule of Law and Right of Property.

Article 377 – Ucadia Property

1437. ***Ucadia Property*** is the highest form of valid and legitimate Property Rights, consistent and in accord with the most sacred Covenant *Pactum De Singularis Caelum*:-

    (i)   *Ius Divinum Proprietatis* exists as the highest Divine Rights of Ownership of Use or Fruits of Use of Property; and

    (ii)   *Ius Ecclesiae Proprietatis* exists as the highest Ecclesiastical Rights of Ownership of Use or Fruits of Use of Property, as inherited from the Divine Rights *Ius Divinum Proprietatis*; and

    (iii)   *Ius Regnum Proprietatis* exists as the highest Sovereign Rights of Ownership of Use or Fruits of Use of Property, as inherited from the Ecclesiastical Rights *Ius Ecclesiae Proprietatis*; and

    (iv)   *Ius Administrationis Proprietatis* exists as the highest Administrative Rights of Ownership of Use or Fruits of Use of Property, as inherited from the Sovereign Rights *Ius Regnum Proprietatis*.

1438. Ucadia Property including (but not limited to) any and all trusts, estates, property, accounts, assets and all deposits and other funds entrusted to it shall be immune in time of peace and in time of war from any measure such as expropriation, requisition, distress, seizure, confiscation, prohibition or restriction or any other similar measures by a Non-Ucadia Entity.

Article 378 – Non-Ucadia Property

1439. ***Non-Ucadia Property*** is an inferior claim of Property formed under Non-Ucadia Laws by a Non-Ucadia Person, Entity, Body or Corporation. Non-Ucadia Property is always inferior under valid law to Ucadia Property.

1440. In general reference to Non-Ucadia Property:-

    (i)   By definition Non-Ucadia Property relates to claims of Non-Ucadia Rights and therefore things that have no proper inheritance to Divine Rights or Divine Law; and

    (ii)   Non-Ucadia Property frequently relates to claims of rights connected to morally repugnant statutes, misrepresentations, deceptions, perfidy, fraud and Bad Faith that render such claims absurd and without validity or effect under any notion of

Civilised Rule of Law; and

(iii) Non-Ucadia Property is always inferior in every way to Ucadia Property Rights and whenever a challenge exists concerning a Property Right within both jurisdictions, Ucadia Property Rights shall always have greater authority and validity and supersede any claimed Non-Ucadia Property claim; and

(iv) As Non-Ucadia Property is prone to corrupt, fraudulent, deceptive and morally repugnant claims, Ucadia reserves the absolute right to record any and all Property into valid and proper Ucadia Registers as the first, primary and highest registers of Property Rights within both Ucadia and Non-Ucadia Jurisdictions; and

(v) Ucadia shall at all times possess the absolute right to issue any and all forms of certificates, instruments and money in Ucadia currency or the public currency of Non-Ucadia jurisdictions against any and all Property Rights duly recorded within valid Ucadia Registers; and

(vi) Where a formal treaty exists for the exchange of instruments and currencies between authorised and mandated Ucadia Entities, Foundations and Bodies and a Non-Ucadia Government, such Ucadia Entities shall not seek to register or monetize the values of Non-Ucadia Property without prior agreement.

1441. Starting with the Law of Property Act 1925 (15 & 16 Geo. 5 c. 20), the laws of Property were deliberately and intentionally corrupted across many Non-Ucadia Jurisdictions via the creation of the "legal and equitable interests" system:- *[Deliberate and Intentional Corruption of Property Laws in Non-Ucadia Jurisdictions]*

(i) The Act introduced the notion of "psuedo-rights" in the form of Interests being "a right to have the advantage accruing from anything; and any right in the nature of property, but less than title"; and

(ii) "*Legal Interest*" defined a registered and enforceable right or interest in a property that is recognized by law and can be legally protected and enforced as a right in a court of law; and

(iii) "*Equitable Interest*" defined a registered and enforceable right or interest enforceable by right in a court of equity, as opposed to a purely legal interest that is enforceable at law. Equitable Interests were defined to arise when there is an arrangement, trust, or specific agreement that creates a duty on the part of one party (the legal owner or trustee) to hold and manage the property for the benefit of another party (the equitable owner or beneficiary); and

(iv) The concept of "Interests" intentionally created (a) ***circular reasoning*** (i.e. an interest means an interest); and (b) ***contradictions*** (i.e. an interest is not strictly a right but in all senses it functions as a right); and (c) ***lawful corruption*** (i.e. a trustee or agent gaining an interest in the very property they are supposed to manage for another; and (d) ***absurdity*** (i.e. conditions and arguments where interests are considered irrevocable; and (e) ***institutional fraud*** (i.e. parties gaining interests against property of another without consent and in bad faith); and (f) ***conditions for future anarchy*** (i.e. interests do not need to operate under good faith, or trust, yet are still treated as property and rights); and

(v) The Act more than any other has led to the complete breakdown in competence, reason and function of Non-Ucadia Forums of Law when it comes to matters of Property, whereby such "Interests" must be brought forward as Rights, yet such forums then permit governments and agencies to circumvent their fiduciary obligations concerning Property Rights and the enforcement of Interests as effectively "Rights in Bad Faith" by numerous agencies and institutions.

Article 379 – False, Absurd & Prohibited Property

1442. ***False, Absurd & Prohibited Property*** is any claim of Property created in Bad Faith, Bad Conscience and Bad Actions in contradiction to the present Maxims and the most sacred Covenant *Pactum De Singularis Caelum*.

False, Absurd & Prohibited Property

1443. Any denial that a valid Interest in Property must by definition be recognised as a Right, therefore invalidates such an Interest:-

Denial that an Interest in Property is a Right invalidates such an Interest

(i) All language in defining the nature of an Interest, ultimately defines a Right. There is no such thing in law as a Pseudo Right or Part Right; and

(ii) For an Interest to be "enforceable" in a valid forum of law, it must logically and sensibly relate to at least one Right; and

(iii) Regardless of any acts or laws to the contrary, no Interest can be obtained in Bad Faith or Bad Conscience or Bad Action; and

(iv) Regardless of any acts or laws to the contrary, holding an Interest in any form of Property makes the holder a Fiduciary and subject to the obligations of acting in Good Faith.

12.2 – Funds

Article 380 - Funds

1444. A ***Fund*** is a sum of equal units representing certain Property Rights of monetary value, recorded in one or more designated accounts of a Body; and set apart for a term of years and one or more specific purposes; and available for the payment of debits, debts, legacies and claims in accord with these Maxims and the most sacred Covenant *Pactum De Singularis Caelum*. Fund

1445. In respect of the character, purpose and nature of a Fund:- Character, Purpose and Nature of Fund

  (i) The Instrument of formation and of guiding the character, purpose and nature of one or more Funds is a Trust Covenant as a Fund Constitution issued and approved by a valid Body; and

  (ii) The underlying Rights and Property used to derive the value of a Fund must be set aside and sealed in its own Trust in accord with the Trust Covenant to protect the integrity of the Fund and prevent any re-transfer or re-conveyance that might threaten the value of the Fund. This means, the only ownership of rights of property that may be conveyed or discharged against the underlying Rights and Property are Claims, also known as "Charges"; and

  (iii) The life or operation of a Fund (the period it conducts business) shall be the 128 year maximum as specified by the most sacred Covenant *Pactum De Singularis Caelum*, unless otherwise required by law to be the Western-Roman custom of a maximum of 70 years; and

  (iv) A Fund may be actual money, or notes, or certificates, or securities or stocks able to be converted or negotiated for monetary value, providing the nature and monetary value of each element is clearly outlined within the accounts of the Fund; and

  (v) The terms of negotiation of the Stock of a Fund for other stock, or actual money, or notes, or certificates, or other securities is determined on a Fund by Fund basis, including whether a particular Fund is able to purchase the Stock of another Fund, to what maximum and other conditions (if any); and

  (vi) A Fund is never the original Assets themselves, but the Derivation of the value of the underlying Property, as recorded in the accounts and ledgers of the Fund, to permit the remission, remittance, settlement and discharge of debits, debts and obligations; and

(vii)   When the term of a Fund expires, it is absolutely forbidden to conduct any more new business. However, it may continue to manage and administer existing business and obligations until all such existing obligations and settlements expire or are balanced or dissolved or liquidated; and

(viii)   The property and assets held in Trust are absolutely forbidden to be released from such a Trust underwriting a Fund until after the term of a Fund expires and after all obligations and settlements are balanced and the fund dissolved or liquidated and the purpose of the Trust is fulfilled and the Trust dissolved; and

(ix)   A Fund ceases to exist when it is properly liquidated or dissolved by an action in accord with the instrument of its creation, or after the expiry of its term. In accord with these Maxims, the administrators of a valid Fund are morally obligated to ensure the timely dissolution of the Fund as soon as practical after such a valid event.

1446.   The Capital Stock of a Fund is divided into equal and indivisible units of account called "Stocks", whereby such units of value shall grant a valid and registered holder ("Stockholder") certain Rights to participate in the management of the Fund and to share in its net profits or earnings.   *Capital Stock of Fund*

Article 381 – Ucadia Fund

1447.   A ***Ucadia Fund*** is a proper and valid Fund formed by a Ucadia Person, Entity, Body or Corporation in accord with the present Maxims.   *Ucadia Fund*

1448.   Ucadia at all times shall possess the absolute and immutable Rights to create Funds derived from Property duly recorded and registered within Ucadia Registers, whether such Property is directly in control of a Ucadia Entity, or still in the control of a Non-Ucadia Government, Entity, Body or Person:-   *Right of Ucadia Funds*

(i)   Ucadia shall at all times have the absolute and unfettered Rights to create sums of equal units of a Ucadia Fund in the denomination and currency values of a Non-Ucadia Jurisdiction and Government, where such a Non-Ucadia Body has no proper treaty with Ucadia and continues to hold Property duly registered within the valid Registers of Ucadia; and

(ii) Ucadia shall at all times have the absolute and unfettered Rights to trade, exchange and use such units of Funds in the denomination and currency values of a Non-Ucadia Jurisdiction as legal tender for the discharge of all debts and obligations, where no formal treaty exists with Ucadia.

1449. For the purpose of any rules or directives, from time to time, concerning the registration of any Trust or Fund associated with a Ucadia Body or Entity as registered in a Non-Ucadia Jurisdiction:-

Registration of Funds or Trusts

(i) Any and all Trusts associated with Funds are deemed to be exempt and excluded from requiring to be registered to the extent that no public offering, or public advertising, media, news or notice is permitted concerning the offering or purchase of any Stock or Securities of such Funds, as it is intended that all such Stock and Securities shall be for private application, referral and invitation only; and

(ii) Any such Stock or Securities of any Fund associated with a Trust shall only be offered to qualified investors in addition to a limited number of persons.

Article 382 – Non-Ucadia Fund

1450. A ***Non-Ucadia Fund*** is a Fund (or claim of Fund) formed under Non-Ucadia Laws by a Non-Ucadia Person, Entity, Body or Corporation. A Non-Ucadia Fund is always inferior under valid law to a Ucadia Fund.

Non-Ucadia Fund

Article 383 – False, Absurd & Prohibited Funds

1451. A ***False, Absurd & Prohibited Fund*** is any claim or Fund created in Bad Faith, Bad Conscience and Bad Actions in contradiction to the present Maxims and the most sacred Covenant *Pactum De Singularis Caelum*.

False, Absurd & Prohibited Funds

Title XIII – Associations & Relations

13.1 – Association

Article 384 - Association

1452. An ***Association*** is an assembly of persons for some common lawful purpose or objective, who freely choose to be bound together according to some governing instrument and rules.

Association

1453. In reference to the general elements of an Association:-

    (i) ***Purpose***: Associations may have a wide range of lawful purposes, from professional development and advocacy to social and recreational activities; and

    (ii) ***Formation***: Associations are typically formed by individuals or entities that share a common interest, goal, or purpose; and

    (iii) ***Legal Personality***: Depending on the jurisdiction, associations may have legal personality, meaning they can enter into contracts, own property, sue, and be sued in their own name; and

    (iv) ***Management***: Associations usually have a leadership structure, such as a board of directors or executive committee, responsible for making decisions and overseeing the Organisation's activities; and

    (v) ***Membership***: Associations have members who typically have rights, responsibilities, and sometimes voting privileges within the Organisation; and

    (vi) ***Liability***: The liability of association members may be limited to their investment or contribution to the association in some cases, especially in non-profit associations; and

    (vii) ***Nonprofit vs. For-Profit***: Associations can be non-profit or for-profit entities. Non-profit associations are organized for charitable, educational, or other non-commercial purposes and may enjoy tax benefits; and

    (viii) ***Regulation***: The formation and operation of associations are often subject to legal regulations and requirements that vary by jurisdiction.

General Elements of an Association

1454. A ***Governing Instrument*** refers to the legal document or set of documents that establish the structure, rules, and governance framework for an Association. It serves as the foundational document that outlines how the association is structured, how it operates, and how it makes decisions. The specific content and format of a Governing Instrument may vary by jurisdiction and the nature of the association. Examples include (but are not limited to):-

Governing Instrument of Association

Lex Positivum: Maxims of Positive Law

    (i)   ***Articles of Incorporation***: In many countries, associations are required to file articles of incorporation (also known as a certificate of incorporation or a charter) with the relevant government authority. These articles formally create the association as a legal entity and typically include information such as the association's name, purpose, registered office address, and the names of its initial directors or officers; and

    (ii)   ***Charter or Agreement***: Depending on the type of association and its specific legal structure, the governing instrument might be referred to as a charter or agreement. These documents outline the association's objectives, membership criteria, and governance provisions; and

    (iii)   ***Trust Deed***: In some cases, especially for charitable Organisations or trusts, a trust deed may serve as the governing instrument. A trust deed outlines the purpose of the Organisation, the roles and responsibilities of trustees, and how the Organisation's assets are to be managed; and

    (iv)   ***Bylaws***: Bylaws are a crucial part of the governing instrument. They provide detailed rules and procedures for how the association will operate. Bylaws typically cover matters such as membership requirements, board composition and responsibilities, meeting procedures, voting processes, and other internal governance matters. Bylaws are often adopted by the association's initial board of directors or members and can be amended as needed through a formal process outlined in the bylaws themselves; and

    (v)   ***Constitution***: Some associations use the term "constitution" instead of "bylaws" to refer to their governing instrument. While the terminology may vary, the content and purpose are generally similar.

1455. Legal structures for Associations include (but are not limited to):-   *Types of Association*

    (i)   ***Foundation***: Foundations are non-profit organisations established to provide funding and support for charitable, educational, or philanthropic purposes; and

    (ii)   ***Partnership***: A partnership is a business association where two or more individuals or entities join together to operate a business for profit. Partnerships can be general partnerships, limited partnerships, or limited liability partnerships, each with different liability and management structures; and

    (iii)   ***Corporation***: A corporation is a separate legal entity that is owned by shareholders. It provides limited liability protection to its owners; and

(iv) **Limited Liability Company**: A Limited Liability Company combines the limited liability protection of a corporation with the flexibility of a partnership; and

(v) **Non-profit Organisation**: Nonprofits are associations organized for purposes other than profit. They can take various legal forms, including nonprofit corporations, charitable trusts, and unincorporated associations; and

(vi) **Professional Association**: These associations are typically formed by individuals in a specific profession, such as lawyers, doctors, or engineers, to promote their common interests and professional standards; and

(vii) **Trade Association**: Trade associations are formed by businesses or Organisations within a particular industry or trade. They work to advance the interests of their members and the industry as a whole; and

(viii) **Political Association**: Political associations are formed as political parties or to raise and spend money to support or oppose political candidates, parties or issues; and

(ix) **Cooperative (Co-op)**: Cooperatives are associations where members collectively own and operate a business or provide services for mutual benefit. Examples include agricultural cooperatives and consumer cooperatives; and

(x) **Labor Union**: Labor unions are associations formed by workers to negotiate and advocate for better working conditions, wages and benefits on behalf of their members.

Article 385 - Ucadia Association

1456. A *Ucadia Association* is a valid Association duly registered under and subject to Ucadia Laws and Jurisdiction.
Ucadia Association

1457. To pursue and fulfil their proper Objects, Ucadia Associations by innate Right shall acquire, retain, administer and alienate Property and Temporal Goods within its Jurisdiction.
Property and Temporal Goods of the Body Corporate

1458. Valid registered Ucadia Associations can acquire Temporal Goods by every just means of natural or positive law permitted to other bodies politic and corporate.
Acquisition of Temporal Goods

1459. Valid registered Ucadia Associations possess the innate Right to require from its Officers, Agents, Employees, Contractors, Members, Suppliers
Right of support etc.

and Customers, those things, including Temporal Goods, that are necessary for the Objects proper to it; and no temporal body possesses any right or authority or power to impede such Right.

1460. Valid registered Ucadia Associations shall assert their rights that any and all legitimate and valid Charitable and Benevolent Funds formed in accord with the Primary Objects of the Association shall be exempt from any duties, taxation, penalties or alienation by Non-Ucadia Jurisdictions; and that such exemption shall be duly recorded and certified in writing so as to avoid any controversy or injury. *Exemption of Charitable and Benevolent Trusts and Funds*

Article 386 - Non-Ucadia Association

1461. A ***Non-Ucadia Association*** is an Association duly registered under and subject to Non-Ucadia Laws and Jurisdiction. *Non-Ucadia Association*

1462. No Non-Ucadia Association of any kind shall have jurisdiction or authority over a valid and registered Ucadia Association. However, where a formal treaty exists between Ucadia and Non-Ucadia Governments, the treaty may permit matters to be heard in Non-Ucadia forums of law. *Non Jurisdiction of Non-Ucadia Association*

Article 387 - False, Absurd & Prohibited Associations

1463. A False, Absurd & Prohibited Association is an Association formed for unlawful or illegal purposes, contrary to the laws of Ucadia and Civilised Rules of Law. *False, Absurd & Prohibited Associations*

13.2 – Relations

Article 388 - Relation

1464. A ***Relation*** refers to a legally recognised interaction and connection between individuals, entities, or parties, especially concerning their rights, obligations and legal responsibilities toward each other. *Relation*

1465. The key elements associated with any type of *Relation* concerning any legal recognition or any enforceable rights includes (but are not limited to):- *Key Elements of Relations*

   (i) **Relation Classification**: That the Relation in question is able to be properly classified under law (such as familial, marital, contractual, employment, tort (wrong), consumer etc.); and

   (ii) ***Proof of Relation Classification***: That the minimum criteria needed to establish a specific type of Relation is capable of being Proven, or that sufficient evidence exists to file a claim, capable of being proven through an Action within a Forum of Law; and

    (iii) ***Proof of Obligation***: That sufficient evidence exists that one or more rights, obligations or legal responsibilities existed or are still in effect concerning the Relation; and

    (iv) ***Proof of Contact within Jurisdiction***: That sufficient and purposeful contacts relating to any defendant exist or one or more "long-arm" rights exist within the jurisdiction where any claim or action is filed; and

    (v) ***Proof of Claim for Injury or Remedy***: That any necessary and associated claims or proof of injury and proposed remedy exist.

1466. *Relations* encompass a variety of interactions and connections between individuals, entities, or parties, each with its own set of legal implications. Examples include (but are not limited to):-   *Types of Relations*

    (i) ***Familial Relations***: Civil law governs legal relations within families. Examples include parent-child relationships, spousal relations and legal guardianship; and

    (ii) ***Marital Relations***: Civil law includes aspects of marital relations, such as marriage contracts, divorce proceedings and the division of marital assets; and

    (iii) ***Employment Relations***: Employment law regulates the relations between employers and employees. Employment contracts and labour laws establish the rights and responsibilities of both parties; and

    (iv) ***International Relations***: International law deals with the relations between countries, including treaties, diplomatic relations, trade agreements and disputes resolution mechanisms; and

    (v) ***Government-Citizen Relations***: Administrative law defines the legal relations between government entities and citizens, covering issues like regulatory compliance, taxation and government actions; and

    (vi) ***Agency Relations***: Fiduciary law governs the relationship between principals (those who authorize agents to act on their behalf) and agents (those who act on behalf of principals); and

    (vii) ***Trustee-Beneficiary Relations***: Fiduciary law governs the relations between trustees, who manage assets for the benefit of beneficiaries, setting out the trustee's fiduciary duties; and

(viii) **Business Relations**: Company Law encompasses various aspects of business interactions, including relations between partners in a partnership, shareholders in a corporation and participants in joint ventures; and

(ix) **Partnership Relations**: Company Law governs Partnerships, whether general partnerships or limited partnerships, legal relations between partners, defining their roles, liabilities and profit-sharing arrangements; and

(x) **Intellectual Property Relations**: Trade & Intellectual Property Law establishes relations concerning copyrights, trademarks, patents and trade secrets; and

(xi) **Contractual Relations**: These arise when parties enter into a legally binding agreement, known as a contract, which establishes rights and obligations. For example, a lease agreement between a landlord and a tenant creates a contractual relation; and

(xii) **Tort Relations**: Civil Law and Criminal law deals with wrongs and injuries caused by one party to another; and

(xiii) **Debtor-Creditor Relations**: Monetary Law and Civil Law governs Debtor-Creditor Relations. Creditors and debtors have legal relations based on lending agreements, such as loans, credit card contracts or mortgages. Financial laws also govern these relations; and

(xiv) **Real Property Relations**: Civil law governs relations related to real estate, including ownership, leasing, easements and boundary disputes; and

(xv) **Consumer Relations**: Consumer protection laws regulate relations between consumers and businesses, ensuring fairness, transparency and safety in transactions.

Article 389 - Ucadia Relations

1467. ***Ucadia Relations*** are validly classified, recognised and recorded relations between two or more Persons, Bodies, Entities or Associations within Ucadia Jurisdiction. — Ucadia Relations

1468. Where a Legal Relation is duly recorded within a Ucadia Register or Roll, this Relation shall be proof of a Primary Record and Primary Jurisdiction under Ucadia:- — Primary Record of Relation

(i) Ucadia Members and Entities shall at all times have the authority to duly record any and all Relations within Ucadia records, registers and rolls, with or without consent of the other parties; and

(ii) Ucadia shall have the absolute authority to choose to assert primary jurisdiction over any and every Legal Relation recorded and registered within its registers and rolls, with or without the consent of all the parties; or may choose to defer and permit such a Legal Relation to be enforced within a Non-Ucadia Jurisdiction; and

(iii) Where a valid Ucadia entity has a formal treaty with a Non-Ucadia Jurisdiction concerning instruments, records and currencies, a condition of any such treaty shall be that no Legal Relation shall be recorded by either party without notice; and with the right of either the Ucadia entity or Non-Ucadia country or government to assert primary jurisdiction.

Article 390 - Non-Ucadia Relation

1469. A *Non-Ucadia Relation* is one classified, recognised or recorded relation between two or more Persons, Bodies, Entities or Associations within a Non-Ucadia Jurisdiction.

_{Non-Ucadia Relation}

1470. Any record of a Relation entered into a register or roll held by a Non-Ucadia Country, Government, Entity or Agency that relates to a Trust, Person, Estate or Property is first subject to the jurisdiction and Rights of Ucadia in accord with the most sacred Covenant *Pactum De Singularis Caelum*:-

_{Invalid Recorded Relations}

(i) The age of any record of Relation including (but not limited to) land titles, birth certificates and all other instruments is irrelevant to the fact that any such entry made by deception, misrepresentation, omission, error, bad faith, perfidy or fraud renders such a record null and void, without any force or effect whatsoever; and

(ii) Regardless of the date of entry, any record of Relation in a valid Ucadia register or roll shall always and at all times be primary and higher than any record in a Non-Ucadia register or roll.

Article 391 - False, Absurd & Prohibited Relation

1471. A False, Absurd & Prohibited Relation is any Relation listed as unlawful and illegal under Ucadia Laws and the present Maxims.

_{False, Absurd & Prohibited Relation}

Title XIV – Consensus

14.1 – Consensus

Article 392 - Consent

1472. **Consent** is the unilateral, voluntary and informed granting of permission to another Person, to do or refrain from doing some certain act. A concurrence of *Consent* between two or more Persons is called *Consensus*.
Consent

1473. While the concept of *Implied Acceptance* is a legitimate concept associated with the negotiation of written Agreements, the concept of *Implied Consent* is an absurdity, moral repugnant and false. There exists only one proper form of *Consent* within Jurisdictions operating under Civilised Rule of Law.
One form of Consent

1474. The key elements that constitute valid Consent include (but are not limited to) *Capacity, Voluntary, Specificity, Adequacy, Reasonality, Clarity, Evidentiary* and *Revocability*:-
Key elements of valid Consent

    (i) **Capacity**: Consent can only be granted by a Person that has the legal capacity to do so at the time. This typically means they must be of sound mind and, in some cases, meet a minimum age requirement. For example, minors may have limited capacity to provide consent in certain situations; and

    (ii) **Voluntary**: Consent must be granted freely and without coercion, duress, or undue influence. This means that the Person providing consent has the capacity to make a rational decision and has not been pressured or manipulated into agreeing; and

    (iii) **Specificity**: Consent is required to be specific to the particular action or transaction in question at the time. Blanket Consent is an absurdity in law and not legally enforceable as it fails the adequacy test of being able Informed Consent; and

    (iv) **Adequacy**: Consent is required to be informed (Informed Consent) in most cases. This means that the individual providing consent must have a clear understanding of the nature, risks, benefits, and implications of the action they are agreeing to. They should be provided with relevant information to make an educated decision; and

    (v) **Reasonality**: Consent is an act of reason, accompanied with cognitive deliberation as in the mind weighing the balance of pros or cons. It means not just possession but exercise of sufficient mental capacity to make an intelligent choice to grant permission to another to do (or refrain from doing) something; and

(vi) **Clarity**: Consent must be clear. If expressed it must be a yes or affirmative statement of permission. If written it must be a clear and unmistakable approval of permission; and

(vii) **Evidentiary**: Consent in relation to Agreements requires some evidential proof of approval and all the elements necessary for valid Consent; and

(viii) **Revocability**: Consent in relation to Agreements requires revocability up until the Agreement is executed; and then such a right to be the Right of Recission should it be discovered later that one or more of the other parties failed to meet the necessary standards of a valid Agreement.

1475. Within the Legal Model of any Civilised Rule of Law, concepts such as Consent always relate to Persons and never to Living beings such as Men or Women. Thus Consent when expressed or written may be properly defined as the Will or "mind" of a Person. — *Consent as the Expression of the Will of a Person*

Article 393 - Consensus

1476. *Consensus* is a concurrence, accord and harmony of Wills of two or more Persons, also known as a *Meeting of the Minds*. — *Consensus*

1477. The concept of "concurrence" refers to the simultaneous occurrence of two or more elements, factors or circumstances, including signifying that multiple legal conditions are met or that multiple events or actions are happening at the same time. — *Concurrence and Consensus*

1478. *Consensus* is both fundamental and necessary for the validity of any Agreement concerning the Transfer of any Rights, Property, Authority or Powers under Civilised Rules of Law. In the absence of Consensus, no such claim of Transfer of any Rights, Property, Authority or Powers is valid, legitimate or has any force or effect in law. — *Necessity of Consensus in relation to Rights etc.*

1479. Given the concept of *Implied Consent* is an absurdity, moral repugnance and falsity, the concept of Unilateral Consensus is likewise an absurdity, moral repugnance and falsity having no validity under Civilised Rule of Law. — *Absurdity of Unilateral Consensus*

1480. The Consent of two or more parties to the same acts regarding the same Property and Rights in a valid Consensus makes the law. This may be expressed by the Latin maxim: *Consensus facit legem* meaning "consent makes the law". — *Valid Consensus*

1481. When any matter is brought before a court having established proper — *Resolution by a* jurisdiction and when consent has been given by both parties for the matter to be heard by a judge and/or jury, a proper Consensus then exists between all parties to seek resolution by a judgment.

judgement

Article 394 – Bilateral Consensus

1482. ***Bilateral Consensus*** is a term describing Consensus between two Persons concerning one or more Acts - hence bilateral.

What is Bilateral Consensus

1483. The most common forms of Bilateral Consensus Instruments are agreements, alliances, conveyances, compacts, bargains, deeds, arrangements and correspondence.

Common form of Bilateral Consensus Instruments

Article 395 – Trilateral Consensus

1484. ***Trilateral Consensus*** is a term describing Consensus between three Persons concerning one or more Acts – hence trilateral.

What is Trilateral Consensus

1485. An Ecclesiastical Deed Poll is an example of a Trilateral Consensus Instrument between the Divine Creator, the Person and a Tribunal of Witnesses.

Ecclesiastical Deed Poll and Trilateral Consensus

1486. The most common forms of Trilateral Consensus Instruments are charters, covenants, unions, treaties, wills and testaments and concordats.

Common examples of Trilateral Consensus Instruments

14.2 – False, Absurd & Prohibited Consensus

Article 396 - False, Absurd & Prohibited Consensus

1487. False, Absurd & Prohibited Consensus are examples of claimed Consensus that are in fact false, morally repugnant and having no force or effect under Civilised Rule of Law.

False, Absurd & Prohibited Consensus

1488. Examples of False, Absurd & Prohibited Consensus include (but are not limited to):-

Examples of False, Absurd & Prohibited Consensus

   (i) ***Implied Consent***: refers to the deliberately false and absurd notion that proper and valid Consent can be granted by implication; and

   (ii) ***Perfidy & Injury***: Perfidy refers to deceitful or treacherous behaviour, often involving betrayal of trust, while injury denotes harm, damage or physical/mental pain inflicted upon someone or something; and

   (iii) **Misstatement & Misrepresentation**: Misstatement refers to an incorrect or false statement made unintentionally or due to error, whereas misrepresentation involves intentionally presenting false or misleading information to deceive or manipulate others; and

(iv) **Omission & Concealment**: Omission is the act of leaving out or neglecting to include something, often unintentionally, while concealment involves purposefully hiding or keeping information, facts or objects from others; and

(v) **Espionage & Sabotage**: Espionage is the secretive gathering of confidential information or intelligence by individuals or organizations for strategic or illicit purposes, often related to national security, while sabotage involves deliberate actions aimed at damaging or undermining the functioning, integrity, or effectiveness of systems, processes or organizations; and

(vi) **Deception & Fraud**: Deception involves the act of misleading or tricking someone through deceit or falsehoods, while fraud encompasses intentional deception for financial gain or to cause harm, often involving misrepresentation or manipulation of information; and

(vii) **Bribery & Extortion**: Bribery is the act of offering or receiving something of value to influence someone's behavior or decisions, often in an unlawful or unethical manner, while extortion involves obtaining something through threats, coercion, or intimidation, often accompanied by fear of harm or consequences; and

(viii) **Coercion & Duress**: Coercion is the use of force, pressure, or threats to compel someone to do something against their will or better judgment, while duress is a legal concept that refers to threats or unlawful pressure that can void a contract or negate a person's consent due to fear or intimidation.

Article 397 – Implied Consent

1489. *Implied Consent* is an absurd, morally repugnant and false legal concept that refers to a situation in which a person's actions or behaviour suggest that they have given their consent to something, even if they have not explicitly stated their consent in writing or verbally. — Implied Consent

1490. The wickedly evil, corrupt and false notion that *Silence implies Consent* first entered into English culture at the end of the 17th Century, but claimed from much earlier:- — Silence as Consent

(i) The phrase "Silence gives consent" is a statement within the early 17th century Play of William Shakespeare titled "A Man for All Seasons" about the life, trial and execution of Sir Thomas More. The dialogue being: "**Sir Thomas More**: Not so. Not so, Master Secretary. The maxim is "Qui tacet consentire": the maxim of the law is "Silence gives consent". If therefore you wish to construe what my silence betokened, you must construe that I consented, not that I denied"; and

(ii) The key scene within the play directly contradicts the alleged quote by Sir Thomas More as accounted by William Roper in books supposedly available since 1535 being: "**Sir Thomas More**: nor no other Law in the World can punish any Man for his Silence, feeing they can do no more than punish Words or Deeds; 'tis God only that is the Judge of the Secrets of our Hearts. **Attorney**: Sir Thomas, tho we have not one Word or Deed of yours to object against you, yet we have your Silence, which is an evident sign of the Malice of your Heart: because no dutiful Subject, being lawfully ask'd this Question, will refuse to answer"; and

(iii) It is unclear why Shakespeare would so blatantly reverse the meaning and words of Sir Thomas More on such an important point as Divine Law and the repugnancy of "Silence gives consent" nor make the egregious falsehood that such a statement is an ancient maxim; and

(iv) There is no credible evidence whatsoever that "Silence is Consent" was ever a maxim under Roman Law; and overwhelming evidence that such a statement could not possibly have been a doctrine from 8th Century to at least the 13th Century under true Anglo-Saxon and Roman Catholic Law; and clear evidence such an absurd, ignorant and wicked doctrine was not part of Commonwealth (Common) Law under the Commonwealths of Great Britain (1642-1706), Ireland (1642-1691) and New England (America) (1642-1783); and

(v) Despite its presence in Shakespeare, there appears little evidence of judges or juries accepting the notion of "Silence as Consent" to be credible over the past several hundred years; and

(vi) In the 1970s' among Law Academics in the United Kingdom and Australia did launch a concerted effort to argue the efficacy of the notion as valid. However, little direct progress was made. In contrast, some progress was achieved in getting the notion of "implied consent" adopted for certain minor crimes such as drunk and drug driving convictions; and

(vii) The most active promotion of "Silence is Consent" has been via the "Truth Movement" since at least 2005, in combination with other falsities and absurdities of law such as "accepted for value".

Title XV – Agreement

15.1 – Agreement

Article 398 - Agreement

1491. An ***Agreement*** in its widest sense, means a bilateral consensus of common intent between two or more persons with a view to a thing done or that ought to be done, having the effect of altering their rights or powers and obligations. Agreement

1492. *Agreements* always pertain to the permanent or temporary Transfer of one or more Rights of Title and/or Rights of Use of Property:- Rights and Agreements

   (i) In Agreements, a Right may be named according to their function, condition or mode of transfer including (but not limited to): Legal Interest, Equitable Interest, Interest, Authority, Power, License, Benefit, Liberty, Privilege, Possession or Use; and

   (ii) Regardless of the naming and language used, an Agreement is not valid unless all related Rights are clearly defined; and

   (iii) No Right may be Transferred except by Agreement; and

   (iv) No Right may be permanently transferred except by Agreement in writing; and

   (v) The type of Right and Property may require certain formalities to comply with the laws of the relevant jurisdiction; and

   (vi) Failure to comply with the formalities of an Agreement in the relevant jurisdiction may result in the Agreement being null and void as to the Transfer of one or more Rights.

1493. Based upon the fact that *Agreements* always pertain to the permanent or temporary Transfer of one or more Rights of Title and/or Rights of Use of Property, all Agreements may be classified into four main types being *Deed, Deed Poll, Compact* and *Contract*:- Types of Agreements

   (i) **Deed**: A Deed is an Agreement made between two or more Persons of Equal or Unequal Status for the permanent or temporary bilateral Transfer of at least one or more Rights of Title and/or Rights of Use between each of the Parties; and

   (ii) **Deed Poll**: A Deed Poll is an Agreement made by only one Person for the permanent or temporary unilateral Transfer of at least one or more Rights of Title and/or Rights of Use; and

   (iii) **Compact**: A Compact is an Agreement made between two or more Persons of Equal Status for the temporary bilateral Transfer of at least one or more Rights of Title and/or Rights of Use between each of the Parties; and

(iv) **Contract**: A Contract is an Agreement made between two or more Persons of Equal or Unequal Status for the temporary Transfer of at least one or more Rights of Title and/or Rights of Use.

1494. **Status** in the context of Agreements refers to the legal condition, position, or standing of an individual, entity, or subject matter under the law. It is a recognition that in reality Parties to an Agreement may not be exactly the same or equal in terms of their financial or legal capacities, or specific knowledge of the areas covered by an Agreement. The term Status can encompass a wide range of legal attributes, rights, and obligations, and its specific meaning can vary depending on the area of law and the jurisdiction, including (but not limited to):-

Status and Agreements

(i) **Financial Status**: Financial status refers to an individual's or entity's financial condition, position, or standing in relation to their financial assets, liabilities, income and financial affairs; and

(ii) **Property Status**: Property status pertains to the legal ownership, title, and condition of real and personal property, including whether property is subject to liens, encumbrances or easements; and

(iii) **Legal Status**: Legal status pertains to an entity's or individual's position under the law. It can encompass a variety of aspects, such as whether someone is a legal adult or minor, a legal immigrant or non-citizen or a legal entity; and

(iv) **Civil Status**: Civil status typically refers to an individual's legal condition in terms of marital status, citizenship, residency and other personal attributes. For example, one's civil status could include being single, married, divorced, a citizen of a particular country or a resident of a specific jurisdiction; and

(v) **Corporate Status**: Corporate status relates to the legal existence and standing of a business entity, including whether it is in good standing with regulatory authorities, has the necessary licenses and has complied with reporting requirements; and

(vi) **Tax Status**: Tax status refers to an entity's classification for tax purposes, which can affect its tax liability, deductions, and obligations. Examples include tax-exempt status for non-profit organizations and the tax status of different business entities like sole proprietorships, partnerships and corporations.

1495. ***Obligations of Status*** is a fundamental recognition of fairness, negotiations and operation of any Agreement between Parties of unequal Status, whereby a more powerful Party to an Agreement is necessarily held to a higher set of standards and obligations in jurisdictions operating under Civilised Rules of Law:-

    (i) A more powerful Party, especially if they are the Primary Party responsible for drafting the Agreement, must be able to demonstrate and prove the other Party (or Parties) have a full and clear comprehension of the terms, obligations, consequences, penalties and remedies of the Agreement; and

    (ii) A more powerful Party must be seen to be considerate, reasonable and fair to the less powerful Party and avoid the use of legal loopholes, tricks or acts that may be seen as unconscionable, impossible, misleading, deceptive or cruel; and

    (iii) A more powerful Party must be seen to never take advantage of their position and the weaker position of the other Party to gain unfair advantage, especially in the determining of prices, or fees and other conditions; and

    (iv) Contrary to jurisdictions that operate under Uncivilised and Absurd Rules of Law, within proper Civilised Systems of Law and Forums of Law, the Obligations of Status means that the more powerful Party must necessarily be in a weaker position should a dispute or litigation arise, simply because within any authentic Forum of Law genuine Justice is obligated to place the more powerful Party to a higher standard of proof and performance; and

    (v) Any Forum of Law, or Government Agency or Body that grants greater benefits or powers to a more powerful Party in a Dispute of Agreement, disqualifies any subsequent action from being a genuine action in law. Rather, such an action constitutes a deliberate abuse of power or an acknowledgment that such a jurisdiction does not function according to Civilised Rules or the proper Rule of Law.

Obligations of Status

1496. From the foundation of modern Western Civilisation in the 8th Century CE by the Holly (Holy) Bloodlines directed by the Holly Carolingians and Holly Irish Academics, there have been fundamental Maxims guiding the formation, operation and adjudication of Agreements. No Civilised Society has ever corrupted or rejected these fundamental Maxims concerning Agreements

Founding Maxims of Agreements

including (but not limited to):-

- (i) *In bona fide* meaning "(all agreements are made) in good faith"; and
- (ii) *A verbis legis non est recedendum* meaning "(in agreements) from the language of the law there must be no departure"; and
- (iii) *Dictum meum pactum* meaning "my spoken word [is] my covenant"; and
- (iv) *Pacta sunt servanda* meaning "agreements are to be kept"; and
- (v) *Conventio non vincit legem* meaning "an agreement cannot usurp the law"; and
- (vi) *Nemo contra factum suum venire potest* meaning "no man may contradict his own agreement"; and
- (vii) *Cujus est dare ejus est disponere* meaning "he who has a right to give, has the right to dispose of the gift"; and
- (viii) *Locum pactum regit actum* meaning "The place of the agreement governs the act"; and
- (ix) *Pactum nulla res est non valet* meaning "An agreement of a non-existent thing is not valid"; and
- (x) *Nihil oritur in consensu sine conditiones* meaning "No action arises on an agreement without conditions"; and
- (xi) *Mala grammatica non vitiat pactum* meaning "Bad grammar does not vitiate an agreement"; and
- (xii) *Consensus facit pactum* meaning "Consent makes the agreement (valid)"; and
- (xiii) *Nemo tenetur ad impossibile* meaning "No one is bound to an impossibility"; and
- (xiv) *Nemo est, nisi sciat cum quod convenit* meaning "no one is present unless he knows with what he agrees".

1497. In any discussion, opportunity, investigation, potential business dealing or negotiation where Ucadia is likely to be the first or leading or primary grantor, giftor, devisor, delegator, licensor, transferor or trustor of any right, property, power or authority of Ucadia or a valid entity, body, person or company, it shall be the sole obligation of the Ucadia entity, body, person or company to make and write the Agreement and then provide such drafts of the Agreement to the satisfaction of other parties for its acceptance, signing and execution.

Obligation of Ucadia to Write Agreement

1498. Where another party makes demands, conditions or assertions as to their right to make and write an agreement whereby Ucadia is likely to be the first or leading or primary grantor, giftor, devisor, delegator, licensor, transferor or trustor of any right, property, power or authority of Ucadia or a valid entity, body, person or company, the relevant Ucadia entity, body, person or company by its obligations shall be forbidden from accepting any such drafts or entering into such an agreement.

Must not breach Obligations

1499. Ucadia warrants that for every Agreement made and written by one or more authorised Officers of Ucadia regarding any right, property, power or authority of Ucadia for which it is designated within the Agreement as the first or leading or primary grantor, giftor, devisor, delegator, licensor, transferor or trustor, Ucadia accepts liability as the author of the Agreement to the extent and limit of any and all limited liability and conditions expressed therein or by these Maxims.

Warranty of Agreements of Corporation

1500. Where Ucadia or a valid entity, body, person or company is not the first or leading or primary grantor, giftor, devisor, delegator, licensor, transferor or trustor of any right, property, power or authority, a duly authorised Officer of Ucadia or a valid entity, body, person or company may enter into a written agreement made and written by some other party, providing such agreement complies to the fundamental and minimum requirements of any valid Agreement.

Acceptance of Agreement made by other party

1501. Notwithstanding Ucadia Law, no agreement may be entered into by Ucadia or a valid entity, body, person or company, nor signed by a duly authorised Director, or Officer, or Agent, or Employee or Contractor if the wording of such agreement in any way may be reasonably implied or construed, or interpreted, or read to mean a transfer, or gift, or deposit, or surrender, or forfeit, or grant, or delivery, or alienation, or consignment, or conveyance, or arrest, or capture, or seizure, or resignation of any Rights or Property of Ucadia to a Non-Ucadia entity, body, agency, person or company whatsoever, if this is not a primary and fully disclosed purpose of such an agreement.

Forbidden to sign agreements that imply transfer of Rights or Property within wording.

1502. Notwithstanding Ucadia Law, no agreement may be entered into by Ucadia or a valid entity, body, person or company, nor signed by a duly authorised Director, or Officer, or Agent, or Employee or Contractor if the wording of such agreement in any way may be reasonably implied or construed, or interpreted, or read to mean that Ucadia or a valid entity, body, person or company in the relation of a Debtor to the other Party as Creditor and fair and reasonable consideration has not been fully disclosed, or the nature of the liability or the full consequences of such obligation.

Forbidden to sign agreements that imply Ucadia entities as Debtor for no consideration

1503. All signed, sealed and executed Agreements of Ucadia or a valid entity, body, person or company must be duly registered within Ucadia Jurisdiction immediately upon execution, with the relevant registrar then required to hold all originals in the appropriate chancery and then providing certified or notarised copies back to the appropriate Officers.

All Agreements held by Ucadia Registry

Article 399 – Terms and Conditions

1504. **Terms and Conditions** are any special meanings or any clauses in an Agreement that has for its object to suspend, rescind, or modify any principal obligation under certain events.

Terms and Conditions

1505. A **Condition** refers to a specific requirement or provision that must be met or satisfied for the agreement to be valid, enforceable, or for certain rights and obligations to take effect. Conditions are often used in contracts to specify the circumstances under which the parties' obligations become effective or can be terminated. There are generally two types of possible Conditions in valid Agreements:-

Condition

   (i) **Condition Precedent**: This type of condition is something that must occur or be fulfilled before the parties' obligations under the contract are triggered. Until the condition precedent is satisfied, the contract may not be binding, and the parties are not required to perform their obligations. If the condition is not met, the contract may be voided or terminated; or

   (ii) **Condition Subsequent**: A condition subsequent is a provision in a contract that, if it occurs, can terminate or modify the parties' rights and obligations under the contract after they have already been established. In other words, it's a condition that, if met, can end the contract or change its terms.

1506. **Terms of Negotiation**, also known as **Terms of Reference** and **Negotiation Terms** are non-binding conditions by which parties intending in Good Faith, Good Conscience and Good Action to form a valid Agreement, agree to work together to achieve such a shared goal, within reasonable limits. The purpose of any properly formed Terms of Negotiation is to reduce the risk of miscommunication, unnecessary delays, conflicts and potential controversies that may cause the finalisation of mutually satisfactory agreement, or possibly cause such negotiations to cease entirely.

Terms and Conditions Agreement

1507. The general requirements and elements of any Terms of Negotiation are:-

General Requirements of Terms of Negotiation Document

   (i) A listing of all the Parties; and

(ii) A brief set of Warranties by which the Parties agree to move forward in relation to negotiations; and

(iii) A summary of the documents provided and associated with the negotiation; and

(iv) A summary of negotiation procedural steps by which all Parties shall communicate, raise issues and agree to respond; and

(v) A signature by all Parties on the Terms of Negotiation document that they agree to use the terms for negotiation, or some written confirmation of such fact.

Article 400 - Deed

1508. A ***Deed*** is the first of four possible types of Agreements in the permanent or temporary Transfer of Rights being an Agreement made between two or more Persons of Equal or Unequal Status for the permanent or temporary bilateral Transfer of at least one or more Rights of Title and/or Rights of Use between each of the Parties.

Deed

1509. The word *Deed* was first created into Law in the 8th Century CE within the whole context of modern law including (but not limited to) Rights, Law, Tort, Droit, Courts etc. during the formation of modern Western Civilisation under the Holly (Holy) Bloodlines directed by the Holly Carolingians and Holly Irish Academics:-

Origin of the Word Deed

(i) Similar to the word "right" originating from the Holly Irish ***ríghte*** meaning "gift from the kings head", the word "deed" comes to Anglaise from the Holly Irish ***déid*** meaning "to express agreement" with ***dé*** meaning "puff, breath" and ***id*** meaning "I do, I agree"; and

(ii) From the beginning of modern Western Civilisation, the permanent and temporary Transfer of Rights could only legally and lawfully be done through a Deed. This fundamental system of law remained in place up until the Great Death (Outbreak of Haemorrhagic Fever) from 1300s that killed more than 85% of the population in Europe, North Africa, Middle East and Asia Minor; and

(iii) The concept of Deeds being the only valid medium to Transfer Rights returned as a legal mechanism in many countries. However, by the 1520s when the Venetian nobility sought refuge to England, they immediately sought to dismantle such systems of lawful transfer of Rights by poisoning the meaning of Deed to mean "insensible, void of meaning, utterly and absolutely void". This is the true origin of the modern English word of **Dead**, and why despite several attempts at false etymology there remains the memory of *Deed* somehow meaning *Dead* and vice versa; and

(iv) There is no credible evidence that the legal system of Deeds being the primary and only valid means of Transfer of Rights returned to the Laws of England (now Great Britain) until the Subscription of Deeds Act around 1681. At the same time, a completely fake and absurd history was created by "backdating" the alleged legitimacy of Deeds under English Law to 1540 under Henry VIII – around the same time Henry VIII destroyed the use of Deeds in his own kingdom by turning the word Deed into what we now know as the meaning of Dead; and

(v) The final return and formality of Deeds as the primary and only valid means of Transfer of Rights occurred in the first half of the 19th Century with no fewer than 150 Acts related to Deeds and their registration, compared to less than 5 Acts for the whole of the 18th Century; and

(vi) The introduction of Contracts in the 20th Century under Western Law has seen the gradual decline and knowledge in the use of Deeds to the point that many jurisdictions now permit the absurdity and corruption of Civilised law via allowing Contracts to be used for the permanent Transfer of Rights as "Powers".

1510. From the beginning of the creation of valid Deeds in the 8th Century, a Deed needed to be written on parchment, vellum or paper; and be delivered to all other parties; and contain the following elements being *Incipio, Oratio, Recitatio, Condicio, Decretio, Insignio and Testificatio* :- Ancient Elements of Deed

(i) ***Incipio*** (Beginning) being the first sentence or words, usually in majuscule (capitals) and in Latin; and

(ii) ***Oratio*** (Prayer) as the opening words before any actual gift, grant or permission, also usually in Latin. By the 10th Century, many Deeds carried the same Incipio and Oratio being *Omnibus Christi fidelibus ad quos presents littere peruenerint salutem sempiternam* meaning "To all the faithful of Christ to whom these present letters shall come everlasting greeting"; and

(iii) ***Recitatio*** (Recitals) being a clear and brief summary of the grant or conveyance and promise and parties; and

(iv) ***Condicio*** (Conditions) being the listing of at least one binding obligation or promise of performance in relation to the Transfer of one (or more) Rights; and

(v) ***Decretio*** (Decree) being a decree that the instrument had been handed (delivered) to all parties; and

(vi) ***Insignio*** (Seal and Sign) also known as the "*signati recordis*" being usually a wax seal of their distinguishing mark, seal, badge, decoration or name connected by red and/or gold cord to the linen; and

(vii) ***Testificatio*** (Attestation) usually in Latin being the testification of the maker at a time and place that it is their wish reflected in the Deed.

1511. Modern Deeds from the 19th Century and 20th Century still need to be written on parchment, vellum or paper; and be delivered to all other parties; and contain the following elements being Recitals, Conditions, Delivery, Affirmation and Seal and Sign:- Modern Elements of Deed

(i) ***Recitals***: Being a clear and brief summary of the grant or conveyance and promise and parties; and

(ii) ***Conditions***: Being the listing of at least one binding obligation or promise of performance in relation to the Transfer of one (or more) Rights; and

(iii) ***Delivery***: Being an assurance that the instrument has been handed (delivered) to all parties upon execution; and

(iv) ***Affirmation***: Being a clear acknowledgment by all parties who sealed and signed the Agreement that it is firm and binding; and

(v) ***Seal and Sign***: Being a seal and the distinguishing marks of those party or witness to the Agreement.

1512. The nature and type of Deed, including the Civilised Jurisdiction may have additional requirements that Deeds must meet, especially in the transfer and conveyance of Real Property. However, some of the more common additional requirements historically include (but are not limited to):- Additional Requirements of Modern Deeds

(i) ***Money must be written in words and capitalised to be operative***: Meaning any amount of money expressed in a Deed must be written in capital words to be operative, while its numeric equivalent can be included in brackets; and

(ii) ***Address of property or rights to be conveyed must be written in words and capitalised to be operative***:

Meaning any location or plot of land must be capitalised and in words, not numbers; and

(iii) ***Specific Language confirming nature of Transfer***: Means that almost all laws of Deeds require the presence of specific words and language to validate a Transfer (e.g. "grant" or "give and grant"); and

(iv) ***Names of parties must be capitalised***: But may be then redefined by a word in Proper case; and

(v) ***The official addresses of parties must be clearly listed***: But can be written in numbers and sentence case; and

(vi) ***The names of signatories must be clear***: Underneath any signatures; and

(vii) ***The date and location of execution must be in words***: So that the day, month and year must be expressed in words, usually capitalised. However, many jurisdictions no longer make this a condition of a valid Deed.

1513. Examples of Types of Deeds include (but are not limited to):- *Examples of Types of Deeds*

(i) ***General Warranty Deed***: This type of deed provides the highest level of protection to the grantee (buyer). The grantor (seller) warrants that they have clear title to the property and will defend the title against any claims. It typically includes covenants of seisin (ownership), right to convey, against encumbrances, quiet enjoyment, and warranty forever; and

(ii) ***Quitclaim Deed***: A quitclaim deed conveys the grantor's interest in the property, if any, without making any warranties. It offers the least amount of protection to the grantee, as the grantor makes no guarantees about the quality of title. Quitclaim deeds are often used in situations where the parties have an existing relationship or when transferring property between family members; and

(iii) ***Bargain and Sale Deed***: This type of deed conveys the property with no warranties against encumbrances, but it implies that the grantor holds title and possession. It's common in some jurisdictions and may include language such as "grant and bargain"; and

(iv) ***Executor's Deed/Administrator's Deed***: These deeds are used by executors or administrators of estates to convey property from the estate of a deceased person. They typically contain warranties similar to a special warranty deed; and

(v) **Trustee's Deed**: Trustee's deeds are used when property held in a trust is transferred. The trustee conveys the property according to the terms of the trust, and the deed may contain specific warranties or limitations as outlined in the trust instrument; and

(vi) **Grant Deed**: Grant deeds are commonly used in some Non-Ucadia Jurisdictions. They imply that the grantor has not conveyed the property interest to anyone else and has not encumbered the property, but they do not make the same extensive warranties as a general warranty deed; and

(vii) **Life Estate Deed**: This type of deed conveys ownership of property for the duration of a person's life. The person holding the life estate is known as the life tenant and has the right to possess and use the property during their lifetime; and

(viii) **Easement Deed**: An easement deed grants a specific right to use someone else's property for a particular purpose, such as access, utilities, or drainage. It does not transfer ownership of the property but grants a limited interest in it; and

(ix) **Copyright Assignment Deed**: This document is used to transfer ownership or specific rights related to a copyrighted work from the creator or current owner to another party. It can include terms about exclusive or non-exclusive rights, territorial limitations, and compensation; and

(x) **Mineral Rights Deed**: In addition to real estate deeds, mineral rights deeds are used to convey ownership or rights to minerals, oil, gas, or other subsurface resources. These deeds specify the rights granted, any royalties, and restrictions on extraction.

1514. A **Trust Deed** is a Deed by a Trustor that defines the parameters, scope and constraints of authority in relation to the Trustee. A Trust Deed is not the actual instrument that conveys certain Rights and Property, but the Deed that creates the "container" for such transfer to be effected. However, a Trust Deed is permitted to define the agreement for vesting and transfers to occur upon or after the execution of the Trust Deed. Trust Deed

1515. A **Vesting Deed** is a Deed that effects the transfer of a Right or Property into a Trust. By definition, the Trust must already exist, via a Trust Deed. The general and logical reason that a Vesting Deed cannot occur until a Trust is formed, is a Vesting Deed is in essence a Deed Poll executed by a Grantor, Giftor, Assignor or Delegator, whereas a Trust Deed is an agreement between a Trustor and Vesting Deed

Trustee.

Article 401 – Deed Poll

1516. A ***Deed Poll*** is the second of four possible types of Agreements in the permanent or temporary Transfer of Rights being an Agreement made by only one Person for the permanent or temporary unilateral Transfer of at least one or more Rights of Title and/or Rights of Use.

Deed Poll

1517. The name Deed Poll comes from the fact that such unilateral Deeds historically required the seal to be the thumbprint of the Grantor to be effective. As validation to this tradition, the word "Poll" comes from the Latin ***pollex*** meaning 'thumb'.

Origin of Name Deed Poll

1518. Examples of Deed Polls include (but are not limited to):-

Examples of Deed Polls

    (i) ***Name Change Deed Poll***: One of the most common uses of a deed poll is to officially change one's name. If an individual wishes to adopt a new name or revert to a previous name, they can execute a name change deed poll to record and formalize the change. This is often done for personal, cultural, or religious reasons; and

    (ii) ***Change of Business Name Deed Poll***: In the business context, companies may use a deed poll to officially change their registered business name. This is often required when a company undergoes a rebranding or restructuring; and

    (iii) ***Change of Signature Deed Poll***: Sometimes, individuals may want to change their signature for various reasons, such as to update their legal signature on bank accounts, contracts, or other documents. A change of signature deed poll can be used to make this change official; and

    (iv) ***Dissolution of Partnership Deed Poll***: When a business partnership is dissolved, partners may use a deed poll to formally declare the dissolution and the distribution of assets and liabilities; and

    (v) ***Declaration of Solvency Deed Poll***: In certain legal contexts, such as bankruptcy proceedings, an individual may use a declaration of solvency deed poll to declare that they are solvent and able to meet their financial obligations; and

    (vi) ***Ecclesiastical Deed Poll***: Is a valid Form of Deed Poll whereby a True Person first expresses, affirms and conveys certain rights to a Non-Ucadian Official who is then morally, legally and lawfully required to acknowledge it as a record of fact.

Article 402 - Compact

1519. A ***Compact*** is the third of four possible types of Agreements in the temporary Transfer of Rights being an Agreement made between two or more Persons of Equal Status for the temporary bilateral Transfer of at least one or more Rights of Title and/or Rights of Use between each of the Parties. Compact

1520. A *Compact* by all known Civilised Rule of Law cannot be a medium for the permanent Transfer of one or more Rights of Title and/or Rights of Use. Thus, any Compact that is written to such an effect is null and void, having no force or effect from the beginning. Compact can never seek to permanently transfer rights

1521. All property land conveyances as Trusts for Sale require purchase and Agreement in Equality and are therefore strictly Compacts and not Contracts. Land and Trusts for Sale as Compacts

Article 403 - Contract

1522. A ***Contract*** is the fourth of four possible types of Agreements in the temporary Transfer of Rights being an Agreement made between two or more Persons of Equal or Unequal Status for the temporary Transfer of at least one (or more) Rights of Title and/or Rights of Use. Contract

1523. A Contract by all known Civilised Rule of Law cannot be a medium for the permanent Transfer of one or more Rights of Title and/or Rights of Use. Thus, any Contract that is written to such an effect is null and void, having no force or effect from the beginning. Contract can never seek to permanently transfer rights

1524. Contracts may be generally classified according to the following including (but not limited to):- Classification of Contracts

    (i)   ***Unilateral Contract***: In a unilateral contract, one party makes a promise or an offer that can be accepted only through the performance of a specific act or condition. The contract is formed when the act is completed. If the act is not performed, no contract is created; and

    (ii)   ***Trespass Contract***: A trespass contract or tort contract is a unilateral contract where one party asserts one or more claims and obligations over property held by another (obligor); and then by lapse of time, silence, belligerence or refusal to resolve by arbitration, a contract is formed with the obligor then having one or more obligation or duty to perform; and

    (iii)   ***Bilateral Contract***: In a bilateral contract, both parties exchange promises to perform certain acts or provide

(iv) **Executed Contract**: An executed contract is one in which all parties have fully performed their obligations, and nothing further remains to be done; and

(v) **Executory Contract**: In an executory contract, one or both parties have not yet completed their obligations. There are future actions or performances expected from one or both parties; and

(vi) **Adhesion Contract**: Also known as a "take-it-or-leave-it" contract, an adhesion contract is a standardized agreement offered by one party to a weaker party, who has little to no bargaining power. The terms are usually non-negotiable; and

(vii) **Option Contract**: An option contract gives one party the right (but not the obligation) to enter into a contract with another party at a later time, typically for a specified consideration.

1525. An ***Implied Contract*** is a false and prohibited form, absurd in Civilised Law that fails to meet the minimum standards of enforceable Contract Law. It is based on the spurious notion that some form of enforceable Contract may be implied from the conduct or actions of the parties or "implied" promises or obligations. — *Falsity of Implied Contracts*

1526. Ucadia and its valid entities, bodies and corporations shall at all times have the absolute right to monetize the value of any and all Trespass Contracts issued against one or more Non-Ucadia Officials concerning property and rights in their control where no treaty is in place with the relevant Non-Ucadia Government or Agency; and to use such instruments as underwriting for the issuance of Non-Ucadia and foreign legal tender, foreign currencies, or as bonds and other instruments for sale to the equivalent value of the property unlawfully withheld by Non-Ucadia Officials and entities. — *Right to Monetize Trespass Contracts*

1527. In terms of the origin of the modern concept of Contracts:- — *Origin of Contracts*

(i) One of the first genuine mentions of the concept of Contracts in English Law is the *Sale of Farming Stock Act 1816* (56Geo3 c.50) whereby poor people attached to farms and plantations could be converted into "Stock"; and that they as well as their "Chattels" could be sold in matters of bankruptcy, except where existing Contracts were already in place concerning the use of People as "Stock"; and

(ii) The first genuine mention of the concept of Contracts in English Law is the Slave Trade Act 1824 (5 Geo4 c.113) that did not abolish slavery as many falsely claim and assume, but merely made "the purchase, sale, or contract for slaves declared unlawful", with the Crown (Corporation) owed financial restitution as the ultimate owner of the slaves should anyone be found to have unlawfully contravened the Act; and

(iii) The claim that the concept and word Contract was used as early as the Statute of Frauds 1677 (29 Car2. c.3) is contradictory and inconsistent with the history and evolution of Deeds and subsequent takeover of Contracts in the late 19th Century and into the 20th Century; and

(iv) As demonstration and proof that Contracts are a relatively recent invention, one of the first statutes to define the proper form and style of contracts is the Sale of Goods Act 1893 (56 & 57 Vict. c.71) whereby "a contract of sale of goods is a contract by which the seller transfers or agrees to transfer the property in goods to the buyer for a money consideration, called the price"; and this is the first example in history of statute defining the form of Contract; and

(v) As further demonstration that the formality and use of Contracts is a modern invention, there are no more than 11 claimed Acts listed between 1600 and 1700 mentioning the word "contract" with none defining form; and the same number (11) between 1700 and 1800; and then 36 Acts mentioning "contract" between 1800 and 1850 with none defining their formality; and then suddenly over 150 Acts between 1850 and 1900 mentioning "contracts".

15.2 – Agreement Elements

Article 404 – Agreement Elements

1528. ***Agreement Elements*** refer to the fundamental components or requirements that must be present for a legally binding agreement to be valid and enforceable under Civilised Rules of Law.

Agreement Elements

1529. The following twelve (12) elements are considered fundamental elements for an Agreement (such as a contract or deed) to be legally enforceable:-

Fundamental Elements of an Agreement

(i) ***Legal Capacity***: Both parties must have the legal capacity to enter into the Agreement. This typically means that they must be of sound mind, of legal age, and not under the influence of drugs or alcohol. Minors and individuals with certain mental incapacities may lack legal capacity; and

(ii) ***Legality of Purpose***: The purpose of the Agreement must be legal. Contracts that involve illegal activities or contravene public policy are generally not enforceable; and

(iii) ***Intention to Create Legal Relations***: Both parties must intend for the Agreement to be legally binding. In some cases, Agreements between friends or family members may not be considered legally binding if they lack this intention; and

(iv) ***Good Faith, Good Conscience & Good Actions***: The ancient and fundamental requirement that all valid Agreements are formed under Good Faith, Good Conscience and Good Actions; and

(v) ***Free Will & Consent***: The consent of the parties must be freely given, without duress, fraud, undue influence or misrepresentation; and

(vi) ***Certainty & Possibility of Performance***: The terms of the Agreement must be sufficiently certain and capable of being performed. Vague or ambiguous terms can render a contract unenforceable; and

(vii) ***Consideration***: Consideration is something of value exchanged between the parties. It can be money, goods, services, a promise to do something, or a promise to refrain from doing something. Consideration demonstrates that each party is giving something up or incurring a legal detriment in exchange for what the other party is offering; and

(viii) ***Proper Form***: Some Agreements, such as those involving real estate may need to be in writing to be enforceable. These requirements vary by jurisdiction and the nature of the contract; and

(ix) ***Offer***: An offer is a clear and definite proposal made by one party (the offerer) to another party (the offeree) expressing an intention to enter into a Agreement under certain terms and conditions; and

(x) ***Acceptance***: Acceptance occurs when the offeree agrees to the terms of the offer, unconditionally and without any material modifications. The acceptance must correspond exactly to the terms of the offer; and

(xi) ***Mutual Assent***: Both parties must have a mutual understanding and agreement about the essential terms and subject matter of the Agreement. If there is a material misunderstanding between the parties, the contract may not be enforceable; and

(xii) **Execution & Ratification**: An Agreement must be executed and ratified by all parties to be effective. Typically, ratification for a simple Agreement requires an exchange of signed and executed copies (as in the necessary case for Deeds). However, with more complex Agreements, such as Treaties, ratification may require the Treaty be passed and assented by the political body of a Sovereign country before it becomes law.

1530. A key element for any Agreement to be legally enforceable within Ucadia Jurisdiction is that an Agreement be in writing, within the form prescribed under Ucadia Law and duly registered with the correct Register:- *[Agreements in Writing as Key Element within Ucadia Jurisdiction]*

(i) Unlike many Non-Ucadia Jurisdictions, a valid proper and legally enforceable Agreement within Ucadia Law is one that is in writing, using the correct form prescribed for the particular type of Agreement; and

(ii) Under Ucadia Law all valid Agreements must be duly registered with the correct Ucadia Register. In most cases, an unregistered Agreement even if it is in writing, the prescribed form that is unregistered will not be legally enforceable.

Article 405 - Legal Capacity

1531. *Legal Capacity* is the first of twelve fundamental elements of any valid Agreement. *Legal Capacity* refers to a person's mental competence and legal ability to understand and enter into an Agreement. It encompasses the individual's ability to comprehend the terms, consequences and obligations of the contract. Lack of legal capacity, such as due to age, mental incapacity or coercion can render an Agreement void or voidable. *[Legal Capacity]*

1532. *Legal Capacity* refers to a person's ability to understand, appreciate, and make informed decisions about their legal rights and responsibilities. The key elements associated with legal capacity typically include (but are not limited to):- *[Key Elements of Legal Capacity]*

(i) **Age**: Individuals must typically reach a certain age (often 18 or 21) to have full legal capacity. Minors may have limited capacity and may require a guardian or parent to make decisions for them; and

(ii) **Mental Capacity**: Individuals must have the mental ability to understand the nature and consequences of their actions. Those with severe mental impairments may have limited legal capacity; and

(iii) **Guardianship**: In cases where an individual lacks capacity due to mental incapacity or other factors, a legal guardian may be appointed to make decisions on their behalf; and

(iv) ***Freedom from Intoxication***: Entering into legal agreements while under the influence of drugs or alcohol may impair one's capacity, potentially rendering the agreement voidable; and

(v) ***Voluntary***: Decisions and agreements must be made voluntarily, without coercion or undue influence. Coerced or forced agreements may be voided due to a lack of voluntary nature; and

(vi) ***Free Will***: Individuals must have the freedom to make choices without external constraints. Threats, duress, or fraud can undermine free will and therefore legal capacity; and

(vii) ***Understanding of the Transaction***: Parties must understand the terms and implications of the contract or agreement they are entering into. Lack of comprehension can indicate a lack of capacity.

Article 406 - Legality of Purpose

1533. ***Legality of Purpose*** is the second of twelve fundamental elements of any valid Agreement. *Legality of Purpose* means that the objective of an Agreement must be lawful. The contract must not involve illegal activities or go against public policy. Agreements made in Bad faith, Bad Conscience or Bad Action are void from the beginning having no force or effect in Law.

Legality of Purpose

Article 407 - Intention to Create Legal Relations

1534. ***Intention to Create Legal Relations*** is the third of twelve fundamental elements of any valid Agreement. *Intention to Create Legal Relations* signifies the parties' genuine intent for their Agreement to be legally binding. Agreements entered into with this intent are enforceable, while social or domestic arrangements typically lack this intention and are not legally binding.

Intention to Create Legal Relations

1535. The requirement for clear *Intention to Create Legal Relations* is one of the primary reasons Implied Contract are a fraud and absurdity against proper and Civilised law:-

Lack of Clear Intention to Create Relations and Implied

(i) The absence of any clear Intention to Create Legal Relations should be sufficient to void and nullify any and all arguments of Implied Contracts within Non-Ucadia Jurisdictions; and

(ii) The fact that so many claimed forums of law within Non-Ucadia Jurisdictions uphold Implied Contracts, despite the glaring absence of this fundamental element for a valid Agreement, is overwhelming evidence of corruption and collusion of the entire fabric of law and order itself in such places; and

(iii) Any penalty derived from the enforcement of an Implied Contract stands as a profound injury against fairness, good faith, decency and the proper rule of law; and

(iv) Any Non-Ucadia official that permits the enforcement of Implied Contracts is directly liable, without any protection of immunity, for any subsequent penalties and damages should such a Non-Ucadia Jurisdiction rediscover and start applying the ancient concept of Civilised Rule of Law.

Article 408 - Good Faith, Good Conscience & Good Actions

1536. ***Good Faith, Good Conscience & Good Actions*** is the fourth of twelve fundamental elements of any valid Agreement. *Good Faith, Good Conscience & Good Actions* implies an honest and fair approach by parties. It involves a commitment to acting honestly and not undermining the purpose of the Agreement. Good faith is a fundamental principle in any Lawful Agreement, encouraging fair dealings and cooperation between parties to fulfil the Agreement's objectives.

Article 409 - Free Will & Consent

1537. ***Free Will & Consent*** is the fifth of twelve fundamental elements of any valid Agreement. *Free Will & Consent* signify that parties willingly and without undue influence or coercion enter into Agreements. It implies that the Agreement is the result of voluntary choices by all involved parties. Agreements formed under these conditions are legally valid, while those obtained through force, fraud, or manipulation may be voidable.

Article 410 - Certainty & Possibility of Performance

1538. ***Certainty & Possibility of Performance*** is the sixth of twelve fundamental elements of any valid Agreement. *Certainty & Possibility of Performance* refer to the requirement that Agreement terms must be clear and definite. Parties should be able to understand their obligations, and the contract must be capable of being carried out. Vague, ambiguous, or impossible terms may render an Agreement unenforceable.

1539. The most frequent example of Impossible and Unenforceable Terms are found in Finance and Financial Services Agreements, commonly known as an *Acceleration Clause*, or *Default Clause* or *Due on Demand Clause* whereby the lender "legally" demands the full repayment of a loan if the borrower violates certain terms or conditions:-

    (i)   Given the overwhelming cause of violation of certain terms or conditions of Finance and Financial Services Agreements is failure to make a payment due to an inability to make a regular repayment, this example is a perfect "textbook" case of an Impossible and Unconscionable Agreement; and

    (ii)   The most shocking and evil revelation of this perfect example of Impossible and Unconscionable Agreement that should be immediately rescinded by any competent forum of law, the direct opposite appears to be standard practice within Non-Ucadia Jurisdictions as such unconscionable and impossible conduct continues to be rewarded and upheld.

Article 411 – Consideration

1540. *Consideration* is the seventh of twelve fundamental elements of any valid Agreement. *Consideration* is the Offer of something possessing value given as incentive or recompense for a previous promise which then causes the promise to become binding as a Consensus if accepted.

1541. *Consideration* is a fundamental element in the formation of a legally binding Agreement. It refers to something of value that is exchanged between the parties to the Agreement. The key elements of consideration in respect of Agreements include (but are not limited to):-

    (i)   ***Something of Value***: Consideration involves a promise, an act, or a forbearance of an act that has some value. It can be money, goods, services, property, or any other legal benefit; and

    (ii)   ***Bargained-for Exchange***: Consideration must be the result of a bargain or negotiation between the parties. It should not be something given as a gift or a donation; and

(iii) **Legal Value**: The consideration exchanged must have legal value, which means it must be something that the law recognizes as having value. Illegal or morally unacceptable consideration is not valid; and

(iv) **Adequacy**: Consideration does not require that the value exchanged be equal or fair; it only needs to be sufficient.

1542. Generally, past consideration (something that has already been done before the Agreement) is not valid consideration. Consideration must be contemporaneous with the Agreement. — *Past Consideration*

1543. A promise to perform an act in the future can be valid consideration if it is binding and enforceable when the time comes. However if a party is already legally obligated to perform an act, promising to do the same act cannot serve as valid consideration. However, if the party promises to do something different or additional, it may be valid consideration. — *Future Consideration*

1544. A token or nominal consideration may be sufficient to make an Agreement legally binding, as long as the other elements of consideration are present. — *Nominal Consideration*

Article 412 - Proper Form

1545. **Proper Form** is the eighth of twelve fundamental elements of any valid Agreement. Proper Form indicates adherence to legal formalities and requirements. It involves following specific rules, such as writing, signing, or witnessing, depending on the type of Agreement and jurisdiction. Agreements that do not meet the required form may be unenforceable or invalid. — *Proper Form*

Article 413 - Offer

1546. **Offer** is the ninth of twelve fundamental elements of any valid Agreement. *Offer* is a clear and specific proposal made by one party to another, expressing the intent to enter into an Agreement under certain terms. It is a critical element, initiating the Agreement formation process. Once accepted, it creates a binding Agreement, and any deviations from the offer typically constitute a counteroffer, altering the Agreement terms. — *Offer*

1547. An *Offer* is a crucial element in the formation of an Agreement. An offer typically represents a promise by one party to do something or refrain from doing something in exchange for something of value from another party. The key elements of Offer in respect of Agreements include (but are not limited to):- — *Key elements of Offer*

(i) **Intention to Create Legal Relations**: The offeror must intend to create a legally binding Agreement; and

(ii) **Definiteness and Certainty**: The offer must be clear and definite in its terms. It should specify the essential terms and conditions of the Agreement, such as the subject matter, price, quantity, and the parties involved; and

(iii) **Communication**: The offer must be communicated to the offeree (the party to whom the offer is made). An offer cannot be accepted if the offeree is unaware of its existence; and

(iv) **Acceptance**: To form an Agreement, the offeree must accept the offer as it was presented, without any material changes. Acceptance creates a binding Agreement.

1548. Advertisements, price lists, and catalogue listings are generally not considered offers but rather invitations to treat. They invite potential buyers to make an offer, which the seller can accept or reject. *Invitations to Treat not Offer*

1549. As the original and true definition of Judgement is to "bind together the mind (and person)" most Judgments of Non-Ucadia Jurisdictions and Forums of Law since the end of the 19th Century are typically an Offer requiring unanimous Consent of all the parties, usually through the interpretation of absence of objection:- *Most Non-Ucadian Judgements are an Offer*

(i) The reason that most Judgements of Non-Ucadia Jurisdictions and Forums of Law are typically an Offer is that since the 2nd half of the 19th Century (see Judicature Acts), most Justices became merely "recorders in ecclesiastical and admiralty matters" requiring Consent of all parties to enter into the registers and rolls of the court. By the mid 1950's many lower western courts became arbitration courts that further required unanimous Consent of all parties to render a Judgement effective; and

(ii) Many Justices and Magistrates in Non-Ucadia Jurisdictions unlawfully use coercive and threatening tactics to force defendants under duress to surrender Consent. Not only is this an injury of law, but within any Civilised System of Law should be grounds for any sentence to be overturned and reviewed; and

(iii) In some cases Justices and Magistrates in Non-Ucadia Jurisdictions falsely and criminally misrepresent their powers in fraudulently claiming they still possess dictatorial powers to enter a judgment without the consent of the defendant. This is a further example of frequent injury of the law in broken courts, and further examples of illegal coercive and threatening tactics.

Article 414 - Acceptance

1550. ***Acceptance*** is the tenth of twelve fundamental elements of any valid Agreement. Acceptance is the unequivocal and unqualified agreement by one party to the terms of an offer made by another. It indicates the willingness to be bound by the terms proposed. Once accepted as offered, a Agreement is formed. Any changes to the terms generally create a counteroffer, requiring acceptance by the original offeror to establish a new Agreement.

Acceptance

Article 415 - Mutual Assent

1551. ***Mutual Assent*** is the eleventh of twelve fundamental elements of any valid Agreement. *Mutual Assent* also known as a "meeting of the minds," signifies that both parties involved in a contract have a shared understanding and agreement on the essential terms and obligations. It confirms that both parties genuinely consent to the terms, forming a legally binding contract when all other required elements are met.

Mutual Assent

Article 416 - Execution & Ratification

1552. ***Execution & Ratification*** is the twelfth of twelve fundamental elements of any valid Agreement. *Execution & Ratification* refers to the formal act of signing or performing an Agreement, signalling its creation. Ratification occurs when a party accepts or approves an Agreement after it has been executed, either explicitly or through their actions. It confirms the Agreements validity and enforces the obligations contained within it.

Execution & Ratification

15.3 – Agreement Penalty, Remedy & Enforcement

Article 417 – Agreement Penalty, Remedy and Enforcement

1553. ***Agreement Penalty, Remedy and Enforcement*** refers to those Agreement provisions and their enforcement where parties agree upon a predetermined course of action in event of any Breach or Default by one (or more) of the Parties.

Agreement Penalty, Remedy and Enforcement

Article 418 - Breach of Agreement

1554. ***Breach of Agreement*** is when one party fails to perform its obligations as specified in a legally binding Agreement.

Breach of Agreement

1555. A Breach of Agreement can take various forms, including (but not

Examples of

limited to):-   *forms of Breach of Agreement*

- (i) **Material (Major) Breach**: This is a significant or substantial violation of the Agreements terms that goes to the core of the Agreement. It typically entitles the non-breaching party to seek damages or terminate the Agreement; and

- (ii) **Minor Breach**: Also known as a partial breach or immaterial breach, this is a relatively minor violation of the Agreements terms that does not significantly affect the overall purpose of the Agreement. The non-breaching party may still have a claim for damages, but it may not be as extensive as in the case of a material breach; and

- (iii) **Anticipatory Breach**: This occurs when one party indicates, either through words or actions, that they do not intend to fulfil their written obligations in the future. The non-breaching party can often treat this as an immediate breach and seek remedies; and

- (iv) **Fundamental Breach**: Some Agreements include a specific clause that defines certain breaches as "fundamental" or "repudiatory". A fundamental breach is a serious violation that gives the non-breaching party the right to terminate the Agreement and seek damages.

1556. Generally under Ucadia Law, valid Agreements require clarity and definition as to what constitutes a Material (Major) Breach and what constitutes a Minor Breach:-   *Clarity and Definition of Types and Levels of Breach*

- (i) In the absence of clarity of major and minor breach, including evidence of remedy as well as penalty, an Agreement may be unenforceable; and

- (ii) Under Ucadia Law, what constitutes a breach must be defined within the terms of a valid Agreement. Furthermore, for each defined breach, there must be one defined for each party; and

- (iii) The presence of a one-sided Agreement in the definition of breaches is evidence of an unconscionable and therefore unenforceable agreement.

1557. Within Ucadia Law and many Non-Ucadia Jurisdictions a claim of breach and therefore grounds for a possible right of action is only valid if:-   *General process for Establishing Breach*

- (i) A valid Agreement is duly completed and registered and contains clear and unambiguous terms that specify the rights and obligations of each party; and

(ii) The valid Agreement specifies clearly in writing what constitutes a breach on the part of one party; and

(iii) The valid Agreement specifies at least one Penalty and one Remedy clause concerning the specific type or nature of breach; and

(iv) Sufficient evidence exists of the breach; and

(v) Proper notice of the breach has been communicated to the offending party with sufficient time to remedy.

Article 419 - Penalties for Breach of Agreement

1558. ***Penalties for Breach of Agreement*** refer to punitive measures established in Agreements representing adverse consequences from a breach or default of an Agreement. *(Penalties for Breach of Agreement)*

1559. The term Penalties is used to encompass all potentially adverse consequences from a breach or default of an Agreement. Therefore, under this comprehension, Penalties include (but are not limited to):- *(Use of the term Penalties)*

(i) Damages and Liquidated Damages; and

(ii) Conditions for Termination of Agreement; and

(iii) Conditions for Delay, Hold or Reversal of Performance; and

(iv) Conditions for Loss of one or more Rights; and

(v) Forfeiture being a penalty and loss of rights and interest in property; and

(vi) Fees for failure to perform an obligation.

1560. Unlike authorised government bodies such as courts, Penalties defined within a valid Agreement are never permitted to be punitive in nature:- *(Penalties never punitive under valid Agreements)*

(i) Punitive Penalties means they are designed to punish the party that has breached the contract or committed a wrongful act. The intention is not to compensate the injured party for actual losses but to deter future breaches or violations. Such clauses are illegal and unlawful under Ucadia Law and many Non-Ucadia Jurisdictions; and

(ii) Punitive measures included in an Agreement are grounds to invalidate and void it under Ucadia Law; and it is an offence to attempt to register an Agreement with such Punitive Penalties; and

(iii) Valid Agreements can never include Fines. A Fine is a punitive monetary fee imposed by a government authority as a consequence of a violation (breach) of an Agreement.

Article 420 - Remedies for Breach of Agreement

1561. ***Remedies for Breach of Agreement*** are legal actions or solutions available to parties when the terms of an Agreement are claimed to be violated.

1562. Under Ucadia Law and some Non-Ucadia Jurisdictions, a valid Agreement must pair a Remedy to any defined Penalty concerning any possible breach:-

(i) From the very beginning of modern Western Civilisation in the 8th Century under the Holly Bloodlines until the collapse of Civilisation in the 1300's, valid Agreements always required a Remedy to any stated Penalty. This notion was finally reintroduced into Non-Ucadian Law by the end of the 18th Century, especially through the alleged works of William Blackstone. However, by the second half of the 19th Century and into the 20th Century, the observance of ethical and moral law making concerning the pairing of Remedy and Penalty was largely abandoned again; and

(ii) The absence of a Remedy to a Penalty or condition of Breach renders an Agreement void and unenforceable. Similarly, the presence of a one-sided agreement whereby only Penalties are defined for one party, while the other party is given Remedy is considered morally repugnant and unconscionable.

Article 421 - Obligation of Mitigation

1563. ***Obligation of Mitigation*** is a legal principle requiring parties who have suffered harm due to a breach of Agreement to take reasonable steps to minimise their losses. This means they must make efforts to reduce the damages they incur as a result of the breach. Failure to do so can affect the amount of compensation or remedies they are entitled to in any Right of Action within a Forum of Law concerning a Breach of Agreement.

Article 422 - Legal Enforcement of Penalties or Remedies

1564. ***Legal Enforcement of Penalties or Remedies*** pertains to the process whereby courts or legal authorities uphold and enforce the penalties and remedies specified in Agreements.

1565. When a party breaches an Agreement, the non-breaching party may seek the intervention of the legal system to ensure that the agreed-upon penalties or remedies, such as monetary damages or specific performance, are enforced in accordance with the Agreement terms and applicable laws.

Agreement Terms

1566. The highest standards as required for the registration of a valid and enforceable Agreement under Ucadia Law is to ensure its efficient and fair enforcement for all parties:-

Efficient & Fair Justice & Necessary Standards of Valid Ucadia Agreements

    (i)   Clarity of key terms and conditions and their entry into registration enables many of the key procedures and steps of breach notification, remedy and penalty to be streamlined and automated under Ucadia Law; and

    (ii)   As far as possible, Ucadia seeks at all times to ensure the enforcement of valid Agreement represents a natural extension of the function of Justice and Civilised Rule of Law for all members.

15.4 – Agreement Dispute or Extinction

Article 423 - Agreement Dispute or Extinction

1567. ***Agreement Dispute or Extinction*** refers to situations where the terms of a legally enforceable Agreement are contested or the Agreement is terminated, cancelled or voided due to disagreements, breaches, or other reasons.

Agreement Dispute or Extinction

1568. The most common examples of Disputes of Agreement include (but are not limited to):-

Common Examples of Agreement Dispute

    (i)   ***Interpretation***: Parties may disagree on the meaning or interpretation of specific terms or clauses within an Agreement, leading to disputes about their respective rights and obligations; and

    (ii)   ***Breach of Agreement***: One party alleges that the other party failed to fulfil their obligations under the Agreement, such as payment, delivery of goods or services, or meeting specific deadlines; and

    (iii)   ***Termination***: One party seeks to invoke a right to terminate the Agreement, without necessarily citing a particular breach; and

    (iv)   ***Frustration***: Sometimes unforeseen events occur, making it impossible to fulfil a term of the Agreement, through no fault of the parties; and

    (v)   ***Force Majeure***: Events beyond the parties' control, such as natural disasters or unforeseen circumstances, can trigger a force majeure clause, affecting the performance of the Agreement; and

(vi) **Repudiation**: One party communicates that they refuse or are unable to continue to perform their obligations of the Agreement.

1569. Parties in Dispute over an Agreement may Settle, or Abandon a Dispute without Litigation in certain circumstances:- *(Settlement by Non-Litigation of Agreement Dispute)*

(i) Ucadia Law and most Non-Ucadia Jurisdictions require any parties in dispute to first seek Non-Litigation means such as Arbitration before being permitted to file an Action in Court. The only exception is where there exists grounds and claims of perfidy, fraud or deception on the part of one party; and

(ii) Parties to a dispute may may find a resolution through Arbitration mitigating the need to proceed to full litigation; and

(iii) A Party may choose not to contest a dispute or claim of repudiation or termination given the high costs in most Non-Ucadia Jurisdictions for pursuing a litigated remedy.

1570. Ucadia and some Non-Ucadia Jurisdictions provide low cost options for semi-litigation or "automated" remedies for settling disputes:- *(Semi-Litigation Options for Settling Agreement Dispute)*

(i) Ucadia provides a number of automated low cost remedies for the recovery of monies, issuance of penalties and settlement of disputes; and

(ii) Some Non-Ucadia Jurisdictions have introduced simple methods of recovery where a Default is perfected, allowing Government mandated Debt Recovery to recover funds under such disputes.

1571. Parties willing to risk the cost of Full Litigation may have a range of options for enabling the court to enforce their Rights of Actions and Rights for Remedy under a disputed Agreement, including (but not limited to):- *(Full Litigation Options for Settling Agreement Dispute)*

(i) **Declaratory Judgment**: In some cases, a party may seek a declaratory judgment from the court to determine the parties' rights and obligations under an Agreement without seeking monetary damages or specific performance; and

(ii) **Summary Judgement**: Is a judgment rendered by a court when there are no genuine disputes of material fact, and the legal issues in the case can be decided as a matter of law. A judgement in favour of a perfected default (as Default

Judgement) is a textbook example of a Summary Judgment; and

(iii) **_Reformation_**: Reformation is a remedy used to correct errors or ambiguities in the language of an Agreement. A court may reform the Agreement to reflect the true intent of the parties; and

(iv) **_Damages_**: Damages are a common remedy in Agreement disputes and are designed to compensate the innocent party for their financial losses resulting from the breach of Agreement; and

(v) **_Restitution_**: Restitution is a remedy aimed at restoring or compensating for unjust enrichment that occurs when one party benefits at the expense of another, often as a result of an Agreement of Undue Influence of one party over the other; and

(vi) **_Rescission_**: Rescission is a remedy that aims to restore the innocent party to their pre-Agreement position by requiring the fraudulent party to return any gains or benefits they obtained as a result of the Agreement; and

(vii) **_Voidance_**: In cases of fraudulent misrepresentation, the Agreement may be deemed void from the outset, meaning it was never legally binding. In such cases, the contract is treated as if it never existed.

Article 424 - Default

1572. **_Default_** refers to a claim of utter failure by a party to answer and provide a reasonable explanation or defence as to a claim of fundamental or material breach of their legal obligations under a valid and enforceable Agreement. In this sense, Default is an unrefuted claim having the effect in any subsequent Right of Action of strongly inferring to the court the defendant has no real defence. Default

1573. Upon clear evidence of a material breach, the non-breaching party usually has the right to send notice to the breaching party of the claim of material breach via a **_Notice of Default_**, also known as **_Default Notice_**. A clear process is then expected to follow beginning with a valid *Notice of Default* including (but not limited to):- Notice of Default

(i) **_Details of Breach_**: A valid Notice of Default should clearly state the specific provisions or terms of the Agreement that have been breached. It outlines the details of how the breaching party has failed to meet their obligations; and

(ii) ***Reasonable Actions to Cure***: A valid Notice of Default will demand that the breaching party take corrective actions to remedy the breach as specified in the valid Agreement; and that no greater burden or demands are placed on the breaching party; and

(iii) ***Deadline to Cure***: The Notice of Default must include a deadline whereby the breaching party must address the breach. This deadline must allow the breaching party a reasonable period to cure the default or take corrective action. The length of this period can vary depending on the terms of the Agreement and applicable laws, but generally be not less than fourteen days from receipt of the Notice; and

(iv) ***Consequences of Failure to Cure***: The Notice of Default must outline the potential consequences of failing to rectify the breach within the specified time frame. These consequences may include further legal action, such as a lawsuit for damages or a request for specific performance.

1574. *Default* only takes effect after the deadline passes without Cure or Remedy as stated in a valid Notice of Default. The creation and issue of such a Notice is never the earliest date of Default itself. Furthermore, a defective, false or ineffective Notice of Default invalidates any subsequent claim of Default.

_{Default only takes effect after the deadline passes on a valid Notice of Default without Cure}

1575. A *Notice of Default* shall be defective, false and ineffective if it contains any of the following elements:-

_{Defective, False, Ineffective Notice of Default}

(i) ***Unclear or Deceptive Title of Notice***: A Notice of Default must clearly state itself to be what it is. Any use of confusing or deceptive language, renders such a notice, letter or electronic communication null and void in terms of being a valid Notice of Default; and

(ii) ***Absence of Details of Breach***: The absence of a clear material breach detailed in a claimed Notice renders such an instrument ineffective as a Notice of Default; and

(iii) ***Unreasonable or Impossible Actions to Cure***: The introduction, presence or demand of an unreasonable or impossible action to cure renders not only the Notice of Default as ineffective but evidence itself for the alleged breaching party to seek via Right of Action their own remedy to have such an Agreement rescinded as Impossible and Unconscionable. However, it is important to note that many Non-Ucadia alleged forums of law no longer follow any resemblance of Civilised Rule of Law, nor their own alleged principles of property law and contracts; and

(iv) ***Unreasonable or Missing Deadline to Cure***: An unreasonable or missing deadline is grounds for the invalidation of any claimed Notice of Default; and

(v) ***Unclear of Missing Consequences of Failure to Cure***: Unclear or missing consequences can sometimes lead to the invalidation of a Notice of Default.

1576. The consequences and options once a Default is perfected include (but are not limited to):- *Consequence of Perfected Default*

(i) In Ucadia and most Non-Ucadia Jurisdictions, Default implies a level of dishonesty against the breaching party; and

(ii) The non-breaching party is then able to file a motion and hearing for a Summary Judgment, being effectively a "Default" Judgment in favour of a proven Default.

1577. Under Ucadia Law and most Non-Ucadia systems of law, a valid Agreement does not provide for the issuance of Notices of Default from two or more parties against one another. Thus the alleged breaching party is limited to the conditions of remedy of the Agreement itself or available Right of Action under the relevant form of law:- *Right of Action of alleged breaching party to allegations of Default*

(i) A valid Notice of Default is a technical document relating specifically to the available remedy and penalties of the Agreement itself. If an alleged breaching party believes the Agreement itself should be rescinded or terminated because of defect or some other issue, then such a claim must be tested under a Right of Action with the alleged breaching party as Plaintiff; and

(ii) A rebuttal of a Notice of Default generally has no force or effect in Ucadia Law or most Non-Ucadia Jurisdictions, as such an answer does not respond properly to the technical nature of such a Notice; and

(iii) Generally, an alleged breaching party has the right to initiate a Right of Action as plaintiff against the other party (or parties) of an Agreement even after Default has been perfected against them. Furthermore, Ucadia Law and many Non-Ucadia Jurisdictions permit the joining of two separately launched cases together. However, it is important to consider that in a number of Non-Ucadia jurisdictions, the party that perfected the Default will be the claimant and the other party will be the cross-claimant and defendant in any counter suit.

Article 425 - Force Majeure

1578. ***Force Majeure*** is a legal provision that excuses a party from fulfilling its contractual obligations when unforeseen and uncontrollable events, like natural disasters or emergencies, make performance impossible or impractical. It allows parties to temporarily suspend or terminate the contract without liability for non-performance. Force majeure clauses vary by contract and jurisdiction, and their applicability depends on the specific language and circumstances. — Force Majeure

1579. *Force Majeure* is never a Right but an optional clause as part of any valid Agreement. However, in the absence of such a clause or a clear clause, a party may have no excuse from fulfilling its contractual obligations when unforeseen and uncontrollable events, like natural disasters or emergencies, make performance impossible or impractical. — Force Majeure is not a Right but Optional Clause

Article 426 - Frustration

1580. ***Frustration*** is a legal doctrine that applies when unforeseen events occur, making it impossible to fulfil a contract's terms, through no fault of the parties. It may lead to the contract being considered void and the parties relieved from their obligations. Frustration is a defence against claims of breach when circumstances drastically change, rendering the contract's purpose unattainable. — Frustration

1581. Whilst the legal concept of Frustration is supposed to afford a reasonable defence against claims of breach, in practice it may provide little remedy against a Default Notice and subsequent Motion for Summary Judgment. Frustration is therefore more appropriately and effective expressed as an affirmative action under a Right of Action of Voidance. — Frustration as Defence against Default

Article 427 - Termination

1582. ***Termination*** signifies the act of ending or discontinuing a contractual or legal relationship, agreement or employment. — Termination

1583. Termination can be initiated for various reasons, such as breach of contract, expiration of terms, mutual consent, or as provided for in the agreement itself. It results in the cessation of rights, obligations, and responsibilities previously established between the parties involved. — Conditions for Termination

1584. An Agreement involving registered Security, such as a Mortgage, or where the other party refuses consent may render the concept of — Limitations on Termination

Termination invalid as a remedy:-

(i) Strictly, some Agreements are not permitted to be simply Terminated, even with mutual consent. For example, a Redemption of Mortgage has the effect of terminating an Agreement only after certain steps and notifications have been given and the discharge of any security; and

(ii) A demand for Termination on one or more claims of false or prohibited clauses for an Agreement may have little or no effect against the other party, except to potentially trigger a Default against the party demanding Termination; and

(iii) If grounds exist for Termination or Voidance, then a party is expected to be affirmative with their Rights in pursuing a Right of Action and not passive.

Article 428 - Voidance

1585. ***Voidance*** is a term used to describe the process whereby part or all of an Agreement is terminated or rendered void within a valid Forum of Law. When part or all of an Agreement is voided, it is treated as if it never existed, and the parties are released from their obligations under the previous Agreement. Voidance can occur for various reasons, such as a contract being found to be void *ab initio* (void from the beginning) due to illegality, fraud, duress, or lack of capacity. Voidance

1586. While both the Actions of Voidance and Rescission address the remedy of voiding, a successful Action of Rescission always results in the complete Void Ab Initio (Void from the Beginning) of an Agreement, whereas a successful Action of Voidance may leave some of an Agreement in force and effect or may choose a date sometime after the beginning to be the point the Agreement is void. Voidance vs Rescission

1587. Given the potential different outcomes of an Action of Voidance, it is important to understand the key elements and consequences of such a remedy:- Key elements of Voidance

(i) An Action for Voidance of an Agreement does not mean a whole Agreement will be made Void if successful. Nor can it be assumed that the Agreement will be Void Ab Initio (from the beginning). Therefore, it is possible a competent Forum of Law will leave some clauses effective and enforceable; and

(ii) If an Agreement is deemed ***Void*** by a Court, neither party can enforce from the moment it was formed (*Ab Initio*) and the Court will treat it as though it never existed; and

(iii) If an Agreement is Voided some time after its commencement, it will be considered **Voidable**, whereby one or more parties may still have enforceable rights up to the date and time the Agreement is considered Voided; and

(iv) A competent Forum of Law may choose to simply render one (or more) offending clauses Void via such an Action thereby preserving the main enforceability elements of the Agreement still in effect.

Article 429 - Damages

1588. **Damages** refer to the monetary compensation that one party may be entitled to receive from the other party due to a breach of the Agreement or some other wrongful act or omission. Damages are a legal remedy that is designed to compensate the non-breaching party for any losses or harm they have suffered as a result of the breach of Agreement.

Damages

1589. There are different types of Damages that can be awarded in Agreement cases, including (but not limited to):-

Types of Damages

   (i) **Compensatory Damages**: These are the most common type of damages awarded in Agreement cases. They are intended to compensate the non-breaching party for the actual losses they have incurred as a result of the breach. Compensatory damages aim to put the injured party in the position they would have been in if the contract had been performed as agreed; and

   (ii) **Consequential Damages (Special Damages)**: These are damages that result indirectly from the breach and were foreseeable at the time the Agreement was formed. These damages compensate the non-breaching party for losses that are not a direct result of the breach but are a consequence of it; and

   (iii) **Nominal Damages**: In some cases, the non-breaching party may be awarded a small amount of money (often a symbolic amount, like $1) as a form of recognition that their rights were violated, even if they did not suffer significant actual losses; and

   (iv) **Liquidated Damages**: In some Agreements, the parties may include a provision that specifies a predetermined amount of damages to be paid in the event of a breach. These are known as liquidated damages and must be a reasonable estimate of the actual damages that could result from a breach; and

(v) **Punitive Damages**: Punitive damages are not typically awarded in Agreement cases but are more common in cases involving intentional wrongdoing or misconduct. They are meant to punish the breaching party rather than compensate the injured party.

Article 430 - Reformation

1590. **Reformation** refers to a remedy used to correct errors or ambiguities in the language of an Agreement. A court may reform the Agreement to reflect the true intent of the parties. However, Reformation is considered a remedy of last resort, and both Ucadia and competent Non-Ucadia courts typically require a high standard of proof to grant it.

Reformation

1591. The key elements of the legal remedy of Reformation in relation to Agreements includes (but is not limited to):-

Key elements of Reformation

(i) **Mutual Mistake or Error**: Reformation is generally granted when there is a mutual mistake or error in the written contract. This means that both parties to the contract must have made a mistake regarding the terms of the agreement. The mistake could be related to a typographical error, a clerical error, or a misunderstanding about the intentions of the parties at the time the contract was formed; and

(ii) **Clear and Convincing Evidence**: The party seeking reformation must provide clear and convincing evidence that there was a mutual mistake or error in the contract. This evidence may include documents, correspondence, or witness testimony that supports the claim that the written contract does not accurately reflect the parties' true intentions; and

(iii) **Intention of the Parties**: The evidence presented must also demonstrate what the parties actually intended the contract to say. In other words, it must show what the contract would have said had it not been for the mistake or error. This can be a complex factual determination for the court; and

(iv) **No Prejudice to Third Parties**: Courts will generally grant reformation only if it does not unfairly prejudice the rights of third parties who have acquired interests in the contract without knowledge of the mistake. If third parties would be adversely affected by the reformation, the court may be less inclined to grant it; and

(v) **Statute of Limitations**: There may be a statute of limitations that limits the time within which a party can seek reformation. The time frame for seeking reformation varies by jurisdiction and can be influenced by factors such as when the mistake was discovered.

Article 431 - Restitution

1592. ***Restitution*** is a legal remedy aimed at restoring or compensating for unjust enrichment that occurs when one party benefits at the expense of another, often as a result of an Agreement of Undue Influence or Adhesion of one party over the other. — Restitution

1593. ***Quantum Meruit*** is a form of remedy similar to *Restitution* whereby a party has partially performed under an Agreement before the other party breaches, they may be entitled to recover the reasonable value of the work or services rendered, even if the Agreement is not fully performed. — Quantum Meruit

1594. The key elements and legal principles related to *Restitution* include (but are not limited to):- — Key elements of Restitution

   (i) **Benefit Received**: The party seeking *Restitution* must have conferred a benefit or value upon the other party under the Agreement. This benefit can take various forms, such as goods, services, money, promissory notes or other property; and

   (ii) **Unjust Enrichment**: *Restitution* is fundamentally based on the principle of preventing unjust enrichment. The enriched party must have received a benefit that would be unjust for them to retain without providing compensation; and

   (iii) **Unenforceability of Agreement**: *Restitution* usually requires evidence of an Unenforceable Agreement due to illegality, undue influence, unconscionable conduct, deception, misrepresentation, fraud, mistake, or other reasons, or when one party has breached the Agreement; or

   (iv) **Restitution as a Remedy**: *Restitution* can be a standalone remedy or sought in addition to other remedies, such as damages, specific performance, or rescission, depending on the circumstances of the case; and

   (v) **Exceptions and Defences**: The party against whom *Restitution* is sought may raise defences or exceptions to the remedy, such as arguing that they did not receive an unjust benefit of enrichment, or that the claimant has already been compensated, or that there was no misrepresentation, fraud or mistake.

Article 432 - Rescission

1595. ***Rescission*** is a legal remedy that allows a party to cancel or void a contract, restoring the parties to their pre-Agreement positions. It is typically invoked due to fraud, misrepresentation, duress, or other factors that render the Agreement unfair or unlawful. *Rescission* aims to undo the effects and obligations of the former Agreement, as if the Agreement had never existed.

Rescission

1596. The key elements of the legal remedy of Rescission in relation to Agreements includes (but is not limited to):-

Key elements of Rescission

(i) ***Grounds for Rescission***: *Rescission* is generally available in situations where there is a valid legal reason to cancel the Agreement such as Misrepresentation or Fraud, Mistake, Duress and Undue Influence, Illegality or Lack of Capacity; and

(ii) ***Notice***: The party seeking *Rescission* often needs to provide notice to the other party of their intention to rescind the Agreement. This notice should specify the grounds for *Rescission;* and

(iii) ***Timeliness***: Generally, the party directly seeking *Rescission*, rather than a form of relief as part of an overall action (e.g. Restitution), must act promptly and within a reasonable time after discovering the grounds for *Rescission*. Delay in seeking *Rescission* may affect the availability of the remedy; and

(iv) ***Restitution***: Upon *Rescission*, the parties are generally required to restore each other to their pre-Agreement positions, including returning any consideration received under the Agreement. This ensures that both parties are placed in the same position they were in before the Agreement was formed; and

(v) ***Third-Party Rights***: The rights of third parties who may have acquired interests in the Agreement could be affected by *Rescission*. Courts normally consider the impact on any such third parties when deciding whether (or not) to grant *Rescission*; and

(vi) ***Exceptions and Defences***: The party against whom *Rescission* is sought may raise defences or exceptions to the remedy, such as arguing that the Agreement should be upheld or that there was no misrepresentation or mistake, deception or fraud.

15.5 – False & Prohibited Agreements

Article 433 - False & Prohibited Agreements

1597. **False & Prohibited Agreements** are Agreements formed under false and prohibited conditions, or containing false information or operate under false and prohibited conditions. — False & Prohibited Agreements

1598. Agreements that contain one or more of any of the following are considered, false and prohibited and without force or effect in law:- — Examples of False and Prohibited Agreements

   (i)   Perfidy or Intentional Injury; or

   (ii)   Undue Influence or Unconscionability; or

   (iii) Misstatement or Misrepresentation; or

   (iv)   Omission or Concealment; or

   (v)   Frustration or Impossibility; or

   (vi)   Espionage or Sabotage; or

   (vii) Deception or Fraud; or

   (viii) Bribery or Corruption; or

   (ix)   Extortion or Unjust Enrichment; or

   (x)   Collusion or Restraint of Trade; or

   (xi)   Coercion or Duress.

1599. False & Prohibited Agreements are defective and voidable; and by their nature subject to Rescission within a competent Forum of Law. They represent some of the worst attempts to injure the law, given such False & Prohibited Agreements attempt to use the colour and cover of law for unlawful and often criminal offences. False & Prohibited Agreements may also cause the offending party to be criminally liable with the affected party able to receive damages. — False & Prohibited Agreements Subject to Rescission etc.

Article 434 - Agreements of Perfidy or Intentional Injury

1600. **Agreements of Perfidy or Intentional Injury** are false and prohibited Agreements where evidence exists of deliberate bad faith, betrayal or intentional harm and injury against one or more parties to an Agreement. — Agreements of Perfidy or Intentional Injury

1601. **Perfidy** refers to a deliberate and dishonest breach of trust or violation of the terms of the contract. It involves deceitful actions or misrepresentations by one party to gain an unfair advantage, leading to a breach of the agreement's fundamental principles of honesty and good faith. — Perfidy

1602. ***Intentional Injury*** refers to a deliberate and purposeful act by one party that causes harm or damage to the other party's rights or interests, typically violating the contractual obligation of good faith and fair dealing.

Intentional Injury

Article 435 – Agreements of Undue Influence or Unconscionability

1603. ***Agreements of Undue Influence or Unconscionability*** are false and prohibited Agreements where evidence exists of undue influence by a more powerful party or the inclusion of terms of unconscionable nature within an Agreement.

Agreements of Undue Influence or Unconscionabllity

1604. ***Undue Influence*** refers to a situation where one party exerts improper and unfair pressure or persuasion on another, causing them to enter into a contract against their free will or judgment.

Undue Influence

1605. ***Unconscionability*** signifies a contract that is so one-sided and oppressive that it shocks the conscience and fairness standards. Courts may deem such contracts unenforceable if one party had significantly more bargaining power, and the terms were unfairly favourable to them. This concept aims to protect parties from exploitation and unfairness in contracts.

Unconscionabllity

1606. Common examples of Agreements of Undue Influence and Unconscionability or Misrepresentation include (but are not limited to):-

Examples of Undue Influence or Unconscionabllity

   (i) ***Bank Account Agreements***: Many bank agreements are standard adhesion contracts, containing numerous unconscionable clauses allowing banks to freeze accounts, freeze transactions, raise costs and sell or transfer the data of their customers with little or no rights for the customer; and

   (ii) ***Home Loan Agreements***: Many home loan agreements are "boiler plate" adhesion contracts that allow lenders to seize and sell property at an unfair advantage in the event of a default by the borrower; and

   (iii) ***Utility (Energy & Water) Agreements***: Are another example of adhesion contracts, whereby many energy companies force customers to use proprietary "smart" equipment that increases costs and enables services to be more easily terminated; and

   (iv) ***Car Loan and Lease Agreements***: Many Car Loans charge higher than average interest rates, hidden costs and commissions and allow lenders to seize (repossess) cars even on a single missed payment with little or no recourse for the borrower; and

(v) ***Credit Card Agreements***: Most Credit Card agreements are the most notorious in history for unjust enrichment by charging hidden fees, allowing suppliers to charge hidden fees with little to no rights for the consumer.

Article 436- Agreements of Misstatement or Misrepresentation

1607. ***Agreements of Misstatement or Misrepresentation*** are false and prohibited Agreements where evidence exists of errors or mistakes of misstatement of facts or the deliberate misrepresentation of material information to one or more parties to an Agreement. — Agreements of Misstatement or Misrepresentation

1608. ***Misstatement*** refers to an inaccurate or false statement made by one party during negotiations or in the contract document. If the misstatement influences the other party's decision to enter into the contract and results in harm, legal remedies like rescission or damages may apply. The law aims to uphold truthfulness and integrity in contractual relationships. — Misstatement

1609. ***Misrepresentation*** refers to a false statement or omission of important information made by one party to induce the other party into a contract. When the misrepresentation is relied upon and causes harm, the injured party may seek legal remedies, such as contract rescission or damages. The concept seeks to ensure fairness and honesty in contractual dealings. — Misrepresentation

Article 437 – Agreements of Omission or Concealment

1610. ***Agreements of Omission or Concealment*** are false and prohibited Agreements where evidence exists of errors, mistakes or negligence of omission or the deliberate concealment of material information to one or more parties to an Agreement. — Agreements of Omission or Concealment

1611. ***Omission*** refers to the deliberate exclusion or failure to disclose important information by one party during negotiations or in a contract. If the omission is material and deceives the other party, it can lead to legal consequences, such as the contract being voided or damages awarded to the aggrieved party. This principle promotes transparency and fairness in contractual relationships — Omission

1612. ***Concealment*** refers to intentionally hiding or not disclosing crucial information by one party during negotiations or in a contract. When the concealed information is significant, and its omission deceives the other party, legal remedies like contract voidance or damages may be pursued. The aim is to maintain transparency and fairness in — Concealment contractual transactions.

Article 438 – Agreements of Frustration or Impossibility

1613. ***Agreements of Frustration or Impossibility*** are false and prohibited Agreements where evidence exists of deliberate frustration or the creation of impossible terms or conditions.   *Agreements of Frustration or Impossibility*

1614. ***Frustration*** occurs when unforeseen events render the contract impossible to perform, significantly altering its purpose or making it unlawful. In such cases, the contract may become void, releasing both parties from their obligations. Frustration applies when circumstances beyond the parties' control disrupt the contract's core objectives, making performance unreasonable or illegal.   *Frustration*

1615. ***Impossibility*** refers to a situation where it becomes objectively and entirely impossible for one party to fulfil their contractual obligations. This can result from events beyond their control, rendering performance utterly unattainable. In such cases, the affected party may be excused from their duties, and the contract may be discharged.   *Impossibility*

Article 439 – Agreements of Espionage or Sabotage

1616. ***Agreements of Espionage or Sabotage*** are false and prohibited Agreements where evidence exists of espionage or sabotage to the detriment of one or more parties to the Agreement.   *Agreements of Espionage or Sabotage*

1617. ***Espionage*** refers to the covert and unlawful act of gathering sensitive or classified information on behalf of a foreign government or entity, often for purposes of national security or economic advantage. It is illegal in most jurisdictions and can lead to severe criminal penalties for those engaged in espionage activities. Espionage is a violation of state or national laws and international agreements   *Espionage*

1618. ***Sabotage*** refers to intentional acts aimed at damaging or disrupting the normal operations of a business, organization or infrastructure. These actions may include vandalism, destruction of property, or interference with processes or equipment. Sabotage is typically illegal and can result in criminal charges, civil liability and significant penalties for those responsible. It violates laws and agreements related to property, safety, and security.   *Sabotage*

Article 440 – Agreements of Deception or Fraud

1619. ***Agreements of Deception or Fraud*** are false and prohibited Agreements where evidence exists of deception or fraud.

1620. ***Deception*** refers to intentionally misleading or tricking the other party through false statements, actions, or concealment of material facts during contract negotiations or performance. When deception leads to a contract being formed or harms the deceived party, it can render the contract voidable or result in legal remedies like damages. The principle aims to safeguard the integrity of contractual agreements.

1621. ***Fraud*** refers to a deliberate and deceptive act, involving false representations, concealment, or misleading statements made by one party with the intention of inducing the other party to enter into a contract. When fraud is proven, the contract may be voided, and the injured party can seek legal remedies such as damages. Fraudulent actions undermine the integrity of contractual relationships.

Article 441 – Agreements of Bribery or Corruption

1622. ***Agreements of Bribery or Corruption*** are false and prohibited Agreements where evidence exists of bribery or corruption.

1623. ***Bribery*** refers to the offering, giving, receiving, or soliciting of something of value with the intent to influence or manipulate the actions or decisions of a party to a contract. It is typically illegal and undermines fair and honest contractual dealings. Bribery can lead to criminal charges, civil liability, and contract nullification. It contravenes laws and ethical standards.

1624. ***Corruption*** refers to dishonest or illegal practices involving the misuse of power, authority, or influence to gain unfair advantages or benefits in contractual transactions. This can include bribery, embezzlement, and other unethical activities that compromise the integrity of agreements. Corruption is illegal and subject to both criminal and civil penalties, as well as contractual nullification.

Article 442 – Agreements of Extortion or Unjust Enrichment

1625. ***Agreements of Extortion or Unjust Enrichment*** are false and prohibited Agreements where evidence exists of extortion or plans or actual unjust enrichment.

1626. ***Extortion*** refers to the unlawful act of compelling someone to enter into a contract or perform specific actions through the use of threats, coercion or intimidation. It involves gaining an unfair advantage by instilling fear or duress in the other party. Extortion is illegal and can result in criminal charges, civil liability, and contract invalidation. It violates laws against coercion and unlawful influence.

1627. ***Unjust Enrichment*** refers to a situation where one party benefits unfairly at the expense of another, typically due to an absence of a valid contract. When this occurs, the party receiving the benefit may be required to compensate the disadvantaged party to restore fairness. It aims to prevent one party from profiting unfairly or without legal justification.

_{Unjust Enrichment}

Article 443 – Agreements of Collusion or Restraint of Trade

1628. ***Agreements of Collusion or Restraint of Trade*** are false and prohibited Agreements where evidence exists of Collusion in terms of artificial fixing of prices to control a market or restrain trade in a market.

_{Agreements of Collusion or Restraint of Trade}

1629. ***Collusion*** refers to a secret, unlawful agreement between two or more parties to manipulate or deceive others, often to gain an unfair advantage or distort competition. It is typically illegal and can lead to civil or criminal penalties. Collusion undermines fair and transparent contractual dealings and is subject to legal prohibition.

_{Collusion}

1630. ***Restraint of Trade*** refers to contractual clauses or agreements that limit a party's ability to engage in certain business activities or professions after the contract's termination. Such restrictions must be reasonable to be enforceable, and they aim to protect legitimate business interests while avoiding undue limitations on trade and competition. Violations of reasonable restraint of trade agreements may result in legal actions.

_{Restraint of Trade}

Article 444 – Agreements of Coercion or Duress

1631. ***Agreements of Coercion or Duress*** are false and prohibited Agreements where evidence exists of Coercion or Duress during the creation phase.

_{Agreements of Coercion or Duress}

1632. ***Coercion*** refers to the use of threats, force, or intimidation to compel someone to enter into a contract against their will. Contracts formed under coercion are typically considered voidable, as they lack genuine consent. Coercion undermines the voluntary nature of contractual agreements and may result in legal remedies such as contract annulment or damages.

_{Coercion}

1633. ***Duress*** refers to the use of threats, violence, or undue pressure to force someone into a contract, causing them to act against their free

_{Duress}

will. Contracts formed under duress are typically voidable, as they lack voluntary consent. Duress undermines the integrity of contractual agreements and may lead to legal remedies like contract annulment or damages.

Article 445 – Agreements of Criminal Enterprise

1634. ***Agreements of Criminal Enterprise*** are false and prohibited Agreements between criminal organisations for the purpose of furthering illegal and unlawful activities. Agreements of Criminal Enterprise

1635. Criminal Enterprise refers to an organized and ongoing criminal operation involving multiple individuals or entities collaborating in unlawful activities. These activities often include illegal businesses, such as drug trafficking, racketeering, or money laundering. Criminal enterprises are subject to criminal prosecution and severe penalties under the law, including asset forfeiture and imprisonment for those involved. Criminal Enterprise

Title XVI – Powers & Authority

16.1 – Authority

Article 446 – Authority

1636. ***Authority*** is a temporary or permanent Right of Office to do or act, or refrain from doing or acting in a way that they could not lawfully otherwise do:-

    (i)   All forms of valid and proper *Authority* are derived from the necessary acceptance and promise to perform one or more obligations in *relation* to a particular Office in *Bona Fidei* (Good Faith), *Bona Conscientia* (Good Conscience) and *Bona Acta* (Good Actions); and

    (ii)   All forms of valid temporary or permanent *Authority* are vested into an Office and not the Person. A "Power" in respect of an Agent is equivalent to an Authority to an Officer; and

    (iii)   All forms of valid temporary or permanent *Authority* must be unilaterally given or delegated without financial consideration or interest; and must be held and executed without financial consideration or interest; and

    (iv)   A permanent *Authority* is always donated into an Office, while a temporary *Authority* is always delegated into an Office; and

    (v)   The *Scope* of an Authority of Office is always limited and constrained by the Rights of the one giving or delegating the Right to the Office; and

    (vi)   In the absence of Good Faith, Good Conscience and Good Actions, an Officer holds no Authority or Power whatsoever.

[margin: Authority]

1637. The word authority comes from two (2) Latin words *auctor* and *ritus*:

    (i)   *Auctor* meaning "progenitor, founder of deeds, composer of writings, historian of knowledge, investigator, teacher, instigator of action, adviser of measures, promoter of laws, proposer of laws, supporter or ratifier of laws, person of influence in public life, leader of conduct, guarantor of witness, guarantor of bail, seller of property, guardian of minors or champion of others"; and

    (ii)   *Ritus* meaning "ecclesiastical ritual or ceremony, custom, right of usage (property)".

[margin: Origin of word Authority]

1638. In reference to the key elements of *Authority*:-

    (i)   All Authority concerns Rights and is ultimately derived through the inheritance of Rights from the Divine Right of *Ius*

[margin: Key Elements of Authority]

Lex Positivum: Maxims of Positive Law

> *Divinum*, in accord with the most sacred Covenant *Pactum De Singularis Caelum*; and
>
> (ii) There is no such thing as an *Authority* that is not derived from a Right. Any such claim to the contrary is an absurdity and falsity of law; and
>
> (iii) In the absence of a properly defined Right as inherited from *Ius Divinum*, in accord with the most sacred Covenant *Pactum De Singularis Caelum*, no proper and valid Right of *Authority* exists; and
>
> (iv) The Scope of a proper and valid Right of Authority of an Officer can never exceed the scope of the Authority of the one that gifted, granted, assigned or delegated it; and
>
> (v) Similar to every proper and valid Right, a Right of Authority must be accepted, held and executed in *Bona Fidei* (Good Faith), *Bona Conscientia* (Good Conscience) and *Bona Acta* (Good Actions); and
>
> (vi) A Right of *Authority* normally carries the ancillary Right of Immunity when an Officer or Agent performs their obligations in *Good Faith, Good Conscience* and *Good Actions*; and
>
> (vii) In the absence of *Good Faith, Good Conscience* and *Good Actions*, an Officer holds no Authority and has no Immunity whatsoever.

1639. All Authority is by definition limited in Scope and may be defined into six (6) levels consistent with the structure of Rights under the most sacred Covenant *Pactum De Singularis Caelum*, being:- Levels and Scope of Authority

> (i) **Ius Divinum** (Divine Rights) being the highest Rights and the highest Authority; and
>
> (ii) **Ius Naturale** (Natural Rights) being the second highest Rights and the second highest Authority; and
>
> (iii) **Ius Ecclesiae** (Ecclesiastical Rights) being the third highest Rights and third highest Authority; and
>
> (iv) **Ius Regnum** (Sovereign Rights) being the fourth highest Rights and fourth highest Authority; and
>
> (v) **Ius Publicum** (Official Public Rights) being the fifth highest Rights and fifth highest Authority; and
>
> (vi) **Ius Administrationis** (Administrative Rights) being the sixth highest Rights and sixth highest Authority.

1640. The Primary Maxims of Authority consistent with the most sacred Primary Maxims of Authority

Covenant *Pactum De Singularis Caelum*, are:-

(i) **Divina Summa Iustitia** means "The Divine is the Highest Right (Authority); and

(ii) **Ius Ecclesiae Non Maior Divina** means "The Right of the Church is not Greater than the Divine"; and

(iii) **Ius Regnum Non Maior Ecclesiae** means "The Right of the Sovereign (Kingdom) is not Greater than the Church"; and

(iv) **Ius Publicum Non Maior Regnum** means "Public Rights are not Greater than the Sovereign (Kingdom)"; and

(v) **Ius Administrationis Non Maior Publicum** means "The Right of (Public) Administration is not Greater than the Public"; and

(vi) **Princeps Non Delegare Ius Maius Quam Habet** means "A Principal cannot Delegate a Greater Right than they have"; and

(vii) **Ius Agentis Non Maior Principis** means "The Right of the Agent is not Greater than that of the Principal".

1641. There exists multiple levels and functions of Administrative Authority essential for the function of a Civilised Society, being:

(i) **Administrative Authority**: In administrative law, authority often refers to the power and jurisdiction of government agencies and administrative bodies. These agencies are granted authority to make and enforce rules and regulations within their specified areas of responsibility; and

(ii) **Judicial Authority**: This refers to the power and jurisdiction of courts and judges to interpret and apply the law, make legal decisions, and render judgments. Judicial authority is essential for the administration of justice; and

(iii) **Police Authority**: Police officers and law enforcement agencies have the authority to enforce laws, investigate crimes, and make arrests. Their authority is derived from the laws and regulations of their jurisdiction.

1642. Authority is always vested into an Office and not to the Person occupying an Office.

1643. Once Authority is legitimately vested, an Officer is said to have a mandate. The Officer may then grant temporary commissions of authority to others called delegation. However, an officer may not delegate the same authority to the same place at the same time, except with all such temporary commissions requiring an expiry date within the scope of the delegating Officers mandate.

1644. As Authority is by definition ultimately Divine Property, an Officer vested into Office can only exercise the Authority granted by such Office if they remain in Honour under Oath in Good Faith, Good Conscience and Good Action. As soon as they are in dishonour or bad faith or fail to abide by their sacred oath, their dishonour immediately prevents any Authority being present in their actions. This is called "Excommunication from Office" and is an automatic Divine Action. *[Officers Authority]*

1645. There is no such thing as supreme secular Authority nor any other claimed form of legitimate Authority except through Divine Right. Therefore all claims of Authority that denounce Ecclesiastical and Divine source, or the obligation of honour, duty and oath is an absurdity of law and without validity, therefore null and void from the beginning. *[No legitimate Authority than through Divine Right]*

1646. By definition, any Official who refuses to produce their oath and be bound by it, have no Authority. *[Refusal of Oath voids Authority]*

1647. *Implied Authority* is a concept in agency law of certain Non-Ucadia Jurisdictions that allows an Agent to take actions on behalf of a Principal that are not explicitly mentioned in the agency agreement but are considered "reasonably necessary" to carry out the agent's express authority or to fulfil the principal's expectations. Implied Authority is forbidden under Ucadia Law and Jurisdiction. *[Concept of Implied Authority]*

1648. While *Implied Authority* may first appear a useful legal principle, it is ripe for abuse, including (but not limited to):- *[Why Concept of Implied Authority is False & Prohibited]*

    (i) **Lack of Clarity**: Implied Authority can be vague and lack the clarity of express authority. Because it relies on what is "reasonably necessary," determining the scope of implied authority can be subjective and may lead to disputes; and

    (ii) **Potential for Abuse**: In some cases, agents might overreach their authority by claiming that certain actions were reasonably necessary when they may not have been. This can lead to disputes and concerns about abuse of implied authority; and

    (iii) **Inconsistent Application**: The application of implied authority can vary from one case to another, leading to inconsistencies in legal decisions. What one court considers reasonable and necessary in a particular context may differ from another court's interpretation; and

    (iv) **Unauthorized Actions**: Implied authority can result in agents taking actions that the principal did not intend or want to be taken. This can lead to unintended consequences and harm the principal's interests; and

(v) **Risk for Principals**: Principals may be exposed to legal liability for actions taken by their agents under the concept of implied authority, even if they did not expressly authorize those actions. This can be seen as a risk for principals who may not have intended to be bound by certain actions.

16.2 – Power

Article 447 – Power

1649. *Power* is a temporary or permanent *Right* of Authority of an Agent, conveyed to them by a Principal, that enables the Agent to do or act, or refrain from doing or acting in a way that they could not lawfully otherwise do:-

(i) All forms of valid and proper *Powers* are derived from the necessary acceptance and promise to perform one or more obligations in *Bona Fidei* (Good Faith), *Bona Conscientia* (Good Conscience) and *Bona Acta* (Good Actions) creating an Agency; and

(ii) All forms of valid temporary or permanent *Power* when accepted and performed in Good Faith, Good Conscience and Good Action, are held in an Agency and not by the Person as Agent. A valid *Power* can never be given, or accepted or performed in Bad Faith, or Bad Conscience or Bad Action; and

(iii) All forms of valid temporary or permanent *Power* must be unilaterally given or delegated by the Principal without financial consideration or interest; and must be held and executed without financial consideration or interest; and

(iv) A permanent *Power* is always donated to an Agency, while a temporary *Power* is always delegated to an Agency. However, unlike an Authority to an Office, any permanent *Power* must be fully revocable, as there is no such valid concept in Civilised Law as an "irrevocable power"; and

(v) The *Scope* of any *Power* is always limited and constrained by the Rights of the Principal giving or delegating the Right; and

(vi) In the absence of Good Faith, Good Conscience and Good Actions, an Agent has no Agency and holds no Power whatsoever.

1650. All Powers are inherently revocable by their very nature, while a

Principal still holds Legal Capacity:- — *revocable while Principal holds Legal Capacity*

(i) Even if a Legal Instrument is executed to appoint an Agent to one or more permanent Powers, also known as enduring powers, a Principal always holds the absolute and unfettered right to be able to revoke in writing such a grant of Powers; and

(ii) So long as a Principal retains Legal Capacity and Sound Mind, they have the right to revoke in writing any and all agreements of Powers in respect of one or more Agents; and

(iii) While an Agent may request more time or process be permitted in the winding up of an Agency, no Agent has any right whatsoever to deny, obstruct or repudiate a properly executed revocation of a Power.

1651. Any notion or claim that a Power may be granted irrevocably, or with certain interest that prevents its revocation is a profound corruption, injury and falsity against Civilised Law and absolutely prohibited under Ucadia Law:- — *Irrevocable Powers are false and nullify validity of Power from beginning*

(i) The claim of irrevocability contradicts the very nature of Fiduciary Duty and the valid formation of an Agency in the first instance. Any claim or inclusion of clauses giving effect to irrevocability in an instrument seeking to grant one or more Powers nullifies and invalidates any such Authority from the beginning; and

(ii) Any claimed forum of law that permits the corruption of the notion of Fiduciary Duty by permitting the enforcement of claims of irrevocability cannot then credibly be a court of law under Civilised Law; and

(iii) Any additional claim that an agreement cannot be revoked because an Agent was granted an interest in the Power transferred to them is a profound example of corruption, conflict of interest and criminal behaviour. If such claims and clauses are endorsed or permitted by a Non-Ucadia Jurisdiction, then such an action declares no proper rule of law exists.

1652. A Permanent Power, also known as an Enduring Power can still be revoked even after the Principal no longer holds Legal Capacity:- — *Permanent Powers can be revoked for Bad Faith even if Principal no longer holds Legal Capacity*

(i) If the Agent ceases to perform their Fiduciary Duties in Good Faith, Good Conscience and Good Actions; and

(ii) If an Action of Revocation of Powers is brought by a trusted friend or family member of the Person against the actions of the Agent.

1653. Whilst the term *Power* has a narrow and specific meaning, since the 20th Century the term *Powers* commonly refers to a much broader meaning as the authority or rights granted to an individual, entity, or government body to perform certain actions or make specific decisions within the framework of the law:-

    Power and General Notion of Powers

- (i) Regardless of the narrow or broader meaning of *Power* or *Powers*, all legitimate and valid Powers are derived from proper Authority being a Right, not the other way around; and

- (ii) The confusion of meanings concerning *Powers* across Non-Ucadia Societies is the consequence of a deliberate strategy from the 1920's beginning with the Law of Property Act 1922 (12&13 Geo5 c.16) and then the Law of Property Act 1925 (15 Geo5 c.20) to create a form of "pseudo-rights" capable of being used in potential bad faith, without the constraints of good conscience and action associated with trusts and rights; and enabling agents to claim "irrevocable" powers and interests in the very property they are supposed to manage at arms length; and

- (iii) The consequence of this deliberate strategy by Non-Ucadia governments and their officials has been the continuous and accelerating breakdown in property and agreement law.

1654. In reference to the key elements of a *Power*:-

    Key Elements of Power

- (i) All *Powers* concerns Rights and are ultimately derived through the inheritance of Rights from the Divine Right of *Ius Divinum*, in accord with the most sacred Covenant *Pactum De Singularis Caelum*; and

- (ii) There is no such thing as a *Power* that is not derived from a Right. Nor can a *Power* exist unless it has been given or delegated to an Agent by an authorised Principal. Any such claims to the contrary is an absurdity and falsity of law; and

- (iii) In the absence of a properly defined Right as inherited from *Ius Divinum*, in accord with the most sacred Covenant *Pactum De Singularis Caelum*, no proper and valid *Power* exists; and

- (iv) The Scope of a proper and valid *Power* of an Agent through their Agency can never exceed the scope of the Authority of the Principal that gifted or delegated it; and

- (v) Similar to every proper and valid Right, a *Power* must be accepted, held and executed in *Bona Fidei* (Good Faith), *Bona Conscientia* (Good Conscience) and *Bona Acta* (Good Actions); and

(vi) Unlike Authority of an Office, a valid Power can never carry the Right of Immunity, only the Promise of Indemnity being a form of Assurance or Insurance, contingent on the Agent performing their obligations in *Good Faith, Good Conscience* and *Good Actions*. There is no such thing in Civilised Law as Indemnity for *Bad Faith, Bad Conscience or Bad Actions*; and

(vii) In the absence of *Good Faith, Good Conscience* and *Good Actions*, an Agent holds no Authority and has no Indemnity whatsoever.

1655. When a *Power* is conferred without specific conditions, it is said to be a **General Power**; and when a Power is conferred with certain terms and conditions is it said to be a **Special Power**:-

General Powers and Special Powers

(i) **General Power**: Refers to a broad and comprehensive authority granted to a Person to manage or make decisions regarding certain matters. A General Power is all-encompassing and provides the Agent with broad control or discretion over specific actions. It allows the Agent to exercise authority without significant restrictions; and

(ii) **Special Power**: Refers to a specific and limited authority or permission granted to a Person to perform certain actions or make particular decisions within a defined scope. A Special Power is restricted in its scope and applicability. It only authorizes the Agent to exercise authority over specific matters or actions as defined in the legal document granting the Power.

1656. There is no such thing in Civilised Law or Ucadia Law as an *Implied Power*. Therefore any claim of Authority by virtue of an Implied Power is false and prohibited.

No such thing in Civilised Law as an Implied Power

16.3 – Powers Creation

Article 448 – Powers Creation

1657. A proper and legitimate *Power* is created from the conveyance of a temporary or permanent *Right* of Authority by a Principal to an *Agency* of an Agent through a valid legal instrument of proper form:-

Powers Creation

(i) A proper and legitimate *Power* must always be created in writing and can never be verbally expressed or implied from a Principal to an Agent; and any such claim in law is false and without force or effect under Civilised Law; and

(ii) There is no such thing as an Implied Power or a *Power* being legitimately conveyed via an Implied Contract. Both such claims are absurdities, falsities and corruptions of Civilised Law; and

(iii) An *Agency* of an Agent is a temporary Office created and bound by the original Fiduciary Duty owed to the Principal through the legal instrument that first conveyed the Right. Thus, under Civilised Law an Agency (and therefore an Agent) is not transferable or conveyable to another as property as any such transaction would necessarily dissolve the original Fiduciary Duty and thus the Agency itself. However, nothing precludes a bona fide Agent from appointing one or more Sub-Agents under the same terms and conditions of the Agency.

1658. A *Power* can never be created as a Right of Title over Property, only ever a Right of Use. Any claimed Power effectively as Title or part ownership is false, absurd and prohibited under Civilised Law.

<small>Power can never create Right of Title</small>

1659. A *Power* can never be legitimately or validly created by argument of an Implied Contract. Such a claim or assertion is an abuse of law and absolutely prohibited under Ucadia Law and those societies that operate under Civilised Rule of Law.

<small>Power Cannot be Created by Implied Contract</small>

1660. The key elements of creating a valid and legitimate *Power* include (but are not limited to):-

<small>Key Elements of Creation of Power</small>

(i) ***Capacity of Principal***: That the Principal must be of sound mind and have the legal capacity to be able to transfer a Right to create a Power; and

(ii) ***Authority of Principal***: That the Principal legitimately and lawfully possesses the particular Right that is the Authority to be transferred and created as a Power; and

(iii) ***Full Disclosure and Declaration of Principal***: That the Principal fully understands and has declared in writing their understanding of the implication of appointing the Agent under the particular proper form of Legal Instrument; and the scope of the Power being temporarily or permanently transferred; and

(iv) ***Proper Form of Legal Instrument***: That the proper form of legal instrument is used for the appropriate creation of the Power; and

(v) ***Nature of Power(s)***: That the Legal Instrument makes clear whether the Power (or Powers) are enduring meaning they may exist beyond the capacity of the Principal, or limited meaning they will cease when the capacity or authority of the Principal ceases; and

(vi) ***Capacity of Agent***: That the Agent must be of sound mind and have the legal capacity to be able to perform their duties as an Agent; and

(vii) **Full Disclosure and Declaration of Agent**: That the Agent fully understands and has declared in Good Faith, Good Conscience and Good Actions their understanding in writing of the implication of being bound by Fiduciary Duty as an Agent under the particular proper form of Legal Instrument; and the scope of the Power being temporarily or permanently transferred to them; and

(viii) **Witness and Notarisation**: That in some jurisdictions, the proper Form must be witnessed and signed; and that this may also include notarisation; and

(ix) **Notice and Revocation of Previous Agent Powers**: In most jurisdictions, proper Notice is required to be sent revoking any previous Agent Powers that relate to the new Agent Powers; and

(x) **Registration**: That in many jurisdictions, a Power is only effective once it has been registered with the proper government departments.

1661. A Power cannot be legitimately or validly created where a document claims or implies that one of more Powers shall be irrevocable or that the Agent shall be granted some form of interest in property or rights associated with the Power:- A Power Cannot be Created with claim of Irrevocability or Agent Interest

(i) Clauses that state a Power may be enduring, or lasting or durable does not in anyway infer or mean irrevocability. Instead, irrevocability means that the principal is somehow prevented from revoking the grant of one or more Powers transferred to an Agency in Good Faith, Good Conscience and Good Action; and

(ii) Irrevocability is an absurdity and falsity in law and prohibited under Ucadia Jurisdictions and those Jurisdictions that respect and function under Civilised Rule of Law; and

(iii) The claim or assumption that an Agent may be granted some interest in the very property or rights they are supposed to administer is in complete contradiction to the inherit concept of Powers, as a valid valid temporary or permanent *Power* must be unilaterally given or delegated by the Principal without financial consideration or interest to the Agent; and must be held and executed by the Agent without financial consideration or interest.

1662. Examples of Proper Forms of Legal Instruments for the Transfer of   Examples of Proper Forms

Authority and creation of Powers includes (but is not limited to):- *of Legal Instruments for Powers*

(i) **_Deed of Power of Attorney_**: A Power of Attorney is a legal instrument that allows one person (the principal as donor) to grant authority to another person (the attorney or agent) to act on their behalf. A Power of Attorney can be broad or limited in scope, and they can cover various matters, such as financial, healthcare, or specific transactions; and

(ii) **_Guardianship or Conservatorship Order_**: Is a legal instrument issued by a court as an order in cases where a person is unable to manage their affairs due to incapacity. The court order appoints a guardian or conservator who is then granted legal authority by the court order to make decisions on the person's behalf; and

(iii) **_Letters Patent_**: Is a formal legal instrument usually issued by a Sovereign Authority in the appointment of senior agents such as an Attorney General or Governor General; and

(iv) **_Letters of Administration or Letters Testamentary_**: Is a legal instrument issued by a court as a letter of authority in probate cases and grants authority to an executor or administrator to manage the affairs of a deceased person's estate. **_Letters of Administration_** are typically used when there is no will, while **_Letters Testamentary_** are used when there is a valid will; and

(v) **_Letter of Authorisation_**: Is a simple written document that grants limited authority to an individual or organisation to perform specific actions on behalf of the authorising party. It is often used for one-time or short-term purposes; and

(vi) **_Letter of Appointment_**: Is a formal document issued by an organization, entity, or individual to formally offer and confirm someone's appointment to a specific position, role, or task. It typically outlines the details of the appointment, including the person's name, the position or role they are being appointed to, the effective date of the appointment, and any specific terms or conditions associated with the appointment; and

(vii) **_Corporate Resolutions and Agency Agreements_**: Is a resolution adopted by the board of directors or shareholders that creates an Authority; and then the associated agreement that establishes the relationship and powers of an agent representing the corporation as principal. Examples include banking authority, legal authority, sales or distribution representation; and

(viii) **Mandate or Direct Debit Authorisation**: Is a simple written document that grants a financial institution or service provider the authority to automatically debit funds from an individual's bank account for specified payments, such as loan repayments or utility bills; and

(ix) **Beneficiary Designation Form**: Is a form that allows the account holder to name a beneficiary who will receive the assets or benefits upon the account holder's death. It conveys the right to inherit or receive these assets; and

(x) **Authorization for Release of Information**: Is a form that grants permission for one party to share specific information or records with another party, such as medical records, employment records or educational records.

Article 449 – Power of Attorney

1663. *Power of Attorney* or *Powers of Attorney* is a formal legal instrument that grants one Person (the *Agent* or **Attorney**) the authority to act on behalf of another Person (the *Principal*) in specific or general legal, financial, health or other personal matters.

Power of Attorney

1664. Key elements of Power of Attorney include (but are not limited to):-

Key Elements of Power of Attorney

(i) **No Personal Gain or Financial Advantage**: A Power of Attorney is only valid and legal under Civilised Law when the Agent receives no personal gain or financial advantage from it – hence the one who accepts the role of Attorney is a pure Fiduciary and that such transactions must be done in full disclosure, without coercion, or inducement, or threat or promise in good faith, good conscience and good actions; and

(ii) **General or Special Powers**: A Power of Attorney agreement may grant broad powers to the Agent (**General**), or specific and limited powers (**Special**) but not both; and

(iii) **Enduring (Durable or Lasting) or Limited (Temporary or Ordinary)**: A Power of Attorney agreement may be **Enduring** even when the Principal is unable to make choices any more of their own, or **Limited** meaning the Power of Attorney expires when the capacity and authority of the Principal expires.

1665. Types of Power of Attorney (POA) Agreements include (but are not limited to):-

Types of Powers of Attorney Agreements

(i) **Enduring Power of Attorney (EPA)**: An Enduring Power of Attorney is a specific type of POA that remains in effect even if the principal becomes mentally incapacitated. It is often used for long-term financial or healthcare decision-making; and

(ii) ***Durable Power of Attorney for Healthcare or Healthcare Proxy***: This document grants an agent the authority to make medical decisions on behalf of the principal if the principal is unable to make healthcare choices. It is commonly used for end-of-life care and medical treatment decisions; and

(iii) ***Advance Healthcare Directive or Living Will***: An Advance Healthcare Directive allows an individual to specify their healthcare preferences, including end-of-life decisions, in advance. It often designates a healthcare agent to make decisions in accordance with the individual's wishes if they become unable to communicate their preferences; and

(iv) ***General Power of Attorney***: A General Power of Attorney grants broad authority to the agent to act on the principal's behalf in various financial and legal matters; and

(v) ***Special Power of Attorney***: A Special Power of Attorney is similar to a Limited POA and grants the agent authority for specific, limited purposes. It is often used for situations like real estate transactions or handling specific legal matters.

Article 450 – Attorney

1666. An *Attorney* is an duly appointed Agent, authorised to act on behalf of another Person (the *Principal*) in specific or general legal, financial, health or other personal matters, in accord with the laws of the relevant jurisdiction. — Attorney

1667. The word *Attorney* originates in the 8th Century as *Attíornaí* (Attiorné in Anglaise) under the creation of modern Western Civilisation (Anglo-Saxon Law and the Catholic Church) by the Holly Carolingians and Irish Scholars meaning literally "to be together with the young, vulnerable and innocent through a test of heat or fire (of law)":- — Origin of Meaning of Attorney

(i) The word *Attorney* originally comes directly from the ancient pre-8th Century Holly Irish legal word *Attíornaí* from *at* meaning "with, together", *tíor* meaning "test of heat or fire" and *naí* meaning young, innocent or vulnerable". Under Holly Irish Law, a person incapable of defending themselves against an accusation was entitled to an advocate of law called an *Attíornaí* who was then solemnly bound to guide them through the trials and tribulations of law; and

(ii) When first forming modern Western Civilisation in the 8th Century, the Anglaise (Old French) word of Attiorné was created in honour of the ancient Irish legal practice of providing a legal advocate for the young, vulnerable and ignorant of law procedure; and

(iii) The claim that the word Attorney is derived from Latin is absurd as the prefix "at" does not exist and the combination of a+tornos produces the nonsensical meaning of "not a lathe". Hence most credible dictionaries accept the origin of the word from Old French and no longer try to argue a Latin connection; and

(iv) The use of Attorneys under Anglo-Saxon Law persisted until the great death from 1300s that saw more than 85% of the population of Europe, North Africa, Middle East and Asia Minor die from the return of Haemorrhagic Fever; and

(v) The claim that a person called Laurence Del Brok was the earliest "attorney of the crown of England" in 1243 is a complete falsity and absurdity as the Venetian City states had no interest in Anglo-Saxon Law or the Rule of Law in general until 1660 and the seizure of England back from the democratic nation known as the Commonwealth of Great Britain (1641-1660 but 1706 in Scotland); and

(vi) The first credible presence of representatives or agents of law returning to English law was the 17th Century word **Lawyer**, from *lawe* (law) and *yere* (belongs, belonging to me) meaning "one versed in law, one whose profession is suits in court" and **Solicitor** from Latin *solicito* meaning "one who manages the business of another"; and

(vii) In the 18th Century in England and the reintroduction of local common courts through Alehouses, a new common law position was created of **Barrister** from common Gaelic barro (mud, waste) and stere (control, guide) meaning literally "one who controls (guides) the waste"; and

(viii) In 1843 (6&7 Vict. c.73) the UK laws of Attorneys and Solicitors were consolidated under major changes that required for the first time that a person be "admitted and enrolled or otherwise duly qualified to act as an Attorney or Solicitor". In 1877 (40&41 Vict. c.25), the Private Law Guild(s) were granted the exclusive power of first examination if a person be suitable to be admitted; and by 1888 (51&52 Vict. c.65) the public courts were effectively "privatized" by granting custody and control of the rolls of Attorneys and Solicitors to the Private Law Guild(s); and

(ix) In the second half of the 19th Century, the role of Attorney finally started to appear more frequently across acts of parliament culminating in creation of the first Powers of Attorney Act 1882 (45 & 46 Vict. c. 75), while the function of the Attorney General changed to being "the only legal representative of the crown in the courts; and principal counsel of the crown"; and

(x) In the 20th Century, the Law of Property Act 1922 (12&13 Geo5 c.16) and then the Law of Property Act 1925 (15 Geo5 c.20), place the concept of Powers and Attorneys as central elements to the revisions to laws of estates and property. Today, the concept of Powers of Attorney is present in the laws of virtually every country, in international law and virtually all key legal and property contracts; and

(xi) Several Acts and Statutes of different countries refer to Powers of Attorney (e.g. UK Powers of Attorney Act 1971) in the plural, while modern legal dictionaries and documents refer to it in the singular as "Power of Attorney". The difference appears more than cosmetic as a Powers of Attorney document implies more than one power, whereas Power of Attorney in the singular, infers only a single power. This appears to be the most common form.

1668. Consistent with the origin of the laws of modern Western Civilisation (Anglo-Saxon Law and the Catholic Church) since the 8th Century, Ucadia shall permit the enrolment to Ucadia Courts of suitably qualified and competent Persons as Attorneys and other Offices:- *Special Guardian Attorney*

(i) A Person not properly certified and enrolled as an Attorney under Ucadia Law, shall be culpable of a serious criminal offence should they seek to be employed in representing or advising or practising matters of law under Ucadia Law, Forms, Knowledge and Procedures. At all times, Ucadia entities, bodies and persons shall have the right to fully indemnify and notify Non-Ucadia jurisdictions and authorities of any person suspected of such criminal offences both under Ucadia Laws and Non-Ucadia Laws; and

(ii) At all times, a competent and certified and enrolled Ucadia Attorney or Ucadia Law Officer shall possess the unquestionable rights to represent, advise or practice matters of law under all forms of Civilised Law; and for various Private Bar Guilds, Justices and Law Officers of Non-Ucadia Jurisdictions to recognise such rights without controversy.

16.4 – False, Absurd & Prohibited Powers

Article 451 – False, Absurd & Prohibited Powers

1669. ***False, Absurd & Prohibited Powers*** are claimed or asserted *Powers* that are false or absurd in their claim or assertion and therefore prohibited under Ucadia Law and Civilised Law.

False, Absurd & Prohibited Powers

1670. By definition a Power of Attorney Clause in a contract can only ever be a claim, even if such a contract states it to be "irrevocable" and "enduring". Similar to any contract containing unreasonable, unconscionable, or impossible clauses and any associated misleading, coercive, malicious, vexatious or false behaviour, it is up to the aggrieved party to point out the wrong-doing and have it set aside in a competent forum of law. In most cases, even though such contracts may be fraudulent and unconscionable, through the participation of the other party, their default and the court process is sufficient to exonerate any such errors and perfect the Claim into a Right. This is the case with many unconscionable contracts such as the action by finance companies of Foreclosure or Credit Card Default actions.

Power of Attorney Clauses

Title XVII – Jurisdiction

17.1 – Jurisdiction

Article 452 – Jurisdiction

1671. ***Jurisdiction*** refers to the Authority of a court or other government entity to review legal matters, make legal decisions and enforce the law of a given Body Politic and Corporate or Civilised Society. — Jurisdiction

1672. The word *Jurisdiction* comes from combing two (2) ancient Latin words *iuro* meaning "to make an oath" and *dicio* meaning "power, influence, authority of word; to speak, to argue". Therefore, Jurisdiction by definition is dependent upon the making of a sacred oath associated with speech or argument first before "some authority or power capable of determining the validity of such speech or argument". — Origin of word Jurisdiction

1673. ***Ucadia is judged by no one***. Ucadia Law is judged by Ucadia and its duly appointed Officers and Agents and no one else. — Ucadia has no judge

1674. Under Ucadia Law, all duly registered Ucadia Entities, Bodies, Corporations and Societies possessing proper mandate shall have jurisdiction concerning Ucadia Law. — Absolute Jurisdiction

1675. The key elements in law concerning *Jurisdiction* include (but are not limited to):- — Key elements of Jurisdiction

    (i) ***Authority***: Jurisdiction is based on the authority of a court or government entity to exercise legal power over a particular matter or dispute. This authority is typically derived from constitutions, statutes, regulations, or other legal sources that define the jurisdictional scope of the entity; and

    (ii) ***Territorial Limits***: Territorial Jurisdiction defines the geographic boundaries whereby a court or government entity may exercise its authority. Courts are typically limited to hearing cases that arise within their territorial jurisdictional boundaries, whether at the local, regional, national or international level; and

    (iii) ***Subject Matter***: Subject Matter Jurisdiction refers to the authority of a court to hear cases involving specific types of legal issues or subject matters. Courts are typically classified based on the types of cases they have the authority to handle. For example, family courts have jurisdiction over family law matters, while criminal courts have subject matter jurisdiction over criminal cases; and

    (iv) ***Personal Jurisdiction***: Personal Jurisdiction concerns the authority of a court over the persons involved in a case. Courts must have the legal authority over the persons to compel individuals or entities to appear before them and be subject to their rulings. Personal Jurisdiction is often based on factors such as residency, physical presence, or minimum contacts within the jurisdiction; and

(v) **Consent**: In almost all cases, the valid consent of the parties is considered essential for a court to proceed on a legal matter. If consent is not granted, then a court typically must prove consent has been granted or may be implied by other legal means and arguments.

1676. A valid and proper court must secure **Perfected Jurisdiction**, being Personal Jurisdiction, Subject Matter Jurisdiction and Territorial Jurisdiction to have any authority to review, judge or enforce a matter of law:-

[margin: Perfected Jurisdiction]

(i) *Personal Jurisdiction* is typically claimed through consent or through *lex situs* as "laws of the place where the property is situated" over a Person. Once perfected, a court is said to have *jus in rem* being "right against some property or thing" and *jus in personam* being "right against a person". Ucadia courts have *Personal Jurisdiction* over all Persons, Property and Things, whereas Non-Ucadia courts only have *Personal Jurisdiction* over Non-Ucadia Persons, Property and Things; and

(ii) *Subject Matter Jurisdiction* is usually claimed once *jus in rem* and *jus in personam* are perfected through *lex specialis* being "laws governing a specific subject matter" over the subject of the legal questions involved; and

(iii) *Territorial Jurisdiction* is usually claimed through *jus gentium* as "law of nations" and *lex loci* meaning "laws of the place" confined to a bounded space, including all those Persons, Property and Things residing therein and any events which occur there. Once *jus in rem* and *jus in personam* are perfected, Territorial Jurisdiction is assumed perfected.

1677. No Non-Ucadia Court shall hold any proper or valid authority or power of Personal Jurisdiction whatsoever over a Ucadia Person, unless written permission from an authorised Ucadia Official is granted on a case by case basis:-

[margin: No Personal Jurisdiction of Non-Ucadia Courts over Ucadia Persons without permission]

(i) At all times, a competent, certified and enrolled Ucadia Attorney or Ucadia Law Officer shall possess the unquestionable rights to appear for any form of Person under all forms of Civilised Law; and for various Private Bar Guilds,

Justices and Law Officers of Non-Ucadia Jurisdictions to recognise such rights without controversy; and

(ii) Should a competent, certified and enrolled Ucadia Attorney or Ucadia Law Officer appear for a Person, Property or Thing in a Non-Ucadia court, the respectful recognition and any necessary enrolment and certifications shall therefore signify an agreement Personal Jurisdiction concerning the conduct of the Ucadia Official and any Persons they represent; and

(iii) In the absence of respectful agreement or recognition of a competent, certified and enrolled Ucadia Official, a competent and duly registered Ucadia Person may at any time give notice of Appearance and Appear in any Non-Ucadia court, forum or setting in relation to any directly related Non-Ucadia Person, Property or Thing not otherwise concerning an alleged serious criminal offence carrying a penalty of greater than ten years imprisonment.

1678. Common Issues concerning *Jurisdiction* include (but are not limited to):-

Common Issues Concerning Jurisdiction

(i) **Consent Challenges**: Many parties in legal matters mistakenly assume that Consent can only be achieved by their tacit and willing approval and not by other established legal means and arguments. In Criminal Cases, Consent in Non-Ucadia courts is often given under the authority of Guardian Laws by the Magistrate or Judge in their capacity both Custodian and Guardian over a belligerent "infant". However, in Civil Cases, clear and willing Consent by all parties is still seen as fundamental; and

(ii) ***Jurisdictional Challenges***: Parties in a legal dispute may raise jurisdictional challenges to contest the authority of the court to hear the case. These challenges can involve questions about whether the court has proper subject matter jurisdiction or personal jurisdiction over the parties, or whether it is the appropriate forum to resolve the dispute; and

(iii) ***Waiver of Jurisdiction***: In some cases, parties may voluntarily waive objections to jurisdiction, allowing a court to hear their dispute even if it would not ordinarily have jurisdiction; and

(iv) **Forum Selection Clauses**: Contracts and agreements often include forum selection clauses that specify which court or jurisdiction will have the authority to hear disputes related to the contract. These clauses can be enforceable if they meet certain legal criteria.

1679. By definition, any Official who refuses to produce access to their public record of oath and be bound by it, has no Jurisdiction. — Refusal to produce oath

Article 453 - Personal Jurisdiction

1680. *Personal Jurisdiction* refers to a court's authority over the parties involved in a legal dispute. It determines whether a court can assert its authority over a particular individual or entity. Personal jurisdiction can be based on factors such as residency, location of business operations, or the defendant's contacts with the jurisdiction where the court is located. — Personal Jurisdiction

1681. *Jus in Rem* is Latin for "right against a thing" and according to Non-Ucadia Law means "a claim of right enforceable against anyone in the world interfering with that claim founded on some specific relationship, status or particular property accorded legal protection from interference by anyone". Thus, when *Jus in Rem* is repudiated by appearance of a Ucadia Person under Ucadia Law, *Jus in Rem* of a Non-Ucadia court has no force or effect as a false claim. — Meaning of Jus in Rem in Non-Ucadia Law

1682. Under Non-Ucadia Law, in the absence of willing Consent, *Jus In Rem* is often applied as the primary claim to Personal Jurisdiction on the basis that a Person was born or naturalized within the boundaries of the state and therefore a record of birth was created including a set of Cestui Que Vie Trusts or "secret testamentary trusts". Therefore, because the state claims "ownership" of the register and the trusts, it claims "ownership" of the man or woman as property evidenced by their 'holding' a Birth Certificate. — Jus In Rem as claim to Personal Jurisdiction

Article 454 - Territorial Jurisdiction

1683. *Territorial Jurisdiction* refers to the geographical area over whereby a court or government entity has the authority to hear and decide cases. Different courts and government bodies have jurisdiction over specific geographic regions. For example, a state court typically has jurisdiction over cases that arise within the boundaries of that state, while federal courts have jurisdiction over matters that involve federal law or disputes between parties from different states. — Territorial Jurisdiction

1684. Under Non-Ucadia Law, *Jus Gentium* is often applied as the primary claim to Personal Jurisdiction on the basis that a person was born or naturalized within the boundaries of the state. — Non-Ucadia Law claim to Territorial Jurisdiction

Article 455 - Subject Matter Jurisdiction

1685. ***Subject Matter Jurisdiction*** relates to the authority of a court or administrative agency to hear cases involving specific types of legal issues or subject matters. For example, family courts typically have jurisdiction over divorce and child custody matters, while bankruptcy courts have jurisdiction over bankruptcy cases. — Subject Matter Jurisdiction

1686. The word ***Subject*** comes from the Latin *subjectum* meaning "to put under, bring under, to submit, subordinate, answer or to substitute". Hence when a judge or magistrate asks if an accused "understands?" they are inviting them to consent to being a subject of the court and "stand under, submit" to court authority. — Derivation and meaning of the word Subject

1687. ***Lex Specialis*** is the shortening of the Latin phrase *Lex specialis derogat legi generali* meaning "law governing a specific subject matter" and is founded on a doctrine for interpreting the laws of the state that a law governing a specific subject matter (lex specialis) overrides a law which only governs general matters (lex generalis). — Lex Specialis

1688. By its form, existence and specificity, Ucadia has innate and superior Subject Matter Jurisdiction over all Civilised forms of Law. — Ucadia and Subject Matter Jurisdiction

1689. Where Subject Matter Jurisdiction has not been established by consent of one or more of the parties, the use of trickery in language such as "do you understand?" does not constitute consent under any moral, sensible or Civilised Law. However, where Personal Jurisdiction is established and there is no dispute a court can hear such specific matters of law, Subject Matter Jurisdiction is automatically assumed. — Subject Matter Jurisdiction cannot be implied or established by trickery

Article 456 - Original & Appellate Jurisdiction

1690. ***Original Jurisdiction*** refers to the authority of a court to hear a case for the first time, while ***Appellate Jurisdiction*** allows a higher court to review the decisions of a lower court. Some courts have both original and appellate jurisdiction, while others have only one or the other. — Original & Appellate Jurisdiction

1691. By innate rights, the competent courts and forums of Ucadia possess absolute, supreme and first authority of *Original Jurisdiction* to review, hear and decide any and all matters of law of any and all Persons, Property and Things:- — Ucadia Courts and Original Jurisdiction

  (i) When a competent Ucadia court or forum of law duly registers a case, issue or some legal matter for the first time, such a court or forum of law shall be the court of Original Jurisdiction, unless challenged under Ucadia Law for the matter to be heard in a different Ucadia court or forum of law;

and

(ii) No Non-Ucadia court or forum of law shall ever possess Original Jurisdiction over a matter duly registered and recorded within a competent Ucadia court or forum of law, unless such jurisdiction is granted under the conditions of a formal treaty; and

(iii) In all communication with Non-Ucadia entities, governments, courts and agencies, the registered number within Ucadia shall serve as proof as the matter being within the Original Jurisdiction of Ucadia and nowhere else. However, should a matter fail to be registered within Ucadia after thirty days notice by a Non-Ucadia entity, person or agency, then such a right shall lapse; and

(iv) A competent, certified and registered Ucadia Attorney or Ucadia Officer shall have at all times the right to give notice and file as a courtesy within a Non-Ucadia court or forum to have a matter vacated and transferred to a Ucadia Court as the proper court of jurisdiction. However, to avoid controversy, this shall not apply to matters currently before a Non-Ucadia Court where the alleged criminal offence carries a maximum sentence of 10 years or more in prison; and

(v) A Non-Ucadia Court or Non-Ucadia Official that fails to acknowledge and grant a motion to vacate and transfer to a matter duly registered as Original Jurisdiction of a Ucadia Court shall be culpable of obstruction of justice, malfeasance and incompetence and shall have no immunity in any further prosecution and sanctions in relation to the relevant Non-Ucadia Society.

1692. By Divine Right and Authority, the *Supreme Court of One Heaven*, also known as *Curia Divina* and any lesser court granted such spiritual and temporal Authority and Powers is the absolute, supreme and highest possible court of appeal and review:-

Supreme Court of One Heaven

(i) No court or forum of law may claim or possess Divine Authority whatsoever, unless it has been conveyed in accord with the most sacred Covenant *Pactum De Singularis Caelum*; and

(ii) A judicial review, decision, judgment or order issued under *Curia Divina* in accord with the most sacred Covenant *Pactum De Singularis Caelum* possesses the absolute highest authority of any court or forum. All lesser Ucadia and Non-Ucadia courts and forums are therefore bound to take notice and be bound by any such judicial review, decision, judgment or order; and

(iii) Under a comprehensive treaty, Ucadia reserves the right to grant for a time being the proper authority of *Curia Divina* to the highest court of the particular Non-Ucadia Society.

Article 457 - Exclusive & Concurrent Jurisdiction

1693. ***Exclusive Jurisdiction*** means that only one court or government entity has the authority to hear cases of a particular type. ***Concurrent Jurisdiction*** means that multiple courts or entities can hear cases of the same type. In cases of concurrent jurisdiction, plaintiffs often have the choice of which court to file their case in.

Exclusive & Concurrent Jurisdiction

Article 458 - Foreign & International Jurisdiction

1694. ***Foreign Jurisdiction*** refers to the legal authority or control exercised by a country or a specific geographic region over matters that pertain to individuals, entities, or activities outside of its own borders. ***International Jurisdiction*** refers to the authority or legal power that a country or a legal entity has in matters that extend beyond its own national borders and involve international relations or foreign parties.

Foreign & International Jurisdiction

1695. Given all proper and valid Rights, Authority and Powers originate from Ucadia in accord with the most sacred Covenant *Pactum De Singularis Caelum*, Ucadia possesses the absolute, supreme and highest Foreign and International Jurisdiction over all bodies, persons, entities, associations and agencies:-

Ucadia and Foreign & International Jurisdiction

(i) No Non-Ucadia entity, person, body, association or agency may legitimately or validly claim Jurisdiction over Ucadia, or equal or higher Jurisdiction than Ucadia; and

(ii) Ucadia and its duly authorised courts, persons, bodies and agencies may assert authority and powers over any Person, Property or Thing in any Non-Ucadia Country; and

(iii) Ucadia and its duly authorised courts may hear and adjudicate cases related to specific subject matters with international elements concerning any Person, Property or Thing in any Non-Ucadia Country; and

(iv) Under a comprehensive treaty, Ucadia reserves the right to grant for a time being the proper authority of *Foreign and International Jurisdiction* to the highest court of the particular Non-Ucadia Society.

Article 459 - Ecclesiastical & Supreme Jurisdiction

1696. ***Ecclesiastical Jurisdiction*** refers to the legal authority and control exercised by religious organizations or ecclesiastical bodies over matters related to their faith, religious practices and members. ***Supreme Jurisdiction*** refers to the highest level of authority or decision-making power possible or within a particular legal or governmental system.

_{Ecclesiastical & Supreme jurisdiction}

1697. In reference to key elements associated with Supreme Jurisdiction including (but not limited to):-

_{Elements of Supreme Jurisdiction}

    (i) ***Religious or Spiritual Context***: In some religious or spiritual contexts, "supreme jurisdiction" may refer to the highest religious authority within a religious organization or belief system; and

    (ii) ***Autonomy and Self-Governance***: In certain contexts, "supreme jurisdiction" may be used to emphasize the highest level of autonomy or self-governance that an entity or organization possesses; and

    (iii) ***Supreme Court Jurisdiction***: In some countries "supreme jurisdiction" may refer to the highest court's authority to make final and binding decisions on legal matters; and

    (iv) ***Sovereign State Authority***: In international law, the concept of "supreme jurisdiction" can be associated with the sovereign authority of a nation-state within its own territory. It signifies that a state has the ultimate authority and control over its internal affairs and legal matters, subject to the principles of international law.

1698. Given the Divine Nature of Ucadia and the meaning of Ucadia, there exists no higher jurisdiction than Ucadia.

_{No higher jurisdiction}

1699. By Divine Right and Authority, the *Supreme Court of One Heaven*, also known as *Curia Divina* and any lesser court granted such spiritual and temporal Authority and Powers is the absolute, supreme and highest possible Supreme Jurisdiction and Ecclesiastical Jurisdiction.

_{Supreme Court of One Heaven Highest Court}

Title XVIII – Occurrence, Drama & Fact

18.1 – Occurrence

Article 460 - Occurrence

1700. ***Occurrence*** is a collection of two or more *Instances* of *Time* and *Place* experienced by one or more Persons in accordance with the present Maxims of Law. — Occurrence

1701. As Ucadia Time is the oldest, the first and only true measurement system of time and space in accordance with valid Divine Law, Natural Law and Positive Law, all claims by any person, aggregate, corporation or other body to own or control any aspect of time and space is a fraud and null and void from the beginning. — Ucadia Time

1702. No two observers may experience Time under exactly the same conditions and location, therefore no two observers will have the precise same experience of an Occurrence. Therefore, even in the presence of fact and evidence, there is no absolute truth of experience or memory of a singular collective Occurrence. — Uniqueness of Occurrence

Article 461 - Instance

1703. An ***Instance*** is the unique experience of a unit of time and space (an *Instant*) of Ucadian Time by a single Observer. A collection of Instances by one or more Observers represents an *Occurrence*. — Instance

1704. No two Observers may experience Time under exactly the same conditions and location; therefore no two Observers will have the precise same experience of an Instant. — Uniqueness of an Instant

1705. The perceived duration of an Instance is relative; the greater the density of objects and interactions, the shorter an Instance will appear; the lesser the density of objects and interactions, the longer an Instance will appear. — Relativity of Instance

18.2 – Drama

Article 462 - Drama

1706. A ***Drama*** is a formal framework and composition for the reenactment of two or more *Occurrences*, real or imagined, performed by one or more *Actors* in relation to a *Plot*. A Court Case in Civilised Law is commonly referred to as a ***Legal Drama***. — Drama

1707. The word *Drama* is derived from the 5th Century BCE Ancient Greek word Δρᾶμα (Drama) originally meaning "action or deed":- — Origin of Concept of Drama

    (i)   The term for theatrical performances, and the place where they took place and the viewing or spectating of them was θέατρον (théatron), not the word Drama; and

(ii) τραγῳδία (tragōidia): *Tragedy*, one of the two main genres of Greek theatre, is referred to as "τραγῳδία." It is derived from "τράγος" (tragos), meaning "goat," and "ᾠδή" (ōidē), meaning "song." Tragedy often featured serious and somber themes; and

(iii) κωμῳδία (kōmōidia): *Comedy*, the other main genre of Greek theatre, is referred to as "κωμῳδία." It is derived from "κῶμος" (kōmos), which originally meant a revel or festivity, and "ᾠδή" (ōidē), meaning "song." Greek comedies were known for their humour and satirical elements; and

(iv) The word Drama did not then acquire its formal meaning as "an act, theatrical play; a fictional composition" until the early 16th Century CE and the works of the Jesuit College of English published under the name William Shakespeare.

1708. The most significant formal structure of Drama both in fictional plays and legal drama is the adoption of a classic "three-act structure" of three (3) parts being the Setup, Confrontation and the Resolution:- *[Classic Structure of Drama]*

(i) The **First Act** of a Drama is usually to establish the main characters, their relationships and the pressing controversy that confronts the main character (Protagonist). The first act usually ends upon the "first dramatic turning point" where the full crucible facing the Protagonist is laid bare by the Antagonist; and

(ii) The **Second Act** of a Drama, also referred to as "rising action", normally sees the Protagonist respond to the crucible in some form of defence of attack. However, the efforts only normally make things worse as the Antagonist(s) appear superior in skill, in knowledge, while the Protagonist struggles to find their competence that can only be solved through a higher sense of self awareness, or "epinoia"; and

(iii) The **Third and Final Act** of a Drama sees the resolution of the story. The climax, also known as the "second dramatic turning point" is when all the outstanding threads of the story are brought to their most intense moment and the key question(s) resolved, leaving the protagonist and other characters with the benefit of knowledge of hindsight and self awareness.

1709. Unlike other forms of fiction, Drama in the classic Greek style of tragedy often ends with the Protagonist suffering some great loss, sacrifice, punishment or even death at the end of the Third Act. *[Tragic nature of classic Greek Drama]*

1710. Apart from the classic "Three Act" structure of Drama, other key *[Additional Key Elements]*

elements of form and structure include (but are not limited to):- of a Drama

(i) **Stage**: A Stage is a designated area, typically in a theatre or performance space, where actors perform for an audience; and

(ii) **Scene**: A Scene is a segment of an Act that takes place in a specific place and time, with a particular set of Characters and Actions, that then advance the Plot; and

(iii) **Actors (Personae)**: A Drama always involve one or more Personae (Actors), with the word *persona* originally meaning mask in Latin; and

(iv) **Cast of Actors (Dramatis Personae)**: A Drama always involve a Cast of at least one or more Actors, with each inhabiting at least one character or different parts of the same character; and

(v) **Plot**: A Plot is the sequence of events that make up the storyline of a Drama, including the central conflict, character actions, and their consequences, designed to engage and entertain the audience and ultimately reveal Motive; and

(vi) **Protagonist**: The Protagonist is the central character of the Drama, often the hero or main character around whom the story revolves; and

(vii) **Deuteragonist**: The Deuteragonist is the secondary character or a key supporting character who interacted closely with the protagonist; and

(viii) **Tritagonist**: Tritagonist is the third important character in a Drama, though never as central as the protagonist and deuteragonist; and

(ix) **Chorus**: The Chorus is a group of actors who function as a collective character. They provide commentary on the events of the Drama, offer moral and thematic insights, and sometimes participated in the action; and

(x) **Appearance**: Throughout a Drama, different Actors appear in various capacity. By tradition, notice was given to the audience to assist in comprehending the context of the Character; and

(xi) **Motive**: Motive is the existence of a clear and definable intention previously possessed by an Actor capable of being connected to observed Actions such that the intention may be claimed as the cause of the action; and

(xii) **Fate**: Fate is the moral lesson and consequence of the revealed Plot and Motive of the Drama, often seen as predetermined destiny due to the course of actions.

1711. There is nothing inherently immoral, repugnant or unsound in considering the formalities associated with Drama as the fabric for Legal Drama and the conduct of matters of law:-

    (i) **Law is always about events in the past**: All valid legal matters pertain to at least one or more Occurrences in the past; and

    (ii) **Law is necessarily about re-enacting certain events from the past**: All valid trials pertain in some way to having to re-enact or re-imagine one or more Occurrences in the past, in order to ascertain the actions, mind and potential culpability of the accused; and

    (iii) **Law always pertains to a Plot and Motive**: The necessary components to prove a criminal offence of *actus reus* (guilty act) and *mens rea* (guilty mind) are ideally suited to the framework of Drama; and

    (iv) **Law always requires persons to assume certain characters**: The nature and complexity of Criminal and Civil Cases requires that one or more persons assume certain characters in order for the Law to function, whether it be the Prosecutor or Plaintiff as Protagonist, or the Defendant as the Antagonist or the Chorus as the Jury.

The Moral Nature of Drama and Legal Drama

1712. When the framework of a Drama is not explained, or deliberately corrupted, or when actions are secretive and collusion between the various actors, then the law itself becomes corrupted.

Corruption of Drama is corruption of the Law

Article 463 – Stage

1713. A **Stage** is a designated area, typically in a theatre or performance space, where actors perform for an audience. In a Legal Drama as a court case, the Stage is the Court Room.

Stage

1714. Since the time of Ancient Greek and Roman Drama, a Stage was divided into designated parts. These parts then formed the basis of key parts of a Modern Court including (but not limited to):-

Designated Parts of the Stage

    (i) **Orchestra (pit)**: The central, circular performance area at the lowest (ground) level where the chorus sang, danced, and interacted with the actors. This area is called the **well** in a court room and is where the legal counsel for both parties (plaintiff and defendant) sit during proceedings, separate to the jury box; and

    (ii) **Skene**: The "skene" was a building or structure located behind the orchestra. It served as a backdrop for the action and provided a separate area for actors to change characters and prepare for a new scene. In a courtroom, this narrow space is called ***chambers*** and the backdrop is simply called the ***wall***; and

(iii) ***Theatron***: The "theatron" referred to the seating area for the audience. It was typically built into the hillside or elevated to provide a clear view of the orchestra and skene. In a courtroom this is typically called the ***gallery***; and

(iv) ***Altar (Thymele)***: The altar, as a raised platform located in the centre of the orchestra, was a focal point for religious rituals and ceremonies. In a courtroom it is called the ***bench*** where the judges sit during proceedings; and

(v) ***Proskenion***: The "proskenion" or Pulpitum (in Latin) was an additional raised platform or stage area in front of the skene. It allowed actors to perform at a higher level than the orchestra and provided more visibility for the audience. In a courtroom this is the origin of the ***podium*** and ***witness box***.

1715. Following Queen Elizabeth I (1558-1603) expulsion of most intellectuals and writers from England in 1570, many found refuge at the newly formed Jesuit College of English including William Breakspeare (Shakespeare). From 1600's the work of the English Jesuits placed the concept of the Stage as central to viewing life, including (but not limited to):- English Venetian Law and Concept of Stage

(i) From the Play *As You like It* "All the world's a stage, And all the men and women merely players; They have their exits and their entrances, And one man in his time plays many parts, His acts being seven ages."; and

(ii) From the Play *Macbeth* "Life's but a walking shadow, a poor player That struts and frets his hour upon the stage And then is heard no more. It is a tale Told by an idiot, full of sound and fury Signifying nothing.".

Article 464 - Scene

1716. A ***Scene*** is a segment of an Act that takes place in a specific place and time, with a particular set of Characters and Actions, that then advance the Plot. Scene

1717. The word scene is derived from the Ancient Greek σκηνή (skēnē) meaning "the part of a theater (stage) on which the acting is normally performed". Origin of word Scene

Article 465 - Dramatis Personae (Cast)

1718. The **Dramatis Personae** is a list or cast of the characters of a Drama, arranged in order of first appearance.

1719. The phrase is constructed from two Latin words being *dramatis* meaning "drama, play" and *personae* being the plural of person or "persons".

1720. Within a classic Drama as well as a Legal Drama, the Actors may play different characters or divisions or "parts" of the same character. This is the origin of the use of the word "Party" when describing a person connected to a legal matter that they are playing a "part" of a whole.

1721. The word Party originates from the Latin word *partis* meaning "share, fraction, side, direction, respect, degree, role, duty, function".

1722. Within an ancient Drama and a modern Legal Drama there needs to be a minimum cast of three main Actors being the Accuser (Protagonist), the Accused (Deuteragonist) and a Witness (Tritagonist):-

(i) This model in modern law equates to the three essential parts of the Person (1st (I, me), 2nd (you, he, she, him, her) and 3rd (we, they). When all three are presented this is literally the hidden underlying meaning of Joinder; and

(ii) In modern law the Parties of a cast also equates to the three parties to a trust (trustor, trustee and beneficiary along with the res of the trust).

Article 466 - Persona (Actor)

1723. A **Persona** refers to a mask worn by Actors in ancient Greek and Roman theatre. These masks symbolized the characters they played and gave rise to the modern usage of the term to describe roles or identities. Hence the connection between the word Persona (mask), Person (character) and Actor.

1724. The word **Actor** comes from the Ancient Greek word ακτωρ (aktōr) meaning "a leading performer".

1725. In a Legal Drama, the comprehension of the names of the Characters reveal if they are stand alone characters or parts of a greater character or person:-

(i) **Prosecutor** is the name of a Legal Party from Latin **pro-** meaning "bringing forth", **se** "my, oneself" and **cutis** meaning "skin" meaning literally "bringing forth in his/her skin"; and

(ii) **Accused** is the name of a Legal Party from Latin **ac** meaning "to", ***cuso*** meaning "stricken, beaten, stamped or marked" and *-ed* meaning "possession of a thing or feature" meaning literally "to have possession of a stricken, beaten, stamped or marked thing".

Article 467 – Protagonist

1726. The ***Protagonist*** is the central character of the Drama, often the hero or main character around whom the story revolves. It is the account of the actions and decisions of the Protagonist that by tradition are key to the development of the Plot. In Law, it is the *Plaintiff* or *Prosecutor* that usually acts as the *Protagonist* in a Court Case, never the Defendant.

_{Protagonist}

1727. The word *Protagonist* originates from Ancient Greek word Πρωταγωνιστής (*Prōtagōnistēs*) meaning "a chief actor", itself from πρωτος (protos) meaning "first" and αγωνιστής (agōnistēs) meaning "actor, competitor".

_{Origin of Protagonist}

Article 468 – Deuteragonist

1728. The ***Deuteragonist*** is the secondary character or a key supporting character who interacted closely with the protagonist. They often played a significant role in the unfolding of the plot.

_{Deuteragonist}

1729. The word *Deuteragonist* originates from Ancient Greek word Δευτεραγωνιστής (*Deuteragōnistēs*) meaning "second actor", itself from δεύτερος (deuteros) meaning "second" and αγωνιστής (agōnistēs) meaning "actor, competitor".

_{Origin of Deuteragonist}

1730. The word *Antagonist* originates from Ancient Greek word ανταγωνιστής (antagonistes) meaning "opponent" itself from αντί (anti) meaning "against" and αγωνιστής (agōnistēs) meaning "actor, competitor".

_{Antagonist}

Article 469 – Tritagonist

1731. A ***Tritagonist*** is the third important character in a Drama, though never as central as the protagonist and deuteragonist. They sometimes have their own subplots or storylines.

_{Tritagonist}

1732. The word *Tritagonist* originates from Ancient Greek word Τριταγωνιστής (*Tritagōnistēs*) meaning "third actor", itself from τρίτος (trítos) meaning "third" and αγωνιστής (agōnistēs) meaning "actor, competitor".

_{Origin of Tritagonist}

Article 470 – Chorus

1733. The ***Chorus*** is a group of actors who function as a collective character. They provide commentary on the events of the Drama, offer moral and thematic insights, and sometimes participated in the action. The chorus also performed choral odes and dances. — Chorus (Narrator & Jury)

1734. The word *Chorus* originates from Ancient Greek word Χορός (*Khorós*) meaning "a group of singers and dancers in a theatrical performance who comment and judge the main performance in speech or song". — Origin of Chorus

Article 471 - Appearance

1735. ***Appearance*** refers to the notification, announcement and presence of a character or actor on the stage during a specific scene or moment in the performance. An *Appearance* typically signifies that a character enters the stage, interacts with other characters or the environment, and then exits the stage. — Appearance

1736. ***Legal Appearance***, or simply *Appearance* is both (1) the formal written memorandum whereby a defendant submits himself to the jurisdiction of the court; and (2) the coming to court as a party to a suit:- — Legal Appearance

   (i) In the primary sense of the word, appearing or entering an appearance is memorandum and form written and submitted by a defendant (or their agent) to any action after they have been served with the writ of summons: its object is to intimate to the plaintiff that the defendant intends to contest his claim, or contest the jurisdiction of the court; and

   (ii) In the secondary sense of the word, the parties to a proceeding or application (petition, motion, summons) are said to appear on it when they are present before the Court or judge when it is heard; and

   (iii) If a defendant fails to accomplish both these mandatory requirements, then it is said that they "failed to appear" and a default judgement may be issued against the party who failed to appear, even if they physically appeared on the day of the hearing.

1737. *Appearance* of a Defendant (and their Agent) may be either *General* or *Special*:- — General & Special Appearance

   (i) *General Appearance* is simple and unqualified or unrestricted submission to the jurisdiction of the court; and

(ii) *Special Appearance* is a submission to the jurisdiction for some specific purpose only, not for all purposes of a suit. The most common reason is to contest the jurisdiction of the court.

1738. The ***Character of Appearance*** is both the written notice and actual presentment on the day of the hearing as to whether a party will appear as themselves, or be represented by an agent:-

    (i) ***Appearance without Counsel***: For individuals will either be *in propria persona* meaning "In one's own person" in Civil matters or *pro se* "For oneself as a thing" for Criminal matters. Under Non-Ucadia Law, the Accused is always treated as a form of disputed property in custody or "res", no matter what is written or claimed when self representing. Thus in any Non-Ucadia criminal matter, it is vital a defendant always has competent representation. Corporations are not permitted to represent themselves and must appear by Attorney/Counsel; and

    (ii) ***Appearance by Attorney/Counsel***: Is the most common and balanced form of appearance whereby a competent, qualified and enrolled Attorney or Counsel appears on behalf of the defendant; and

    (iii) ***Appearance by Special Attorney/Counsel***: Is the rarest form of appearance whereby a competent, qualified and registered Ucadia Attorney or Counsel that is not enrolled on the court rolls of members of a Private Bar Guild appears on behalf of the defendant. This usually requires additional notifications and assurances and including preparedness to submit to any examinations to avoid controversy. A Person who attempts this without proper written authorisation from Ucadia is committing a serious criminal offence.

Article 472 – Plot

1739. A ***Plot*** is the sequence of events that make up the storyline of a Drama, including the central conflict, character actions, and their consequences, designed to engage and entertain the audience and ultimately reveal Motive.

1740. The role of Plaintiff or Prosecutor possess a natural advantage in any Legal Drama as the primary drivers of the unfolding plot in three or four Acts:-

    (i) It is the Plaintiff or Prosecutor that has the initial advantage in setting out the Plot of any Case in terms of alleged Facts and Narrative; and

(ii)   The advantage however may be soon be lost if it can be shown that the alleged Facts do not stand and that the Narrative does not hold firm.

Article 473 - Motive

1741. ***Motive*** is the existence of a clear and definable intention previously possessed by an Actor capable of being connected to observed Actions such that the intention may be claimed as the cause of the action. — Motive

1742. A Drama is incomplete without the Motive of the Protagonist being revealed. — Drama and Motive

Article 474 - Fate

1743. ***Fate*** is the moral lesson and consequence of the revealed Plot and Motive of the Drama, often seen as predetermined destiny due to the course of actions. — Fate

18.3 – Fact

Article 475 - Fact

1744. A ***Fact*** is any *Event, Action, Circumstance, Attribute* or *Relation* that is provable in Reality to be true or false. In law, a fact is a statement or assertion that can be proven to be true or false. — Fact

1745. The word *Fact* comes from the Latin *factus* meaning "done, made, having been done or made". — Origin of the word Fact

1746. Common aspects of Facts include (but are not limited to):- — Common Aspects of Facts

   (i)   An *Event*: an actual occurrence; a thing done; an actual happening in time space or an event mental or physical; that which has taken place; and

   (ii) An *Action*: an action performed or an incident transpiring; and

   (iii) A *Circumstance*: an existence; a state of things that is; a motion that is; an actual and absolute reality as distinguished from mere supposition or opinion; and

   (iv) An *Attribute*: the quality of being actual; a physical object or appearance, as it usually exists or existed; and

   (v)   A *Relation*: a truth, as distinguished from a fiction or error.

1747. While it may first appear that commonly accepted Facts and Facts in Law are the same, there are significant differences:- — Difference between common concept of Fact and a

   (i)   Facts in day to day life may appear "self evident".

Furthermore, certain events, actions or circumstances may be simply claimed as Factual and often believed by the community without deeper investigation; and

_{Fact in Law}

(ii) In contrast, all statements or assertions of Fact in Law must include evidence and reliable testimony to be considered; and are therefore set to a higher standard; and

(iii) A whole array of Facts may be claimed in day to day life concerning an event, whereas in Law, there are specific standards and procedures of relevancy, specificity and admissibility that may greatly limit what evidence is admitted in a legal matter.

1748. To establish a fact in a legal context, several key elements should typically be present including (but not limited to):-

Testimony and Fact in Law

(i) **Relevance**: The fact must be relevant to the legal issue or dispute at hand. It should have a direct bearing on the central questions in the case; and

(ii) **Competence and Authenticity**: The fact should come from a reliable and competent source or witness. Evidence and testimony that lack credibility or authenticity may not be accepted as facts; and

(iii) **Admissibility**: The fact should be presented in a legally admissible manner. This means it must conform to the rules of evidence and be permissible under the applicable laws and regulations; and

(iv) **Specificity**: A fact should be specific and clearly defined. Vague or ambiguous statements may not be accepted as facts by the court; and

(v) **Materiality**: The fact must be material, meaning that it has a significant impact on the legal issues in the case. Immaterial or irrelevant facts may not be considered by the court; and

(vi) **Consistency**: A fact should be consistent with other known facts and evidence in the case. Inconsistencies or contradictions may raise doubts about the fact's accuracy; and

(vii) **Corroborating Evidence**: In some cases, a single piece of evidence or testimony may not be sufficient to establish a fact. Corroborating evidence or multiple witnesses may be required to support the fact's validity.

1749. In law, facts can be categorized into various types or categories, depending on their relevance and role in a legal case. Common

Categories of Facts in Law

categories of facts in legal proceedings include:-

(i) **_Material Facts_**: Material facts are facts that are directly related to the legal issues at hand and have a significant impact on the outcome of the case. These facts are crucial for determining liability, culpability or the resolution of a legal dispute; and

(ii) **_Immaterial Facts_**: Immaterial facts are facts that, while true, do not have a significant bearing on the legal issues in the case and are not considered relevant by the court; and

(iii) **_Evidentiary Facts_**: Evidentiary facts are facts that serve as evidence or support for the material and ultimate facts. They are used to establish the truth of the central claims or defenses in a case; and

(iv) **_Circumstantial Facts_**: Circumstantial facts are facts that do not provide direct proof of a claim or defense but can be used to infer the existence of certain material or ultimate facts. They are often used to build a persuasive case when direct evidence is lacking; and

(v) **_Statutory Facts_**: Statutory facts refer to facts that are established by a statute or law and are relevant to the legal issues being considered; and

(vi) **_Historical Facts_**: Historical facts are facts about past events or circumstances that are pertinent to the legal issues being considered. They can be crucial in cases involving contracts, property rights and historical context; and

(vii) **_Stipulated Facts_**: Stipulated facts are facts that both parties in a legal case agree upon, eliminating the need to prove them through evidence. These facts are often presented in a stipulated or agreed-upon statement; and

(viii) **_Undisputed Facts_**: Undisputed facts are facts that both parties agree upon, and there is no dispute or controversy regarding their accuracy or relevance; and

(ix) **_Presumed Facts_**: Presumed facts are facts that the law assumes to be true in the absence of evidence to the contrary. These presumptions can vary depending on the legal jurisdiction and the specific legal issue; and

(x) **_Procedural Facts_**: Procedural facts pertain to the steps and actions taken during the legal process, such as the timing of filings, notices and court orders. These facts are relevant to the conduct of the legal proceedings; and

(xi) ***Collateral Facts***: Collateral facts are facts that are not directly related to the central issues of the case but may be introduced for various purposes, such as impeachment of witnesses or establishing credibility; and

(xii) ***Adjudicative Facts***: Adjudicative facts are facts that are determined by the court during the legal proceedings, such as a judge's findings of fact in a bench trial.

1750. By virtue of the ratification of these Maxims by the Founding Members of Ucadia, the Founding Members hereby solemnly testify that these Maxims are True and Factual. *(Ratification of Maxims as Fact)*

1751. The publishing of any Proclamation, Order, Regulation or Notice within the Gazette of Ucadia is the highest acknowledgement of a Fact and Truth, not subject to dispute or dishonour. *(Gazette Notices as Fact)*

1752. The provision of any valid Ucadia Instrument and Form of Ucadia is Fact and Truth in itself and not subject to dispute or dishonour by any Non-Ucadian person, entity, forum, association or body. *(Instruments and Forms of Ucadia as Fact)*

1753. Any Edict, Decree, Command, Demand, Order, Judgement, Opinion that contradicts one or more of these Maxims cannot be Fact. *(Contradictions to Maxims not Fact)*

1754. When anyone references, writes or speaks of a "Fact", "True Fact", or "Absolute Fact" it shall mean these Maxims and no other. *(True Facts)*

Article 476 - Reality

1755. In accord with Divine Law, Reality is one of a Binary pair of Models constructed upon certain Rules of Form and Meaning, enabling a certain degree of stability necessary for the existence and function of two or more Theoretical or Real Objects. The opposite Model is Unreality. *(Reality)*

1756. In Relation to Reality and Theoretical or Real Objects within Dimension: *(Reality within Dimension)*

(i) All Models of Reality are by definition Theoretical. This is because all forms of Reality (and Unreality) are Models; and

(ii) While all Models of Reality are Theoretical, a Model of Reality may be described as Real to the extent that is presents a comprehensive and well-formed Standard Model of Universal Laws, consistent with the Principle of Relativity and the present Sacred Maxims; and

(iii) The binary opposite to a Real Model (**R**) of Reality may be defined as Perfectly Unreal Model (**U**) to the extent that it belongs as the opposite to such a Standard Model of Universal Laws and properly completes a consistent conceptual set of all possible Theoretical and Real Objects; and

(iv) A Model of Reality that seeks to deliberately contradict the present Sacred Maxims, or obstinately or belligerently persist with false and absurd Concepts that cannot possibly form a Standard Model nor reasonable Universal Laws is said to be a Delusional Model of Reality, or simply a "Delusion".

1757. All Civilised Rules of a Society exist within a Set and Dimension of Form and Meaning defined as a Reality:- Civilised Rules & Reality

(i) A Model of Reality in relation to any Society is always bound as a Binary Pair to a particular Model of Unreality. By definition and necessity, a Model of Reality can only exist when its constituent Model of Unreality also exists under the same System of Rules; and

(ii) Any argument in support of a Social Model of Reality, that fails or denies its Binary relation and dependence to the existence of an opposite Model of Unreality, is therefore an absurdity and sign of delusion; and

(iii) The definition of any alternate Social Reality that is inconsistent with the present sacred Maxims and the most sacred Covenant *Pactum De Singularis Caelum* is automatically delusional, false, null and void from the beginning.

Article 477 - Truth

1758. ***Truth*** and ***True*** is three fundamental qualities: Honest and consistent Testimony; or Reasonable and Logical acceptance of one or more claimed facts or statements as having objective Reality; or a steadfast Fidelity and Loyalty to such Testimony and Facts conclusively found to be True: Truth

(i) As to the first quality, the highest Truth has always been honest and consistent Testimony under solemn Oath and Vow in acknowledgement of a Supreme Divine Creator of all the Universe and all Heaven and Earth. The first meaning of Truth, therefore is openness and without concealment, or secrecy or hiding. Occult therefore can never be truthful as the very meaning of occult is opposed to this first notion of Truth. Furthermore a statement without a proper and solemn Oath and Vow to the Divine Creator of all Existence cannot be reasonably regarded as Truth, only opinion or information; and

(ii) As to the second quality of Truth, any claimed fact or statement can only be considered as True if it is both Reasonable and Logical. Therefore a claimed fact or statement born from prejudice, or fraud, or coercion must always be considered unreasonable and therefore cannot be True. Similarly, a claimed fact or statement that is Incoherent, Fallacious, Irrelevant, Malicious, Perfidious, Unproven, Unasserted, Circular, Verbose, Absurd, Repetitive or Defamatory cannot logically be concluded as True; and

(iii) As to the third and final quality of Truth, it is the essential preservation of Truth, such that once a Testimony or Fact or Statement is found to be True, it is properly recognised and preserved; and then used as a reliable "stepping stone" for other discoveries and conclusions. However, a steadfast adherence or orthodoxy to claimed statements and alleged facts that contradicts a quality of Truth cannot therefore, then be considered "true" as this would mean that Truth contradicts itself.

1759. By virtue of the ratification of these Maxims by the Founding Members of Ucadia, the Founding Members hereby solemnly testify that these Maxims are true; and that these Maxims are Reasonable and Logical and collectively represent the embodiment of Truth itself. *Ratification of Maxims as Truth*

1760. Any Edict, Decree, Command, Demand, Order, Judgement, Opinion that contradicts one or more of these Maxims cannot be Truth. *Contradiction to Maxims cannot be Truth*

Article 478 – Source of Fact

1761. ***Source of Fact*** is the primary person, place, thing from where a Fact has come or is acquired. *Source of Fact*

1762. When the source of a claimed Fact is obtained through documentation, it may be classed as a source text and such information must be referred by Citation. *Citation and Source Texts*

1763. There are three forms of source text being *Primary, Secondary* and *Tertiary*:- *Forms of Source Texts*

(i) A ***Primary Source Text*** is first hand written evidence and testimony made at the time of the events by an actor or witness to such events and whereby the provenance of such evidence is verifiable; and

Lex Positivum: Maxims of Positive Law

(ii) A ***Secondary Source Text*** is written accounts or references based upon Primary Source Texts or a claimed reprint or approximate reproduction of an alleged Primary Source Text; and

(iii) A ***Tertiary Source Text*** is written accounts or references based upon Secondary Source Texts of a claimed reprint or approximate reproduction of an alleged Primary Source Text.

1764. Given the return after 770 years of the Three Great Black Death (Haemorrhagic Fever) Pandemics (1314-1321, 1346-1353 and 1400-1408) that killed more than 85% of the population of Europe, North Africa, Middle East and Asia Minor; and that only France, Ireland and the Moor-Venetian cities survived with any semblance of civilisation, not a single Non-Ucadian Primary Source, Secondary Source or Tertiary Source of history claimed to have been written from 13th Century to the 16th Century can be relied upon as trusted, authentic or fact:-

(i) Not a single genealogy or chart of any and all noble family lines can be relied upon as trusted, authentic or fact, except those found in *Lebor Clann Glas* and other Ucadia Primary Sources; and

(ii) Not a single claimed chronology of history, or biography written or "discovered" during this period can be relied upon as trusted, authentic or fact, except those found in *Lebor Clann Glas* and other Ucadia Primary Sources.

1765. Not a single Primary Source Text allegedly written in "Old English", or "Middle English" prior to the 16th Century, nor any Secondary or Tertiary Source Text claiming that the English Language existed prior to the 16th Century can be relied upon as trusted, authentic or fact:-

No claim of English Language existing prior to 16th Century reliable as Fact

(i) English is an early 16th Century artificially formed phonological language created by Venetian and Dutch language and printing experts to standardise all forms of information for political and commercial purposes; and then first imposed as an official language starting in Britain, to improve the control and profitability of printing and media; and to reduce the long term influence of Anglaise (Old French), Gaelic and Norse; and

(ii) By 1500, Europe had a population of around 60 million and a literacy rate of around 10% (yet 25% in England and 40% in Ireland), with over 100 printing and publishing houses having printed more than 1 million books and pamphlets. Yet the biggest challenge wasn't the technology of publishing, but the lack of suitable standards of spelling and grammar, as well as a narrow market, making costs much higher and profits lower for the media (publishing) industry; and

(iii) By 1514, the Venetian exiled families in England created a plan to form a new language to transform the profitability of global printing and at the same time control most of the information of the world, in the creation of the "English Language" as a standard for spelling, grammar and typeface. However, by the year 1560 only 7,500 to 12,000 words in English had been created and the language had utterly failed, with literacy in England plummeting to less than 5% following the wholesale destruction of the network of 800+ monasteries across England, Wales and Scotland; and

(iv) By 1590, the plays in English by the Jesuit College of English via William Shakespeare introduced no less than 12,000 new words into the language transforming it into the leading European language for law, commerce and science; and single handedly saved the English Language Project of the English-Venetian nobility from extinction. Since then, the English nobility have never once acknowledged the role of the Jesuit College of English and have consistently played down the number of words created under "Shakespeare" to less than 1,200.

1766. Not a single English Statute or Secondary or Tertiary Source text referencing or quoting English statute prior to 19th Century can be relied upon as trusted, authentic or fact:- *(No English statute prior to 19th Century reliable as Fact)*

(i) ***1642 Palace of Green Witch (Greenwich) Fire***: Statutes, Rolls and Records of Henry VII, Henry VIII, Elizabeth I, James I and Charles I destroyed in fire by Parliamentary Forces; and

(ii) ***1666 Palace of West Minster Fire***: Statutes, Rolls and Records of Commonwealth Parliaments (1642-1660) destroyed in suspicious fire by Charles II; and

(iii) ***1698 Palace of White Hall Fire***: Statutes, Rolls and Records of Charles II destroyed in suspicious fire along with key land records and surviving pre 17th Century statutes, texts & rolls; and

(iv) ***1731 Palace of Westminster Fire***: 66 years after 1st fire, key texts, Rolls and Records destroyed in suspicious fire in "Cotton Library"; and

(v) ***1809 Palace of St James Fire***: Key Statutes, Rolls and

Lex Positivum: Maxims of Positive Law

              Records of Hanover's destroyed in suspicious fire; and

      (vi)   ***1834 Palace of Westminster Fire***: Palace completely destroyed in suspicious fire along with all records; and

      (vii)   ***1941 Palace of Westminster (Bombing) Fire***: Palace Records badly damaged and unknown original records destroyed by war time bombing.

1767. In 1642, the first Democratic Parliaments and Nations of the Commonwealth of Great Britain (1642-1706), Commonwealth of Ireland (1642-1691) and Commonwealth of New England (1642-1783) were formed. Given these facts were deliberately removed and remain suppressed under Non-Ucadia history to the present day, not a single Non-Ucadian Primary, Secondary or Tertiary Source historical or political text referencing or quoting British, Irish or American history can be relied upon as trusted, authentic or fact:- *[No English, Irish or American history after 1642 reliable as Fact]*

      (i)   "Common Law" is another name for Commonwealth Law being the attempt to resurrect Holly Anglo-Saxon; and not Venetian Admiralty and Merchant-Pirate Law; and

      (ii)   The Commonwealth of Great Britain was not extinguished as a democratic nation until the final defeat in Scotland by 1706. The Scottish flag remains the original flag of the Commonwealth of Great Britain; and

      (iii)   The Commonwealth of Ireland was not finally defeated until 1691 and the green background and white ensign suppressed as a flag. However, the Parliament of Ireland was permitted to continue until being dissolved in 1800, causing a mass revolt of Irish nobles; and

      (iv)   The Commonwealth of New England, (using a red background and white ensign as its flag) was not comprehensively attacked until 1776 when the United Company of Merchants funded by Dutch Wall Street Banks commenced a major campaign to defeat the democratic nation so that wholesale black African slavery could commence and turn the Americas into a highly profitable set of plantations. In 1783 in London, the defeated Commonwealth representatives were forced to accept the repayment of war damages to the crown, but were granted semi-autonomy as the United States of America with Philadelphia remaining its parliament and capital until 1861 and the Civil War.

1768. A Non-Ucadia Source Text cannot be considered to be a Primary Source Text if the text is a claimed reprint or approximate reproduction, or the text is derived from an extract of a Secondary *[Missing Non-Ucadia Primary Source Text]*

1768. Source Text to imply the existence of a Primary Source but the original is missing.

1769. A Non-Ucadia Source Text cannot be considered to be a Secondary Source Text if the text is a claimed reprint or approximate reproduction, or the text is derived from an extract of a Tertiary Source Text to imply the existence of a Secondary Source but the original is missing.
Missing Non-Ucadia Secondary Source Text

1770. A claimed Fact derived from a valid Ucadia Primary Source Text shall always have higher standing than a claimed Fact derived from a Ucadia Secondary Source Text. Similarly, a claimed Fact derived from a valid Ucadia Secondary Source Text shall always have higher standing than a claimed Fact derived from a Ucadia Tertiary Source Text.
Facts from Primary Source Texts

1771. No Non-Ucadian source text deemed a fraud in part or whole, in accordance with these Maxims may be used as a valid source text in Law.
Non-Ucadia unreliable texts forbidden

Article 479 - Citation

1772. A ***Citation*** is an abbreviated identification of another document source within a body of text including a complete and formal identification at the end of the text.
Citation

1773. A valid Citation is any Reference that conforms in Form to the requirements prescribed by these Maxims in accordance with the most sacred Covenant *Pactum De Singularis Caelum*.
Valid Citation

1774. There is no higher form of authority of valid Citation than these Maxims. When anyone references, writes or speaks of "Citation", "Valid Citation", or "Highest Authority Citation" it shall mean these Maxims and no other.
Citation and these Maxims

1775. Excluding the sacred covenants, charters, scripture, codes and Maxims of Ucadia and One Heaven, no text of historic significance, or of more than twenty (20) words that represents an exact likeness of an earlier source may be included within a more recent text without valid Citation. Failure to provide valid Citation is an offence known as plagiarism.
Plagiarism

1776. All valid Citations comprise three (3) elements: an inserted abbreviated reference within the body of some text known as a ***Cito***, a more formal and complete reference at the end of a page, chapter or division of the document known as a ***Profero*** and a comprehensive summary of all sources as an appendix to the document known as a ***Summarum***.
Valid Citation

1777. When considering the three (3) elements of any valid Citation, an author may choose one of two valid systems of Citation to use throughout their work: Notational Citation and Parenthetical Citation. Only one system may be used throughout a whole document.

Choice of Citation Method

1778. ***Notational Citation*** is a system of valid citation whereby the use of Cito within the body of text is as superscript sequential numbers, corresponding to a correspondingly numbered Profero at the bottom of each page or at the end of the chapter or division and then the Summarum at the end of the document.

Notational Citation

1779. ***Parenthetical Citation*** is a system of valid citation whereby the use of Cito within the body of text is through short abbreviated text within correct brackets or parenthesis, corresponding to alphabetically or time arranged Profero at the end of the chapter or division and then the Summarum at the end of the document.

Parenthetical Citation

17.4 – Evidence

Article 480 - Evidence

1780. ***Evidence*** is any accepted means in Argument employed for the purpose of proving one or more alleged Facts, whereby the Truth is established or disproven. Evidence may be Judicial (public) or Extra-Judicial (private or personal).

Evidence

1781. The *Law of Evidence* states that the Facts in any Dispute or Argument may be defined as either *Principal Facts* (*facta probanda*) or *Evidentiary Facts* (*facta probantia*):

Law of Evidence

   (i) ***Principal Facts*** (*facta probanda*) or "Facts in Issue" are those facts required to be proved. They are called Facts in Issue because these facts are usually the backbone of any matter of controversy and therefore essential to be proven; and

   (ii) ***Evidentiary Facts*** (*facta probantia*) or "Facts in Evidence" are those facts given in evidence with the view of proving Facts in Issue. These are facts normally entered during the course of a hearing or trial and not part of the initial disclosure with any citation, complaint or petition. Circumstantial evidence is therefore a more common description of *facta probantia* or "Facts in Evidence" whereby one or more inferences may be concluded via circumstantial evidence leading to the logical conclusion of a Principal Fact (*facta probanda*).

1782. The provision of any valid Certificate of Title to Land, Property and

Certificate of Title from

Rights as an authentic extract of a record from a valid Ucadia Register shall be *Prima Facie* Evidence of Proof of Original Title. Ucadia Register Proof of Original Title

1783. As all Ucadia digital services, websites and products require acknowledgement by the *User* that they are bound by an *End User Licence Agreement*, any reference or copies of material from Ucadia digital services, websites and products or services controlled by Ucadia shall be legal notice and acceptance of a contractual arrangement; and acceptance of any liabilities and penalties for any breach of such agreement. Reference of Extract from Ucadia site as Proof of Contract

1784. All Members, Officers, Agents, Contractors or Employees shall first ensure their Affidavits as Testimony and Evidence are duly recorded and registered within the Registers of Ucadia first, before an extract is supplied to any foreign body in relation to any dispute or matter. Affidavits as Testimony and Evidence

1785. Only three valid classes of evidence exist: Physical, Testimonial and Inferential:- Classes of Evidence

   (i) ***Physical Evidence*** is any physical object which may be considered relevant to an Argument in that it provides physical support or rebuttal to a statement of fact; and

   (ii) ***Testimonial Evidence*** is any sworn testimony by a witness having been given either in an open court, video recording or written statement; and

   (iii) ***Inferential Evidence*** is any combination of admissible physical and/or testimonial evidence which when taken as a whole through the use of Logic, Reason and Inference implies the existence of further evidence which is unable to be physically submitted at the time of proceedings.

Article 481 – Physical Evidence

1786. ***Physical Evidence***, also defined as "real evidence" is any form or parts of a physical object intended to support or rebut a Fact associated with an Argument. Physical Evidence

1787. There are six (6) broad categories of Physical Evidence being *Object, Material, Chemical, Biological, Documentary* and *Digital* namely:- Categories of Physical Evidence

   (i) ***Object*** is complete or self contained objects whether instruments, firearm, powered, non-powered, clothes etc.; and

   (ii) ***Material*** is parts of any material such as fibre, metal, stone etc.; and

   (iii) ***Chemical*** is part of any chemical reaction, residue, gunpowder, fingerprint reaction etc.; and

(iv) **Biological** is any biological culture, sample, body part or whole; and

(v) **Documentary** is any printed documents; and

(vi) **Digital** is any digital files, audio, video, transactions and recordings.

Article 482 - Testimonial Evidence

1788. **Testimonial Evidence** is a form of evidence obtained from a witness who makes a solemn statement or declaration of fact under oath or affirmation. — Testimonial Evidence

1789. The validity and therefore admissibility of Testimonial evidence relevant to an Argument is dependent upon four major qualities being Competency, Integrity, Authenticity and Objectivity, namely:- — Validity of Testimonial Evidence

(i) **Competency** is that the witness is capable of comprehending questions and capable of answering truthfully without influence; and

(ii) **Integrity** is the context that the witness has not been offered any financial benefit or that reward has been offered to a witness for their testimony, nor has the witness been threatened or coerced; and

(iii) **Authenticity** is that the words of the witness are their own and that they have not been coached in any way by any third party on what to say or not to say; and

(iv) **Objectivity** that the answers are first-hand knowledge of fact and not hearsay.

1790. No Testimonial Evidence may be taken in court by a court official unless they themselves have agreed and declared themselves to be operating under oath. — Testimonial Evidence and Oath

Article 483 - Inferential Evidence

1791. **Inferential Evidence** is any evidence "inferred" through the application of the tools of Logic and Reason based on prevailing physical and/or testimonial evidence. — Inferential Evidence

1792. The validity and therefore admissibility of Inferential Evidence relevant to an Argument is dependent upon four (4) major qualities being *Induction, Reduction, Deduction* and *Conclusion*, namely:- — Test of Inferential Evidence

(i) **Induction** is the derivation of general principles from specific instances of at least three (3) forms of Physical Evidence or

Testimonial Evidence; and

(ii) **Reduction** is the logical elimination of possible alternatives to the conclusion derived from Induction to validate the Inductive conclusion is sound; and

(iii) **Deduction** is the testing of both induction and reduction conclusions by the determination of a conclusion from existing known truths; and

(iv) **Conclusion** is a summary of all three (3) methods of Induction, Reduction and Deduction to validate the consistency of any postulation.

Article 484 – Disclosure of Evidence

1793. **Disclosure of Evidence** is the acknowledgement, notification and presentment of Evidence in the due process of any argument or dispute.
Disclosure of Evidence

1794. Prior to the commencement of any formal proceedings, all parties are required to fully disclose all Physical Evidence they plan to present in a formal index of citation properly and uniquely numbered so that the court and any opposing parties may refer to it by number or by subject name.
Requirement of Disclosure

1795. Prior to the commencement of any formal proceedings, either party may lodge an Application for Discovery of Evidence in which specific requests for documents reputedly in the possession of another party material to the proceedings is believed to possess or control. The party receiving such a request is then obliged to respond within a reasonable time to the request or give good cause as to why such documents cannot be produced or specific requests are unreasonable or mistaken.
Application for Discovery of Evidence

1796. Prior to the commencement of any formal proceedings, either party may lodge an Application for Interrogatory Evidence in which specific requests to answer certain questions are put to the other party material to the proceedings. However, no question may be put that directly accuses the other party of an offence. The party receiving such a request is then obliged to respond within a reasonable time to the request or give good cause as to why such questions cannot be answered. By default, unanswered questions of a valid Application for Interrogatory Evidence are always answered in the affirmative at the commencement of proceedings.
Application for Interrogatory Evidence

1797. Prior to the commencement of any formal proceedings, either party may lodge Documentary Evidence providing it conforms to the form
Prior to Start of Formal Proceedings and

accepted by the relevant competent forum of law. — Disclosure

1798. Excluding Testimonial and Inferential Evidence, Physical Evidence is generally excluded from being entered into a formal proceeding after it has commenced after pleadings unless the knowledge of such Physical Evidence is divulged through Testimonial Evidence and it can be reasonably argued that such evidence would have been presented as part of defence or prosecution if its existence were known. — After Start of Formal Proceedings and Disclosure

1799. The deliberate withholding of relevant and material evidence either by the prosecution or the legal investigators that would otherwise favour the defendant is a criminal offence and grounds for dismissal in favour of the defendant. — Failure to Disclose Evidence Favourable to the Defendant

Article 485 - Admission of Evidence

1800. ***Admission of Evidence*** or "admissibility" is the formal acceptance by adjudication of any evidence presented as part of an Argument. — Admission of Evidence

1801. ***Admissible Evidence*** is relevant evidence that complies with the rules of relevance and integrity of existence defined by these Maxims. Only admissible evidence may be presented in all Ecclesiastical, Civil and Criminal Matters. — Admissible Evidence

1802. The ***Admissibility of Evidence*** relevant to an Argument is dependent upon seven major qualities being Relevance, Authenticity, Chain of Custody, Method of Collection, Competence of Witnesses, Hearsay and Privilege, including (but not limited to):- — Admissibility of Evidence

    (i) ***Relevance***: Evidence must be relevant to the issues in the case. Relevant evidence tends to prove or disprove a fact that is of consequence in the case. Irrelevant evidence is usually not admissible; and

    (ii) ***Authenticity***: The party offering the evidence must establish that it is what it purports to be. This includes proving that documents are genuine, that physical evidence has not been tampered with, and that testimony accurately reflects events; and or statements; and

    (iii) ***Chain of Custody***: For physical evidence, there must be a clear and unbroken chain of custody to establish that the evidence has not been tampered with or altered since it was collected; and

    (iv) ***Method of Collection***: For physical and testimonial evidence, the way that the evidence was collected, especially that the evidence was obtained legally and without threat, or torture is critical to its admissibility. Evidence obtained unlawfully must be excluded from admissibility; and

(v) **Competence of Witnesses**: Witnesses must be competent to testify. This means they must have the capacity to understand the questions asked and give coherent answers. Additionally, certain individuals, such as children or those with severe mental impairments, may require special considerations; and

(vi) **Not Hearsay**: Hearsay is generally not admissible unless it falls within an exception. Hearsay is an out-of-court statement offered to prove the truth of the matter asserted. Common exceptions include statements made by unavailable declarants against their interest or statements made for medical diagnosis or treatment; and

(vii) **Not Privileged**: Certain communications are protected by privilege and cannot be introduced as evidence. Common privileges include attorney-client privilege, doctor-patient privilege and spousal privilege.

1803. The Method of Collection is an essential quality affecting the validity and therefore admissibility of Physical Evidence. As a result, there are several essential criteria that must be met in order for Physical Evidence to be accepted and admitted as valid evidence, namely:- *(Method of Collection of Evidence)*

(i) That the date of obtaining and recording the evidence, or the act/event in question does not exceed the statutory limit of charges and/or suits been brought for such a civil or criminal offence; and

(ii) That the collection and/or submission of evidence has been properly recorded in a record of evidence and witnessed by a clerk of a court independently of formal investigators; and

(iii) That the evidence has been collected using proper forensic methods and has been properly sealed and stored securely.

1804. The Integrity of the object/evidence is an essential quality affecting the validity and therefore admissibility of Physical Evidence. As a result, there are several essential criteria concerning Integrity of the storage and protection of Evidence, namely:- *(Integrity of the Evidence)*

(i) That all reasonable efforts have been made to ensure the evidence has not been accessed or handled other than through the formal proceedings to which it relates; and

(ii) That its authenticity may be examined by a formal expert called by either the prosecutor or defence of a formal proceeding; and

(iii) That it may be represented to formal proceedings on request; and

(iv) The forensic procedures by which evidence is collected must be able to prove that in its obtaining and in its processing it has not been contaminated by external sources that may potentially account for its existence; and

(v) All evidence obtained forensically must be recorded properly and able to be subject to scientific/expert testimony and cross examination.

1805. Where the accused in a suit has an active criminal record, physical evidence from previous criminal convictions, including the details and circumstances of the previous convictions(s) are automatically admissible. — Previous Active Criminal Record

1806. Where the same two parties have previously been engaged in a Civil suit (trial or hearing), the physical evidence from the previous dispute is automatically admissible. — Previous Evidence

Article 486 – Acceptance of Evidence (Proof)

1807. **Proof**, is when a valid and competent Forum of Law is convinced of the Truth of an allegation of Fact in accord with the present Maxims and the most sacred Covenant
Pactum De Singularis Caelum. Such allegation is then said to be "proved". — Proof

1808. When a Person who makes an allegation is bound to prove it, the burden or onus of proof (*onus probandi*) is said to initially rest upon them. — Burden of Proof

1809. When a Person on whom the burden of proof lies, adduces Evidence sufficient to raise a presumption that what is said is true, they are said to shift the burden of proof to the other party. — Shifting Burden of Proof

1810. A Certificate of Exemplification as a formal Certificate issued under an Official Seal of Ucadia or an Authorised related entity and referring to the extract of a Matter and then Certified by a Principal and Witness under Oath as being true shall be *Prima Facie* proof in any jurisdiction where there exists the Rule of Law and competent forums of Law. The refusal of a foreign or external body to accept a proper Certificate of Exemplification is a confession of perfidy, incompetence and heresy against all forms of Law. — Certificate of Exemplification as Prima Facie Proof

Article 487 – Dispute of Evidence

1811. ***Dispute of Evidence*** refers to a situation in legal proceedings where the parties involved in a case disagree or dispute the admissibility, relevance, or accuracy of certain pieces of evidence that are being presented in court.
Dispute of Evidence

1812. Common arguments in Dispute of Evidence include (but are not limited to):-
Common Arguments in Dispute of Evidence

    (i) ***Admissibility of Evidence***: One party may argue that certain evidence should not be allowed in court because it was obtained illegally, or unfairly withheld from the other party, or it is irrelevant to the case, or it violates the rules of evidence; and

    (ii) ***Relevance of Evidence***: Parties may dispute whether a particular piece of evidence is relevant to the case. Evidence must be relevant to the issues being litigated, and if it is not, it may be excluded; and

    (iii) ***Authenticity of Evidence***: A party may dispute the authenticity of documents or other physical evidence, alleging that they have been forged, tampered with, or are otherwise not what they appear to be; and

    (iv) ***Expert Testimony***: Disputes can also arise regarding the qualifications and credibility of expert witnesses and the admissibility of their opinions or reports; and

    (v) ***Hearsay Objections***: Hearsay is a type of evidence where an out-of-court statement is offered in court to prove the truth of the matter asserted. Parties may dispute whether a statement qualifies as hearsay or falls under an exception to the hearsay rule.

www.ingramcontent.com/pod-product-compliance
Lightning Source LLC
Chambersburg PA
CBHW060332010526
44117CB00017B/2807